An eye witness of McCheyne:

'He preached with eternity stamped upon his brow. I think I yet can see his seraphic countenance, and hear his sweet and tender voice. I was spell-bound, and would not keep my eyes off him for a moment. He announced his text - Paul's thorn in the flesh. What a sermon! I trembled, and never felt God so near. His appeals went to my heart, and, as he spoke of the last great day in the darkening twilight, for once I began to pray.'

Duncan Matheson
Scottish Evangelist

From The Preacher's Heart

From The Preacher's Heart

R. M. McCheyne

Christian Focus Publications

© Christian Focus Publications

ISBN 1-85792-025-2

Originally published in 1846 with the title
Additional Remains of the Rev. Robert Murray McCheyne.

This edition published in 1993 and reprinted in 2001
by
Christian Focus Publications
Geanies House, Fearn, Ross-shire,
IV20 1TW, Scotland, Great Britain.

www.christianfocus.com

Cover design by Owen Daily

Printed and bound by WSOY, Finland

Contents

LECTURES

Preface to original edition

The very favourable reception which the Christian public has given to the 'Memoir and Remains' of the author, by the Rev Andrew A Bonar, has induced the editor of this volume, with the sanction and approbation of a clerical friend of great eminence and piety, intimately acquainted with the author and his writings, and by whom the greater part of the work has been revised, to publish these *Additional Remains,* consisting of a selection from the various Sermons and Lectures delivered by Mr McCheyne in the course of his ministry. Like those annexed to Mr Bonar's Memoir, they are printed from the author's MS notes, written as preparations for the pulpit, but not intended for publication, or revised by him with that view.

This volume contains specimens of Discourses delivered in all the years of the author's ministry; and the places and dates of delivery are given at the close of each Discourse, wherever they have been marked. The demand for their publication by members of his flock and other friends, many of whom own him as their spiritual father, has been loud and urgent. To all such the book will be acceptable, as helping 'to stir up their pure minds by way of remembrance'; and notwithstanding many imperfections, which, in the circumstances of its publication, have been unavoidable, the editor hopes that, by the blessing of God, it may be useful to others also into whose hands it may fall.

Edinburgh
November 1846

Preface to this Edition

Robert Murray M'Cheyne (1813-1843) belongs to that rare class of Christian ministers whose writings deserve to be always in print. It is a matter for thankfulness to God that his *Additional Remains*, which appeared within a few years of their author's early death in 1843, are now happily republished. They are again made available to the many thousands who love the name of M'Cheyne still to this day. The scarcity of this book on the second-hand market is easily accounted for by the fact that those who have it will not readily be willing to part with it. It is therefore timely that this new edition should now appear. Already in the past few years Andrew Bonar's *Memoir and Remains of R. M. M'Cheyne* has been greatly appreciated in a recent edition. Also M'Cheyne's affectionate and magnetising preaching has made its impact on many modern readers in a newly-issued and choice collection of his sermons entitled *A Basket of Fragments*.

It was clearly not the will of his Heavenly Father that Robert Murray M'Cheyne's words should be lost. Like the words of Samuel, God 'let none of them fall to the ground'. As a consequence we have, largely through the devoted labours of his bosom-friend Andrew Bonar, a remarkably full and complete record of the brief yet meteoric ministry of this young Scottish preacher. The Memoir was at once judged to be one of the best in the English language. To complete his picture of M'Cheyne, Andrew Bonar included sixty-one *Letters* and twenty-eight *Sermons*, together with other pieces of both prose and poetry from his pen.

The spirituality and forcefulness of those first-published Sermons was so much appreciated that there was 'a loud and urgent' request for more of them to be made available. As a consequence, the volume which the reader now holds in his hands was first prepared for the press - evidently not directly by Bonar himself - from M'Cheyne's own manuscript sermon notes. It is no doubt a pity that the spiritual treasure comprised in these sermons was obscured in the old edition by their being published under the drab title of *Additional Remains*. The fact is, however, that they are the workmanship of a M'Cheyne, exquisite sermons in miniature, the fruits of a spiritual genius. The new title is an improvement.

The justification for publishing again a volume of sermons by a now long-dead preacher might lie in their fine quality as specimens of what sermons ought to be today. Or it might lie in the blessing of God which accompanied their delivery at the time when they were first preached. Or it might lie in both, as in this case. They are sermons which are in many ways models for us today and they were attended with wonderful power and fruitfulness at the time when first preached. 'I do not think I can speak a month in this parish [St. Peter's, Dundee] without winning some souls', wrote M'Cheyne to a correspondent in 1841, when his race was nearing its end. 'Hundreds look to me as a [spiritual] father', he could say in reference to the blessed unction of God's grace upon his pulpit and pastoral labours. So then, these *Additional Remains*, like the other sermons of his, are a representative sample of a ministry which God conspicuously blessed.

Andrew Bonar tells us in his transparently honest *Diary* that he began to write the *Memoir of M'Cheyne* on Saturday, September 30, 1843, just seven months after the latter's death on March 25. He finished it in just three months on Friday morning of December 22 the same year. He was conscious of the prayers of many as he set about his responsibility of preserving the rare fragrance of so choice a Christian and pastor. To us it may well appear remarkable today that Bonar was enabled to perform his task as M'Cheyne's biographer so rapidly as well as so inspiringly.

Part of the explanation for the excellence of the Memoir and its deservedly great influence lies in the attachment of the two friends to one another. Those who know Bonar's Diary will have noticed how scrupulously he marks each passing anniversary of his deceased friend's death and how conscientiously he chides himself for not being more like him: 'I have not improved Robert M'Cheyne's death' (1844); 'Memorable anniversary of Robert M'Cheyne's death' (1849); 'Stood by Robert M'Cheyne's grave' (1866).

Indeed, just as the lives of David and Jonathan, Paul and Timothy, Augustine and Alypius were bound together in the bundle of life and come down to us now as spiritual friendships forged by Heaven, so, too, was the friendship between Bonar and the author of these *Additional Remains*. Bonar was to enjoy 'a long life of perfect health' (his own words just shortly before his death) and was to survive his bosom friend by almost fifty years till he was laid at length to rest in the Sighthill Cemetery, Glasgow, a century ago on January 4, 1893.

During all of those years Andrew Bonar made it his practice to keep ever before his mind the inspiring life of Robert M'Cheyne. The diary entries of Bonar reveal his innermost soul and heart. 'There was no friend whom I loved like him'. 'When [just after his death] I gazed upon Robert's face, I cannot tell what agony it was to think he was away; 'I dreamed two nights ago that I was at the side of his coffin again, and woke in tears'.

As the years went by, he rejoiced to hear of the *Memoir* being blessed to one here and another there of its readers both at home and abroad. In his lifetime it was translated into at least two languages, Dutch and Gaelic. From that day to this M'Cheyne's name has been held in the highest esteem by Christians in the Scottish Highlands and beyond in places to which copies of his life or sermons have providentially travelled.

However, the bond of love between these two men of God is only a part of the explanation for the influence which the life and sermons of M'Cheyne have had. Still more importantly we need to appreciate that Robert Murray M'Cheyne was one of the greatest Christians Scotland has ever had. This was certainly the opinion of M'Cheyne's later biographer, Alexander Smellie. Writing in 1913 Smellie quotes these words about M'Cheyne: 'Love to Christ was the great secret of all his devotion and consistency; and, since the days of Samuel Rutherford, I question if the Church of Scotland has contained a more seraphic mind, one that was in such a constant flame of love and adoration toward *Him that liveth and was dead'*. The words are those of M'Cheyne's friend, James Hamilton of Regent Square, London, but Alexander Smellie quotes him here with full approval. 'That is the right estimate and the fitting word', he affirms.

Just how it is that God makes one Christian in every so many thousand to be so inspirational is not easy to say. It must illustrate God's sovereignty in a marked way and prove the practical reality of those words in the Westminster Confession which assert that at times God works 'above means'. By a happy concurrence of divine actions and providences it pleased God to make M'Cheyne 'a burning and a shining light' such that even those who knew him best were at times mystified. 'I can't understand M'Cheyne,' said R. S. Candlish, 'grace seems to be natural to him.' Even Andrew Bonar, when he had completed the Memoir had to admit: 'It humbles me. My heart often sinks in me.' If this conspicuous spirituality in R. M. M'Cheyne was inexplicable to those who knew him well, it was at times arresting and fascinating to men who met him for the very first time. 'Ye're nae common man', said two workmen to him one day as they worked beside a fire in a quarry and listened to the Dundee pastor who had reminded them of a greater fire to come. Again there is a similarly moving story of how he appeared to a hostile crowd in a part of Scotland notorious then for its Moderatism, or spiritual deadness. The narrative ought to be given in the words of Andrew Bonar, and they relate to the period just two months before M'Cheyne's death:

> 'His eminently holy walk and conversation, combined with the deep solemnity of his preaching, was specially felt. The people loved to speak of him. In one place, where a meeting had been intimated, the people assembled, resolved to cast stones at him as soon as he should begin to speak; but no sooner had he begun, than his manner, his look, his words, riveted them all, and they listened with intense eagerness; and before he left the place, the people gathered round him, entreating him to stay and preach to them. One man, who had cast mud at him, was afterwards moved to tears on hearing of his death'.

From what we have said so far it is clear that R. M. M'Cheyne's influence and authority as a preacher were intimately related to his own personal character as a holy man. Too much cannot be made of this fact. He himself believed that holiness was the gospel minister's supreme need. Indeed, his personal diary, which is extensively quoted by Bonar in the *Memoir*, is replete with observations, prayers and resolutions which breathe the very atmosphere of love to Christ and love of holiness. Some of his sayings have become household words on the subject. 'A holy minister is an awful weapon in the hand of God'. 'My people's greatest need is my own personal holiness'. Like most Christians he believed this; unlike most he strove with might and main to practise it.

The temper of M'Cheyne's soul was evidently placid and joyful. In this respect he contrasts with Dr John Duncan, a contemporary and a man equal to M'Cheyne in spirituality. A. Moody-Stuart is surely correct to say that Dr Duncan was not 'joyful enough for him'. The learned Duncan soared higher and plunged far lower than most Christians have ever done. His soul craved to know the reasons of things and he was never so happy as when he had traced a doctrine up to its source, so far as such a mind as even his might go. M'Cheyne, on the other hand, had an intensely practical concern in his study of theology. It was the matter of his preaching to others and the rule of life for himself. The two men met and knew each other. Moody-Stuart, who was a close friend of both, could go so far as to say: 'The holiness of Robert M'Cheyne, if not so deep, was more equal [than Duncan's] and more thoroughly leavened the character hour by hour'. 'There were giants in the earth in those days'.

As a preacher in the Presbyterian Church of Scotland, Robert M'Cheyne lived in a time of immense importance. The dreary age of Moderatism which had blighted the religious life of the national church throughout most of the eighteenth century had given way to a spring-time of evangelical awakening. This was especially so among the young ministerial students who studied in Edinburgh under the eminent Dr Thomas Chalmers, their supreme theological mentor. This band of men whose hearts God had touched included Andrew and Horatius Bonar, A. N. Somerville, John Milne, A. Moody-Stuart, Robert Macdonald, James Hamilton and, of course, M'Cheyne himself. They were all intimate friends and kept up a very warm correspondence over the later years of their ministries.

In spiritual terms they were all eminent and all did great things for God in the respective spheres of their calling. Somerville, for instance, was to travel all over the world preaching the gospel in such far distant places as Spain, India, Australasia, Russia and among the Jews of Eastern Europe. M'Cheyne, always frail in health, spoke once of his own readiness to go to Australia to preach to the neglected convicts there. They all had the spirit of the missionary.

The lifetime of M'Cheyne, therefore, was a period of transition from the frosty days of the recent past to a season of spiritual refreshing. Showers of blessing were falling in Scotland in many places. Already in 1812 there had been notable revivals in Arran and Skye. Lewis was gloriously visited with an outpouring of grace in the 1820s. A wonderful series of such showers was to attend the preaching of William C. Burns in 1839, first in his father's parish of Kilsyth and then in St Peter's (Dundee) and elsewhere.

At length the Ten Years' Conflict came to an end and the principles of evangelical and biblical religion prevailed in the national church once again for the first time in over a century. A company of faithful preachers was now going out into the gospel ministry whose sole aim in life was to win sinners to Christ. They all knew and loved R. M. M'Cheyne and all looked up to him as men naturally do to one who is born to be their leader and their life-long hero.

As God would have it, Robert M'Cheyne was not to be allowed to remain in this world long enough to see his thirtieth birthday. A brief assistantship in Larbert and Dunipace, near Stirling, proved the prelude to his now famous and historic ministry of less than eight years in Dundee. But what years they were! He saw the whole parish of some 4000 souls stirred to its depths by the Spirit of God. The parish church had from the first held 1,100 persons. But latterly the church could scarcely accommodate all who came to hear their seraphic pastor. They stood in the aisles. They sat on the pulpit steps. Men and women, boys and girls wept as they heard the Word of life from his lips. It is said that there grew up thirty nine prayer meetings in the parish in the latter part of his ministry.

Such were the days which witnessed the close of M'Cheyne's brief ministry in Dundee. Of his work in home mission and church extension, his zeal to promote missionary outreach to the Jewish people, and his clear conviction that the coming inevitable Disruption of May 1843 (which he never saw) was fully justified, we cannot here speak. He delivered his last sermons in his beloved St Peter's on March 12, 1843 after recently completing an extensive preaching itinerary in the North East parts of Scotland. His final illness brought delirium to his mind but among the last words caught by those at his bedside were these: 'This parish, Lord, this people, this whole place!' On Saturday morning of March 25 he passed forever into the presence of the Lord.

We have here spoken at greater length about the life of M'Cheyne than about the sermons which form the substance of this book. It is surely right that we should do so because it is our settled conviction that the secret of his excellence in the pulpit lay not so much in what he said as in the man he was. It would, however, be misleading to suppose that M'Cheyne placed all his emphasis on personal preparation. He prepared his sermons with great care. Our final concern then must be to draw attention to some of the main characteristics of the excellent sermons here given to the reader.

First, the *doctrine* of these sermons is that good old evangelical theology which was taught by the apostles, by Calvin, by the Puritans and by Jonathan Edwards. M'Cheyne himself had been awakened through reading the *Sum of Saving Knowledge* attached to the *Westminster Confession* and *Catechisms*. From this theology he never deviated. It was in such books as those of Baxter, Edwards and the Puritans that he imbibed his sense of the sovereignty of God and the urgency of the minister's task. All M'Cheyne's sermons reflect his awareness of the brevity of life, the preciousness of man's immortal soul, the reality of hell, the sole sufficiency of Christ to save the sinner and the absolute necessity of the new birth.

In *method* M'Cheyne is scriptural, direct and clear. He is a textual preacher whose concern is to open up the principal heads of doctrine and to develop the main aspects of the central thought of his text. But doctrine is never left in mid air. His burden is to apply it with all the energy of his soul to the mind, heart and conscience of his hearers. In this it is evident that he excelled. The doctrine, however, came first. He was careful not to let preaching degenerate into vague exhortations. Each sermon is a unit and a whole. The sermon was for M'Cheyne what it is generally not to the average modern preacher - the means for moving his hearers from sin to God. He aimed to affect them at the time, to stir their emotions to the depths by the searching and probing action of the preached Word of God. There is no show of cleverness, no needless illustration, no light-heartedness, absolutely nothing like entertainment or mirth. All is truth and gospel.

In *diction* M'Cheyne is elegant and charming. He was naturally poetical and had the delightful gift of expressing his thoughts in perfectly-chosen words. This natural gift was certainly improved and enhanced by the excellent classical education he had enjoyed at High School and at University in his native city of Edinburgh. Those were the days when it was a virtue to know Latin and Greek authors and to select one's vocabulary to promote accuracy of thought and forcefulness of argument. However, M'Cheyne never affected a learned style. He was far too earnest about his Master's work to use any but simple, plain speaking. His words therefore are as lucid as those of any preacher we have met with. Nothing must detract from the great task which he set himself of conveying the glorious news of Christ's gospel to every hearer's attention, even the youngest. Like Richard Baxter, he preached 'as a dying man to dying men'. Language to this real preacher is but the handmaid to man-fishing and soul-saving.

It is the fervent hope of the Publishers that this book of M'Cheyne's sermons may be used of God to draw attention in our day to the great spiritual subjects of which it speaks. No greater blessing could come to Scotland or the world than for its preachers to proclaim with life and unction the old gospel truths which form the substance of this volume. O that the God of our fathers may, in this the 150th anniversary of the Disruption and of M'Cheyne's death, lighten our darkness once more! If that should happen we shall be blessed with preachers who, like Robert Murray M'Cheyne, preach *from a pastor's heart.*

Maurice Roberts
Ayr,
January, 1993

SERMONS

1. Turn you at my reproof

Wisdom crieth without; she uttereth her voice in the streets: she crieth in
the chief place of concourse, in the openings of the gates; in the city she
uttereth her words, saying, How long, ye simple ones, will ye love simplicity? and the scorners delight in their scorning, and fools hate
knowledge? Turn you at my reproof: behold, I will pour out my Spirit unto
you, I will make known my words unto you (Proverbs 1:20-23).

That none other than our Lord Jesus Christ is intended to be painted to
us under the majestic figure of Wisdom in the Book of Proverbs, is
evident from the passage before us. Of whom but the Saviour could it
be said so truly that he stood with outstretched hands in the streets, in
the markets and in the openings of the gates, crying after the simple
ones, the publicans and sinners; and the scorners, the Scribes and
Pharisees; and those haters of knowledge, the Jewish priesthood? And
again, of whom but the Saviour could it be said, with any truth at all, that
he offered to '*pour out his Spirit*' upon the returning sinner, and to make
known his words unto him? Christ alone '*hath ascended up on high*,
leading captivity captive; and hath received gifts for men, yea, even for
the rebellious, that the Lord God *might dwell among them.*'

Before pressing home upon you, brethren, this earnest and soul-
piercing call of the Saviour, there are two explanations which I
anxiously desire you to bear in mind.

First, that the call of the Saviour, in the words before us, and the
promise with which it is accompanied, are addressed to *sinners*, and not
to saints. Nay more, they are not addressed to sinners promiscuously.
They are not addressed to those who have been awakened to know their
sin and danger, and are crying out, 'Men and brethren, what shall we
do?' But they are addressed to the simple ones, who are loving their
simplicity; to the scorners, who delight in their scorning; to the fools,
that hate knowledge.

The Bible is full of most precious promises to Christ's 'hidden ones'
- his peculiar people, his body, his bride; and there are many pressing
calls and most winning encouragements to those in whom God hath
begun the good work by convincing them of sin. But the words before
us belong to neither of these. They are addressed to those who are dead
in trespasses and sins, to those who are so much lost that they do not

know that they are lost, to those who are happy and comfortable in their sins, to those who have not a doubt as to the sufficiency of their worldly decency and respectability as a righteousness before God, and who do not so much as move the question whether they are saved or unsaved - the simple ones loving their simplicity, the scorners who delight in scorning, the fools who hate knowledge.

Is there none of you who has a secret suspicion that he may be just one of these characters which we have described? I would beseech that man to feel that *he*, then, is this day addressed by the Saviour, not in the accents of wrath, but of tenderest kindness. It is *to you* that Jesus stretches out these beseeching hands. It is to you that Jesus speaks these gentle words. Oh, how blinded you are to the bowels and compassions of the Saviour! Oh, how you dishonour him every day by your hard and blasphemous thoughts of him! You think that because you delight in going away from him, therefore he hath nothing but messages of anger and of coming judgment for you. But oh, how much wiser to gather his thoughts towards you from his own words: '*Turn you at my reproof.* Behold, I will pour out, [not "judgment"] - but, my Spirit unto you, I will make known my words unto you'!

My *second* explanation is, that the call of Christ is to an immediate conversion. He doth not say: *Why* will ye love your simplicity, but, '*How long* will ye love your simplicity?' And again he doth not say, Turn *at any time*, and I will pour out my Spirit unto you; but '*Turn at my reproof*'; that is, Turn t*his day while I am reproving you.* Immediate turning unto God, immediate application to the blood of Christ, immediate acceptance of the righteousness of God, a movement this day, conversion this day, this, and nothing but this, is the *doctrine* of the text. Let none of you say, I will take the gracious offer into consideration, I will take up the question *some day soon* with all due deliberation, I will set apart *some future day* for the very purpose of settling it. That man of you is as effectually casting a mockery on the words of the Saviour as if he were to say, I will have neither part nor lot in this matter. It is not resolutions for the future that Christ asks of you, and to which he attaches the promise of the Spirit; it is a turning *this day* - conversion *this day* - whilst he is reproving you.

Having premised these things, it is now my desire to press home upon you the call of the Saviour by means of three arguments.

1. The call of the Saviour ought to be obeyed by you, because of the rich promise with which it is seconded: 'Turn you at my reproof: behold, I will pour out my Spirit unto you, I will make known my words unto you.'

Often in the Bible are sinners entreated to turn and believe on Jesus, for the sake of the peace and the pardon to be found in believing; but the argument here is a more rare, and perhaps a still more moving one. Here you are besought to turn and believe, that you may be made new creatures: 'Turn you at my reproof: behold, I will pour out my Spirit unto you.'

1. Think how essential such a change is to your well-being: 'Except a man be born again, he cannot see the kingdom of God;' 'Without holiness no man shall see the Lord'. To dwell in the new heavens and the new earth, we must be made new creatures. There will be exquisite scenery in heaven, when the pearly gates of the New Jerusalem appear; but a blind man could not enjoy it. There will be exquisite melody in heaven, from the golden harps of angels and the redeemed; but a man without an ear for music could not enjoy it. And just so there will be spotless holiness in heaven - it will be the very atmosphere of heaven - how, then, could an unholy soul enjoy it? 'Marvel not that I said unto you, Ye must be born again.' But if this be an essential change -

2. Think how impossible it is with man. Search every sect and system of philosophy - search every plan of education - search from one end of the earth to another - where will you find a power to make you holy?

> 'The depth saith, It is not in me:
> And the sea saith, It is not with me.
> It cannot be gotten for gold,
> Neither shall silver be weighed for the price thereof ...
> No mention shall be made of coral, or of pearls;
> For the price of Wisdom is above rubies.'

A man may be able to change his sins, but, ah! what man can change his heart? The reason why this is utterly impossible with man is that he is not only fond of the objects of sin, but he is fond of his sinful heart; he is not only simple, but he loves his simplicity; not only scornful, but delights in scorning; not only a fool, but he hates the very knowledge that would make him wise unto salvation. Which of you, then, does not feel the power of the Saviour's tenderness in the offer which he makes this day to the most careless and unawakened of you all: 'Turn at my reproof: behold, I will pour out my Spirit unto you'? If you will only turn and accept of Christ this day, he offers to give you that Spirit which alone can make you a new creature - which alone can give you a heart that will do for heaven.

You utterly mistake the matter, if you think that Christ here offers to put you under a system of strictness and restraint. You utterly mistake the matter, if you think the gift of the Spirit is to make you walk in ways of preciseness and of pain; for the whole Bible testifies, that the ways in which the Spirit leads us are ways of pleasantness and peace.

Suppose a man happened to be so foolish and inconsiderate as to have an invincible relish for some poisonous drug, because of the sweetness and agreeableness of the taste; and had formed the habit of making such constant use of it that death would, through time, be the inevitable consequence. I can imagine two ways in which the friends of that inconsiderate man, anxious for his life, might cure him of his strange and most destructive appetite. *First*, they might forcibly restrain and keep him away from the use of the poison, forbidding it even to be brought within his sight. This would be the system of restriction - *the appetite would remain*, but it would be crossed and denied. Or, *secondly*, instead of forcibly taking away the poison, they might bring new and wholesome objects before him, the taste of which was far more agreeable and excellent; so that, when once he had tasted these, there would be no fear of his so much as desiring the poison any more. A new taste has been introduced, so that the drug which seemed sweet and agreeable before, seems now no longer palatable.

Now, though this illustration be a very imperfect one, yet it shows distinctly the one feature in sanctification which I wish to bring into view, namely, *its pleasantness*. The Spirit which Christ offers sanctifies us, never in the first way, but always in the second way - not by restraining us, but by making us new. By nature we love sin - the world and the things of the world - though we know that the wages of sin is death. Now, to cure this, I can imagine a man setting himself down deliberately to cross all his corrupted passions - to restrain all his appetites - to reject and trample on all the objects that the natural heart is set upon. This is the very system recommended by Satan, by Antichrist and the world. But there is a far more excellent way, which the Holy Ghost makes use of in sanctifying us - not the way of changing the objects, but the way of changing the affections - not by an *external* restraint, but by an *internal* renewing. As it is said in Ezekiel: 'A new heart also will I give you, and a new spirit will I put within you. And I will take away the stony heart out of your flesh, and will give you an heart of flesh; and I will put my Spirit within you, and cause you to walk in my statutes, and ye shall keep my judgments and do them.'

Ah! then, brethren, if there be one poor sinner here who has been deceived by the detestable heresy of the world - as if the keeping of the commandments by the saints were a grievous and unwilling service - let that man this day open his eyes to the true nature of gospel holiness - that God does not offer to work in you to *do*, without first working in you to *will*. He does not offer to pluck from you your favourite objects, but he offers to give you a new taste for higher objects; and just as the boy finds it no hardship to cast away the toys and trifles that were his bosom friends in childhood, so the believer feels no hardship in casting away the wretched playthings that so long amused and cheated the soul; for, behold, a new world hath been opened up by the Spirit of God, to his admiring, enamoured gaze.

Behold, then, ye simple ones, that are loving your simplicity, what an argument is here to move you to immediate conversion - to immediate acceptance of Jesus! If you will only put on Christ, behold, he offers this day to begin the work of creating you anew - not of crossing and restraining you, and tying you down to services which you loathe, but of giving you a taste and delight in objects which angels, which all holy and happy beings, delight in. 'Turn you at my reproof.'

2. The call of the Saviour to *turn now* ought to be obeyed by us, because conversion becomes harder every day.
There is no law of our nature that works with a surer and more silent power than the law of habit. That which at first we find the utmost difficulty in accomplishing, becomes easier upon every trial, till habit becomes, as it were, a second nature. Thus, in learning to read, how slow and how gradual is the progress made until, trained by oft-repeated trial, the stammering tongue becomes the tongue of grace and fluency. Nay, so easy does the art become, that we at length forget to notice the very letters which compose the words we read. Just similar is the growth of habit in sinning.

Depraved as is the natural heart, yet the ingenuous mind of youth finds something painful and revolting in acquiring the first oath which fashion or companionship obliges him to learn. The loose jest and the irreligious sneer will generally summon up the blush of indignation in the cheek of the simple-hearted boy, newly ushered into the busy world. But who does not know the power of habit in rubbing off the fine varnish of the delicate mind? Who has not, within a few months, heard the oath drop as with native vivacity from the tongue? Who has not seen vice and profanity pass unreproved, even by the silent blush of shame?

As it is with these sins, so is it with the greatest sin of which humanity is guilty - the sin of rejecting the Saviour. There is a time in youth when the mind seems peculiarly open to the reception of a Saviour. There is a time when the understanding and the affections suddenly burst forth into maturity, like the rose-bud bursting into the full-blown rose; a time when all the passions of our nature spurn control, and break forth with a reckless impetuosity; and all experience testifies that this is the time when conviction of sin may most easily be wrought in the sou, the time when the work and sufferings of the Saviour may with greatest hope of success be presented to the mind. It is then that the whole scene of gospel truth flashes upon the mind with a freshness and a power which, in all human probability, it never will do again. The tenderness of a Saviour's love, if resisted then, will every day lose more of its novelty and of its power to touch the heart, the habit of resistance to the word and testimony of a beseeching God will every day become more predominant, the stony heart will every day become more adamant, the triple brass of unbelief will every day become more impenetrable.

Oh! my friends, it is fearful to think how many among us are every hour subjecting our hearts to this sure and silent process of hardening. Look back, brethren, as many of you may do, to the time when Christ and his sufferings had first an awakening interest to your souls. Look back to the first death in your family, or the first time you prepared to sit down at the holy sacrament. Were there not arousing, quickening feelings stirred in your breast, which now you have not? Had you not some struggle of conscience - something like a felt *kicking against the pricks* - in rejecting Christ, in putting away the tenderness of the tenderest of beings? But you were successful in the struggle, you smothered every disquieting whisper, you lulled every pang of uneasiness. The Spirit was striving with you, but you quenched his awakening influences. And now, do you not feel that these days of feeling are well-nigh past, that spirit-stirring seasons are becoming every year rarer and rarer to you? Deaths are more frequent around you, but they speak with

less power to your conscience. Every sacrament seems to lose something of its affecting energy; every Sabbath becomes more dull and
monotonous.

It is true you may *not* feel all this. There is a state of the conscience
in which it is said to be *past feeling*. But if there be any truth in the Bible,
and any identity in human nature, this process of hardening is going on
day after day in every unconverted mind. Oh! it is the saddest of all
sights that a godly minister can behold, to see his flock, Sabbath after
Sabbath, waiting most faithfully on the stirring ministrations of the
Word, and yet going away unawakened and unimpressed; for well he
knows that the heart that is not turned is all the more hardened.

How simple and how mighty an argument is here to persuade you to
turn to God *this day*! This day we hold out to you all the benefits to be
found in Christ, *forgiveness* through his blood, *acceptance* through his
righteousness, *sanctification* by his Spirit. Reject them, and you add not
only another act of sin to the burden of your guilt, but you add another
hardening crust to your impenetrable heart. *This day* refuse Christ, and
by all human calculation, you will more surely refuse him *the next day*.
So that, without at all meaning to question the sovereignty of the Spirit
of God, who worketh whensoever and on whomsoever it pleaseth him,
the only conclusion that any reasonable man has a right to come to is,
that this day, of all days between this and judgment, is the best and
likeliest for your conversion; and your dying day - that sad season of
tossings and heavings, before the spirit is torn from its earthly tenement
- is, in all human calculation, the worst day of your life for turning unto
God. When the minister of Christ pulls aside the curtains of your bed,
to speak the word of Jesus Christ, the ear that for a whole lifetime had
heard the glad message of salvation all unmoved, will, in that hour, hear
as if it did not hear. The heart that has so long turned aside the edge of
the Word of Life, will then be like the nether mill-stone. '*Today*, then,
if ye will hear his voice, harden not your hearts.'

3. The call of the Saviour to turn now ought to be obeyed by us, because the Saviour will not always call.

'My Spirit will not always strive with man,' was the warning of God
given to the antediluvian world. 'Now they are hid from thine eyes,' was
a similar warning given by the Saviour to Jerusalem. The passage
immediately following the text expresses the same sentiment in still
more fearful language. And who does not see the solemnity and power

which it gives to the call of the Saviour, that the time is at hand when he will *not* call any more?

Behold yon majestic figure bearing on his body the marks of the Man of Sorrows, but bearing in his eye and words the aspect of him 'who liveth, and was dead, and, behold, he is alive for evermore.' Behold, how he stands in an attitude of unmingled tenderness to sinners, even the chief! Behold, how the beseeching hands are stretched out! Hearken to the soft accents of mercy, of invitation, of promise: '*I will pour out my Spirit unto you*'.

But remember that attitude of mercy is but *for a time*; these beseeching hands are stretched out only *for a time*; these accents of gentleness are but *for a time*. The day is at hand when he shall come 'with clouds, and every eye shall see him, and they also which pierced him; and all kindreds of the earth shall wail because of him.' This is Christ's *attitude of judgment*. No more are the inviting hands stretched out beseechingly; for the rod of iron is in his right hand, and his enemies are before him as a potter's vessel. His right hand teacheth him terrible things; his arrows are sharp in the hearts of the King's enemies, whereby the people fall under him. And, oh! how fearfully shall his accents of tenderness be changed!

> I also will laugh at your calamity;
> I will mock when your fear cometh;
> When your fear cometh as desolation;
> And your destruction cometh as a whirlwind;
> When distress and anguish cometh upon you.

Oh! what a day will it be, when the tender-hearted Jesus, that wept at the grave of Lazarus, shall laugh at your calamity, and mock at your terrors! The contrast between these two representations is so striking that it cannot escape the notice of anyone. But what I wish you to observe is, that it is not only a very striking change, but *a very sudden one*. The transition from kindness to indignation is here not gradual, like the change from day into night. There is no twilight, as it were; the transition is as sudden as it is terrible. May not this be intended to teach us that God frequently ceases to strive with men, not gradually, but *suddenly*? Not only that death is frequently sudden, and that the coming of the Son of Man shall surely be sudden, as a thief in the night, but that the withdrawing of the beseeching Saviour, from living men who long resist his call, is often sudden and irremediable?

Awake, then, brethren, those of you who think it is all one when you repent and embrace the Saviour, provided it be done before you die. Awake, those of you who say: 'A little more sleep, and a little more slumber; a little more folding of the hands to sleep.' The sun of grace may set not like the sun of nature; there may be no calm and tranquil twilight, when thou mightest bethink thee of the coming darkness, and flee to him who is the *light of the world*. However this may be, there is enough surely in the fact, *that the Spirit withdraws from those who resist* him, whether suddenly or gradually, to move every one of you *this day* to immediate conversion. It must be *now*, or it may be *never*.

On a winter evening, when the frost is setting in with growing intensity, and when the sun is now far past the meridian, and gradually sinking in the western sky, there is a double reason why the ground grows every moment harder and more impenetrable to the plough. On the one hand, the frost of evening, with ever-increasing intensity, is indurating the stiffening clods. On the other hand, the genial rays, which alone can soften them, are every moment withdrawing and losing their enlivening power. Oh! brethren, take heed that it be not so with you. As long as you are unconverted, you are under a double process of hardening. The frosts of an eternal night are settling down upon your souls; and the Sun of Righteousness, with westering wheel, is hastening to set upon you for evermore. If, then, the plough of grace cannot force its way into your *ice-bound hearts today*, what likelihood is there that it will enter in *tomorrow*? Amen.

Larbert, November 15, 1835

2. A son honoureth his father

A son honoureth his father, and a servant his master: if then I be a father, where is mine honour? and if I be a master, where is my fear? saith the Lord of hosts unto you (Malachi 1:6).

The first conviction that is essential to the conversion of the soul is conviction of sin. Not the general conviction that all men are sinful, but the personal conviction that I am an undone sinner. Not the general conviction that other men must be forgiven or perish, but the personal conviction that *I* must be forgiven or perish.

Now, there is no greater barrier in the way of this truth being impressed on the soul than the felt consciousness of possessing *many virtues*. We cannot be persuaded that the image of God has so completely been effaced from our souls as the Bible tells us, when we feel within ourselves, and see exhibited in others, what may almost be termed godlike virtues. The heroes of whom we have read in history, with their love of country and contempt of death, their constancy in friendship and fidelity in affection, seem to rise up before us to plead the cause of injured humanity. And what is far more baffling, our everyday experience of the kindness of hospitality, the flowings of unbounded generosity, the compassion that weeps because another weeps; and all this among men that care not for Christ and his salvation seems to raise a barrier impregnable against the truth, that man is conceived in sin and shapen in iniquity.

When we enter one cottage door, and see a whole company of brothers and sisters melted into tears at the sight of a dying sister's agonies; or when we enter another door, and see the tenderness of a mother's affection toward the sick infant in her bosom; or when we see, in a third family, the cheerful obedience which the children pay to an aged father; or, in a fourth family, the scrupulous integrity with which the servant manages the affairs of an earthly master, we are ready to ask, Is this indeed a world of sin? Is it possible that the wrath of God can be in store for such a world?

It will be very generally granted, that there are some men so utterly worthless and incorrigible, so far gone in the ways of desperate wickedness, that nothing else is to be expected for them, but an eternity of hopeless misery. There is a crew of abandoned profligates, who scoff at the very name of God and religion. There are atheists, who openly deny his very being; infidels, who openly deny that Christ came in the flesh. There are cold-blooded murderers, and worse than murderers, who are confessed by all to be a disgrace to the name of man. For these, few would dare to plead exemption from the awful vengeance that awaits the ungodly. So that there is a felt reasonableness in the dreadful words: 'The abominable, and murderers, and whoremongers, and sorcerers, and idolaters, and all liars, shall have their part in the lake which burneth with fire and brimstone.'

But that the obedient child, the faithful servant, the tenderly affectionate mother, the hospitable and generous neighbour, the man of intelligence and good feeling, that all these should ever be bound up in the same bundle of destruction, and consigned to the same eternal flames, merely because they do not believe in Jesus - this is the rock of offence on which thousands stumble and fall, to their inevitable ruin.

There is, perhaps, no way more commonly used by man to repel all the personal convictions of sin which the Word of God would cast on us. For do I not feel within me all the tender affections of humanity, all the honesties and integrities of our nature? Do not I feel pleasure in being honest and fair-dealing, in being compassionate, and generous, and hospitable? How plainly, then, may I say to my soul: 'Soul, take thine ease. These virtues of thine are a sure token that thou art born for a blessed eternity'?

Ah! my friends, is it not a most blessed thing that, in the passage now before us, God wrests from our hand the very weapon wherewith we would defend ourselves, and turns it with a shaft to pierce our worldly consciences? And, oh! if we had minds as intelligent as when Adam walked with God in Paradise, nothing more would be necessary to carry to our hearts the overwhelming conviction of sin than the repetition of the words: 'A son honoureth his father, and a servant his master: if then I be a father, where is mine honour? and if I be a master, where is my fear? saith the LORD of hosts unto you.'

There is a power and a pathos in this argument, which might well break down the hardest and most unfeeling mind; it is as if God had said, as he elsewhere doth: 'Come and let us reason together.' You say that you have many excellent virtues, that you have tender and beautiful affections; you say that filial and parental love occupy a master-place in your bosom, that integrity and unsullied honesty beat high in your breast. And do I deny all this? Shall I detract from the glory of my own handiwork, so beautiful, even in ruins? No, it is all true; the son does honour his father, the servant is faithful to his master; all is beautiful, when I look only to the earthly relationships.

But that is the very thing which shows the utter derangement of all the heavenly relationships; for, 'If *I* then be a father, where is *mine* honour? if *I* be a master, where is *my* fear? saith the LORD of hosts unto you.' I see that you honour your earthly fathers, and serve faithfully your earthly masters; but that is the very thing which shows me that I am the exception. I see that there is not a father in the whole universe that is deprived of the love of his children, but me. There is not a master under heaven that is robbed of the honour and service of his domestics as I am.

If, brethren, you and I were sunk into actual brutality - if we had no love for parents, no honesty to masters - then God might have had cause to say of us, that nothing better could be expected from such wretches, than that we should forget our heavenly Father and Master. But, oh! when there are such tender affections in our bosoms towards our earthly relations, is not our sin written as with an iron pen, and with lead in the rock for ever, that we make God the exception - that we are godless in the world?

I would, with all affection and tenderness, beseech every one of you to search his own heart, and see if these things be not so - see if that which you generally take for the excuse of your sins, be not the very essence of them. What would you not do, what would you not suffer, for the sake of an earthly parent? And yet you will not expend so much as a thought, or the breathing of a desire, for your heavenly Parent. God is not in all your thoughts. You will toil night and day in behalf of an earthly master; yet you will not do a hand's turn for your heavenly Master. God is the only parent whom you dishonour; God is the only master whom you wrong. 'If you were blind, you should have no sin; but now it is plain you see, therefore your sin remaineth.' If you were incapable of affection or fidelity, then you should have no sin; but now it is plain you are capable of both, therefore your sin remaineth.

Imagine a family of brothers and sisters all bound together by the ties of the closest amity and affection. Oh! it is a good and pleasant sight to see brethren dwell together in unity. 'It is like precious ointment upon the head, that ran down upon the beard, even Aaron's beard, that went down to the skirts of his garments. It is as the dew of Hermon, that descended upon the mountains of Zion.' What will they not do for each other? What will they not suffer for each other? But imagine, again, that all this unity, which is so much like the temper of heaven, was maintained among them, whilst all the while they were united in despising the tender mother that bore them, in turning away from, and forsaking the grey-haired father that had brought up every one of them. Would not this one feature in the picture change all its beauty and all its interest? Would it not make their unity more like that of devils than that of angels? Would you not say, that their affection for one another was the very thing which made their disaffection to their parents hateful and most unnatural?

Oh! brethren, the picture is a picture of us: 'A son honoureth his father, and a servant his master: if then I be a father, where is mine honour? and if I be a master, where is my fear? saith the LORD of hosts unto you.'

Oh! it is a fearful thing, when our very virtues, to which we flee for refuge against the wrath of God, turn round most fiercely to condemn us. What avail your honesties, what avail your filial attachments, what avail your domestic virtues, which the world so much admire, and praise you for, if, in the sight of God, these are all the while enhancing your ungodliness?

Let no man misunderstand me, as if I had said that it was a bad thing to be honest, to be faithful, and just, and affectionate to parents. Every sensible man knows the value of these earthly virtues, and how much they are invigorated and enlarged, and begin a new life, as it were, when the worldly man becomes a believer. But this I do say, that if thou hast nothing more than these earthly virtues, they will, every one of them, rise in the judgment only to condemn thee. I say only what the mighty Luther hath said before me - that these virtues of thine, whereby thou thinkest to build thy Babel tower to heaven, are but the splendid sins of humanity; and that they will only serve to cast thee down into tenfold deeper condemnation.

God doth not charge you, brethren, with dishonesty, with disobedience to parents. The only charge which he brings against you here is, the one long sin of the natural man's life - *ungodliness*. God is not in all your thoughts. He admits that you have earthly virtues; but these just make blacker and more indelible your sins against heaven.

1. I infer from this passage, that our worldly virtues will not atone for sin, or make us acceptable in the sight of God.
Humanity is a ruin; but it is beautiful even in ruins. And just as you may wander through some magnificent ruin, over which the winter storms of whole centuries have passed, and stand with admiring gaze beside every fluted column, now broken and prostrate, and luxuriate with antiquarian fancy amid the half-defaced carving of Gothic ages - as you may do all this without so much as a thought of the loss of its chief architectural glory, the grand proportions of the whole towering majestically heavenward, with bastion and minaret, all now lying buried in their own rubbish - so may you look upon man. You may wander from one earthly affection and faculty to another, filled with admiration of the curious handiwork of him who is indeed the most cunning of artists; you may luxuriate amidst the exquisite adaptations of man to man, so nice

as to keep all the wheels of society running smoothly and easily forward; you may do all this, as thousands have done before you, without so much as a thought of the loss of man's chiefest glory - the relation of man to his God - without thinking that while many amid the rubbish of this world are honest, and fair-dealing, and affectionate to parents, *there is not one that seeketh after God.*

Let us imagine for an instant that these worldly virtues could take away sin; and just look to the consequences. Where would you find the man altogether destitute of them? Where is salvation to stop? If honesty and generosity are to blot out one sin, why not all sin? In this way you can fix no limit between the saved and the unsaved; and, therefore, all men may live as they please, for you never can prove that one man is beyond the pale of salvation.

Again, if worldly virtues could blot out sin, Christ is dead in vain. He came to save his people from their sins. Angels ushered him into the world as the Saviour of sinners. John bade men behold in him the Lamb of God that taketh away the sins of the world; and the whole Bible testifies, that 'through this man is preached unto you the remission of sins'. But if the everyday honesties, and kindnesses, and generosities of life, could avail to take away sin, what needed Christ to have suffered? If anything so cheap and common, as earthly virtues are, could avail to the blotting out of sin, why needed so inestimably precious a provision to be made as the blood of the Son of God? If, with all our honesties and all our decencies and respectabilities in the world, we do not stand in need of everything, why doth Christ counsel us to buy of him gold tried in the fire, that we may be rich?

Nothing that is imperfect can make us perfect in the sight of God. Hence the admirable direction of an old divine: 'Labour after sanctification to the utmost; but do not make a Christ of it; if so, it must come down, one way or another. Christ's obedience and sufferings, not thy sanctification, must be thy justification.'

The matter seems a plain one. God is yet to judge the world in righteousness - that is, by the strictest rule of his holy law. If we are to be justified in his sight on that day, we must be perfect in his sight. But that we cannot be, by means of our own sanctification, which is imperfect. It must be through the imputing of a perfect righteousness, then - even the perfect obedience of Christ - that we are to be justified in that day. We are complete only in Christ; we are perfect only in Christ Jesus. But, ah! brethren, if our sanctification will not do for a righteousness in that day, much less will our worldly virtues do. If your honesties and worldly decencies are to be enough to cover your nakedness, and make you comely in the sight of God, why needed Christ to have fulfilled all righteousness, as a surety in the stead of sinners? Why does he offer to make poor sinners the righteousness of God in him? Why does he say of his saved ones: 'Thou wast perfect in beauty, through my comeliness which I put upon thee'?

2. I infer from this passage that earthly virtues may accompany a man to hell.

I desire to speak with all reverence and with all tenderness upon so dreadful a subject. The man who speaks of hell should do it with tears in his eyes. But, oh! brethren, is it not plain, that if the love of earthly parents, and honesty to earthly masters, be consistent with utter ungodliness upon earth, they may also be consistent with the utter ungodliness of hell?

Which of you does not remember the story of the rich man and Lazarus? When the rich man lifted up his eyes in hell, being in torments, and when he prayed Abraham to send Lazarus to dip his finger in water and cool his tongue, what was the one other desire which in that fearful hour racked the bosom and prompted the prayer of the wretched man? Was it not love for his brethren? 'I pray thee, therefore, father, that thou wouldest send him to my father's house; for I have five brethren; that he may testify unto them, lest they also come into this place of torment' (Luke 16:27,28).

Ah! my brethren, does not this one passage remove a dreadful curtain from the unseen world of woe? Does it not reveal to you some eternal pains which you never dreamed of? There will be brotherly affection in hell. These parching flames cannot burn out that element of our being. But, oh! it will give no ease, but rather pain. The love of children will be there; but, oh! what agonies shall it not cause, when the tender mother meets the children on whose souls she had no pity, the children whom she never brought to the Saviour, the children unprayed for, untaught to pray for themselves! Who shall describe the meeting of the loving wife and the affectionate husband in an eternal hell?

Those that never prayed with one another, and for one another, those that mutually stifled each other's convictions, those that fostered and encouraged one another in their sins? Ah! my friends, if these, the tenderest and kindest affections of our nature, shall be such fierce instruments of torture, what shall our evil affections be?

I would now speak a word to those of you who are counting upon being saved, because you are honest and affectionate. Oh! that you would be convinced this day by Scripture and common sense, that these, if you be out of Christ, and therefore not at peace with God, do but aggravate your ungodliness, and will add torment inexpressible to your hell. If, then, our very virtues condemn us, what shall our sins do? If the ungodly shall meet with so fearful a doom, where shall the open sinner appear?

But there is a fountain opened up in Zion, to which both the ungodly and the sinner may go; and if only you will be persuaded to believe that you are neither more nor less than one of these lost and undone creatures, I know well how swiftly you will run to plunge yourself into these atoning waters. But if you will still keep harping upon the theme of your many excellent qualities - your honesty, your uprightness, your filial and parental affection, your exactness in equity, your kindness in charity, and will not be convinced by the very words of God, that though the son honour his father, and the servant his master, these do but add a deeper and more diabolical dye to your forgetfulness and contempt of God - if you still do this, then we can only turn away from you with sadness, and say: 'The publicans and harlots enter into heaven before you.'

Larbert, November 22, 1835.

3. The difficulty and desirableness of conversion

I waited patiently for the LORD; and he inclined unto me, and heard my cry. He brought me up also out of an horrible pit, out of the miry clay, and set my feet upon a rock, and established my goings. And he hath put a new song in my mouth, even praise unto our God; many shall see it, and fear, and shall trust in the LORD (Psalm 40:1-3).

There can be little doubt that the true and primary application of this psalm is to our Lord Jesus Christ; for though the verses we have read might very well be applicable to David, or any other converted man, looking back on what God had done for his soul, yet the latter part of the psalm cannot, with propriety, be the language of any but the Saviour. And, accordingly, the 6th, 7th and 8th verses are directly applied to Christ by the apostle in the tenth chapter of Hebrews: 'Sacrifice and offering thou wouldest not, but a body hast thou prepared me: in burnt-offerings and sacrifices for sin thou hast had no pleasure. Then said I, Lo, I come (in the volume of the book it is written of me) to do thy will, O God.'

The whole psalm, therefore, is to be regarded as a prayerful medita-tion of the Messiah when under the hiding of his Father's countenance; for how truly might he who knew no sin, but was made sin for us - he on whom it pleased the Father to lay the iniquities of us all - how truly might *he* say, in the language of verse 12, 'Innumerable evils have compassed me about: mine iniquities have taken hold upon me, so that I am not able to look up; they are more than the hairs of mine head: therefore my heart faileth me.'

According to this view, verses one to three are to be regarded as the recalling of a former deliverance from some similar visitation of darkness, in order to comfort himself under present discouragement. And who can doubt that he who was a man of sorrows, and acquainted with grief, experienced many more seasons of darkness and of heaven-sent relief than that which is recorded in the garden of Gethsemane? His so frequently retiring to pray alone seems to prove this. But as it is quite manifest that his description of his iniquities laying hold upon him is expressed in words most suitable to any burdened but awakened sinner, so the verses of my text are every way suitable to any converted soul looking back on the deliverance which God hath wrought out for him. 'Waiting, I waited for Jehovah' (as verse 1 may be most literally rendered), expresses all the intense anxiety of a mind aroused to know the danger he is in, and the quarter whence his aid must come. 'And he inclined unto me' expresses the bodily motion of one who is desirous to hear, bending forward attentively. 'And he heard my cry.'

> He brought me up also out of an horrible pit,
>   Out of the miry clay,
> And set my feet upon a rock;
>   And established my goings.
> And he hath put a new song in my mouth,
>   Even praise unto our God;
> Many shall see it, and fear,
>   And shall trust in the LORD.

He expresses the state of an unconverted man under the striking imagery of one who is in an horrible pit, and sinking into miry clay; while the change at conversion is compared to setting his feet upon a rock, and establishing his goings, and putting a new song in his mouth. Regarding, then, my text as a true and faithful picture of that most blessed change in state and character which, in Bible language, is called conversion, I proceed to draw from these words two simple but most important conclusions:

1. The difficulty of conversion.

So difficult and superhuman is the work of turning a soul from sin and Satan unto God, that God only can do it; and accordingly in our text, every part of the process is attributed solely to him. '*He* brought me up out of an horrible pit, *he* took me from the miry clay, *he* set my feet upon a rock, *he* established my goings, and *he* put a new song in my mouth.' God, and God alone, then, is the author of conversion. He who created man at first, alone can create him anew in Christ Jesus unto good works. And the reason for this we shall see clearly by going over the parts of the work here described.

The first deliverance is imaged forth to us in the words: '*He brought me up out of an horrible pit;*' and the counterpart or corresponding blessing to that is, '*He set my feet upon a rock.*'

There can hardly be imagined a more hopeless situation than that of being placed, like Joseph, in a pit, and especially an horrible pit, or a pit of destruction, as the Psalmist calls it. Hemmed in on every side by damp and gloomy walls, with scarce an outlet into the open air, in vain you struggle to clamber up to the light and fresh atmosphere of the open day; you are a prisoner in the bowels of the earth, the tenant of a pit of horrors. Such is your state, if you be unconverted. You are lying in a pit of destruction; you are dead while you live - buried alive, as it were; *dead* in trespasses and sins, whilst yet you *walk* in them. You cannot possibly ascend to the light of day, and the fresh atmosphere above you; for the pit in which you are is indeed your prison-house; and except you be drawn up from it by the cords of grace, it will usher you into that yawning pit which the Bible says is bottomless.

Such is your state, if you be unconverted. You are under the curse; for 'cursed is every one that continueth not in all things written in the book of the law to do them;' and you have never continued in *any* of these things - doing them from the heart, as unto the Lord, which only can be called doing them. You have never savingly believed on the Son of God; and therefore you are '*condemned already.*' You have never been lifted out of the pit of condemnation. '*He that believeth on the Son hath everlasting life; but he that believeth not the Son shall not see life, but the wrath of God abideth on him;*' that is, it is never lifted off him. The pit of wrath and destruction, in which you are by nature, is never exchanged by you until you leave it for the pit of wrath eternal.

Since this horrible pit, then, represents the state of wrath and condemnation in which we are by nature, how impossible is it that we can extricate ourselves from it! To escape from the prison-house of earthly kings is a hard and daring enterprise; but who shall break loose from the prison-house of the eternal God? Who shall clamber up from the pit of condemnation in which he confines the soul? Who can work out a pardon for past offences? Who can blot out the sin of his past life? Look back upon your lives, brethren, spent in forgetfulness of God, in desires and deeds contrary to God; and then, remembering that he is infinitely just - that he cannot lie, that he cannot repent, say if you think it an easy thing, or a possible thing, to deliver yourselves from the fearful pit in which you are now reserved for his wrath.

But if you cannot save yourself from the pit, and set your feet upon a rock, much less can you extricate yourself from the miry clay, and establish your own goings. The pit of destruction represents the *wrath* you are in by nature; the miry clay represents the *corruption* you are in by nature. To be standing in a dry pit, as Joseph was, is bad enough; but how hopeless and wretched when you are standing in miry clay! To be under condemnation for past sins, one would think to be misery sufficient; but your case is far more desperate, for you are also sinking daily under the power of present corruptions. Every struggle which you make to get up from your wretched condition only makes you sink deeper in the miry clay; and every hour you remain where you are, you are sinking the deeper; your ever getting out becomes more hopeless.

How truly does the growth of sinful habits in you resemble the sinking of your feet in miry clay! Which of your habits does not grow inveterate by exercise? How does the habit of swearing grow upon a man until he is absolutely its slave, and so with those more refined sins whose seat is in the heart! Every day gives them new power over the soul, every new indulgence binds your feet more indissolubly than ever in the evil way; and though you may, nay, in the course of nature, you must, change your lusts, your passions and desires, yet every change is but like extricating one foot from the miry clay, only to set it down in another spot to sink again.

Ah! the undoneness of an unconverted heart - what imagination is bold enough to paint all its horrors? Look in upon your own hearts, ye who are unchanged in heart and life; and if the Spirit of grace may but use the passage we are speaking of to convince you this day of your sin, you shall see how truly there is within you a dark chamber of imagery - a depth of spiritual wretchedness and inability either to forgive your own self, or to make your heart new, either to set your feet upon a rock or to establish your goings - which can be described only by such ideas as those of an horrible pit, and sinking in miry clay.

A third step in conversion you cannot take for yourself; and that is, the putting *a new song* in your mouth. A song is the sign of gladness and light-heartedness, and hence James saith: 'Is any merry? let him sing psalms.' And the spoilers of Jerusalem, when they would put mockery on the sorrows of the exiled Israelites, required of them *mirth*, saying: 'Sing us one of the songs of Zion.' But to sing a *new* song, even praise to our God, is a privilege of the believer alone. To be merry and glad in heart, whilst a holy God is before the thoughts - that is a privilege only of him whose feet are settled on the Rock, Christ.

It is true the unconverted world have a mirth of their own; and they, too, can sing the song of gladness. But here lies the difference: they can be glad and merry only when God is not in all their thoughts, only when a veil of oblivion is cast over the realities of death and judgment. Keep away all serious thought of these things, and they can revel - like Belshazzar and his thousand lords, when they drank wine, and praised the gods of gold and silver. But unveil to their eyes the grand realities of a holy and omnipresent God, of death at the door, and after death the judgment, and then is their countenance changed (as was Belshazzar's at the appearance of the mysterious hand). Their thoughts trouble them, so that the joints of their loins are loosed, and their knees smite one against another.

But to the believer a holy God is the very subject of his song - 'Praise to our God'; and the views of death and judgment do not break in upon this divine melody. On his dying bed he may begin the song which shall be finished only when he wakes up in glory. Now, what unconverted man has the power to put this supernatural song in his mouth, this strange joy in his heart? Gladness cannot be forced, and least of all the Christian's gladness. If thou be unforgiven, unjustified, still at enmity with God, how canst thou raise one note of praise to him? In the fourteenth chapter of Revelation, where the redeemed sing, as it were, a new song before the throne, and before the four beasts and the elders, it is added: 'And no man could learn that song, but the hundred and forty and four thousand which were redeemed from the earth.' None but *new* creatures can learn this new song. Angels cannot join in it; for it is the hymn of the *redeemed* - of those who were sinners, and have been made *new*. And, oh! if angels cannot, how much less can *un*converted, *un*redeemed sinners join in that eternal harmony.

In every way, then, how unspeakably hard a work is conversion! How *impossible* with man! But with God all things are *possible*. He hath provided the Rock, Christ; and his ear is not heavy that it should not hear, if we but cry; his arm is not shortened that it cannot save, if only we will inquire of him for this.

2. From this picture of a true conversion I deduce, not only the difficulty, but also the *desirableness of conversion*.

If you can imagine the delight of being lifted out of the horrible pit, where wrath only awaited us, and having our feet set upon the Rock, where our foundation is firm and solid as the everlasting hills, and we are raised high above the reach of enemies - for 'our defence is the munition of rocks' - then, my friends, you have some notion of what it is to be taken out of wrath into peace, to be translated from being under the curse to the privilege of standing on the righteousness of Christ - a standing on which you are justified, so that neither man, nor angel, nor devil, can bring accusation against you.

And, again, if you can imagine the delight of being carried out of the miry clay, where your feet were continually sinking deeper and deeper every hour, and of having your goings established, a straight path set before you, and solid ground beneath you - then you have some notion of what it is to be taken out of your worldly lusts, and desires, and cares, and thoughts, and anxieties, and habits of sin, in which every new day found you sinking deeper and deeper, and always with less hope of recovery, and to be enabled to love God and the things of God , 'to set your affection on things above', 'to bring every thought into captivity to the obedience of Christ.'

And still further, if you can imagine the delight of exchanging the groan of the prisoner bound in affliction and iron, for the song of the captive who has been set free - the emancipated slave - then you have some notion of what it is to exchange the sullenness and cheerlessness of an unrenewed spirit for the joy and light-heartedness of the redeemed, and the new song of praise which they only can sing.

But when you have imagined all these things, you will have a notion merely, and nothing more, of the desirableness of conversion. The riches of Christ are unsearchable. I might ransack all nature for images. I might bring all conditions of misery and sudden peace and happiness into contrast. Yet would I fail to give you a just idea of the blessings received in conversion; for, indeed, 'eye hath not seen, nor ear heard, nor hath it entered into the heart to conceive, the things which God hath prepared in this world, aye, in the hour of believing for all them that love him.' But leaving images borrowed from nature, which may only confuse, let me simply lay before you the realities which these images signify.

The first thing to be had in conversion is *peace with God*. 'Justified by faith, we have peace with God.' This is the immediate effect of standing on the Rock, Christ. Sin-laden man, dost thou see no desirableness in peace with an offended, forgotten, despised God? Art thou so enamoured of the horrible pit of enmity and condemnation, that thou hast no desire to be out of it? Then, indeed, it is in vain to tell you of a Saviour; you can see no beauty in Christ.

The second thing to be had in conversion is *a holy life*: 'To as many as receive Christ, he giveth power to become sons of God.' Depraved man, whose heart is wrinkled with habitual sins, dost thou see no desirableness in a holy life? I do not ask thee if it would be pleasant to thee this moment to restrain and cross all thine appetites, and desires, and indomitable lusts - I know it would appear to thee intolerable. But I do ask thee if thou seest no desirableness in having these very appetites and desires changed or taken away in their power, so that strictness and holiness of life would no longer appear irksome, but pleasantness and peace? Art thou so delighted, not with the objects which gratify thy passions, but with these very passions themselves, that thou hast no wish to be made new? Then, indeed, it is needless to tell thee of the Sanctifier.

The third good thing to be had in conversion is *a joyful and thankful heart*: 'We joy in God, through our Lord Jesus Christ.' This is the song of the redeemed. The mirth of heaven is thankfulness and praise. The mirth of heaven upon earth - that is, of the converted soul - is the same, even praise to our God. If, then, cheerfulness and thankfulness, which will endure even amid all the gloominess of the death-bed, and the dark valley, and the awful insignia of judgment - if these be desirable gifts, they all join to prove the desirableness of conversion.

But to many of you I know it is in vain that I talk of the desirableness of conversion; for you do not yet feel the misery of being *unconverted*, the wretchedness of being a child of wrath, and a slave of corruption. When we tell you the unjustified are in an horrible pit, that the unsanctified are sinking in miry clay, you tell us that you never felt any horror about your situation. Nay, you have many pleasures, and you are comfortable and at ease. Ah! most wretched of all unconverted men, you are in the horrible pit; yet you are insensible to its horrors. You are in the miry clay, sinking every step you take; yet you feel no alarm. You know that you never savingly believed in Christ; yet you have no horror when the Bible tells you you are '*condemned already*'. You know that your heart has never been *made new, born again*; and yet you do not tremble when the Bible tells you that '*without holiness no man shall see the Lord.*'

You remind me of nothing so much as of a man travelling in a snow storm. He wanders far from home and shelter. Every step he takes his feet sink the deeper in the drifted snow. A strange insensibility creeps over his mind. Death itself has lost its horrors. As his danger increases, his fears diminish. A deep slumber is quickly descending on every faculty, till he sinks down quietly to sleep, but never to rise again. In like manner, your insensibility, instead of being a sign that there is no danger, increases the danger and horror of your situation a thousand-fold.

As the Bible is true, the state of every unconverted man is so awful, that could you see it as God sees it, the words, *an horrible pit and miry clay*, would seem too feeble to express it. *The sorrows of death and the pains of hell* might, perhaps, come nearer your view of it. Ah! then, strive hard to know the misery of being unconverted. Be determined to know the worst of yourself; for thus only will you see the desirableness of conversion - the excellency of Christ.

And now, then, laying together the two conclusions which I have drawn from our text - the difficulty of conversion, so great that God himself must be its author; and the desirableness of conversion, so great that peace, holiness and joy, all depend upon it - suffer the word of exhortation - to seek it in the only way in which the Psalmist found it: '*Waiting, I waited for Jehovah*' - that is, *I waited anxiously* - '*and he inclined unto me, and heard my cry*'. He is more ready to hear, than thou to ask. The Rock is already laid. Christ hath died, and thou art this day besought to stand upon his righteousness; and being in Christ, you shall every day become more a new creature; and being a new creature, you shall sing a new song of praise to him who hath loved us.

One word to those of you who can look back upon an experience like that described in my text - who can say that God hath brought you out of an horrible pit and the miry clay, and set your feet upon a rock, and established your goings, and put a new song in your mouth. Take you heed that the following words be also realised: *Many shall see it and fear, and shall trust in the Lord.* How many on every hand of you are yet unconverted - both in the pit and in the clay! Let them see, then, how great things God hath done for your souls, that they may fear lest they die unconverted, lest this glorious change never come to them, lest they die *old creatures*, tenants of the horrible pit, to remove only to the pit eternal, lest they be altogether swallowed up in the miry clay; and that thus, moved by fear, they may be persuaded to trust in God, as you have done, to rest on the Rock, Christ, for righteousness.

'Let your light *so* shine before men, that they, seeing your good works, may glorify your Father which is in heaven.' Amen.
Dunipace, August 2, 1835

4. The love of Christ

For the love of Christ constraineth us; because we thus judge, that if one died for all, then were all dead (2 Corinthians 5:14).

Of all the features of St Paul's character, untiring activity is the most striking. From his early history, which tells us of his personal exertions in wasting the infant Church, when he was a 'blasphemer, and a persecutor, and injurious,' it is quite obvious that this was the prominent characteristic of his natural mind. But when it pleased the Lord Jesus Christ to show forth in him all long-suffering, and to make him 'a pattern to them which should afterwards believe on him', it is beautiful and most instructive to see how the natural features of this daringly bad man became not only sanctified, but invigorated and enlarged; so true is it that they that are in Christ are a new creation: 'Old things pass away, and all things become new.'

'*Troubled* on every side, yet not distressed; *perplexed*, but not in despair; *persecuted*, but not forsaken; *cast down*, but not destroyed' - this was a faithful picture of the life of the converted Paul. 'Knowing the terrors of the Lord', and the fearful situation of all who were yet in their sins, he made it the business of his life to 'persuade men', striving if, by any means, he might commend the truth to their consciences. 'For [saith he] whether we be beside ourselves, it is to God; or whether we be sober, it is for your cause' (verse 13). Whether the world think us wise or mad, the cause of God and of human souls is the cause in which we have embarked all the energies of our being.

Who, then, is not ready to inquire into the secret spring of all these supernatural labours? Who would not desire to have heard from the lips of Paul what mighty principle it was that impelled him through so many toils and dangers? What magic spell has taken possession of this mighty mind, or what unseen planetary influence, with unceasing power, draws him on through all discouragements; indifferent alike to the world's dread laugh, and the fear of men, which bringeth a snare; careless alike of the sneer of the sceptical Athenian, of the frown of the luxurious Corinthian, and the rage of the narrow-minded Jew? What saith the apostle himself?

We have his own explanation of the mystery in the words before us: '*The love of Christ constraineth us.*'

That Christ's love to man is here intended, and not our love to the Saviour, is quite obvious, from the explanation which follows, where his dying for all is pointed to as the instance of his love. It was the view of that strange compassion of the Saviour, moving him to die for his enemies - to bear double for all our sins, to taste death for every man - it was this view which gave Paul the impulse in every labour - which made all suffering light to him, and every commandment not grievous. He 'ran with patience the race that was set before him'. Why? Because, 'looking unto Jesus', he lived as a man 'crucified unto the world, and the world crucified unto him.' By what means? By looking to the cross of Christ.

As the natural sun in the heavens exercises a mighty and unceasing attractive energy on the planets which circle round it, so did the Sun of Righteousness, which had indeed arisen on Paul with a brightness above that of noon-day, exercise on his mind a continual and an almighty energy, *constraining* him to live henceforth no more unto himself, but to him that died for him and rose again. And observe, that it was no temporary, fitful energy, which it exerted over his heart and life, but an abiding and a continued attraction; for he does not say that the love of Christ *did once* constrain him; or that it *shall yet* constrain him; or that in times of excitement, in seasons of prayer, or peculiar devotion, the love of Christ *was wont* to constrain him; but he saith simply, that the love of Christ *constraineth* him. It is the ever-present, ever-abiding, ever-moving power, which forms the main-spring of all his working; so that, take that away, and his energies are gone, and Paul is become weak as other men.

Is there no one before me whose heart is longing to possess just such a master-principle? Is there no one of you, brethren, who has arrived at that most interesting of all the stages of conversion in which you are panting after a power to make you new? You have entered in at the strait gate of believing. You have seen that there is no peace to the unjustified; and therefore you have put on Christ for your righteousness; and already do you feel something of the joy and peace of believing. You can look back on your past life, spent without God in the world, and without Christ in the world, and without the Spirit in the world. You can see yourself a condemned outcast, and you say: 'Though I should wash my hands in snow-water, yet mine own clothes would abhor me.' You can do all this, with shame and self-reproach it is true, but yet without dismay and without despair; for your eye has been lifted believingly to him who was made sin for us, and you are persuaded that, as it pleased God to count all your iniquities to the Saviour, so he is willing, and hath always been willing, to count all the Saviour's righteousness to you.

Without despair, did I say? Nay, with joy and singing; for if, indeed, thou believest with all thine heart, then thou art come to the blessedness of the man unto whom God imputeth righteousness without works which David describes, saying: 'Blessed are they whose iniquities are forgiven, and whose sins are covered. Blessed is the man to whom the Lord imputeth not sin.' This is the peace of the justified man.

But is this peace a state of perfect blessedness? Is there nothing left to be desired? I appeal to those of you who know what it is to be just by believing. What is it that still clouds the brow, that represses the exulting of the spirit? Why might we not always join in the song of thanksgiving: 'Bless the Lord, O my soul, and forget not all his benefits, who forgiveth all thine iniquities'? If we have received double for all our sins, why should it ever be needful for us to argue as doth the Psalmist: 'Why art thou cast down, O my soul; and why art thou disquieted in me?' Ah! my friends, there is not a man among you, who has really believed, who has not felt the disquieting thought of which I am now speaking. There may be some of you who have felt it so painfully, that it has obscured, as with a heavy cloud, the sweet light of gospel peace, the shining in of the reconciled countenance upon the soul. The thought is this, 'I am a justified man; but, alas! I am not a sanctified man. I can look at my past life without despair; but how can I look forward to what is to come?'

There is not a more picturesque moral landscape in the universe than such a soul presents. Forgiven all trespasses that are past, the eye looks inwards with a clearness and an impartiality unknown before, and there it gazes upon its long-fostered affections for sin, which, like ancient rivers, have worn a deep channel into the heart; its periodic returns of passion, hitherto irresistible and overwhelming, like the tides of the ocean; its perversities of temper and of habit, crooked and unyielding, like the gnarled branches of a stunted oak. Ah, what a scene is here! What anticipations of the future! What forebodings of a vain struggle against the tyranny of lust, against old trains of acting, and of speaking, and of thinking! Were it not that the hope of the glory of God is one of the chartered rights of the justified man, who would be surprised if this view of terror were to drive a man back, like the dog to his vomit, or the sow that was washed to wallow again in the mire?

Now it is to the man precisely in this situation, crying out at morning and at evening, 'How shall I be made new? What good shall the forgiveness of my past sins do me, if I be not delivered from the love of sin?' that we would now, with all earnestness and affection, point out the example of Paul, and the secret power which wrought in him. '*The love of Christ* [says Paul] *constraineth us.*' We, too, are men of like passions with yourselves. That same sight, which you view with dismay within you, was in like manner revealed to us in all its discouraging power. Nay, ever and anon the same hideous view of our own hearts is opened up to us. But we have an encouragement which never fails. The love of the bleeding Saviour constraineth us. The Spirit is given to them that believe; and that almighty Agent hath one argument that moves us continually - *the love of Christ.*

My present object, brethren, is to show how this argument, in the hand of the Spirit, moves the believer to live unto God, how so simple a truth as the love of Christ to man, continually presented to the mind by the Holy Ghost, should enable any man to live a life of gospel holiness. And if there be one man among you whose great inquiry is, How shall I be saved from sin? how shall I walk as a child of God? - that is the man, of all others, whose ear and heart I am anxious to engage.

1. The love of Christ to man constraineth the believer to live a holy life, because that truth takes away all his dread and hatred of God. When Adam was unfallen, God was everything to his soul; and everything was good and desirable to him, only in so far as it had to do with God. Every vein of his body, so fearfully and wonderfully made, every leaf that rustled in the bowers of Paradise, every new sun that rose, rejoicing like a strong man to run his race, brought him in every day new subjects of godly thought and of admiring praise; and it was only for that reason that he could delight to look on them. The flowers that appeared on the earth, the singing of birds, and the voice of the turtle heard throughout the happy land, the fig tree putting forth her green figs, and the vines with the tender grapes giving a good smell - all these combined to bring in to him *at every pore* a rich and varied tribute of pleasantness.

And why? Just because they brought into the soul rich and varied communications of the manifold grace of Jehovah. For, just as you may have seen a child on earth devoted to its earthly parent, pleased with everything when he is present, and valuing every gift just as it shows more of the tenderness of that parent's heart, so was it with that genuine child of God. In God he lived, and moved, and had his being; and not more surely would the blotting out the sun in the heavens have taken away that light which is so pleasant to the eyes, than would the hiding of the face of God from him have taken away the light of his soul, and left nature a dark and desolate wilderness. But when Adam fell, the fine gold became dim. The system of his thoughts and likings was just reversed. Instead of enjoying God in everything, and everything in God, everything now seemed hateful and disagreeable to him, in as far as it had to do with God.

When man sinned, then he feared and hated him whom he feared; and fled to all sin, in order to flee from him whom he hated. So that, just as you may have seen a child who has grievously transgressed against a loving parent, doing all it can to hide that parent from its view, hurrying from his presence, and plunging into other thoughts and occupations, to rid itself of the thought of its justly offended father - in the very same way when fallen Adam heard the voice of the Lord God walking in the garden in the cool of the day - that voice which, before he sinned, was heavenly music in his ears - *then did Adam and his wife hide themselves from the presence of the Lord, among the trees of the garden*. And in the same way does every natural man run from the voice and presence of the Lord - not to hide under the thick embowering leaves of Paradise, but to bury himself in cares, and business, and pleasures, and revellings. Any retreat is agreeable, where God is not. Any occupation is tolerable, if God be not in the thoughts.

Now I am quite sure that many of you may hear this charge against the natural man with incredulous indifference, if not with indignation. You do not feel that you hate God, or dread his presence; and, therefore, you say it cannot be true. But, brethren, when God says of your heart that it is 'desperately wicked', yea, unsearchably wicked - who can know it? God alone claims for himself the privilege of knowing and trying the heart - is it not presumptuous in such ignorant beings as we are, to say that that is not true, with respect to our hearts, which God affirms to be true, merely because we are not conscious of it?

God saith that *the carnal mind is enmity against God* - that the very grain and substance of an unconverted mind is hatred against God, absolute, implacable hatred against him in whom we live, and move, and have our being. It is quite true that we do not feel this hatred within us; but that is only an aggravation of our sin and of our danger. We have so choked up the avenues of self-examination; there are so many turnings and windings, before we can arrive at the true motives of our actions; that our dread and hatred of God, which first moved man to sin, and which are still the grand impelling forces whereby Satan goads on the children of disobedience - these are wholly concealed from our view, and you cannot persuade a natural man that they are really there. But the Bible testifies, that out of these two deadly roots - dread of God and hatred of God - grows up the thick forest of sins with which the earth is blackened and overspread. And if there be one among you, brethren, who has been awakened by God to know what is in his heart, I take that man this day to witness, that his bitter cry, in the view of all his sins, has ever been: '*Against thee, thee only,* have I sinned.'

If, then, dread of God, and hatred of God, be the cause of all our sins, how shall we be cured of the love of sin, but by taking away the cause? How do you most effectually kill the noxious weed? Is it not by striking at the root? In the love of Christ to man, then - in that strange unspeakable gift of God, when he laid down his life for his enemies; when he died the just for the unjust, that he might bring us to God - do not you see an object which, if really believed by the sinner, takes away all his dread and all his hatred of God? The root of sin is severed from the stock. In his bearing double for all our sins, we see the curse carried away, we see God reconciled. Why should we fear any more? Not fearing, why should we hate God any more? Not hating God, what desirableness can we see in sin any more? Putting on the righteousness of Christ, we are again placed as Adam was - with God as our friend. We have no object in sinning; and, therefore, we do not care to sin.

In the sixth chapter of Romans, Paul seems to speak of the believer sinning, as if the very proposition were absurd: 'How shall we that are dead to sin' - that is, who in Christ have already borne the penalty - 'how shall we live any longer therein?' And again he says very boldly: 'Sin *shall not* have dominion over you' - it is impossible in the nature of things - 'for ye are not under the law, but under grace'. Ye are no longer under the curse of a broken law, dreading and hating God; ye are under grace, under a system of peace and friendship with God.

But is there anyone ready to object to me, that if these things be so - if nothing more than that a man be brought into peace with God is needful to a holy life and conversation - how comes it that believers do still sin? I answer, it is indeed too true that believers do sin; but it is just as true that unbelief is the cause of their sinning. If, brethren, you and I were to live with our eye so closely on Christ bearing double for all our sins, freely offering to all a double righteousness for all our sins; and if this constant view of the love of Christ maintained within us - as assuredly it would, if we looked with a straightforward eye - the peace of God which passeth all understanding, the peace that rests on nothing in us, but upon the completeness that is in Christ - then, brethren, I do say, that frail and helpless as we are, we should never sin, we should not have the slightest object in sinning.

But, ah! my friends, this is not the way with us. How often in the day is the love of Christ quite out of view! How often is it obscured to us, sometimes hid from us by God himself, to teach us what we are! How often are we left without the realising sense of the completeness of his offering, the perfectness of his righteousness, and without the will or the confidence to claim an interest in him! Who can wonder, then, that where there is so much unbelief, dread and hatred of God should again and again creep in, and sin should often display its poisonous head?

The matter is very plain, brethren, if only we had spiritual eyes to see it. If we live a life of faith on the Son of God, then we shall assuredly live a life of holiness. I do not say, *we ought to do so*, but I say we shall, as a matter of necessary consequence. But, in as far as we do not live a life of faith, in so far we shall live a life of unholiness. It is through faith that God purifies the heart; and there is no other way.

Is there any of you, then, brethren, desirous of being made new, of being delivered from the slavery of sinful habits and affections? We can point you to no other remedy than the love of Christ. Behold how he loved you! See what he bore for you! Put your finger, as it were, into the prints of the nails, and thrust your hand into his side; and be no more faithless, but believing. Under a sense of your sins, flee to the Saviour of sinners. As the timorous dove flies to hide itself in the crevices of the rock, so do you flee to hide yourself in the wounds of your Saviour; and when you have found him like the shadow of a great rock in a weary land, when you sit under his shadow with great delight, you will find that he hath slain all the enmity, that he hath accomplished all your warfare. God is now for you. Planted together with Christ in the likeness of his death, you shall be also in the likeness of his resurrection. Dead unto sin, you shall be alive unto God.

2. The love of Christ to man constraineth the believer to live a holy life; because that truth not only takes away our fear and hatred, but stirs up our love.

When we are brought to see the reconciled face of God in peace, that is a great privilege. But how can we look upon that face, reconciling and reconciled, and not love him who hath so loved us? Love begets love. We can hardly keep from esteeming those on earth who really love us, however worthless they may be. But, ah! my friends, when we are convinced that God loves us, and convinced in such a way as by the giving up of his Son for us all, how can we but love him in whom are all excellences - everything to call forth love?

I have already shown you that the gospel is a restorative scheme; it brings us back to the same state of friendship with God which Adam enjoyed, and thus takes away the desire of sin. But now I wish to show you that the gospel does far more than restore us to the state from which we fell. If rightly and consistently embraced by us, it brings us into a state far better than Adam's. It constrains us by a far more powerful motive. Adam had not this strong love of God to man shed abroad in his heart; and, therefore, he had not this constraining power to make him live to God. But our eyes have seen this great sight. Before us Christ hath been evidently set forth crucified. If we really believe, his love hath brought us into peace, through pardon; and because we are pardoned and at peace with God, the Holy Ghost is given to us. What to do? Why, just to shed abroad this truth over our hearts, to show us more and more of this love of God to us, that we may be drawn to love him who hath so loved us - to live to him who died for us and rose again.

It is truly admirable, to see how the Bible way of making us holy is suited to our nature. Had God proposed to frighten us into a holy life, how vain would have been the attempt! Men have always an idea, that if one came from the dead to tell us of the reality of the doleful regions where dwell, in endless misery, the spirits of the damned, that that would constrain us to live a holy life. But, alas brethren, what ignorance does this show of our mysterious nature! Suppose that God should this hour unveil before our eyes the secrets of those dreadful abodes where hope never comes. Nay, suppose, if it were possible, that you were actually made to feel for a season the real pains of the lake of living agony, and the worm that never dies, and then that you were brought back again to the earth, and placed in your old situation, among your old friends and companions - do you really think that there would be any chance of your walking as a child with God?

I doubt not you would be frightened out of your positive sins, the cup of godless pleasure would drop from your hand, you would shudder at an oath, you would tremble at a falsehood, because you had seen and felt something of the torment which awaits the drunkard, and the swearer, and the liar, in the world beyond the grave. But do you really think that you would live to God any more than you did, that you would serve him better than before? It is quite true you might be driven to give larger charity, yea, to give all your goods to feed the poor, and your body to be burned; you might live strictly and soberly, most fearful of breaking one of the commandments, all the rest of your days. But this would not be living to God. You would not love him one whit more. Ah! brethren, you are sadly blinded to your curiously formed hearts, if you do not know that love cannot be forced; no man was ever frightened into love, and, therefore, no man was ever frightened into holiness.

But thrice blessed be God - he hath invented a way more powerful than hell and all its terrors, an argument mightier far than even a sight of those torments. He hath invented a way of *drawing us* to holiness. By showing us the love of his Son, he calleth forth our love. He knew our frame, he remembered that we were dust, he knew all the peculiarities of our treacherous hearts; and, therefore, he suited his way of sanctifying to the creature to be sanctified. And thus, the Spirit doth not make use of terror to sanctify us, but of love: *'The love of Christ constraineth us.'* He draws us by *'the cords of love, by the bands of a man.'* What parent does not know that the true way to gain the obedience of a child, is to gain the affections of the child? And think you God, who gave us this wisdom, doth not himself know it? Think you he would set about obtaining the obedience of his children, without first of all gaining their affections? To gain our affections, brethren, which by nature rove over the face of the earth, and centre anywhere but in him, God hath sent his Son into the world to bear the curse of our sins. 'Though he was rich, yet for our sakes he became poor, that we, through his poverty, might be made rich.'

And, if there is but one of you who will consent this day, under a sense of undoneness, to flee for refuge to the Saviour, to find in him the forgiveness of all sins that are past, I know well, that from this day forth you will be like that poor woman which was a sinner, which stood at Christ's feet behind him, weeping, and began to wash his feet with tears, and wipe them with the hairs of her head; kissing his feet, and anointing them with the ointment. Forgiven much, you will love much. Loving much, you will live to the service of him whom you love. This is the grand master-principle of which we spoke; this is the secret spring of all the holiness of the saints.

The life of holiness is not what the world falsely represents it - a life of preciseness and painfulness, in which a man crosses every affection of his nature. There is no such thing as self-denial, in the popish sense of that word, in the religion of the Bible. The system of restrictions and self-crossings is the very system which Satan hath set up as a counterfeit of God's way of sanctifying. It is thus that Satan frightens away thousands from gospel peace and gospel holiness; as if to be a sanctified man were to be a man who crossed every desire of his being, who did everything that was disagreeable and uncomfortable to him. My friends, our text distinctly shows you that it is not so.

We are constrained to holiness by the love of Christ. The love of him who loved us, is the only cord by which we are bound to the service of God. The scourge of our affections is the only scourge that drives us to duty. Sweet bands, and gentle scourges! Who would not be under their power?

And, finally, brethren, if Christ's love to us be the object which the Holy Ghost makes use of, at the very first, to draw us to the service of Christ, it is by means of the same object that he draws us onwards, to persevere even unto the end. So that if you are visited with seasons of coldness and indifference, if you begin to be weary, or lag behind in the service of God, behold here is the remedy: look again to the bleeding Saviour. That Sun of Righteousness is the grand attractive centre, around which all his saints move swiftly, and in smooth harmonious concert - *not without song.*

As long as the believing eye is fixed upon his love, the path of the believer is easy and unimpeded; for that love always constraineth. But lift off the believing eye, and the path becomes impracticable, the life of holiness a weariness. Whosoever, then, would live a life of persevering holiness, let him keep his eye fixed on the Saviour. As long as Peter looked only to the Saviour, he walked upon the sea in safety to go to Jesus; but when he looked around, and saw the wind boisterous, he was afraid, and, beginning to sink, cried, 'Lord, save me!'

Just so will it be with you. As long as you look believingly to the Saviour, who loved you and gave himself for you, so long you may tread the waters of life's troubled sea, and the soles of your feet shall not be wet; but venture to look around upon the winds and waves that threaten you on every hand, and, like Peter, you begin to sink, and cry, 'Lord, save me!' How justly, then, may we address to you the Saviour's rebuke to Peter: 'O thou of little faith, wherefore didst thou doubt?'! Look again to the love of the Saviour, and behold that love which constraineth thee to live no more to thyself, but to him that died for thee and rose again. *College Church, August 30, 1835*

5. Arise, shine

> Arise, shine; for thy light is come, and the glory of the LORD is risen upon thee. For, behold, the darkness shall cover the earth, and gross darkness the people: but the LORD shall arise upon thee, and his glory shall be seen upon thee. And the Gentiles shall come to thy light, and kings to the brightness of thy rising (Isaiah 60:1-3).

These words are yet to be fulfilled in Jerusalem. It has been long trodden down by the Gentiles, its walls are desolate, its temple burnt, and the Mosque of Omar raised over it in cruel mockery. The ways of Zion do mourn; because none come to the solemn feasts. No sunbeam pours upon the dark brow of Judah; no star of Bethlehem sparkles in their sky. But another day is at hand. The time is coming when a voice shall be heard saying to Jerusalem: 'Arise, shine; for thy light is come, and the glory of the LORD is risen upon thee.'

Observe:

1. *It shall be a time when the world is in darkness*: 'For, behold, the darkness shall cover the earth, and gross darkness the people.' The whole Bible bears witness that the time when the Jew is to be enlightened is to be a time when the world is dark and unenlightened. Paul says plainly that the world will be dead - one great dead mass - when God gives life to the Jews: 'If the casting away of them has been the reconciling of the world, what shall the receiving of them be, but life from the dead?'

2. *In that time of darkness, the Lord Jesus shall reveal himself to the Jews* - the veil shall be taken away and that glorious Bridegroom shall come forth to them: 'The LORD shall arise upon thee, and his glory shall be seen upon thee.' Like the rising sun appearing above the hills, tinging all Mount Olivet with living gold, then pouring down upon the prostrate ruins of Jerusalem, till the holy hills smile again in its cheering ray; so shall it be with desolated Judah. Christ shall arise upon their souls - the day shall dawn, and the day-star arise on their hearts. Christ shall appear beautiful and glorious, and they shall submit with joy to put on his imputed righteousness. His glory, his beauty, his comeliness shall be seen upon them.

3. *The command of God to the enlightened Jews:* 'Arise, shine.' Hitherto they have been sitting on the ground, desolate, in darkness; but when Christ is revealed to them, they shall give life to the dead world - they shall be the lights of a dark world. The word is, 'Arise, shine.' As Christ rises upon them, so they must rise on the dark world; as Christ shines upon them, so they must reflect his beauty and his brightness all around. Even as the moon, in itself dark and desolate, does not drink in the rays of the sun, but arises and shines, reflecting his beams on the dark earth; so shall it be with the enlightened Jews.

4. *The effect*: 'The Gentiles shall come to thy light, and kings to the brightness of thy rising.' When the songs of the ransomed Israelites are heard in their native mountains, their mouth filled with laughter and their tongue with singing, then shall the nations say: 'The Lord hath done great things for them.' Ten men out of all languages of the nations

shall take hold of the skirt of him that is a Jew, saying: 'We will go with you; for we have heard that God is with you.' When the psalms of Israel rise from under their vine and their fig tree, even kings shall lay by their crowns, and come to learn of them the way to peace.

Dear brethren, pray for the Jews! Pray for the peace of Jerusalem. Oh! hasten the happy day. The Lord will hasten it in his time.

Doctrine. Christ arises and shines upon souls, in order that they may arise and shine.

1. By nature men are in a state of darkness: 'Darkness covers the earth, and gross darkness the people' (v.2). When Christ arises upon a soul, he finds it in utter darkness.

1. *A natural man does not know himself.*
A man in the dark cannot see himself - he cannot see his own hand before him, he cannot tell whether his hands are filthy or clean; so is it with all of you who are in an unconverted state. You do not know yourselves. Your fingers are defiled, your garments are stained; but you know it not. Impure desires are written in your heart; but you cannot read what is there. You say: 'Peace, peace, when there is no peace.'

2. *A natural man shrinks from the light.*
A person who has been long in a dark dungeon, cannot bear the glaring light; it hurts the eyes; he starts back into his darkness: so is it with all unconverted souls. You love the darkness rather than the light, because your deeds are evil. When the light of God's holy law is brought upon you, you shrink back from it. When Jesus, who is the light of the world, is preached unto you, you shut your eyes closer than before. Is there none of you who has felt that when Christ is fully preached to you, when you have been compelled for a little to bear the light of his lovely countenance shining through the Word, when you have gone home, did you not creep back with delight to other thoughts of sin and worldliness? The more that sun shone, the more you have closed your eyes. Oh! how plainly you are in darkness, and a lover of it.

3. *A natural man gropes after salvation.*
A man in the dark gropes like the blind. If he wants to find the door, he is obliged to feel for it; he gropes about, not knowing where to place his hand; often he goes in the very opposite direction. So is it with natural

men seeking salvation - they grope for it in the dark. 'We grope for the wall like the blind, and we grope as if we had no eyes: we stumble at noonday as in the night; we are in desolate places as dead men' (Isaiah 59:10). Do you not remember a time when you were alarmed about your soul, when a sudden threatening of death, or the near approach of a sacrament awakened you to tremble for your soul? And where did you go for peace? You did not know where to go; you groped for it; you did not know where to turn yourself. You were directed to Jesus; but you could not comprehend him: 'The darkness comprehended it not.' How plain that you are in gross darkness!

4. *They know not at what they shall stumble.*
A man in the dark does not know what he may come against. His next step may be over a precipice, or upon dark mountains. So is it with Christless souls: 'The path of the wicked is as darkness; they know not at what they shall stumble.' Oh! poor blinded souls, that walk so boldly in sin; ye know not what ye do. You that know you have never come to Christ, and yet walk with a light, confident step, as if you were to walk on a smooth carpet for ever - awake, dear souls! Do not rush on in the dark; for fear, and the pit, and the snare are in the way, and many bold sinners have gone down quick into hell. Give glory to the Lord before your feet stumble on the dark mountains, and while ye look for light, he turn it into the shadow of death, and make it gross darkness.

2. Learn how a soul is brought into light and peace: 'The LORD shall arise upon thee, and his glory shall be seen upon thee.'

1. *It is by Christ rising upon the soul.*
The image here is taken from the rising of the sun. When the sun rises, then all is light; so when Christ rises upon the soul, all is light. When God first awakens a soul, he finds himself sitting in gross darkness and the shadow of death; he fears he shall soon be cast into outer darkness. He says, I must make my way to light; so he struggles to justify himself, he tries to blot out his past sins by repentance, he tries to mend his life; but he is met by the word: 'Behold, all ye that kindle a fire, that compass yourselves about with sparks, walk in the light of your fire and in the sparks that ye have kindled; this shall ye have of mine hand, ye shall lie down in sorrow.'

So he sits down in agony, in more midnight darkness than before.

But man's extremity is God's opportunity. The soul is sitting, as it were, in a dungeon; he sees no way of peace. The Spirit opens the Word, and Christ shines through - Christ the Son of God, the Lord our Righteousness. The heart of Christ is revealed - his love to the lost, his undertaking for them, his suretyship obedience, his suretyship sufferings. Glorious Christ! Precious Christ! He shines like a new sun; the soul gazes and says: 'Truly light is sweet, and a pleasant thing it is for the eyes to behold the sun.'

Has Christ risen upon you? Has he been revealed to you - that better Sun? Oh! if not, you are of all men most miserable; you are sitting in darkness and the shadow of death. Oh! what are all the sparks of worldly pleasure, what are all the fires and torches of the world's kindling? They are like the glow-worm's deceitful blaze - they are leading you to ruin; they will soon go out, and leave you to the blackness of darkness for ever.

Anxious souls, learn to look out for peace. Oh! how anxiously you search that bosom, to see if there is any change there which may give you peace. Now, change your plan. No more gaze into that foul dungeon, but look out upon the glorious Sun. Look upon Christ: one look to him gives peace.

Learn to wait for light. Be like those that wait for the morning. You can no more bring yourself into peace than you can change the course of the sun. Feel your vileness, feel your helplessness, and wait on his hand to take the veil away. 'I wait for the LORD, my soul doth wait, and in his word do I hope. My soul waiteth for the Lord more than they that watch for the morning' (Psalm 130:5,6).

2. *Christ's glory is put upon the soul*: 'His glory shall be seen upon thee.'
It has long been discovered that colour is nothing in the object, but is all thrown upon it by the sun, and reflected back again. The beautiful colours with which this lovely world is adorned all proceed from the sun. His glory is seen upon the earth. It is all the gift of the sun that the grass is of that refreshing green, and the rivers are lines of waving blue. It is all the gift of the sun that the flowers are tinged with their thousand glories, that the petal of the rose has its delicate blush, and the lily, that neither toils nor spins, a brightness that is greater than Solomon's. Now, my dear souls, this is the way in which you may be justified. You are dark, and vile, and worthless in yourselves; but Christ's glory shall be seen on you.

Observe it is his glory. If you only consent to take Christ for your surety, his divine righteousness is all imputed to you; his sufferings, his obedience are both yours. Tell me, anxious soul, what are you seeking? 'I am seeking to make myself appear better in the sight of God.' Well, then, do you think you will ever make yourself appear as lovely and glorious as Jesus Christ in the sight of God? 'No; I have no hope of that.' Ah! then, look here. Christ himself is offered you for a covering; put on the Lord Jesus Christ, and his glory shall be seen upon thee. Oh! that God would open some heart to believe the word concerning Jesus. Oh! to see dust and ashes clothed in the brightness and beauty of Christ! Oh! to see a weary sinner perfect in beauty, through Christ's comeliness. This is the loveliest sight in all the world. 'His glory shall be seen upon thee.'

3. The command to all in Christ: 'Arise, shine.'

There never yet was a man saved for himself. God never yet made a Christian to be a selfish being. 'Ye are the salt of the earth.' But salt is not for itself, but to be used. A city set on an hill cannot be hid; so a Christian is set upon God's holy hill not to be hid. No man lighteth a candle and putteth it under a bushel or a bed, but on a candlestick, and then it gives light to all that are in the house. But here is a more wonderful comparison still: 'Arise, shine.' Christians are to become like Christ - little suns, to rise and shine upon the dark world. He rises and shines upon us, and then says to us: 'Arise, shine.' This is Christ's command to all on whom he has arisen: 'Arise, shine.' Dear Christians, ye are the lights of the world. Poor, and feeble, and dark, and sinful, though you be, Christ has risen upon you for this very end, that you might 'Arise and shine.'

1. *Be like the sun, which shineth every day, and in every place.*
Wherever he goes he carries light; so do you. Some shine like the sun in public before men, but are dark as night in their own family. Dear Christians, look more to Christ, and you will shine more constantly.

2. *Shine with Christ's light.*
The moon rises and shines, but not with her own light - she gathers all from the sun. So do you. Shine in such a way that Christ shall have all the glory. They shine brightest who feel most their own darkness, and are most clothed in Christ's brightness. Wherever you go, make it manifest that your light and peace all come from him, that it is by looking

unto Jesus that you shine, that your holiness all comes from union with him. 'Let your light so shine before men.'

3. *Make it the business of your life to shine.*

If the sun were to grow weary of running his daily journey, and were to give over shining, would you not say it should be taken down, for did not God hang it in the sky to give light upon the earth? Just so, dear Christians, if you grow weary in well-doing, in shining with Christ's beauty, in walking by Christ's Spirit, you, too, should be taken down and cast away - for did not Christ arise upon you for this very end, that you might be a light in the world? Ah! think of this, dark, useless Christians, who are putting your candle under a bushel. I tremble for some who will not lay themselves out for Christ. Ah! you are wronging yourselves and dishonouring Christ. Your truest happiness is in shining; the more you shine for Christ, the happier you will be. 'To me to live is Christ; and to die, gain.'

4. *Shine far and near.*

You are this day besought to help your brethren in the colonies - to send them the gospel, that the Sun of Righteousness may rise upon them.

Objection: Better help the heathen at home.

Answer: It is quite right to help the heathen at home, but it is just as right to help the heathen abroad. Oh! that God would free you from a narrow mind, and give you his own divine Spirit. Learn a lesson from the sun. It shines both far and near; it does not pour its beams all into one sunny valley, or on one bright land. No; it journeys on from shore to shore, pours its rich beams upon the wide ocean, on the torrid sands of Africa, and the icy coasts of Greenland. Go you and do likewise. Shine as lights in the world.

Shine in your closet in secret prayer. Ah! let your face shine in secret communion with God. Shine in your family; that without the word you may gain their souls. Shine in your town; that, when you mingle with the crowd, it may be as if an angel shook his wings. Shine in the world, embrace every shore with the beams of living love. Oh! let your heart's desire and prayer be, that every soul may be saved. Be like Christ himself, who is not willing that any should perish. And whenever a soul sinks into the dark lake of eternal agony, may you be able to lift up your tearful eyes and say: Father, I have prayed to the last, and spoken to the last. 'Even so, Father; for so it seemed good in thy sight.'

6. Melting the betrayer

When Jesus had thus said, he was troubled in spirit, and testified, and said, Verily, verily, I say unto you, that one of you shall betray me (John 13:21).

There are many excellent and most Christian men who think that the feast of the Lord's Supper should never be sullied or interrupted by allusions to those who may be eating and drinking unworthily. They think that when men have, by their own solemn act and deed, deliberately seated themselves at the table of the Lord - that table to which none but believers in Jesus are invited - for the time being, at least, it is the part of that charity which hopeth all things, to address them as if all were the genuine disciples of Jesus, and children of God.

These good men know well that there are always many intruders into that holy ordinance; they know that many come from mere custom, and a sense of decency, and from a dislike to be marked out as openly irreligious and profane. And though they feel, in addressing the whole mass as Christians, many a rise of conscience within, many a sad foreboding that the true guests may be the little flock, while the intruders may be the vast majority, yet they do not feel themselves called upon to disturb the enjoyment of the believing flock, however few they may be, by insinuating any such dark suspicion as that there may be some there who have already sold their Lord for their sins - some who, though they may eat bread with him, yet lift up the heel against him.

Now, a most complete answer to the scruples of these good men is to be found in the example of our blessed Lord. In that night, so much to be remembered, in which he instituted the Lord's Supper, a night in which nothing but kindness and tenderness flowed from his blessed lips, we find that no fewer than five times over did he begin to speak about his betrayer. In many respects that was the most wonderful evening that ever was in the world, and that upper room in Jerusalem the most wonderful room that ever was in the world. Never did the shades of evening gather round a more wonderful company. Never did the walls of an upper chamber look upon so wonderful a scene. Three strange events were crowded into that little space.

First, there was the washing the disciples' feet - the Lord of glory stooping as a servant to wash the feet of poor worms!

Second, there was the last Passover, eating of the lamb and the bitter herbs, which had been the memorial of the dying Saviour to all believing

Jews, but which was now to come to an end.

Third, there was the first Lord's Supper - the breaking of bread and pouring out of wine, and the giving and the receiving of it; which was to be the memorial of his dying love even to the end of the world.

Oh, what an assemblage of love was here! What a meeting together of incidents, each one more than another picturing forth the inexpressible love of Jesus! Oh, what an awfully tender hour was this! What an awfully tender joy was now thrilling through the bosoms of his believing disciples! Oh, brethren, what an exulting gladness would now fill the bosom of the courageous Peter! What an adoring love the breast of the Israelite indeed, the simple-hearted Nathaniel! And what a breathing of unspeakable affection in the heart of the beloved John, as he leaned on the dear Saviour's bosom!

Oh, who would break in on such an hour of holy joy with harsh and cruel words about the betrayer? Who would dare to ruffle the calm tranquillity of such a moment by one word of dark suspicion? Hush, brethren, it is the Saviour that speaks: '*Verily, verily, I say unto you, that one of you shall betray me.*'

I trust, then, my friends, you see plainly, from the example of our blessed Lord, that the awfully solemn warning of the text, instead of being a rash and unwarrantable intrusion upon the joyous feelings with which every true disciple should encompass the table of the Lord, is, of all other Scriptures, the most appropriate, and the most like what Jesus would have us to say upon this solemn occasion. It is not, then, with the harshness of unfeeling man, but it is with the tenderness of the compassionate Jesus, that we repeat these words in your hearing: 'Verily, verily, I say unto you, that one of you shall betray me.'

There is a cruel kindness, almost too cruel, one would think, for this cruel world, which is sometimes practised by the friends of a dying man, when from day to day they mark the approaches of death upon his pallid cheek, and yet they will not breathe a whisper of his danger to him. They flatter him with murderous lies - that he is getting better, and will yet see many days - when his days are numbered. But ten thousand times more cruel, more base and unfeeling, would that minister be, who, set over you by God to care for your never-dying souls, should yet look upon those of you who surround so willingly the table of the Lord, but whose whole life, and walk, and conversation, proclaim you to be the betrayers of that Lord, and not once lift up the warning cry: 'Ye are not all clean. Verily, verily, I say unto you, that one of you shall betray me.'

Question: What could be Christ's reason for so often and so solemnly speaking of his betrayer?

Answer: I can see no other reason for it but that he might make one last effort to melt the heart of his betrayer.

Doctrine: Christ is earnestly seeking the salvation of those unconverted persons who sit down at his table.

There are two arguments running through the whole of this scene, by means of which Jesus tried to melt the betrayer. *First, his perfect knowledge of him.* As if he had said: I know thee, Judas; I know thy whole life and history; I know that thou hast always been a thief and a traitor; I know that thou hast sold me for thirty pieces of silver; I know all thy plans and all thy crimes. In this way he tried to awaken the traitor - to make him feel himself a lost sinner. *Second, his anxious love for him.* As if he had said: I love thee, Judas; I have left the bosom of the Father just for lost sinners like thee; I pitied thee before the world was; I am quite willing still to be a Saviour to thee. In this way he tried to win the traitor - to draw him to himself.

1. All the Saviour's dealings with Judas were intended to convince him that he knew his whole heart: 'I know thee, Judas, and all thy crimes.'

(1) This was plainly his intention when washing the disciples' feet, and telling them, that if they be bathed in his blood, they need nothing more than to have their feet washed - their daily sins wiped off daily: 'Ye are clean every whit.' He then adds, *'But ye are not all clean.'* This was evidently intended as a hint to Judas, to awaken his guilty conscience.

(2) And then, when he had sat down again, to partake of the Passover with them, and had sent round the cup of the Passover, saying, as we are told in Luke: 'Take this and divide it among yourselves,' he would not let Judas slumber, as if he were unknown to him; but declares more plainly than before: 'I know whom I have chosen; but that the Scripture may be fulfilled, He that eateth bread with me hath lifted up his heel against me.' This was evidently intended as a plainer intimation to Judas, that, however concealed he might be to others, he was naked and laid open to the eyes of the Saviour, with whom he had to do.

(3) And, *thirdly*, when he was about to put the bread and wine into their hands, to institute the holy ordinance of the Supper, he would not do it without a still more convincing proof to the conscience of Judas that he knew him perfectly: 'As they did eat, he said, Verily I say unto

you, that one of you shall betray me: and they were exceeding sorrowful, and began every one of them to say unto him, Lord, is it I? And he answered, He it is that dippeth his hand with me in the dish; he it is that betrayeth me. And Judas answered and said, Lord, is it I? He said unto him, Thou hast said.' Here we find the Saviour no longer deals in hints and intimations, but tells him plainly he is the man.

Oh! my friends, if we did not know the deceitfulness of the natural heart, how it evades the most pointed declarations of the Word, we would be amazed that the heart of Judas was not overwhelmed with the conviction: 'Thou, Lord, seest me.' But no; the arrows of the Saviour, so faithfully directed, yet strike off from his heart as from a flinty rock, and Judas sits still at the table of the Lord, still secure, to receive with his bloody hands (those hands which so lately had received the thirty pieces of silver, the price of blood) the symbols of the Saviour's broken body, which he himself was to betray. Ah! my friends, are there no hearts here like Judas', from which the plainest arrows of conviction, having written on them: 'thou art the man', glance off, without even wounding? Are there none of you who sit, Judas-like, with unclean hands to receive the memorials of the Saviour whom you are betraying?

(4) And, last of all, when the feast of love was over - when Judas, with unaffected conscience, had swallowed down the bread and wine, whose sacred meaning he did not, and could not, know - Jesus, deeply affected, 'being troubled in spirit', made one last effort, more pointed than all that went before, to thrust the arrow of conviction into the heart of Judas. When the beloved John, lying on Jesus' breast, saith unto him: 'Lord, who is it? Jesus answered, He it is to whom I shall give a sop when I have dipped it. And when he had dipped the sop, he gave it [unseen it would appear by all the rest] 'to Judas Iscariot, the son of Simon. And Jesus said unto him, That thou doest, do quickly.'

That this pointed word of the Lord was intended to awaken Judas, and for no other reason, is plain from the fact that 'no man at the table knew for what intent he spake this unto him. For some of them thought, because Judas had the bag, that Jesus had said unto him, Buy those things that we have need of against the feast; or, that he should give something to the poor.' So secretly, but so powerfully, did the Saviour seek to awaken the slumbering conscience of the traitor. How was it possible he could miss the conviction that Christ knew all the thoughts and intents of his heart? How did he not fall down and confess that God was in him of a truth? Or, like the Samaritan woman: 'Come, see a man that told me all things that ever I did. Is not this the Christ?' But Satan had his dark mysterious hold upon him; and not more dark was the gloomy night which met his eyes as he issued forth upon his murderous errand, than was the dark night within his traitorous breast.

Now, brethren, the same Saviour is this day in the midst of us. He walks in the midst of the seven gold candlesticks, his eyes are like a flame of fire, and he searcheth the reins and the hearts. *Think of this, you that are open sinners*, and yet dare to sit down at the table of Christ - swearers, drunkards, Sabbath-breakers, unclean. Ministers and elders may not know your sins; they are weak and short-sighted men. Your very neighbours may not know your sins; you may hide them from your own family. It is easy to deceive man; but to deceive Christ is impossible. He knows your whole history. He is present at every act of dishonesty - of filthiness - of folly. The darkness and the light are both alike to him.

Think of this, you that live in heart-sins, rolling sin beneath your tongue as a sweet morsel; you that put on the outward cloak of seriousness and sobriety, that you may jostle and sit down among the children of God; you that have the speech of Canaan in your lips, but hatred and malice, and the very breath of hell in your hearts; you that have the clothing of sheep, but inwardly are ravening wolves; you that are whited sepulchres, beautiful without, but within full of dead men's bones and all uncleanness.

Think of this, you that know yourselves unconverted, and yet have dared to sit down at the table of Christ. Christ knows you. Christ could point to you. Christ could name you - Christ could give the sop to you. You may be hidden to all the world, but you are naked and open to the eyes of him with whom you have to do. Oh! that you would fall down beneath his piercing glance, and say: 'God be merciful to me, a sinner!' Oh! that every one of you would say: 'Lord, is it I?'

2. The second argument which Christ made use of to melt and win the heart of Judas was his love: I have loved thee, Judas, and came to save thee.

This was plainly his intention when washing the disciples' feet. He did not shrink from the traitor's feet. Yes, he not only stooped to wash the feet of those who were to forsake him and flee - he not only washed the feet of Peter, who was before cock-crow to deny him with oaths and curses - but he also washed the feet of Judas, the very feet which had gone, two days before, to the meeting of priests in Caiaphas' palace, where he sold the Saviour for thirty pieces of silver, the value of a slave; and it was in his hearing he spoke the gentle words: 'If I wash thee not, thou hast no part with me.'

If then, the Saviour's washing the feet of the eleven was so blessed a proof of his tenderness to his own disciples, how much more is his washing the feet of him who (he knew) had betrayed him, a proof of his love to sinners, even the chief! He willed not the death of Judas. He wills not the death of any one of you.

You think that, because you have betrayed the Saviour, and come to the feast without any warrant or title, an unbidden intruder, therefore Jesus cannot love you. Alas! this shows your own heart, but not Christ's heart. Behold Jesus washing the feet of Judas, and wiping them with the towel wherewith he was girded! Behold his anxiety to awaken and to win the heart of the traitor Judas! And then think how, the more you are a traitor and a betrayer, the more does Jesus pity you, and wait upon you, willing still to wash and to save you, saying, 'Turn ye, turn ye, why will ye die?'

The *second* instance of Jesus' love to the traitor is, when he had sat down again, and was eating the Passover along with the other eleven, he did not shrink from eating meat with the traitor. Yes; he not only sat down to eat with the eleven who were to forsake him and flee; he not only allowed John to recline on his bosom, and Peter to sit at the table; but he suffered Judas to dip his hand in the very same dish with him, even when he knew that he was fulfilling that prophecy which is written: 'He that eateth bread with me, hath lifted up his heel against me.' It was a blessed proof of the Saviour's love to his believing disciples, as is recorded by Luke, when he said: 'With desire have I desired to eat this Passover with you before I suffer.'

One would have thought that to the eye of the Saviour this Passover must have appeared covered with threatening clouds, involved in the deep gloom of the garden of Gethesemane, and the bloody cross from which the sun himself hid his beams. You always find, that when you are in immediate expectation of some calamity, it renders gloomy and uninviting every event that bespeaks its near approach. You would have thought, then, that the human soul of Jesus must have shrunk back from this Passover with horror. But no; he felt the shrinking of humanity which more plainly showed itself in the garden; yet his love for his own disciples was stronger than all beside, and made him look forward to this Passover, when he was to picture out to them his dying love more clearly than ever, with intense desire: 'With desire have I desired to eat this Passover with you before I suffer.' But how much more wonderful is the proof of the Saviour's love to the unbelieving - to those who care not for him, but are his betrayers and murderers - when, with such divine complacency, he dips his hand in the same dish with Judas, and tells him, at the same time, that he does it not through ignorance, but that the prophecy might be fulfilled: 'He that eateth bread with me, hath lifted up the heel against me.'

Ah! my unbelieving friends, I know well the dark suspicions that lurk in your bosoms. Because you have done everything against Christ, you think that he cannot have any love for you. But behold, dark and proud sinners, how lovingly, how tenderly, he tries, if it may be, to awaken and to win over the heart of Judas! And then think how anxious he is this day to win and awaken you, though you are of sinners the chief - to bow that brazen neck, to break that heart of adamant, to wring a tear from those eyes that never wept for sin.

The *third* instance of Jesus' love to the traitor is, his faithful declaration of his danger to him: 'The Son of man goeth, as it is written of him; but woe unto that man by whom the Son of man is betrayed! It had been good for that man if he had never been born.' In the two former instances Jesus had shown his love, by showing how willing he was to save him to the very uttermost - that he would bear all things to save him. But now he uses another way - he shows him the terror of the Lord, tells him that if he will persist, 'it had been good for him that he had not been born.' As a mother, when she wishes her child to take some wholesome medicine, first wins upon its love, and then, if that will not do, tries to win upon its fears; with the same more than mother's tenderness did Jesus first try to win upon the affections, and now upon the fears of Judas.

And he is the same Saviour this day in the upper chambers of the universe that he was that night in the upper chamber at Jerusalem; and he sends his messengers to you to carry the same messages of kindness and of love. It is only in love that he threatens you. And, oh! that in love we might speak the threatening to you - that if you have no part in Jesus, and yet, by sitting down at his table, are becoming guilty of the body and blood of our Lord, it were better for you that you had not been born.

It is a happy thing to live; there is a blessedness which cannot be expressed in having life. The fly that lives but for a day, the veriest worm or insect that crawls upon the ground, has an amount of blessedness, in the very fact that it lives, which it is far beyond the skill of man to calculate. To breathe, to move, to feel the morning sun and the evening breeze, to look out upon the green world and the blue sky; all this is happiness immense, immeasurable. It never can be said of a fly or worm, that it were better never born; but, alas! it may be said of some of you: if you are living, but not living united to Christ; if you are sitting at the table of Christ, and yet unconverted - it had been good for you that you had not been born.

Ah! my friends, there was once a heathen man who always wept, and got the name of the Weeping Philosopher. One would almost think that he had known this truth which we preach unto you - that if that union which you make with the bread and wine at the holy table be not a picture and a seal of the union between your soul and the Saviour of sinners, you had far better never have been born. Better not to be, than to be only in hell. 'They shall wish to die, and shall not be able; they shall seek to die, and death shall flee from them.'

The *fourth* and last instance of Jesus' love to the traitor is the most touching of all. After the supper was over, *Jesus was troubled in spirit*, and testified and said: 'Verily, verily, I say unto you, that one of you shall betray me.' It was but a few days before that he came riding down the declivity of Mount Olivet upon an ass's colt; and his disciples, behind and before, were all rejoicing and praising God, crying 'Hosanna!' and Jesus - what was he doing? He was weeping: 'When he came near, he beheld the city, and wept over it, saying, If thou hadst known, even thou, at least in this thy day, the things that belong unto thy peace! but now they are hid from thine eyes.' He wept over the very city which he doomed to destruction.

And just so here: when his disciples on every hand were filled with a holy joy, and John most of all rejoicing, for he lay in the bosom of Immanuel, what was Christ doing - the author of all their joy? He was heavy and troubled in spirit. He was always the man of sorrows, and acquainted with grief, but now a ruffle of deeper sorrow came over the placid calm of his holy features. He was troubled in spirit, and said, 'Verily, verily, I say unto you, One of you shall betray me.' He had tried all arguments to move his betrayer; he had unbosomed the tenderness of his love; he had shown the dreadfulness of his anger; but when he saw that all would not do to move his hard heart, when he saw the heartless unconcern with which Judas could swallow down the bread, and share in the blessed cup, the spirit of the Saviour sank within him; and the last effort of his love to awaken the impenitent murderer was to unbosom the depth of his sorrows, and to breathe out, with many sighs, the words: 'Verily, verily, I say unto you, that one of you shall betray me.'

My friends, there may be some within these walls with a heart as hard as that of Judas. Like Judas, you are about to partake of the most moving ordinance the world ever saw; like Judas, you may eat of the bread and drink of the wine; and like Judas, your heart may grow harder, and your life more sinful than ever. And you think, then, that Jesus is your enemy? But what does the Bible say? Look here: he is troubled in spirit; he weeps as he did over Jerusalem. Yes; he that once shed his blood for you, now sheds his tears for you. Immanuel grieves that ye will not be saved. He grieved over Judas, and he grieves over you. He wept over Jerusalem, and he weeps over you. He has no pleasure that you should perish - he had far rather that you would turn and have life.

There is not within these walls one of you so hard, so cruel, so base, so unmoved, so far from grace and godliness, so Judas-like, that Jesus does not grieve over your hardness, that you will still resist all his love, that you will still love death, and wrong your own soul. Oh! that the tears which the Saviour shed over your lost and perishing souls might fall upon your hearts like drops of liquid fire; that you might no more sit unmelted under that wondrous love that burns with so vehement a flame, which many waters cannot quench, which all your sins cannot smother - the love which passeth knowledge. Amen.

Larbert , August, 1836

7. I the LORD have called thee in righteousness

Thus saith God the LORD, he that created the heavens, and stretched them out; he that spread forth the earth, and that which cometh out of it; he that giveth breath unto the people upon it, and spirit to them that walk therein: I the LORD have called thee in righteousness, and will hold thine hand, and will keep thee, and give thee for a covenant of the people, for a light of the Gentiles; to open the blind eyes, to bring out the prisoners from the prison, and them that sit in darkness out of the prison-house. I am the LORD; that is my name: and my glory will I not give to another, neither my praise to graven images (Isaiah 42:5-8).

In this passage we have some of the most wonderful words that ever were uttered in the world. It is not a man speaking to a man. It is not even

God speaking to a man. It is God speaking to his own Son. Oh, who would not listen? It is as if we were secretly admitted into the counsel of God, as if we stood behind the curtains of his dwelling-place, or were hidden in the clefts of the rock, and overheard the words of the eternal Father to the eternal Son. Now sometimes when you overhear a conversation on earth, between two poor perishing worms, you think it is worth treasuring up; you remember what they said; you repeat it over and over again. Oh! then, when you overhear a conversation in heaven, when God the Father speaks, and God the Son stands to receive his words, will you not listen? Will you not lay up all these sayings in your heart?

God tells the Son: (1) That he had called him to this service - had passed over all his angels, and chosen him for this difficult work. (2) He tells him that he is not to shrink from the difficulties of it. There is an ocean of wrath to wade through, but fear not; I will hold thee by the hand - I will keep thee. (3) He tells him that he must be given as a covenant Saviour. However dear to his heart, still, says God, 'I will give thee.' (4) He encourages him by the great benefit to be gained - that he would be a light to whole nations of poor, blind, captive sinners. (5) That in all this he would have his glory: 'My glory will I not give to another, nor my praise to graven images.'

Doctrine: God has provided the Saviour, and alone can reveal him; and he will keep his glory to himself.

1. God provided the Saviour.

He says here: 'I have called thee in righteousness.' The meaning is: I have called thee to do this work of righteousness, to work out this salvation, which shall show me to be a righteous God. God did, as it were, look round all the creatures, to see whom he would call to this great work, of being a Saviour of lost sinners. *He looked upon the earth*, through all its families; but there was none that understood, there was none that did seek God. Every man had his own curse to bear; no man could give a ransom for the soul of his brother, for the ransom of the soul was precious. *He looked round all the blooming angels*, as if to say, Who will go for me? Seraphim and cherubim all stood, veiling their faces with their wings; but he saw that none of them could bear infinite wrath. They are only creatures; they would be crushed eternally under the weight of my wrath. These will not do. *He looked into his own bosom*. There was his eternal Son, his dear Son, his well-beloved Son.

Oh, this will do! I have found a ransom; I have laid help on one who is mighty. My Son, I have called thee in righteousness.

Learn how complete a Saviour Christ is. God did not choose a man to this great work. He did not choose an angel. He passed by them all, and chose his Son. Why? Because he saw none other could be a sufficient Saviour. If Christ had not been enough, God never would have called him to it. God knew well the weight of his own wrath; and, therefore, he provided an almighty back to bear it. Trembling sinner, do not doubt the completeness of Christ. God knew all your sins and your wrath when he chose Christ - that they were both infinite; and therefore he chose an almighty, an infinite Saviour. Oh! hide in him, and you are complete in him.

2. God upheld the Saviour.

'I will hold thine hand, and will keep thee.' The figure here seems taken from a father and his little child. When a little child has to go over some very rough road, or to travel in the darkness, or to wade through some deep waters, he says to his father, 'I fear I shall be lost; I shall not be able to go through.' 'Nay, do not fear,' the father answers: 'I will hold thine hand; I will keep thee.' Such are the words of the Father to his dear Son. I would not have dared to have imagined them, if I had not found them in the Bible.

When God called his Son to the work, it could not but be a fearful work in his eyes. Christ knew well the infinite number of men's sins; for he is the searcher of hearts and trier of reins. He knew also the infinite weight of God's anger against these sins; he saw the dark clouds of infinite vengeance that were ready to burst over the head of sinners; he saw the infinite deluge of eternal wrath that was to drown for ever the guilty world. And, oh! how dreadful his Father's anger was in his eyes; for he had known nothing but his infinite love from all eternity. Oh! how could he bear to lie down under that wrath? How could he bear to exchange the smile of his Father's love for the dark frown of his Father's anger? How could he bear, for the sake of vile sinners, to exchange the caresses of that God who is love, for the piercings and bruisings of his almighty hand? Surely the very thought would be agony. God here comforts his Son under the view: Yon sea of wrath is deep, its waves are dreadful; but 'I will hold thine hand; I will keep thee.'

Learn from this how dreadful the sufferings of Christ were. He needed God to hold his hand. He was God himself, thought it no robbery to be equal with God. He had the Spirit given to him without measure: 'I have put my Spirit upon him'. But all that would not do - God the Father must hold his hand too. Oh! think what a weight must have been crushing and bruising the Lamb of God, when Father, Son and Holy Ghost combined their force to hold him up. Oh! think what a depth of agony must have been upon him, when he cried: 'What shall I say? Father, save me from this hour; but for this cause came I unto this hour. My soul is exceeding sorrowful, even unto death. Take away this cup from me;' and when the Father answered him: 'I will hold thine hand, I will keep thee.' Oh, my friends, this is a great deep! Cry, 'O the depth of the riches, both of the wisdom and knowledge of God! How unsearchable are his judgments, and his ways past finding out!'

Learn the greatness of your sins. Remember Christ had no sins of his own. No wrath was due to himself; all that wrath he bore was ours. You that are believers, you have but a small sense of the greatness of your sins. Oh! look here; see God holding the hand of his Son, while he wades through that sea of wrath! Oh! surely a look at a suffering Christ should keep you in the dust for ever. You must never open your mouth any more. And, oh! will you not love him who so loved you, who lay down under these surges and billows of God's wrath for you?

You that are unconverted, see here the dreadful wrath that is over your souls. You think your sins are very few, and God will not be very angry. This is natural; all natural men think this; and yet see here how dreadful the wrath is that is over you. Even Christ trembled and started back when he came to bear it: and how will you do? You are not the Son of God. You have no divinity within you, as Christ had: how will you be able to bear the bruisings and lashings of God's infinite anger? You have not the Spirit of God given to you as Christ had, without measure: how will you be able to stand under the outpourings of his eternal indignation? You have not God to take you by the hand. God is not your God, not your friend; he has nowhere said that he will hold you by the hand: ah! how will you wade through an eternal and bottomless sea of wrath? How will you contend and fight against the fiery billows, where there is no creature, in heaven or in earth, to hold you by the hand?

Oh! my friends, it is because you are blind that you have no fears. Christ saw all that is before you, and it made him tremble; you do not see it, and therefore you do not tremble. You can be happy, and smile, and sleep, and enjoy yourselves; but your day of trembling is at hand. Ah! woe is me; how will you stand upon the shore of that fiery sea? How will you hang back, and wish you had some one to hold you by the hand; but it will be all in vain. Oh! that you were wise, that you would remember your latter end, that you would consider this.

Learn God's great hand in Christ's work. When a father guides his child through some dark part of the road, or through some rapid stream, holding him by the hand, this shows that the father is interested in the journey of the child; so, when God says, 'I will hold thee by the hand', this shows that God has a great hand in Christ's work. In writing, if you hold a child's hand, and guide the pen, then you have a great hand in the writing. Just so did God hold the hand of the Saviour. The work is God's as much as Christ's. Oh! that we might give him all the glory! Remember, he will not give his glory to another.

3. God gave Christ for a covenant.

'I will give thee for a covenant of the people.' 'God so loved the world, that he gave his only begotten Son, that whosoever believeth on him should not perish'. 'Herein is love; not that we loved God.' God not only provided the Saviour, and upheld him, but he gave him - gave him away, to be a covenant Saviour of the people, and a light to lighten the Gentiles. When Abraham bound his son Isaac upon the altar and lifted up the knife to strike, this was giving away his son at the command of God. This is just what God did. He took his Son out of his bosom, and gave him away to be bound, to be a covenant Saviour of the people. There are not more wonderful words in the whole Bible than these: 'I will give thee.' 'God spared not his own Son, but freely delivered him up to the death for us all.' The Son was infinitely dear to the Father. God cannot but love that which is perfectly holy and beautiful. Now, such was Christ. From all eternity there had been the outgoings of love and infinite admiration from the bosom of the Father towards his well-beloved Son. Canst thou part with me? Canst thou give me up to the garden and the cross? 'I will give thee.' Sinners were infinitely vile in the sight of the Father. God cannot but hate that which is enmity and rebellion to himself. 'He is of purer eyes than to behold iniquity.' How loathsome and hateful this world must have been in his eyes, where every heart was enmity against him! Canst thou give me up for such sinners, for the sake of such vile worms? 'Yes, I will give thee.'

Learn the intense love of God for sinners. He spared not his own Son. Herein is love. He loved the happiness of his Son; but he loved the salvation of sinners more. He loved to have his Son in his bosom; but he loved more to have sinners brought into his bosom. He cast out his Son, in order to take us in. Oh! sinner, how will you escape, if you neglect so great a salvation?

Learn that God must have the glory of this. He will not give his glory to another. Some awakened persons look to God as an angry inexorable judge, but to Christ as a smiling Saviour, that comes between us and an angry Father. Now, remember you will never come to peace as long as you think this. This is robbing God of his glory. You must believe in Christ and believe in God. God wishes you to honour the Son even as you honour the Father; but not more than you honour the Father. You will never come to peace till you look to Christ as the gift of God, till you see that the heart of God and Christ are one in this matter, till God open a window in his breast, and show you the love which provided, upheld, and gave up the Son.

4. God gave Christ for a light.

'I will give thee for a light.' It is God that causes the sun to rise every morning, so that the dark shades of evening are scattered before him; so it is God that makes Christ rise upon the soul of a sinner.

(1) By nature, men have blind eyes. They do not know the beauty of Christ. They read of him in the Word, hear him preached, talked of; they see no form nor comeliness in him, no beauty that they should desire him. They have eyes, but they see not.

(2) By nature, men are bound in prison. They serve diverse lusts and pleasures; they are bound to selfishness, and pride, and luxury, and lust: these things compass them about as with a chain.

(3) By nature, men sit in a dark prison-house. They are bound, but do not see that they are bound; they do not see their misery. They sit; they do not strive to get free, but sit contented and happy in their darksome dungeon. Oh! unconverted souls, what a picture this is of your condition. Blind, in prison, contented in the dark dungeon. You will say: I feel it not; I am contented and happy. Ah! does not this just show that this word is true: you are blind; you do not see your misery? When a blind man is in darkness, he feels no pain from it. You are chained; you do not struggle; you sit still in the prison-house. I have often thought that your very ease and contentment might awaken you to think that all is not right.

Now, learn how a change comes: 'I will give thee for a light of the Gentiles.' It is all the gift of God. Oh! I fear we little understand this.

There is much robbing God of his glory, even among Christians. When God causes the sun to rise, then nothing can make darkness. The mists and fogs cannot keep back the beams of the sun; so, when God causes Christ to rise on the soul, then there is light. Revealing Christ does the whole work for the soul. It awakens; it wins; it draws; it makes free; it makes holy.

Question: Has Christ been made to rise upon your soul? If not, then you are still blind, still in chains, and in the dark dungeon; you have neither peace nor holiness. Oh! seek it from God; cry to him, that Christ may give you light.

But, if Christ has been made to rise on your soul, happy are you. You were sometime darkness, but now you are light in the Lord. Walk as children of the light. See who did it, and give him the praise. It is the Lord. God gave Christ to be a light to thy soul. Give him, and him alone, the glory. 'My glory I will not give to another.' (1) Do not give the praise to yourself. Do not say, my own wisdom or my own prayers have gotten me this. It was all undeserved mercy to the chief of sinners. 'My glory I will not give to another.' (2) Do not give the glory to ministers. They are often the instruments of bringing souls to Christ, but they cannot make Christ arise on the soul, any more than they can make the sun to rise on the earth. We can point to the sun, though we cannot make it rise; so, we can point you to Christ, but cannot make him rise on your soul. The work is God's, and he will have the glory. I believe the work is greatly hindered amongst us from the cause mentioned.

Plead with God to fulfil his word, that Christ may be a light to the nations. It is as easy with God to make Christ rise on many souls as upon one. Show him that it is for his glory that a nation be born in a day. Give him no rest till he pour down the Spirit on all our families, till there be a great looking unto Jesus, and rejoicing in him. Take thine own glory, O Lord; give it to no other, neither thy praise to graven images.

St Peter's, January 7, 1838

8. Return unto me

Remember these, O Jacob and Israel; for thou art my servant: I have
formed thee; thou art my servant: O Israel, thou shalt not be forgotten of
me. I have blotted out, as a thick cloud, thy transgressions, and, as a cloud,
thy sins: return unto me; for I have redeemed thee (Isaiah 44:21-22).

In these words God contrasts the happy condition of his chosen people
with that of the poor blind idolaters whom he had been describing in the
verses before. Ah! my friends, to the eye of man, there may be little
difference between the children of the wicked one and the children of
God; but, to the eye of God, they are as different as the chaff from the
wheat, as the lily from the thorn. Of you that are Christless, God says:
'He feedeth on ashes' (verse 20); but to you that are his children:
'Remember these, O Jacob.' May God open our eyes to see wonders out
of his scripture!

1. All that have come to Christ are forgiven: 'I have blotted out, as
a thick cloud, thy transgressions, and, as a cloud, thy sins' (verse 22).

1. *Observe the completeness of their forgiveness*: 'I have blotted out as
a thick cloud.' This complete forgiveness is in many ways showed forth
in the Bible.

First, it is compared to the change produced on clothes by washing
or dyeing them: 'Though your sins be as scarlet, yet shall they be as
white as snow' (Isaiah 1:18); and again: 'Unto him that loved us, and
washed us from our sins in his blood.'

Second, again, to something covered over: 'Blessed is the man
whose transgression is forgiven, whose sin is covered.' And Jesus says:
'Buy of me white raiment, that thou mayest be clothed, and that the
shame of thy nakedness do not appear.'

Third, again, it is compared to something lost. Hezekiah says: 'Thou
hast cast all my sins behind thy back'; Micah: 'Thou wilt cast all their
sins into the depths of the sea.' But still they may be near at hand? No:
'As far as east is distant from the west' (Psalm 103:12). But if God were
to seek for them? 'In those days, and in that time ... shall the iniquity of
Israel be sought for, and there shall be none; and the sins of Judah, and
they shall not be found' (Jeremiah 50:20).

Fourth, to something forgotten: 'Thy sins and thine iniquities will

I remember no more'; 'All his transgressions that he hath done, they shall not be mentioned unto him.'

Fifth, to something blotted out. Although they be washed, covered, lost, forgotten, yet they will still remain in God's record? Yes, they will; but how? - *Blotted out.*

Any of you that believe in Jesus, do you take the Son of God as your Surety? Take this word to yourself. See what the page will be like on which thy sins are written. It will be one great blot, one thick cloud. When you look on the clouds, can you read anything written there? No more can God read any of thy sins, O believer in Jesus.

2. *Observe, it is present forgiveness.* It is not, I will blot out; but, 'I have blotted out.' Some say: I hope God will forgive me. Ah! my friends, you greatly mistake the Bible. A present forgiveness is offered to you. The moment a soul closes with Christ, that moment is this word true of him: 'I have blotted out.' 'There is now no condemnation to them that are in Christ Jesus.'

Question: Has God blotted out your sins?

First, most say, I don't know; I never inquired. Oh! sinner, if you never inquired, then I will answer for you: there is not one of them blotted out. Every evil thought, word and deed you have done is written against you - you will meet them all another day. A deceived heart hath turned thee aside, and thou dost not know that there is a lie in thy right hand.

Second, some say, It is impossible to tell. I never saw the book of God's remembrance. How can I tell? True, you never saw the book of God's remembrance; and yet there is another book, and if you would search it much, and believe the word concerning Jesus, you would come to know that you are forgiven. Oh, yes! It is quite possible. David tasted it, and thousands since David have blessed God for forgiving all their iniquities. The woman that touched the hem of Christ's garment felt in herself that she was made whole. She was no physician, and yet she knew that she was well. When a man has a burden on his back, if you lift it off, he knows it at once; so does the heavy-laden soul that comes to Jesus. He finds rest.

3. *Observe who blots*: 'I, even I, am he that blotteth out thy transgressions' (Isaiah 43:25).

First, some try to blot out their own sins: I will be grieved, and sorry for my sins, says one. I will blot them out with tears. I will pray to God, and cover my past sins with my earnest prayers, says another. I will mend my life, and cover my naked soul with good deeds, says another. But no; this is all vain - God alone can blot out. Either he will do it, or it will not be done: 'I, even I, am he.' *Second, some hope that Christ will blot out their sins*, unknown to the Father. They think that Christ is very willing to be a Saviour, but not so the Father. But no; Christ and the Father are one. If you come to Christ, God himself will do it, and will tell you: 'I have done it.'

Speak to unforgiven souls: Unhappy man! You have many pleasures, and many friends; but one thing you want - the forgiveness of sins. Do you think you would not be happier, lighter in heart, if you were forgiven? Oh! how miserable are all your daily employments and pleasures, when you know that hell is opening its mouth for you. God has never blotted out your sins; yet you might be forgiven: 'Unto you, O men, I call; and my words are to the sons of men.' Come to Christ, and God will abundantly pardon.

2. All that have come to Christ are God's servants.

'Thou art my servant.' Two reasons are given: (1) 'I have redeemed thee'; (2) 'I have formed thee.'

First, because redeemed

When a man consents that Christ shall be his Surety, he feels that he is not his own, but bought with a price. So David felt: 'Truly I am thy servant; I am thy servant, and the son of thine handmaid: thou hast loosed my bonds.' So Paul felt, when he lay gasping on the ground: 'Lord, what wilt thou have me to do?' Before conversion, the unconverted thinks that he is his own: may I not do what I will with mine own? He was the willing slave of the devil. But when he sees the price laid down for him, he feels that the Lord has redeemed him out of the house of bondage. Now he says: I am the Lord's. Now he is more the servant of the Lord than ever he was of the devil. Oh! dear Christians, would that I could see more of this among you - a devoting of yourselves unto the Lord: 'For thou art my servant.'

Second, because formed by God: 'I made thee, and formed thee from the womb' (Isaiah 44:2).

The whole work of grace is the Lord's doing, and wondrous in our eyes. Paul says: 'It pleased the Lord, who separated me from my mother's womb, to reveal his Son in me;' and God to Jeremiah: 'Before I formed thee in the belly, I knew thee; and before thou camest out of the womb, I sanctified thee.' God marks his own from their mother's womb. When infants, God treasures up every prayer for them. Every mother's tears he puts into his bottle; her sighs into his book. In boyhood, he preserves their souls from death, gives them times of awakening, fixes words in their memory: 'I girded thee, though thou hast not known me.' When his time comes, he guides them to some fitting ministry; or, by some sore trial, awakens, leads to Christ, draws, wins, comforts, builds the soul. He is a faithful Creator. 'Sing, O heavens, for the Lord hath done it.' That soul becomes a servant indeed.

Some of you know that God has formed you. You can trace his hand, guiding you ever since you were born, girding you when you did not know him, in the mother that wrestled for you, in dear ones that prayed for you, now in their lonely grave, in the ministers that you have been brought to, in the texts they have been guided to. O be the Lord's servant! Let him bore thine ear. Bear in your body the marks of the Lord Jesus.

3. Souls in Christ shall not be forgotten of God.
'Thou shalt not be forgotten of me.' The children of God often think their God has forgotten them. Often, when they fall into sin and darkness, they feel cut off from God - as if his mercies were clean gone for ever. But learn here that God never forgets the soul that is in Christ Jesus.

(1) So it was with Moses in the land of Midian. For forty years he thought God had forgotten his people. He wandered about as a shepherd in the wilderness for forty years, sad and desolate. But had God really forgotten his people? No; he appeared in a flaming fire in a bush, and said, 'I have seen, I have seen the affliction of my people, and I have heard their groaning, and am come down to deliver them; for *I know their sorrows.*' God knows thy sorrows, O soul in Christ.

(2) So it was with David, in Psalm 77, 13 and 31.

(3) So it was with Hezekiah, when God told him he must die. Hezekiah wept sore: 'Like a crane or a swallow, so did I chatter; I did mourn as a dove: mine eyes fail with looking upward: O LORD, I am oppressed; undertake for me' (Isaiah 38:14). Did God forget him? No; God said this word to him: 'I have heard thy prayer, I have seen thy tears:

I will add unto thy days fifteen years.' God never forgets the soul in Christ.

(4) So shall it be with God's ancient people: 'Zion said, The LORD hath forsaken me, and my Lord hath forgotten me. Can a woman forget her sucking child, that she should not have compassion on the son of her womb? Yea, they may forget, yet will I not forget thee' (Isaiah 49: 14,15).

(5) So it is in the words of the text: 'Thou shalt not be forgotten of me.' The world may forget thee; thy friends, thy father, thy mother, may forsake thee; yet 'thou shalt not be forgotten of me.'

A word to souls in Christ. The Lord cannot forget you. If you stood before God in your own righteousness, then I see how you might be separated from his love and care; for your frames vary, your goodness is like the morning cloud and the early dew. But you stand before him in Christ: and Christ is the same yesterday, today, and for ever. You shall be held in everlasting remembrance. The world may forget you; your friends may forget you: for this is a forgetting world. You may not have a tombstone over your grave; but God will not forget you. Christ will put your name beside that of his faithful martyr, Antipas. In life, in death, in eternity, thou 'shalt not be forgotten of me.'

4. A redeemed soul should return unto God: 'Return unto me.'

The sin and misery of every natural soul is in going away from God. Adam hid himself from the presence of God. So Isaiah complains: 'They have provoked the Holy One of Israel to anger: they are gone away backward.' And God says: 'What iniquity have your fathers found in me, that they are gone far from me?'; 'Can a maid forget her ornaments, or a bride her attire? Yet my people have forgotten me days without number.' But when a soul has come to Christ, there is no more reason why he should return unto God. 'Return unto me, for I have redeemed thee'; 'Through Jesus, we both have access by one Spirit unto the Father'; 'I am the way; no man cometh unto the Father but by me.'

Dear brethren in Christ, let me entreat you to return unto the Father. *Come into the arms of his love.* When God has redeemed a soul, he wants to have him in his arms; he wants to fall upon his neck and kiss him. See how he tries to win the soul! - tells all that he has done for him, all that he will do; and adds: 'Return unto me; for I have redeemed thee.' Oh! why are ye fearful, ye of little faith? Why do you hang back, and will not venture near to God? Why do you not run to him? Some say: I am afraid of past sins. Oh! but hear his word: 'I have blotted them out. Return unto me, for I have redeemed thee.' Some say: I am afraid he cannot wish such a sinful, weak thing as I beside him! Oh! foolish, and slow of heart to believe his own word. Does he not speak plain enough and kind enough? 'Return unto me; for I have redeemed thee.'

Come into communion with him; daily walk with him. Enoch walked with God. Once Adam walked with God in Paradise, as easily, Herbert says, 'as you may walk from one room to another'. He talked with him concerning his judgments. Oh! come unto thy God, redeemed, forgiven soul. Acquaint thyself with God, and be at peace. Come to him; do not rest short of him. You think it a great thing to know a lively Christian; oh! how infinitely better to know God. It is your infinite blessedness. You will get more knowledge in one hour with God, than in all your life spent with man. You will get more holiness from immediate conversing with God, than from all other means of grace put together. Indeed, the means are empty vanity, unless you come to God in them. 'Return unto me; for I have redeemed thee.'

To the backslider. Guilty soul, you have been within the veil; you know the peace that Jesus gives, you know the joy of the smile of God. But you have left all this, and gone away backward. Guilty soul, you have done worse than the world. Worldly men never served Christ as you have done. They have spat on him, and buffeted him, and crucified him; but you have wounded him in the house of his friends: 'It was not an enemy that reproached me; then I could have borne it; but thou, my friend and mine acquaintance.' Guilty soul, what says God unto thee? 'Depart, thou cursed?' No; 'Return unto me; for I have redeemed thee;' 'Return, O backsliding daughter; for I am married unto you.' Return, sinner, thy God calleth thee - the God that chose thee, the Saviour that died for thee, the Comforter that renewed thee. 'Return unto me; for I have redeemed thee.'

St Peter's, July 8, 1838

9. I will pour water

> For I will pour water upon him that is thirsty, and floods upon the dry
> ground: I will pour my Spirit upon thy seed, and my blessing upon
> thine offspring: and they shall spring up as among the grass, as
> willows by the water courses (Isaiah 44:3,4).

These words describe a time of refreshing. There are no words in the
whole Bible that have been oftener in my heart and oftener on my tongue
than these, since I began my ministry among you. And yet, although
God has never, from the very first day, left us without some tokens of
his presence, he has never fulfilled this promise; and I have taken it up
today, in order that we may consider it more fully, and plead it more
anxiously with God. For, as Rutherford said, 'My record is on high, that
your heaven would be like two heavens to me; and the salvation of you
all, like two salvations to me.'

1. Who is the author in a work of grace? It is God: '*I will pour.*'
(1) It is God who *begins* a work of anxiety in dead souls. So it is in
Zechariah 12:10: 'I will pour out the Spirit of grace and supplications,
and they shall look upon me whom they have pierced, and mourn.' And
so the promise is in John 16:8,9: 'When he is come, he will convince the
world of sin; because they believe not on me.' And so is the passage of
Ezekiel 37:9: 'Come from the four winds, O breath, and breathe upon
these slain, that they may live.' If any of you have been awakened, and
made to beat upon the breast, it is God, and God alone, that hath done
it. If ever we are to see a time of widespread concern among your
families, children asking their parents, parents asking their children,
people asking their ministers, 'What must I do to be saved?'; if ever we
are to see such a time as Mr Edwards speaks of, when there was scarcely
a single person in the whole town left unconcerned about the great
things of the eternal world - God must pour out the Spirit: 'I will pour.'
(2) It is God who *carries* on the work, leading awakened persons to
Christ. 'I will pour out my Spirit upon all flesh, and whosoever shall call
upon the name of the LORD shall be delivered' (Joel 2:28,32). And again,
in John 16:8: 'He shall convince the world of righteousness.' If ever we
are to see souls flying like a cloud, and like doves, to Jesus Christ, if ever
we are to see multitudes of you fleeing to that city of refuge, if ever we
are to see parents rejoicing over their children as new-born, husbands

rejoicing over their wives, and wives over their husbands - God must pour out the Spirit. He is the author and finisher of a work of grace: 'I will pour.'

(3) It is God who *enlarges* his people. You remember, in Zechariah 4, how the olive-trees supplied the golden candlesticks with oil; they emptied the golden oil out of themselves. If there is little oil, the lamps burn dim; if much oil, the lamps begin to blaze. Ah! if ever we are to see you who are children of God greatly enlarged, your hearts filled with joy, your lips filled with praises, if ever we are to see you growing like willows beside the water-courses, filled with all the fullness of God, God must pour down his Spirit. He must fulfil his word; for he is the Alpha and Omega, the author and finisher of a work of grace: 'I will pour.'

First Lesson - Learn to look beyond ministers for a work of grace. God has given much honour to his ministers: but not the pouring out of the Spirit. He keeps that in his own hand: 'I will pour.' 'It is not by might, nor by power, but by my Spirit, saith the Lord of hosts.' Alas! we would have little hope, if it depended upon ministers; for where are our men of might now? God is able to do it today as he was at the day of Pentecost; but men are taken up with ministers and not with God. As long as you look to ministers, God cannot pour; for you would say it came from man. Ah! cease from man, whose breath is in his nostrils. One would think we would be humbled in the dust by this time. In how many parishes of Scotland has God raised up faithful men, who cease not day and night to warn every one with tears! And yet still the heavens are like brass, and the earth like iron. Why? Just because your eye is on man, and not on God. Oh! look off man to him, and he will pour; and his shall be all the glory.

Second Lesson - Learn good hope of revival in our day.

Third Lesson - Learn that we should pray. We are often for preaching to awaken others; but we should be more concerned with prayer. Prayer is more powerful than preaching. It is prayer that gives preaching all its power. I observe that some Christians are very ready to censure ministers, and to complain of their preaching, of their coldness, their unfaithfulness. God forbid that I should ever defend unfaithful preaching, or coldness, or deadness, in the ambassador of Christ! May my right hand sooner forget its cunning! But I do say, Where lies the blame of unfaithfulness? Where, but in the want of faithful praying? Why, the very hands of Moses would have fallen down, had they not been held up by his faithful people. Come, then, ye wrestlers with God, ye that climb Jacob's ladder, ye that wrestle Jacob's wrestling - strive you with God, that he may fulfil his word: 'I will pour.'

2. God begins with thirsty souls: 'I will pour water upon him that is thirsty.'

1. Awakened persons.
There are often souls that have been a long time under the awakening hand of God. God has led them into trouble, but not into peace. He has taken them down into the wilderness, and there they wander about in search of refreshing waters; but they find none. They wander from mountain to hill seeking rest, and finding none; they go from well to well, seeking a drop of water to cool their tongue; they go from minister to minister, from sacrament to sacrament, opening their mouth, and panting earnestly: yet they find no peace. These are thirsty souls. Now, it is a sweet thought that God begins with such: 'I will pour water upon him that is thirsty.'

The whole Bible shows that God has a peculiar tenderness for such as are thirsty. Christ, who is the express image of God, had a peculiar tenderness for them: 'The Lord God hath given me the tongue of the learned, that I should know how to speak a word in season to him that is weary.' 'Come unto me, all ye that are weary and heavy-laden, and I will give you rest.' 'If any man thirst, let him come unto me and drink.' Many of his cures were intended to win the hearts of these burdened souls. The woman that had spent all upon other physicians, and was nothing better, but rather worse, no sooner touched the hem of his garment than she was made whole. Another cried after him: 'Lord, help me,' yet he answered not a word; but at last said: 'O woman, great is thy faith; be it unto thee even as thou wilt.' Another was bowed down eighteen years; but Jesus laid his hands on her, and immediately she was made straight.

Weary sinner, (1) This is Jesus; this is what he wants to do for you: 'I will pour water upon him that is thirsty.' Only believe that he is willing and able, and it shall be done.

(2) Learn that it must come from his hand. In vain you go to other physicians; you will be nothing better, but rather worse. Wait on him; kneel and worship him, saying: 'Lord, help me.'

(3) Oh! long for a time of refreshing, that weary souls may be brought

into peace. If we go on in this every-day way, these burdened souls may perish, may sink uncomforted into the grave. Arise, and plead with God that he may arise and fulfil his word: 'I will pour water upon him that is thirsty.'

2. *Thirsty believers.* All believers should be thirsty; alas! few are. Signs:
(1) *Much thirst after the Word.*
When two travellers are going through the wilderness, you may know which of them is thirsty, by his always looking out for wells. How gladly Israel came to Elim, where were twelve wells of water, and seventy palm trees! So it is with thirsty believers: they love the Word, read and preached; they thirst for it more and more. Is it so with you, dear believing brethren? In Scotland, long ago, it used to be so. Often, after the blessing was pronounced, the people would not go away till they heard more. Ah! children of God, it is a fearful sign to see little thirst in you. I do not wonder much when the world stays away from our meetings for the Word and prayer; but, ah! when you do, I am dumb. My soul will weep in secret places for your pride. I say, God grant that we may not have a famine of the Word ere long.

(2) *Much prayer.*
When a little child is thirsty for its mother's breast, it will not keep silence; no more will a child of God who is thirsty. Thirst will lead you to the secret well, where you may draw unseen the living water. It will lead you to united prayer. If the town were in want of water, and thirst staring every man in the face, would you not meet one with another, and consult, and help to dig new wells? Now, the town is in want of grace - souls are perishing for lack of it, and you yourselves are languishing. Oh! meet to pray. 'If two of you shall agree on earth as touching anything that they shall ask, it shall be done for them of my Father which is in heaven.'

(3) *Desire to grow in grace.*
Some persons are contented when they come to Christ. They sink back, as it were, into an easy chair, they ask no more, they wish no more. This must not be. If you are thirsty believers, you will seek salvation as much after conversion as before it. 'Forgetting those things which are behind, and reaching forth unto those things which are before, press toward the mark for the prize of the high calling of God in Christ Jesus.'

To thirsty souls.
Dear children, I look for the first drops of grace among you, in answer
to your prayers, to fill your panting mouths. Oh, yes, he will pour. 'A
vineyard of red wine, I the LORD do keep it; I will water it every moment:
lest any hurt it, I will keep it night and day' (Isaiah 27:2,3). 'With joy
shall ye draw water out of the wells of salvation' (Isaiah 12:3).

3. God pours floods on the dry ground.
The dry ground represents those who are dead in trespasses and sins.
Just as you have seen the ground, in a dry summer, all parched and dry,
cracking and open, yet it speaks not; it asks not the clouds to fall: so is
it with most in our parishes. They are all dead and dry, parched and
withered, without a prayer for grace, without even a desire for it. Yet
what says God? 'I will pour floods upon them.' Marks:

1. *They do not pray.*
I believe there are many in our parishes who do not make a habit of secret
prayer, who, neither in their closet nor in the embowering shade, ever
pour out their heart to God. I believe there are many who are dropping
into hell who never so much as said: 'God, be merciful to me a sinner.'
Ah! these are the dry ground. Oh! it is sad to think that the souls that are
nearest to hell are the souls that pray least to be delivered from it.

2. *They do not wish a work of grace in their souls.*
I believe many of you came to the house of God today who would rather
lose house, home and friends, than have a work of grace done in your
heart. Nothing would terrify you so much as the idea that God might
make you a praying Christian. Ah! you are the dry ground; you love
death.

3. *Those who do not attend to the preached Word.*
I have heard anxious persons declare that they never heard a sermon in
all their life until they were awakened, that they regularly thought about
something else all the time. I believe this is the way with many of you.
You are the dry ground. What will God pour out on you? Floods - floods
of wrath? Oh! the mercy of God - it passes all understanding. You
deserve the flood that came on the world of the ungodly, but he offers
floods of blessing. You deserve the rain of Sodom; but, behold, he offers
floods of his Spirit.

First Lesson - Learn how much you are interested that there should be a work of grace in our day. You are the very persons who do not care about lively preaching, who ridicule prayer-meetings, and put a mock on secret prayer; and yet you are the very persons that are most concerned. Ah! poor dry-ground souls, you should be the first to cry out for lively ministers; you should go round the Christians, and on your bended knees, entreat them to come out to our prayer-meeting. You, more than all the rest, should wait for the fulfilment of this word; for if it come not, oh! what will become of you? Poor dead, dead souls, you cannot pray for yourselves! One by one, you will drop into a sad eternity.

Second Lesson - Learn, Christians, to pray for floods. It is God's word - he puts it into your mouth. Oh! do not ask for drops, when God offers floods. 'Open thy mouth and I will fill it.'

4. Effects.

1. *Saved souls will be like grass.*
They shall spring up as grass. So, in Psalm 72: 'They of the city shall be like grass of the earth.' Many will be awakened, many saved. At present, Christ's people are like a single lily amongst many thorns; but in a time of grace they shall be like grass. Count the blades of grass that spring in the clear shining after rain: so many shall Christ's people be. Count the drops of dew that come from the womb of the morning, shining like diamonds in the morning sun: so shall Christ's people be in a day of his power. Count the stars that sparkle in night's black mantle: so shall Abraham's seed be. Count the dust of the earth: so shall Israel be in the day of an outpoured Spirit. Oh! pray for an outpoured Spirit, ye men of prayer, that there may be many raised up in our day to call him blessed.

2. *Believers shall grow like willows*
There is nothing more distressing in our day than the want of growth among the children of God. They do not seem to press forward, they do not seem to be running a race. When I compare this year with last year, alas! where is the difference? - the same weakness, the same coldness; nay, I fear, greater languor in divine things. How different when the Spirit is poured out! They shall be like willows. You have seen the willow, how it grows - ceases not day or night, ever growing, ever shooting out new branches. Cut it down - it springs again. Ah! so would you be, dear Christians, if there were a flood-time of the Spirit, a day of Pentecost.

(1) Then there would be less care about your business and your workshop, more love of prayer and of sweet praises. (2) There would be more change in your heart - victory over the world, the devil, and the flesh. You would come out, and be separate. (3) In affliction, you would grow in sweet submission, humility, meekness.

There was a time in Scotland when Sabbath-days were growing days. Hungry souls came to the Word, and went away filled with good things. They came like Martha, and went away like Mary. They came like Samson, when his locks were shorn, and went away like Samson when his locks were grown.

3. *Self-dedication*

'One shall say, I am the Lord's.' Oh! there is no greater joy than for a believing soul to give himself all to God. This has always been the way in times of refreshing. It was so at Pentecost. First they gave their own selves unto the Lord. It was so with Boston, and Doddridge, and Edwards, and all the holy men of old.

'I have this day been before God,' says Edwards, 'and have given myself - all that I am and have - to God; so that I am in no respect my own. I can challenge no right in myself - in this understanding, this will, these affections. Neither have I right to this body, or any of its members - no right to this tongue, these hands, these feet, these eyes, these ears. I have given myself clean away.'

Oh! would that you knew the joy of giving yourself away. You cannot keep yourself. Oh! this day try and give all to him. Lie in his hand. Little children, O that you would become like him who said, 'I am God's boy altogether, mother!' Write on your hand: 'I am the Lord's.'
St Peters, July 1, 1838

10. God let none of his words fall to the ground

> Samuel grew, and the LORD was with him, and did let none of his words fall to the ground (1 Samuel 3:19).

It has long been a matter of sad and solemn inquiry to me, what is the cause of the little success that attends the preaching of the gospel in our

day, and in particular in my own parish. Many reasons have risen up
before me.

1. There are reasons in ministers.

(1) The flocks are too large to be cared for by the shepherd. My own
flock is just four times the size a flock used to be in the days of our
fathers, so that I am called upon to do the work of four ministers, and
am left like Issachar, couching down between two burdens.

(2) Again, there is little union in prayer amongst ministers. Heart-
burnings and jealousies, and cold suspicions, seem to put a sad bar in
the way to this so necessary union.

(3) Again, comparing ministers now with ministers long ago, it is to
be feared there is not that longing for the conversion of their people
which there used to be - little weeping between the porch and the altar,
little wrestling with God in secret for a blessing on the Word, little
travailing in birth till Christ be formed in their people the hope of glory.
It is said of the excellent Alleine, that he was 'infinitely, insatiably
greedy of the conversion of souls'. It is to be feared there is little of this
greediness now. Matthew Henry used to say: 'I would think it a greater
happiness to gain one soul to Christ, than mountains of gold and silver
to myself.' We have few Matthew Henrys now. Samuel Rutherford used
to say to his flock: 'My witness is above, that your heaven would be two
heavens to me; and the salvation of you all as two salvations to me.' O
that God would give us something of this spirit now!

2. There are reasons in Christians.

(1) There seems *little appetite for the Word among Christians*. I do not
mean that there is little hearing - oh, no, this is an age for hearing
sermons; but there is little hearing the Word for all that. 'One says I am
of Paul; and another, I of Apollos; and I of Cephas; and I of Christ.' You
come to hear the word of man, but not the Word of God. You go away
judging and criticising, instead of laying it to heart. Oh, for the time
when Christians, like new-born babes, would desire the sincere milk of
the Word, that they might grow thereby!

(2) *Little prayer*. Two farmers possessed two fields that lay next each
other. The one had rich crops, the other very scanty ones. 'How comes
it,' says the one to the other, 'that your field bears so well, and mine so
poorly, when my land is as good as yours?' 'Why, neighbour,' said the
other, 'the reason is this - you only sow your field, but I both sow mine

and harrow in the seed.' Just so, my dear friends, there is little fruit
among Christians, because there is little harrowing in by prayer. I think
I could name many Christians among you who do not know one another,
and never pray one with another. What wonder that there is little fruit!

3. There are reasons in unconverted men.

(1) There is much keeping away from the house of God. I suppose there
are at least a thousand persons in my parish who never enter the house
of God. Ah! how shall we catch these souls, when they keep so far from
the net?

(2) Again, many only come in the afternoons. The very souls that
have most need to hear are those who come but once. How do you expect
a work of God, when you cast such open contempt upon his ordinance?

(3) Again, how many keep out of the way when we visit in your
houses, lest some word should strike upon your conscience, and you
should convert and be healed! How often, when I preach in your houses,
do I find ten women for every man! Have the men no souls, that they
keep away from God's holy ordinance?

(4) Again, there is an awful profaning of the two sacraments of
baptism and the Lord's Supper. The whole Bible declares that they are
intended only for those who have been born again; yet how many rush
forward to them with mad and daring hand, drawing down the curse of
a seared conscience and a stony heart!

These are painful truths - enough to break the heart of any Christian
man that labours among you. Ah! where is the wonder that God should
be a stranger in the land, and like a wayfaring man, that turns aside to
tarry for a night?

And yet this word comes like a beam of sunshine in a storm - God
be praised for it! - 'Samuel grew, and the LORD was with him, and did
let none of his words fall to the ground.' Samuel was young in years, and
it pleased God to cast him in days just as wicked as ours. And how did
God encourage him? In two ways.

First, God was with him - God stood at his right hand, so that he
could not be moved.

Second, God did let none of his words fall to the ground. May the
Lord give us both these encouragements this day!

Doctrine - God will not let one word of his ministers fall to the
ground.

1. The Word often works visibly.

In most cases a work of grace is very visible.

(1) When the Spirit awakens a soul to know its lost condition, there are very generally evident marks of awakening. The jailer trembled, and sprang in, and fell down, and said, 'What must I do to be saved?' So it is commonly. This is not to be wondered at. If a man be in danger of losing all his money, his wife or his child, he will often weep, and tremble, and wring the hands, and cry, Woe is me, I am undone! And is there less cause for weeping and trembling, if a man be in danger of losing his own soul?

(2) When the soul is brought to peace, there is in general an evident change. 'The woman stood behind Christ's feet weeping. She washed them with her tears, and wiped them with the hairs of her head, and kissed them.' So it is commonly. The bosom is brought to rest, the eyes are filled with tears of joy; there is a lively attendance on the Word of God, an exultation in singing his praises; the Sabbath is now plainly honoured and kept holy; sinful companions are forsaken. Ah! my dear friends, it is my heart's desire and prayer, that these outward marks of a work of grace were more common in the midst of you. I fear there can be no extensive work of grace where these are wanting.

2. The Word may be working unseen.

In some cases the work of grace is quite invisible. I believe that God, for wise reasons, sometimes carries on a work of grace in the heart, secretly and unknown to all the world but to himself. There are three things that make me think so:

(1) Christ compared the kingdom of heaven in the heart to leaven and to seed: 'The kingdom of heaven is like unto leaven, which a woman took and hid in three measures of meal till the whole was leavened.' Now, you know that the process of leavening goes on a long time in the heart of the meal quite unseen; so may the work of grace. Again: 'So is the kingdom of God as if a man should cast seed into the ground, and should sleep, and rise night and day, and the seed should spring and grow up, he knoweth not how' (Mark 4:27). Now you know the growing of the seed beneath the clod is all unseen; so is it often with the work of grace.

(2) Who is the workman in conversion? It is the Spirit of God. Now he works unseen, like the wind: 'The wind bloweth where it listeth, and thou hearest the sound thereof, but canst not tell whence it cometh, or

whither it goeth; so is every one that is born of the Spirit.' He works like
the dew: 'I will be as the dew unto Israel.' Now, no man ever yet heard
the dew falling. He works like the well. 'The water that I shall give him
shall be in him a well of water springing up into eternal life.' If the Spirit
work so secretly, no wonder if his work is sometimes unseen.

(3) So it has been in fact: Elijah cried, 'I, even I, am left alone.' How
surprised was he to find seven thousand who had never bowed the knee
to Baal! So shall it be in the latter day: 'Then shalt thou say in thine heart,
Who hath begotten me these, seeing I have lost my children, and am
desolate, a captive, and removing to and fro? And who hath brought up
these? Behold I was left alone; these, where had they been?' (Isaiah
49:21).

This may afford encouragement to godly parents, and teachers, and
ministers. I know some of you have long been watching for a work of
grace in your children's hearts. Learn this day that God will not let one
word fall to the ground. His word shall not return to him void. But you
say, Alas! I see no marks of grace. Go to the dough when the leaven has
been thrust in, and it is covered up. Do you see any marks of leavening?
No, not one. Still the work is going on beneath. So it may be in your
child. Go to the field when the seed has been covered in. Do you see any
marks of growing? No, not a green speck. Still the work is going on.
Turn up the clod, and you will see the seed sprouting. Have patience;
weary not in well-doing. Be instant in prayer. God will be faithful to his
promise. He will not let one word fall to the ground.

3. The Word may take effect another day.

(1) It is a curious fact in natural history, that seeds may be preserved for
almost any length of time. Seeds that have been kept in a drawer for
many years, yet, when sown in their proper season, have been known
to spring up, as if they had been but a year old. So it may sometimes be
with the seeds of grace. They may be kept long in the soul without in
the least affecting it, and yet may be watered by the Spirit, and grow up
many days after.

(2) In general it is not so. It is the testimony of an old divine, who
was indeed a master in Israel that 'the main benefit obtained by
preaching is, by impression made upon the mind at the time, and not by
remembering what was delivered' (Edwards). And what says the
Scripture? 'Is not my Word like as a fire, and like a hammer that breaketh
the rock in pieces?' Now you know that if the fire burns not when it is

applied, it will not burn afterwards. If the rock does not break when the hammer strikes, it is not likely to break afterwards. Oh! my dear friends, today, while it is called today, harden not your hearts. If your hearts do not break under the hammer today, I fear they will never break. If they melt not now, under the fire of his love, I fear they will never melt.

(3) In some cases, the Word takes effect another day. One faithful man of God laboured in his parish for many a long year; and though greatly blessed elsewhere, yet died without, I believe, knowing one of his people brought to the knowledge of the Saviour. Another servant now stands in his room; and souls have been gathered in crowds, every one declaring that it is the word of their departed minister that comes up into their heart, and makes them flee. Ah! God is a faithful God. He will not let any of his words fall to the ground.

The excellent John Flavel was minister of Dartmouth in England. One day he preached from these words: 'If any man love not the Lord Jesus Christ, let him be *anathema maranatha.*' The discourse was unusually solemn, particularly the explanation of the curse. At the conclusion, when Mr Flavel rose to pronounce the blessing, he paused, and said: 'How shall I bless this whole assembly, when every person in it who loves not the Lord Jesus is *anathema maranatha?*' The solemnity of this address deeply affected the audience.

In the congregation was a lad named Luke Short, about fifteen years old, a native of Dartmouth. Shortly after he went to sea, and sailed to America, where he passed the rest of his life. His life was lengthened far beyond the usual term. When a hundred years old, he was able to work on his farm, and his mind was not at all impaired. He had lived all this time in carelessness and sin; he was a sinner a hundred years old, and ready to die accursed. One day, as he sat in his field, he busied himself in reflecting on his past life. He thought of the days of his youth. His memory fixed on Mr Flavel's sermon, a considerable part of which he remembered. The earnestness of the minister, the truths spoken, the effect on the people, all came fresh to his mind. He felt that he had not loved the Lord Jesus; he feared the dreadful anathema; he was deeply convinced of sin, was brought to the blood of sprinkling. He lived to his one hundred and sixteenth year, giving every evidence of being born again. Ah! how faithful God is to his Word. He did let none of his words fall to the ground.

Be of good cheer, Christian mothers, who weep over your unawakened children. They may be going far from you, perhaps across the seas, and you tremble for their souls. Remember God can reach them everywhere. A believing mother never prayed in vain. Be instant in prayer. God will not forget his Word. He will let none of his words fall to the ground.

4. The Word may harden.

In some cases, I believe, the Word of God is sent to harden souls; and so it will not return void, but prosper in the thing whereunto he sent it. That was an awful message God sent by his prophet: 'Hear ye indeed, but understand not; and see ye indeed, but perceive not' (Isaiah 6:9). I fear there are many such messages in our day.

Question: Does God not wish men to be saved? Answer: O yes; God willeth all men to be saved. I believe there is not one soul that the Saviour does not yearn over as he did over Jerusalem; and the Father says: 'O that they had hearkened unto me, and Israel had walked in my ways!' But still, when Jerusalem resisted the word of Christ, Christ said: 'Now they are hid from thine eyes.' And if you refuse the Word of Christ, and neglect this great salvation, I firmly believe that he shall soon come to you with Isaiah's dreadful message: 'Hear ye indeed, but understand not.'

Oh! how dreadful a thought it is, that though we be the savour of life to some, we are the savour of death unto death to most. How dreadful, that the very words of love and mercy which we bring, should be making some souls only more fit for the burning! And yet it must be so. How often have I heard men of God complain that their greatest fruit was when they entered first upon their ministry! I do begin to fear that it is going to be so with us - that God hath chosen out his firstfruits, and the rest are to be hardened. Why is this? Because the people are hardened by the constant preaching of the truth.

My dear friends, remember this word: 'God did let none of his words fall to the ground.' I have gone among you for more than a year, preaching the gospel of the kingdom. Remember the Word was not mine, but his that sent me. I would have been ashamed to stand up and speak my own words. If the hammer does not break, it makes the iron into steel. Every blow makes it harder. If the fire does not melt, it hardens the clay into brick, as hard as stone. If the medicine does not heal, it poisons. If the word concerning Christ does not break your heart, it will make it like the nether millstone.

5. The Word will be a witness.

That is an awful word in Matthew 24:14: 'And this gospel of the
kingdom shall be preached in all the world for a witness unto all
nations.' Ah! my dear friends, God's Word cannot return unto him void.
Every drop of rain has its errand from God. These driving showers of
snow are all fulfilling his word. And do you really think that the word
concerning his Son shall be spoken without any end? Ah, no! even
though not one soul should be saved by it, it shall be for a witness.

When Moses lifted up the brazen serpent in the wilderness, if the
Israelites had been unwilling to look, I can easily imagine the haste with
which he would go round the camp, crying to every dying man: Look here!
look here! Two things would be in his mind: *first*, to get his people healed;
second, to give glory to his God, by bearing witness to them of the love
of God; as if he had said, Now, if you perish, it is your own blame; God
is clear of your blood.

So it is with the Christian minister. You remember Paul, how he was
'instant in season and out of season, teaching publicly, and from house
to house, warning every one day and night with tears; in labours more
abundant, in stripes above measure, in prisons more frequent, in deaths
oft.' Why all this? *Answer*: For two reasons: *first*, he wanted souls to be
saved. 'He was infinitely and insatiably greedy for the conversion of
souls.' *Second*, he sought the honour of God. He wanted to preach the
gospel for a witness, to leave every man without excuse for remaining
in his sins; as if he had said, Now if you perish, it is your own blame -
God is clear of your blood.

Ah! my dear friends, such is our ministry to many of you. It is for a
witness. God, who knows my heart, knows that I seek your salvation
night and day. 'My record is above, that your heaven would be two
heavens to me; and your salvation as two salvations to me.' Yet if you
will not learn, I will be a witness against you in that day. The words that
we have spoken in weakness and much trembling, will rise to condemn
you in that day. How fain would I see you gathered with the ransomed
flock on the right hand of the throne! How fain, in that day, would I see
you smiled on by the lovely Saviour, whose smile is more bright than
the summer sun! But, if it may not be, I will say with the angels:
'Hallelujah!' 'Even so, Father; for so it seemed good in thy sight.'
Amen.

St Peter's, February 25, 1838

11. The work of the Spirit

And the Spirit of God moved upon the face of the waters (Genesis 1:2).

There is, perhaps, no subject upon which there is greater ignorance than that of the Spirit of God. Most people, in our day, if they answered truly, would say as those twelve men at Ephesus: 'We have not so much as heard if there be any Holy Ghost' (Acts 19:2). And yet, if ever you are to be saved, you must know him; for it is all his work to bring a poor prisoner to Christ. A little boy, when dying, said: 'Three persons in the Godhead. God the Father made and preserved me; God the Son came into the world and died for me; God the Holy Ghost came into my heart, and made me love God and hate sin.' My dear friends, if you would die happy, you must be able to bear the same dying testimony.

You know it is said by John, that '*God is love.*' This is true of God the Father in his giving up his Son for sinners; this is true of God the Son, in his becoming man and dying for sinners; this is true of God the Holy Ghost, in his whole work in the hearts of sinners. At present I wish to show you the love of the Spirit, by observing all that he has ever done for men in the world. Today I will show you his work at creation, at the flood, and in the wilderness.

1. At Creation.
'The Spirit of God moved upon the face of the waters' (Genesis 1:2). The expression is taken from a dove brooding over its nest. 'Thou sendest forth thy Spirit, they are created; and thou renewest the face of the earth' (Psalm 104:30). Here the Spirit is said to have renewed the face of the earth. He made every blade of grass to spring, every flower to open, every tree to put forth blossoms. 'By his Spirit he hath garnished the heavens' (Job 26:13). Here God does, as it were, lead us forth to look upon the midnight sky; and when we gaze upon its spangled maze, studded with brilliant stars, he tells us that it was the loving Spirit that gave them all their brightness and their beauty.

Observe, then, that whatever beauty there is in the glassy sea, in the green earth or in the spangled sky, it is all the work of the Holy Spirit. God the Father willed all, God the Son created all, God the Holy Ghost garnished, and gave life and loveliness to all.

Oh! What a lovely world that unfallen world must have been - when God the Son walked with Adam in Paradise, when God the Holy Ghost watered and renewed the whole every moment, when God the Father looked down well pleased on all, and said that it was very good. Learn:

The love of the Spirit.
He did not think it beneath his care to beautify the dwelling-place of man. He wanted our joy to be full. He did not think it enough that we had a world to live in, but he made the waters full of life and beauty. He made every green thing to spring for man, and made a shining canopy above, all for the joy of man. Whatever beauty still remains on earth, or sea, or sky, it is the trace of his almighty finger. You should never look on the beauties of the world without thinking of the Holy Spirit that moved upon the face of the waters, that renewed the face of the earth, that garnished the heaven with stars.

The holiness of the Spirit.
From the very beginning he was the *Holy* Spirit, of purer eyes than to behold iniquity. It was a sinless world. The sea had never been defiled by bearing wicked men upon its bosom. The green earth had never been trodden by the foot of a sinner. The spangled sky had never been looked upon by one whose eye is full of adultery, and cannot cease from sin. It was a holy, holy, holy world - a temple of the living God. The lofty mountains were the pillars of it; the glittering heavens its canopy. The far-resounding ocean sang his praise. The hills broke forth into singing, and all the trees of the field clapped their hands. As the cloud which so filled Solomon's temple that the priests could not stand to minister by reason of the cloud, so the Holy Spirit filled this world - a holy, sinless temple to the Father's praise.

When man fell into sin, and the very ground was cursed for his sake, then the Holy Spirit, in great measure, left his temple; he could not dwell with sin. And never do you find him coming back, as before, till he lighted on the head of a sinless Saviour; for the Holy Ghost descended upon him like a dove, and abode upon him.

Just so it is with the soul. As long as your soul is guilty, polluted, vile in the sight of the Spirit, he cannot make his abode in your heart. He is a loving Spirit, full of a tender desire to make you holy. But as long as you are guilty in his sight, it is contrary to his nature that he should dwell in you. But come to the blood of Jesus, sinner; come to the blood that makes you white as snow. Then will the Spirit see no iniquity in you, and he will come and dwell in your heart, as he dwelt at first in the sinless world. As he moved on the face of the waters, like a dove over its nest, so he will make his nest in your heart, and brood there. As he renewed the face of the ground, so will he renew your heart. As he garnished the heavens, so will he beautify your soul, till he make you shine as the stars for ever and ever.

2. At the flood.

'My Spirit shall not always strive with man, for that he also is flesh [fading]: yet his days shall be an hundred and twenty years' (Genesis 6:3). What a different scene we have here! Yet here also we shall learn that the Holy Spirit is a loving Spirit. At the creation we found him beautifying the world, dwelling in it as in a temple; the earth, the sea, the sky, all proclaiming that it was a sinless world. But now fifteen hundred years had passed away, and the whole earth was covered with a race of godless men - giants in body and giants in wickedness.

'God looked upon the earth, and it was corrupt.' It was all one putrid mass. 'From the sole of the foot to the crown of the head there was no soundness in it;' for all flesh had corrupted his way. Just as a putrid body is loathsome in the sight of man, so the earth was loathsome in the sight of God. Nay, more; the earth was filled with violence. The few children of God that remained were hated and persecuted, hunted like the partridge on the mountains. It repented the Lord that he had made man, and it grieved him at his heart.

How is the Holy Spirit engaged?

Answer: (1) He does not dwell with sinful men. He cannot dwell with unpardoned sinners; for he is the Holy Spirit.

(2) But still he strives with men, and strives to the very end. The men were giants in sin. Every imagination of their heart was only evil continually. But this is the very reason he strives. He sees the flood that is coming; he sees the hell that is beneath them: therefore does he strive. In the preaching of Noah he pleaded with them; he pricked their hearts - made them think of their danger, their sin, their misery. In the preparing the ark he pleaded with them - showed them the way of safety, and said: 'Yet there is room.' He made every stroke of the hammer speak to their hearts. 'The Spirit and the Bride said, Come.' Learn:

1. *That he is a striving Spirit.*

O! let those of you that are living in sin, learn what a loving Spirit is now striving with you. Some of you, who are living in sin, think that God is nothing but an angry God; therefore you do not turn to him. True, 'he is angry with the wicked every day'; still he is striving with the wicked every day. He sends the Holy Spirit to strive with you. Oh! what a loving Spirit he is, that does not at once turn you into hell, but pleads and strives, saying: Turn ye, turn ye; why will ye die?'

Some may say: I am a giant in wickedness; I am corrupt; I am a violent against God's children. True; yet still see here how he strove with giants in wickedness. The whole earth was corrupt and filled with violence; yet he strove. So he strives with you in whatever state you are. He is a loving Spirit. He strives by ministers, Bibles, providences. Sometimes, when you are all alone, that Spirit wrestles with you, brings your sin to remembrance, and makes you tremble; or, like the angels at Sodom, strives to make you flee from destruction. Oh! what love is here, to strive with hell-deserving worms. 'Oh! ye stiff-necked and uncircumcised in heart and ears, ye do always resist the Holy Ghost: as your fathers did, so do ye.'

2. *A long-suffering Spirit.*
One hundred and twenty years he strove with the men before the flood. He never ceased till the flood came. Some of you remember a time when God's Spirit was striving with you at the Sabbath School, or your first sacrament. You wept for your soul, and prayed; but the world has come on you since then, and now you fear he strives no more. Learn, he is a long-suffering Spirit - he strives with you yet. 'He that hath ears, let him hear what the Spirit saith unto the churches.'

3. *He will not always strive.*
Observe, the Spirit strove till the flood came, but no longer; for the flood came, and carried them all away. So it is with you, my dear friends. As long as our ministry lasts he strives with you; but when death comes, or when the Saviour comes, he will strive no more. Ah! you will have no awakening, inviting, striving sermons in hell - not one invitation more. Oh! how sad it is to think that so many, who have the Spirit of God striving with them, should perish after all.

3. In the wilderness.
Nearly 1,000 years after the flood, we find God choosing a peculiar people to himself, and keeping them separate from all others, in the wilderness. Here the Spirit shows himself still more as the loving Spirit.

The glorifier of Christ.
Bezaleel and Aholiab, by his guidance, made the tabernacle, the mercy-seat, the altar, the high priest's garments (Exodus 31:1-11). All these typify Christ. The Spirit here enables these men to show forth the Saviour to the many thousands of Israel. Although they often vexed the Holy Spirit, and grieved him in the desert, yet, see here how lovingly he sets forth Christ in the midst of them, that he may lead them to peace and holiness! This is exactly what Christ said of him afterwards: 'He shall glorify me; for he shall receive of mine, and shall show it unto you.'

Dear friends, has the Spirit glorified Christ to you? He is still the great revealer of Christ. He shines into our heart, to give us the light of the knowledge of the glory of God, in the face of Christ. Has he led you to the altar, to the Lamb of God, that taketh away the sin of the world? Has he clothed you in the high priest's garments? Has he brought you within the veil, to the mercy-seat? This is his delightful work. Oh! it is a sweet work to be the minister on earth that leads souls to Christ - that points, like John, and says: 'Behold the Lamb of God!' But O how infinitely more loving is that Holy Spirit of God to lead trembling souls to Jesus! Oh! praise him that has done this for you. Oh! love the Spirit of God. 'Thy Spirit is good: lead me to the land of uprightness.'

He purifies all that believe: 'Thou shalt set the laver between the tent of the congregation and the altar' (Exodus 40:7).

This brazen laver, containing water, was set up in the wilderness to typify the Holy Spirit; and observe the place where it was put - between the altar and the tabernacle of God. The first thing that the sinner came up to was the altar with the bleeding lamb. He laid his hands upon the head of the lamb and confessed his sins, so that they were all carried away in the blood of the lamb. Forgiven and justified, he advanced a few paces further to the brazen laver; there he washed his feet and hands. This represented the Holy Spirit washing and renewing his heart. And then he entered into the holy place of God.

'Whatsoever things were written aforetime were written for our learning, that we, through patience and comfort of the scripture, might have hope.' Dear friends, has the Holy Spirit purified you? If you have laid your sins upon the Lamb of God, have you come to this laver of living water? Are you really washing there, and preparing to enter the holy place made without hands, eternal in the heavens? 'Without holiness no man can see the Lord;' and without the Spirit you will have no holiness. Oh! is he not a loving Spirit who thus delights to prepare the believer for glory, who comes into our vile heart, and 'creates a clean heart, and renews a right spirit within us'? Oh! love him who thus loves you; and ask for him, you that are his children. The Father delights to give him. 'If ye, being evil, know how to give good gifts to your children, much more will your heavenly Father give the Holy Spirit to them that ask him.'

He upholds the life of believers: 'They all drank of that Rock which followed them; and that Rock was Christ' (1 Corinthians 10: 4.). This was a third way in which the Spirit showed himself in the wilderness.

A river. This was to show Israel how refreshing and supporting he is to the weary soul, and that there is abundance in him. Drink, and drink again. You will not drink a river dry: so there is infinite fullness of the Spirit.

Flowing from a smitten rock. This shows that he is given by a wounded Saviour, that it is only when we hide in that Rock that we can receive the Holy Ghost. 'I will send him unto you.'

It followed them. This was to show that, wherever a believer goes, the Holy Spirit goes with him: 'I will pray the Father, and he will give you another Comforter, that he may abide with you for ever' - a well within, springing up into everlasting life.

My dear friends, have you received the Holy Ghost, since you believed? It appears to me that few Christians realise this river flowing after them. Oh! what inexpressible love and grace there is in this work of the Spirit. Is there any of you weak and faint, and ready to perish under a wicked heart, and raging lusts? or, have you got a thorn in the flesh, a messenger of Satan to buffet you, and you are driven to pray that it may be taken from you? See here the answer to your prayer. A river of living water flows from Christ. There is enough here for all your wants: 'My grace is sufficient for thee; for my strength is made perfect in weakness.' Some of you are afraid of the future; you fear some approaching temptation, you fear some coming contest. See here the river flows after you - the Spirit will abide with you for ever. Oh! what love is here. Notwithstanding all your sinfulness, weakness and unbelief, still he abides with you, and will for ever. He is 'a well of water springing up into everlasting life' (John 4:14).

Oh! love the Spirit, then, who so loves you. Grieve not the Holy Spirit of God, whereby you are sealed unto the day of redemption.
St Peter's, December 16, 1836

12. Moses and Hobab

And Moses said unto Hobab, the son of Raguel the Midianite, Moses'
father-in-law, We are journeying unto the place of which the LORD
said, I will give it you: come thou with us, and we will do thee good:
for the LORD hath spoken good concerning Israel (Numbers 10:29)

The children of Israel had been nearly a year encamped in the wilderness
that surrounds the rocky peaks of Mount Sinai. But now the cloud rose
from off the tabernacle - the signal that God wished them to depart - and
so Israel prepared for the march in regular order. Upon a rocky
eminence, that overlooked the marshalled thousands of Israel, stood
Moses and his brother-in-law, Hobab. The heart of Moses grew full at
the sight, when he looked upon their banners floating in the wind, when
he looked at the pillar-cloud towering over them like some tall angel
beckoning them away, when he thought of God's good words concerning Israel, and the good land to which they were hastening. He felt that
his loins were girt with truth, and on his head he had the helmet of
salvation, and in his hand the sword of the Spirit. He could not bear that
any he loved should leave them now; and, therefore, while Hobab stood
lingering, uncertain which way to go, Moses spoke thus: 'We are
journeying toward the place of which the LORD hath said, I will give it
you: come thou with us, and we will do thee good.'

Such are the feelings of every child of God. Whenever a soul is
brought to Jesus Christ, to wash in his blood and to stand in his
righteousness, he is brought to feel two things: *first*, that now he is
journeying to a good land, his sins are blotted out, the Spirit is within
him, God is his guide, heaven is before him; *second*, he wishes all he
loves to come along with him.

Doctrine. The children of God are on a journey, and wish all they
love to come along with them.

1. This world is not the home of a Christian.

When Israel was travelling through the wilderness, they did not count
it their home. Sometimes they came to places, like Marah, where the
waters were bitter; they would not rest there. Sometimes they came to
sweet, refreshing places, like Elim, with its seventy palm trees and
twelve wells of water; and yet they would not sit down and say: 'This
is my rest.' It was sweet when the manna fell round the camp every

morning, and when the water followed them; yet it was a wilderness and a land of drought, and the shadow of death. 'We are journeying,' said Moses. So is this world to a true Christian - it is not a home. Sometimes he meets with bitter things - disappointments, losses, bereavements - and he calls the waters Marah; for they are bitter. Sometimes, too, he comes to refreshing spots, like Elim; yet he does not rest in them.

(1) *There are the sweet joys of home and of kindred*, when the family ring is still unbroken, when not a chair is empty by the hearth, when not a link is wanting in the chain, when not even a lamb is carried off from the flock. These are very pleasant and lovely to the child of God; yet he does not, he cannot, rest in them. He hears a voice saying: 'Arise, depart, this is not thy rest; for it is polluted.'

(2) *Christian friends are sweet to the Christian*. Those that are sharers of our spiritual secrets, those who mingle prayer with us before the throne, those who never forget us when within the veil - oh, there is something cheering in the very light of their kindly eye! It is an intercourse of which the world knows nothing. We have them in our heart, inasmuch as they are partakers of one grace, washed in one fountain, filled with the same Spirit, having one heart, members one of another - yet our rest is not among these. This is a taste of heaven, but not heaven. They often disappoint us - go back and become colder, or they are taken from us before, and leave us to journey on alone. 'We are journeying.'

(3) *Ordinances are sweet to the Christian*. They are the manna and the waters in the wilderness, the rain that fills the pools in the Valley of Baca. How sweet is the Sabbath morning! The sun shines more brightly than on any other day. How amiable are thy tabernacles, O Lord! the singing of psalms, how pleasant! the prayers, how solemn, when we stand within the veil! the doctrine, how it distils like the dew! the blessing, how full of peace! the sacraments especially, how sweet to the Christian - wells of salvation, Bethels, trysting-places with Christ! What sweet days of pleasure, love, and covenanting with Jesus! Still not our home, not our rest. They are *defective*; always something human about them to mar the sweetest ordinances. There is a bunch of grapes, but oh! it is not enough to satisfy. They are *polluted*; always some fly to spoil the fragrant ointment; always so much sin in the minister and in the hearer. 'We are journeying unto the place.'

Learn firstly, *to look with a traveller's eye upon the world*. When a traveller is journeying, he sees many fine estates, beautiful houses, and lawns and gardens; but he does not set his heart on them. He admires, and passes on. So must you do, dear Christians. Ye are a little flock, travelling through the wilderness. Twine not your affections round any one thing here. Do not set your affections on home, or on kindred, or houses, or lands. Be like Abraham, and Isaac, and Jacob, who lived in tents, declaring plainly that they sought a better country. 'If ye be risen with Christ, seek those things which are above, where Christ sitteth'. 'Set your affections on things above, not on things of the earth.'

Learn secondly, *not to mourn over the loss of Christian friends*, as those who have no hope. Some of you have lost little children, who died in the Lord. Some of you have lost near friends, who fell asleep in Jesus. Some of you have lost aged parents, who have committed their spirit into the hand of Jesus. Now, you cannot but weep; and yet, if they were in Christ you need not. They have got to their journey's end, and we are on the way. A voice seems to rise from their grave, saying: 'Weep not for me, but weep for yourselves and your children.' They are at rest, and 'we are journeying'.

2. The Christian's home is nearer every step.

When Israel was travelling the wilderness they came nearer to the good land every step they took. They had a long wilderness to pass through, still every day's journey brought them nearer to the end. So it is with all that are in Christ Jesus. Every step is bringing them nearer to heaven. Every day they are coming nearer and nearer to glory. 'Now it is high time to awake out of sleep; for now is our salvation nearer than when we believed'. 'The night is far spent, the day is at hand.' Every sheep that is really found, and on the shoulder of the shepherd, is coming nearer to the heavenly fold every day. Every soul that is carried on the wings of the eagle is flying towards the rest that remaineth. The hours fly fast; but as fast flies that divine eagle. In running a race, every step brings you nearer to the end of it, nearer to the prize, to the crown.

Question: Are you fitter for heaven every day?

Ah! my dear Christians, I tremble for some of you who are on your way to glory, and yet are not turning fitter for glory. Oh! that you would forget the things that are behind, and, reaching forth to those that are before, press towards the mark for the prize of the high calling of God in Christ Jesus.

Some of you are just beginning the journey to heaven. Dear little children, wax stronger and stronger; pray more, read more, hear more, love more, do more every day. Let your sense of sin grow, like the roots of trees, downwards, deeper and deeper. Let your faith grow, like the branch of the vine, stronger and stronger every year. Let your peace grow, like a river, broader and broader. 'We are journeying.'

Some are well-nigh through the wilderness. Some of you are on the top of Pisgah. The time draws nigh when you must die. Dear aged Christians, how soon your eyes will see him whom, having not seen, you love! How soon your heart will love him as you wish to do! How soon you will grieve him no more for ever! Do not be afraid, but meekly rejoice. Live more above the world; care less for its pleasures. Speak plainer to your friends, saying, 'Come ye with us.' Be oftener within the veil. Soon you shall be a pillar, and go no more out.

Unconverted, you are nearer hell every day. You, too, are journeying to the place of which God hath said: 'I will give it you.' 'For the fearful, and unbelieving, and the abominable, and murderers, and whoremongers, and sorcerers, and idolaters, and all liars, shall have their part in the lake which burneth with fire and brimstone, which is the second death' (Revelation 21:8).

Oh! stop, poor sinner; stop and think! Wherever you are, and whatever you are engaged in, you are travelling thither. The most go in at the wide gate. When you are sleeping, you are posting thither. When you take a journey of pleasure, you are still advancing on that other journey. When you are laughing and talking, or in the full enjoyment of your sin, you are still hurrying on. You have never stopped since you began to live. You never stand a moment to take breath. You are nearer hell this afternoon than in the forenoon. O stop and think! 'Come thou with us, and we will do thee good.'

3. This journey is the great concern of a Christian.

Their journey was the great concern of Israel. They did not care much for doing anything else. They did not take to another occupation. When they came to a green spot, they did not take to the plough, to try and cultivate it. Their journey was their great concern. So it should be with those of you who are children of God. Your journey to heaven should be your great concern.

Dear friends, judge of everything in this way - whether it will help you on in your journey or no. In choosing a profession, or trade, choose it with regard to this - will it advance or hinder your heavenward journey? will it lead you into sore temptations, or into wicked company?

Oh! take heed. What is the use of living, but only to get on in our journey to heaven?

Choose your abode with regard to this. Christian servants, choose your place with regard to this. Remember Lot. He chose the Plain of Jordan, because it was well watered; but his soul was all but withered there.

In choosing connections or friends, O choose with regard to this - will they help or hinder your prayers? will they go with you, and help you on your journey? or will they be a drag upon your wheels? In going into companies, in reading books, choose with regard to this - will they fill your sails for heaven? If not, go not near them. In yielding to your affections, especially if you find them hindering your journey, drop them instantly. Never mind the consequences.

'If thy right hand offend thee, cut it off, and cast it from thee. It is better to enter into life maimed, than having two hands to be cast into hell-fire.'

'Wherefore let us lay aside every weight, and the sin that doth so easily beset us, and let us run with patience the race that is set before us, looking unto Jesus.'

4. All true Christians wish others to journey along with them: 'Come thou with us, and we will do thee good.'

So it was with Moses. Hobab had been his friend for forty years, in the land of Midian, where Moses married his sister, and lived in his father Raguel's house. In that time, I doubt not, Moses had told him much of Israel's God, and Israel's coming glory. Many a time, while they fed their flocks in this very wilderness, Moses had reasoned with him of righteousness, temperance and judgment to come, till Hobab trembled.

Still it would seem Hobab was not quite convinced. He doubted, he lingered. He had been awed by the terrors of Sinai, but not won by the love of Calvary. He did not know whether to go or stay. But the hour of decision came. He must decide now. Now was the heart of Moses stirred in him: 'Come thou with us, and we will do thee good; for the LORD hath spoken good concerning Israel.'

So it was with Paul, when he himself had tasted the joy and peace of believing; then says he: 'My heart's desire and prayer to God for Israel is, that they might be saved.'

So it was with Andrew: 'Andrew first findeth his own brother

Simon, and saith unto him, We have found the Christ.'

So it was with the poor maniac whom Jesus healed: 'Go home, tell thy friends how great things the Lord hath done for thee, and how he hath had compassion on thee.'

So it was with the poor slave in Antigua, who used to pray that there might be a full heaven and an empty hell.

Question: Is it so with you? Have you asked your friends to come with you? Have you a father whom you love? a mother that carried you at her breast? Have you a brother or a sister? Are they lingering like Hobab? Oh! Will you not put in a word for Christ, and say: 'Come thou with us, and we will do thee good'? Have you a friend whom you love much, who knows nothing of Christ and of God, who is willing to die in the wilderness? Oh! Will you not win him to go with you to Israel's God and Israel's glory?

A word to lingering souls. Some of you, like Hobab, are half persuaded to go with Israel. 'Almost thou persuadest me to be a Christian.' Some of you see your children converted, and you not; and yet you are not determined to go with them. Oh! why halt ye between two opinions? Go with them now.

Observe, 1. *This may be the deciding day.* It was so with Hobab. God is pleading hard with you today. He has spoken to you by most solemn providences - by the Bible, by his ministers, and by the tender persuading voice of those you love. 'Come thou with us.' 'Choose you this day, then, whom you will serve.' Remember this may be the deciding day. Tomorrow it may be too late.

2. *You will share in their joys*: 'We will do thee good.' What makes them so anxious for you to go with them, if it be not for your good? You know they love you tenderly; they would not have a hair of your head hurt. You will taste their forgiveness, their peace with God, their joy in the Word and prayer. You will know their God. You will know their heaven. Oh! that God would put it into your heart to cleave to them like Ruth to Naomi, saying: 'Whither thou goest I will go; and where thou lodgest I will lodge; thy people shall be my people, and thy God my God.'

St Peter's, July 22, 1838.

13. Comfort ye

Comfort ye, comfort ye my people, saith your God. Speak ye comfortably to Jerusalem, and cry unto her, that her warfare is accomplished, that her iniquity is pardoned: for she hath received of the LORD's hand double for all her sins (Isaiah 40:1,2).

These words are a blast of the silver trumpet of the gospel. Blessed are the people that know the joyful sound. They are like the words of the angel at Bethlehem: 'I bring you good tidings of great joy, which shall be to all people.' This is the voice of the shepherd, which all his flock know and love.

1. Believers have received double punishment for all their sins: 'She hath received of the LORD's hand double for all her sins' (verse 2). There are two ways in which sinners may bear the punishment of their sins.

1. *In themselves* - on their own body and soul for ever.
This is the way in which all unconverted men, who finally perish, will bear their sins. 'These shall go away into everlasting punishment.' 'Depart from me, ye cursed, into everlasting fire.' Not that they will be able to bear their punishment: 'My punishment is greater than I can bear'. 'The great day of his wrath is come, and who shall be able to stand?' They shall say one to another, 'Who among us can dwell with the devouring flame? Who among us can dwell with everlasting burnings?' And God will say: 'Can thine heart endure, or can thine hands be strong, in the day that I shall deal with thee?'
    This is not the way spoken of in the text; for firstly, it would be a message of woe and not of comfort. Woe, woe, woe, and not, Comfort ye, comfort ye. When God really takes in hand to punish sinners, there will be no comfort in that day. The heart of sinners will sink under insupportable gloom.
    Secondly, sinners never can bear double in themselves. When a poor sinner dies Christless, and goes to bear the punishment of his sins, he never can bear enough. He has sinned against an infinite God; and his punishment, if it be just, must be infinite. His stripes must be eternal, the gnawing worm must never die, the burning flame must never be quenched. In this way, poor Christless souls can never satisfy the justice of God. God will never say, It is enough. He will never pour water on

the flames of hell, nor send a drop to the parched tongues that are tormented there. Instead of suffering double, they will never receive enough at the Lord's hand for all their sins.

Oh! dear friends, it is easy talking of this now; but many of you will probably feel it soon.

2. *In Christ the surety.*

It is according to justice, that sinners may bear their sins in Christ the surety.

(1) This was the very errand that Christ came upon. He thought upon this from all eternity. For this end he came into the world. For this end he became man. 'He himself bare our sins in his own body on the tree.' If it were not a just and righteous thing, that sinners should bear their sins in another, and not in themselves, Christ never would have undertaken it. This is the very way here spoken of.

(2) All the sufferings of Christ were at the hand of his Father: 'It pleased the LORD to bruise him: he hath put him to grief. The LORD hath laid on him the iniquities of us all.' We generally look at the wicked hands that crucified and slew Christ; but we must not forget that it was by the determinate counsel and foreknowledge of God, and that they would have had no power at all against him, except it had been given them from above. Through all the crowd of scoffing priests and bloody soldiers, you must see the Lord's hand making his soul an offering for sin.

This shows that Christ is a Saviour appointed of the Father. Awakened souls are afraid of the avenging hand of God; but in Christ there is a refuge. And you need not fear but Christ will shelter you; for there was an agreement between them, that Christ should suffer these things for sinners, and enter into his glory. Christ finished the work which the Father gave him to do.

(3) When sinners take refuge in Christ, the law takes its course against their sins - not upon their soul, but upon Christ. All their sins, whether they may be many or few, are reckoned his, and he is made answerable; and he has already borne double for them all. How was it just that Christ should bear double?

Answer: He could not suffer at all, without bearing double for all our sins, by reason of his excellency and glory. The sufferings of Christ for a time were, in God's eye, double the eternal sufferings of sinners, by reason of the infinite dignity of his person. God is well pleased for his righteousness' sake; for he magnified the law, and made it honourable. In the death of Christ, the angels saw God to be holy, infinitely better than if all mankind had perished for ever.

Come freely, then to Jesus Christ, O awakened sinner! There you will find a shelter from the wrath due to your sins. Your sins are, indeed, infinite, and the wrath of God intolerable; but in Jesus you may find safety. He came upon this very errand. You need not fear but he will receive you; his heart and his arms are open for you. His Father is willing you should come. Be your sins many or few, it is all one; in Christ you will find that they are all borne, suffered for, in a way glorifying to God and safe to you.

2. All believers are, therefore, in a truly blessed condition.

1. *Their iniquity is pardoned.*

A soul in Christ is a pardoned soul. It matters not how many his sins have been. The iniquity of Jerusalem was very great. The people of Jerusalem had sinned against light and against love. All the prophets had been sent to them; yet they were stoned or killed. The Son of God came to them; they cast him out of the vineyard, and slew him. Their sins had grown up to heaven; yet, no sooner do they betake themselves to Christ than God says: 'Her iniquity is pardoned.'

And observe, *first*, it is *a present pardon.* He does not say, Her iniquity shall be pardoned, but 'Her iniquity is pardoned.' No sooner does a guilty, heavy-laden soul betake himself to Christ, than this sweet word is heard in heaven: '*His iniquity is pardoned.*' 'There is now no condemnation to them that are in Christ Jesus.' Oh! it is no future or uncertain pardon that is offered in the gospel; but a sure and present pardon - pardon now, this instant, to all who believe in Jesus. You are as completely pardoned in the moment of believing as ever you will be. Oh! haste ye, and receive pardon from Christ. Oh! that ye knew the day of your visitation.

Observe, *second*, it is *a holy pardon.* Your iniquity is pardoned, for another has died for your sins. Oh! it is an awful way of pardon. 'There is forgiveness with God, that he may be feared.' It is a pardon to make you tremble, and hate sin with a perfect hatred. Oh! can you ever love that which nailed him to the tree, which bowed down his blessed head? Will you take up sin again, and thus put the spear afresh into the side of Jesus? Some say, I am too vile. Ah! are you viler than Jerusalem? When you take a pebble, and cast it into the deep sea, it sinks, and is entirely covered; so are the sins of those who take refuge in Christ: 'Thou wilt cast all our sins into the depths of the sea.'

2. *Their warfare is accomplished.*
With the law.
An awakened soul has a dreadful warfare with the law of God. The law of God is revealed to his conscience, armed with a flaming glittering sword. It demands the obedience of his heart and life. The sinner tries to obey it; he tries to bring his life up to its requirements; but in vain. The law lifts up its sword to slay him; it hurls its curses at him. This is a dreadful warfare in every awakened conscience; but when the sinner runs into Jesus Christ, his warfare is accomplished. 'The name of the Lord is a strong tower; the righteous runneth into it, and is safe.' In Christ Jesus, the demands of the law are satisfied; for he was made under the law. Its curses are borne; for he was made a curse for us. The glittering sword pierced the side of Jesus. Oh! do you know what it is to have this warfare accomplished?

With the devil.
We wrestle not with flesh and blood. An awakened soul often has an awful warfare with Satan. Satan fights against him in two ways: *first*, by stirring up his corruptions, and making his lusts to flame and burn within him in a fearful manner. *Second*, by accusing him. Satan is the accuser of the brethren. He accuses him in his conscience, in order to drive him away from Christ - to drive him to despair, and to give up all hope of salvation. He says to him: 'Thou art a vile wretch, not fit for a holy Saviour. See what raging lusts are in thy heart. Thou wilt never be saved.' Ah! when the poor sinner runs into Christ, he finds rest there - his warfare is then accomplished. He sees all the accusations of Satan answered in the blood of the Lamb.

With sin.
The awakened soul has a dreadful warfare with his corruptions. His heart appears full of raging lusts, all tearing him to pieces. He is driven hither and thither; but when he comes to Christ, this warfare is accomplished. Indeed, in one sense, the battle is not over, but just begun; but now victory is sure. God is now for him. Greater is he that is for him than all that can be against him. 'If God be for us, who can be against us?'

The Spirit of God is now within him; he will abide with him for ever. The Spirit now reigns in him. *Christ* now fights for him, covers his head in the day of battle, carries him on his shoulder. He is as sure to overcome as if he were already in glory. He says to him: 'Fear not, thou worm Jacob: fear not, for I have redeemed thee; I have called thee by thy name; thou art mine. I will never leave thee, nor forsake thee.' That word, *never leave thee*, reaches through the darkest hours of temptation, the deepest waters of affliction, the hottest fires of persecution; it reaches unto death - through death and the grave, into eternity.

3. Believers should take the comfort of their condition.

1. *God commands it.*

Some say, It is a dangerous thing to be happy. They are afraid of too much joy. They say, It is better to be in deep exercises, better to have deep wadings; it is not good to be of too joyful a spirit. What says the Word of God? 'Comfort ye, comfort ye.' If your joy flow from the cross of Christ, you cannot have too much joy. 'Rejoice in the Lord alway; and again I say, Rejoice.' When Christ truly rises on the soul, he should be like a morning without clouds. If it be true that Christ came into the world to seek and save that which was lost, if you see his freeness and preciousness, I ask, how *can* you do otherwise than rejoice and be comforted? 'Whom, having not seen, we love; in whom, though now we see him not, yet believing, we rejoice with joy unspeakable and full of glory.' May the God of hope fill you brimful with joy and peace in believing!

2. *Examine from whence your comfort flows.*

All true gospel comfort flows from the cross of Christ, from the Man of Sorrows. The comfort of hypocrites flows from themselves. They look to themselves for comfort. They look to the change in their life. They see some improvements there, and take rest from that; or they look deeper - to their concern, their mourning over sin, their convictions, their endeavours after Christ; or they look to their devotions - their delight in prayer, their flowing of affection and words; or to texts of the Bible coming into their minds; or they look to what their friends or ministers think of them, and they take comfort from these. All these are refuges of lies - false Christs, that must be cast away, or they will ruin your soul. Christ's blood and righteousness, and not any work in your own heart, must be your justification before a holy God. True gospel comfort comes from a sight of Christ's bearing double for all our sins. 'Behold the Lamb of God!' Gospel comfort is a stream that flows direct from Calvary.

3. *See how false the comfort of Christ-neglecting souls.*

This sweet word of comfort is only to those who are under the wings of Christ. That little flock alone have got rest for their souls. But most neglect this great salvation. You do not feel your need of an atoning Saviour. You think you can justify yourself before God. You do not feel your need of an almighty Sanctifier. Christ is a tender plant in your eyes. You have not betaken yourself to him. Ah! my friend, woe to you. Your warfare is not accomplished. The law, with its curses and its flaming sword, stands in your way. Satan also accuses you, and you have nothing to answer him. Sin rages in you, and you have no power against it. Your iniquity is not pardoned - not one sin is blotted out. All is naked and laid open to the eyes of him with whom you have to do. Your comfort is all a lie; your peace is Satan's peace - it is the slumber that ends in perdition. You will yet bear your own sins. When the great day of his wrath is come, you will not be able to stand. 'Can thine heart endure, or can thine hands be strong, in the day that I shall deal with thee?'

Oh! Sirs, you think it a small thing to be Christless this day. You can talk lightly of it, and jeer and jest about it; you can sleep soundly withal - but there is a day coming, when your bitter cry will be heard throughout all the caverns of hell: Woe is me! I am Christless, I am Christless!

14. Can a woman forget?

> But Zion said, The LORD hath forsaken me, and my Lord hath forgotten me. Can a woman forget her suckling child, that she should not have compassion on the son of her womb? Yea, they may forget; yet will I not forget thee (Isaiah 49:14, 15).

These words apply, first of all, to God's ancient people, the Jews. Before their final conversion, I believe their eyes will be opened to see their sin and misery. They will look upon him whom they have pierced, and mourn. When they hear the glorious offers of mercy, they will not be able to believe them: 'Zion will say, The LORD hath forsaken me, and my God hath forgotten me.' But God will answer them, that notwithstanding all their past sins and afflictions, still he will love them, and be their God: 'Can a woman forget her sucking child, that she should not have compassion on the son of her womb? Yea, they may forget; yet will I not forget thee.' These words are equally true of all believers.

1. Let us inquire into those times when believers think themselves forsaken.

1. *In time of sore affliction.*

So it was with Naomi. She had lost her beloved husband and her two sons in the land of Moab. And now, when she returned, leaning on her daughter-in-law up the hill of Bethlehem, the whole town was moved, and they said: 'Is this Naomi? But she said unto them, Call me not Naomi; call me Mara; for the Lord hath dealt very bitterly with me: I went out full, and the Lord hath brought me home again empty. Why then call ye me Naomi, seeing the Lord hath testified against me, and the Almighty hath afflicted me?'

So with Hezekiah. When the Lord said to him: 'Set thine house in order, for thou shalt die, and not live,' Hezekiah turned his face to the wall, and prayed to the Lord; and Hezekiah wept sore. Like a crane or a swallow so did I chatter; I did mourn as a dove; mine eyes fail with looking upward. O Lord, I am oppressed; undertake for me.'

So with Job. When Job lost his flocks and herds and his ten children in one day, when his bodily health was destroyed, and he sat down among the ashes - then Job opened his mouth, and cursed his day: 'Let the day perish wherein I was born. Wherefore is light given to him that is in misery, and life to the bitter in soul? O that I might have my request, and that God would grant me the thing that I long for: even that it would please God to destroy me, that he would let loose his hand, and cut me off.'

Ah! it is a sad thing when the soul *faints* under the rebukes of God. They were intended to lead you deeper into Christ, into a fuller enjoyment of God. Faint not when thou art rebuked of him. When a soul comes to Christ, he expects to be led to heaven in a green, soft pathway, without a thorn. On the contrary, he is led into darkness. Poverty stares him in the face, or bereavement writes him childless, or persecutions embitter his life; and now his soul remembers the wormwood and the gall. He forgets the love and wisdom that are dealing with him; he says:

'I am the man that hath seen affliction. The Lord hath forsaken me, and my God hath forgotten me.'

2. *When they have fallen into sin.*

As long as a believer walks humbly with his God, his soul is at peace. The candle of the Lord shines on his head. He walks in the light as God walks in the light, and the blood of Jesus Christ his Son cleanseth him from all sin. But the moment that unbelief creeps in, he is led away into sin - like David, he falls very low. A believer generally falls lower than the world; and now he falls into darkness.

When *Adam* fell, he was afraid; and he hid himself from God among the trees of the garden, and made a covering of leaves. Alas! when a believer falls, he is also afraid - he hides from God. Now he has lost a good conscience, he fears to meet with God; he does not love the house of prayer; his heart is filled with suspicions. He says to himself: 'If I had been a child of God, would God have given me up to my own heart's lusts?' He refuses to return. 'There is no hope: no; for I have loved strangers, and after them will I go.' Though God has never been a wilderness or a land of darkness to the soul, yet he says: 'We are lords; we will come no more unto thee.' 'The Lord hath forsaken me, and my God hath forgotten me.' Ah! this is the bitterest of all kinds of desertion. If you put away faith and a good conscience, you will make shipwreck.

3. *In a time of desertion.*

Desertion is God withdrawing from the soul of a believer, so that his absence is felt. The world knows nothing of this, and yet it is true. God has ways of revealing himself to his own in another way than he does to the world: 'The secret of the Lord is with them that fear him, and he will show them his covenant.'

Jesus is often with his own. They feel his presence, they hear his words, their hearts burn within them. They sometimes feel that he fulfils that word: 'I will not leave you orphans; I will come to you.' *The Father* is the refuge of his own. They feel his everlasting arms underneath them, they feel his love pouring down on them like a stream of light from heaven. *The Holy Spirit* is within them. They sometimes feel his breathing, they sometimes feel that they have the Spirit within them crying, 'Abba, Father.' Oh ! this is heaven upon earth - full, satisfying joy.

Sometimes it pleases God to withdraw from the soul, chiefly, I believe, *first*, to humble us in the dust; *second*, to discover some corruption unmortified; *third*, to lead us to hunger more after him.

Such was the state of *David* when he wrote the 42nd Psalm: 'I will say unto God my Rock, Why hast thou forgotten me? ... As with a sword in my bones, mine enemies reproach me, while they say daily unto me, Where is thy God?'. 'As the hart panteth after the water-brooks, so panteth my soul after thee, O God.' Ah! far more than the natural thirst of the wounded deer for the clear-flowing brook, is the spiritual thirst of the deserted soul after God.

Such was the feeling of Job when he cried: 'The arrows of the Almighty are within me;' and again: 'Oh that I knew where I might find him; oh that it were with me as in months past!' He has a bitter remembrance of his past enjoyment, a bitter sense that means cannot bring his soul back again to rest.

Such was the feeling of the bride: 'By night on my bed I sought him whom my soul loveth: I sought him, but I found him not' (Song 3:1).

Ah! brethren, if ever you have known anything of this, you will know something of the wretched feeling of distance from God, of having mountains between the soul and him, implied in these words: 'The Lord hath forsaken me, and my God hath forgotten me.'

2. God cannot forget a soul in Christ: 'Can a woman forget her sucking child, that she should not have compassion on the son of her womb? Yea, they may forget; yet will I not forget thee.'

1. It is like a mother's love.
There is no love in this world like a mother's love. It is a free, unbought, unselfish love. However much pain she has suffered on her child's account, however many troubles she has to bear for it, by night and by day, while it hangs upon her breast, still it is more precious than gold. There is something in her heart that clings to her weak, sickly, nay, even to her idiot boy. God's love to a soul in Christ is stronger than this love. The Psalmist compares it to a father's: 'Like as a father pitieth his children, so the Lord pitieth them that fear him.' And Malachi 3:17: 'I will spare them, as a man spareth his own son that serveth him.' Again, Isaiah 66:13: 'As one whom his mother comforteth, so will I comfort you.'

This love of a mother to her child is natural to her. She cannot account for it. You cannot change it. You must break to pieces the mother's heart before you can change her love to her child. And yet there are some poor souls so disfigured by Satan, their hearts so brutalized, that they can forget their children. The Indian mother can dance over her infant's grave, and the murderess can lift her hand against the life of her little one: Ah! *'They* may forget; yet will I not forget thee.'

The love of God to a soul in Christ is a natural love. It is a love engrained in his nature. The Father loves the Son; and it is the same love with which he loves the soul that is in Christ. He cannot forget him. He loves him because he is altogether lovely. He loves him because he is worthy to be loved. He loves him because he laid down his life for the sheep. All that is in God binds him to love his Son - his holiness, his justice, his truth; and so that all that is in God binds him to love the soul that is in Christ.

Be not cast down, brethren in affliction. Deserted souls, God's love cannot change unless his nature change. Not till God cease to be holy, just and true, will he cease to love the soul that hides under the wings of Jesus.

2. *The Father's love is full love.*

A mother's love is the fullest love which we have on earth. She loves with all her heart. But there is no love more full than that of God toward his Son; God loves Jesus fully. The whole heart of the Father is, as it were, continually poured down in love upon the Lord Jesus. There is nothing in Christ that does not draw the infinite love of God. In him God sees his own image perfectly, his own law acted out, his own will done. The Father loves the Son fully; but when a soul comes into Christ, the same love rests on that soul: 'That the love wherewith thou hast loved me may be in them' (John 17:26).

True, a creature cannot receive the love of God as Jesus can; but it is the same love that shines on us and him - full, satisfying, unbounded love. When the sun pours down its beams on the wide ocean and on a little flower at the same time, it is the same sunshine that is poured into both, though the ocean has vastly larger capacity to receive its glorious beams. So, when the Son of God receives the love of his Father, and a poor guilty worm hides in him, it is the same love that comes both on the Saviour and the sinner, though Jesus is able to contain more.

How can God forget what he fully loves? If God fully loves thee, he has not forgotten thee - he cannot forget thee. A creature's love may fail, for what is a creature? - a clay vessel, a breath of wind that passeth away, and cometh not again. But the Creator's love cannot fail. It is full love toward an object infinitely worthy of his love, in which thou sharest.

3. *It is an unchanging love.*
A mother's love is, of all creature-love, the most unchangeable. A boy leaves his parent's roof, he crosses a thousand seas, he labours beneath a foreign sky; he comes back, he finds his aged mother changed, her head is grey, her venerable brow is furrowed with age; still he feels, while she clasps him to her bosom, that her heart is the same. But ah! far more unchanging is the love of God to Christ, and to a soul in Christ: 'I am the Lord; I change not.' The Father that loves has no variableness. Jesus, who is loved, is the same yesterday, today, and for ever. How can that love change? It flowed before the world was; it will flow when the world has passed away.

If you are in Christ, that love shines on you: 'I have loved thee with an everlasting love.' 'I am persuaded, that neither death, nor life, nor angels, nor principalities, nor powers, nor things present, nor things to come, nor height, nor depth, nor any other creature, shall be able to separate us from the love of God, which is in Christ Jesus our Lord.'

Let the remembrance of these things comfort downcast believers. Many of you may be cast down, and your souls disquieted. You think God has dealt bitterly with you - he has written you childless; or he has met you as a lion, and as a bear bereaved of her whelps; or he has blasted your gourd; or he has deserted you, so that you seek him, and find him not. Look still to Jesus. The love of God shines on him. Nothing can separate Jesus from that love - nothing can separate you. At the very time Zion was saying: 'My God hath forgotten me,' at that moment God was saying: 'I will not forget thee.'

Your afflictions and desertions only prove that you are under the Father's hand. There is no time when the patient is an object of such tender interest to the surgeon, as when he is under his knife; so, you may be sure, if you are suffering from the hand of God, his eye is all the more bent on you. 'The eternal God is thy refuge, and underneath are the everlasting arms.'

Encourage poor sinners to come and taste of this love. It is a sweet thing to be loved. I suppose the most of you have tasted a mother's love. You know what it is to be rocked in her arms, to be watched by her gentle eye, to be cheered by her smile; but, oh! brethren, this is nothing to the love of your God. That dear mother's eye will close in death, that dear mother's arm will moulder in the dust. Oh! come and share the love of Him who cannot die. There is one spot alone on which the love of God continually falls unclouded - it is the head of Jesus: 'The Father loveth the Son.' He loves him from his very nature, so that the perfections of God must change before this love can change. He loves him fully. The whole treasures of love that are in the infinite bosom of Jehovah are pouring continually into the bosom of the Son. He loves unchangingly; no cloud can ever come between - no veil - no distance.

But what is this to me? Everything to you, sinner. Jesus stands a refuge for sinners - ready to receive even thee. Flee into him, sinner; abide in him, and that love shall abide on you. You are a worm; but you may enter into the joy of your Lord. You may share the love of God with Jesus in a way that holy angels cannot do. Oh! sinner, had you rather remain under the wrath of God? 'He that believeth not the Son shall not see life; but the wrath of God abideth on him.' 'God is angry with the wicked every day.' But, ah! 'This is a faithful saying, and worthy of all acceptation, that Christ Jesus came into the world to save sinners, of whom I am chief.'

Oh! it is sweet to pass from wrath to love, from death to life. That poor murderess would leap in her cell, when the news came that she was not to die the murderer's death; but, ah! ten thousand times sweeter would it be to you, if God were, this day, to persuade you to embrace Jesus Christ freely offered in the gospel.

15. Thanksgiving obtains the Spirit

It came even to pass, as the trumpeters and singers were as one, to make one sound to be heard in praising and thanking the LORD; and when they lifted up their voice with the trumpets and cymbals and instruments of music, and praised the LORD, saying, For he is good; for his mercy endureth for ever: that then the house was filled with a cloud, even the house of the LORD; so that the priests could not stand to minister by reason of the cloud; for the glory of the LORD had filled the house of God (2 Chronicles 5:13, 14).

The day here spoken of appears to have been a day of days. It seems to have been the day of Pentecost in Old Testament times, a type of all the glorious days of an outpoured Spirit that ever have been in the world, a foretaste of that glorious day when God will fulfil that amazing, soul-satisfying promise: 'I will pour out my Spirit upon all flesh.'

My dearly beloved flock, it is my heart's desire and prayer that this very day might be such a day among us - that God would indeed open the windows of heaven, as he has done in times past, and pour down a blessing, till there be no room to receive it.

Let us observe, then, how thanksgiving brings down the Spirit of God.

1. How the people were engaged: 'In praising and thanking the Lord.' Yea, you have their very words: 'For he is good; for his mercy endureth for ever.' It was thus the people were engaged when the cloud came down and filled the house.

They had been engaged in many other most affecting duties. The Levites had been carrying the ark from Mount Zion and placing it under the wings of the cherubim. Solomon and all his people had been offering sacrifices, sheep and oxen, which could not be told for multitude. Still no answer came from heaven. But when the trumpeters and singers were as one in praising and thanking the Lord, when they lifted up their voices, saying: 'For he is good; for his mercy endureth for ever' - then the windows of heaven were opened. Then the cloud came down and fill the whole temple.

My dear flock, I am deeply persuaded that there will be no full, soul-filling, heart-ravishing, heart-satisfying, outpouring of the Spirit of God, till there be more praise and thanking the Lord. Let me stir up your hearts to praise.

(1) *He is good.*
Believers should praise God for what he is in himself. Those that have never seen the Lord cannot praise him. Those that have not come to Christ, have never seen the King in his beauty. An unconverted man sees no loveliness in God. He sees a beauty in the blue sky, in the glorious sun, in the green earth, in the spangling stars, in the lily of the field; but he sees no beauty in God. He hath not seen him, neither known him; therefore there is no melody of praise in that heart.

When a sinner is brought to Christ, he is brought to the Father. Jesus gave himself for us, 'that he might bring us to God.' O! what a sight breaks in upon the soul - the infinite, eternal, unchangeable God! I know that some of you have been brought to see this sight.

Oh! praise him, then, for what he is. Praise him for his *pure, lovely holiness*, that cannot bear any sin in his sight. Cry, like the angels, 'Holy, holy, holy, Lord God Almighty.' Praise him for his *infinite wisdom* - that he knows the end from the beginning. In him are hid all the treasures of wisdom and knowledge. Praise him for his *power* - that all matter, all mind, is in his hand. The heart of the king, the heart of saint and sinner, are all in his hand. Hallelujah! for the Lord God Omnipotent reigneth. Praise him for his *love*; for God is love. Some of you have been at sea. When far out of sight of land, you have stood high on the vessel's prow, and looked round and round - one vast circle of ocean without any bound. Oh! so it is to stand in Christ justified, and to behold the love of God - a vast ocean all around you, without a bottom and without a shore. Oh! praise him for what he is. Heaven will be all praise. If you cannot praise God, you never will be there.

(2) *For his mercy - for what he has done for us.*
The Lord has done much for me since we parted. We were once in perils of waters; but the Lord saved the ship. Again and again we were in danger of plague. We nightly heard the cry of the mourner; yet no plague came near our dwelling. Again and again we were in peril of robbers. The gun of the murderous Arab has been levelled at us; but the Lord stayed his hand. I have been at the gates of death since we parted. No man that saw me would have believed that I could be here this day; yet he hath healed our diseases, and brought me back to open once more to you the unsearchable riches of Christ. I, then, have reason to praise him; for his mercy endureth for ever.

The Lord has done much for you since we parted. My eyes filled with tears when I left you; for I thought he had done it in anger. I thought it was anger to me, and I thought it was anger to you; but now I see it was all love. It was all mercy to unworthy you and to unworthy me. The Lord gave you my dear brother to care for your souls; and far better than that - for to give you a man only would have been a poor gift - he has given you his Holy Spirit. 'Bless the Lord, O my soul!' Praise him, O my people! for he is good; for his mercy endureth for ever.

Are there not some of you brands plucked out of the burning? You were in the burning; the pains of hell were actually getting hold on you. You had a hell in your own hearts, you had a hell yawning to receive you; but the Lord snatched you from the burning. Will you not praise him?

Are there not some of you whom I left blind, and deaf, and dumb, and dead? You saw no beauty in him who is fairer than the children of men; you saw no glory in Immanuel - God manifest in flesh. But the Lord has said: 'Go, wash in the pool of Siloam;' and whereas you were blind, now you see. Oh! praise him that hath done it. In heaven, they praise God most of all for this: 'Worthy is the Lamb that was slain.' Oh! have you no praise for Jesus for all his love, for the Father, for the Spirit?

Some of you cannot sing: 'No man could learn that song but those that were redeemed from the earth.' Some of you are worse than when I left you. You have resisted me, you have resisted my brother, and, oh! worse than all, you have resisted the Holy Ghost. You are prayerless yet - Christless yet. Ah! unhappy souls! unredeemed, unrenewed, remember it will be too late to learn to praise when you die. You must begin now.

I will tell you what a dear friend of mine once said before dying. She desired all the servants to be brought in, and she said very solemnly: 'There's nothing but Christ between me and weeping, and wailing, and gnashing of teeth. Oh! if you have not Christ, then there is nothing between you and weeping, and wailing, and gnashing of teeth.' You that will not praise Christ now, shall wail because of him soon.

2. The manner of their praise.

They were 'as one.'

Their hearts were all as one heart in this exercise. There were a thousand tongues, but only one heart. Not only were their harps, and cymbals, and dulcimers all in tune, giving out a harmonious melody, but their hearts were all in tune. God had given them one heart, and then the blessing came down.

The same was the case on the day of Pentecost; they were all with *one accord* in one place; they were looking to the same Lamb of God. The same thing will be the case in that day prophesied of in the 133rd Psalm: 'Behold, how good and how pleasant it is for brethren to dwell together in unity! ... There the LORD commands the blessing, even life for evermore.'

This is the very thing which Jesus prayed for in that prayer which none but God could have asked, and none but God could answer: 'Neither pray I for these alone, but for them also which shall believe on me through their word; that they all may be one; as thou, Father, art in me, and I in thee, that they also may be one in us; that the world may believe that thou hast sent me.' And then follows the blessing: 'And the glory which thou gavest me I have given them; that they may be one, even as we are one: I in them, and thou in me, that they may be made perfect in one; and that the world may know that thou has sent me, and hast loved them, as thou hast loved me.'

Dear children of God, unite your praises. Let your hearts no more be divided. You are divided from the world by a great gulf. Soon it will be an infinite gulf. But you are united to one another by the same Spirit. You have been chosen by the same free, sovereign love. You have been washed in the same precious blood. You have been filled by the same blessed Spirit. Little children, love one another. He that loveth is born of God. Be one in your praises. Join in one cry: 'Worthy is the Lamb that was slain. Thou art worthy to open the book - thou art worthy to reign in our hearts.'

And, oh! be fervent in praise. Lift up your voices in it. Lift up your hearts in it. In heaven they wax louder and louder. John heard the sound of a great multitude; and then it was like many waters, and then it was like mighty thunderings, crying: 'Hallelujah! Hallelujah!' I remember Edwards' remark, that it was in the singing of praises that his people felt themselves most enlarged, and that then God was worshipped somewhat in the beauty of holiness.

Let it be so among yourselves. Learn, dearly beloved, to praise God heartily, to sing with all your heart and soul in the family and in the congregation. But, oh! remember that even your praises must be sprinkled with blood, and can be acceptable to God only by Jesus Christ.

3. Effects.
1. *The cloud filled the house.*
This cloud is the very same which led them through the Red Sea, and went before them forty years in the wilderness. It was a pillar of cloud by day, to shade them from the heat; it was a pillar of fire by night, to guide Israel on their way to the promised rest; and now it came and filled the holiest of all and the holy place. Such was the wonderful effect which followed their united fervent praises. God himself came down, and filled every chamber of the house with his presence. 'This is my rest for ever: here will I dwell; for I have desired it.'

Now, my dear friends, we are not now to expect that God will answer our prayers, or follow our praises with a pillar of cloud or a pillar of fire. These were but the shadows; now we receive the reality - the substance. If ye will but unite in unanimous and heartfelt praises, then am I persuaded that God will give his Holy Spirit to fill this house - to fill every heart in the spiritual temple.

How glorious this will be *for the children of God.*

Are there not some of you who have come to Christ, and nothing more? Guilty, weary, heavy-laden, you have found rest, redemption through his blood, even the forgiveness of sins. Oh! do not stop there. Do not rest in mere forgiveness. Cry for the indwelling of the Holy Ghost, the Comforter. Forgiveness is but a means to an end. You are justified in order that you may be sanctified. Remember, without holiness you will never see the Lord; and without this indwelling Spirit, you never will be holy.

Are there not some of you groaning under a body of sin and death, and crying, with the apostle, 'Oh! wretched man, who shall deliver me from the body of this death?' Do you not feel the plague of your own heart? Do you not feel the power of your old nature? How many in this state lean upon themselves, trust in their resolutions, attempt, as it were, by force, to put down their sins! But here is the remedy. Oh! cry for the flood-tide of God's Spirit, that he may fill every chamber of your heart, that he may renew you in the spirit of your mind.

Are there not many who are cold, worldly Christians, those who were long ago converted, but have fallen sadly back, under the power of the world - either its gaiety or its business, its mirth or its money - and they have got into worldly habits, deep ruts of sin? Ah! see what you need. He that created man in his own image at first, must create you over again. You need an almighty indwelling Comforter. Oh! it is he only who can melt your icy heart, and make it flow out in love to God, who can fill you with all the fullness of God.

Are there not some who read the Bible, but get little from it? You feel that it does not sink into your heart, it does not remain with you through the week. It is like the seed cast in the wayside, easily plucked away. Oh! it is just such an outpoured Spirit you require, to hide the Word in your heart. When you write with a dry pen, without any ink in it, no impression is made upon the paper. Now, ministers are the pens, and the Spirit of God is the ink. Pray that the pen may be filled with that living ink, that the Word may remain in your heart, known and read of all men - that you may be sanctified through the truth.

How glorious this will be *for the unconverted.*

So it was in the day of Pentecost - the Spirit came first upon the small company of disciples, and then on the three thousand. You have seen the hills attracting the clouds, and so drawing down the shower into the valleys. So do God's children, having their heads within the veil, obtain the Spirit of God in fullness, and dispense it to all around. You have seen some tall tree or spire catching the lightning, and conveying it down into the ground. So does the fire of God's Spirit come first upon the trees of righteousness, and from them descends to the dead souls around them.

A word to dead souls. Keep near to God's children at such a time as this. Do not separate from them, do not mock at them; you may yet receive the grace of God through them. Dear believers, for the sake of the dead souls around you, for the sake of this great town, full of wickedness, for the sake of our land, filled with formality and hypocrisy - oh! unite in prayer, and unite in praise, and prove the Lord, if he will not pour out a blessing. Not for your own sakes only, but for the sake of those perishing around you, let us wrestle and pray for a fuller time of the Spirit's working than has ever been seen in Scotland yet.

2. *The priests could not stand to minister.*

Before the cloud came down, no doubt the priests were all busily engaged burning incense and offering sacrifices; but when the cloud came down, they could only wonder and adore. So it ever will be when the Lord gives much of his Spirit; he will make it evident that it is not the work of man.

If he were to give only a little, then ministers would begin to think they had some hand in it; but when he fills the house, then he makes it plain that man has nothing to do with it. David Brainerd said, that when God awakened his whole congregation of Indians, he stood by amazed, and felt that he was as nothing - that God alone was working.

Oh! it is this, dear friends, that we desire and pray for - that the Lord the Spirit would himself descend, and with his almighty power tear away the veil from your hearts, convincing you of sin, of righteousness, and of judgment; that Jesus himself would take his sceptre and break your hard hearts, and take all the glory, that we may cry out: 'Not unto us, Lord, not unto us, but unto thy name give glory.'

St Peter's, November 24, 1839 (after returning from Palestine)

16. An exceeding good land

And they spake unto all the company of the children of Israel, saying,
The land, which we passed through to search it, is an exceeding good
land. If the LORD delight in us, then he will bring us into this land, and
give it us, a land that floweth with milk and honey' (Numbers 14:7,8).

When the children of Israel arrived at the border of the promised land,
Moses, at the command of God, sent twelve men to spy out the good
land. They searched it for forty days from the one end to the other, and
then returned, bringing a bunch of grapes, borne between two on a staff,
from the fruitful valley of Eshcol. But ten of the spies brought an evil
report of the land. The land, they said, was good; but the inhabitants
were giants, and the cities walled up to heaven; and the conclusion they
came to was: 'We are not able to go up against the people, for they are
stronger than we' (Numbers 13:31).

Joshua and Caleb alone tried to still the people. They did not deny
that the men were tall, and that the cities were walled; but they pointed
to the pillar-cloud to answer all objections: 'The Lord is with us', and
we shall subdue the people as easily as we eat bread. 'The land which
we passed through to search it is an exceeding good land.'

Doctrine: If God delight in a soul, he will bring it into the good land.

1. Show who they are that God delights in.

God has no delight in a natural soul.

'If thou shouldest mark iniquities, O Lord, who shall stand?' 'Thou art
not a God that delightest in wickedness; neither shall evil dwell with
thee.' 'Thou art of purer eyes than to behold evil, and canst not look on
iniquity.' 'Surely thou wilt slay the wicked, O God.' Eli's sons
hearkened not unto the voice of their father, for the Lord would slay
them. It is God's very nature to loathe and turn away from that which
is sinful. A person with a fine ear for music cannot delight in a jarring
discord. It is impossible, from his very nature. So it is impossible for
God to delight in a naked sinner. And when naked sinners and God meet
in the judgment, God will have no mercy, neither will his eye spare. He
will say: 'Bind them hand and foot, and cast them into outer darkness.'

Oh! you that are covered over with sin, think of this. You that are
uncovered with the pure robe of the righteousness of Jesus, prepare to
meet your God. How will you come into the presence of one who abhors

sin, when he puts your most secret sins in the light of his countenance, when he brings to light all the hidden works of darkness, when you shall give account of every idle word? Ah! where will you appear?

He delights in one sprinkled with the blood of Christ.
When a hell-deserving sinner is enlightened in the knowledge of Christ - when he believes the record that God hath given concerning his Son, and joyfully consents that the Lord Jesus should be his surety, then the blood of Christ is, as it were, sprinkled over that soul. When Aaron and his sons were set apart for the priesthood, the blood of the ram was put upon the tip of their right ear, and the thumb of their right hand, and the great toe of their right foot, to signify that they were dipped in blood from head to foot; so when God looks upon a soul in Christ, he sees it dipped in the blood of the Saviour. He looks upon that soul as having suffered all that Christ suffered; therefore he delights in it.

His sense of justice is pleased. God has an infinite sense of justice. His eyes behold the things that are equal. Now when he sees the blood of his Son sprinkled upon any soul, he sees that justice has had its full satisfaction in that soul, that that man's sins have been more fully punished than if he had borne them himself eternally.

His sense of mercy is pleased. He delighteth in mercy. Even when justice was crying out, 'Thou shalt surely slay the wicked,' his mercy was yearning over sinners, and he provided a ransom. And now when the sinner has laid hold on the ransom, mercy is poured down in forgiveness. God delighteth in mercy; he delights to forgive. It is sweet to notice how Jesus loves to forgive sins. In the story of the woman that washed his feet, how he seems to dwell on it! 'Her sins, which are many, are forgiven.' And again he said unto her: 'Thy sins are forgiven thee.' And again, a third time: 'Go in peace.' And so God loves to forgive: 'There is joy in heaven over one sinner that repenteth.'

Trembling sinners, come to Jesus. Some of you are trembling under a sense of being exposed to God's wrath. Which of his commandments have you not broken? Your case is, indeed, a dismal one. Your fears are most just and reasonable; and if you saw your condition fully, they would be ten thousand times greater. Yet here is a fountain opened for sin and uncleanness. If only you are willing to come to the Lord Jesus, you do not need to remain another moment out of God's favour. You see how completely safe you would be, if you would take this blood. A just and merciful God would rejoice over you to forgive you. It is all in vain that you try your own righteousness - it will never make God delight in you, for it is filthy rags in his sight. But the blood of atonement, the blood of the Lamb - it speaketh peace.

God delights in the sanctified.
You remember, in the Book of Revelation, how often Jesus says, 'I know thy works.' He says it with delight in the case of Smyrna: 'I know thy works and tribulation and poverty; but thou art rich.' When God brings a soul into Christ, he makes him a new creature; then God loves the new creature. Just as when God made the world, he saw all that he had made, and smiled, for all was very good; so, when God makes a new creation in the heart, God delights in it. He says, It is all very good.

Objection: My graces are all imperfect. They do not please me - how can they please God? I cannot do the things that I would.

Answer: All true; yet God loves his own workmanship in the soul. His Spirit prays in you, lives in you, walks in you. God loves the work of his own Spirit. Just as you love flowers of your own planting, as you love a spot that you have laid out much on; so God loves his children, not for anything of their own, but for what he has done for them, and in them. They are dear-bought; he has bought them with his own blood. He waters them every moment, lest any hurt them; he keeps them by night and by day, and how can he but love them? He loves the place where his Spirit dwells. Just as God loved the temple: 'This is my rest; here will I dwell, for I have desired it;' not for any good in it, but because it was the place of his feet, because he had done so much for it; so God loves his Christians, just because he dwells in them, and has done so much for them. Just as it was with Aaron's rod: it was a dry stick, like any other rod; but God made it bud forth, and bloom blossoms, and bear ripe almonds; and therefore he caused it to be laid up in the holiest of all. So is a Christian - naturally a dry tree. But God makes him bear fruit, and loves the work of his own hands.

Dear Christians, walk after the Spirit, and please God more and more. He saveth such as be of a contrite heart. His countenance doth behold the upright: 'I love them that love me.'

2. God will bring all his people to glory.
There are many difficulties in the way. So it was with Israel. The cities were walled, and very great. The inhabitants were gigantic and strong. Israel felt before them like grasshoppers. So it is with God's children.

They have many and great enemies - the devil and his angels, once the brightest and highest of all created intelligences, now the great enemies of souls. They are against the Christian. The world is full of giants all opposing God's children. The persecutions of the ungodly, the allurements of pleasure - these are great enemies in the way. They are giant lusts in the heart: the lust of praise, the lust of the flesh, the lust of the eye, the pride of life. Before these the soul feels like a grasshopper, without strength: 'We are not able to go up against the people, for they are stronger than we.'

Argument: If he delight in us, he will bring us into this land.

He is able: 'If God be for us, who can be against us?'

God is stronger than Satan.

Satan is nothing in his hand. It is easier for God to crush Satan under our feet, than for you to crush a fly. God is infinitely stronger than Satan. Satan can no more hinder God from carrying us to glory than a little fly can, which you crush with your foot. 'He shall bruise Satan under your feet shortly.' Submit yourselves to God. Resist the devil, and he will flee from you.

God is stronger than the world.

The world often comes against us like armed men; but, if God be for us, who can be against us? 'The people shall be like bread.' It is as easy to overcome all opposition when God is with us, as for a hungry man to eat bread. It was God that girded Cyrus, though he did not know him. So he does still: worldly men are a rod in God's hand. God puts it this way or that way, to fulfil all his pleasure; and when he has done with it, he will break it in pieces, and cast it into the fire. 'So fear not them that kill the body, and after that, have no more that they can do.' Oh! Christian, if you would live by faith, you might live a happy life!

God is stronger than our own heart.

There is many a Jericho in our own heart walled up to heaven, many a fortress of sin, many giant lusts, which threaten our souls. 'O wretched man that I am, who shall deliver me from the body of this death?' 'If the Lord delight in us, he will bring us into the good land.' 'By faith the walls of Jericho fell down after they were compassed about seven days.' God made the walls of Jericho fall flat, by a mere breath of wind, a noise; so he is able still. Settle it in your hearts: there is no Jericho in your hearts which God is not able to make fall in a moment. You have seen a shepherd carrying a sheep on his shoulder. He meets with many a stone in the way, many a thorn, many a stream; yet the sheep feels no difficulty, it is carried above all. So is it with every soul that yields itself to God; the only difficulty is to lie on his shoulder.

Apply to young Christians.
Learn where your sanctification lies - in God: 'With thee is the fountain of life.' 'Your life is hid with Christ in God.' Your holiness does not depend on you, but on him. It is a hard lesson to learn, that you cannot sanctify yourself, that you cannot overcome these giants, and scale these walls. You have learned one humbling lesson, that you have no righteousness, that nothing you have done, or can do, will justify you. Now, learn another humbling lesson - that even when pardoned you have no strength. It is the most humbling of all things to lie like a sheep on his shoulders; but, oh! it is sweet. Be like Aaron's rod - a dry stick in yourself till he shall make you bud, and blossom, and bear fruit. Say, like Ephraim: 'I am a green fir tree;' and hear God say, 'From me is thy fruit found.'
Apply to fallen Christians
Some of you may have fallen into sin. The reason was just this: you forgot where your strength lay. It was not the force of passion, nor the power of Satan, nor the allurement of the world, that made you fall - it was unbelief. You did not lie in his hand.

Apply to aged Christians
You have come to the border of the promised land, and still your enemies seem like giants, and the cities walled up to heaven, and you feel like a grasshopper. Still, if the Lord delight in you, he will keep you in the love of God. He that saved you out of the mouth of the lion, and out of the paw of the bear, will save you out of the hand of this Philistine. Trust God to the end. Even in the valley of the shadow of death, look back over all your deliverances; look over all the Ebenezers you have raised, and say:

> After so much mercy past,
> Canst thou let me sink at last?

17. Family government

*For I know him, that he will command his children and his household after him, and they shall keep the way of the L*ORD*, to do justice and judgment; that the L*ORD *may bring upon Abraham that which he hath spoken of him (Genesis 18:19).*

There are three things very remarkable in these words.

(1) *That Abraham used parental authority in governing his family:* 'I know him, that he will command his children and servants after him.' He did not think it enough to pray for them, or to teach them, but he used the authority which God had given him. He commanded them.

(2) *That he cared for his servants as well as his children.* In Genesis 14:14, we learn that Abraham had 318 servants born in his house. He lived after the manner of patriarchal times, as the Arabs of the wilderness do to this day. His family was very large, and yet he did not say, 'They are none of mine.' He commanded his children and his household.

3. *His success.* 'They shall keep the way of the Lord.' It is often said that the children of good men turn out ill. Well, here is a good man, and a good man doing his duty by his children - and here is the result. His son Isaac was probably a child of God from his earliest years. There is every mark of it in his life. And what a delightful specimen of a believing, prayerful servant was Eliezer! (Genesis 24)

It is the duty of all believers to rule their houses well.

1. The spring of this duty.
Love to souls.

As long as a man does not care for his own soul, he does not care for the souls of others. He can see his wife and children living in sin, going down to hell. He does not care. He does not care for missions, gives nothing to support missionaries. But the moment a man's eyes are opened to the value of his own soul, that moment does he begin to care for the souls of others. From that moment does he love the missionary cause. He willingly spares a little to send the gospel to the Jew and the perishing Hindus. Again, he begins to care for the church at home, for his neighbours, all living in sin. Like the maniac at Decapolis, he publishes the name of Jesus wherever he goes. And now he begins to care for his own house. He commands his children and his household after him.

How is it with you? Do you rule well your own house? Do you worship God, morning and evening, in your family? Do you deal with your children and servants touching their conversion? If not, you do not love their souls. And the reason is, you do not love your own. You may make what outward profession you please; you may sit down at sacraments, and talk about your feelings, etc.; but if you do not labour for the conversion of your children, it is all a lie. If you but felt the preciousness of Christ, you could not look upon their faces without a heart-breaking desire that they might be saved. This was Rahab's prayer (Joshua 2:13).

Desire to use all talents for Christ.
When a man comes to Christ, he feels he is not his own (1 Corinthians 6:19). He hears Christ say: 'Occupy till I come.' If he be a rich man, he uses all for Christ, like Gaius. If a learned man, he spends all for Christ, like Paul. Now, parental authority is one talent, the authority of a master is another talent, for the use of which men will be judged. He uses these also for Christ. He commands his children and his household after him. How is it with you? Do you use these talents for Christ? If not, you have never given yourself away to him - you are not his.

2. Scripture examples of it.
Abraham. The most eminent example of it - the father of all believers. Are you a child of Abraham? Then walk in his steps in this. Wherever Abraham went, he built an altar to the Lord.

   Job. Upon every one of his son's birthdays Job offered sacrifices, according to the number of them all (Job 1:5).

   Joshua. 'As for me and my house, we will serve the Lord' (Joshua 24:15).

   Eunice. From a child, little Timothy knew the Scriptures; and the reason for this you understand, when you read of the faith of his mother Eunice (2 Timothy 3:15, with 1:5).

   Such was the manner in Scotland in the days of our fathers; and if ever we are to see Scotland again a garden of the Lord, it must be by the reviving of family government.

3. The manner of it.
Worship God in your family.
If you do not worship God in your family, you are living in positive sin;

you may be quite sure you do not care for the souls of your family. If you neglected to spread a meal for your children to eat, would it not be said that you did not care for their bodies? And if you do not lead your children and servants to the green pastures of God's Word, and to seek the living water, how plain is it that you do not care for their souls! *Do it regularly*, morning and evening. It is more needful than your daily food, more needful than your work. How vain and silly all your excuses will appear, when you look back from hell! *Do it fully.* Some clip off the psalm, and some the reading of the Word; and so the worship of God is reduced to a mockery. *Do it in a spiritual, lively manner.* Go to it as to a well of salvation. There is, perhaps, no mean of grace more blessed. Let all your family be present without fail - let none be awanting.

Command - use parental authority.
How awfully did God avenge it upon Eli, 'because his sons made themselves vile, and he restrained them not!' Eli was a good man, and a holy man; and often he spoke to his two wicked sons, but they heeded not. But herein he failed, he did not use his parental authority - he did not restrain them. Remember Eli. It is not enough to pray for your children, and to pray with them, and to warn them; but you must restrain them. Restrain them with the cords of love. From wicked books, from wicked companions, from wicked amusements, from untimely hours, restrain them.

Command servants as well as children.
So did Abraham. Remember you are in the place of a father to your servants. They are come under your roof, and they have a claim on your instructions. If they minister to you in carnal things, it is but fair that you minister to them in spiritual things. You have drawn them away from under the parental roof, and it is your part to see that they do not lose by it. Oh! what a mass of sin would be prevented, if masters would care for their servants' souls.

Deal with each as to the conversion of his soul.
I have known many dear Christian parents who have been singularly neglectful in this particular. They worship God in the family, and pray earnestly in secret for their children and servants, and yet never deal with them as to their conversion. Satan spreads a kind of false modesty among parents, that they will not inquire of their little ones, Have you

found the Lord, or no? Ah! how sinful and foolish this will appear in eternity. If you should see some of your children or servants in hell - all because you did not speak to them in private - how would you look? Begin tonight. Take them aside and ask, What has God done for your soul?

Lead a holy life before them.
If all your religion is on your tongue, your children and servants will soon find out your hypocrisy.

4. The blessings which follows the performing of it.
1. You will avoid the curse.
You will avoid Eli's curse. Eli was a child of God, and yet he suffered much on account of his unfaithfulness. He lost his two sons in one day. If you would avoid Eli's curse, avoid Eli's sin. 'Pour out thy fury ... on the families that call not on thy name' (Jeremiah 10:25). If you do not worship God in your house, a curse is written over your door. If I could mark the dwellings in this town where there is no family prayer, these are the spots where the curse of God is ready to fall. These houses are over hell.

2. Your children will be saved.
So it was with Abraham. His dear son Isaac was saved. What became of Ishmael I do not know. Only I remember his fervent cry: 'O that Ishmael might live before thee!' Such is the promise: 'Train up a child in the way he should go, and when he is old he will not depart from it.' Such is the promise in baptism. Ah! who can tell the blessedness of being the saved father of a saved family?

Dear believers, be wise. Surely if anything could mar the joy of heaven, it would be to see your children lost through your neglect. Dear unconverted souls, if one pang could be more bitter than another in hell, it would be to hear your children say 'Father, mother, you brought me here.'

18. The gospel feast

And in this mountain shall the LORD of hosts make unto all people a feast of fat things, a feast of wines on the lees, of fat things full of marrow, of wines on the lees well refined. And he will destroy in this mountain the face of the covering cast over all people, and the veil that is spread over all nations. He will swallow up death in victory; and the Lord GOD will wipe away tears from off all faces; and the rebuke of his people shall he take away from off all the earth: for the LORD hath spoken it (Isaiah 25:6-8).

These words are yet to be fulfilled at the second coming of the Saviour. It is true that the Lord of hosts has long ago prepared this feast, and sent out his servants, saying: 'Come, for all things are ready.' But it is just as true that the veil that is spread over all nations is not yet taken away; and Paul tells us plainly, in 1 Corinthians 15:54, that it is in the resurrection morning that these words shall be quite fulfilled: 'He hath swallowed up death in victory.'

Still these words have been in some measure fulfilled wherever there has been a peculiar outpouring of the Spirit upon any place. Often at sacrament seasons in our own land these words have been fulfilled. God has made Christ a feast of fat things to hungry souls. The veil of unbelief has been torn from many hearts, and the tears wiped away from many eyes. It is my humble but earnest desire that next Sabbath day (the Communion Sabbath) may be such a day in this place. I want to engage all of you who are the children of God to secret and united prayer that it may be so; and I have, therefore, chosen these words by which to stir you up to pray. (1) Consider the feast. (2) The tearing away of the veil. (3) The effects of it.

1. The feast.

1. *Where is it? Answer*: 'In this mountain.'

(a) *Moriah?* Ah! it was here that Abraham offered up Isaac. It was here that the Passover lamb used to be slain. It was here that Jesus stood and cried, 'If any man thirst, let him come to me and drink.'

(b) *Mount Olivet?* It was here that Jesus said, 'I am the true vine.' It was here that Jesus had the cup of wrath set down before him, in that night in which he was betrayed.

(c) *Mount Calvary?* It was here that they crucified Jesus, and two thieves, one on each hand. It was here that the passers-by wagged their heads, the chief priests mocked, and the thieves cast the same in his teeth. It was here that there was three hours' darkness. It was here they pierced his hands and feet. It was here that God forsook his own Son. It was here that infinite wrath was laid upon an infinite Saviour: 'In this mountain shall the LORD of hosts make unto all people a feast of fat things.'

To anxious souls
The world tries to cheer you. They bid you to go into company, see more of the world, enjoy pleasure, and drive away these dull thoughts. They spread a feast for you in some lighted hall, with brilliant lamps; and the pipe and the tabret, and wine are in their feasts. Oh! anxious soul, flee these things: remember Lot's wife. If you are anxious about your soul, flee from the feasts of the world. Stop your ears, and run. Look here how God tries to cheer you - he, too, prepares a feast. But where? On Calvary. There is no light; it is all darkness round the cross; no music, but the groan of a dying Saviour: 'Eli! Eli! - My God! my God!' Oh! anxious soul, it is there you will find peace and rest. 'Come unto me, all ye that labour and are heavy laden, and I will give you rest.' The darkest hour that ever was in this world gives light to the weary soul. The sight of the cross brings within sight of the crown. That dying sigh which made the rocks to rend, alone can rend the veil, and give you peace. The Place of a Skull is the place of joy.

2. *What is it?* 'A feast of fat things, of wines on the lees.'
(a) *A feast.* It is not a meal, but a feast. At a meal, it is well if there be enough for all who sit round the table; but at a feast, there should be more than enough - there is a liberal abundance. The gospel is compared to a feast: 'Come, eat of my bread, and drink of the wine that I have mingled' (Proverbs 9:5). Again in the Song of Songs: 'He brought me to the banqueting house, and his banner over me was love.' 'Stay me with flagons, comfort me with apples; for I am sick of love.' Again, in Matthew 22:4: 'Tell them which are bidden, Behold, I have prepared my dinner; my oxen and my fatlings are killed, and all things are ready: come unto the marriage.'

So it is in Jesus: there is bread enough and to spare. He came that we might have life, and might have it more abundantly. There is a feast in a crucified Jesus. His dying in the stead of sinners is enough, and more than enough, to answer for our sins. It is not only equal to my dying, but it is far more glorifying to God and his holy law than if I had suffered a hundred deaths. 'Comfort ye, comfort ye; ye have received at the Lord's hand double for all your sins.' His obeying in the stead of sinners is enough, and more than enough, to cover our nakedness. It is not only equal to my obeying, but it is far more glorifying to God than if I had never sinned. His garment not only clothes the naked soul, but clothes from head to foot; so that no shame appears - only Christ appears, the soul is hid. His Spirit is not only enough, but more than enough, to make us holy. There is a well in Christ which we never can exhaust, rivers of grace which we never can drink dry.

Christians, learn to feed more on Christ: 'Eat, O friends! drink, yea, drink abundantly, O beloved!' When you are asked to a feast, there is no greater affront you can put upon the entertainer than by being content with a crumb below the table. Yet this is the way the Christians of our day affront the Lord of glory. Oh, how few seem to feed much on Christ! How few seem to put on his white flowing raiment! How few seem to drink deep into his Spirit! Most are content with a glimpse now and then of pardon - a crumb from the table, and a drop of his Spirit. Awake, dear friends! 'These things have I spoken unto you, that your joy may be full.'

(b) A feast of fat things, of wines on the lees. The fat things full of marrow are intended to represent the richest and most nourishing delicacies; and the wines on the lees well refined, to represent the oldest and richest wines; so that not only is there abundance in this feast, but abundance of the best. Ah! so it is in Christ.

First, there is forgiveness of all past sins. Ah! this is the richest of all delicacies to a heavy-laden soul. As cold water to a thirsty soul, so is good news from a far country. A good conscience is a perpetual feast. Oh! weary sinner, taste and see. 'I sat down under his shadow with great delight, and his fruit was sweet to my taste.' These are the apples that a weary soul cries out for: 'Comfort me with apples; for I am sick of love.'

Second, there are the smiles of the Father. The Father himself loveth you . Oh, to pass from the frown of an angry God into the smile of a loving Father! This is a feast to the soul. This is to pass from death unto life.

Third, the droppings of the Spirit into the soul - ah! it is this which comforts the soul. This is the oil of gladness that makes the face to shine.

This makes the cup run over. This is the full well rising within the soul, . at once comforting and purifying. Dear friends, be not filled with wine, wherein is excess; but be filled with the Spirit. These are the flagons that stay the soul. May you be in the Spirit on the Lord's Day!

3. *For whom is it?*

'Unto all people.' 'The gospel is the power of God unto salvation to every one that believeth; to the Jew first, and also to the Greek!' 'Go ye into all the world, and preach the gospel to every creature.' Ah! there is not a creature under heaven for whom the feast is not prepared. There is not a creature from whom we can keep back the message: 'All things are ready; come to the marriage.'

Dear anxious souls, why do you keep away from Christ? You say Christ is far from you; alas! he has been at your door all day. Christ is as free to you as to any that ever came to him. Come hungry, come empty, come sinful, come as you are to feed on glorious Jesus. He is a feast to the hungry soul.

Dear dead souls, that never felt one throb of anxiety, that never uttered one heartfelt cry to God, this message is for you. The feast is for all the people. Christ is as free to you as to any other: 'How long, ye simple ones, will ye love your simplicity?' 'The Spirit and the Bride say, Come.'

2. The tearing away of the veil.

1. *Observe, there is a veil over every natural heart, a thick, impenetrable veil.*

(a) There was a veil in the temple over the entrance to the holiest of all, so that no eye could see the beauty of the Lord within.

(b) There was a veil over the face of Moses, when he came down from the mount, for something of the brightness of Christ shone in his countenance. When the veil was down they could not see his glory.

(c) So there is a veil upon the hearts of the Jews to this day, when Moses and the Prophets are read to them.

(d) So is there a veil over your hearts - so many of you as are in your natural state - a thick, impenetrable veil. Its name is unbelief. The same veil that hid the beauty of the promised land from Israel in Kadesh-barnea - 'for they could not enter in, because of unbelief' - that veil is over your hearts this day.

Learn the great reason of your indifference to Christ. The veil is upon your heart. God may lay down all the riches of his bosom on the table, the unsearchable riches of Christ; yet so long as that veil is over you, you will not move. You see no form nor comeliness in Christ: 'And when we shall see him, there is no beauty that we should desire him' (Isaiah 53:2). 'The natural man receiveth not the things of the Spirit of God: for they are foolishness unto him: neither can he know them, because they are spiritually discerned' (1 Corinthians 2:14).

2. *Who takes the veil away?*
Answer: 'The Lord of hosts'; he that makes the feast is he that tears the veil away. Ah! it is a work of God to take away that covering. We may argue with you till midnight, telling you of your sin and misery; we may bring all the sweetest words in the Bible to show you that Christ is fairer than the children of men. Still you will go home and say, We see no beauty in him. But God can take away the veil. Sometimes he does it in a moment, sometimes slowly; then Christ is revealed, and Christ is precious. There is not one of you so sunk in sin and worldliness, so dull and heartless in the things of God, but your heart would be overcome by the sight of an unveiled Saviour. Oh! let us plead this promise with God: 'He will destroy in this mountain the face of the covering cast over all people, and the veil that is spread over all nations.' Come and do it, Lord. 'I will pour out my Spirit unto you.' Pour quickly, Lord.

3. *Where?*
'In this mountain' - in the same place where he makes the feast. He takes the soul to Calvary. Ah! yes; it is within sight of the crucified Saviour that God takes every veil away.

Anxious souls, wait near the cross. Meditate upon Christ, and him crucified. It is there that God tears the veil away. Be often at Gethsemane. Be often at Golgotha. Oh! that next Sabbath he may reveal himself to all in the breaking of bread. As easy to a thousand as to one soul!

3. Effects.
1. *Triumph over death.*
(a) Even here this is fulfilled. Often the fear of death is taken away in those who trembled before. The soul that has really had the veil taken away can go through the valley, if not singing, at least humbly trusting, and can say at the end, 'Lord Jesus, receive my spirit!' Ah! nothing but

a real sight of Christ can cheer in death. Worldly people can die stupidly and insensibly; but the unveiled Christian alone can feel in death that the sting is taken away.

(b) In resurrection. When we stand like Christ in body and soul, 'when the sea has given up the dead that are in it, and death and hell the dead that are in them,' 'when this corruptible shall have put on incorruption - then shall be brought to pass the saying that is written, Death is swallowed up in victory.'

Dear friends, what solemn scenes are before us! Ah! nothing but a sight of Christ as our own Surety and Redeemer can uphold us, in sight of opening graves and reeling worlds. We shall remember his own words and be still: 'I will ransom them from the power of the grave; I will redeem them from death. O death, I will be thy plagues; O grave, I will be thy destruction.' 'Father, I will that they also whom thou hast given me be with me where I am, that they may behold my glory.'

2. Triumph over sorrow.

(a) Even here, God wipes away the tears of conviction, the tears of sin and shame, by revealing Christ. A work of grace always begins in tears; but when God takes the soul to Calvary - look here: there are thy sins laid upon Immanuel; there the Lamb of God is bearing them; there is all the hell that thou shalt suffer. Oh, how sweetly does God wipe away the tears! Anxious souls, may God do this for you next Sabbath day!

(b) Complete fulfilment after. There will always be tears here, because of sin, temptation, sorrow; but there 'they shall hunger no more, neither thirst any more; neither shall the sun light on them, nor any heat. For the Lamb which is in the midst of the throne shall feed them, and shall lead them unto living fountains of waters, and God shall wipe away all tears from their eyes.'

3. Triumph over reproaches.

Even here God lifts his people above reproaches. He enables them to bless, and curse not: 'Love your enemies; bless them that curse you, do good to them that hate you, and pray for them that despitefully use you and persecute you.' But there shall be full triumph yonder. He will clear up our character. Here we may endure reproaches all the way! Christians are slighted, despised, trampled on, here; but God will acknowledge them as his jewels at last. The world will stand aghast.

19. The heart deceitful

The heart is deceitful above all things, and desperately wicked: who can know it? I the LORD search the heart, I try the reins, even to give every man according to his ways, and according to the fruit of his doings (Jeremiah 17:9, 10).

1. The state of the natural heart (verse 9).

This is a faithful description of the natural heart of man. The heart of unfallen Adam was very different. 'God made man upright.' His mind was clear and heavenly. It was riveted upon divine things. He saw their glory without any cloud or dimness. His heart was right with God. His affections flowed sweetly and fully towards God. He loved as God loved, hated as God hated. There was no deceit about his heart then. It was transparent as crystal. He had nothing to conceal. There was no wickedness in his heart, no spring of hatred, or lust, or pride. He knew his own heart. He could see clearly into its deepest recesses; for it was just a reflection of the heart of God.

When Adam sinned, his heart was changed. When he lost the favour of God, he lost the image of God. Just as Nebuchadnezzar suddenly got a beast's heart, so Adam suddenly got a heart in the image of the devil. And this is the description ever since: 'The heart is deceitful above all things, and desperately wicked' (verse 9).

It is 'deceitful above all things.'
Deceit is one of the prime elements of the natural heart. It is more full of deceit than any other object. We sometimes call the sea deceitful. At evening the sea appears perfectly calm, or there is a gentle ripple on the waters, and the wind blows favourably; during the night a storm may come on, and the treacherous waves are now like mountain billows, covering the ship. But the heart is deceitful *above all things* - more treacherous than the treacherous sea. The clouds are often very deceitful. Sometimes, in a time of drought, they promise rain; but they turn out to be clouds without rain, and the farmer is disappointed. Sometimes the clouds appear calm and settled; but, before the morning, torrents of rain are falling. But the heart is deceitful above all things. Many animals are deceitful. The serpent is more subtle than any beast of the field; sometimes it will appear quite harmless, but suddenly it will put out its deadly sting, and give a mortal wound. But the natural heart is more

deceitful than a serpent - *above all things*. It is deceitful in two ways -
in deceiving others and itself.

(1) *In deceiving others*. Every natural man is a hypocrite. He is
different in reality from what he appears to be. I undertake to say, that
there is not a natural man present here today in his true colours. If every
natural man here were to throw off his disguise, and appear as he really
is, this church would look more like the gate of hell than the gate of
heaven. If every unclean man were to lay bare his heart, and show his
abominable, filthy desires and thoughts; if every dishonest man were
now to open his heart, and let us see all his frauds, all his covetous, base
desires; if every proud, self-conceited one were now to show us what is
going on below his coat, or below that silk gown, to let us see the paltry
schemes of vanity and desire of praise; if every unbeliever among you
were openly to reveal his hatred of Christ and of the blessed gospel - O
what a hell would this place appear!

Why is it not so? Because natural men are deceitful. Because you
draw a cloak over your heart, and put on a smooth face, and make the
outside of a saint cover the heart of a fiend. Oh! your heart is deceitful
above all things. Every natural man is a flatterer. He does not tell other
men what he thinks of them. There is no plain, honest dealing between
natural men in this world. Those of you who know anything of this
world, know how hollow most of its friendships are. Just imagine for
a moment that every natural man were to speak the truth when he meets
his friends; suppose he were to tell them all the bitter slanders which he
tells of them a hundred times behind their back; suppose he were to
unbosom himself, and tell all his low, mean ideas of them, how worldly
and selfish they are in his eyes'- alas! what a world of quarrels this would
be. Ah, no! natural man, you dare not be honest. You dare not speak the
truth one to another. Your heart is so vile that you must draw a cloak over
it, and your thoughts of others so abominable that you dare not speak
them out. 'The heart is deceitful above all things'.

(2) It shows itself in another way - *in self-deceit*. Ever since my
coming among you I have laboured with all my might to separate
between the precious and the vile. I have given you many marks by
which you might know whether or not you have undergone a true
conversion, or whether it has only been a deceit of Satan, whether your
peace was the peace of God or the peace of the devil, whether you were
on the narrow way that leads to life, or on the broad way that leads to
destruction. I have done my best to give you the plainest Scripture marks

by which you might know your real case; and yet I would not be in the least surprised, if most of you were found at the last to have deceived yourselves. Often a man is deeply concerned about his soul; he weeps and prays, and joins himself to others who are inquiring. He now changes his way of life, and changes his notions; he talks of his experience, and enlargement in prayer; perhaps he condemns others very bitterly. And yet he has no true change of life. He walks after the flesh still, not after the Spirit. Now, others think this man a true Christian, and he believes it himself; yea, he thinks he is a very eminent Christian; when, all the time, he has not the Spirit of Christ, and is none of his. Ah! 'the heart is deceitful above all things'.

2. 'Desperately wicked.'
This word is borrowed from the book of the physician. When the physician is called to see a patient past recovery, he shakes his head and says, This is a desperate case. This is the very word used here. 'The heart is desperately wicked' - past cure by human medicine.

Learn that you need conversion, or a new heart. When we speak of the necessity of a change to some people, they begin to be affected by it, and so they put away some evil habits, as drinking, or swearing, or lying; they put these away, and promise never to go back to them; and now they think the work is done, and they are in a fair way for heaven. Alas, foolish man! it is not your drinking, or your swearing, or your lying that are desperately wicked - but your heart. You have only been cutting off the streams. The source remains polluted. The heart is as wicked as ever. It is the heart that is incurable. It is a new heart that you need. Nothing less will answer your need.

Learn that you must go to Christ for this. When the woman had spent her all upon physicians, and was nothing better, but rather worse, she heard of Jesus. Ah! said she, if I may but 'touch the hem of his garment I shall be made whole'. Jesus said to her: 'Daughter, be of good comfort, thy faith hath made thee whole.' Come, then, incurable, to Christ. Leprosy was always regarded as incurable. Accordingly, the leper came to Jesus, and worshipping, said, Lord if thou wilt thou canst make me clean. Jesus said, I will, be thou clean. And immediately his leprosy was cleansed. Some of you feel that your heart is desperately wicked; well, kneel to the Lord Jesus, and say: 'Lord, if thou wilt, thou canst make me clean.' You are a leper - incurable; Jesus is able - he is also willing to make you clean.

3. Unsearchably wicked: '*Who can know it?*'
No man ever yet knew the badness of his own heart. We are sailing over a sea the depths of which we have never fathomed.

Unawakened persons have no idea of what is in their hearts. When Elijah told Hazael what a horrible murderer he would be, Hazael said: 'Is thy servant a dog, that he should do this thing?' The seeds of it were all in his heart at that moment; but he did not know his own heart. If I had told some of you, when you were little children playing beside your mother's knee, the sins that you were afterwards to commit, you would have said, 'Am I a dog, that I should do this thing?' and yet you see you have done them. If I could show each of you the sins that you are yet to commit, you would be shocked and horrified. This shows how ignorant you are of your own heart. I suppose that most of you think it quite impossible you should ever be guilty of murder, or adultery, or apostasy, or the sin against the Holy Ghost. This arises from ignorance of your own black heart: '*Who can know it?*'

Some awakened persons have an awful sight given them of the wickedness of their own hearts. They see all the sins of their past life, as it were, concentrated there. They see that their past sins all come out of their heart, and that the same may come out again. And yet the most awakened sinner does not see the ten thousandth part of the wickedness of his heart. You are like a person looking down into a dark pit. You can only see a few yards down the sides of the pit; so you can only see a little way down into your heart. It is a pit of corruption which is bottomless: 'Who can know it?'

Some children of God have amazing discoveries given them of the wickedness of their own hearts. Sometimes it is given them to see that the germs of every sin are lodging there. Sometimes they see that there never was a sin committed, in heaven, in earth, or in hell, but it has something corresponding to it in their own heart. Sometimes they see that if there were not another fountain of sin, from which the fair face of creation might be defaced, their own heart is a fountain inexhaustible - enough to corrupt every creature, and to defile every fair spot in the universe. And yet even they do not know their own hearts. You are like a traveller looking down into the crater of a volcano, but the smoke will not suffer you to look far. You see only a few yards into the smoking volcano of your own heart.

Learn to be humbled far more than you have ever been. None of you have ever been sufficiently humbled under a sense of sin, for this reason:

that none of you have ever seen fully the plague of your own heart. There are chambers in your heart you have never yet seen into, there are caves in that ocean you have never fathomed, there are fountains of bitterness you have never tasted. When you have felt the wickedness of your heart to the uttermost, then lie down under this awful truth: that you have only seen a few yards into a pit that is bottomless, that you carry about with you a slumbering volcano, a heart whose wickedness you do not and cannot know.

4. The witness of the heart.

1. *'I, the Lord.'*
We have seen that we do not know one another's hearts; for 'the heart is deceitful'. Man looks on the outward appearance. We have seen that no man knows his own heart - that most know nothing of what is there; and those who know most, see but a short way down. But here is an unerring witness. He that made man knows what is in man.

2. *Observe what a strict witness he is*: 'I, the LORD, search the heart, I try the reins.'
It is not said, I know the heart, but, I *search* it. The heart of man is not one of the many objects upon which God turns his all-seeing eye, but it is one which he singles out for investigation: 'I search the heart.' As the astronomer directs his telescope upon the very star he wishes to examine, and arranges all his lenses, that he may most perfectly look at it, so doth God's calm eye pore upon the naked breast of every man. As the refiner of silver keeps his eye upon the fining-pot, watching every change in the boiling metal, so doth God's eye watch every change in the bosom of man. Oh! natural man, can you bear this? How vain are all your pretences and coverings! God sees you as you are. You may deceive your neighbour, or your minister, or yourself - but you cannot deceive God.

3. *Observe, he is a constant witness.*
He does not say, I have searched, or, I will search it - but, I *search*. I do it now, and always. Not a moment of our life but his pure, calm searching eye has been gazing on the inmost recesses of our hearts. From childhood to old age his eye rests on us. The darkness hides not from him. The darkness and the light are both alike to him.

4. *Observe his end in searching*: 'Even to give every man according to his ways, and according to the fruit of his doings' (verse 10).

In order to know the true value of an action, you must search the heart. Many a deed that is applauded by men, is abominable in the sight of God, who searches the heart. To give an alms to a poor man may be an action either worthy of an eternal reward, or worthy of an eternal punishment. If it be done out of love to Christ, because the poor man is a disciple of Christ, it will in no wise lose its reward. Christ will say: 'Inasmuch as ye did it to the least of these my brethren, ye did it unto me.' If it be done out of pride or self-righteousness, Christ will cast it from him; he will say, 'Depart, ye cursed; ye did it not unto me.'

The reason, then, why Christ searches the heart is, that he may judge uprightly in the judgment. Oh, sirs! how can you bear this, you that are Christless? How can you bear that eye on your heart all your days, and to be judged according to what his pure eye sees in you? Oh! do you not see it is a gone case with you? 'Enter not into judgment with thy servant; for in thy sight shall no flesh living be justified.' Oh! if your heart be desperately wicked, and his pure eye ever poring on it, what can you expect, but that he should cast you into hell? Oh! flee to the Lord Jesus Christ for shelter, for blood to blot out past sins, and righteousness to cover you. 'See God, our shield.'

Learn the amazing love of Christ

He was the only one that knew the wickedness of the beings for whom he died. He that searches the hearts of sinners died for them. His eye alone had searched their hearts; ay, was searching at the time he came. He knew what was in men; yet he did not abhor them on that account - he died for them. It was not for any goodness in man that he died for man. He saw none. It was not that he saw little sin in the heart of man. He is the only being in the universe that saw all the sin that is in the unfathomable heart of man. He saw to the bottom of the volcano - and yet he came and died for man. Herein is love! When publicans and sinners came to him on earth, he knew what was in their hearts. His eye had rested on their bosoms all their life. He had seen all the lusts and passions that had ever rankled there. Yet in no wise did he cast them out. So with you. His eye hath seen all your sins - the vilest, darkest, blackest hours you have lived, his pure eye was resting on you. Yet he died for such, and invites you to come to him, and will in no wise cast you out. Amen.

20. Trust in the LORD

Trust in the LORD with all thine heart; and lean not unto thine own
understanding (Proverbs 3:5).

When an awakened soul is brought by God to believe on Jesus, he enjoys
for the first time that calm and blessed state of mind which the Bible
calls *peace in believing*. The sorrows of death were compassing him,
and the pains of hell getting hold on him; but now he can say: 'Return
unto thy rest, O my soul.' It is not to be wondered at, that when this
heaven upon earth is first realised in the once anxious bosom, the young
believer should often imagine that heaven is already gained, and that he
has bid farewell to sin and sorrow for evermore. But, alas! it may need
but the passing away of one little day to convince him that heaven is not
yet gained; that though the Red Sea may be passed, yet there is a wide
howling wilderness to pass through, and many an enemy to be overcome, before the soul can enter into the land of which it is said, that 'the
people are all righteous'.

The first breath of temptation from without, or the first rise of
corruption from within, awakens new and strange anxieties within the
believing bosom. He had just put on the breastplate of the Redeemer's
righteousness, but these noxious vapours tarnish and bedim its bur-
nished steel. Alas! he cries, what good will it do me to be rid of all
accusations from past sins, if I am not secure from raising up new
accusers in the days to come? What good will the forgiveness of past
sins do me, if, every step of my life, I am to fall into new sin?

The young believer in this state of mind is just like a traveller in the
midst of a dangerous wood. He has been brought into a place of perfect
security for the present. He can hear the cry of the wolves behind him
without the least alarm, for he is brought into a fortress, a strong tower,
where he is safe; but when he thinks of his farther journey, when he
remembers that he is still in the midst of the wood, and still far from
home, alas! he knows not how to move; he knows not which path will
lead him right, and which will lead him wrong. When the lost sheep was
found by the good shepherd, it was safe in that moment, as safe as if it
were already in the fold; and yet it was doubtless in great perplexity how
to get back again for it had wandered so far over the mountains, and
down into the valleys, and across the brooks, and through the thorny
brakes, that it was impossible the bewildered sheep could find its way

back; and therefore it is said that the good shepherd laid it on his shoulders rejoicing. And just so is it with the soul that is found by Christ. Washed in his blood, he may feel as secure and as much at peace as if he were already in heaven; but when he looks to the thousand entanglements into the midst of which he has wandered - the evil habits, the evil companions that lay snares for him on every hand, alas! he is forced to cry: How shall I walk in such a world as this? I thought I was saved; but, alas! I am only saved to be lost again. So real and so painful is this state of mind, that some young believers have actually wished to die that they might be rid of these tormenting anxieties. But there is a far more excellent way pointed out in the words before us:

> Trust in the LORD with all thine heart;
> And lean not to thine own understanding.
> In all thy ways acknowledge him,
> And he shall direct thy paths.

This is a word in season to the bewildered believer; and 'a word spoken in due season, how good is it!'

First of all, consider what this grace is that is here recommended: 'Trust in the LORD with all thine heart.'

When the Philippian jailer cried out: 'What must I do to be saved?' the simple answer was: 'Believe on the Lord Jesus Christ, and thou shalt be saved.' His great anxiety was to escape from under the wrath of the God of the earthquake; and, therefore, they simply pointed to the bleeding Lamb of God. He looks to Jesus doing all that we should have done, and suffering all that we should have suffered; and while he looks, his anxiety is healed, and a sweet heavenly peace springs up within - the peace of believing.

But the inquirer who is spoken to in the text is one who already enjoys the peace of a justified man, but wants to know how he may enjoy the peace of a sanctified man. A new anxiety hath sprung up within his bosom, as to how he shall order his steps in the world; and unless this anxiety also can be healed, it is to be feared his joy in believing will be sadly interrupted. How seasonable, then, is the word which points at once to the remedy! And how amazing is the simplicity of the gospel method of salvation, when the soul is directed just to look again at Jesus; 'Trust in the LORD with all thine heart!'

When you came to us weary and heavy laden with guilt, we pointed you to Jesus; for he is the Lord our righteousness. When you come to us again, groaning under the power of indwelling sin, we point you again to Jesus; for he is the Lord our strength. It is the true mark of a false and ignorant physician of bodies, when to every sufferer, whatever be the disease, he applies the same remedy. But it is the true mark of a good and faithful physician of souls, when, to every sick and perishing soul, in every stage of the disease, he brings the one, the only remedy - the only balm in Gilead.

Christ was anointed not only to bind up the broken-hearted, but also to proclaim liberty to the captives; so that, if it be good and wise to direct the poor broken-hearted sinner, who has no way of justifying himself, to Jesus, as his righteousness, it must be just as good and wise to direct the poor believer, groaning under the bondage of corruption, having no way to sanctify himself, to look to Jesus as his wisdom - his sanctification - his redemption. Thou hast once looked unto Jesus as thy covenant head, bearing all wrath, fulfilling all righteousness in thy stead, and that gave thee peace; well, look again to the same Jesus as thy covenant head, obtaining by his merits gifts for men, even the promise of the Father, to shed down on all his members; and let that also give thee peace. 'Trust in the LORD with all thine heart.' Thou hast looked to Jesus on the cross, and that gave thee peace of conscience; look to him now upon the throne, and that will give thee purity of heart. I know of but one way in which a branch can be made a leafy, healthy fruit-bearing branch; and that is by being grafted into the vine, and abiding there. And just so I know of but one way in which a believer can be made a holy, happy, fruitful child of God; and that is by believing in Jesus, abiding in him, walking in him, being rooted and built up in him.

And observe it is said: 'Trust in the LORD *with all thine heart.*' When you believe in Jesus for righteousness, you must cast away all your own claims for pardon; your own righteousness must be filthy rags in your eyes, you must come empty, that you may go away full of Jesus. And just so, when you trust in Jesus for strength, you must cast away all your natural notions of your own strength; you must feel that your own resolutions, and vows, and promises are as useless to stem the current of your passions, as so many straws would be in stemming the mightiest waterfall. You must feel that your own firmness and manliness of disposition, which has so long been the praise of your friends and the boast of your own mind, are as powerless, before the breath of temptation, as a broken reed before the hurricane. You must feel that you wrestle not with flesh and blood, but with spirits of gigantic power, in whose mighty grasp you are feeble as a child; then, and then only, will you come with all your heart to trust in the Lord your strength. When the believer is weakest, then is he strongest. The child that knows most its utter feebleness, entrusts itself most completely into the mother's arms. The young eagle that knows, by many a fall, its own inability to fly, yields itself to be carried on the mother's mighty wing. When it is weak, then it is strong; and just so the believer when he has found out, by repeated falls, his own utter feebleness, clings, with simplest faith, to the arm of the Saviour and leans on his Beloved, coming up out of the wilderness, and hears with joy the words: 'My grace is sufficient for thee; my strength is made perfect in weakness.'

But, *secondly*, consider how this grace of trusting hinders the believer from leaning to his own understanding.

> Trust in the LORD with all thine heart;
> And lean not to thine own understanding.

Well may every soul that is untaught by the Spirit of God exclaim: 'This is a hard saying, who can hear it?' And, indeed, there is perhaps no truth that calls forth more of the indignant opposition of the world than this blessed one, that they who trust in the Lord with all their heart do not lean to their own understanding. The understanding, here, plainly includes all the observing, knowing, and judging faculties of the mind, by which men ordinarily guide themselves in the world; and, accordingly, it is with no slight appearance of reasonableness that the world should brand with the name of fanatics a peculiar set of men, who dare to say that they are not to lean upon these faculties, to guide them in their every-day walk and conversation.

But surely it might do something to moderate, at least, the opposition of the world (if they would but listen to us), to tell them that we never refuse to *be guided by* the understanding, although we altogether refuse *to lean* upon it. Every enlightened believer, however implicitly he depends upon the breathing of the Holy Ghost, without whose almighty breathing he knows that his understanding would be but a vain and useless machine, leading him into darkness, and not into light, yet follows the guidance of the understanding as scrupulously and as religiously as any unconverted man is able to do. Therefore, it ought never to be said, by any man who has a regard for truth, that the believer in Jesus casts aside the use of his understanding, and looks for miraculous guidance from on high. The truth is this, that he trusts in a divine power enlightening the understanding, and he therefore follows the dictates of the understanding more religiously than any other man.

When a man comes to be in Christ Jesus, he becomes a new creature, not only in heart, but in understanding also. The history of the world, the history of missions, and individual experience fully prove this; and it may not be difficult to point out what may be called natural reasons for the change.

When a man becomes a believer, a new and untried field is opened up for the understanding to penetrate into. It is true that unconverted men have made dives into the character of God, his government, his redemption. But the unconverted man never can gaze on these things with the love of one interested in them; and, therefore, he cannot know them at all; for God must be loved in order to be known. But reconcile a man to God, and the intelligence springs forward with a power unfelt before, and feels that this is life eternal, to know God, and Jesus Christ whom he hath sent.

When a man becomes a believer, he enters into every pursuit impelled by heavenly affections. Before, he had none but earthly motives to impel him to gather knowledge; but now, a holy inquisitiveness is instilled into his mind, and a retentiveness which he never had before. He looks with new eyes upon the fields, the woods, the hills, the broad resplendent rivers, and says: *My Father made them all.*

But if these are natural reasons for the change, there is one supernatural reason which is greater than all. The believer's understanding is new; for the Spirit of God is now a dweller in his bosom. He leans upon this almighty guest - trusts in the Lord the Spirit with all his heart, and leans not to his own understanding. In the prophet Hosea, the gift of the Spirit is compared to dew: 'I will be as the dew unto Israel.' Now, it is peculiarly true of the dew that it moistens everything where it falls; it leaves not one leaf unvisited, there is not a tiny blade of grass on which its diamond drops do not descend, every leaf and stem of the bush is burdened with the precious load. Just so it is peculiarly true of the Spirit, that there is not a faculty, there is not an affection, a power or passion of the soul on which the Spirit does not descend, working through all, refreshing, reviving, renewing, recreating all.

And if we are really in Christ Jesus, abiding in him by faith, we are bound to expect this supernatural power to work through our understanding; for if we be not led by the Spirit, we are none of his. But the more implicitly we lean on this loving Spirit, is it not plain as day that we all the more implicitly follow the guidance of our understanding? We do not lean upon our own understanding; for we lean upon the Spirit of grace and of wisdom, who has promised to guide us into all truth and guide our footsteps in the way of peace. But we do not throw away our own understanding; because it is through that understanding alone that we look for the guidance of the Spirit.

In a mill where the machinery is all driven by water, the working of the whole machinery depends upon the supply of water. Cut off that supply, and the machinery becomes useless. Set on the water, and life and activity is given to all. The whole dependence is placed upon the outward supply of water; still it is obvious that we do not throw away the machinery through which the power of the water is brought to bear upon the work. Just so in the believer; the whole man is carried by the Spirit of Christ, else he is none of his. The working of every day depends upon the daily supply of the living stream from on high. Cut off that supply, and the understanding becomes a dark and useless lump of machinery; for the Bible says that unconverted men have the understanding darkened. Restore the divine Spirit, and life and animation is given to all - the understanding is made a new creature. Now, though the whole leaning or dependence here is upon the supply of the Spirit, still it is obvious that we do not cast away the machinery of the human mind, but rather honour it far more than the world.

Now, however difficult it may be to explain all this to the world, it is most beautiful to see how truly it is acted on by the simplest child of God.

If you could overhear some simple cottage believer at his morning devotions - how simply he brings himself in lost and condemned, and therefore cleaves to Jesus, the divine Saviour - how simply he brings himself in dark, ignorant, unable to know his way - unable to guide his feet, his hands, his tongue throughout the coming day, and, therefore, pleading for the promised Spirit to dwell in him, to walk in him, to be as the dew upon his soul, and all this with the earnestness of a man who will not go away without the blessing - you would see what a holy contempt a child of God can put upon his own understanding, as a refuge to lean upon. But, again, if you could watch him in his daily walk in the field and in the market place among the wicked world and see how completely he follows the guidance of a shrewd and intelligent mind, you would see with what a holy confidence a child of God can make use of the faculties which God hath given him. You would see the happy union of the deepest piety and the hardest painstaking. You would know the meaning of these words: 'Trust in the Lord with all thine heart; and lean not unto thine own understanding.'

Dundee Presbytery, 1836

21. Formality not Christianity

> He is not a Jew, which is one outwardly; neither is that circumcision, which is outward in the flesh: but he is a Jew, which is one inwardly; and circumcision is that of the heart, in the spirit, and not in the letter; whose praise is not of men, but of God (Romans 2:28,29).

Formality is, perhaps, the most besetting sin of the human mind. It is found in every bosom and in every clime; it reigns triumphant in every natural mind; and it constantly tries to re-usurp the throne in the heart of every child of God. If we were to seek for proof that fallen man is 'without understanding', that he hath altogether fallen from his primitive clearness and dignity of intelligence and that he hath utterly lost the image of God in knowledge after which he was created, we would point to this one strange, irrational conceit by which more than one-half of the world are befooled to their eternal undoing: that God may be pleased with mere bodily prostrations and services, that it is possible to worship God with the lips, when the heart is far from him.

It is against this error, the besetting error of humanity, and preeminently the besetting error of the Jewish mind that Paul directs the words before us. And it is very noticeable, that he does not condescend to argue the matter. He speaks with all the decisiveness and with all the authority of one who was not a whit behind the very chiefest of the apostles, and he lays it down as a kind of first principle to which every man of ordinary intelligence, provided only he will soberly consider the matter, must yield his immediate assent - that 'he is not a Jew, which is one outwardly; neither is that circumcision which is outward in the flesh: but he is a Jew, which is one inwardly; and circumcision is that of the heart, in the spirit, and not in the letter; whose praise is not of men, but of God.'

In the following discourse I shall show very briefly, *first*, that external observances are of no avail to justify the sinner; and, *second*, that external observances can never stand in the stead of sanctification to the believer.

1. External observances are of no avail to justify the sinner.

In a former discourse I attempted to show several of the refuges of lies to which the awakened soul will run, before he can be persuaded to betake himself to the righteousness of God; and in every one of them we saw that he that compassed himself about with sparks of his own kindling received only this of God's hand, to lie down in sorrow. First of all, the soul generally contents himself with slight views of the divine law, and says: 'All these have I kept from my youth up'; then, when the spirituality of the law is revealed, he tries to escape by undermining the whole fabric of the law; when that will not do, he flies to his past virtues to balance accounts with his sins; and then, when that will not do either, he begins a work of self-reformation, in order to buy off the follies of youth by the sobrieties of age. Alas! how vain are all such contrivances, invented by a blinded heart - urged on by the malignant enemy of souls.

But there is another refuge of lies which I have not yet described, and to which the awakened mind often betakes itself with avidity, to find peace from the whips of conscience and the scorpions of God's law; and that is, a form of godliness. He will become a religious man, and surely that will save him. His whole course of life is now changed. Before, it may be, he neglected the outward ordinances of religion. He used not to kneel by his bed-side; he never used to gather his children and servants around him to pray; he never used to read the Word in secret or in the family; he seldom went to the house of God in company with the multitude that kept holy day; he did not eat of that bread which, to the believer, is meat indeed, nor drink of that cup which is drink indeed.

But now his whole usages are reversed, his whole course is changed. He kneels to pray even when alone; he reads the Word with periodical regularity; he even raises an altar for morning and evening sacrifice in his family; his sobered countenance is never awanting in his wonted position in the house of prayer. He looks back now to his baptism with a soothing complacency, and sits down to eat the children's bread at the Table of the Lord.

His friends and neighbours all observe the change. Some make a jest of it, and some make it a subject of rejoicing; but one thing is obvious, that he is an altered man; and yet it is far from obvious that he is a new man, or a justified man. All this routine of bodily exercise, if it be entered on before the man has put on the divine righteousness, is just another way of going about to establish his own righteousness, that he may not be constrained to submit to put on the righteousness of God. Nay, so utterly perverted is the understanding of the unconverted, that many men are found to persevere in such a course of bodily worship of God, while, at the same time, they persevere as diligently in some course of open or secret iniquity.

Such men seem to regard external observances not only as an atonement for sins that are past, but as a price paid to purchase a licence to sin in time to come. Such appears to have been the refuge of lies which the poor woman of Samaria would fain have sat down in, when the blessed Traveller, sitting by the well, awakened all the anxieties of her heart, by the searching words: 'Go call thy husband, and come hither.' Her anxious mind sought hither and thither for a refuge, and found it. Where? *In her religious observances:* 'Our fathers worshipped in this mountain, and ye say that in Jerusalem is the place where men ought to worship?'

She thrusts away the pointed conviction of sin by a question as to her outward observances. She changes her anxiety about the soul into anxiety about the place where men ought to worship, whether it should be Mount Zion or Mount Gerizim. Oh! if he would only settle that question, if he would only tell her on which of these mountains God ought to be worshipped, she was ready to worship all her lifetime in that favoured place. If Zion be the place, she would leave her native mountain and go and worship there, that that might save her. Oh! how fain she would have found here a refuge for her anxious soul.

With what divine kindness, then, did the Saviour sweep away this refuge of lies, by the answer: 'Woman, believe me, the hour cometh and now is, when ye shall neither in this mountain, nor yet in Jerusalem, worship the Father. God is a Spirit, and they that worship him, must worship him in spirit and in truth.'

Now it is with the very same object, and with the very same kindness, that Paul here sweeps away the same refuge of lies from every anxious soul, in these decisive words: 'He is not a Jew, which is one outwardly; neither is that circumcision, which is outward in the flesh: but he is a Jew, which is one inwardly; and circumcision is that of the heart, in the spirit, and not in the letter; whose praise is not of men, but of God.'

Is there any of you whom God hath awakened out of the deadly slumber of the natural mind? Has he drawn aside the curtains, and made the light of truth to fall upon your heart, revealing the true condition of your soul? Has he made you start to your feet alarmed, that you might go, and weep as you go, to seek the Lord your God? Has he made you exchange the careless smile of gaiety for the tears of anxiety, the loud laugh of folly for the cry of bitter distress about your soul? Are you asking the way to Zion with your face directed thitherward? Then take heed, I beseech you, of sitting down contented in this refuge of lies. Remember, he is not a Jew which is one outwardly - remember, no outward observances, no prayers, or churchgoing, or Bible-reading can ever justify you in the sight of God.

I am quite aware that when anxiety for the soul enters in, then anxiety to attend ordinances will also enter in. Like as the stricken deer goes apart from the herd to bleed and weep alone, so the sin-stricken soul goes aside from his merry companions, to weep, and read, and pray, alone. He will desire the preached Word, and press after it more and more; but remember, he finds no peace in this change that is wrought in himself. When a man goes thirsty to the well, his thirst is not allayed merely by going there. On the contrary, it is increased every step he goes. It is by what he draws out of the well that his thirst is satisfied. And just so it is not by the mere bodily exercise of acting on ordinances that you will ever come to peace; but by tasting of Jesus in the ordinances - whose flesh is meat in deed, and his blood drink indeed.

If ever, then, you are tempted to think that you are surely safe for eternity, because you have been brought to change your treatment of the outward ordinances of religion, remember, I beseech you, the parable of the marriage feast, where many were called and invited to come in, but few, few were found having on the wedding garment. Many are brought within the pale of ordinances, and read and hear, it may be, with considerable interest and anxiety about the all things that are ready - the things of the kingdom of God; but of these many, few are persuaded to abhor their own filthy rags, and to put on the wedding garment of the Redeemer's righteousness. And these few alone shall sit still to partake of the feast - the joy of their Lord. The rest shall stand speechless, and be cast out into outer darkness, where there shall be weeping, and wailing, and gnashing of teeth. You may read your Bible, and pray over it till you die; you may wait on the preached Word every Sabbath-day, and sit down at every sacrament till you die; yet, if you do not find Christ in the ordinances - if he do not reveal himself to your soul in the preached

Word, in the broken bread and poured-out wine; if you are not brought to cleave to him, to look to him, to believe in him, to cry out with inward adoration: 'My Lord and my God, how great is his goodness! How great is his beauty!'; then the outward observance of the ordinances is all in vain to you. You have come to the well of salvation, but have gone away with the pitcher empty; and however proud and boastful you may now be of your bodily exercise, you will find in that day that it profits little, and that you will stand speechless before the King.

2. External observances can never stand in the stead of sanctification to the believer.

If it be a common thing for awakened minds to seek for peace in their external observances, to make a Christ of them, and rest in them as their means of acceptance with God , it is also a common thing for those who have been brought into Christ, and enjoy the peace of believing, to place mere external observances in the stead of growth in holiness. Every believer among you knows how fain the old heart within you would substitute the hearing of sermons, and the repeating of prayers, in the place of that faith which worketh by love, and which overcometh the world. Now, the great reason why the believer is often tempted to do this, is, that he loves the ordinances.

Unconverted souls seldom take delight in the ordinances of Christ. They see no beauty in Jesus, they see no form nor comeliness in him, they hide their faces from him. Why should you wonder, then, that they take no delight in praying to him continually - in praising him daily - in calling him blessed? Why should you wonder that the preaching of the cross is foolishness to them, that his tabernacles are not amiable in their eyes, that they forsake the assembling of themselves together? They never knew the Saviour, they never loved him; how, then, should they love the memorials which he has left behind him?

When you are weeping by the chiselled monument of a departed friend, you do not wonder that the careless crowd pass by without a tear. They did not know the virtues of your departed friend, they do not know the fragrance of his memory. Just so the world care not for the house of prayer, the sprinkled water, the broken bread, the poured-out wine; for they never knew the excellency of Jesus.

But with believers it is far otherwise. You have been divinely taught your need of Jesus, and therefore you delight to hear Christ preached. You have seen the beauty of Christ crucified; and therefore you love the place where he is evidently set forth. You love the very name of Jesus - it is as ointment poured forth; therefore you could join for ever in the melody of his praises. The Sabbath day of which you once said: 'What a weariness is it!' and 'When will it be over, that we may set forth corn?' is now a 'delight' and 'honourable' - the sweetest day of all the seven. The ordinances, which were once a dull and sickening routine, are now green pastures and waters of stillness to your soul; and surely this is a blessed change.

But still you are in the body - heaven is not yet gained. Satan is hovering near; and since he cannot destroy the work of God in your soul, therefore he tries all the more to spoil it. He cannot stem the current; therefore he tries to turn it aside. He cannot drive back God's arrow; and therefore he tries to make it turn awry, and spend its strength in vain. When he finds that you love the ordinances, and it is in vain to tempt you to forsake them, he lets you love them; ay, he helps you to love them more and more. He becomes an angel of light - he helps in the decoration of the house of God, he throws around its services a fascinating beauty, hurries you on from one house of God to another, from prayer-meetings to sermon-hearing, from sermons to sacraments.

And why does he do all this? He does all this just that he may make this the whole of your sanctification - that outward ordinances may be the all in all of your religion, that in your anxiety to preserve the shell, you may let fall the kernel.

If there be one of you, then, in whose heart God hath wrought the amazing change of turning you from loathing to loving his ordinances, let me beseech you to be jealous over your heart with godly jealousy. Pause, this hour, and see if, in your haste and anxious pursuit of the ordinances, you have not left the pursuit of that holiness without which the ordinances are sounding brass and a tinkling cymbal. I have a message from God unto thee. It is written: 'He is not a Jew, which is one outwardly; neither is that circumcision, which is outward in the flesh: but he is a Jew which is one inwardly; and circumcision is that of the heart, in the spirit, and not in the letter; whose praise is not of men, but of God.' He is not a Christian which is one outwardly, neither is that baptism which is merely the outward washing of the body; but he is a Christian which is one inwardly, and true baptism is that of the heart - when the heart is washed from all filthiness of the flesh and of the spirit; whose praise is not of men, but of God.

Remember, I beseech you, that the ordinances are means to an end;

they are stepping-stones, by which you may arrive at a landing-place. Is your soul sitting down in the ordinances, and saying, It is enough? Are you so satisfied that you can enjoy the ordinances of Christ, that you desire no higher attainments? Remember the word that is written: 'This is not your rest.' Would you not say he was a foolish traveller, who should take every inn he came to for his home - who should take up his settled rest, and instead of preparing himself for a hard journeying on the morrow, should begin to take the ease and enjoyment of the house as his all? Take heed that you be not this foolish traveller. The ordinances are intended by God to be but the inns and refectories where the traveller Zion-ward, weary in well-doing, and faint in faith, may betake him to tarry for a night, that, being refreshed with bread and wine, he may, with new alacrity, press forward on his journey home as upon eagles' wings.

Take, then, this one rule of life along with you, founded on these blessed words: 'He is not a Jew which is one outwardly': that if your outward religion is helping on your inward religion; if your hearing of Christ on the Sabbath-day makes you grow more like Christ through all the week; if the words of grace and joy which you drink in at the house of God lead your heart to love more, and your hand to do more; then, and then only, are you using the ordinances of God aright.

There is not a more miserably deceived soul in the world than that soul among you who, like Herod, lives in sin. You love the Sabbath-day, you love the house of God. You love to hear Christ preached in all his freeness and in all his fullness; yes, you think you could listen for ever if only Christ be the theme. You love to sit down at sacraments, and to commemorate the death of your Lord. And is this all your holiness? Does your religion end here? Is this all that believing in Jesus has done for you?

Remember, I beseech you, that the ordinances of Christ are not means of *enjoyment*, but means of *grace*; and though it is said that the travellers in the Valley of Baca dig up wells, which are filled with the rain from on high, yet it is also said: 'They go from strength to strength.' Awake, then, my friends, and let it no more be said of us, that our religion is confined to the house of God and to the Sabbath-day. Let us draw water with joy from these wells, just in order that we may travel the wilderness with joy and strength, and love and hope - blessed in ourselves, and a blessing to all about us.

And if we speak thus to those of you whose religion seems to go no farther than the ordinances, what shall we say to those of you who contradict the very use and end of the ordinances in your lives? Is it possible you can delight in worldliness, and vanity, and covetousness, and pride, and luxury? Is it possible that the very lips which are so ready to sing praises, or to join in prayers, are also ready to speak the words of guile, of malice, of envy, of bitterness? Awake, we beseech you; we are not ignorant of Satan's devices. To you he hath made himself an angel of light.

Remember it is written: 'If any among you seemeth to be religious, and bridleth not his tongue, but deceiveth his own heart, this man's religion is vain. Pure religion, and undefiled before God and the Father is this, To visit the fatherless and widows in their affliction, and to keep himself unspotted from the world.' 'For he is not a Jew, which is one outwardly; neither is that circumcision which is outward in the flesh: but he is a Jew, which is one inwardly, and circumcision is that of the heart, in the spirit, and not in the letter; whose praise is not of men, but of God'! Amen.

Preached before the Presbytery of Dundee, November 2, 1836

22. Christ's compassion on the multitudes

And Jesus went about all the cities and villages, teaching in their synagogues, and preaching the gospel of the kingdom, and healing every sickness and every disease among the people. But when he saw the multitudes he was moved with compassion on them, because they fainted, and were scattered abroad, as sheep having no shepherd. Then saith he unto his disciples, The harvest truly is plenteous, but the labourers are few; pray ye therefore the Lord of the harvest, that he will send forth labourers into his harvest (Matthew 9:35-38).

I. '*When Jesus saw*, he was moved with compassion.'
From Matthew 4:23, we learn that, when Jesus first entered on the ministry, Galilee was the scene of his labours: 'He went about all Galilee, teaching in their synagogues, and preaching the gospel of the kingdom, and healing all manner of sickness and all manner of disease among the people.' And we learn also (verse 25) that great multitudes

followed him. Chapters 5, 6 and 7, contain a specimen of what he taught and preached; chapters 8 and 9, of the manner in which he healed; and now, at verse 35, we are told that he had gone over all the cities and villages of Galilee - he had finished his survey; and 'when he saw the multitudes, he was moved with compassion.' Galilee was at that time a thickly populated country - its towns and villages swarmed with inhabitants; so that it got the name of 'Galilee of the nations' or populous Galilee. What I wish you to observe then, is, that it was an actual survey of the crowded cities - of the over-peopled villages - of the crowds that followed him - it was an actual sight and survey of these things that moved the Saviour's compassion. His eye affected his heart: 'When he saw, he was moved with compassion.'

This shows that Christ was truly man.
The whole Bible shows that Christ was truly God :'he was with God, and was God;' he was 'God over all, blessed for ever'. But this event shows that he was as truly man.

It is the part of a man to be overcome by what he sees. When you sit by the fire on a winter evening, hearing the pelting of the pitiless storm, the rain and the sleet driving against the window, if you think of some houseless, homeless wanderer, your heart is a little moved, you heave a passing sigh and utter a passing expression of sympathy. But if the wanderer comes to your door - if you open the door, and see him all wet and shivering, the sight affects the heart, your heart flows out in a thousandfold greater compassion, and you invite him to sit before the fire. When the full bloom of health is upon your cheek, if you hear of some sick person, you are a little affected; but if you go and see, if you lift up the latch of the door, and enter in with quiet step, and see the pale face, the languid eye, the heaving breast; then does the eye affect the heart, and your compassion flows like a mighty river. This is humanity - this is the way with man.

This was the way with Christ: when he saw, he was moved with compassion. Once they brought him to the grave of a dearly loved friend. They said: 'Come and see'; and it is written, 'Jesus wept'. Another time he was riding on an ass' colt across Mount Olivet, the hill that overhangs Jerusalem: and when he came to the turn of the road, where the city bursts upon the view - 'when he came near, and beheld the city, he wept over it'. And just so here. He had gone round the cities and villages of Galilee; he had looked upon the poor, scattered multitudes, hastening on to an undone eternity: 'And when he saw the multitudes, he was moved with compassion.'

Let me speak to believers. *Jesus is your elder brother.* He says to you as Joseph said to his brethren: 'I am Joseph, your brother.' In all your afflictions he is afflicted. For he is not an high priest which cannot be touched with a feeling of our infirmities; but he was in all points tempted like as we are, yet without sin. Some of you have little children pained, and tossing in fever. Jesus pities them; for he was once a little child. Little children, if you would take Jesus for a Saviour, then you might carry all your griefs to him; for Jesus knows what it is to be a little child. Grown believers, you know the pains of weariness, and hunger, and thirst, and nakedness. Tell these things to Jesus, for he knew them too. You know the pains of inward heaviness: of a drooping heart, exceeding sorrowful, even unto death; of the hidden face of God. Jesus knew them too. Go to Jesus then, and he will heal them all.

This shows that Christians should go and see.
Many Christians are content to be Christians for themselves - to hug the gospel to themselves, to sit in their own room, and feast upon it alone. This did not Christ. It is true he loved much to be alone. He once said to his disciples: 'Come into a desert place, and rest a while.' He often spent the whole night in prayer on the lone mountain-side; but it is as true that he went about continually. He went and saw, and then he had compassion. He did not hide himself from his own flesh.

You should be Christ-like. Your word should be: 'Go and see.' You should go and see the poor; and then you will feel for them. Remember what Jesus said to all his people: 'I was sick, and in prison, and ye visited me.' Be not deceived, my dear friends; it is easy to give a cold pittance of charity at the church door, and to think that that is the religion of Jesus. But, 'Pure religion and undefiled, before God and the Father is this, To visit the fatherless and widows in their affliction, and to keep yourself unspotted from the world.'

2. What it was that Jesus saw.

He saw the multitudes.
He had gone through the crowded cities and villages of populous Galilee; and O how many faces he had looked upon! This made him sad. There is something very saddening to a Christian too look upon a

multitude. To stand in the crowded streets of a large metropolis, and to see the current of human beings flowing onward to eternity, brings an awful sadness over the spirit. Even to stand in the house of God, and look upon the dense mass of assembled worshippers, fills the bosom of every true Christian with a pitiful sadness.

Why is this? Because the most are perishing souls. Ah! it was this that filled the bosom of the Redeemer with compassion. Of all the bustling crowds that hurry through the streets of your town, of all the teeming multitudes that issue forth from your crowded factories - ah! how few will stand on the right hand of Jesus. Nay, to come nearer still, of the hundreds now before me in this house of God - souls committed to my care and keeping - willing and anxious as you are to hear, yet how few believe our report! How few will be to me a crown of joy and of rejoicing in the day of the Lord Jesus!

Just think how dreadful, my friends, if there be one soul here that is to perish - one body and soul with us, in health and strength today, that is to be with devils in a short while, feeling the worm, and the flames, and the gnashing of teeth. If there were but one in the whole town, I do think it would be enough to sadden the soul. But, ah! does not the Bible say: 'Many are called, but few are chosen?' Ah! then, you will know why Jesus was moved with compassion; and surely you will never look upon a crowd but the same feeling will rise in your breast.

He saw the multitudes fainting.
Perhaps for hunger - poor, weak, frail men! There is something most moving in the sight of weak men, when they are in an unconverted condition. What would a spider be, if it were thrown into one of your great blast-furnaces? It would be as it were nothing - so weak, so miserable, so unable to resist the scorching flame. Just such was the sight Jesus saw - poor frail men fainting for lack of food, and yet perishing for lack of knowledge; and he thought, Alas! if they be unable to bear a little bodily want, how will they bear my Father's anger, when I shall tread them in mine anger, and trample them in my fury? Oh! no wonder Jesus was sad. Think of this, you who are very feeble and frail - unable to bear hunger or a little sickness. Think what a poor thing you are in a fever, when you need some one to turn you in your bed; how will you bear to die Christless, and to fall into the hands of the living God? If you cannot contend with God now, how do you think you will contend with him after you die?

He saw them scattered abroad.

When the sheep have been driven away from the fold, they do not all go in a flock; but they are scattered over the mountains - they run every one to his own way. This is what Jesus saw in the multitudes - they were all scattered, turning every one to his own way. In the cities and villages he saw men going every one after different things. One set of men were going after money, making it their chief good; toiling night and day over their work yet not enjoying the money they made. Another set went after pleasure - the dance, the song, the pipe, and the tabour. Another set went after the joys of the deep carousal - their bellies were their god, and they gloried in their shame. Like the leech, they said: 'Give, give.' Another set went after still darker and more abominable things, of which it is a shame even so much as to speak. Jesus saw all - the hearts of all - and had compassion; because they were all thus scattered - none seeking after God. Observe, Jesus was not angry - Jesus did not threaten. Jesus was moved with compassion.

Let me speak to the unconverted. You are thus scattered, every one to his own way. Each of you have got your favourite walk in life - your favourite footpath. You all go different ways; and yet all away from God. I do not know what it is that your heart loves most; but this I know, that you love to go away from Christ and from God. Christ's eye is upon you all - your histories, your hearts. He knows every step you have taken, every sin you have committed, every lust that reigns in your heart. His eye is now on this assembly. I will ask you a question. What does Jesus feel when he looks upon you? Some will say, Anger, some will say, Revenge. What does the Bible say? Compassion. Christ pities you. He does not wish you to perish. Oh, the tender pity of Jesus! He would often have gathered you, as a hen gathers its chickens; but you would not.

As sheep having no shepherd.

This was the saddest thing of all. If the sheep be driven away from the fold, fainting and scattered upon the mountains, and if there be a number of shepherds to seek the lost, and bring them back to the fold, the sight is by no means so painful; but when they are sheep that have no shepherd, then the case is desperate. So it was with the people of Galilee in Christ's day. If they had had pastors after God's own heart, then their case would not have been so bad; but they were like sheep that had no shepherd. This made Jesus sad.

Jesus Christ is the same yesterday, today, and for ever. Just as he went through the towns and villages of Galilee, beholding the multitudes, so does he now go through the towns and villages of our beloved land; and, oh! if his heart was moved with compassion over the thousands of Galilee, surely it must be breaking with intensest pity over the tens of thousands of Scotland.

There may be some of you who can look coldly and carelessly on the fifty thousand of Edinburgh that never cross the threshold of the house of God. There may be some of you who can hear unmoved of the eighty thousand of Glasgow who know neither the melody of psalms nor the voice of prayer. There may be some of you who can look upon the haggard and vice-stricken countenances of the mill-population of your own town, thousands of whom show, by their dress, and air, and open profligacy, that they are utter strangers to the message of a preached Saviour. Some of you may look on them, and never shed one tear of pity, never feel one prayer rising to your lips. But there is one above these heavens, whose heart beats in his bosom at the sight of them; and if there could be tears in heaven, that tender Saviour would weep; for he sees the multitudes fainting and scattered, and, oh! worst of all - as sheep that have no shepherd.

Some of you have no compassion on the multitudes. Some of you think we have enough of ministers. See here, how unlike you are to Christ. You have not the Spirit of Christ in you - you are none of his. Some of you know the Lord Jesus, and tremble at his Word. Learn this day to be like-minded to Jesus: 'Let this mind be in you which was also in Christ Jesus.' Christ had compassion on the multitudes; and, oh! will you have none? Christ gave himself for them; what will you give? Surely the stones of this house will rise against you in judgment, and condemn you, if you be not like Christ in this: 'Freely ye have received, freely give.'

3. The remedy.

More labourers.

'The harvest truly is plenteous, but the labourers are few.' Christ looked upon the towns of Galilee as upon a mighty harvest - field after field ready for the sickle. He and his apostles seemed like a small band of reapers. But what are they to such a harvest? The ripe corn will be shaken, and shed its fruit upon the ground, before it can be cut down and gathered in. The word of Christ, then, is: 'Pray ye, therefore, the Lord of the harvest, that he will send forth labourers into his harvest.'

There is a striking resemblance between this day and Christ's day. (1) Our cities and villages are crowded like those of Galilee, and the little band of faithful ministers are indeed nothing to such a harvest. (2) The people are willing to hear. Wherever men of God have been sent, they have gathered around them multitudes, eager to hear the words of eternal life. The harvest is ripe - ready to be gathered in. Oh! then, do not say it is a scheme of man's devising - do not say we are seeking to enrich ministers - do not say we are seeking our own things. We are doing what Christ bids us do: 'Pray ye the Lord of the harvest.'

Labourers sent of God.

(1) This shows we should seek *ordained ministers* - men sent out or thrust out by God. Some well-meaning people are satisfied if we can get private Christians, or unordained men, to do the work of the ministry. This is a deep snare into which Satan leads good men. Does not the whole Bible bear witness that no man taketh this honour to himself, but he that is called of God, as was Aaron? And even Christ glorified not himself to be made an high priest. Woe be to them that run unsent! It was a good wish in Uzzah to hold up the ark; yet Uzzah died for it.

(2) It shows we should seek *converted ministers*. If men may not run without an outward call, far less without an inward call. There were crowds of ministers in Christ's day. At every corner of the street you might have met them. But they were blind leaders of the blind. So we may have plenty of ministers raised amongst us, and yet be as sheep that have no shepherd.

Ah! you that know Christ, and love him - ye Jacobs who wrestle with God till morning light, wrestle ye with God for this. Give him no rest until he grant it. I have a sweet persuasion in my own breast, that if we go on in faith and prayer, building up God's altars that are desolate, God will hear the cry of his people, and give them teachers according to his own heart, and that we shall yet see days such as have never before shone upon the Church of Scotland - when our teachers shall not be removed into corners any more, when the great Shepherd shall himself bless the bread, and give it to the under shepherds, and they shall give to the multitudes; and all shall eat, and be filled.

St Peter's, November 12, 1837

23. Christ's love to the church

Husbands, love your wives, even as Christ also loved the church, and
gave himself for it; that he might sanctify and cleanse it with the
washing of water by the word, that he might present it to himself a
glorious church, not having spot, or wrinkle, or any such thing; but
that it should be holy and without blemish (Ephesians 5:25-27).

In this passage the apostle, under the guidance of the Spirit, is teaching
wives and husbands their duties to one another. To the wives he enjoins
submission - a loving yielding to their husbands in all lawful things; to
the husbands, love; and he puts before them the highest of all patterns
- Christ and his Church.

1. Christ's love to his Church.

The object of his love.
The Church - all who are chosen, awakened, believing, justified,
sanctified, glorified ; all who are finally saved - all who shall stand with
the Lamb, the hundred and forty and four thousand redeemed ones, all
looked on as the bright company; the Church - all who are awakened and
brought to Christ, all who shall sit down at the marriage supper.

I believe Jesus had compassion for the whole world. He is not willing
that any should perish. He willeth all men to be saved. He shed tears over
those who will finally perish.

Still, the peculiar object of his love was the Church. He loved the
Church. On them his eye rested with peculiar tenderness before the
world was. He would often say: These shall yet sit with me on my
throne; or, as he read over their names in his book of life, he would say:
These shall yet walk with me in white. When they lived in sin, his eye
was upon them. He would not let them die, and drop into hell: 'I have
much people in this city.' I have no doubt, brethren, Christ is marking
some of you, that are now Christless, for his own. When they came to
Christ, he let out his love toward them on the land where they dwelt -
a delightsome land. His eye rests on the houses of this town, where his
jewels live. Christ loves some streets far better than others - some spots
of earth are far dearer to him than others.

Christ loved his Church. Just as a husband at sea loves the spot where
his dear wife dwells, so does the Lord Jesus: 'I have graven thee upon

the palms of my hands' (Isaiah 49:16). He loves some in one house far more than others. There are some apartments dear to Christ - where he is often present - where his hands are often on the door: 'Open to me, my love.'

The state of the Church when first loved.
(1) They were *all under the curse of God* - under condemnation - exposed to the just wrath of God - deserving nothing but wrath; for 'he gave himself for it'. The Church had no dowry to attract the love of Jesus, except her wrath and curse.

(2) *Impure.* For he had to 'sanctify and cleanse it'; unholy within - opposed to God - no beauty in the eye of Jesus: I am black, spotted, and wrinkled.

(3) *Nothing to draw the love of Christ.* Nothing that he could admire in them. He admires whatever is like his Father. He had eternally gazed upon his Father, and was ravished with that beauty; but he saw none of this - not a feature - no beauty at all. Men love where they see something to draw esteem - Christ saw none.

(4) *Everything to repel his love:* 'Polluted in thine own blood' - cast out - loathsome (Ezekiel 16); yet that was the time of his love. Black - uncomely: 'Thou hast loved me out of the pit of corruption.'

(5) *Not from ignorance.* Men often love where they do not know the true character, and repent after. But not so Christ. He knew the weight of their sins - the depths of their wicked heart.

Nothing is more wonderful than the love of Christ. *Learn the freeness of the love of Christ.* It is unbought love. 'If a man would give all the substance of his house for love, it would be utterly contemned' (Song 8:7). He drew all his reasons from himself: 'I knew that thou wast obstinate.' You have no cause to boast. He loved you, because he loved you - for nothing in you. O what a black soul wast thou, when Christ set his love upon thee!

The greatness of that love: 'He gave himself.'
This is unparalleled love. Love is known by the sacrifice it will make. In a fit of love, Herod would have given away the half of his kingdom. If you will sacrifice nothing, you love not. Hereby we know that men love not Christ - they will sacrifice nothing for him. They will not leave a lust - a game - a companion, for Christ. 'Greater love than this hath no man.' But Christ gave himself. Consider what a self. If he had created

ten thousand millions of worlds, and given them away, it had been great love. Had he given a million of angels; but he gave the Lord of angels, the Creator of worlds. 'Lo, I come.' He gave the pearl of heaven. O what a self! - Jesus! - all loveliness!

What he gave himself to.
He gave himself to be put in their place - to bear their wrath and curse, and to obey for them. We shall never know the greatness of this gift. He gave himself to bear the guilt of the Church. There cannot be a more fearful burden than guilt, even if there be no wrath. To the holy soul of Jesus, this was an awful burden. He was made sin: 'mine iniquities have taken hold upon me, so that I am not able to look up' (Psalm 40:12). 'For mine iniquities are gone over mine head: as a heavy burden, they are too heavy for me' (Psalm 38:4). He endured the cross, despising the shame. He laid his soul under their guilt - shame and spitting; silent like a lamb.

To bear their wrath. A happy soul shrinks from suffering. Ask one that has always been in the love of God, what for would he cast himself out of that love - bear as much wrath as he is bearing love - receive the lightning instead of the sunshine? Not for ten millions of worlds. Yet this did Jesus. He became a curse for us: Pour it out on me. See how he shrunk back from it in the garden. Yet he drank it.

'God commendeth his love to us, in that, while we were yet enemies, Christ died for us.' Pray to know the love of Christ. It is a great ocean, without bottom or shore.' ('It is as if a child could take the globe of earth and sea in his two short arms' Samuel Rutherford.) In the broken bread you will see it set forth so that a child may understand: 'This is my body, broken for you.' 'This is my blood, shed for many.'

2. His purpose in time (verse 26).
Christ's work is not done with a soul when he has brought it to pardon - when he has washed it in his own blood. Oh, no! the better half of salvation remains - his great work of sanctification remains.

Who is the author?
He that gave himself for the Church - the Lamb that was slain. God having raised his Son Jesus, sent him to bless you, in turning every one of you away from your iniquities. He is exalted by the right hand of God, and, having obtained the promise of the Father, sheds him down. There is no hand can new-create the soul, but the hand that was pierced. Many

look to a wrong quarter for sanctification. They take pardon from Christ, then lean on themselves - their promises, etc. - for holiness. Ah, no! you must take hold of the hand that was pierced - lean on the arm that was racked - lean on the Beloved coming up from the wilderness. You might as well hold up the sun on its journey as sanctify yourself. It needs divine power. There are three concerned in it. The Father - for this is his will; the Son - he is the Shepherd of all he saves; the Holy Ghost.

The means.

'The Word.' I believe he could sanctify without the Word, as he created angels and Adam holy, and as he sanctifies infants whose ear was never opened; but I believe in grown men he never will, but through the Word. When Jesus makes holy, it is by writing the Word in the heart: 'Sanctify them through thy truth.' When a mother nurses her child, she not only bears it in her arms, but holds it to her breast, and feeds it with the milk of her own breast; so does the Lord. He not only holds the soul, but feeds it with the milk of the Word. The words of the Bible are just the breathings of God's heart. He fills the heart with these, to make us like God. When you go much with a companion, and hear his words, you are gradually changed by them into his likeness; so when you go with Christ, and hear his words, you are sanctified. Oh, there are some whom I could tell to be Christ's, by their breathing the same sweet breath! Those of you that do not read your Bible cannot turn like God - you cannot be saved. You are unsaveable; you may turn like the devil, but you never will turn like God. Oh, believers, prize the Word!

3. *The certainty of it.*

Some are afraid they will never be holy: 'I shall fall under my sin.' You shall be made holy. *It was for this Christ died.* This was the grand object he had in view. This was what was in his eye - to build a holy Church out of a world of lost sinners; to pluck brands out of the fire, and make them trees of righteousness; to choose poor, black souls, and make them fair brothers and sisters round his throne. Christ will not lose this object.

Look up, then - be not afraid. He redeemed you to make you holy. Though you had a million of worlds opposing you, he will do it: 'He is faithful, who also will do it.'

3. His purpose in eternity - twofold.

Its perfection: 'A glorious Church.'
At present believers are sadly imperfect. They have on the perfect righteousness that will be no brighter above; but they are not perfectly holy; they mourn over a body of sin - spots and wrinkles. Neither are they perfectly happy. Often crushed; waves go over them; like the moon waning. But they shall be perfectly glorious. Perfect in righteousness - white robes, washed in the blood of the Lamb. Perfect in holiness - filled with the Holy Spirit. Perfect in happiness - this shall be. It is all in the covenant.

He will present it to himself.
He will be both father and bridegroom. He has bought the redeemed - he will give them away to himself. The believer will have great nearness, he shall see the King in his beauty. Great intimacy - walk with him, speak with him. He shall have oneness with him: 'All that I have is thine'.
St Peter's, January, 1841 (Action Sermon)

24. Christ became poor for sinners

For ye know the grace of our Lord Jesus Christ, that, though he was rich, yet for your sakes he became poor, that ye through his poverty might be rich (2 Corinthians 8:9).

In these words, there is brought before you the amazing grace of the Lord Jesus Christ. In the broken bread and poured-out wine you will this day see the same thing brought before your eyes. Before your eyes Jesus Christ is this day to be evidently set forth crucified. It is the most awakening sight in all this world. Oh! pray that many secure sinners may this day be brought to look on him whom they have pierced, and to mourn. It is the most peace-giving sight in this world. O! pray that the Holy Spirit may be poured upon awakened souls, that they may look to a crucified Jesus, and be saved. It is the most sanctifying sight in this world. Oh! pray that all God's children may look upon this gracious Saviour, till they are changed into his image.

1. The Lord Jesus was rich.

The riches here spoken of are not the riches which he now possesses as Mediator, but the riches which he had with the Father before the world was. He was full of all riches.

He was rich in the love and adoration of all the creatures.

All holy creatures loved and adored him. This is shown in Isaiah 6: 'I saw also the LORD sitting upon a throne, high and lifted up, and his train filled the temple. Above it stood the seraphim: each one had six wings; with twain he covered his face, and with twain he covered his feet, and with twain he did fly. And one cried unto another, and said, Holy, holy, holy, is the LORD of hosts; the whole earth is full of his glory. And the posts of the door moved at the voice of him that cried, and the house was filled with smoke.' John 12:41 tells us: 'These things said Esaias when he saw his glory, and spake of him.'

It was from all eternity the will of God that every creature should honour the Son even as they honour the Father. The brightest seraphs bowed down before him. The highest angels found their chief joy in always beholding his face. He was their Creator: 'By him were all things created, that are in heaven, and that are in earth, visible and invisible, whether they be thrones, or dominions, or principalities, or powers; all things were created by him, and for him' (Colossians 1:16). And, therefore, it was little wonder that they poured out their perpetual adorations before him. Now there is great joy in being loved by one holy creature - it fills the heart with true joy; but every holy creature loved Jesus with their whole heart and strength. This, then, was part of his riches - part of his infinite joy.

He was rich in the love of the Father.

This is shown in Proverbs 8:22,30: 'The LORD possessed me in the beginning of his way, before his works of old. Then I was by him, as one brought up with him: and I was daily his delight, rejoicing always before him.' To be loved by God is the truest of all riches. The love of the creatures is but poor love - it may soon die; but the love of God is undying, unchanging love. The creatures may love us, and yet not be able to help us; but God's love is a satisfying portion.

But none ever enjoyed the love of God as Jesus did. True, God's love to the holy angels is infinite; and he says, in John 17:26, that he loves believers with the same love with which he loves Christ: 'That the love wherewith thou hast loved me may be in them'; still there is this infinite difference between believers and Christ, that they can contain but a few drops of the love of God; they are but vessels - they cannot open their mouth wide enough.

But Jesus could contain all the infinite ocean of the love of God. In the Son there was an object worthy of the infinite love of the Father; and if the Father's love was infinite, so the bosom of the Son was infinite also. From all eternity there was the flowing of infinite love from the bosom of the Father into the bosom of the Son: 'The Father loveth the Son' - 'Rejoicing always before him.' This was the greatest riches of the Lord Jesus. This was the infinite treasure of his soul. If a man has the love of God, he can well want all other things. If a man want food and raiment - if he be like Lazarus at the rich man's gate, full of sores - still, if he be lying in the love of God, he is truly rich. Much more the well-beloved Son of God, the only begotten of the Father, was rich in the full outpouring of the Father's love from all eternity.

He was rich in power and glory.
He was the Creator of all worlds: 'Without him was not anything made that was made.' He was the Preserver of all worlds: 'By him all things consist', and hang together. All worlds, therefore, were his domain - he was Lord of all. He could say: 'Every beast of the forest is mine, and the cattle upon a thousand hills. I know all the fowls of the mountains: and the wild beasts of the field are mine. If I were hungry, I would not tell thee: for the world is mine, and the fullness thereof' (Psalm 50:10-12). All lands sang aloud to him: the sea roared his praise, the cedars bowed before him in lowly adoration. Nay, he could say: 'All things that the Father hath are mine' (John 16:15); and he could speak to his Father of the glory which he had with him before the world was. Whatever of power, glory, riches, blessedness, the Father had, dwelt with equal fullness in the Son; for he was in the form of God, and thought it no robbery to be equal with God. This was the riches of the Lord Jesus.

Oh, brethren! can you trust your salvation to such an one? You heard it was he that undertook to be the surety of sinners, and died for them. Can you trust your soul in the hands of such an one. Ah! surely if so rich and glorious a being undertake for us, he will not fail nor be discouraged, 'till he have set judgment in the earth; and the isles shall wait for his law'.

2. Christ became poor.
He was in the form of God, and thought it no robbery to be equal with God; but he made himself of no reputation, and took upon him the form of a servant, and was made in the likeness of men: and being found in fashion as a man, he humbled himself, and became obedient unto death, even the death of the cross. He became poor in all those things wherein he had been rich.

At his birth.
He laid aside the adoration of the creatures. He left the hallelujahs of the heavenly world for the manger at Bethlehem. No angel bowed before the infant Saviour; no seraph veiled his face and feet before him. The world knew him not. A few shepherds from the fields of Bethlehem came and kneeled to him, and the wise men saw and adored the infant King; but the most despised him. His mother wrapped him in swaddling clothes and laid him in a manger, for there was no room for them in the inn: 'He became poor'.

He left the love of God. The moment that babe was born, he became the surety of a guilty world. He was born of a woman, made under the law. The law took hold of him, even in infancy, as our surety. From the cradle to the cross he was bearing the sins of many; and therefore he says: 'I am afflicted and ready to die from my youth up; while I suffer thy terrors, I am distracted' (Psalm 88:15). Ah! what a change was here, from the infinite joy of his Father's love to the misery and terror of his Father's frown: 'He became poor'.

He left the power and glory that he had. Instead of wanting nothing, he became a helpless child, in want of everything. Instead of saying: 'If I were hungry, I would not tell thee', he needed now the milk of his mother's breast. Instead of holding up worlds with his arm, he needed now to be supported - to be wrapped in swaddling clothes, and laid in a manger, watched by a mother's tender eye: 'He was rich, and became poor.'

In his life.
He that was adored by the myriads of heaven was lightly esteemed. Few believed on him; they called him glutton - wine-bibber - deceiver. Once

they sought to cast him over the rocks; often they plotted to kill him. He that before received the full love of God, now received his full frown. The cloud became every day darker over his soul. Many of the hills and valleys of this world re-echoed with his cries and bitter agony. Gethsemane was watered with his blood. He that had all things as his domain now wanted everything. Certain women ministered to him of their substance (Luke 8:3). He had no money to pay the tribute, and a fish of the sea had to bring it to him (Matthew 17:27). The creatures of his hand had a warmer bed than he: 'The foxes have holes, and the birds of the air have nests, but the Son of Man hath not where to lay his head' (Matthew 8:20). Every man went to his own home - Jesus went to the Mount of Olives. And again, we are told, as they sailed, Jesus was asleep on a pillow. Another time he sat wearied at the well, and said: 'Give me to drink.' He that was God over all, blessed for ever, could say, 'I am a worm, and no man'. 'He became poor.'

In his death most of all he became poor.
(a) Once his ear was filled with the holy songs of angels, hymning their pure praises: 'Holy, holy, holy'; now his ears are filled with the cry of his creatures: 'Not this man, but Barabbas' - 'Crucify him, crucify him'. Once every face was veiled before him; now rulers deride him - soldiers mock him - thieves rail on him. They shoot out the lip - they wag the head - they give him vinegar to drink. 'He became poor' indeed.

(b) Once God loved him without a cloud between; now not a ray of divine love fell upon his soul; but instead of it a stream of infinite wrath. He that once said: 'The Lord possessed me; I was daily his delight', now cried: '*Eloi, Eloi, lama sabachthani*'. Ah! this was poverty!

(c) Once he gave being to unnumbered worlds - gave life to all - he was the Prince of life; but now he bowed his head, and gave up the ghost. He lay down in the grave among worms. He became a worm, and no man.

This is what is set before you in bread and wine today: The Son of God became poor. He takes simple bread, to show you it is a poor man that is set before you - broken bread, to show that he is a crucified Saviour. Ah! sinners, whilst you gaze on these simple elements, remember the sufferings of him who was Lord of glory, and who died for sinners. 'This do in remembrance of me.'

3. For what end? 'For your sakes - that ye through his poverty might be rich.'

The persons for whom: 'For your sakes'.

Corinth was one of the most wicked cities that ever was on the face of the world. It lay between two seas; so that luxury came flowing in from the east and from the west. These Corinthians had been saved from the deepest abominations, as you learn from 1 Corinthians 6:11: 'Such were some of you'; and yet it was for the sake of such that the Lord of glory became poor - 'For your sakes'. In like manner, Paul, writing to the Romans, says: 'When we were without strength, in due time Christ died for the ungodly' (5: 6). Ah! see what names are here given to those for whom Christ died: *without strength* - unable to believe, or to think a right thought; *ungodly* - living as if there were no God; *sinners* - breaking God's holy law; *enemies* - hating and opposing a holy God of love.

Oh, brethren! this is good news for the most wicked of men. Are there some of you who feel that you are like a beast before God, or all over sin, like a devil? Some of you have lived in the abominations of Corinth. Some of you are like the Romans - without strength, ungodly, sinners, enemies; yet for your sakes Christ became poor. He left glory for souls as vile as you. He left the songs of angels, the love of his Father, and the glories of heaven for just such wretches as you and me. He died for the ungodly. Do not be afraid, sinners, to lay hold upon him. It was for your sakes he came. He will not, he cannot cast you out.

Oh, sinners! you are poor indeed; but he will make you rich. All the riches he left he is ready to raise you to. He will make you rich in the love of God - rich in the peace that passeth all understanding, if you truly lay hold on him. The wrath of God will pass away from you, and he will love you freely. The love wherewith God loves Christ shall be on you. He will make you rich in holiness. He will fill you with all the fullness of God. He will make you rich in eternity. You will behold his glory - you will enter into his joy - you will sit with him on his throne.

4. The grace in all this: 'Ye know the grace'.

There is much to be seen in this amazing work. There is deep wisdom, 'the wisdom of God, the hidden wisdom which God ordained before the world unto our glory.' There is power, 'the power of God unto salvation.' But most of all, grace is to be seen in it from beginning to end: 'Ye know the grace of the Lord Jesus.'

When Jesus washed the disciples' feet, when he came to Peter, Peter said, 'Lord, dost thou wash *my* feet?' Three things amazed him: (1) The glorious being that knelt down before him: 'Thou'. (2) The lowly action he was going to perform: 'Dost thou wash?' (3) The vile wretch whose feet were to be washed: '*My* feet'. He was amazed at the grace of the Lord Jesus. So in this amazing work you may see a threefold grace: (1) The glorious being that undertook for sinners: 'He who was rich'. (2) The depth to which he stooped: 'He became poor'. (3) The wretches whose souls were to be washed: 'For your sakes'. Ah! well may you be amazed this day, and cry out: 'Dost thou wash my soul?'

5. The sin and danger of not knowing.

I would speak to those who do not know the grace of the Lord Jesus. I fear the most of you are still ignorant of Christ: 'The natural man receiveth not the things of the Spirit of God; for they are foolishness unto him.' Ah, brethren! think this day who it is you are lightly esteeming. Did you ever see the son of a king lay by his robes, and his glory, and become a poor man, and die in misery - and all this for nothing? Do you think the Lord Jesus left his Father's love, and the adoration of the angels, and became a worm, and died under wrath, and all for no purpose? Is there no wrath lying upon you? Have you no need of Christ? Ah! why, then, do you not flee unto him?

> Ungrateful sinners! whence this scorn
> Of God's long-suff'ring grace?
> And whence this madness, that insults
> Th'Almighty to his face?

Ah! remember as long as you come not to Christ, you are despising the grace of the Lord Jesus, and sinning against the love of God. What though you make a show of coming to Christ? What though you pretend it by coming to his table, and doing honour to the poor bread and wine? The poor Papist adores the bread, while he denies the Saviour; and so you may waste your honour on the bread and wine, while you are all the time rejecting and despising the grace of the Lord Jesus.

I would welcome poor sinners to Jesus Christ.
He became poor for such as you. He did not come for those 'who are rich and increased in goods, and stand in need of nothing'. Do not say you are too vile for such a Saviour. If you have all the pollutions of a

Corinthian - all the wicked heart of a Roman - he came on purpose for
such as you. You are the very souls he came to seek and save. His
salvation is all of grace. Free favour to those that deserve hell! Do not
deny the grace of the Lord Jesus. It is false humility that keeps any back
from Christ; for 'there is no difference between the Jew and the Greek,
for the same Lord over all is rich unto all that call upon him.' 'Ho, every
one that thirsteth, come ye to the waters, and he that hath no money
come: let him buy wine and milk without money and without price.'

To you that know Jesus and his grace
Oh! study him more. You will spend eternity in beholding his glory -
spend time in beholding his grace. That you may know your own
vileness, that you may abhor yourself, that you may see what a poor hell-
deserving creature you are, oh! study the grace of the Lord Jesus. That
your peace may be like a river, full, deep, and lasting, learn more of the
grace of the Lord Jesus. Come and declare with joy at the Lord's table
all that he has done for your soul. Oh! learn more. Few know much of
Christ. You have infinitely more to learn than you have ever known.
St Peter's, April 18, 1841 (Action Sermon)

25. Enemies reconciled through death

And you, that were sometime alienated and enemies in your mind by
wicked works, yet now hath he reconciled in the body of his flesh
through death, to present you holy, and unblameable, and
unreprovable in his sight: if ye continue in the faith grounded and
settled, and be not moved away from the hope of the gospel
(Colossians 1:21-23).

1. The past condition of all who are now believers: 'You that were
sometime alienated and enemies in your mind by wicked works.'
When two families have quarrelled, they become alienated from one
another; they do not visit one another any more - their children are not
allowed to speak together as formerly - if they meet in the street they
look another way. So it is with unconverted sinners and God: they are

alienated from God - they do not visit God - they do not seek his presence
- they do not love to meet his children - they like neither their words nor
their ways. When God meets them in a pointed sermon or providence,
they try to look another way, that they may not meet God's eye.

Alienated.
This word is used three times: 'Ye were aliens from the commonwealth
of Israel' (Ephesians 2:12). 'Alienated from the life of God' (Ephesians
4:18). And again here. In all, it paints to the life the true character of
every unconverted man. It is vain to conceal it, dear unconverted
brethren. You may pretend the greatest love to ministers - to sacraments
- to meetings of Christians; still the true state of your heart is estrangement from God. Ah! I fear there are many of you come to the church,
and even to the sacrament, with the name of Christ on your lips, and a
cold, estranged heart in your breast: 'They did flatter him with their
mouth, and they lied unto him with their tongues; for their heart was not
right with God' (Psalm 78:36).

Enemies in your minds.
This is more than estrangement. You may be strange to a man, and yet
not hate him, but unconverted souls hate God. The whole Bible bears
witness that all unconverted men hate God. In Romans 1:28 it is said:
'They did not like to retain God in their knowledge' so that God gave
them up to a reprobate mind, so that they became *haters of God.* In
Exodus 20:5, God says: 'I the Lᴏʀᴅ thy God am a jealous God, visiting
the iniquity of the fathers upon the children to the third and fourth
generation of them that hate me.' And again: 'Know ye not that the
friendship of the world is enmity against God? Whosoever, therefore,
will be a friend of the world, must be the enemy of God' (James 4:4).

   Would God say this if it were not the case? God knows best what is
really in the heart of man. It is true you may not show this hatred in your
words, or in your manner - you may not curse God, not even in a
whisper; but God says it is in your mind. It is at the bottom of that muddy
pool. In hell, where all restraints are lifted away, you will curse God
through all eternity.

   The most amazing trial of this that could be, was when God came
into this world. God was manifest in the flesh. In him dwelt all the
fullness of the Godhead bodily. All the perfections of God flowed
through his bosom. There was not a feature of God but it was shining

through his glorious countenance, yet softened to human eyes by all the perfections of his manhood. Did men love him when they saw him? Let Isaiah 53:3 answer: 'He is despised and rejected of men.' Or, hear his own words: 'The world cannot hate you; but me it hateth, because I testify of it that the works thereof are evil' (John 7:7). And again: 'He that hateth me hateth my Father also. If I had not done among them the works which none other man did, they had not had sin; but now have they both seen and hated both me and my Father' (John 15:23,24). How did they deal with him? They slew him, and hanged him on a tree - they buffeted him and spat on him - they scourged and crucified him - they nailed and pierced him. They were no worse than other men - men of like passions as we are; and yet the opportunity showed what is in man.

It is vain for you to conceal it, dear unconverted brethren, that your heart is full of enmity to God - that you are haters of God. Although it is fearful to think of, yet it is true, that all of you who are friends of the world are enemies of God; and though I believe in my heart there is not one of you here present that would wantonly kill a fly or a worm, yet I fear there are many who, if you could, would kill God.

What is the reason of this enmity? Answer: 'By wicked works.' It is the love of their sins that makes men hate God. Jesus himself tells you this: 'Me it hateth, because I testify of it that the works thereof are evil.' You could hardly imagine it possible that any one could hate the Lord Jesus. 'He is altogether lovely.' There is no perfection in God but it dwelt in him; there is no loveliness in man but it shone in him. And then his errand was one of purest love. He came to seek and to save that which was lost. He healed all that came - spoke lovingly to all. Even his threatenings were mingled with tears of compassion. How could they hate him? He told them of their sins - that these sins were sinking them to hell. He said: 'Ye shall die in your sins, and whither I go ye cannot come.' He offered to save them from their sins - to give them rest - rest from the weary load of guilt - rest from the tossing of a wicked heart. It was this which enraged them. They loved their wicked works - they did not want to be saved out of them; therefore they hated Jesus.

So is it still. Many of you, when you first heard the gospel, said: 'This is very fine; we will hear thee again of this matter.' The offer of pardon and heaven, a crown and a harp, and freedom from hell - all this sounded well. But when you found out that you must 'break off your sins by righteousness', 'that Christ will save his people from their sins' - then you began to linger, to ponder, to hesitate, to turn back and hate God.

When you saw that Christ would part you from your glass, from your oaths, from your cards and dice, from your lusts - then you hated him. Alas! what a sad choice you have made! - loved your sin, and hated the Saviour! 'They that hate me love death.'

Children of God, this was *your* state. Eat bitter herbs with your Passover this day. Oh! do not forget your sin. You were sometime alienated and enemies of God by wicked works. Can you look back without being confounded?

2. The reconciliation.
'Yet now hath he reconciled in the body of his flesh through death' (verse 21). This is the amazing work of the Lord Jesus Christ, and this is the blessed state into which he brings every saved soul.

He took on him a body of flesh.
Out of pure love to hell-deserving worms, 'he that was in the form of God, and thought it no robbery to be equal with God, emptied himself, and took upon him the form of a servant, and was made in the likeness of men.'

In order to be the Saviour of sinners, he must obey the law, which we had never obeyed - he must live a lifetime of sinless obedience; but how shall the great God who made the law do this? He was made of a woman, made under the law, that he might redeem them that were under the law.

Again: if he will save sinners, he must drink their cup of suffering. He must bear their stripes - their sins - on his own body. But how shall the infinitely holy, happy, and unchangeable God, suffer this? Because the children were of flesh, he himself likewise took part of the same. He became united to a weak, frail, human soul and body; so that he could suffer, weep, groan, bleed, die. 'Great is the mystery of godliness, God was manifest in the flesh.'

Again: if he will be the Saviour and elder brother of sinners, if he will know their sorrows, and be their tender shepherd, he must have a human heart, a breast filled with all the milk of a mother's tenderness. But how can this be, when he is infinitely holy, wise, just and true? Ah! he became bone of our bone, and flesh of our flesh. 'When all the tribes of Israel came to David to Hebron, they said, Behold we are thy bone and thy flesh' (2 Samuel 5:1); and so can we in going to Christ: 'He is one that can be touched with a feeling of our infirmity.'

Ah! to all eternity the incarnation of Jesus will be the theme of our wonder and praise. Brethren, you will all see that face. Some of you will wail when you see it. When that lovely countenance gleams through the clouds, you will call on rocks and mountains to cover you. It is the Saviour you have rejected and despised.

He died: 'Through death.'
The death of Christ is the most amazing event that ever took place in the universe; and therefore the Lord's Supper is the most amazing of all ordinances.

The angels desire to look into it. I doubt not that angels hover around the communion table, and sing their sweetest praises to the Lamb, when they see that bread broken and that wine poured out.

If the incarnation of Jesus was wonderful, far more wonderful was his *dying*. This was the highest summit of his obedience: 'Obedient unto death.' It was the lowest depth of his humiliation. He stood silent under our accusations; he lay down under our curse; he bore our hell, and died our death.

He was the great Lawgiver, the judge of all before whom every creature must stand and be judged; and yet he consented to come and stand at the bar of his wicked creatures, and to be condemned by them!

He was adored by every holy creature - their sweetest praises were poured out at his feet; and yet he came to be spit upon and reviled, to be mocked, and nailed, and crucified by the vilest of men!

'In him was life.' He was the Prince of life: the author of all natural and spiritual life. He gave to all, life and breath and all things; and yet they killed him. He gave up the ghost; he lay in the cold grave.

The Father loved him infinitely, eternally without beginning, or intermission, or end; and yet he was made a curse for us - bore the same wrath that is poured upon damned spirits.

Ah! brethren, herein was infinite love. Infidels scoff at it, fools despise it; but it is the wonder of all heaven. The Lamb that was slain will be the wonder of eternity. Today Christ is evidently set forth crucified among you. Angels, I doubt not, will look down in amazing wonder at that table. Will you look on with cold, unmoved hearts? It is a sight of the Lamb slain that moves the hosts of heaven to praise (Revelation 5:8). When the Lamb as it had been slain appears, they fall down before him, having every one of them harps, and golden vials full of odours. Will *you* not praise?

He hath reconciled us: 'Yet now hath he reconciled.'

Sinners, we are not reconciled in the day of our election, nor at the death of Christ, but in the hour of conversion. Oh! that is a precious now: '*Now* hath he reconciled.' It is a happy moment, when the Lord Jesus draws near to the sinful soul, and washes him clean in his precious blood, and clothes him in his white raiment, and so reconciles him to God.

A double reconciliation takes place in the hour of believing.

(1) *God becomes reconciled to the soul.* When the soul is found in Christ, the Father says: 'I will heal his backsliding, I will love him freely; for mine anger is turned away from him' (Hosea 14:4). The soul replies to God: 'I will praise thee: though thou was angry with me, thine anger is turned away, and thou comfortedst me' (Isaiah 12:1). God does not impute to that soul his trespasses; he reckons to him the obedience of the Lord Jesus. God justifies him: 'He will save, he will rejoice over thee with joy; he will rest in his love; he will joy over thee with singing' (Zephaniah 3:17).

(2) *The soul is reconciled to God.* The Holy Spirit, who bends the soul to submit to Jesus, changes the heart to love him. When the beasts came into the ark, their natures were changed - they did not tear one another to pieces, but lovingly entered two and two into the ark; the lion did not devour the gentle deer, nor did the eagle pursue the dove. So, when sinners come to Christ, their heart is changed from enmity to love.

Dear brethren, has he reconciled you to God? You were sometime afar off; have you been brought nigh? You were sometime darkness; have you been made light in the Lord? You were sometime alienated and enemies in your mind; has he reconciled you? Has he brought you into the light of God's reconciled countenance? Is God's anger turned away from you? Can you sing: 'O LORD, I will praise thee: though thou wast angry with me, thine anger is turned away, and thou comfortedst me' (Isaiah 12:1); or, 'Bless the LORD, O my soul, and forget not all his benefits: who forgiveth all thine iniquities; who healeth all thy diseases; who redeemeth thy life from destruction' (Psalm 103:2-4)? Have you been changed to love God? Do you love his Word - his people - his way of leading you?

3. The future object in view: 'That he might present you holy, and unblameable, and unreprovable in his sight.'

Sacrament days are holy days; but there is a more solemn day at hand, even at the door. Here, we meet to teach you and feed you, and get you to meet with Christ, and to live upon him; there, we shall meet to present you as a chaste virgin to Christ. In that day Christ will take those of you whom he has redeemed and reconciled, and present you to himself a glorious Church. He will confess your name before his Father, and present you faultless before the presence of his glory with exceeding joy. There is a double perfection the saints will have in that day.

You will be perfectly righteous. You will be 'unreprovable'. Satan will accuse you, and the world, and conscience; but Christ will say: 'The chastisement of their peace was upon me.' Christ will show his scars, and say: 'I died for that soul.'

You will be perfectly holy: 'Holy and unblameable'. The body of sin you will leave behind you. The Spirit who dwells in you now will complete his work. You will be like Jesus - for you will see him as he is. You will be holy as God is holy - pure as Christ is pure.

Everyone whom Christ reconciles he makes holy, and confesses before his Father: 'Whom he justified, them he glorified'. If Christ has truly begun a good work in you, he will perform it to the day of Christ Jesus. Christ says: 'I am Alpha and Omega, the beginning and the ending.' Whenever he begins, he will make an end. Whenever he builds a stone on the foundation, he will preserve it unshaken to the end. Only make sure that you are upon the foundation - that you are reconciled - that you have true peace with God, and then you may look across the mountains and rivers that are between now and that day, and say: 'He is able to keep me from falling.' You have but two shallow brooks to pass through - sickness and death; and he has promised to meet you, and go with you, foot for foot. A few more tears - a few more temptations - a few more agonizing prayers - a few more sacraments, and you will stand with the Lamb upon Mount Zion!

4. Perseverance is needful to salvation.

'If ye continue in the faith grounded and settled, and be not moved away from the hope of the gospel' (verse 23). All whom Christ reconciles will be saved; but only in the way of persevering in the faith. He grounds and settles them in the cleft rock, and keeps them from being moved.

Dear believers, see that you continue in the faith. Remember you will be tried.

You may be tried by false doctrine. Satan may change himself into an angel of light, and try to beguile you by another gospel. 'Hold fast the form of sound words.'

You will be tried by persecution. The world will hate you for your love to Christ. They will speak all manner of evil against you falsely.

You will be tried by flattery. The world will smile on you. Satan will spread his paths with flowers; he will perfume his bed with myrrh, and aloes, and cinnamon.

Will you continue in the faith? Will you not be moved away? Can you withstand all these enemies? Remember perseverance is needful to salvation, as needful as faith or as the new birth. True, every one that believes in Christ will be saved; but they will be saved through perseverance: 'If a man abide not in me, he is cast forth as a branch, and is withered; and men gather them, and cast them into the fire, and they are burned' (John 15:6). Behold, in Jesus there is strength for that perseverance. This bread and wine today are a pledge of that. Seek persevering grace today. Ask this when you take that bread and wine.

Hypocrites! you will one day be known by this. Many of you seem to be united, who truly are not. All who have had convictions of sin which have passed away; all who have the outward appearance of Christians, but have within an unconverted heart; all who attend ordinances, but live in some way of sin; you will soon be discovered. You put on an appearance, you pretend that you do cleave to Christ, and get grace from Christ. Oh! how soon you will be shown in your true colours. Oh! that the thought may pierce your heart, that even now, though you came with a lying profession in your right hand, you may be persuaded to cleave to Jesus in truth. Amen.

St Peter's, August 1, 1841 (Action Sermon)

26. My God, my God

My God, my God, why hast thou forsaken me? (Matthew 27:46).

These are the words of the great Surety of sinners, as he hung upon the accursed tree. The more I meditate upon them, the more impossible do I find it to unfold all that is contained in them. You must often have observed how a very small thing may be an index of something great going on within. *The pennant* at the mast-head is a small thing; yet it shows plainly which way the wind blows. *A cloud* no bigger than a man's hand is a small thing; yet it may show the approach of a mighty storm. *The swallow* is a little bird; and yet it shows that summer is come. *So is it with man.* A look, a sigh, a half-uttered word, a broken sentence may show more of what is passing within than a long speech. *So it was with the dying Saviour.* These few troubled words tell more than volumes of divinity. May the Lord enable us to find something here that will feed your souls.

1. The completeness of Christ's obedience.

Words of obedience. 'My God, my God.'
He was obedient unto death. I have often explained to you how the Lord Jesus came to be a doing as well as a dying Saviour - not only to suffer all that we should have suffered, but to obey all that we should have obeyed - not only to suffer the curse of the law, but to obey the commands of the law. When the thing was proposed to him in heaven, he said: 'Lo, I come to do thy will, O my God!' - 'Yea, thy law is within my heart.' Now, then, look at him as a man obeying his God. See how perfectly he did it - even to the last!

God says: Be about my business - he obeys: 'Wist ye not that I must be about my Father's business?'

God says: Speak to sinners for me - he obeys: 'I have meat to eat that ye know not of; my meat is to do the will of him that sent me, and to finish his work.'

God says: Die in the room of sinners - wade through a sea of my wrath for the sake of enemies - hang on a cross, and bleed and die for them - he obeys: 'No man taketh my life from me.'

The night before he said: 'The cup which my Father hath given me, shall I not drink it?' But perhaps he will shrink back when he comes to the cross? No; for three hours the darkness had been over him, yet still he says: 'My God, my God.' Sinner, do you take Christ as your surety? See how fully he obeyed for thee! The great command laid upon him was to die for sinners. Behold how fully he obeys!

Words of faith. 'My God, my God.'
These words show the greatest faith that ever was in this world. Faith in believing the Word of God, not because we see it to be true, or feel it to be true, but because God has said it. Now Christ was forsaken. He

did not see that God was his God - he did not feel that God was his God; and yet he believed God's Word, and cried: 'My God, my God.'

(1) *David* shows great faith in Psalm 42:7,8: 'Deep calleth unto deep at the noise of thy water spouts: all thy waves and thy billows are gone over me. Yet the LORD will command his lovingkindness in the day time, and in the night his song shall be with me, and my prayer unto the God of my life.' He felt like one covered with a sea of troubles. He could see no light - no way of escape; yet he believed the Word of God, and said: 'Yet the Lord will.' This is faith - believing when we do not see.

(2) *Jonah* showed great faith: 'All thy billows and thy waves passed over me: then I said, I am cast out of thy sight; yet I will look again toward thy holy temple' (Jonah 2:3,4). He was literally at the bottom of the sea. He knew no way of escape - he saw no light - he felt no safety; yet he believed the Word of God. This was great faith.

(3) *But, ah! a greater than Jonah is here.* Here is greater faith than David's - greater faith than Jonah's - greater faith than ever was in the world, before or after. Christ was now beneath a deeper sea than that which covered Jonah. The tossing billows of God's anger raged over him. He was forsaken by his Father - he was in outer darkness - he was in hell; and yet he believed the Word of God. 'Thou wilt not leave my soul in hell.' He does not feel it - he does not see it - but he believes it, and cries: 'My God.' Nay, more, to show his confidence, he says it twice: 'My God, my God.' 'Though he slay me, yet will I trust in him.' Dear believer, this is your surety. You are often unbelieving - distrustful of God; behold your surety - he never distrusted; cling to him - you are complete in him.

Words of love. 'My God, my God.'
Those were words of sweet submission and love which Job spake, when God took away from him property and children: 'Naked came I out of my mother's womb' etc. Sweet, that he could bless God even in taking away from him. Those were words of sweet submissive love which old Eli spake when God told him that his sons should die: 'It is the Lord, let him do what seemeth him good.' The same sweet temper was in the bosom of the Shunammite who lost her child, when the prophet asked: 'Is it well with thee? - is it well with thy husband? - is it well with the child? And she answered, It is well.'

But, ah! here is greater love - greater, sweeter submission, than that of Job, or Eli, or the Shunammite - greater than ever was breathed in this cold world before. Here is a being hanging between earth and heaven - forsaken by his God - without a smile - without a drop of comfort - the agonies of hell going over him; and yet he loves the God that has forsaken him. He does not cry out, Cruel, cruel Father! No, but with all the vehemence of affection, cries out: 'My God, my God.'

Dear, dear souls, is this your surety? Do you take him as obeying for you? Ah! then, you are complete in him. You have very little love for God. How often you have murmured, and thought God cruel in taking things away from you; but, behold your surety, and rejoice in him with exceeding joy. All the merit of his holy obedience is imputed to you.

2. The infinity of Christ's sufferings.

He was forsaken by God: 'My God, my God, why hast thou forsaken me?' The Greek Liturgy says: 'We beseech thee, by all the sufferings of Christ, known and unknown.' The more we know of Christ's sufferings, the more we see that they cannot be known. Ah! who can tell the full meaning of the broken bread and poured-out wine?

He suffered much from his enemies.
(a) He suffered in *all parts of his body.* In his head that was crowned with thorns, and smitten with the reed. In his cheeks for they smote him on the face, and he gave his cheeks to them that plucked off the hair: 'I hid not my face from shame and spitting'. In his shoulders that carried the heavy cross. In his back: 'I gave my back to the smiters.' In his hands and feet: 'They pierced my hands and my feet.' In his side for a soldier thrust a spear into his side. Ah! how well he might say: 'This is my body, broken for you.'

(b) He suffered in *all his offices.* As a prophet: 'They smote him on the face and said, Prophesy who smote thee?' As a priest: they mocked him when offering up that one offering for sins. As a king: when they bowed the knee, and jesting said, 'Hail! King of the Jews.'

(c) He suffered from *all sorts of men* - from priests and elders, from passers-by and soldiers, from kings and thieves: 'Many bulls have compassed me; strong bulls of Bashan have beset me round;' 'Dogs have compassed me;' 'They compassed me about like bees.'

(d) He suffered much *from the devil:* 'Save me from the lion's mouth.' His whole suffering was one continued wrestling with Satan; for he spoiled principalities and powers, and made a show of them openly, triumphing over them in his cross.

He suffered much from those he afterwards saved.
How bitter would be the scoffing of the thief who that day was to be forgiven and accepted! How bitter the cries of the three thousand who were so soon brought to know him whom they crucified!

From his own disciples.
They all forsook him and fled. John, the beloved, stood far off, and Peter denied him. It is said of the camomile flower, that the more you squeeze and tread upon it, the sweeter is the odour it spreads around. Ah! so it was in our sweet Rose of Sharon. It was the bruising of the Saviour that spread sweet fragrance around. It is the bruising that makes his name as ointment poured forth.

From his Father.
All other sufferings were nothing in comparison with this: 'My God, my God, why hast thou forsaken me?' Other sufferings were finite - this alone was an infinite suffering. It was little to be bruised by the heel of men or devils; but, ah! to be trodden by the heel of God: 'It pleased the Father to bruise him.'

Three things show the infinity of his sufferings.

Who it was that forsook him.
Not his people Israel, not Judas the betrayer, not Peter his denier, not John that lay in his bosom; he could have borne all this. But, ah! it was his Father and his God. Other things little affected him compared with that. The passers-by wagged their heads - he spoke not. The chief priests mocked him - he murmured not. The thieves cast it in his teeth - he was a deaf man who heareth not. God brought a three hours' darkness over him, the outward darkness being an image of the darkness over his soul, ah! this was infinite agony: 'My God, my God, why hast thou forsaken me?'

Who it was that was forsaken. 'Me.'
(a) One infinitely dear to God. Thou lovedst me before the foundation of the world, yet thou hast forsaken me. I was always by thee - rejoicing always before thee. I have basked in the beams of thy love. Ah! why this terrible darkness to me? 'My God, my God.'

(b) One who had an infinite hatred of sin. How dreadful to an innocent man to be thrust into the cell of a condemned criminal! But, ah!

how much more dreadful to Christ, who had an infinite hatred of sin, to be regarded by God as a sinner.

(c) One who had an infinite relish of God's favour. When two friends of exalted minds meet together, they have an intense relish of one another's love. How painful to meet the cold averted looks of one in whose favour you find this sweet joy! But, ah! this is nothing to Christ's pain.

What God did to him - forsook him.
Dear friends, let us look into this ocean through which Christ waded.
(a) He was without any comforts of God: no feeling that God loved him, no feeling that God pitied him, no feeling that God supported him. God was his sun before - now that sun became all darkness. Not a smile from his Father, not a kind look, not a kind word.

(b) He was without a God - he was as if he had no God. All that God had been to him before was taken from him now. He was Godless - deprived of his God.

(c) He had the feeling of the condemned, when the Judge says: 'Depart from me, ye cursed' - 'who shall be punished with everlasting destruction from the presence of the Lord, and from the glory of his power.' He felt that God said the same to him. Ah! this is the hell which Christ suffered. Dear friends, I feel like a little child casting a stone into some deep ravine in the mountain side, and listening to hear its fall - but listening in vain; or like the sailor casting the lead at sea, but it is too deep - the longest line cannot fathom it. The ocean of Christ's sufferings is unfathomable.

3. Answer the Saviour's why.
Because he was the surety of sinners, and stood in their room.

He had agreed with his Father, before all worlds, to stand and suffer in the place of sinners: Every curse that should fall on them, let it fall on me. Why should he be surprised that God poured out all his fury? 'Why hast thou forsaken me?' Because thou didst covenant to stand in the room of sinners.

He set his face to it: 'He set his face like a flint'; 'He set his face steadfastly'. God set down the cup before him in the garden, saying, 'Art thou willing to drink it, or no?' He said: 'The cup which my Father hath given me, shall I not drink it?' 'Therefore it pleased the Lord to bruise him.' Why? Because thou hast chosen to be the surety - thou wouldst not draw back.

He knew that either he or the whole world must suffer. It was his pity for the world that made him undertake to be a Saviour: 'He saw that there was no man, and wondered that there was no intercessor. Therefore his arm brought salvation unto him, and his righteousness it sustained him.' Why? Either thou or they - hell for thee or hell for them.

Lesson to Christless persons.
Learn your danger. Wherever God sees sin he will punish it. He punished it in the rebellious angels, in Adam, in the old world, in Sodom. And when he saw sins laid on Christ, he forsook his own Son. You think nothing of sin. See what God thinks of it. If so much as one sin be upon you uncovered, you cannot be saved. God says: 'Though thou wert the signet on my right hand, though thou wert the son of my bosom, yet would I pluck thee hence.' Oh, let me persuade you, this day, to an immediate closing with Jesus Christ!

Lesson to the people of Christ.
Admire the love of Jesus. Oh, what a sea of wrath did he lie under for you! Oh, what hidings did he bear for you, vile, ungrateful soul! The broken bread and poured-out wine are a picture of his love. Oh, when you look on them, may your heart break for longing towards such a Saviour!

We would say to all who close with Jesus Christ, he was forsaken in the room of sinners. If you close with him as your surety, you will never be forsaken. From the broken bread, and poured-out wine seems to rise the cry: 'My God, my God, why hast thou forsaken me?'

For *me* - for *me*. May God bless his own Word!
(Action Sermon)

27. Death of Stephen

And they stoned Stephen, calling upon God, and saying,
Lord Jesus, receive my spirit (Acts 7:59).

Stephen was the first to die as a martyr in the cause of Christ; and he seems to have resembled the Saviour more than any that followed after. His very face appeared like the face of an angel. His irresistible wisdom in arguing with the Jews was very like Christ. His praying for his enemies with his dying breath nearly in the same words as the Saviour, and his recommending his soul into the hands of the Lord Jesus, were in the same spirit of confidence as that in which Christ said: 'Father, into thy hands I commend my spirit.' There cannot be a doubt that it was by looking unto Jesus that he became thus Christ-like. And the last view which he got of Christ seems especially to have given him that heavenly composure in dying which is so much above nature.

Two things are to be noticed: (1) that it was a sight of Christ at the right hand of God; (2) that it was a sight of Christ standing there. Christ being at the right hand of God is mentioned sixteen times in the Bible; thirteen times he is described as seated there, twice as being there; but here only is he spoken of as standing. This appears to have made a deep and lively impression on the mind of Stephen, for he cries out: 'Behold, I see the heavens opened, and the Son of Man standing on the right hand of God'; and then, with a sweet assurance that Christ's hands were stretched out to receive him, he cried: 'Lord Jesus, receive my spirit.'

Doctrine: Since Christ is at the right hand of God, and since he rises up to receive the dying believer, believers should commend their spirit to the Lord Jesus.

1. If Christ be at the right hand of God, the believer's sins must be pardoned, so that he can peacefully say: 'Lord Jesus, receive my spirit.'
If the grave had closed over the head of Christ for ever - if the stone had remained at the mouth of the sepulchre to this day - then we might well be in doubt whether he had suffered enough in the stead of sinners. 'If Christ be not risen, your faith is vain - you are yet in your sins.' But is it true that Christ is at the right hand of God? Then the stone has been rolled away from the sepulchre. God has let him go free from the curse

that was laid on him. The justice of God is quite satisfied.

If you saw a criminal put into prison, and the prison doors closed behind him, and if you never saw him come out again, then you might well believe that he was still lying in prison, and still enduring the just sentence of the law. But if you saw the prison doors fly open, and the prisoner going free; if you saw him walking at large in the streets, then you would know at once that he had satisfied the justice of his country, that he had suffered all that it was needful to suffer, that he had paid the utmost farthing. So with the Lord Jesus; he was counted a criminal - the crimes of guilty sinners against God were all laid at his door, and he was condemned on account of them. He was hurried away to the death of the cross, and the gloomy prison-house of his rocky sepulchre where the stone was rolled to the mouth of the grave. If you never saw him come out, then you might well believe that he was still enduring the just sentence of the law. But, lo! 'he is risen - he is not here' - 'Christ is risen indeed'. God, who was his judge, hath raised him from the dead, and set him at his own right hand in the heavenly places; so that you may be quite sure he has satisfied the justice of God. He has suffered everything that it was needful for him to suffer - he has paid the utmost farthing.

Now, is there any of you hearing me who cleaves to the Lord Jesus? Is this the Saviour whom you take to be your surety? 'Be of good cheer, thy sins are forgiven thee.' For if your surety is free, then you are free. It was this which gave such a tranquil peace to the dying Stephen. He had the same vile nature which you have, he had committed the same sins as you, he had the same condemnation over him. But when he saw Jesus Christ, whom he had taken as his surety, standing free at the right hand of God, then he felt that the condemnation had been already borne, that God's anger was quite turned away from his soul. And thus being inwardly persuaded of pardon, he committed his spirit into the hand of Christ: 'Lord Jesus, receive my spirit.'

Oh! brethren, cleave to the same Lord Jesus. He is still as free as he was when Stephen died. He always will be free; death hath no more power over him for he hath suffered all. Take him as your surety, cleave to him as your Saviour, and you may this day have the same peace that Stephen had; and may die with the same peaceful breast, saying: 'Lord Jesus, receive my spirit.'

2. If Christ be at the right hand of God, then the believer is accepted with God, and may peacefully say with Stephen: 'Lord Jesus, receive my spirit.'

The Son of God came to be a surety for men in two respects: firstly, in suffering the wrath which they deserved to suffer; and, secondly, in rendering the obedience which men had neglected to render. If he stood as surety in suffering, then every dying sinner that cleaved to him was to be freed from the curse of God. If he stood as surety in obeying, then he and every sinner that cleaved to him was to be rewarded with a place in glory.

Now, if Christ had not risen from the dead, then it would have been manifest that God had not accepted his obedience as worthy of eternal life. But if Christ is risen, and not only so, but if he be at the right hand of God, the place of highest glory in heaven, where are pleasures for evermore, then I am quite sure that God is satisfied with Christ as a surety for man.

If you saw some peer of the realm sent away by the king upon a distant and hazardous undertaking, with the promise that, if he succeeded, he should be advanced to the seat nearest the throne - if you never saw that peer return to claim his reward, then you would say at once that he had failed in his undertaking. But if you saw him return, amid the applause of assembled multitudes, and if you saw him received into the palace of the king, and seated on the right hand of majesty, then you would say at once that he had succeeded in that which he undertook, and that the king upon the throne was well pleased with him for it.

Just so, dear brethren, if you had been in heaven on that most wonderful day that ever was, of which the Christian Sabbath is an ever-enduring monument, when Christ ascended to his Father and our Father; had you seen the smile of ineffable complacency wherewith God received back into glory the surety of men, saying: 'Thou art my Son, this day have I begotten thee'; as if he said: 'Never till this day did I see thee so worthy to be called my Son'; and again: 'Sit thou at my right hand, till I make thine enemies thy footstool;' had you seen all this, then you would have known how excellent the obedience of Christ is in the eyes of the Father. But all this obedience was endured, not for himself, but as a surety for men. He was accepted himself before he left heaven. He was infinitely near and dear to the Father, and did not need to become man to obey for himself.

Everything that Jesus Christ did or suffered was as a surety in the stead of sinners. Do you take him for your surety? Do you cleave to the Lord Jesus, because you have nothing of your own to recommend you to God? Then look up with the eye of faith, and see him at the right hand of God. If you cleave to him, you are as much accepted with God as Christ is, you are as near to God as your surety is. Ah! it was this that gave the dying Stephen such calm tranquillity. He had the same vile nature that you have, he had as little obedience to God as you have, he was a naked sinner as you are; but he took the Lord Jesus to be his surety, the man in his stead; so that, when he saw him at the right hand of God, he felt that Christ was accepted, and that he also was accepted in the Beloved. And thus, being inwardly persuaded that in Christ he had a safe way to the Father, he cried, with dying breath: 'Lord Jesus, receive my spirit.'

Oh! trembling, naked sinner, cleave to the Lord Jesus. He is as much offered to you as he was to Stephen. Take him as your surety - cleave to him as your Saviour, and you may this day have the same sense of acceptance which Stephen had, and you may die with the same sweetly confiding cry: 'Lord Jesus, receive my spirit.'

3. If Christ stands up to receive the dying believer, this gives the believer great confidence, so that he may peacefully say: 'Lord Jesus, receive my spirit.'

When believing souls seek for peace and joy in believing, they do very generally confine their view to Christ upon the earth. They remember him as the good Shepherd seeking the lost sheep, they look to him sitting by the well of Samaria, they remember him saying to the sick of the palsy: 'Be of good cheer, thy sins are forgiven thee.' But they too seldom think of looking where Stephen looked - to where Jesus is now,, at the right hand of God.

Now, my friends, remember, if you would be whole Christians, you must look to a whole Christ. You must lift your eye from the cross to the throne, and you will find him the same Saviour in all, 'the same yesterday, and today, and for ever'. I have already observed, that wherever Christ is mentioned as being at the right hand of God, he is spoken of as seated there upon his throne; here, and here only, are we told that he is standing. In other places he is described as enjoying his glory, and entered into his rest; but here he is described as risen from his throne, and standing at the right hand of God.

He rises to intercede: 'He is able to save to the uttermost all that come unto God by him, seeing he ever liveth to make intercession for them.'

How often would a believer be a castaway, if it were not for the great Intercessor! How often faith fails! - 'flesh and heart faint and fail'; but see here, Christ never fails. On the death-bed, often the mind is taken off the Saviour, by pains of body and distress of mind; but, oh! happy soul that has truly accepted Christ. See here, he rises from his throne to pray for you, when you cannot pray for yourself. Look up to him with the eye of faith, and cry: 'Lord Jesus, receive my spirit.'

He rises to defend.

(a) The world is a sore enemy to the believer - by temptation on the one hand, and persecution on the other. Oh! how hard it strives to cast him down. Happy believer, you are safe in a dying hour! *Firstly*, because the world cannot reach beyond death. The sneering tongue cannot spit its venom beyond the grave. The stone of violence may kill the body, but it hath no more that it can do. *Secondly*, even if it were possible that some arrow of the world might reach beyond the grave, Jesus hath risen up to defend. His everlasting arms are underneath the departing soul.

(b) The devil is a worse enemy in that hour. He stands close by the dying bed. He often molests, but he cannot destroy, if you be cleaving to Jesus. Christ has all power in heaven and in earth, and he rises up to defend your soul. 'Be not afraid,' he says, 'it is I.' Ah! dear brethren, cleave to the Lord Jesus now, if you would have him to stand up for you in a dying hour - if you would cry with confidence: 'Lord Jesus, receive my spirit.'

He rises to receive the departing soul.

This is the sweetest of all comforts to the godly. It is a sweet thought, that the holy angels are waiting to receive the believing soul. When Lazarus died, the good angels carried him into Abraham's bosom. But, oh! it is sweeter far, to think that Jesus looks down upon the dying bed, and stands up to receive the soul that loves him. Oh! dear brethren, he is the same kind Saviour in death that he is through life.

(a) Once you lived without prayer, without God, without Christ in the world; did Christ not stretch out the hands all the day, even then?

(b) Once you were lying under convictions of sin; you felt yourself worthy of hell, and that God would be just if he never had mercy on your soul; did not Christ draw near to your soul, saying: 'Peace be unto you?'

(c) Again, you were groaning under the power of temptation, crying against indwelling sin: 'O wretched man! who shall deliver me from the body of this death?' Did not Christ draw near and say: 'My grace is sufficient for thee; my strength is made perfect in weakness'?

(d) Once more: you may yet groan under the weight of dying agonies. The last enemy is death. It may be a hard struggle, it may be a dark valley. Yet look where Stephen looked; and, lo! Jesus is standing at the right hand of God, waiting to receive you to himself. Oh! sweet death, when God is with you, the Spirit within you, and Christ waiting to receive you. Behold! he stretches out his hands to receive your departing spirit. Breathe it into his hand, saying: 'Lord Jesus, receive my spirit.'

Learn that death is no death to the Christian: 'He that liveth and believeth on me, shall never die.' It is only giving the soul into the hand of Christ. He knows its value; for he died for it.

Learn that to die is, to the believer, better than to live
If Christ rises up to receive the soul, then the soul goes to be with Jesus. But to be with Christ, is to be in glory; therefore it is far better. Oh! be willing, Christians, to be absent from the body, and present with the Lord. There you shall be free from pain of persecuting stones - no more sneering, cruel friends; no more doubts about your soul; no more sin within your heart. 'Oh, that I had the wings of a dove, that I might flee away and be at rest!'

Learn the dreadfulness of having no interest in Jesus Christ
You must die; and yet how will you die, poor Christless soul? To whom will you commend your dying spirit? (a) There will be no good angels waiting round your bed - no gentle hands of ministering spirits stretched out to receive your trembling soul. (b) You will have no Christ rising up to receive you. You never washed in his blood - you would not come to him to have life; he often stretched out his hands, but you pushed them away; and now he will have no pity for you. (c) You will have no God. God will not be your God - he will not be your friend. You have always been his enemy. Your proud heart would not be reconciled to him; and now you will find him an enemy indeed.

Where will you go? Die you must. Your breath must cease. These eyes that look on me this day must close in death - that heart which you feel beating in your bosom must cease to beat. And what will you do with your soul? To whom will you commend it - a naked, guilty, shivering thing, with the wrath of God abiding on it? None of the angels will dare to shelter it. No rocks, or caves, or mountains can hide it. Hell itself will not be a hiding-place from the just wrath of God. Oh! be wise now: 'Turn ye, turn ye, why will ye die?'

Learn, if you have lost any friends in Christ, to be comforted over them. It is true they are gone from you; but remember they have gone into far tenderer hands. You stood up to bend over their dying body; but the Lord Jesus stood up to receive their undying soul. Your feeble but affectionate hands were stretched out to smooth their dying pillow; but the almighty hands of the Saviour formed a sweeter, softer bed for their departing soul. Follow their faith - look to the same Saviour; and when you come to die, you will use with your heart, or with your tongue, the same sweet words: 'Lord Jesus, receive my spirit.'
St Peter's, Dundee, August 13, 1837

28. Time is short

> But this I say, brethren, the time is short: it remaineth, that both they
> that have wives be as though they had none; and they that weep, as
> though they wept not; and they that rejoice, as though they rejoiced
> not; and they that buy, as though they possessed not; and they that use
> this world, as not abusing it: for the fashion of this world passeth away
> (1 Corinthians 7:29-31).

In this chapter the apostle is discoursing concerning marriage. The mind of God upon this subject seems to be:

(1) *That in ordinary times marriage is honourable in all, provided it be in the Lord.* There are some who seem to imagine that there is peculiar holiness about an unmarried life; but this seems quite contrary to the Word of God. In the sinless world before man fell, God said: 'It is not good for man to be alone'; and the closest walker with God in Old

Testament times was a married man: 'Enoch walked with God three hundred years, and begat sons and daughters'.

(2) *That in a time of distress and trouble to the Church it is better not to marry*: 'I suppose therefore that this is good for the present distress' (verse 26). When the ark of God is in danger, as at present in our Church, it seems the mind of the Spirit that all who can should keep themselves as much as possible disentangled from earthly engagements. When the wife of Phinehas heard that the ark of God was taken, she travailed in birth, and died, calling her child Ichabod - the glory is departed. So, brethren, it does not become those who love Zion to be marrying and giving in marriage when the ark of God is in danger.

(3) *That even in such times it is lawful to marry*: 'But and if thou marry, thou hast not sinned' (verse 28). I doubt not, brethren, the days are near when they shall say: 'Blessed are the barren, and the wombs that never bare, and the paps that never gave suck.' Still, if any will venture to meet these times, and if you think the faith of two may bear you up better than the faith of one, 'I spare you'. I would lay no snare upon you. You have not sinned.

Having opened up this subject, the apostle proceeds with this affecting statement, suitable to all, married or unmarried: 'But this I say, brethren, the time is short: it remaineth that both they that have wives be as though they had none; and they that weep, as though they wept not; and they that rejoice, as though they rejoiced not; and they that buy, as though they possessed not; and they that use this world as not abusing it: for the fashion of this world passeth away.' In these words there is:

(1) *A statement made*: 'the time is short'; and again: 'the fashion of this world passeth away.' The time to be spent in this world is very short; it is but an inch of time, a short half-hour. In a very little, it will be all over; and all that is here is changing. The very hills are crumbling down, the loveliest face is withering away, the finest garments rot and decay. 'The fashion of this world passeth away.'

(2) *A lesson drawn from this*: believers should sit loose to everything here. Believers should look on everything in the light of eternity. Value nothing any more than you will do then. Sit loose to the objects, griefs, joys, occupations of this world; for you must soon change them for eternal realities.

Doctrine: The shortness of time should make believers sit loose to all things under the sun.

1. Show the shortness of time. True in two respects.

The time a believer has to live in this world is very short.
(a) *The whole lifetime is very short.* From the cradle to the grave is but a short journey: 'The days of our years are threescore years and ten; and if by reason of strength they be fourscore years, yet is their strength labour and sorrow; for it is soon cut off, and we fly away.' The half of men die before the age of twenty. Even when men lived for many hundred years, it was but a short life - a moment, compared to eternity. Methuselah lived nine hundred and sixty-nine years, and he died.

Men are short-lived, like the grass. 'All flesh is as grass'; and the rich and beautiful are like the flower of the field - a little fairer and more delicate. 'The grass withereth, the flower fadeth; because the Spirit of the LORD bloweth upon it' (Isaiah 40:7). 'For what is your life? It is even a vapour, that appeareth for a little time, and then vanisheth away' (James 4:14). You know how swiftly a weaver's shuttle flies; but your life flies more swiftly: 'My days are swifter than a weaver's shuttle' (Job 7:6). 'My days are swifter than a post; they are passed away as the swift ships; as the eagle that hasteth to the prey' (Job 9:25,26).

(b) *How much is already passed away.* Most believers spent their first days in sin. Many hearing me gave their best days to sin and the world. Many among you have only the lame, and the torn, and the sick, to give to God. All of you can look on the past as a sleep, or as a tale that is told. The time since I came among you appears to me just like a dream.

(c) *What remains is all numbered.* All of you hearing me have your Sabbaths numbered - the number of sermons you are to hear. The last one is already fixed upon. Your years are numbered. To many this is the last year they shall ever see in this world. Many will celebrate their next new year in glory. The disease is now in the body of many of you that is to lay you in the dust; and your grave is already marked out. In a little while you will be lying quietly there. Yes, dear brethren, 'the time is short'.

The time of this world's continuance is short.
'The end of all things is at hand.' 'The fashion of this world passeth away.' A believer stands on a watch-tower: things present are below his feet - things eternal are before his eyes. A little while, brethren, and the day of grace will be over; preaching, praying will be done. Soon we shall give over wrestling with an unbelieving world. Soon the number of

believers shall be complete, and the sky shall open over our heads, and Christ shall come. His parting cry was: 'Surely I come quickly.' Then we shall see him 'whom, having not seen, we loved.' A little while, and we shall stand before the great white throne; a little while, and the wicked shall not be for we shall see them going away into everlasting punishment; a little while, and the work of eternity shall be begun. We shall be like him; we shall see him day and night in his temple; we shall sing the new song, without sin and without weariness, for ever and ever. In a little moment, brethren, all this shall be: 'For a small moment have I hid my face from thee; but with everlasting mercies will I gather thee.'

2. The believer should learn from this to sit loose to all things under the sun.

Sit loose to the dearest objects of this world: 'It remaineth, therefore, that they who have wives be as though they had none.'

Marriage is honourable in all. Husbands should love their wives, even as Christ loved the Church. 'So ought men to love their wives as their own bodies.' Still it must not be idolatry. A married believer should be, in some respects, as if he were unmarried - as if he had no wife.

'Honour thy father and thy mother, that thy days may be long in the land which the Lord thy God giveth thee.' You cannot be too kind, too gentle, too loving, to the parents whom God has given you; yet be as though you had none.

Parents, love your children, and bring them up in the nurture and admonition of the Lord; yet feel that the time is short. They are only a loan from the Lord. Be not surprised if he take his own.

Esteem your ministers highly in love, for their work's sake; yet be as if you had none. Lean as entirely on Christ as if you had never seen or heard a minister.

Brainerd mentions an instance of one woman, who, after her conversion, was resigned to the divine will in the most tender points: 'What if God should take away your husband from you - how do you think you would bear that?' She replied: 'He belongs to God, and not to me; he may do with him just what he pleases.' When she longed to die, to be free from sin, she was asked what would become of her infant; she answered, 'God will take care of it; it belongs to him - he will take care of it.'

Rutherford says: 'Build your nest upon no tree here; for you see God hath sold the forest to Death, and every tree whereon we would rest is ready to be cut down, to the end we may flee and mount up, and build upon the Rock, and dwell in the holes of the Rock.'

Set not your heart on the flowers of this world; for they have all a canker in them. Prize the Rose of Sharon and the Lily of the Valley more than all; for he changeth not. Live nearer to Christ than to the saints, so that when they are taken from you, you may have him to lean on still.

Sit loose to the griefs of this world.
They that weep should be as though they wept not. This world is the vale of tears. There are always some mourning. No sooner is the tear dried up on one cheek than it trickles down another. No sooner does one widow lay aside her weeds, than another takes them up.

Those that are in Christ should weep as though they wept not; 'for the time is short'. Do you weep over those that died in the Lord? It is right to weep: 'Jesus wept'. Yet weep as though you wept not; 'for the time is short.' They are not lost, but gone before. The sun, when it sets, is not lost; it is gone to shine in another hemisphere; and so have they gone to shine in a brighter world.

It is self-love that makes you mourn for them; for they are happy. You would not mourn if they were with a distant friend on earth - why do you mourn that they are with the sinner's Friend? 'They shall hunger no more, neither thirst any more, neither shall the sun light upon them, nor any heat; for the Lamb which is in the midst of the throne shall feed them, and shall lead them unto fountains of living waters; and God shall wipe away all tears from their eyes' (Revelation 7:16,17). 'The time is short'; and you will follow after. A few days, and you may be leaning together on the bosom of Jesus; you are nearer them today than you were yesterday. 'The time is short'; and you will meet with all the redeemed at the right hand of Christ. We shall mingle our voices in the new song, and wave together the eternal palm! 'Weep as though you wept not.'

Do you weep over those that died out of the Lord? Ah! there is deeper cause for weeping here; and yet the time is short, when all this will be explained to you, and you will not be able to shed a tear over the lost. A little while, and you will see Jesus fully glorified, and you will not be able to wish anything different from what has happened. When Aaron lost his two sons, he held his peace.

Do you mourn over bodily pain, and poverty, and sickness, and the troubles of the world? Do not murmur: 'The time is short.' If you have believed in Christ, these are all the hell you will ever bear. Think you the dying thief would complain of his pains when he was within a step of paradise? So it is with you. Your hell is dried up, and you have only these two shallow brooks to pass through - sickness and death. And you have a promise that Christ shall do more than meet you - he will go with you foot for foot, and bear you in his arms. When we get to the presence of Jesus, all our griefs shall look like children's griefs: a day in his presence will make you remember your miseries no more. Wherefore take courage, and run with patience.

Sit loose to the enjoyments of this world.
It is quite right for a believer to use the things of this world, and to rejoice in them. None has such a right as the believer has to rejoice and be happy. He has a right to use the bodily comforts of this world - to eat his meat 'with gladness and singleness of heart, praising God'. He has a right to all the joys of home, and kindred, and friendship. It is highly proper that he should enjoy these things. He has a right to all the pure pleasures of mind, of intellect, and imagination; for God has given him all things richly to enjoy.

Still, he should 'rejoice as though he rejoiced not, and use this world as not abusing it'; for 'the time is short'. In a little while, you will be at your Father's table above, drinking the new wine with Christ. You will meet with all your brothers and sisters in Christ - you will have pure joy in God through ceaseless ages.

Do not be much taken with the joys that are here. I have noticed children, when they were going out to a feast, they would eat but sparingly, that they might have a keener appetite for the coming dainties. So, dear friends, you are going to a feast above, do not dull your appetite with earthly joys. Sit loosely to them all; look upon them all as fading. As you walk through a flower garden, you never think of lying down, to make your home among its roses; so, pass through the garden of this world's best joys. Smell the flowers in passing; but do not tarry. Jesus calls you to his banqueting house - there you will feed among the lilies on the mountains of spices.

Oh! it ill becomes a child of God to be fond of an earthly banquet, when you are looking to sitting down so soon with Jesus. It ill becomes you to be much taken up with dress and show, when you are so soon to see the face that was crowned with thorns. Brethren, if you are ever so much taken up with any enjoyment that it takes away your love for prayer or for your Bible, or that it would frighten you to hear the cry:

'The Bridegroom cometh'; and you would say: Is he come already? then you are abusing this world. Oh! sit loose to this world's joy: 'The time is short.'

Sit loose to the occupations of the world.
It is right for Christians to be diligent in business. I often wonder how unconverted souls can be so busy - how, when you are bustling along, filling up all your time with worldly things, it never occurs to you that there will be none of this in eternity. How can I be so busy for my body, when my poor soul is unprovided for? But those in Christ may well be diligent.

(a) They have a good conscience - that oils the wheels. 'A merry heart doeth good like a medicine.' A light heart makes easy work.

(b) They love to honour their Lord. They would not have it said that a believer in Jesus was an idler or a sluggard - the love of Jesus constrains them to all that is lovely. And yet a believer should 'buy as though he possessed not'; for 'the time is short.'

Oh! believers, ye cannot be misers; for you are but stewards. All that you possess here is your Lord's; and the day is at hand when he will transfer you to take care of another property in a brighter land. You are but servants. It would not do if you were to set your hearts on the things of this lower room; for in a few days the Master is to call you to serve in his own dear presence.

Dear believers, be ready to leave your loom for the golden harp, at a minute's warning; be ready to leave the market below, for the street of the new Jerusalem, where the redeemed shall walk. If you were in a sinking ship, you would not cling hard to bags of money - you would sit loose to all, and be ready to swim. This world is a like a sinking ship, and those who grasp at its possessions will sink with it. Oh! 'buy as though you possessed not'; for 'the time is short'.

3. What the unconverted should learn from the shortness of time.

Learn your folly in having lost the past.
Although life be very short, it is all saving time. This is the reason for which God has given it to us. The long-suffering of God is intended for our salvation. God gives men time to hear the gospel - to pray - to get saving conversion. But unconverted souls have wasted all the past.

Think how much time you have lost in idleness. How many golden opportunities for prayer, and hearing the Word, and meditation, have you lost! How much time have you spent uselessly in your bed, or in idle talk, or in loitering about your doors! If you saw how short your time is, and how death and hell are pursuing you, you would have fled to Christ; but you have not.

Think how much you have spent in sin, at the tavern, or in vain company, or in dances, or in night walking, or in sins of which it is a shame even to speak. God gave you time for saving your soul, and you have spent it in ruining your soul. God gave you time to flee to Christ; and you have spent it in business, without one thought for eternity.

Think how you have lost your best time. Youth is your best time for being saved. Many of you have lost it. Time of awakening - Sabbaths - holy time - years of Sabbaths have now gone over many of you. 'The harvest is past, the summer is ended; and we are not saved.'

Consider what value they put on time who are now in hell.
Once, brethren, they cared as little for it as you - once, they could see their years pass away without caring - once, they could let their Sabbaths slip away; but now they see their folly. What would they not give, brethren, for such an opportunity as you have this day? What would they give for another year of grace - for another week - for another day? It is probable that some of your friends or companions, now in hell, are wishing they could come back to tell you how precious is an inch of saving time!

Oh! brethren, be wise. 'Why stand ye all the day idle?' It has come to the eleventh hour with some - your unconverted head is grey - your feet are tottering. If you saw a man condemned to die, lying in chains, who had but three hours to live; if you saw that man playing at dice, or singing wanton songs, would you not be shocked? You would say he was a hardened wretch.

Ah! Are there none among you the same? You are condemned already. Your days are numbered. You are hanging by a thread over the mouth of hell. And yet you are cutting and slashing at the hand that holds you. In a little moment, brethren, it will be all over. Throughout the never-ending ages of eternity you will remember the few days we spent together. Ah! The remembrance will add fuel to the flame, and be a never-dying worm in your poor soul!

29. We would see Jesus

And there were certain Greeks among them that came up to worship at the feast; the same came therefore to Philip, which was of Bethsaida of Galilee, and desired him, saying, Sir, we would see Jesus. Philip cometh and telleth Andrew: and again Andrew and Philip tell Jesus. And Jesus answered them, saying, The hour is come that the Son of Man should be glorified. Verily, verily, I say unto you, Except a corn of wheat fall into the ground and die, it abideth alone: but if it die, it bringeth forth much fruit. He that loveth his life shall lose it; and he that hateth his life in this world shall keep it unto life eternal. If any man serve me, let him follow me; and where I am, there shall also my servant be; if any man serve me, him will my Father honour (John 12: 20-26).

1. Observe here, the manner in which these Greeks sought the Lord Jesus.

They came not direct to Christ, but in a roundabout manner: 'The same came to Philip' (verse 21).

Had they felt the intolerable burden of sin that lay upon them, or had they seen the grace and suitableness of the Lord Jesus, they would have run to his feet; but their concern was very slight indeed. When the publicans and sinners were awakened about their souls, it is said they drew near to Jesus. They did not go to Philip, or to Andrew, or to any man, but they pressed near to Christ. They saw that he was the fountain for their guilty souls, and all the world could not keep them back from him. When the woman which was a sinner knew that Jesus sat at meat in the Pharisee's house, she came to his feet. She did not ask leave - she could not stay, but cast her guilty soul at his feet, washed them with her tears, and wiped them with the hairs of her head. So it is still. If you felt the burden of sin as you ought to feel it, if you felt the free grace of Christ as you ought, you would press through the crowd to come to Jesus. You would say: Make a lane, that I may come to him. He calls me - he calls the chief of sinners. Here, Lord, am I; wash me in thy blood, or else I die. If you feel the crimson colour of your soul, and believe the freeness and fullness of the fountain, you will ask no man's leave, but go direct to Jesus.

They asked only to see Jesus: 'Sir, we would see Jesus.'
This shows how little they were in earnest to be saved by Christ. For the

same cause Zaccheus climbed up into the sycamore tree, to see Jesus, who he was. For the same cause Herod wished long to see Jesus; for he hoped to see some miracle done by him; just as you would like to see some juggler or fortune-teller, out of an earthly, worldly curiosity. Some are spoken of: 'Ye seek me, because ye did eat of the loaves, and were filled' (John 6:26). Ah! How different when men are truly awakened by the Spirit. When Job was under soul concern, his cry was: 'Oh! that I knew where I might find him, that I might come even to his seat.' How different the cry of the Bride: 'I held him, and would not let him go. My beloved is mine, and I am his.' How different the cry of Paul: 'I count all things but dung, that I may win Christ, and be found in him.'

Oh! brethren, if you are under the teaching of the Spirit, no mere outward sight of Christ will satisfy your soul. You must have a heart sight and heart relish of him. You must taste and see that the Lord is gracious. Many of you like to hear about Jesus - you like to be entertained by fine descriptions of Jesus; but if you are under the teaching of the Spirit, nothing will satisfy you but to sit down under his shadow - to be found in him - to be the dove hidden by his own hand 'in the clefts of the rock and in the secret places of the stair' - to be washed in his blood, and new-created by his Spirit.

One reason of their little concern was fear of man.
The rage of Christ's enemies was waxing hotter and hotter. A few days before, they had come to the solemn resolution of putting him to death. Nay, we are told they consulted how they might put Lazarus also to death, so bloodthirsty were they grown (verse 10). We are told that many of the chief rulers also believed on him; but because of the Pharisees they durst not confess him (verse 42); for they loved the praise of men more than the praise of God. There can be no doubt, then, that the heat and anger of Christ's enemies greatly damped the concern of these Greeks. It was probably this that made them apply first to Philip. It made them cautious in their words: 'Sir, we would see Jesus.' How truly is it said: 'The fear of man bringeth a snare!' The roaring of the lion has driven many a soul away from Christ.

Is this not the case among you? What will my family say, what will my companions say, what will the world say, if I should go to Christ, and give up all for him? These three roars of the lion have ruined many souls. How many of you have felt a real desire sometimes to be saved? Perhaps you fell on your knees and prayed sincerely to be delivered. But some companion came in, some merrymaking was proposed, and you had not courage to say, No. You wished to say, I have begun to seek the Lord, I have been on my knees, I have been praying that I may be saved. But you could not say it. Your tongue stuck to your jaws; and so you went back to your vomit, and to wallow in the mire. Alas! you loved the praise of men more than the praise of God. 'How can ye believe, which receive honour one of another, and seek not the honour that cometh from God only?' What a foolish thing it is to fear the frown of a worm of the dust more than the frown of the infinite God! - to fear the laugh of the scorner more than the sentence of Christ: 'Depart, ye cursed!' 'Fear not them who can kill the body, but are not able to kill the soul; but rather fear him who is able to destroy both soul and body in hell.'

2. Christ's answer.

He shows them that he must die before men will seek him in earnest: 'The hour is come that the Son of Man should be glorified' (verse 23).

There is something very deep and solemn in this answer of Christ. He saw that these Greeks had no piercing sense of their need of him; and he explains to the disciples that it is only a discovery of him as a crucified Christ that will draw men to him: as if he should say, I am like a corn of wheat - if it be not put into the earth and die, it will abide alone; but if it be sown, and die, it bears much fruit. So if I die not, no men will be drawn to me; but if I die for sinners, and lie down in the grave for them, then they will be drawn to me.

(a) *The dying of the Lord Jesus is the most awakening sight in the world.* Why did that lovely one that was from the beginning the brightness of his Father's glory, and the express image of his person, degrade himself so much as to become like a small corn of wheat, which is hidden under the earth and dies? Why did he lie down in the cold rocky sepulchre? Was it not that there was wrath infinite and unutterable lying upon men? Would Christ have wept over Jerusalem if there had been no hell beneath it? Would he have died under his Father's wrath if there were no wrath to come? Oh! secure sinners , triflers with the gospel, polite hearers, who say often: 'Sir, we would see Jesus', but who never find him, go to Gethsemane, see his unspeakable agonies; go to Golgotha, see the vial of wrath poured upon his breaking heart; go to the sepulchre, see the corn of wheat laid dead in the ground. Why all this suffering in the spotless one if there be no wrath coming on the unsheltered unbelieving head? Oh! the corn of wheat in the ground is the most awakening sight in the universe.

(b) *It is the most drawing sight*: 'I, if I be lifted up from the earth, will draw all men unto me.' These poor Greeks did not feel much their need of Christ, but still less did they see his suitableness to their need. Had they but seen what shelter there was to be in his wounds for sinners - had they seen how abundant room there would be for the chief of sinners - they would have burst through every difficulty, and come to Jesus. Nothing in the world could have kept them back from Christ. The fear of man would have been like a straw; they would have cried, not, 'Sir, we would see Jesus', but, 'Draw me, and I will run after thee;' 'Hide me in the clefts of the rock;' 'Cause me to sit under the shade of the apple tree.' It was this sight that drew three thousand to Jesus on the day of Pentecost. The corn of wheat dying for us is the true loadstone to draw iron hearts after him. In the natural loadstone the iron may be drawn away again, but the soul once drawn to Christ can never be drawn away any more.

Oh! pray for a drawing discovery of the Lord Jesus. Some of you are in this condition. The Lord Jesus is on one side of you, and Satan on the other, and you in the midst, and both are drawing at your soul. Oh! pray that the Lord Jesus may overcome. His open arms on the cross are drawing you - his wound in the side is inviting you. 'In me ye shall have peace.'

He shows them that men must cleave to him at whatever cost: 'He that loveth his life shall lose it; and he that hateth his life in this world shall keep it unto life eternal' (verse 25).

These poor Greeks were under the fear of man. They were afraid they would be put out of the synagogue, or perhaps that they would be called Galileans or Nazarenes, or perhaps that they would be laughed at, and lose the praise of men; and this made them very cautious in their approach to the Saviour. Now, the Lord Jesus shows them that this is not the way in which awakened souls must seek him; as if he should say, Go and tell them that in coming to me they are coming for eternal life, and therefore every other consideration must be laid aside. I am the one thing needful - I am the pearl of great price. They that seek me must push aside everything that stands in the way. Even if they lose their life in coming to me, they would find life eternal. 'He that loseth his life for my sake shall find it.' Those that know the real worth of Christ will make everything subordinate to their finding him. Those who will not, never will find him.

(a) *Consider how precious Christ is*: 'In him is life eternal.' In him there is pardon for the vilest of sinners. In him there is sweet peace of conscience - peace with God. In him there is rest for the weary soul - the way to the Father - an open door into the fold of God. In him there is a fountain of living waters, unsearchable riches, full supplies of grace and truth for weak and weary souls. In him there is acquittal at the judgment-day, and a glorious crown. Oh! should you not leave all for this? Shall a lust, or a pleasure, or a game, or the smile of a friend, keep you from all this? 'Eye hath not seen, nor ear heard, nor hath it entered into the heart of man to conceive, the things which God hath prepared for them that love him.'

(b) *Consider how sad your case is without him.* The number of your sins is infinite: 'Innumerable evils have compassed me about.' Your heart is as full as ever, ready to gush out with sin to all eternity. God is angry with you every day. There is no refuge but Christ. If you do not get into him, you will never be saved. You will be outside the ark when the flood comes. You will knock, and cry, Lord! Lord! But it will be too late. God will be your enemy. The great day of his wrath will be come, and who will be able to stand? Some of you have felt a little touch of concern about the awfulness of a lost eternity - you have never felt the millionth part of what is the truth. Oh! then, will you let some poor lust, or pride, or love of dress - some Herodias - keep you away from Christ?

Be entreated to cleave to him at whatever cost. If any business comes between, takes up too much time, disturbs your Sabbaths, hinders you from coming to Christ - let it go. If any pleasure comes between, lulls your convictions, deadens you at prayer and Bible, quickens your desire for the world and sin - let it go. If any friend comes between you and Christ; if their company indisposes you for seeking Christ - takes off your mind; if their ridicule or vain talk brings you back to the world - let them go. Never mind though they laugh and sneer - think you odd - ridiculous - call you Methodist; it matters not - one thing is needful - Christ is precious - eternity is near. If you do not, you will lose your soul. Like Paul, count all things but loss.

If we would be Christ's, we must give up ourselves to his service for ever. The poor Greeks said: 'Sir, we would see Jesus.' Jesus here tells them that a mere sight of him will not do: 'If any man serve me, let him follow me.' Many people are willing to be saved from hell; but they are not willing to give themselves up to Christ to be his servants and followers; but every one who is under the teaching of the Spirit, gives himself up to be the Lord's. So Matthew. The Lord said: 'Follow me; and he arose and left all, and followed Jesus.' One who is truly taught of God feels indwelling sin a greater burden than the fear of hell: 'In me, that is in my flesh, there dwelleth no good thing.' 'O wretched man that I am! Who shall deliver me from the body of this death?' Therefore, that soul is willing to be Christ's servant for ever - willing to have his ear bored to the door of Christ's house.

This will discover hypocrites. Are you willing to be Christ's servant - to follow him in hard duties - to be brought under the rules of the gospel? If not, you are a hypocrite. *Count the cost of coming to Christ.*

3. The reward.

You will be with Christ.
You may be cast out by men - father and mother - you may be regarded as the offscouring of all things: 'Today shalt thou be with me in paradise' - be with the Lamb on mount Zion. Sit with me on my throne: 'Father, I will that they also whom thou hast given me be with me where I am, that they may behold my glory.'

The Father will honour you.
You will lose the praise of men, perhaps of some you esteem; but you will gain the honour of God.

(1) *In this world.* Ye shall be a peculiar treasure. He will guide you with his eye, hear your prayer, be with you in trouble, fill you with his Spirit, give his angels charge over you, be with you in death.

(2) *In eternity.* He will receive you, show you his salvation, wipe off tears from your eyes, be your God and portion. Jesus will confess you before his Father: This soul followed me.

30. The soul of the believer a garden

*Thou that dwellest in the gardens, the companions hearken to thy voice;
cause me to hear it. Make haste, my beloved, and be thou like to a roe or
to a young hart upon the mountains of spices (Song 8:13,14).*

I. The description of the Church, or of the believing soul: 'Thou that
dwellest in the gardens.' This is true of the believer in two ways.

He is enclosed and separated from the world.
'A garden enclosed is my sister, my spouse' (Song 4:12). All believers
dwell within an enclosure. Just as the gardens in the East are enclosed
with a fence of reeds, or of prickly pear, or by a stone wall; so all that
are Christ's are enclosed out of the world. Jesus says: 'If ye were of the
world, the world would love its own: but because ye are not of the world,
but I have chosen you out of the world, therefore the world hateth you.'
Paul says, he was 'separated unto the gospel of God.' And again, John
says: 'The world knoweth us not, even as it knew him not.' Great
mistakes are made here. There are many hedges that are none of Christ's
planting. Many are separated, but not unto the gospel of God.

(a) Some are separated by education. They are brought up far away
from the noise and bustle of the world. They see little of its vices, and
hear little of its profanity. They are never allowed to come within its
magic ring. They are a kind of separated people. But, ah! they have the
world in their own heart.

(b) Some, again, are separated from the world by worldly griefs and
distresses, or by sickness of body. Their proud spirit is broken. Their
heart used madly to follow the world; but now it sickens and dies within
them - desire fails. They have no more heart for their idols. These are
a kind of separated people. But, ah! they dwell not in the gardens - that
is the separation of nature, not of grace.

(c) Some have a haughty separation from the world, like those that
said: 'Stand by, for I am holier than thou;' like the Pharisee, who would
not speak to the publican. These are known by their little compassion
for the world. Ah! these do not dwell in Christ's garden.

(d) There is a nominal separation from the world. These people have
a name to live, and are dead. They belong, it may be, to a peculiar
congregation, and to a peculiar prayer-meeting; they have a Christian
name and a Christian appearance; they often speak as Christians, and are

spoken of as Christians; the world are afraid of them, and treat them as if they were believers. But all the time beneath that mantle there beats an unchanged, unbelieving, ungodly heart. Ah! brethren, this is a separation of Satan's making.

But all that are truly Christ's are dwellers in the gardens. They are separated from the world by an infinite, impassable chasm.

First, *by blood.* Just as the houses of Israel were separated from the houses of the Egyptians by having the doors sprinkled with blood; so there are a set of men in this world, the doors of whose hearts have been sprinkled with blood. The blood of Christ upon their conscience marks them out as pardoned men. They had the same nature as other men - the same enmity to God, and desperate departure from him. They had the same love of idols as other men. They spent their youth in the same sins as other men - many of them went into the lowest depths of sin. But the Lord Jesus loved them, and washed them from their sins in his own blood. 'Justified by faith, they have peace with God.' These are they who dwell in the gardens. Ah! brethren, have you been separated by blood?

Second, *by his Spirit.* All that are truly Christ's are separated from the world by the indwelling of the Holy Spirit. 'If any man be in Christ Jesus, he is a new creature.' He has got new desires given him. Once he desired what other men do - praise of men, a name, power, money, pleasure. These were the chief objects set before him. Now these have lost their power over him. The world is become crucified. Now he desires more nearness to God - more complete change of heart. He desires to spread the knowledge of Jesus over the world. He is separated unto the gospel of God. He has got new sorrows. Once all his sorrows were worldly sorrows, he wept at the loss of friends or this world's possessions; but now these sorrows are light afflictions. His heaviest grief now is when he is deserted of God, when he wants the presence of Christ and the smile of God; or perhaps the absence of the Spirit and the burning of corruption within, or sin abounding around him, makes him sigh and cry; or the ark of God makes his heart tremble. That man is separated - he dwells in the gardens.

Dear souls, have you been thus separated from the world? 'We are bound always to thank God for you, beloved; because he hath from the beginning chosen you to salvation; through sanctification of the Spirit and belief of the truth.' Ah! brethren, does the blood of Christ separate you from the unpardoned world? Does the Spirit of Christ separate you from the unregenerate world? Is there a real, eternal separation between you and the world? If not, you will perish with the world.

Dwelling in the gardens seems also to mean dwelling in delight.
When God made man at the first, he planted a garden eastward in Eden; and out of the ground made the Lord God to grow every tree that is pleasant to the sight and good for food - the tree of life also, in the midst of the garden. And the Lord God took the man and put him into the garden of Eden, to dress and to keep it. That garden was a sweet type of the delight of Adam's soul; and there, day by day, he heard the voice of God walking in the garden, in the cool of the day. When Adam fell, God drove him out of the garden into this bleak world, covered with thorns and thistles, to earn his bread by the sweat of his brow. Man no more walked with God in a garden of delights.

But when a sinner is brought to Christ, he is brought into Christ's garden: 'We who believe, do enter into rest.' He says: 'I sat down under his shadow with great delight, and his fruit was sweet to my taste.' He becomes one that dwells in the gardens. True, he is one coming up from the wilderness. This world is a wilderness to the believer - full of pain, sickness, sighing, death - a world that crucified his Lord, and persecutes him - a cold, unbelieving, ungodly world. Still the soul dwells in the gardens: 'His soul shall dwell at ease.' True, a believer has his times of desertion, and clouds, and doubts, and deep waters. At such times, his cry is: 'O wretched man!' Still when his eye rests on Jesus, his soul dwells in a garden of delights.

Oh! brethren, have you been brought into Christ's garden? Have you found great delight in him - a better Eden - a right to the tree of life that is in the midst of the paradise of God? Many of you think it a dull thing to become a Christian. You look upon their outside - their quiet humble walk through the world. You think them dull, morose, severe. But, O man! you are only looking at the shell. Could you see what is felt within, could you see the sunshine of heaven that rests upon that soul, could you taste for a moment the pleasure of being at peace with God, you would feel that all your pleasures are but the husks which the swine are eating.

> Happy is the man that findeth wisdom,
> And the man that getteth understanding.
> She is more precious than rubies:
> And all the things thou canst desire are not to be compared unto her.

> Length of days is in her right hand;
> In her left hand riches and honour.
> Her ways are ways of pleasantness,
> And all her paths are peace.
> She's a tree of life to them that lay hold upon her:
> And happy is every one that retaineth her.

Ah! brethren, go and learn the hymn that begins:

> Shall men pretend to pleasure
> That never knew the Lord?
> Can all the worldling's treasure
> True peace of mind afford?

2. The complaint of Christ: 'The companions hearken to thy voice: cause me to hear it.'

The soul in Christ has many sweet companions - brothers and sisters in Christ Jesus. The soul that is united to the Vine-tree is united to all the branches: 'We know that we are passed from death unto life, because we love the brethren.' 'I am a companion of all them that fear thee.'

Believers have many things to say to one another; as John says to Gaius: 'I had many things to write unto thee, but I will not with ink and pen write unto thee: but I trust I shall shortly see thee, and we shall speak face to face.' So did believers in the days of Malachi: 'Then they that feared the LORD spake often to one another: and the LORD hearkened and heard' (3:16). And so do believers still. They may tell of their past experiences modestly, humbly, with self-loathing, and for the glory of Christ; as Jesus told the maniac: 'Return to thine own house, and show how great things God hath done unto thee' (Luke 8:39); and as David speaks: 'Come and hear, all ye that fear God, and I will declare what he hath done for my soul' (Psalm 66:16).

They speak to one another in their distresses, as it is written: 'Wherefore comfort one another with these words.' Not comfort yourselves, but comfort one another. It is God's ordinance that comfort should be ministered by believer to believer - that the gentle hand of love should bring the cup of consolation. They speak to one another of Jesus: 'Saw ye him whom my soul loveth?' 'Whither is thy Beloved gone, O thou fairest among women? whither is thy Beloved turned aside, that we may seek him with thee?' They exhort one another daily, while it is called today.

Ah! this is a true mark of all true believers: 'The companions hearken to thy voice.' How many of you may know that you are not in Christ by this, that you have never learned the pure language of Canaan. True, there are many who have the outward phrase of Christians, and who have much talk, who will turn out to be clouds without rain - foolish virgins, having a lamp, and wick, and flame - no drop of oil within. Still, if you have not the speech of Canaan, if you have not a word for those who are journeying toward glory, I fear that you belong not to that company.

Christ complains that we speak more to one another than to him: 'Cause me to hear it.' This is too often the case, especially with young believers. When the bosom is filled with joy, the believer pours it out before his companions, rather than before the Lord. In sorrow, when clouds have covered the soul, Christ is forgotten, and some companion sought out to hear your complaints. In difficulty, how often the believer runs first to some companion on earth for counsel! Now the word of Christ is: 'Cause me to hear it.' Run first to me.

(1) *Because Christ is a jealous Saviour.* 'I, the Lord thy God, am a jealous God.' When Christ took us to himself, he said: 'Thou shalt call me Ishi, and shalt call me no more Baali; for I will take away the names of Baalim out of her mouth.' Remember how he said: 'Lovest thou me more than these?' And we said to him: 'What have I to do any more with idols?' Now, the Lord Jesus cannot bear that we should have a nearer friend than himself. He must be our next of kin. We must lean on the Beloved: 'Cause me to hear it.'

(2) *Because in him is the full supply of all our need.* True, the companions are lovely and pleasant in their lives; but where did they get all the grace that made them so? Was it not from Christ? Perhaps we love their gentleness and meekness - their holy wisdom, to advise us in difficult circumstances. But, ah! where did they get all that? From Jesus. They are but cisterns - Christ is the fountain. They are but candles - Christ is the sun. They are but creatures - Christ is the creator. We must leave them, and betake ourselves to him. 'Cause me to hear it.'

(3) *Communion with Christ is always sanctifying.* Communion with men, even with good men, often hardens and hurts the soul. Are you telling experiences? You are apt to be man-pleasing, to seek to appear something wonderful, very humble, or very believing, you are apt to seek the praise of men more than the praise of God. Are you seeking comfort? You are apt to lean on the creature, and to forget the only Comforter. But communion with Christ is always sanctifying. Oh! it is

good for the soul to meet with Jesus. Oh! if you would go to Jesus and tell him all, if you would cause him to hear it, how much happier lives you would lead! Let there be the utmost frankness between your soul and Christ. Cover no sin before him; pour out every joy; unbosom every grief; seek counsel in every perplexity. See here, he bids you come and tell him all: 'Cause me to hear it.'

3. The believer's prayer.

He prays for a swift return of Christ to his own soul.
It is the presence of Christ with the soul that gives true peace and true holiness. It is not circumstances, nor ministers, nor place, nor time, but Jesus present. To sit under his shadow, gives great delight. To lean upon the Beloved alone supports his faltering steps. A true believer cannot be satisfied while Christ is away: 'Make haste, my Beloved.' One that is not a wife may be content with other lovers; but the faithful bride longs for the return of her Lord. The ordinances are all cold and barren till he return. Ministers speak, but not to the heart. The companions cannot give rest nor ease. Oh! brethren, do you know what it is to long for himself - to cry, 'Make haste, my Beloved'?

He prays for a swift return of Christ to the Church.
It is the presence of Christ that makes a sweet time of refreshing in a Church. When he comes leaping on the mountains, skipping upon the hills, the flowers immediately appear on the earth. The Lord's people are quickened in all their graces; they begin to sing songs of deliverance; anxious souls spring up like the grass, and the whole garden of the Lord sends out spices. Ah! if the Lord Jesus were to come in here with power, I would preach and you would hear in another way than we do. I could not be so hard-hearted, and you would be melted under his Word. Oh! will you not pray, 'Make haste, my Beloved, and be thou like to a roe, or to a young hart upon the mountains of spices.' Is not such a time desirable?

He prays for the glorious second coming of Christ.
It is the real visible coming and presence of Jesus, the king, in his beauty, that will perfect the joy of his believing people.

(1) *The love of the soul will then be satisfied.* At present we are tossed with many doubts. Am I really converted? Am I in Christ? Will I

persevere to the end? The soul has oftentimes a hungering after Christ, and cannot get its fill. But when we shall see him as he is, the shadows will all flee away. We shall never have another doubt for ever - we shall be ever with the Lord.

(2) *Jesus shall then be fully glorified.* At present he is scorned and spit upon. His enemies have the upper hand. Kings despise him, and most men lightly esteem him. But then he shall come to be glorified in his saints, and admired in all them that believe. All his saints shall then bless him. Men shall be blessed in him. All nations shall call him blessed.

Ah! my friends, can you honestly say you long for that day? Is it a blessed hope to you? Those only who can say: 'My Beloved', can desire his coming. 'Woe unto you that desire the day of the Lord! To what end is it for you? The day of the Lord is darkness, and not light.' Ah! brethren, when Jesus comes in the clouds of heaven, every eye shall see him; and most of you, I fear, will wail because of him. Ah! there he is! The Saviour we rejected -neglected all our life - despised; there he comes to take vengeance on us that know not God, and obeyed not the gospel. Those of you that can say: 'My Beloved', are not in darkness, that that day should overtake you as a thief. Your prayer is: 'Make haste, my Beloved and be thou like to a roe, or to a young hart upon the mountains of spices.'

31. The wells of salvation

And in that day thou shalt say, O LORD, I will praise thee: though thou wast angry with me, thine anger is turned away, and thou comfortedst me. Behold, God is my salvation; I will trust, and not be afraid: for the LORD Jehovah is my strength and my song; he also is become my salvation. Therefore with joy shall ye draw water out of the wells of salvation (Isaiah 12:1-3).

These words do first apply to God's ancient people, the Jews; but they are no less applicable to ourselves.

Observe the time spoken of: 'In that day' - the day spoken of in the chapter before: 'It shall come to pass in that day, that the Lord shall set his hand again the second time to recover the remnant of his people, which shall be left, from Assyria, and from Egypt, and from Pathros, and from Cush, and from Elam, and from Shinar, and from Hamath, and from the islands of the sea. And he shall set up an ensign for the nations, and shall assemble the outcasts of Israel, and gather together the dispersed of Judah from the four corners of the earth' (verses 11,12). It is in the day when God restores the Jews to their own land, and converts their souls.

Observe what they will do: 'I will praise thee.' They will then be a praising people. At present they are a melancholy people. There is no joy in their service - they are like a company of dry bones; but in that day their voices will be loud in God's praise.

Observe the ground of it: 'Though thou wast angry with me, thine anger is turned away, and thou comfortedst me. Behold, God is my salvation; I will trust, and not be afraid; for the LORD Jehovah is my strength and my song; he also is become my salvation.' The ground of their joy is, that God's anger is turned away from them - they have found a divine Saviour: 'Behold, God is my salvation.' They have found a divine Sanctifier: 'The LORD Jehovah is my strength and song.' Ah! this is the truest ground of joy and praise in the whole world.

Observe the consequences: 'Therefore with joy shall ye draw water out of the wells of salvation' (verse 3). The wells of salvation appear to be the divine ordinances - God's Word and sacraments. The saved Jews will now find all their springs in Zion - they will be joyful hearers of God's Word, they will be joyful partakers in the Lord's Supper. With joy shall they draw water out of the wells of salvation.

Doctrine: Saved souls draw water with joy out of the wells of salvation.

Many among ourselves find no joy in ordinances. Some despise them altogether. They come not at all. They spend the Sabbath morning in their bed - the Sabbath evening in the pleasures of idleness. The most in this parish have no joy in drawing water. Some come to the house of God; but, oh! it is a weariness - when will it be over? If it were a game of cards, or a merry company, you would not weary; but you know not what it is to have joy in drawing water. Multitudes come to the Lord's Table for a name, for custom, for decency, or to obtain baptism for their children. Alas! alas! they are strangers to drawing water with joy. Some weary souls, anxious about their eternity, go from sermon to sermon, from sacrament to sacrament, seeking rest, but finding none. They go to one well but they find it bitter, to another but it is dry, to another but it is deep, and they cannot draw. These are always learning, and never able to come to the knowledge of the truth. They never draw water with joy out of the wells of salvation. Here is the error: In one and all of these, they do not come as saved souls - they do not come to Christ to get God's anger away. *Saved souls alone draw water with joy.*

1. Observe in these words, the state of the unconverted: 'Thou wast angry with me.' Every redeemed soul can look back to a time when they were under the anger of God. God is at present angry with every unconverted soul. Observe:

Whose anger it is: 'Thou.' It is the anger of God. If all the men in the world were angry with a soul, it would be in a sad condition. If every man you met were full of rage and anger against you - the rich and the poor, kings and captains - you would think yourself in a bad case. If all the wild beasts of the forest - the lions, and wolves, and tigers - were to be enraged against you, and you were in their power, you would be in a desperate case. But these are but creatures. Every unconverted soul among you is under the wrath of the Creator. He that made you is angry with you.

He is always angry: 'God is angry with the wicked every day.' Whatever day of the week it be, weekday or Sabbath Day, God is angry with unconverted souls. Their sins are continually before him, and, therefore, he is continually provoked by them. The smoke of their sins is continually rising into his nostrils. He that believeth not the Son, the wrath of God abideth on him. Not only is God angry every day, but every moment of the day. There is not a moment of an unconverted man's life, but God's wrath abideth on him. When he is at his work or at his play, sleeping or waking, in church or at market, the sword of God's wrath is over his head. Unconverted souls walk and sleep over hell.

It is increasing anger. Unconverted men are treasuring up wrath against the day of wrath. Some unconverted persons think they wipe off many sins by coming to the Lord's Table, whereas, if they knew the truth, they would see that they are heaping up wrath. God's anger is like a river dammed up. It is getting higher and higher, fuller and deeper, every day against every soul that is out of Christ. Every Sabbath your cup is getting fuller; it will soon be full.

It is insufferable anger. Unconverted men sometimes say that if they must go to hell, they will just bear it; but it cannot be borne. If you saw a spider about to be crushed under a great rock, and it should swell out its body in order to bear the shock, it would be miserable folly. Such is the folly of unconverted men saying they will bear the anger of God. How can you bear the anger of your Maker? How can you bear the heel of Omnipotence? 'Can thine heart endure, or can thine hands be strong, in the day that I shall deal with thee?'

Learn from this to flee from the wrath to come. Oh! sirs, if ye but knew your condition, you would rise and flee. I declare to you that I sometimes think myself an Infidel, from the cold manner in which I speak to unconverted souls. This is the state of every one of you who is not born again. However amiable and gentle, and irreproachable in the sight of man, whatever experiences you have gone through, though you may have attended ordinances and kept up prayer, yet, if you are unconverted, God is angry with you every day.

Learn that anxious souls should be ten thousand times more anxious than they are. This is the day of grace - this is saving time. God has infinite pity for you. His anger is infinite against you, and yet his compassion is also infinite. The more he is angry with you, the more he has pity for you. Although his justice cries out for vengeance - sword and bow - on your soul; although his holiness demands that you should be cast out of his sight into the blackness of darkness; yet his compassion cries, Let him alone this year also. There is still room for you under the wings of Christ: 'Kiss the Son, lest he be angry, and ye perish from the way, when his wrath is kindled but a little. Blessed are all they that put their trust in him.'

2. The way of salvation: 'Thine anger is turned away.'

Pardon.

(a) *There is abundant provision for the pardon and peace of the sinner*; for God's anger is turned away on the head of Christ. The thing which troubles the conscience of awakened souls is the anger of God. It is this which makes them tremble, by night and by day, in public and in secret. An awakened soul feels that he has broken God's law, and is exposed every moment to his wrath. He can find no rest in his bed, no peace at his meals, no joy in his friends; the heavens are black above his head, the earth is ready to open and devour him. If God be a just and holy God, he will fulfil all his threatenings. If such a soul would take Christ as his surety, he would find abundant peace. The anger of God has already been turned away on the head of Christ. All the clouds of wrath have been directed, like a waterspout upon that one head. If you are willing that Christ be your surety, you do not need to fear. The law has had its course, and God does not demand a second punishment. There is no reason for your standing trembling, when there is such a glorious way of pardon. Christ offers himself as a surety to every one of you; and if you accept of him, your wrath is past - it will never fall on you to all eternity.

(b) *This will be still more evident, if you consider that Christ is a divine person*: 'Behold, God is my salvation.' If trembling sinners only knew the person who has undertaken to be a Saviour, it would dispel all their fears. He is the brightness of God's glory, and the express image of his person. He is the peerless, matchless Son of God that has undertaken to stand for us. He is the maker of the world, he that sees the end from the beginning. 'By him were all things made.' He made the sun, moon, and stars, he made the solid earth, he upholds all things by the word of his power.

Do you think he would fail in any undertaking? Do you think, if he engages to be a shield for sinners, that he will not be enough to cover them? Oh! be ashamed of your unbelief, and come under this infinite Shield. 'Behold, God is my salvation; I will trust, and not be afraid.' Come, trembling soul, under this divine Shield, and you will find divine peace. Come under this Rock, and you will find rest for your weary souls. It matters not what sins you have; if you come under Christ, you shall have peace.

Holiness: 'Thou comfortedst me' - 'The LORD Jehovah is my strength and song.'

When a soul comes first to Christ, he does not know that he needs any more comfort; he feels such joy, he thinks he shall never be sad again. Soon he is made to feel his wants. He feels innumerable enemies within and without. His heart he feels to be a very hell within him, corruptions whose black faces he never saw before now raise their heads, his breast appears full of hissing serpents. The man shudders at himself, he feels on the brink of a precipice, the smallest breath of temptation he feels will throw him down. In despair of help, he looks above - to Jesus at the right hand of God, able to save to the uttermost. In Jesus it hath pleased the Father that all fullness should dwell. He sends the Comforter - the Holy Spirit comes into the heart of the trembling, tempted one. 'I will trust and not be afraid: for the LORD Jehovah is my strength and my song.'

Ah! do you know anything of this Comforter, of this strength, of this song? Tell me, what do you rest on for holiness. Do you rest on your good thoughts of yourself? Ah! this is like Hazael: 'Is thy servant a dog, that he should do this thing?' and yet he was the very dog he so much disclaimed. 'A haughty spirit goeth before a fall.' Do you rest on your promises to man, or your vows to God? Ah! this is like Peter: 'Though all men forsake thee, yet will not I', and yet his promise was like a breath of wind. No, nothing short of Jehovah can be the strength of thy soul, nothing short of the Lord Jehovah. Creatures cannot hold up creatures. The hand that guides the stars alone can hold thy feet from falling. Is he your strength? Then he is able to keep you from falling. Though the world had ten thousand times more temptation than it has - though your heart were ten thousand times more full of lusts - though Satan and his angels had ten million times more power - they cannot cast down the soul that leans upon Jehovah. Wait on the Lord, be of good courage, and he shall strengthen thine heart. The same hand that holds the sun in his journey holds up the souls of his people. Sing, then, weak, trembling, tempted disciple - sing aloud: 'I will trust, and not be afraid.'

3. Joy in ordinances: 'Therefore with joy shall ye draw water out of the wells of salvation' (verse 3). How changed are all the wells of salvation to a poor sinner come to Christ!

The Bible. Once it was a dull, wearisome book. You looked to the end of the chapter when you began it, to see when it would be done. But have you come to Christ? Now the well is a well of salvation - a well of living water.

Prayer. Once it was wholly neglected by you, or a cold form, which you hurried over; now it is a sweet well of delight. Ah! there is no better test of the soul than delight in secret prayer, unobserved and unknown by man.

The house of prayer. Once you despised it, or came for show - to show your best clothes, or to see your companions; now you can say: 'I was glad when they said unto me, Let us go into the house of the Lord.'

The Lord's Supper. Once you sat there another Judas, with stony heart and dry eyes; now you find it a well of salvation indeed. It is a pledge that Christ is yours. When you see the elements, your heart begins to burn; when you touch them, your bands are loosed; when you taste them, your eyes are enlightened; when you eat them, your whole soul is strengthened. As surely as that bread and wine are yours, you feel that Christ is yours.

Oh! come, then, with simple faith, sinners that have come to Christ, and then you will draw water with joy out of this well of salvation. But, ah! have you no saving change in your heart, no faith in Christ, no union to him, no Comforter? Ah! then, it will be a sad day to you. You will sit down at that table with the wrath of God abiding on you: the well of salvation will be a poisoned well to you; the bread of life will be the bread of death to you; the cup of blessing will be the cup of cursing.

32. Look to a pierced Christ

And I will pour upon the house of David, and upon the inhabitants of Jerusalem, the spirit of grace and of supplications: and they shall look upon me whom they have pierced, and they shall mourn for him, as one mourneth for his only son, and shall be in bitterness for him as one that is in bitterness for his first-born... In that day there shall be a fountain opened to the house of David and to the inhabitants of Jerusalem, for sin and for uncleanness (Zechariah 12:10; 13:1).

In these words you have a description of the conversion of the Jews, which is yet to come - an event that will give life to this dead world. But God's method is the same in the conversion of any soul. Conversion is the most glorious work of God. The creation of the sun is a very glorious work - when God first rolled him flaming along the sky, scattering out golden blessings on every shore. The change in spring is very wonderful - when God makes the faded grass revive, the dead trees put out green leaves, and the flowers appear on the earth. But far more glorious and wonderful is the conversion of a soul! It is the creation of a sun that is to shine for eternity; it is the spring of the soul that shall know no winter; the planting of a tree that shall bloom with eternal beauty in the paradise of God.

1. The source of conversion.

The hand of Christ: 'I will pour upon the house of David and upon the inhabitants of Jerusalem the spirit of grace and of supplications; and they shall look upon me whom they have pierced.' The Holy Spirit comes from the very hand that was pierced by the nail to the accursed tree. Indeed the innermost source of the Spirit seems to be the heart of the Father. Jesus calls him 'the Spirit of Truth which proceedeth from the Father'; and, in 1 Corinthians 2:11, he is said to be in the heart of God, as the spirit of a man is in the heart of man. He is the friend that dwelt from eternity in the bosom of the Father and of the Son.

But still it is as true that the Father has given the Spirit to Christ: 'It hath pleased the Father that in him should all fullness dwell.' Jesus has obtained the gift of the Holy Spirit as a reward of his work. It is fitting that he that died for sinners should have the Spirit to dispense to whom he will; and so one of his last words to his disciples was: 'I will send him unto you; and when he is come he will convince the world of sin.'

This teaches awakened souls where their convictions come from.
Do any of you feel that you have been awakened to concern about your souls? You have been pierced through with an arrow of conviction. Look at the arrow; it came out of the bow of Christ. It was Christ that took it out of his quiver. Christ aimed it at your heart, he made it pierce your heart. The feather is marked with the blood of the pierced hand. That arrow came from the hand of love, from the hand that was nailed to the cross.

Ah! then, take it as a proof that Christ wants to save you. He is beginning to deal with you. Ah! do not turn away! Do not tear out the arrow! Do not heal the wound slightly! Go to himself, and the same hand that pierced you will heal. Lord, if I may not have peace from thee, grant I may get it from nothing else.

When you see others sorely wounded, you should acknowledge the hand of Christ.
I find that some acknowledge the hand of the minister, but not the hand of Christ. This is a sore dishonour to our glorious Immanuel! It was said of the Erskines, the fathers of the Secession, that God took away great part of the blessing from their labours, because the people could not see Christ over their heads. I find much of this amongst yourselves. The Lord teach you to look above the heads of ministers, to our glorious

Redeemer, riding on his white horse - sending out his arrows of conviction!

Pray to Christ to do this.
If he pours out the Spirit, then who can hinder? I have no doubt many of you have come up today, who would have stayed away if you thought Christ would this day convert your soul. I fear there are some among you who have shut your eyes, and stopped your ears, and made your heart gross, lest ye should be converted, and Christ should heal you. You would not like to be made a weeping, praying lowly believer in Jesus. But, oh! if Christ pour out the Spirit today, then even you will be melted. Even you will be made to weep and to cry: 'What must I do to be saved?'

In a time when Christ is not pouring the Spirit down, ministers speak and strive, but in vain; it is like speaking to the winds, or the wild waves of the sea. But when Christ rises from his throne and pours the Spirit down, then the weakest means are infinitely mighty. The Word does not come in word only. The jaw-bone of an ass was a very weak sword to kill men with; and yet in the hand of Samson it was mighty. He slew a thousand men with it. A sling and a stone was a very weak weapon to oppose an armed giant; and yet when David slang the stone, it sank into the forehead of the giant, and he fell upon his face to the earth. Oh! pray, dear believers, that the sling and the stone may this day be in the hand of our glorious David, that the Word may sink into the hard hearts of this people, that even giants in sin may be brought down to the very dust.

Ah! I fear that many of you are armed to the teeth against the Word of God; you are armed *cap-a-pie* - armed at all points. You are mocking, perhaps, in your security; yet, look up, dear friends, to the arm of Immanuel - he can bring down the proudest. Pray that he would pour down the Spirit. I believe that the lowly prayers of a single believer may obtain a deep and pure work of God in a town. If there were men among us like Noah, Job and Daniel, we might expect showers of blessings.

2. The Spirit who converts.

The Spirit of grace.
He is so called, because his coming to any soul, and all that he does in the soul, is of free grace. When the Spirit of God first visits a soul, he finds nothing to invite him to come or to stay. He finds the soul like the dry bones in the open valley - without any form or comeliness, without

any desire for life. The natural man has no more comeliness than a dry skeleton - no more desire for grace than a dead carcass. Nay, more, there is everything to drive the Spirit away. He is a holy Spirit; but he finds the heart a sink of corruptions, full of the most loathsome lusts and passions. He is a loving Spirit; but he finds the man's heart full of rebellion and horrid enmity against God. He is a jealous Spirit; but he finds the man's heart a chamber of imagery, full of abominable idols. Oh! I can imagine the Holy Spirit looking into some of your hearts, and saying: 'Why should I come to such a soul? He does not want me to convert him. He wants to be let alone. He had rather serve his lusts; why should I disturb him? I will let him alone.' Stay, stay, blessed Spirit of grace! Come, out of free grace. Come, not because he wants thee, but because thou art gracious. Come and make even these dry bones to rise and call upon the name of Jesus.

Some of you know it was thus he came to you. He found you a rebel, and he has made you an obedient child. Oh, will you ever despair of any, since he turned your heart! There are some among you, dear friends, of whom man would despair: men and women who have lived long in sin; old formalists, to whom betraying the Lord at his table is an old trade. Oh, let us not despair of such! The Spirit is the Spirit of free grace. Invite him to come, poor dead soul.

The Spirit of supplications.

Because he teaches to pray. A natural man can hardly be said to pray. True, he has often a form - often a cry in the time of distress; but 'will he always call upon God'? An anxious soul cannot pray with a form; for he says, None was ever like me. But a man prays in reality when the Spirit comes to his soul.

He drove an ungodly Manasseh to his knees. Manasseh had often bowed in youth at his godly father's knee. He had often prayed to his bloody idols, he had often prayed to the devil. But now, when the Spirit came, he began to pray indeed.

He drove a blaspheming Paul to his knees. Often, doubtless, Paul had prayed at the feet of Gamaliel. In the synagogue, and at the corners of streets, he had made long prayers, for a pretence; but now, awakened by the Spirit of God, 'behold he prayeth'.

Have you been taught to pray by the Spirit of God? You once had a form, or you prayed for a pretence, or you prayed to idols. But have you been driven to pray by the Holy Spirit? Then you may be sure he has begun a work in your heart. If any of you have not been driven to pray in secret, you may be quite sure that you are in the 'gall of bitterness and the bond of iniquity.' A prayerless soul is an unawakened soul, very near to the burning. Some pieces of wood will burn much more easily than others; some pieces are green, and do not readily catch the flame, but a dry piece of wood is easily kindled. Prayerless souls are dry pieces of wood. They are ready for the burning.

3. Where the soul looks in conversion: 'They shall look upon me whom they have pierced.'

When the Spirit of God is really working in the heart, he makes the man look to a pierced Christ. Wherever he goes, this is the prominent object in his eye - Christ whom he has pierced. Satan would make a man look anywhere rather than to Christ. There is such a thing as false conversion. Satan sometimes stirs people up to care about their souls. He makes them look to ministers, or books, or meetings, or duties - to feelings, enlargement in prayer, etc.; he will let them look to anything in the universe except to one object - 'the cross of Christ'. The only thing he hides is the gospel, the glorious gospel of Christ. When it is the Spirit of God, he will not let the soul look to anything else but to Christ, a pierced Christ. What does an awakened soul see there?

That he has pierced the Son of God by his sins.

This gives him an awful sense of the infinite greatness of sin. A natural man thinks nothing of sin. An oath or a lie is as light as a feather on many of your consciences. You feel it no burden, even if there were a million of them lying upon your soul. You can sleep easily under all your sins. But if your eyes were opened to look at a pierced Christ, you would see that the load is infinite. Ah! see there - God did not spare Christ. Though he had no sin of his own, nothing but imputed sin, yet see what infinite wrath was poured upon him! See what arrows pierced his holy soul! The nails pierced his spotless hands and feet, but all the arrows of God were drinking up his spirit. Will God spare you, then, if you die under your own sins, when these sins are your own act and deed?

Think again: Christ was God. That pale sufferer is 'the mighty God, the everlasting Father, the Prince of Peace'; yet see how he sinks under the load; see, in Gethsemane, how he lies trembling, sweating great drops of blood; see him on Calvary, how his bones are out of joint - how his head is bowed in dying agony. You are but a worm. Can you bear that wrath? 'Can thine heart endure, or can thine hands be strong in the day that I shall deal with thee?' Oh! look to Christ, sinners, look to a pierced Christ, and mourn. Nothing will break your heart but a sight of Christ pierced by your sins.

That he has pierced the Son of God by unbelief.
When the Spirit reveals Christ to the soul, this is generally the bitterest pang. An unawakened man thinks nothing of unbelief - he does not care that he has rejected Christ times without number. Ministers have preached till their breath is spent, beseeching him to turn and live. Christ hath stood all the day long with his hands stretched out. God hath waited upon that man, has delayed casting him into hell. Still he is an unmelted rebel. Ah! when the Spirit awakes that man, what a sight he sees in a pierced Christ! Some of you are saying this day: I have despised that glorious one. He would often have gathered me, and I would not. God has been waiting on me for years. Jesus hath been knocking at my door, and I would never let him in; and now I fear he is gone for ever. Yea, some of you may feel that your heart is unwilling to take him, it is so hard and dead. All the more lovely he appears, the more your heart is pierced because you have rejected him. Ah, there is no grief like that of looking to a pierced Christ!

(a) *It is a bitter grief.* Did you ever see parents mourning the loss of their only son, or their firstborn? It is an unspeakable sorrow. Such is the anguish of those who look to a pierced Christ. Indeed, some have deeper agony than others, but all who truly look to Christ are in bitterness.

(b) *It is a lonely grief.* Indeed it will not be restrained anywhere; and they are wrong who condemn rashly intense anxiety breaking forth even in public; but this grief seeks the shade - the stricken soul seeks to be alone with God, or with a few like-minded. David Brainerd mentions that on one occasion, when he was preaching a pierced Christ to his Indians, the power of God came down among them like a mighty rushing wind: 'Their concern was so great, each for himself, that none seemed to take any notice of those about him. They were, to their own apprehension, as much retired as if they had been alone in the thickest desert. Every one was praying apart, and yet all together.'

Oh, dear friends, if you would really look to a pierced Christ, you would be in anguish of soul to obtain an interest in him! Oh, see how you have slighted him in the days gone by. In youth, at the Sabbath-school as little children, how you have refused him! When you first came to the Lord's table, he stood a pierced Saviour before your eyes; yet you neglected him, and trampled him below your feet. And are you coming this day to pierce him over again, to drive the nails again into his hands, the spear into his side, the thorns into his brow? Oh, stop, sinner! You are piercing one who loves you, killing the Prince of Life, neglecting the only Saviour. If you reject him today, you may never see him again till you see him in the clouds of heaven, and wail because of him.

Dear believers, remember how you pierced him; let bitter herbs sweeten your Passover, let a bitter remembrance of past sin make Christ the more precious.

4. A fountain is seen in a pierced Christ.
The first look to Christ makes the sinner mourn; the second look to Christ makes the sinner rejoice. When the soul looks first to Christ, he sees half the truth. He sees the wrath of God against sin, that God is holy and must avenge sin, that he can by no means clear the guilty. He sees that God's wrath is infinite. When he looks to Christ again, he sees the other half of the truth. The love of God to the lost, that God has provided a surety free to all. It is this that fills the soul with joy. Oh, it is strange, that the same object should break the heart and heal it! A look to Christ wounds, a look to Christ heals. Many, I fear, have only a half look at Christ, and this causes only grief. Many are slow of heart to believe all that is spoken concerning Jesus. They believe all except that he is free to them. They do not see this glorious truth: 'That a crucified Jesus is free to every sinner in the world,' that Christ's all is free to all.

When the Spirit is teaching, he gives a full look at Christ, a look to him alone for righteousness. What does the sinner see? The wounds of Christ, a fountain for sin and for uncleanness. Oh, trembling sinners, come and get this look at Christ! Come and see a fountain for sin and for uncleanness, opened on Calvary eighteen hundred years ago. 'I cannot, for my sins are very great.' Are you all sin and uncleanness, nothing but sin, a lump of sin? In your life, in your heart, are you one bundle of lusts? Here is a fountain opened for you; look to a pierced Christ, and weep; look to a pierced Christ, and be glad. 'I cannot wash.' To look is to wash. No sooner is the eye turned than the filthy garments fall.

The fountain is opened up in this house of God today. At the very entrance to the tables, Jesus stands and says: 'Whosoever will, let him take the water of life freely'. Are you willing? Do you look to him alone for righteousness? Then, come thus washed to the Lord's Table , in the very garment you shall wear in glory. Sit with your eye upon the fountain. Oh, prize it highly! What do you not owe to him who saves you from being cast away!

Some would go past the fountain to the table. Take heed, ungodly man! Will you dare to sit there with unpardoned sin upon you? Will you venture to touch the bread, and your soul unwashed? Ah, you will bitterly rue it one day! Some, I trust, will remember this day in glory; some, I fear, will remember this day in hell.

St Peter's, April 19 1840 (Action Sermon)

33. I sleep, but my heart waketh

I sleep, but my heart waketh: it is the voice of my beloved that knocketh, saying, Open to me, my sister, my love, my dove, my undefiled: for my head is filled with dew, and my locks with the drops of the night etc.
(Song 5:2 to the end).

The passage I have read forms one of the dramatical songs of which this wonderful book is composed. The subject of it is a conversation between a forsaken and desolate wife and the daughters of Jerusalem.

She relates to them how, through slothfulness, she had turned away her lord from the door. He had been absent on a journey from home, and did not return until night. Instead of anxiously sitting up for her husband, she had barred the door, and slothfully retired to rest: 'I slept, but my heart was waking'. In this half-sleeping, half-waking frame, she heard the voice of her beloved husband: 'Open to me, my sister, my love, my dove, my undefiled; for my head is filled with dew, and my locks with the drops of the night.' But sloth prevailed with her, and she would not open, but answered him with foolish excuses: 'I have put off my coat; how shall I put it on? I have washed my feet; how shall I defile them?'

She next tells them her grief and anxiety to find her lord. He tried the bolt of the door, but it was fastened. This wakened her thoroughly. She ran to the door and opened, but her beloved had withdrawn himself, and was gone. She listened - she sought about the door - she called - but he gave no answer. She followed him through the streets; but the watchmen found her, and smote her, and took away her veil; and now with the morning light she appears to the daughters of Jerusalem, and anxiously beseeches them to help her: 'I charge you, if ye find him whom my soul loveth, that ye tell him that I am sick of love.'

The daughters of Jerusalem, astonished at her extreme anxiety, ask: 'What is thy beloved more than another beloved?' This gives opportunity to the desolate bride to enlarge on the perfections of her lord, which she does in a strain of the richest descriptiveness, the heart filling fuller and fuller as she proceeds, till she says: 'This is my beloved, and this is my friend, O ye daughters of Jerusalem!' They seem to be entranced by the description, and are now as anxious as herself to join in the search after this altogether lovely one. 'Whither is thy beloved gone, O thou fairest among women? Whither is thy beloved turned aside, that we may seek him with thee?'

Such is the simple narrative before us. But you will see at once that there is a deeper meaning beneath - that the narrative is only a beautiful transparent veil, through which every intelligent child of God may trace some of the most common experiences in the life of the believer: (1) The desolate bride is the believing soul. (2) The daughters of Jerusalem are fellow-believers. (3) The watchmen are ministers. (4) And the altogether lovely one is our Lord and Saviour Jesus Christ.

1. Believers often miss opportunities of communion with Christ through slothfulness.

Observe, Christ is seeking believers.
It is true that Christ is seeking unconverted souls. He stretches out his hands all the day to a gainsaying and disobedient people - he is the Shepherd that seeks the lost sheep. But it is as true that he is seeking his own people also, that he may make his abode with them and that their joy may be full. Christ is not done with a soul when he has brought it to the forgiveness of sins. It is only then that he begins his regular visits to the soul. In the daily reading of the Word, Christ pays daily visits to sanctify the believing soul. In daily prayer, Christ reveals himself to his own in that other way than he doth to the world. In the house of God

Christ comes to his own, and says: 'Peace be unto you!' And in the sacrament he makes himself known to them in the breaking of bread, and they cry out: 'It is the Lord!' These are all trysting times, when the Saviour comes to visit his own.

Observe, Christ also knocks at the door of believers.
Even believers have got doors upon their hearts. You would think, perhaps, that when once Christ has found an entrance into a poor sinner's heart, he would never find difficulty in getting in any more. You would think that as Samson carried off the gates of Gaza, bar and all, so Christ would carry away all the gates and bars from believing hearts; but no, there is still a door on the heart, and Christ stands and knocks. He would fain be in. It is not his pleasure that we should sit lonely and desolate. He would fain come into us, and sup with us, and we with him.

Observe, Christ speaks: 'Open to me, my sister, my love, my dove, my undefiled.' O what a meeting of tender words is here! - all applied to a poor sinner who has believed in Christ.

(a) '*My sister*': for you remember how Jesus stretched his hand toward his disciples, and said: 'Behold my mother and my brethren; for whosoever shall do the will of my Father, the same is my brother, and my sister, and my mother.'

(b) '*My love*': for you know how he loved sinners - left heaven out of love; lived, died, rose again, out of love, for poor sinners; and when one believes on him he calls him, 'My love'.

(c) '*My dove*': for you know that when a sinner believes in Jesus, the holy dove-like Spirit is given him; so Jesus calls that soul, 'My dove'.

(d) '*My undefiled*': strangest name of all to give to a poor defiled sinner. But you remember how Jesus was holy, harmless, and undefiled. He was that in our stead - when a poor sinner believes in him, he is looked on as undefiled. Christ says: 'My undefiled'. Such are the winning words with which Christ desires to gain an entrance into the believer's heart. Oh, how strange that any heart could stand out against all this love!

Observe, Christ waits: 'My head is filled with dew, and my locks with the drops of the night.'

Christ's patience with unconverted souls is very wonderful. Day after day he pleads with them: 'Turn ye, turn ye, why will ye die?' Never did beggar stand longer at a rich man's gate, than Jesus, the almighty Saviour, stands at the gate of sinful worms. But his patience with his own is still more wonderful. They know his preciousness, and yet will not let him in. Their sin is all the greater, and yet he waits to be gracious.

Believers are often slothful at these trysting times, and put the Saviour away with vain excuses.

(a) *The hour of daily devotion* is a trysting hour with Christ, in which he seeks, and knocks, and speaks and waits; and yet, dear believers, how often are you slothful, and make vain excuses! You have something else to attend to, or you are set upon some worldly comfort, and you do not let the Saviour in.

(b) *The Lord's Table* is the most famous trysting-place with Christ. It is then that believers hear him knocking, saying: 'Open to me.' How often is this opportunity lost through slothfulness, through want of stirring up the gift that is in us, through want of attention, through thoughts about worldly things, through unwillingness to take trouble about it! 'I have put off my coat; how shall I put it on? I have washed my feet; how shall I defile them?'

Doubtless, there are some children of God here, who did not find Christ last Sabbath-day at his Table - who went away unrefreshed and uncomforted. See here the cause - it was your own slothfulness. Christ was knocking; but you would not let him in. Do not go about to blame God for it. Search your own heart, and you will find the true cause. Perhaps you came without deliberation - without self-examination and prayer - without duly stirring up faith. Perhaps you were thinking about your worldly gains and losses, and you missed the Saviour. Remember, then, the fault is yours, not Christ's. He was knocking - you would not let him in.

2. Believers in darkness cannot rest without Christ.

In the parable we find that, when the bride found her husband was gone, she did not return to her rest. Oh, no! Her soul failed for his word. She listens, she seeks, she calls. She receives no answer. She asks the watchmen, but they wound her, and take away her veil; still she is not broken off from seeking. She sets the daughters of Jerusalem to seek along with her.

So is it with the believer. When the slothful believer is really awakened to feel that Christ has withdrawn himself, and is gone, he is slothful no longer. Believers remain at ease only so long as they flatter themselves that all is well; but if they are made sensible, by a fall into sin, or by a fresh discovery of the wickedness of their heart, that Christ is away from them, they cannot rest. The world can rest quite well, even while they know that they are not in Christ. Satan lulls them into fatal repose. Not so the believer - he cannot rest.

He does all he can do himself. He listens, he seeks, he calls. The Bible is searched with fresh anxiety. The soul seeks and calls by prayer; yet often all in vain. He gets no answer - no sense of Christ's presence.

He comes to ministers - God's watchmen on the walls of Zion. They deal plainly and faithfully with his backslidden soul, taking away the veil and showing him his sin. The soul is thus smitten and wounded, and without a covering; and yet it does not give over its search for Christ. A mere natural heart would fall away under this - not so the believer in darkness.

He applies to Christian friends and companions - bids them help him, and pray for him: 'I charge you, O ye daughters of Jerusalem, if ye find him whom my soul loveth, tell him that I am sick of love.'

Is there any of you, then, a believer in darkness, thus anxiously seeking Christ? You thought that you had really been a believer in Jesus; but you have fallen into sin and darkness, and all your evidences are overclouded. You are now anxiously seeking Christ. Your soul fails for his Word. You seek, you call, even though you get no answer. You do search the Bible, even though it is without comfort to you. You do pray, though you have no comfort in prayer - no confidence that you are heard. You ask counsel of his ministers; and when they deal plainly with you, you are not offended. They wound you, and take away the veil from you. They tell you not to rely on any past experiences - that they may have been delusive - they only increase your anxiety; still you follow hard after Christ. You seek the daughters of Jerusalem - them that are the people of Christ - and you tell them to pray for you.

Is this your case? As face answers to face, so do you see your own image here? Do you feel that you cannot rest out of Christ? Then do not be too much cast down. This is no mark that you are not a believer, but the very reverse. Say: 'Why art thou cast down, O my soul? Why art thou disquieted in me? Still trust in God; for I shall yet praise him, who is the health of my countenance, and my God.'

Is there any of you awakened, since last Sabbath-day, by some fall into sin, to feel that Christ is away from you? Doubtless, there must be some who, within this little week, have found out that, though they ate bread with Christ, they have lifted up the heel against him. And are you sitting down contented, without anxiety? Have you fallen, and do you not get up and run, that, if possible, you may find Christ again? Ah, then! I stand in doubt of you; or rather, there is no need of doubt - you have never known the Saviour, you are none of his.

3. Believers in darkness are sick of love, and full of the commendation of Christ - more than ever.

In the parable, the bride told the daughters of Jerusalem that she was sick of love. This was the message she bade them carry; and when they asked her about her beloved, she gave them a rich and glowing description of his perfect beauty ending by saying: 'He is altogether lovely.'

So it is with the believer in time of darkness: 'He is sick of love.' When Christ is present to the soul, there is no feeling of sickness. Christ is the health of the countenance. When I have him full in my faith as a complete surety, a calm tranquillity is spread over the whole inner man, the pulse of the soul has a calm and easy flow, the heart rests in a present Saviour with a healthy, placid affection. The soul is contented with him, at rest in him: 'Return unto thy rest, O my soul.' There is no feeling of sickness. It is health to the bones; it is the very health of the soul to look upon him, and to love him.

But when the object of affection is away, the heart turns sick. When the heart searches here and there, and cannot find the beloved object, it turns faint with longing: 'Hope deferred maketh the heart sick.'

When the ring-dove has lost its mate, it sits lone and cheerless, and will not be comforted. When the bird that hath been robbed of its young, comes back again and again, and hovers with reluctant wing over the spot where her nest was built, she fills the grove with her plaintive melodies - she is 'sick of love'.

These are the yearnings of nature. Such also are the yearnings of grace. When Jesus is away from the believing soul it will not be comforted. When the soul reads, and prays, and seeks, yet Jesus is not found, the heart yearns and sickens - he is 'sick of love'. 'Hope deferred maketh the heart sick.'

Did you ever feel this sickness? Did you ever feel that Christ was precious, but not present - that you could not lay hold on Christ as you used to do, and yet your soul yearned after him, and would not be comforted without him? If you have:

Remember it is a happy sickness. It is a sickness not of nature at all, but of grace. All the struggles of nature would never make you 'sick of love'. Never may you be cured of it, except it be in the revealing of Jesus!

Remember it is not best to be 'sick of love.' It is better to be in health, to have Christ revealed to the soul, and to love him with a free, healthy love. In heaven, the inhabitants never say they are sick. Do not rest in this sickness; press near to Jesus to be healed.

Most, I fear, never felt this sickness - know nothing of what it means. Oh! dear souls, remember this one thing: If you never felt the sickness of grace, it is too likely you never felt the life of grace. If you were told of a man that he never felt any pain or uneasiness of any kind all his days, you would conclude that he must have been dead - that he never had any life; so you, if you know nothing of the sick yearnings of the believer's heart, it is too plain that you are dead - that you never had any life.

Last of all, *the believer in darkness commends the Saviour.* There is no more distinguishing mark of a true believer than this. To the unawakened there is no form nor comeliness in Christ - no beauty that they should desire him. Even awakened souls have no true sense of Christ's perfect comeliness. If they saw how Christ answers their need, they could not be anxious. But to believers in darkness there is all comeliness in Christ, he is fairer than ever he was before. And when the sneering world, or cold-hearted brethren, ask: 'What is thy beloved more than another beloved?' he delights to enumerate his perfections, his person, his offices, his everything: he delights to tell that 'he is the chiefest among ten thousand.' 'His mouth is most sweet,' yea, 'he is altogether lovely'.

A word to believers in darkness. There may be some who are walking in darkness, not having any light. Be persuaded to do as the bride did: not only to seek your beloved, but to commend him by going over his perfections.

Because this is the best of all ways to find him. One of the chief reasons of your darkness is your want of considering Christ. Satan urges you to think of a hundred things before he will let you think about Christ. If the eye of your faith be fully turned upon a full Christ, your darkness will be gone in the instant. 'Look unto me, and be ye saved.' Now, nothing so much engages your eye to look at Christ as going over his perfections to others.

Because you will lead others to seek him with you. Oh! dear brethren, the great reason of our having so many dark Christians nowadays is, that we have so many selfish Christians. Men live for themselves. If you would live for others, then your darkness would soon flee away.

Commend Christ to others, and they will go with you. Parents, commend him to your children; children, commend him to your parents, and who knows but God may bless the word, even of a believer walking in darkness, that they shall cry out: 'Whither is thy beloved gone, O thou fairest among women? Whither is thy beloved turned aside, that we may seek him with thee?'
St Peter's, 1837

34. A thorn in the flesh

> And lest I should be exalted above measure through the abundance of the revelations, there was given to me a thorn in the flesh, the messenger of Satan to buffet me, lest I should be exalted above measure. For this thing I besought the Lord thrice, that it might depart from me. And he said unto me, My grace is sufficient for thee: for my strength is made perfect in weakness. Most gladly therefore will I rather glory in my infirmities, that the power of Christ may rest upon me. Therefore I take pleasure in infirmities, in reproaches, in necessities, in persecutions, in distresses for Christ's sake: for when I am weak, then am I strong (2 Corinthians 12:7-10).

What is contained in this passage?

(1) *Paul's wonderful privilege* - caught up into the third heaven, or into paradise, got a day's foretaste of glory, saw and heard wonderful things.

(2) *Paul's humbling visitation* - a thorn in the flesh. He had been in the world of spirits, where is no sin. Now he was made to feel that he had a body of sin, to cry, 'O wretched man that I am! Who shall deliver me from this body of death?' He had been among the inhabitants of heaven. Now one from hell is allowed to buffet him.

(3) *His conduct under it* - fervent repeated prayer. 'I besought (marking his earnestness) thrice' - no answer; still he prayed. Before, he was more engaged in praise, or thinking of telling others; now he is brought to cry for his own soul, lest he should be a castaway. The answer: 'My grace is sufficient for thee.' God does not pluck the thorn away, does not drive the devil back to hell, does not take him out of the

body. No; but he opens his own breast, and says, Look here; here is grace enough for thee, here is strength that will hold up the weakest.

(4) *Paul's resolution* - to go on his way glorying in his infirmities. He is contented to have infirmities, to have a body of sin, in order that Christ may be glorified in holding up such a weak vessel: 'That the power of Christ may rest continually on my soul, that his mighty hand may have one to hold up to his own praise. I take pleasure in all humbling dispensations; for they teach me that I have no strength; and then I am strongest.'

1. Paul's wonderful privilege.

He had a glorious foretaste of heaven given to him. It was a wonderful season to his soul. He was caught up to the third heaven, or to paradise. He was taken to the Father's house with many mansions. He was taken up to be with Jesus and the saved thief in paradise. Much he could not tell. How it was - whether he was in the body or out of the body, he could not tell. The words he heard - the words of the Father, the words of Jesus, the songs of the redeemed, and of the holy angels - they were unspeakable. Still, he could never forget that day. Fourteen years had gone over his head, and yet it was fresh in his remembrance. The sights he saw, the words he heard, he could never forget. It was just a day of glory, a foretaste of heaven.

Dear believers, you also have wonderful privileges. You also have your foretastes of heaven. You may not have the miraculous vision of paradise which Paul here speaks of; yet you have tasted the very joy that is in heaven, drunk of the very river of God's pleasures.

If you have known the Lord Jesus, you know him who is the pearl of heaven, the sun and centre of it. If you have the Father's smile, you have the very joy of heaven. Above all, if you have the Holy Spirit dwelling in you, you have the earnest of the inheritance.

On such days as last communion Sabbath, are not the joys of a Christian unspeakable and full of glory? 'Whom having not seen we love.' Are not such days to be looked back upon? Even fourteen years after, when many will be gone to the Table above, some will look back to last Sabbath as a day spent in his courts - better than a thousand.

To those of you who get no joy on such occasions, what can we say, but that you would get no joy in heaven? If you are not made glad at the table below, you will never, I fear, be made glad at the Table above.

2. Paul's humbling visitation (verse 7).

What was given him.

The thorn in the flesh here spoken of is variously understood by interpreters. (1) Some understand it to have been a bodily disease - some sharp-shooting pains which were given him. Pain and disease are very humbling. They are often used by God to bring down the lofty spirit of man. (2) Some understand by it some remarkable temptation to sin immediately from the hand of the devil, a messenger from Satan, which was like a thorn in his soul. (3) Some understand it to have been some besetting sin - some part of his body of sin of which he complains so sore (Romans 7), some lust of his old man stirred up to activity by a messenger of Satan. It seems most probable that this was the thorn that made him groan.

Whatever it was, one thing is plain, it was a truly humbling visit. It brought Paul to the dust. A little before, he had been in the sinless world - he felt no body of sin - saw the pure spirits before the throne, and the spirits of just men made perfect; now, he is brought down to feel that he has a body of sin and death - he has a thorn in the flesh. A little before, he was among holy angels, trampling hell and the grave below his feet; now, a messenger from hell is sent to buffet him. 'O wretched man!'

Why was this given him?

Lest he should be exalted above measure. This is twice stated. What a singular thing is pride! Who would have thought that taking Paul into paradise for a day would have made him proud? And yet God, who knew his heart, knew it would be so, and therefore brought him down to the dust.

The pride of nature is wonderful. A natural man is proud of anything. Proud of his person - although he did not make it, yet he prides himself upon his looks. Proud of his dress - although a block of wood might have the same cause for pride, if you would put the clothes on it. Proud of riches - as if there were some merit in having more gold than others. Proud of rank - as if there were some merit in having noble blood. Alas, pride flows in the veins. Yet, there is a pride more wonderful than that of nature - pride of grace. You would think a man never could be proud who had once seen himself lost. Yet, alas Scripture and experience show that a man may be proud of his measure of grace - proud of forgiveness, proud of humility, proud of knowing more of God than others. It was this that was springing up in Paul's heart when God sent him the thorn in the flesh.

Dear friends, some of you, last Lord's day were brought very near to God, and filled with joy unspeakable and full of glory. Some, I am persuaded, have since then had Paul's humbling experience. You thought that you were for ever away from sin, but a thorn in the flesh has brought you low. You have fallen into sin during the week or something has brought you low indeed: 'O wretched man!' Why do you thus fall after a communion season?

(a) To make you *humble* - to teach you what a vile worm you are, when you can go to the Lord's table, and yet fall so low; this may well teach you that you are vile. You thought, perhaps, that sin was clean away, but here you see it again. What constant need you have of Jesus' blood!

(b) To make you *long for heaven*. There we shall sin no more for ever. Nothing but holiness there. No unclean thing can enter. Oh, press forward to it! Do not sit down by the way. Look forward to glory.

3. Paul's remedy - prayer.

Here is the difference between a natural man and a child of God. Both have the thorn in the flesh; but a natural man is contented with it. His lusts do not vex and trouble him. A child of God cannot rest under the power of temptation. He flies to his knees. The moment Paul felt the buffetings of Satan's messenger, he fell upon his knees, praying to his Father to take it away from him. No answer came. Again he goes to the throne of grace. Again no answer. A third time he falls on his knees, and will not let God go without the blessing.

The answer comes: 'My grace is sufficient for thee.' Not the thing he asked. He asked: Take this thorn away. Jesus does not pluck it out of his flesh - does not drive Satan's messenger back to hell. He could do this, but he does not. He opens his own bosom, and says: Look here. It hath pleased the Father that in me should all fullness dwell; 'My grace is sufficient for thee.' Here is the Holy Spirit for every need of thy soul. Oh, what a supply did Paul then see in Christ! What unsearchable riches! He had seen much in the third heaven, but here was something more - an almighty Spirit waiting for the need of poor weak sinners.

Dear friends, have you found out this remedy of the tempted soul?

Have you been driven to your knees by temptation? I said, the week before the communion should be a week of prayer; but if you have had Paul's experience, the week after has been one of prayer also.

Oh, tempted soul! be importunate - take no denial. Men ought always to pray, and not to faint. Be like the importunate widow - the Canaanitish woman. If you lie down contented under sin, you may well fear that there is no grace in you.

Take Paul's answer. God may not pluck out the thorn. This is the world of thorns. But look into his breast. There is enough in Jesus to keep thy soul. The ocean is full of drops, but Christ's bosom is more full of grace. Oh! pray either that your lusts may be taken away, or that you may believe the grace that is in Christ Jesus.

4. Paul's determination (verses 9,10).

'Most gladly, therefore, will I rather glory in my infirmities.' When Paul was caught up into paradise he thought he would never again feel his body of sin; but when he was humbled and made to know himself better, and to know the grace that is in Christ, then his glory ever after was, that he had a weak body of sin and death, and that there was power enough in Christ to keep him from falling. From that day he gloried not that he had no sin in him, but that he had an almighty Saviour dwelling in him and upholding him. He took pleasure now in everything that made him feel his weakness; for this drove him to Jesus for strength.

Learn, dear brethren, the true glory of a Christian in this world. The world knows nothing of it. A true Christian has a body of sin. He has every lust and corruption that is in the heart of man or devil. He wants no tendency to sin. If the Lord has given you light, you know and feel this. What is the difference, then, between you and the world? Infinite! You are in the hand of Christ. His Spirit is within you. He is able to keep you from falling. 'Rejoice in the Lord, ye righteous; and shout for joy all ye that are upright in heart.'

St Peter's, April 26, 1840

35. Christ's house and servants - his Second Coming

For the Son of Man is as a man taking a far journey, who left his house, and gave authority to his servants, and to every man his work, and commanded the porter to watch. Watch ye therefore: for ye know not when the master of the house cometh, at even, or at midnight, or at cockcrowing, or in the morning: lest coming suddenly he find you sleeping. And what I say unto you, I say unto all, Watch (Mark 13:34-37).

1. The Church on earth is Christ's house: 'Who left his house' (verse 34). This parable represents the Church on earth as Christ's house or dwelling.

Because he is the foundation stone of it.
Just as every stone of a building rests on the foundation, so does every believer rest on Christ. He is the foundation rock upon which they rest. If it were not for the foundation, the whole house would fall into ruins - the floods and winds would sweep it away. If it were not for Christ, all believers would be swept away by God's anger; but they are rooted and built up in him, and so they form his house.

Because he is the builder.
(1) Every stone of the building has been placed there by the hands of Christ. He has taken every stone from the quarry. Look unto the rock whence ye were hewn, and the hole of the pit whence ye were digged. A natural person is embedded in the world just as firmly as a rock in the quarry. The hands of the almighty Saviour alone can dig out the soul, and loosen it from its natural state.

(2) Christ has carried it, and laid it on the foundation. Even when a stone has been quarried, it cannot lift itself; it needs to be carried, and built upon the foundation. So when a natural soul has been wakened, he cannot build himself on Christ; he must be carried on the shoulder of the great master builder. Every stone of the building has been thus carried by Christ. What a wonderful building! Well may it be called Christ's house, when he builds every stone of it. See that ye be quarried out by Christ; see to it, that ye be carried by him - built on him; then you will be an habitation of God through the Spirit.

Because his friends are in it.

Wherever a man's friends are, that is his home - wherever a man's mother and sister and brother dwell, that is his home; this, then, must be Christ's home, for he stretched forth his hand toward his disciples, and said: 'Behold my mother and my brethren; for whosoever shall do the will of my Father which is in heaven, the same is my brother, and sister, and mother.' As long as this world has a believer in it, Christ will look upon it as his house. He cannot forget, even in glory, the well of Samaria - the garden of Gethsemane - the hill of Calvary. Happy for you who know Christ, and who do the will of his Father; wherever you dwell, Christ calls it his house. You may dwell in a poor place, and still be happy; for Christ dwells with you, and calls it his dwelling - he calls you, 'My brother, sister, mother.'

2. Christ is like a man who has gone a far journey (verse 34). Although the Church on earth be his house, and although he has such affection for it, yet Christ is not here, he is risen - Christ is risen indeed.

He has gone to take possession of heaven in our name.

When an elder brother of a family purchases a property for himself and his brothers, he goes a far journey in order to take possession. So Christ is an elder brother. He lived and died in order to purchase forgiveness and acceptance for sinners. He has gone into heaven to take possession for us. Do you take Christ for your surety? Then you are already possessed of heaven.

How am I possessed of heaven, when I have never been there? Christ your surety has taken possession in your name. If you will realise this, it will give you fullness of joy. A person may possess a property which he has never seen. Look at your surety in the land that is very far off, calling it all his own, for the sake of his younger brethren: 'These things have I spoken unto you, that your joy may be full.'

He has gone to intercede for us.

(a) He has gone to *intercede for unawakened, barren sinners*: 'Lord, let it alone this year also.' Oh, sinner, why is it that you have not died a sudden death? Why have you not gone quite down into the pit? How often the Saviour has prayed for some of you! Shall it be all in vain?

(b) To *intercede for his believing people* - to procure all blessings for them. Often an elder brother of a family goes into a far country, and sends back rich presents to his younger brethren at home. This is what Christ has done. He has gone far above all heavens, there to appear in the presence of God for us, and to ask the very things we need, and to send us down all the treasures of heaven. Of his fullness have we all received, even grace for grace. 'I will pray the Father, and he shall give you another Comforter.' Oh, Christians, believe in a praying Christ, if you would receive heavenly blessings. Believe just as if you saw him, and open the mouth wide to receive the blessings for which he is praying.

He has gone to prepare a place for us.
When a family are going to emigrate to a foreign shore, often the elder brother goes before to prepare a place for his younger brethren. This is what Christ has done. He does not intend that we should live here always - he has gone a far journey in order to prepare a place for us: 'I go to prepare a place for you; and if I go and prepare a place for you, I will come again and receive you to myself, that where I am, there ye may be also.' Oh, Christians! believe in Christ preparing a place for you. It will greatly take away the fear of dying. It is an awful thing to die, even for a forgiven and sanctified soul to enter on a world unknown, unseen, untried. One thing takes away fear: Christ is preparing a place quite suitable for my soul. He knows all the wants and weaknesses of my frame. I know he will make it a pleasant home to me.

3. All Christ's people are servants, and have their work assigned them (verse 34).

Ministers are servants, and have their work assigned them. Two kinds are here mentioned.

(a) *Stewards.* These seem to be the servants to whom he gave authority. All ministers should be stewards: rightly dividing the Word of life, giving to every one of the family his portion of meat in due season. Oh! it is a blessed work, to feed the Church of God, which he hath purchased with his own blood; to give milk to babes, and strong meat to grown men; to give convenient food to every one. Pray for your ministers, that they may be made faithful and wise stewards. There are few such.

(b) *Porters.* He commanded the porter to watch. It is the office of some ministers to stand at the door and invite every sinner, saying:

'Enter ye in at the strait gate.' Some ministers have not the gift of feeding the Church of God and watering it. Paul planted, Apollos watered. Some are only door-keepers in the house of my God. Learn not to despise any of the true servants of God. Are all apostles? Are all prophets? He has appointed some to stand at the door, and some to break the children's bread. Despise neither.

All Christians are servants, and have their work assigned them. Some people think that ministers only have to work for Christ; but see here: 'He gave to every man his work.' In a great house, the steward and the porter are not the only servants; there are many more, and all have their work to do. Just so among the people of Christ. Ministers are not the only servants of Christ; all that believe on him are his servants.

(a) *Learn to be working Christians.* 'Be ye doers of the Word, and not hearers only, deceiving your own souls.' It is very striking to see the uselessness of many Christians. Are there none of you who know what it is to be selfish in your Christianity? You have seen a selfish child go into a secret place to enjoy some delicious morsels undisturbed by his companions? So it is with some Christians. They feed upon Christ and forgiveness; but it is alone, and all for themselves. Are there not some of you who can enjoy being a Christian, while your dearest friend is not; and yet you will not speak to him? See here, you have got your work to do. When Christ found you, he said: 'Go, work in my vineyard.' What were you hired for, if it was not to work? What were you saved for, if it was not to spread salvation? What blessed for? Oh! my Christian friends! How little you live as if you were servants of Christ! How much idle time and idle talk you have! This is not like a good servant. How many things you have to do for yourself! How few for Christ and his people! This is not like a servant.

(b) *Learn to keep to your own work.* In a great house every servant has his own peculiar work. One man is the porter to open the door; another is the steward to provide food for the family; a third has to clean the rooms; a fourth has to dress the food; a fifth has to wait upon the guests. Every one has his proper place, and no servant interferes with another. If all were to become porters, and open the door, then what would become of the stewardship? Or, if all were to be stewards, who would clean the house? Just so is it with Christians. Every one has his peculiar work assigned him, and should not leave it. 'Let every man abide in the same calling wherein he was called.'

Obadiah had his work appointed him in the court of the wicked Ahab. God placed him as his servant there, saying: 'Work here for me.' Does any of you belong to a wicked family? Seek not to be removed, Christ has placed you there to be his servant - work for him. The Shunammite had her work. When the prophet asked: 'Wilt thou be spoken for to the king?' she said: 'I dwell among mine own people.' Once a poor demoniac whom Jesus healed besought Jesus that he might follow after him; howbeit Jesus suffered him not, but saith unto him: 'Go home to thy friends, and tell them how great things the Lord hath done for thee, and how he hath had compassion on thee.'

Learn, my dear friends, to keep to your own work. When the Lord has hung up a lamp in one corner, is there no presumption in removing it to another? Is not the Lord wiser than man? Every one of you have your work to do for Christ where you are. Are you on a sick-bed? Still you have your work to do for Christ there as much as the highest servant of Christ in the world. The smallest twinkling star is as much a servant of God as the mid-day sun. Only live for Christ where you are.

4. Christ is coming back again, and we know not when: 'Watch ye therefore: for ye know not when the master of the house cometh, at even, or at midnight, or at the cockcrowing, or in the morning: lest, coming suddenly, he find you sleeping' (verses 35,36). Two things are here declared.

That Christ is coming back again.
The whole Bible bears witness to this. The master of the house has been a long time away on his journey; but he will come back again. When Christ ascended from his disciples, and a cloud received him out of their sight, and they were looking steadfastly into heaven, the angels said: 'Ye men of Galilee, why stand ye gazing up into heaven? This same Jesus which is taken up from you into heaven, shall so come in like manner as ye have seen him go into heaven.' He went up in a cloud - he shall come in the clouds.

That Christ will come back suddenly.
The whole Bible bears witness to this.

(1) In one place it is compared to a snare which suddenly entraps the unwary wild beast: 'As a snare shall it come on all them that dwell on the face of the whole earth.'

(2) Again, to a thief: 'The day of the Lord so cometh as a thief in the night.'

(3) Again, to a bridegroom coming suddenly: 'At midnight there was a cry made, Behold the bridegroom cometh.'

(4) Again to the waters of the flood.

(5) Again, to the fiery rain that fell on Sodom and Gomorrah.

(6) And here to the sudden coming home of the master of the house: 'Ye know not when the master of the house cometh.'

Now, my dear friends, I am far from discouraging those who, with humble prayerfulness, search into the records of prophecy to find out what God has said as to the second coming of the Son of Man. We are not like the first disciples of Jesus, if we do not often put the question: 'What shall be the sign of thy coming, and of the end of the world?'

But the truth which I wish to be written on your hearts is this: That the coming shall be sudden - sudden to the world - sudden to the children of God: 'In such an hour as ye think not, the Son of Man cometh.' 'Ye know not when the master of the house cometh, at even, or at midnight, or at cockcrowing, or in the morning.'

Oh, my friends! your faith is incomplete, if you do not live in the daily faith of a coming Saviour.

5. Watch: 'And what I say unto you I say unto all, Watch' (verse 37).

Ministers should watch.
This word is especially addressed to the porter: 'Watch ye, therefore.' Ah! how watchful we should be. Many things make us sleep.

(a) *Want of faith.* When a minister loses sight of Christ crucified - risen - coming again - then he cannot watch for souls. Pray that your ministers may have a watching eye always on Christ.

(b) *Seeing so many careless souls.* Ah! you little know how this staggers the ministers of Christ. A young believer comes with a glowing heart to tell of Christ, and pardon, and the new heart. He knows it is the truth of God - he states it simply, freely, with all his heart. He presses it on men - he hopes to see them melt like icicles before the sun. Alas! they are as cold and dead as ever. They live on in their sins, they die in their sins. Ah! you little know how this makes him dull, and heavy, and heart-broken. My friends, pray that we may not sleep. Pray that your carelessness may only make us watch the more.

Christians should watch.
Ah! if Christ is at hand, (a) *take heed lest you be found unforgiven.* Many
Christians seem to live without a realizing view of Christ. The eye
should be fixed on Christ. Your eye is shut. Oh! if you would abide in
Christ, then let him come tonight. At even, or at midnight, or at
cockcrow, or in the morning - he is welcome, thrice welcome! Even so,
come, Lord Jesus.

(b) *Take heed lest you be found in any course of sin.* Many Christians
seem to walk, if I mistake not, in courses of sin. It is hard to account for
it; but so it seems to be. Some Christians seem to be sleeping - in luxury,
in covetousness, in evil company. Ah! think how would you like to be
overtaken thus by the coming Saviour. Try your daily occupations, your
daily state of feeling, your daily enjoyments, try them by this test: Am
I doing as I would wish to do on the day of his coming?

Christless souls, how dreadful is your case!
Death may be sudden - oh! how awfully sudden it sometimes is. You
may have no time for repentance - no breath to pray! The coming of the
Saviour shall be more sudden still. Ye know neither the day nor the hour.
You know not God for you have not obeyed the gospel. Oh! what will
ye do in the day of the Lord's anger?

36. Lot's wife

But his wife looked back from behind him and she became a pillar of salt
(Genesis 19:26).

There is not in the whole Bible a more instructive history than that of
Lot and his family. His own history shows well how the righteous
scarcely are saved. His sons-in-law show well the way in which the
gospel is received by the easy, careless world. His wife is a type of those
who are convinced, yet never converted; who flee from the wrath to
come, yet perish after all; whilst the angels' laying hold on the lingering
family is a type of the gracious violence and sovereign mercy which God
uses in delivering souls.

At present I mean to direct your thoughts to the case of Lot's wife, and to show the following.

Doctrine: Many souls who have been awakened to flee from wrath, look behind, and are lost.

1. Many flee, under terrors of natural conscience; but when these subside, they look back, and are lost.

So it was with Lot's wife. She was not like the men of Sodom - intent upon the world and sin - quite unconcerned about their souls. She was not like her sons-in-law - she did not think her husband mocking. She was really alarmed, and really fled; and yet her terrors were like the morning cloud and the early dew, which quickly pass away. When the angels had brought them out of the gates of Sodom, they said: 'Escape for thy life, look not behind thee; neither stay thou in all the plain; escape to the mountain, lest thou be consumed.'

And as long as these dreadful words were ringing in her ears, doubtless she fled with anxious footstep. The dreadful scene of the past night, the darkness, the anxiety of her husband, the pressing urgency of the noble angels, all conspired to awaken her natural conscience, and to make her flee.

But now the hellish roar of the wicked Sodomites had ceased, the sun was already gilding the horizon, promising a glorious dawn, the plain of Jordan began to smile, well watered everywhere, as the garden of the Lord. Her sons-in-law, her friends, her house, her goods, her treasure were still in Sodom; so her heart was there also. Her anxieties began to vanish with the darkness. She determined to take one look, to see if it were really destroyed. She 'looked back from behind him, and became a pillar of salt'.

So is it with many among us. Many flee under terrors of natural conscience, but when these subside, they look back and are lost.

Some people pass through the world without any terrors of conscience - without any awakening or anxiety about their souls.

Some are like the men of Sodom, intent upon buying and selling, building and planting, marrying and giving in marriage. Or they are greedy upon their lusts, and they have no ears to hear the sounds of coming wrath. As a man working hard at the anvil hears no noise from without, because of the noise of his own hammer, so these men hear nothing of coming vengeance, they are so busy with the work of their hands.

Some are like the sons-in-law of Lot. Yon shrewd, intelligent man of business thinks that ministers do but jest. We seem to them as one that mocks. They are so accustomed to see behind the scenes in other professions, that they think there must be deceit with us too. And when they can point to an insincere, ungodly minister, then their triumph is complete. These shrewd men think that ministers put serious words into their mouths, as other men put on suits of solemn black at funerals, just to look well, and to agree with the occasion. They think that ministers put frightful things into sermons just to frighten weak people, and to make the crowd wonder. Now these shrewd men are seldom, if ever, visited with terrors of conscience. They slip easily through the world into an undone eternity.

Some, again, slumber all their days under a worldly ministry. When God, in judgment, takes away the pure preaching of the Word, and sends a famine of the bread and water of life, their souls grow up quite hard and unawakened. They grow proud, and cannot bear to hear the preaching of Christ. They stop their ears and run for they hate, they detest it. These souls often pass through life without the least awakening, and never know, till they are in hell, that they are lost souls.

But many worldly people have a season of anxiety about their soul. A dangerous illness, or some awful bereavement, or some threatening cloud of Providence, stirs them up to flee from the wrath to come. They are quite in earnest: they lay by their sins, and avoid their sinful companions, and apply diligently to the Bible, and attempt to pray, and seem to be really fleeing out of Sodom. But they continue only for a while, their concern is like the morning cloud and the early dew, it quickly passes away. The sun of prosperity begins to rise, their fears begin to vanish, they look behind and are lost.

Are there none here who can look back on such a course as this? You remember when some providence awakened you to deepest seriousness: some sickness, or the approach of the pestilence, or some fearful dealing of God with your family, or the approach of a sacrament, made you anxiously flee out of Sodom. O how different you were from the gay, laughing unconcerned world! You did not think ministers were mocking then. You read your Bible, and went down on your knees to pray very earnestly. But the storm blew over - the sun began to rise, and everything around you began to smile. You began to think it hard to leave all your friends, your sins, your worldly enjoyments, and that perhaps the wrath of God would not come down. You looked back, and this day you are as hard and immovable as a pillar of salt. 'Remember Lot's wife.'

Learn two things:

(1) *That an awakening by mere natural conscience is very different from an awakening by the Spirit of God.* No man ever fled to Christ from mere natural terror. 'No man can come to me,' saith Christ, 'except the Father which hath sent me draw him.' Seek a divine work upon your heart.

(2) *Learn how far you are from the kingdom of God.* You are quite lost. You are unmoved and unaffected by all we can say. You do not weep - you do not beat upon the breast - you do not flee, though we can prove to you that you are lying under the wrath of the great God that made you. Yet you do not stir one step to flee. Oh! how like you are to the pillar of salt - how likely it is that you will never be saved.

2. Many flee when their friends are fleeing; but they look back, and are lost.

So it was with Lot's wife. Of all the things which helped to awaken the unfortunate woman, I doubt not the most powerful was the anxiety of her husband. If he had not been anxious, I doubt not she would have been as stupid and unconcerned as her neighbours around her. But when she looked upon the anxious countenance of her beloved lord - when she saw how serious and earnest he was in pleading with their sons-in-law, then she could not but share in his anxiety. She had partaken of all his trials, of all his prosperities, and of all his troubles, and she would not leave him now. She clave unto him, she laid hold on the skirt of his garment, determined to be saved, or to perish with her husband. So much for the amiable and interesting affections of nature; but nature is not grace - natural affection carried her out of Sodom, but it did not carry her into Zoar; for she looked behind him, and became a pillar of salt.

Now, there is reason to think that this is true of some in this congregation - that they flee when their friends are fleeing, but look back, and are lost.

Nothing is more powerful in awakening souls than the example of others awakened to flee. It was so in the case of Ruth, when she clave to Naomi, saying: 'Where thou goest I will go.' It was so in the case of the daughters of Jerusalem, when they saw the bride in anxious search of her beloved: 'Whither is thy beloved gone, that we may seek him with thee?' It is foretold that it shall be so in the latter day, when 'ten men shall lay hold on the skirt of him that is a Jew, saying: We will go with you; for we have heard that God is with you.' It was so in the time of John the Baptist, when many of the Pharisees and Sadducees came to be baptized, and John said: 'O generation of vipers, who hath warned you to flee from the wrath to come?'

There is something very moving in the sight of some beloved one going to join the peculiar people of God. When he begins to flee from his old haunts of pleasure - no longer to laugh at wicked jests, no longer to delight in sinful company, when he becomes a reader of the Bible, and prays with earnestness, and waits with anxiety on the preached Word - it is a very moving sight to all his friends. No doubt, some are made bitter against him; for Christ came to set the daughter against her mother, and the daughter-in-law against her mother-in-law; but some are awakened to flee along with him.

Are there none here who were moved to flee because some dear friend was fleeing? Is there no wife that was awakened to flee with her husband, but grew weary and looked back, and is now become like Lot's wife? Is there none here that was made truly anxious by seeing some companions anxious about their soul? They wept, and you could not but weep; they felt themselves lost; and you, for the time, felt along with them. They were very eager in their inquiries after a Saviour, and you joined them in their eagerness. And where is all your anxiety now? It is gone, like the morning cloud and early dew. You looked behind, and are now unmoved as a pillar of salt.

It was quite right to flee with them - it was right to cleave to them; for if not, you would certainly be hardened; if you stand out such moving invitations, nothing else will persuade you. If it was right to flee, it is right to flee still. Why should you look back? They are going to be blessed, and will you not go with them? They are fleeing from wrath, and will you not flee with them? 'Remember Lot's wife.'

Have you made up your mind to separate eternally? If not, why then have you let them go? Why have you given up the first good movement in your breast? Flee still - cleave to them, and say: 'We will go with you.'

3. Some are laid hold of by God, and made to flee, who yet look back, and are lost.

So it was with Lot's wife. Not only were natural means made use of to make her flee, but supernatural means also. Not only was she moved by sudden terror, and by the example of her husband, but she was drawn out by the angels: 'And while he lingered, the men laid hold upon his hand, and upon the hand of his wife, and upon the hand of his two daughters; the LORD being merciful unto him: and they brought him forth, and set him without the city' (verse 16). She shared in the same divine help as her husband - God was merciful to her as he was to her husband. The same mighty hand was put forth to save her, and actually plucked her as a brand out of the burning; but, observe, the same hand did not pull her into Zoar nor lift her away to the cave of the mountain. Grace did something for her, but it did not do everything. She looked back, and became a pillar of salt.

So is it, we fear, with some among us. Some seem to be laid hold of by God, and made to flee, who yet look back, and are lost. Now there are a great many among us of whom we have no right to say or to think that they have ever been laid hold of by God.

There are many among us who seem to live in utter ignorance of their lost condition - who plead the innocence of their lives even when Death is laying his cold hand upon them. There are some poor souls who seem to die willing to be judged by the law. I have lived a decent life, they will say; I have been a harmless, quiet-living man; and I can see no reason why the wrath of the great God should ever come upon me. Oh! brethren, if this is your case, it is very plain that you have never had a divine awakening. The power of God alone could awaken you to flee.

There are many among us who live in the daily practice of sin - some who carry on small dishonesties, or occasionally use minced oaths - who walk in the counsel of the ungodly. O brethren! if this be your case, it is quite plain that you have never had a divine awakening. When a man is made anxious about his soul, he always puts away his open sins.

There are many among us who live much in the neglect of the means of grace. Some who very seldom read the Bible when alone, or never but on Sabbath-days; some who do not pray regularly, nor with any earnestness; some who are very careless about the house of God, contented if they attend it only once on the Sabbath-day; who make no conscience of being up betimes, and ready for the house of God in the morning; who allow the silliest excuses to keep them away; who loiter about on the Sabbath-day, who devote it to most unhallowed visiting, or walking in the fields, making it the most unholy day in the week. Oh! dear souls, if this be your case, then it is quite plain you have never been laid hold on by God. You are as dead and unawakened as the stones you walk upon. You are living in the very heart of Sodom, and the wrath of God abideth on you.

But there are some among us of whom we think that they have been laid hold on by God, and made to flee. There are some who show evident marks that God has been making them flee out of Sodom. The marks are these:

They have a deep sense of their lost condition. They have an abiding conviction that the time past of their lives has been spent under the wrath of the great God that made them; their concern goes with them wherever they go; and anxiety is painted on their very countenance. Is this your condition? Then you have indeed been awakened by God.

They dare not go back to their open sins. They break off quite suddenly from their little dishonesties, their swearing, or evil-speaking; they separate from their wicked companions and filthy conversation - they feel that death is in the cup, and they dare not drink it any longer. Is this your case? Then there is reason to think you have been awakened by God.

They are anxious users of the means of grace. They search the Scriptures night and day, they pray with earnestness, they are unwearied in waiting on ordinances, suffer no trifle to keep them away from the house of God, they seek for the Saviour as for hid treasure, listen for his name as the criminal for the sound of pardon. Is this your case? Then it seems likely that God has been merciful to your soul, that God has been making you flee out of Sodom, and escape for your life.

But the text shows me that many who have been thus awakened look back, and are lost. 'Remember Lot's wife.' She was brought quite out of Sodom, and yet she looked back, and became a pillar of salt. She was awakened, yet never saved. Now, there is reason to fear this may be the case with some amongst us.

Some awakened souls begin to despair of ever finding Christ. They begin to blame God for not having brought them into peace before now; and so they give up striving to enter in at the strait gate. They look behind, and are lost.

Some awakened souls begin to think themselves saved already. They have put away many outward sins, and prayed with much earnestness. Their friends observe the change, and they think they are surely safe now, that there is no need of fleeing any farther; so they look behind, and become a pillar of salt.

Some awakened souls begin to tire of the pains of seeking Christ. They remember their former ease and pleasures - their companions - their walks - their merrymakings; so they look behind and perish.

A word to awakened souls.
Some now hearing me may be at present under the awakening hand of God. You have deep convictions of your lost condition, you have put away outward sins, and wait earnestly on every means of grace. There is every reason to think that God has been merciful to you, and has laid hold upon you. 'Remember Lot's wife.' Learn from her,

(1) *That you are not saved yet.* Lot's wife fled out of Sodom, led by the angel's hand, and yet she was lost. An awakened soul is not a saved soul. You are not saved till God shut you into Christ. It is not enough that you flee, you must flee into Christ. Oh, do not lie down and slumber! Oh, do not look behind you! 'Remember Lot's wife.'

(2) *That God is no ways obliged to bring you into Christ.* God has made but one covenant - that is, with Christ and all in him. But he has nowhere bound himself to men that are out of Christ. He may never bring you to Christ, and yet be a just and righteous God. Do not demand it of God, then, as if he were obliged to save you, but lie helpless at his feet as a sovereign God.

A word to those who are beginning to look back.
There is reason to think that some who were once awakened by God have begun to look back.

Some of you have begun to lose a sense of your wretched and lost condition. Some of you have quite another view of your state from what you had.

Some of you have gone back to old sins - to old habits, especially of keeping company with the ungodly; and some, there is reason to think, are trying to laugh at their former fears.

Some of you have turned more careless of the Bible, and of prayer, and of the ordinances. At last sacrament there were many very eager to hear of Christ; and where are they now? There is reason to fear that much of that concern is gone - that many have lost their anxiety - that some are looking back.

Now, 'remember Lot's wife'.

It will not save you, that you were once anxious - nay, that you were made anxious by God. So was Lot's wife, and yet she was lost.

If you really look back, it is probable you never will be awakened again. Consider that monument of vengeance on the Plain of Jordan. Speak to her, she does not hear. Cry, she does not regard you. Urge her to flee again from wrath, she does not move - she is dead. So will it be with you. If you really turn back now, we may speak, but you will not hear. We may cry, but you will not regard. We may urge you again to flee, but you will not move.

'If any man draw back, my soul shall have no pleasure in him.' 'No man, having put his hand to the plough, and looking back, is fit for the kingdom of God.'

St Peter's, 1837

37. Happy Israel, saved by the Lord

Happy art thou, O Israel: who is like unto thee, O people saved by the LORD, the shield of thy help, and who is the sword of thy excellency! and thine enemies shall be found liars unto thee; and thou shalt tread upon their high places (Deuteronomy 33:29).

These are the last words of Moses, the man of God. He was now an hundred and twenty years old; his eye was not dim, nor his natural force abated. For forty years he had led the people through the wilderness - he had cared for them, and prayed for them, and led them as a shepherd leads his flock. And now, when God had told him that he must part from them, he determined to part from them blessing them. And in this respect, as in many others, did he foreshadow the Saviour, of whom it is written, that 'he led his disciples out as far as Bethany, and he lifted up his hands, and blessed them; and it came to pass, while he blessed them, he was parted from them, and carried up into heaven.'

First of all, we may understand these words *literally* as the blessing of Moses upon the people of Israel. He looked back over the wilderness through which he had led them, and it was all brilliantly studded with the wondrous things which God had wrought for them. He remembered the high hand and outstretched arm with which he had brought them out of Egypt. He remembered how he clave a path for them through the Red Sea, when their enemies sank like lead in the mighty waters. He remembered how he went before them in a pillar of cloud by day, and a pillar of fire by night. He remembered how he had sweetened the waters of Marah, for they were bitter. He remembered how he had fed them with manna from on high, how man did eat angels' food.

He remembered how he had smitten the rock at Rephidim, and

waters gushed forth. How he had held up his hands to the going down of the sun, and Israel prevailed over Amalek. How he had received the law from the very hand of God for them. He remembered how he had again brought water from the flinty rock at Meribah. How he had lifted up the brazen serpent in the wilderness. And, looking back over all this track of forty years' wonders, during which their garments had not waxed old, neither had the sole of their foot swelled, how could he but put a blessing upon them? He felt as Balaam did: 'Blessed is he that blesseth thee, and cursed is he that curseth thee.' And accordingly, when he had gone over each of the tribes separately, leaving each his prophetic blessing, he sums up the whole in these glorious words: 'Who is like unto the God of Jeshurun?'

But, secondly, these words may be understood *typically* as the blessing of Moses upon God's people to the end of time. No man can read the Old Testament intelligently without seeing that the people of Israel were a typical people - that the choosing of them out of Egypt, the bringing them through the Red Sea, and through the wilderness, and into the land of promise - were all typical of the way in which God brings his chosen ones out of their sins, through this world of sin and misery, into the heavenly Canaan - the rest that remaineth for the people of God. If, then, the bondage, the deliverance, the unbelief, the enemies, the journeyings, the guidance, and the rest of the Israelites were all typical of God's dealings with his own people to the end of time, we are quite justified in understanding these words as the blessing of Moses, the man of God, upon all the true children of God.

'Happy art thou, O Israel: who is like unto thee, O people saved by the LORD, the shield of thy help, and who is the sword of thy excellency! and thine enemies shall be found liars unto thee; and thou shalt tread upon their high places.' From these words I draw the following:

Doctrine: That the people of God are a happy people, because they are saved by the Lord.

I. Israel is a happy people, because chosen by the Lord.

This was true of ancient Israel.
Moses tells them plainly: 'The LORD did not set his love upon you, because ye were more in number than any people; for ye were the fewest of all people; but because the LORD loved you, and because he would keep the oath which he had sworn unto your fathers' (Deuteronomy

7:7,8). Here is a strange thing, which the world cannot understand. He loved them because he loved them. Not because they were better, or greater, or worthier than any other nation, but because he loved them. Strange, sovereign, unaccountable love! He gives no account of his matters; so, then, 'it is not of him that willeth, nor of him that runneth, but of God that showeth mercy.'

This is true of all God's people to this day.
David says in Psalm 65:4: 'Blessed is the man whom thou choosest, and causest to approach unto thee.' Christ says in John 15:16: 'Ye have not chosen me, but I have chosen you.' And Paul says in Ephesians 1:3,4: 'Blessed be the God and Father of our Lord Jesus Christ, who hath blessed us with all spiritual blessings in heavenly places in Christ; according as he hath chosen us in him before the foundation of the world, that we should be holy and without blame before him in love.' Ah! yes, my friends, our God is a sovereign God: 'Therefore hath he mercy on whom he will have mercy; and whom he will he hardeneth.'

Every believer is a witness of this. Is there any believer here? Well, I take you to bear witness. You were once dead and careless about your soul - you could be happy with the world, though unforgiven and unsanctified. How was it that you were brought to flee from the wrath to come? Did you waken yourself out of sleep? Ah! no; you know well that if God had let you lie, you would willingly have slept on. Like the sluggard, you would have said: 'A little more sleep, a little more slumber, a little more folding of the hands to sleep'; but he awoke you by his Word, by his ministers, or by his providence; and he would not let you go till you cried: 'What must I do to be saved?' Again: you were brought from conviction of sin to conviction of righteousness, from a troubled conscience to a heart at peace in believing. How was this? Did you come yourself to Jesus, or were you drawn of the Father? Ah! you know well you received it not of man, neither by man - that God brought you within sight of Jesus. He that at first brought light out of darkness shined into your hearts, and stirred you up to act faith on Jesus; and thus you were saved; for 'no man can come to Jesus except the Father draw him'. From beginning to end, then, the work is God's. By grace ye are saved; and blessed, indeed, is 'the man whom thou choosest, and causest to approach unto thee.'

Objection. But someone may object that this doctrine ministers to pride - that to make a man believe himself the chosen favourite of God puffs up that man with pride. To this I answer, that this is the very truth which cuts up pride by the roots. As it is written: 'Who maketh thee to differ from another? and what hast thou that thou didst not receive? Now, if thou didst receive it, why dost thou glory as if thou hadst not received it?' (1 Corinthians 4:7).

If there be one believer among you, I bid him look round upon those of his own family still without Christ, and without God in the world. Perhaps you are the only one in your house that knows and loves the Saviour. Now, I ask you, who made you to differ? Are you by nature any better than your kindred, that you are chosen and they left? How, then, can you be proud? Or, look round on your neighbourhood, you will see drunkenness and pollution - you will hear oaths and profaneness. Now, I ask, who made you to differ? Or, what better were you than they, before God changed your heart? Can you, then, be proud? Or look round on the Popish and heathen world sunk in darkest ignorance - without any to tell them the plain way of salvation by Jesus. Look upon nine-tenths of the world that want the pure light of the gospel, and tell me, who made you to differ? And how can you be proud? Or, look beyond this world's horizon, look down to the realms of darkness and of death eternal, and see the angels that fell:

> Far other once, beheld in bliss -
> Millions of spirits for *one* fault amerced
> Of heaven, and from eternal splendours flung
> For their revolt!

Look upon these majestic intelligences, 'reserved in everlasting chains, under darkness, unto the judgment of the great day,' and tell me, who made you to differ? What better are you by nature than devils? Unconverted men are children of the devil. There is no lust in the heart of the devil that is not in every natural heart; and yet God hath passed them by, and come to save you. God came and wakened you when you were in a natural condition, and no better than devils; yea, he hath passed by the heathen, he hath left your neighbours in their sins, your own children unawakened; but he hath awakened you.

Oh! most mysterious electing love! Well may you cry out with Paul: 'O the depth of the riches both of the wisdom and knowledge of God! how unsearchable are his judgments, and his ways past finding out!' And does this make you proud? Does it not rather make you bury your head in the dust, and never lift up your eyes any more? And does it not make you happy? 'O happy Israel, who is like unto thee, O people saved by the Lord!'

Does it give you no joy to feel that God thought upon you in love before the foundation of the world? That when he was alone from all eternity he gave you to the Son to be redeemed? 'Before I formed thee in the belly, I knew thee; and before thou camest forth out of the womb, I sanctified thee.' Does it give you no joy to think that the Son of God thought on you with love before the world was: 'My delights were with the children of men.' That he came into the world bearing your name upon his heart, that he prayed for you on the night of his agony: 'Neither pray I for these alone, but for all those that shall believe on me through their word'? Does it give you no joy that he thought upon you in his bloody sweat, that he thought of you upon the cross, and intended these sufferings to be in your stead? Oh, little children, how it would lift your hearts in holy rapture above the world, above its vexing cares, its petty quarrels, its polluting pleasures, if you would keep this holy joy within, taking up the very word of your Lord: 'Father, thou lovedst me before the foundation of the world'!

O unbelieving world! ye know nothing of this joy. It is all frantic presumption in your eyes; and this is just what the Bible says: A stranger intermeddles not with the believer's joy. This is just what Christ said: 'Ye believe not, because ye are not of my sheep.' Carry this one thing away with you: 'We were once just what you now are (every believer will tell you) - we were just as senseless and unbelieving as you are. We once despised and laughed at the very persons with whom we are now one in the Lord; but we were awakened by God, and fled to Christ, and are redeemed and happy' - 'knowing our election of God'. Oh! may this be your history, and then you will know the meaning of these words: 'O, happy Israel!'

2. Israel is a happy people, because they are justified by the Lord: 'The eternal God is thy refuge' (verse 27). 'He is the shield of thy help' (verse 29).

First of all, this is true because Christ is our refuge and shield, and Christ is God. It is said of him: 'In the beginning was the Word, and the Word was with God, and the Word was God' (John 1:1). Again it is said of him: 'Thy throne, O God, is for ever and ever: a sceptre of righteousness is the sceptre of thy kingdom' (Hebrews 1:8). Again it is said of him: 'By him were all things created, that are in heaven, and that

are in earth, visible and invisible, whether they be thrones, or dominions, or principalities, or powers: all things were created by him, and for
him: and he is before all things, and by him all things consist'
(Colossians 1:16,17). Again it is said of him, that 'he is over all, God
blessed for ever' (Romans 9:5). Again, Thomas saith unto him: 'My
Lord, and my God' (John 20:28). And he is called, 'God manifest in the
flesh' (1 Timothy 3:16). So, then, he is indeed 'Immanuel, God with us.'
He is the maker of the world - the God of providence - the God of angels.
And this is the being who came to be the Saviour of sinners, even the
chief!

Now, brethren, I wish you to see the use of the Saviour being God,
and how the whole comfort and joy of the believer is founded on it.
Everything that God does is infinitely perfect; he never fails in anything
he undertakes. Everything, therefore, which the Saviour did was
infinitely perfect. He did not, and could not, fail in anything which he
undertook.

He undertook to bear the wrath of God in the stead of sinners. His
heart was set upon it from all eternity; for, before the world was made,
he tells us: 'My delights were with the sons of men.' For this end he took
on him our nature, became a man of sorrows and acquainted with grief.
From his cradle in the manger to the cross, the dark cloud of God's anger
was over him; and especially toward the close of his life, the cloud came
to be at the darkest - yet he cheerfully suffered all. 'How am I straitened
till it be accomplished!' The cup of God's anger was given him without
mixture; yet he said: 'The cup which my Father hath given me, shall I
not drink it?' Now, we may be quite sure, that since he was the Son of
God, he hath suffered all that sinners should have suffered. If he had
been an angel, he might have left some part unfinished; but since he was
God, his work must be perfect. He himself said: 'It is finished'; and
since he was the God that cannot lie, we are quite sure that all suffering
is finished - that neither he nor his body can suffer any more to all
eternity.

But, again, he undertook to obey the law in the stead of sinners. Man
had not only broken the law of God, but he had failed to obey it. And
as the Lord Jesus came to be a complete Saviour, he not only suffered
the curse of the broken law, but he obeyed the law in the stead of sinners.
Through his whole life, he made it his meat and drink to do the will of
God, and since he was the Son of God, we may be sure that he hath done
all that sinners ought to have done. His righteousness is the righteous-

ness of God; so that every sinner who puts on that righteousness is more righteous than if man had never fallen - more righteous than angels - as righteous as God. 'Who shall condemn whom God hath justified?'

O careless sinners! This is the Saviour whom we have always been preaching to you - this is the divine Redeemer whom you have always trodden under foot. You would think it a great thing if the king left his throne, and knocked at your door, and besought you to accept a little gold; but, oh! how much greater a thing is here. The King of kings has left his throne, and died the just for the unjust, and now knocks at your door. Careless sinner, can you still resist?

Awakened, anxious souls! This is the Saviour we have always offered you - this is the refuge - the rock which has followed you. You are anxious for your soul; and why, then, will you not hide here? Do you think that you honour Christ by doubting if his blood and righteousness be enough to cover you? Do you think you honour God by making him a liar, and refusing to believe the record which he hath given of his Son? Oh! doubt him no longer. Another day, and it may be too late. Flee like men who have an eternal hell behind them, and an eternal refuge before them. Take heaven by violence. 'Strive to enter in at the strait gate; for many, I say unto you, will seek to enter in, and shall not be able.'

And you who have fled for refuge to the Saviour: 'O happy Israel: who is like unto thee, O people saved by the LORD!' The eternal God is thy refuge; and of whom can you be afraid? Remember, abide in him. In the hours of sin and temptation, Satan always tries to drive you from this refuge. He will try to make you doubt if Christ be God - if his work be a finished work - if sinners may hide in him - if a backslider may hide in him; but cast not away your confidence. Cleave fast to Christ; and then the eternal God is thy refuge. In the hour of death, you may have a dark valley to pass through - you may lose sight of all your evidences - you may feel all your graces departed, and cry: 'All these things are against me.' Still, as a helpless sinner, flee to the Saviour God. Throw away the question whether you ever believed or not; and say, I will believe now; and thus at evening time it shall be light, and you will die with the eternal God as your refuge. Your eyes will close on this world only to open on the world where there is no doubt, and no fear, and no death.

3. Israel is a happy people, because sanctified by the Lord: 'Underneath are the everlasting arms' - and 'Who is the sword of thy excellency.'

In the chapter before (Deuteronomy 32:11,12), God compares his carrying of Israel to an eagle and her young: 'As an eagle stirreth up her nest, fluttereth over her young, spreadeth abroad her wings, taketh them, beareth them on her wings: so the LORD alone did lead him, and there was no strange god with him.' Again, in Isaiah 63:9, it is said: 'In all their affliction he was afflicted, and the angel of his presence saved them: in his love and in his pity he redeemed them; and he bare them, and carried them all the days of old.' Again, in the story of the lost sheep (Luke 15:3-7), we find that the Saviour not only finds the lost sheep, but 'when he hath found it, he lays it upon his shoulders rejoicing.' This is the very same meaning as the text: 'Underneath are the everlasting arms'; and again: 'He is the sword of thine excellency.'

When a young believer has come to peace in Jesus, he then comes to be anxious about walking holily. No sooner has he found the sweet calm of a forgiven soul, than he begins to know the bitter anxiety of a soul that fears to sin. 'True,' he says, 'I have come to Christ, and should have peace, but now I begin to fear I shall not be able to confess Christ before men. Now I begin to see that the whole world is against me, that all things are tempting me to sin; and I fear I shall go back to the world. I fear I shall be ensnared again. My companions - how can I resist them? And Satan - how can I fight against him?

This is the time when the young believer begins to make a great many resolutions in his own strength. If he could only keep out of the way of temptation, and separate from the world, he thinks he could keep himself holy; but God soon teaches him the insufficiency of his own strength. His resolutions are all broken through - his habits of walking warily and with strictness vanish like smoke before the breath of temptation; and the young child of God sits down to weep over the plague of his own heart, and to cry: 'O wretched man! who shall deliver me from the body of this death?'

If there be any such hearing me, suffer me, I beseech you, to recommend a new plan - a far more excellent way. Give yourself into the everlasting arms. When sin arises, when the world sets in like a flood, when temptation comes suddenly upon you, lean back upon the almighty Spirit, and you are safe. What does the little child do that has been set down upon the ground to walk, when it finds that its little limbs bend under it, that the first breath of wind will overthrow it? Does it not yield itself up into the mother's arms? When it cannot go, it consents to be carried; and so do you, feeble child of God. God hath given you *cleaving faith*, to cleave to Christ alone for righteousness; and that gave you the peace of the justified. Pray now that God would give you resigning faith, that you may trust him alone for strength - that you may yield yourself into the everlasting arms. Go you and learn what this meaneth: Jehovah our Righteousness is the same as Jehovah my Banner. Then, but not till then, will you fully know the meaning of the blessing: 'O happy Israel; who is like unto thee, O people saved by the LORD!'

Objection: I do not see the Spirit, nor hear the Spirit, nor feel the Spirit; and how can I yield myself into his arms?

Answer: This is the very Bible description of the Spirit's work: 'The wind bloweth where it listeth, and thou hearest the sound thereof, but canst not tell whence it cometh, or whither it goeth; so is every one that is born of the Spirit' (John 3:8). You do not see the wind, nor do you understand the machinery by which it blows, and yet you spread the sail to catch the breeze; and thus the tall vessel is borne over many a rough sea to the haven of rest. Just so lean upon the Spirit, though you understand not his working. Though now you see him not, yet believe in him, and you shall rejoice with joy unspeakable and full of glory for you shall be borne over the rough waves of this world to the haven of rest. Again: you do not know how the well springs up, you do not understand the machinery by which the water springs unfailingly; and yet you carry the pitcher to the well, and never come back with it empty. So depend on the unseen supply of the Spirit - get a daily supply for daily wants. Go confidently to the wells of salvation, and ye shall draw water with joy. 'If any man thirst, let him come unto me and drink.' 'O happy Israel: who is like unto thee!' Be of good cheer. We are confident that he which hath begun a good work in you will carry it on to the day of Christ Jesus.

But, ah! poor Christless souls, there is no promise of the Spirit to you. All the promises are yea and amen in Christ. Out of Christ there is no promise - nothing but wrath. You have no everlasting arms underneath you. You are sensual, not having the Spirit. There is no sin into which you may not fall. The sins that make men shudder and turn pale, you may commit. God has nowhere promised to keep you from them. You have not the Spirit - you cannot love God, or do any good work -

you can only sin. O poor souls that are growing still on the stock of old
Adam, you cannot but bear evil fruit: and the end will be death! Oh that
you would go away and weep over your miserable estate, and cry to God
to bring you among his happy Israel - who are chosen, justified,
sanctified - saved by the Lord!
St Peter's, January 29 1837

38. Follow those who follow Christ

And Ruth said, Entreat me not to leave thee, or to return from following
after thee: for whither thou goest, I will go; and where thou lodgest, I
will lodge: thy people shall be my people, and thy God my God
(Ruth 1:16).

In these two women of Moab you see the difference between nature and
grace.

*Orpah appears to have been of a most gentle, affectionate disposi-
tion.* She had been a kind and loving wife for ten years to her now buried
husband. She had been a kind daughter-in-law to Naomi: 'The LORD
deal kindly with you, as ye have dealt with the dead, and with me' (verse
8). She could not bear to part with Naomi. She first determined to go
back with her (verse 6). When Naomi bade them go back, she said:
'Surely we will go with thee.' When Naomi again bade them return, she
lifted up her voice and wept. And she kissed her mother-in-law most
affectionately, and went back to her people and her gods. O how much
of loveliness there is in the gentle affections of nature! Who would
believe that they cover a heart as black as hell?

*Ruth also appears to have been of a kindly, gentle disposition; but
her heart was touched by the Spirit of God also.* Naomi had not only
been her mother-in-law, but the mother of her soul. She had taught her
the way of salvation by the blood of the Lamb; and therefore, when the
day of trial came, that she must part from her people and her gods, or part
from her spiritual instructor, Ruth clave to Naomi: 'And Naomi said,
Behold thy sister-in-law is gone back unto her people and unto her gods:
return thou after thy sister-in-law. And Ruth said, Entreat me not to

leave thee, or to return from following after thee: for whither thou goest I will go: and where thou lodgest I will lodge: thy people shall be my people, and thy God my God' (verses 15,16).

From these words I draw the following lesson: *That we should cleave to our converted friends.*

When God sent me away from you, about eighteen months ago, I think I could then number, in my own mind, more than sixty souls who, I trust, had visibly passed from death unto life during the time I had been among you. Now, I do think I could number many more, ay, twice as many more, of you who have come, by the wonderful grace of God, to choose Israel for your people, and Israel's God for your God. I trust that there is hardly a family in this church who have not some friend or relative really born again. Oh, that God would this day put Ruth's resolution into your heart - to cleave to your converted friends, and to say: 'Where thou goest, I will go' - 'Thy people shall be my people, and thy God my God!'

1. Their God is a precious God.

A sin-pardoning God: 'Who is a God like unto thee, who pardoneth iniquity?'

Unconverted souls have no God: 'Without God, and without hope in the world'; or, like Orpah, they have false gods. Whatever they like best is their god. Their belly is their god - money is their god - or the god of this world is their god. But ah, he is not sin-pardoning! Your converted friends have found a sin-pardoning God that washes out their sins in blood, though red as scarlet. The God and Father of Jesus forgets sins: 'I, even I, am he that blotteth out thy transgressions, for mine own sake, and will not remember thy sins.' 'Thou hast put all my sins behind thy back'; he is the prodigal's Father: 'When he was yet a great way off, his Father saw him.' Should you not cleave to them? They had the same sins as you, perhaps they have sinned along with you. Why should you despair, if they have found mercy? Cleave to the skirt of their garment; for God is with them.

Their God is a faithful God - faithful to them in enabling them to persevere: 'I will never leave thee, nor forsake thee.' 'He who hath begun a good work in you, will perform it until the day of Jesus Christ.' 'Even to old age I am he'.

When once he takes a brand out of the fire, he never lets it fall in again. He will let heaven and earth fall sooner than one of his own. He keeps them night and day. The souls whom God chose four years ago in this place, he has kept to this day. Often they have been ready to die: 'Then the Lord sent from above; he took me, he drew me out of many waters.' 'When the poor and needy seek water, and there is none, and their tongue faileth for thirst, I the Lord will hear them: I the God of Israel will not forsake them.'

Faithful in temptations: 'God is faithful, who will not suffer you to be tempted above that ye are able, but will with the temptation also make a way to escape, that ye may be able to bear it.' Look back, believers, on your temptations. They have been very dreadful. You have been on the brink of ruin. The Lord has delivered you.

Faithful in afflictions: 'When thou passest through the waters, I will be with thee; and through the rivers, they shall not overflow thee.' Do you not see they have a refuge in the storm? Believers in this place have passed through many sore trials within these four years: yet God has been their refuge. He is a strength to the poor, a strength to the needy in his distress. Do you not see in the hour of trial what a rest they found in God, in the Saviour? How they poured out their sorrows into the ear of their High Priest? Cleave you to them.

2. Their people are a happy people.
Naomi was one of the peculiar people of Israel. It was this people that Ruth was going to join. But converted persons amongst us have joined the true Israel - a still more peculiar people. They have been added to the Church - such as have been saved.

(a) *They are a pardoned people*: 'Blessed is the man whose transgression is forgiven.'

They all have this blessedness. Sin is the greatest curse and burden in this world. Sin makes the world groan, makes damned souls shriek, and makes hell blaze. But this people have no unpardoned sin lying upon them. They are washed whiter than snow. They are all fair - without so much as a spot on them. They are as clean in God's pure eye as Christ is. Christ carried all their sins - they carry all his righteousness. Christ has suffered all their hell. They are in the love of God. God delights in them. Are they not a happy people? Are they not happier than you, who have so much sin as would sink a world?

(b) *A holy people.*

All born again - all have received the Holy Spirit. He dwells in them, and will never leave them. They have an old heart; still the Spirit reigns in them. They walk after the Spirit - they love in the Spirit - they pray in the Holy Ghost. Of themselves they cannot pray; but the Spirit teaches them. Heaven is begun in their hearts. They have a little of heaven now. Do you not see that they have left off your carnal pleasures? 'I had rather be a door-keeper in the house of my God, than dwell in the tents of wickedness.' Do you see no difference in their tempers - habits - lives? Are they not calmer, happier, heavenlier, than they were before? Seek what they have found.

(c) *All things work together for their good.*

Perhaps you will say they are an afflicted people. Some in poverty, some bereaved, some groaning on sick-beds. True, God dealeth with them as with sons. Often they cry, These things are against me. But really all is *for* them. If we could see the end as God does, we would see that every event is *for* the believer. When we get to the haven, we will see that every wind was wafting us to glory.

(d) *In death.*

Even wicked Balaam said: 'Let me die the death of the righteous.' 'Mark the perfect man, and behold the upright; for the end of that man is peace.' God calls upon you to mark the death-bed of his children. Sometimes it is triumphant, like Stephen: 'Behold, I see the heavens opened, and the Son of Man standing at the right hand of God. Lord Jesus, receive my spirit.' Almost always peaceful - or, if it be that the sun goes down in a cloud, O how sweet the surprise, when the believer finds himself on the other side of Jordan, at the pearly gate of the New Jerusalem, in the arms of the angels, in the smile of Jesus! 'There is a rest remaining for the people of God.' Will you not cleave to your godly child - parent - brother - sister - friend? You have sported together, you have sinned together - will you not be blessed together? 'Thy people shall be my people, and thy God my God.'

3. They want you to go with them.

It is plain that Naomi wanted Ruth to go with her; only she wanted to go not out of mere natural affection, but out of love to Israel's God. Moses wanted Hobab, his brother-in-law to go with him. Moses knew the value of the soul: 'We are journeying unto the place of which the Lord said, I will give it you. Come thou with us, and we will do thee good.' Jeremiah wanted the Jews of his day to go with him: 'Give glory to the LORD your God, before he cause darkness, and before your feet stumble upon the dark mountains, and while ye look for light, he turn it into the shadow of death, and make it gross darkness. But if ye will not hear it, my soul shall weep in secret places for your pride' (Jeremiah 13:16,17).

Your converted friends want you to go with them. They may not have boldness to tell you so. It is easier to speak to a stranger than to a friend. Do you not see their anxiety in their eyes? Do you not see how anxious they are that you would come to the house of prayer? They pray for you in secret. Often when you are sleeping they are praying for you. They weep for you 'in secret places, for your pride.' Well, if you will not go, you will be left behind. Still weep and pray, dear friends. This earth would be too like heaven if all we love were saved. Oh, what a sad company will be left!

4. If you do not go, there will be an eternal separation between you.
When Orpah turned back from Naomi and Ruth, she little knew she was parting for ever. They had lived together perhaps from infancy. They had played around the same palm tree, sat before the same cottage door, wandered over the same hills of Moab; now, they parted for eternity. So it is amongst us. There are, no doubt, many of us about to be separated for eternity. How strange, that two trees should grow so near - one to flower in paradise, the other to be a firebrand in hell!

Dear friends, do you not see some, whom you love much, really converted and saved? Do you not see they have a peace that passeth understanding, while you are still loaded with guilt? They are growing holier, more fond of prayer, walking more humbly, getting riper for glory. You are riper for hell - your sins getting faster hold. Oh, this separation will be for eternity! You may love them much, but you will go back to your gods. You will be *separated at death*; they will pass into glory, into perfect day - you will lift up your eyes in hell.

Besides all this, you will be *separated at the judgment*. When the Son of Man shall come in his glory, he shall separate the sheep from the goats; those on the right hand shall be solemnly acquitted - rewarded for all the good works you now see them daily performing. All their prayers and tears for you will then be recompensed.

You, on the left hand, shall go away into everlasting punishment. You shall look on that Saviour whom you now despise, and 'wail because of him'. When your eye catches your godly friends, how you will weep and wail! You will then remember all their love, and all your madness. Parents, do you love your converted children? Can you bear to be parted eternally? Will you cleave to Naomi, or go back to your people and your gods? How will you bear to see the fruit of your body on the throne with Christ, and yourself a brand in an eternal hell?
St Peter's, 1840

39. The vision of dry bones

'The hand of the LORD was upon me,' etc. (Ezekiel 37:1-14).

In early life the Prophet Ezekiel had been witness of sieges and battlefields - he had himself experienced many of the horrors and calamities of war; and this seems to have tinged his natural character in such a way that his prophecies, more than those of any other prophet, are full of terrific images and visions of dreadful things. In these words we have the description of a vision which, for grandeur and terrible sublimity, is perhaps unequalled in any other part of the Bible.

He describes himself as set down by God in the midst of a valley that was full of bones. It seemed as if he were stationed in the midst of some spacious battlefield, where thousands and tens of thousands had been slain, and none left behind to bury them. The eagles had many a time gathered over the carcasses, and none frayed them away; and the wolves of the mountains had eaten the flesh of these mighty men, and drunk the blood of princes. The rains of heaven had bleached them, and the winds that sighed over the open valley had made them bare; and many a summer sun had whitened and dried the bones. And as the prophet went round and round to view the dismal scene, these two thoughts arose in his mind: 'Behold, they are very many: and, lo, they are very dry.'

If the place had not been an open valley, it might have seemed to his wondering gaze some vast charnel-house - as if the tombs of all the Pharaohs had been laid bare, by some shock of nature, to the wild winds of heaven - as if the wanton hand of violence had rifled the vast cemeteries of Egypt, and cast forth the mummified bones of other ages to bleach and whiten in the light of heaven. How expressive are the brief words of the seer: 'Behold, they are very many; and, lo, they are very dry!'

No doubt there was an awful silence spread over this scene of desolateness and death; but the voice of his heavenly guide breaks in upon his ear: *'Son of man, can these bones live?'*

How strange a question was this to put concerning dry, whitened bones! When Jesus said of the damsel: 'She is not dead, but sleepeth,' they laughed him to scorn; but here were not bodies newly dead, but bones - bare, whitened bones; nay, they were not even skeletons, for bone was separated from its bone; and yet God asks: 'Can these bones live?' Had he asked this question of the world, they would have laughed a louder laugh of scorn; but he asked it of one who, though once dead, had been made alive by God; and he answered: 'O Lord God, thou knowest.' They cannot live of themselves, for they are dead and dry; but if thou wilt put thy living Spirit into them, they shall live. So, then, thou only knowest.

Receiving this answer of faith from the prophet, God bids him prophesy upon these bones, and say unto them: 'O ye dry bones, hear the word of the LORD. Thus saith the LORD God unto these bones, Behold, I will cause breath to enter into you, and ye shall live; and I will lay sinews upon you, and will bring up flesh upon you, and cover you with skin, and put breath in you, and ye shall live; and ye shall know that I am the Lord.' Had the prophet walked by sight, and not by faith, he would have staggered at the promise, through unbelief. Had he been a worshipper of reason, he would have argued: These bones have no ears to hear, why should I preach to them, 'Hear the word of the Lord?' But no - he believed God rather than himself. He had been taught 'the exceeding greatness of his mighty power'; and therefore he obeyed: *'So I prophesied as I was commanded.'*

If the scene which Ezekiel first beheld was dismal and desolate, the scene which now opened on his eyes was more dismal - more awfully revolting still: 'And as I prophesied, there was a noise, and behold a shaking; and the bones came together, bone to his bone; and when I beheld, lo, the sinews and the flesh came up upon them, and the skin covered them above; but there was no breath in them.' If it were a hideous sight before, to see the valley full of bones, all cleansed by the rains and winds, and whitened in the summer suns, how much more hideous now, to see these slain, bone joined to his bone - sinews, and flesh, and skin upon them; but no breath in them! Here was a battlefield indeed, with its thousands of unburied dead - masses of unbreathing flesh, cold and immovable, ready only to putrefy - every hand stiff and motionless - every bosom without a heave - every eye glazed and lifeless - every tongue cold and silent as the grave.

But the voice of God again breaks the silence: 'Prophesy unto the wind (or Spirit) prophesy, son of man, and say to the Spirit, Thus saith the LORD God, Come from the four winds, O Spirit, and breathe upon these slain that they may live.'

Before, Ezekiel had bent over the dead, dry bones, and preached unto them - a vast but lifeless congregation; but now he lifts his head and raises his eyes; for his word is to the living Spirit of God. Unbelief might have whispered to him, To whom are you going to prophesy now? Reason might have argued, What sense is there in speaking to the viewless wind - to one whom you see not; for it is written: 'The world cannot receive the Spirit of God, because it seeth him not?' But he staggered not at the word through unbelief: *'So I prophesied as he commanded me, and the breath came into them*, and they lived and stood up upon their feet, an exceeding great army.'

The first application made of this vision is to the restoration of the Jews. First, it teaches that at present they are like dry bones in the open valley - *scattered over all lands* - very many, and very dry - without any life to God. Secondly, it teaches that *the preaching of Jesus*, though foolishness to the world, is to be the means of their awakening, and that prayer to the all-quickening Spirit is to be the means of their new life. Thirdly, it teaches that when these means are used with them, God's ancient people shall yet stand up, and be an exceeding great army - shall be as they used to be when they marched through the wilderness, when God went before them in the pillar of cloud; that they shall then be led back to their own land, and planted in their own land, and not plucked up any more. But another, and to us a more important, application of this vision, is to the unconverted souls in the midst of us. Let us go over it with this view.

I. Unconverted souls are like dry bones - very many, and very dry.

They are very many.
When a soul is first brought to Christ, he enjoys a peace in believing which he never knew before; and not only so, but he is quickened from the death of trespasses and sins into a life which he never knew before - he knows the blessedness of living to God.

But even with all this joy, there is an awful feeling of loneliness; for when he looks round upon the world, he feels just like Ezekiel, set down in the midst of a valley full of dry bones. He is alive himself, but this world, once all his joy, looks now like some ancient battlefield, where the remains of the dead are all lying exposed on the open field; and he feels a solitary thing in a world of dead. This world appears now like one vast charnel-house, where whole generations of dead meet, and are jumbled together - all alike fit only for the burning; and he feels himself a solitary living thing, moving over heaps of slain.

He feels like Elijah on the Mount of God, when he complained: 'Lord, they have killed thy prophets, and digged down thine altars, and I, even I, am left alone.'

He feels like our blessed Lord, who was a light shining in darkness, and the darkness comprehended it not. He feels as if he were a feeble 'light in the world, holding forth the word of life' - a lamp suspended in the densest darkness, whose oil is all supplied by grace from on high, and whose rays seem only to make the darkness more visible.

He feels like Paul at Athens; for his spirit is moved in him, to see the whole world given over to idolatry. He feels like Paul at Rome, when he complained: 'I have no man like-minded, who will naturally care for your state; for all seek their own, not the things that are Jesus Christ's.'

He feels like John, when he said so sweetly, yet so sadly: 'We know that we are of God, and the whole world lieth in wickedness.'

To the eye of sense, O what a happy living world this is, with its shops and markets - its compliments and companies - its visits of ceremony and visits of kindness - its mirth and its melody! How living and life-like is the whole world, from morning's dawn till midnight. But to the eye of faith, what a lonely wilderness is this world! For 'the whole world lieth in wickedness.' Is it not so, believing brethren? Is it not like Egypt in that dreadful night when there was a cry heard from every dwelling; for there was not a house where there was not one dead?

Oh, it is more dismal far; for in every house there are many dead souls, and yet there is no cry! Look into your own family - look among the families of your neighbours - look into your native town - are not the many all dead, dead souls? The most are dead, dry bones.

Nay, look into the Christian Church - look among our Sabbath keepers, and those who sit down at sacraments. O, brethren! is it not true that, like the members of the Church of Sardis, most have a name to live and are dead? Do not the most of you live lives of pleasure? Is it not written: 'She that liveth in pleasure is dead while she liveth?' Do not most of you show no love for the brethren? And is it not written: 'He that loveth not his brother abideth in death?' O yes, the most are dry bones! Truly, then, 'they are very many.'

They are very dry.

Dry bones are the farthest of all from the possibility of living: (a) they are without any flesh or comeliness; (b) they are without any marrow or spirit; (c) they are without any activity or power of moving. And, oh! is not this the very picture of poor, unconverted souls - 'They are very dry?'

(a) *They are without any comeliness.* They see no beauty in Christ, and Christ sees no beauty in them - their souls are lean and ill-favoured. Man was made perfect in beauty at the first; for he was made in the image of him who is perfect loveliness; but a fallen, unconverted soul has no beauty - it is like a beautiful building scattered in ruins - it is like a beautiful statue all defaced, not one feature remaining - it is like a beautiful body smitten by death, corrupting in the grave.

(b) *They are without any marrow or spirit.* Man was made to be a habitation of God through the Spirit; and it is only when we are led by the Spirit that we are alive unto God. But the unconverted soul is 'sensual, not having the Spirit.' The Bible says: 'The world cannot receive the Spirit, because it seeth him not, neither knoweth him.' They have no work of the Spirit in their hearts - no awakening work - no convincing of righteousness - no sanctifying work - no sealing of the soul - no walking in the Spirit - no love in the Spirit - no praying in the Holy Ghost.

(c) *They have no activity or motion God-ward.* If we preach the Word of the Lord unto them, they have no heart to attend to the things which are spoken; dry bones have no ears. If we tell them of the wrath of God that is coming upon them, they are not moved to flee; dry bones cannot run. If we tell them of the loveliness of the Lord Jesus - how he offers himself to be their complete Saviour - still they are not moved to embrace him; for dry bones cannot stretch out their arms. Ah, these dry bones are very dry!

Brethren, is it not possible to make you anxious about your souls? Can you sit still and hear how dead and dry they are, and yet go away and forget it all? Can you bear to carry about with you a dead stone in your bosom instead of a heart? Can you bear to have such a cold, icy, wicked heart, as sees no desirableness in the lovely Saviour - no beauty in him who is stretching out his hands to you all the day - 'the chief among ten thousand' - the 'altogether lovely'? Oh, brethren, if you will go away unmoved - and, doubtless, hundreds of you may - what need have we of witnesses? Ye yourselves are the only evidence we need that unconverted souls are 'very many; and, lo, they are very dry'.

2. The second lesson we learn from this vision is, that preaching is God's instrument for awakening the unconverted.

Every intelligent man among you has been puzzled at one time or another by a seeming contradiction which runs through the whole of the Bible. It is written in one place: 'No man can come to me except the Father which hath sent me draw him'; and yet the whole Bible through bids every one of you come to Jesus. Again it is written: 'The natural man receiveth not the things of the Spirit of God, for they are foolishness unto him, neither can he know them'; and yet what are we continually urging upon you, but to receive the things of the Spirit of God? Again, God opened the heart of Lydia to attend to the things which were spoken of Paul - which makes it plain that no natural heart can attend; and yet we do nothing but press these things on your attention.

By nature your hearts are as hard as adamant, and even demonstration will not make you flee from hell; yet, 'knowing the terrors of the Lord, we persuade men'. By nature you cannot so much as comprehend the beauty and loveliness of the Lord Jesus; and yet 'we are determined to know nothing among you but Christ, and him crucified.'

Oh, what a mass of contradiction is here; and yet how easily it is solved! These bones were dead, dry, spiritless, lifeless, without flesh, without ears to hear; and yet God says: '*Prophesy upon these bones, and say unto them, O ye dry bones, hear the word of the Lord.*' And while he prophesied there was a noise, and 'behold a shaking; and the bones came together, bone to his bone; and when I beheld, lo, the sinews and the flesh came up upon them, and the skin covered them, above.'

Just so, my unconverted friends, your souls are like these dry bones
- dead, dry, spiritless, lifeless, without ears to hear, without hearts to
attend to the things which are spoken. You have such blunted consciences, that no words of mine can move you to flee from the wrath to
come; you have such hard, wicked hearts, that no words of mine can
persuade you to embrace the beseeching Saviour; and yet it is by the
foolishness of preaching that it pleases God to save them that believe;
and though our words have no power, yet God can work almightily
through them; and this is his message unto you: '*O ye dry bones, hear
the word of the Lord.*'

I earnestly beseech those of you who care little for the preaching of
the Word to attend to this. You may say, and say truly, that preaching
seems a weak and foolish instrument for such a work. God himself has
called it 'the foolishness of preaching'. You may say, and say truly, that
ministers are but earthen vessels, that they are men of like passions with
yourselves. God himself has called them so before you. But you cannot
say that it is not God's way of converting souls; and it is at the peril of
your own souls if ye despise it. Keep away from the house of God, and
lock up your Bible, and you put away from you the only instruments by
which God can reach you.

**3. The third and last lesson we learn from this vision is, that prayer
must be added to preaching, else preaching is in vain.**
The effects produced by the prophesying of Ezekiel to the dry bones
were very remarkable. The bones came together, bone to his bone - the
flesh, the sinews, the skin came up upon them, and covered them. But
still there was no breath in them - they were as dead as ever. And, oh how
like this is to the effects which often follow on the preaching of the
Word! How often is a people outwardly reformed! Instead of Sabbath
breaking there is Sabbath observance; instead of drunkenness, sobriety;
the form of godliness but none of the power; the bones, and sinews, and
flesh, and skin of godliness, but none of the living breath of godliness.
Ah, my friends, is not this just the way with our congregations at this
day? Abundance of head knowledge, but where is the lowly heart that
loves the Saviour? Abundance of orthodoxy and argument, but where
is the simple faith in the Lord Jesus, and love to all the saints? Does not
the Saviour say, when he looks down on our Churches: 'There is no
breath in them?' Oh then, brethren, let us, one and all, give heed to the
second command to the prophet: 'Prophesy unto the Spirit, son of man;

say, Come from the four winds, O Spirit, and breathe upon these slain, that they may live. So I prophesied as he commanded, and the breath came into them, and they lived, and stood up upon their feet, an exceeding great army.'

Learn two lessons from this.

First, *unconverted friends, what dead hearts you must have* - all the preaching in the world cannot put life into them. What hard hearts yours must be - the heaviest hammer we can lift cannot break them. We speak the weightiest arguments into your ear, yet all will not move you. We must lift up our voice, and prophesy to the Spirit. We must bring down the Almighty Spirit before we can touch your heart.

We try to convince you of sin. We show you how you have broken the law, and that 'cursed is every one that continueth not in all things written in the book of the law to do them' - that you must be under that curse, that you will not be able to bear that curse, that it crushed the Saviour to the earth, and will crush you to the lowest hell. You are somewhat impressed, and we hope that your heart is touched; but your impressions are like impressions on the sand when the tide is out, and the very next tide of the world effaces all.

We try to convince you of righteousness. We tell you of the love of the Saviour, how it passeth knowledge; how there was an ocean of love in that bosom, which no line could fathom - love to lost sinners like you; how he served in the stead of sinners, obeying the law for us; how he suffered in the stead of sinners, bearing the curse for us. We tell you to believe in him, and be saved; you are melted, and the tear stands on your cheek; but it is like 'the morning cloud and early dew - it quickly passes away.'

Ah, brethren, what hard, iron hearts you must have, when all that man can do will not melt them! Your hearts are too hard for us; and we have to go back weeping to our Lord, saying: 'Who hath believed our report?' In all other things we could persuade you by arguments. If your bodies were sick, we could persuade you to send for the physician; if your estate were entangled, we could persuade you to be diligent for your family; oh, how readily you would obey us! But when we demonstrate that you are the heirs, soul and body, of an eternal hell, you will not awake for it all. Even if we could show you the Lord Jesus Christ himself, the bleeding, beseeching Saviour, your wicked hearts would not turn or cleave to him. You need him that made your hearts, to break and bend them. Will you not, each of you, go away, then, beating on the breast, and saying: 'God, be merciful to me, a sinner'?

Learn, secondly, *believing brethren, what need you have to pray.* When God, in the chapter before (Ezekiel 36), promises to give a new heart and a new spirit to Israel - 'to take away the stony heart out of their flesh, and to give them an heart of flesh' - he adds, at verse 37: 'I will yet for this be inquired of by the house of Israel to do it for them.' And when God promises to give to Christ the heathen for his heritage, he only promises it in answer to prayer: 'Ask of me, and I will give thee.' And just so here; when he wishes to give life to these dead carcasses that are lying in the open valley, his word is: 'Prophesy, O son of man, unto the Spirit.'

O believing brethren, what an instrument is this which God hath put into your hands! Prayer moves him that moves the universe. O men of faith and prayer! - Israels, who wrestle with God, and prevail! - righteous, justified men, whose prayers avail much! You may be a little flock, but be you entreated to give the Lord no rest. O pray for the Spirit to 'breathe upon these slain, that they may live!'

And you, selfish Christians, if such a contradiction can exist - you who approach the throne of God only for yourselves, you whose petitions begin and end only for yourselves, who ask no gifts but only for your own peace and joy - go you and learn what this meaneth: 'It is more blessed to give than to receive.' 'Let this mind be in you which was also in Christ Jesus.'

Dundee, December 25, 1836

40. Christ the only refuge

Come, my people, enter thou into thy chambers,
and shut thy doors about thee: hide thyself as it were for a little moment,
until the indignation be overpast (Isaiah 26:20).

This passage is a word in season to God's people in every time of impending calamity. The form of expression is evidently taken from that dreadful night when God passed through the land of Egypt to smite all the firstborn of Egypt, from the firstborn of Pharaoh that sat upon the throne to the firstborn of the captive that sat in the dungeon. 'And Pharaoh arose in the night, he, and all his servants, and all the Egyptians; and there was a great cry in Egypt, for there was not a house where there was not one dead.' But God had commanded his own Israel to kill the paschal lamb, the type of the Lord Jesus Christ, the Lamb of God, and to take the bunch of hyssop, and dip it in the blood, and strike the lintel and the two side posts with the blood: 'And none of you (said he) shall go out at the door of his house until the morning.' As if he had said: 'Come, my people, enter into thy chambers, and shut thy blood-sprinkled doors about thee; hide thyself as it were for a little moment, until the indignation be overpast.'

It may be difficult to determine what time of indignation the prophet here refers to. The prophecy was given in the beginning of Hezekiah's reign, when many a destruction was yet to come upon the land of Israel. The invasion by Sennacherib the Assyrian was just at hand, and may be primarily referred to. The invasion by Nebuchadnezzar, and seventy years' captivity was also coming; and this also may be referred to. And the invasion by the Romans, in which Jerusalem was destroyed, and the Jews finally dispersed over the world, may also be referred to. And in all these coming indignations, God's word to his people was, to hide in their chambers - in the refuge which he had appointed them, till the indignation should be overpast.

But most of all does this prophecy refer to the great storm of indignation which God is yet going to bring upon the world, before the end come - when the Lord Jesus shall come a second time, without sin unto salvation - when he shall come again, no more a poor man, clothed in a seamless garment, but glorious in his apparel, travelling in the greatness of his strength - 'when he shall be revealed from heaven with his mighty angels, in flaming fire, taking vengeance on them that know not God, and obey not the gospel of our Lord Jesus Christ - when he shall come to be glorified in his saints, and admired in all them that believe.' In that day of awful tribulation - in which, except it were shortened, no flesh should be saved - God will gather his own as it were into chambers, and keep them hid till the storm passes over.

As in the flood, he brought his little flock into the ark, and it is written: 'God shut them in' - he shut the doors about them, till the deluge of his wrath was past; as in the destruction of Jericho, the family of Rahab were gathered all within doors, and saved from the wrath that came on all besides; as in the destruction of the firstborn in Egypt, God kept his own Israel safely hid in their dwellings; so, in the last storm that shall fall on this poor perishing world, God will gather his elect safe under the hollow of his hand, saying: 'Come, my people, enter thou into thy chambers, and shut thy doors about thee; hide thyself as it were for a little moment, until the indignation be overpast.'

The doctrine to be learned from this passage is a very plain one, namely, that in every time of calamity God bids us and our families find refuge in Christ. There is no safety anywhere else.

Christ is a complete refuge in every storm. In other parts of the Bible Christ is compared to 'a hiding-place from the wind, a covert from the storm, and the shadow of a great rock in a weary land'; he is compared to 'a fortress, or high tower, into which we may flee and be safe'; he is compared to 'an apple tree amid the trees of the wood, under whose shadow we may sit down, and his fruit be sweet to our taste'. But the comparison here is quite different; he is here compared to our own chamber, with the door shut: 'Come, my people, enter thou into thy chambers, and shut thy doors about thee.'

Now Christ is like our own chamber with the door shut in many respects:

Because there is safety in him. There is no place in all the world to which we look oftener in an hour of danger, as a refuge and place of safety, than our own home - the inner chamber, with the door made fast. Brethren, just such is Christ. There is safety in him: 'There is no condemnation to them that are in Christ Jesus.'

Because there is quietness and rest in him. In the world we look for the bustle and harassment of business; but when we enter into our chamber, and shut the door behind us, we shut out the bustling, noisy world - all is tranquillity and peace. Brethren, just such is Christ. In him the 'weary are at rest'. We are 'without carefulness' - we have 'quietness and assurance for ever'.

Because our home is a ready-made retreat, near and easy of access. When we seek our home, we have not to soar with the eagle to the top of the rugged rocks - nor like the dove that makes its nest in the hole's mouth - neither have we to dig into the earth, that we may hide our head there. Our home is near unto us. Brethren, just such is Christ. He is a ready Saviour - at hand, and not afar off. We have not to ascend, to bring Christ down from above; neither have we to descend into the deep, to bring Christ again from the dead. But the word is nigh thee, even in thy mouth and in thy heart. Oh, he is a near Saviour, he is not far from any one of us.

Now, this is the refuge which God bids his people flee into in every storm: 'Come, my people, enter thou into thy chambers, and shut thy doors about thee; hide thee as it were for a little moment, until the indignation be overpast.' And, oh, it is an all-sufficient refuge in every storm!

1. Christ is a complete refuge in a storm of conscience.

The great mass of unconverted men are living quite securely in their sins, going about from day to day without the least anxiety, though they are abiding under wrath. The reason is, that the vials of wrath are held over their heads, but not yet poured out; the flames of hell are burning up to their very feet, but they are not yet suffered to touch them. God is long-suffering, not willing that any should perish.

But when God awakens a soul to know his true condition, then there arises a storm of conscience within. O brethren, there is no more security to that soul! He does not feel the loathsomeness of sin as a child of God does; but he feels the terribleness of wrath. The Spirit has convinced him of sin. Every sin of his past life rises up behind him, and seems to cry for instant vengeance. All the sins of his hands, his taking things that were not his own, his handling unlawful things, and writing abominable and foolish things. The sins of his feet, swift to shed blood, swift to carry him to the haunts of sin. The sins of his eyes, full of adultery, and that could not cease from sin. The sins of his tongue, loving and making a lie, putting forth words of clamour and evil-speaking, backbiting and bitterness, speaking shameful words in the dark, things of which it is a shame so much as to speak. The sins of his heart, that it should always have been like a fountain, pouring out abominable desires and loath-some affections toward the creature, whilst the Creator was unloved, though the loveliest of all.

Oh, brethren, when a man really feels that the wrath of God is lying on him for a whole lifetime of sin, who can bear that storm? And, worst of all, when the Spirit convinces of sin, 'because he believes not in Jesus'? When the sinner feels that Jesus hath been stretching out his hands all the day, and he hath not regarded; that the gentle Saviour has called, and he has refused, that he has trodden the offers of mercy under his feet, and done despite to the Spirit of grace, oh then does the storm of conscience rise into a whirlwind! The fears of wrath lie hard upon that soul, they are like waves and billows going over him. His wife and children cannot cheer him now. His sinful comrades cannot laugh him from his fears now.

O brethren, if ever you have seen the sad, dejected countenance of a sinner convinced by God, you will not soon forget it! He is not sure but his next step may be into hell. When he falls asleep, he does not know but he may wake up in hell.

Oh, if there be one soul here thus awakened - afflicted, tempest-tossed, and not comforted - hear this word: 'Come, my people, enter thou into thy chambers, and shut thy doors about thee; hide thyself as it were for a little moment, until the indignation be overpast.' True, this is a word chiefly to God's people who have already hidden in Christ; but Christ is as free to you as to them. In him there is perfect safety. In him is quietness and rest. He is a near Saviour. His arms are as open to receive you as is your own home. Come, poor sinners, enter into this chamber. Every one that is now in Christ was once as much tempest-tossed as you are. When a man is overtaken by nightfall on a bleak moor, when the frosty wind blows bitterly upon him and the wreathing snow retards his every footstep, where is it that he longs to be? What spot in all the world comes oftenest across his wishful fancy? It is his home, his inner chamber, with the door made fast. Oh, if he were only there, he would be safe! Oh, poor soul, just such are you, and just such a home is Christ - not afar off, but near! Believe on the Lord Jesus, and thou shalt be saved. Hide in him, for he is a hiding-place from the wind.

2. Christ is a complete refuge in a storm of providence.

When providences are all favourable, it is amazing to see how careless unconverted men grow of God and the things of eternity. When the glow of health has been long upon their cheek, they begin to live as if they were to live for ever, as if there were no death and no hell. When their business goes on prosperously from week to week, they begin to feel like lords of the universe, as if this world were their own, as if their houses, and lands, and money, were all their own, and they could never part company. And, oh, it is still more amazing to see how careless even the children of God will grow in such times of long-continued prosperity ! How death and eternity, and to be with Christ, and to be like Christ, become less desirable things than once they were; how like they become to the world, in supposing that gain is godliness; how the poor, pitiful possessions of this world seem for a time to come between and intercept the view of the inheritance that is incorruptible, undefiled, and that fadeth not away; how the glare and glitter of this present evil world dazzle their eyes, and dim their sight for beholding the King in his beauty, and the land that is very far off.

Now, it is deeply interesting and deeply instructive to mark the panic which comes upon the face of society, when God makes a sudden change of providences - when all of a sudden the sky is overcast, the distant thunder begins to roll, and the storm of providence comes on. When those sudden crashes take place in the commercial world, - when, like the avalanche of the snowy mountains, that comes down upon some hapless village, smothering whole families in the midst of their unthinking gaiety - when those overwhelming catastrophes come down, involving whole families in ruin and penury, oh it is strange to see how the world stand amazed, their wisdom is all dashed and confounded!

Or, when God sends a time of widespread sickness and death, when he seems to poison the very atmosphere, when we are visited by the pestilence that walketh in darkness, and the destruction that wasteth at noon-day, when a thousand fall at our side, and ten thousand at our right hand, oh it is strange to see what a panic comes upon men, and paleness upon all faces! It is like when a set of fishing boats have set out upon an excursion when the wind was fair, and the sun shone happily, and the blue waves curled gently on every side, and all is joy and carelessness in every boat; when suddenly the sky is overcast, the whistling wind rises, a dreadful squall is at hand, and death stares every man in the face. Ah, then what panic seizes upon every boat's crew! What reefing of the sails! What grasping at the helm! How one seeks to run into the shore, another into the deep!

Such is the panic that comes over unconverted men in a time of widespread calamity. And oh, how religious they now become! How they look grave and forsake their jests and loose talking, and think that is religion? They are just like Israel of old: 'When he slew them, then they sought him, and they returned and inquired early after God. And they remembered that God was their rock, and the high God their redeemer. Nevertheless they did flatter him with their mouth, and they lied unto him with their tongues. For their heart was not right with him, neither were they steadfast in his covenant.'

Now, brethren, in such a storm of providence, Christ is a complete refuge; and though the children of God in such times, even they, seem to be in doubt and jeopardy, they know not what to think, they know not where to flee. Yet they may hear the Word of God above the storm: 'Come, my people, enter thou into thy chambers, and shut thy doors about thee; hide thyself as it were for a little moment, until the indignation be overpast.' Just as our own chamber, with the doors shut about us, is the place where we have quietness and rest; and the storm may rage without, but we shall not feel it; and the world may be crying aloud, yet we shall not hear it; so the Lord Jesus is a perfect refuge to the believer from all the storms of providence.

Men are apt to think that the only good of hiding in Christ is to save our souls, that when an awakened sinner hides in the Lord Jesus, he finds pardon of all sin and peace with God, but nothing more. But the whole Bible shows that there is much more in Christ; that when we hide in him, we are saved from *all* our distresses; from our troubles about health, about money, about the world. In the 34th Psalm, it is mentioned four times over, that when we come to Christ we are saved, not out of one trouble, but out of *all* our troubles: 'I sought the LORD; he heard, and delivered me from all my fears' (verse 4). 'This poor man cried, and the LORD heard, and saved him out of all his troubles' (verse 6). 'The righteous cry, and the LORD heareth, and delivereth them out of all their troubles' (verse 17). 'Many are the afflictions of the righteous, yet the LORD delivereth them out of them all' (verse 19). And the reason is plain - when we hide in Jesus, the God of providence becomes our God and Father, and we know he will make all things work together for our good. The Lord is our shepherd, we shall not want. Whatever temporal good may be taken away, we know that our eternal good is secure: 'I know whom I have believed, and am persuaded that he is able to keep that which I have committed unto him against that day' (2 Timothy 1:12).

Oh, my believing friends, why should you be discouraged in this time of widespread sickness and calamity? Why should you be cast down, as if God were covering you with a cloud in his anger? These clouds may be a few drops of God's coming wrath upon the world - they may be like the first of the thunder-shower; but to you they speak in the language of love. God wishes you deeper hid in Christ - he wishes you more separate from the world: 'Come, my people, enter thou into thy chambers, and shut thy doors about thee.'

We never would know so well the blessing of a home, if there were no winter snows and winter winds to make us crowd round the happy hearth. Just so, believer, you would not know the blessing of such a chamber as Christ is, if there were no sicknesses and dark impending providences to make you live more in him. Come then, believer, let every drop of wrath that falls around you speak with new power to your soul, and give new life to that faith by which you cleave to Jesus. Let every sigh you hear, be as it were a voice from God, saying: 'Come, my people, enter thou into thy chambers.'

And you, poor Christless souls, ah, where shall you run - poor sheep that have no shepherd - defenceless and lost in this world's wilderness? You have no home. Enter into your securest room, and shut your door; still vengeance can reach you there. God is against you, his wrath is abiding on you. Oh, the day of the Lord is darkness, and not light to you! Wherever you go, you are a lost soul: 'As if a man did flee from a lion, and a bear met him; or went into the house, and leaned his hand on the wall, and a serpent bit him.' Oh, brethren, ye are men, ye have reason, will ye not flee from the wrath to come? Will these wasting sicknesses not convince you that God is stronger than you - that you will be nothing in the hands of an angry God? Even to you, then, Christ, the door of salvation, is still open, wide open. Come, poor sinner, enter into this chamber, and shut thy doors about thee. 'Hide thyself as it were for a little moment, until the indignation be overpast.'

There are just two remarks I would make in conclusion:

(1) *That this passage bids us hide in Christ, not singly, but in families.* In that deliverance which God wrought for Israel in Egypt he taught this very remarkably; for he did not gather Israel into some great tower where they might be safe, but bade each family remain within their own house, only sprinkling the doors with blood; and so in saving Noah - God saved not single souls, but a whole family; and so in saving Lot - God saved Lot and all that were his; and so in saving Rahab - she and all her household were gathered in and saved. My friends, God is still the God of families, and still does he wish whole families of you to be saved; and he says as much in the words before me: 'Come, my people, enter thou into thy chambers.' Alas, my friends, we live in days when family religion is fallen to the ground. Men are too proud now to be like Abraham, and to command their children and their servants after them. Men nowadays take up the words of Cain, and say: 'Am I my brother's keeper?' Ah, where are our Andrews now? 'Andrew first findeth his own brother, Peter, and saith unto him, We have found the Christ; and he brought him to Jesus.'

What! Is there one of you who thinks himself a child of God, who is yet ashamed to kneel down in the midst of his family, and pray? Alas, my friend, you may dream that you are a child of Abraham, but remember you do not the works of Abraham. Ah, brethren, whole families must be saved; for whole families are in danger of hell.

Oh, then, you that know the Lord, do not your bowels yearn over your perishing kindred? Can you not fall on some contrivance, think you, to win them to Christ? Will you not strengthen our hands, at least, by your words and prayers, and by opening the way for the minister of Christ into the bosom of your unconverted families? Ah, in this time of trouble, will you not lay hands on them, as the angels did on Lot? Hark! The Lord invites you: 'Come, my people, enter thou into thy chambers, and shut thy doors about thee; hide thyself as it were for a little moment, until the indignation be overpast.'

(2) *I observe that the dangers to which the believer is exposed are but for a time.* God says: 'Hide thyself as it were for a little moment, until the indignation be overpast.' It was so in that night, when God smote the firstborn in Egypt. It was but a night that they were to hide in their houses: 'None of you shall go out of his house until the morning.' It was so in the destruction of Jericho - Rahab and her kindred hid themselves seven days till the danger was overpast. And just so the troubles of believers now are for a very short time: 'These light afflictions are but for a moment.' And also the indignation which is coming on the world will be but for a little moment - it will soon be overpast.

(a) *Temporal troubles are but for a moment*; these sad sicknesses and wasting calamities will not last for ever. A short while, and this body will be past the power of pain to grieve it. I know that if any of you have tasted the sweetness of being in Christ, you could be content to hide in him for an eternity. Welcome an eternity of outward troubles, if I have such a hiding-place. But you are not asked to do this: 'Hide thyself as it were for a little moment.' Live but a few years more in faith, and thou shalt live the rest in glory: 'If we suffer with him, we shall also reign with him.'

(b) *The indignation of the latter day will be but for a moment.* Days of wrath are coming such as the world has never known before. My friends, it is vain to conceal it. And if these days were not shortened, no flesh could be saved; but for the elect's sake they shall be shortened - they shall be made as a little moment. Whether these days of trouble shall be in our day I do not know; for we know neither the day nor the hour when the Son of Man cometh. But this I do know, that there is no safety, no, not for another night, for any soul that is not hiding in the

Saviour. I repeat it, my friends, if you lie down in your bed this night out of Christ, the Son of Man may be come before the morning, and you be cut in sunder, and have your portion with the hypocrites where is weeping and gnashing of teeth.

But, O believer, hidden in the cleft Rock, abide in him. As the sky darkens around you, hide deeper in him. It is only for a short time - one dark, dark cloud, and eternal sunshine beyond; one wild wave of vengeance, and an unbounded ocean of glory.

Little children, abide in him, that when he shall appear ye may have confidence, and not be ashamed before him at his coming: 'Come, my people, enter thou into thy chambers, and shut thy doors about thee; hide thyself as it were for a little moment, until the indignation be overpast.'
Dundee, January 15, 1837

41. Will ye also go away?

'From that time many of his disciples went back, and walked no more with him. Then said Jesus unto the twelve, Will ye also go away? Then Simon Peter answered him, Lord, to whom shall we go? thou hast the words of eternal life; and we believe and are sure that thou art the Christ, the Son of the living God' (John 6:66-69).

1. Many who seem to be disciples of Christ, go back, and walk no more with Jesus.

This is a very solemn truth, and may probably answer the case of some who are this day hearing me. Observe, it is said twice over that there were many who went back. If there were many then, it is likely there will be many now.

Many follow Christ for a time, but are stumbled when they hear they must come to personal union with Christ.

(a) *So it was here.* A great many were now following Christ in addition to the twelve apostles. They were evidently much taken with Christ; they called him a prophet; they wanted to make him a king; they followed him across the sea; and yet, when he told them that he was the bread of heaven, they murmured. When he told them that they must eat his flesh and drink his blood to have eternal life, they said: 'This is a hard saying'; and it was for this reason they turned back, and walked no more with Jesus.

(b) *So it is now*. A great many persons are much taken with Christ; they have some anxiety about their souls; they follow anxiously after the preaching of the Word; but when we show them that Christ is the bread of heaven, that they must have a personal closing with Christ, as much as if they were to eat his flesh and drink his blood, these souls say: 'It is a hard saying, who can bear it?' By-and-by, they are offended, they believe not, they go back and walk no more with Jesus. Is any hearing me in this condition? Oh! think again, I beseech you, before you go back. Oh! seek the teaching of God, and he will show you that none of Christ's sayings are hard sayings, but that they are all sweet and easy.' When the heart of a poor Indian was brought under the teaching of God, he said: 'Some people complain that the Bible is a hard book; but I have not read so far as to find it a hard book. To me it is all sweet and easy.'

Many follow Christ for a time, but when they are told that Christ must dwell in them, they go back, and walk no more with Jesus.

(a) *So it was here*. The multitude that followed Christ were pleased with a great many things in him. When he fed them with the five barley loaves and the two fishes, they said: 'Lord, it is good for us to be here.' 'This is in truth that prophet that should come into the world.' And again, when Jesus told them of bread of heaven that would give life, they said most devoutly: 'Lord, evermore give us this bread.' But when Christ said: 'He that eateth my flesh, and drinketh my blood, dwelleth in me, and I in him,' by-and-by they were offended. When he told them that he would be their life, and would dwell in them, they said: 'It is a hard saying, who can bear it?' They believed not - they went back, and walked no more with Jesus.

(b) *So it was in some measure with Nicodemus*. When he regarded Christ as a worker of miracles, this drew the heart of the Jewish ruler, and he said to him: 'Rabbi, we know thou art a teacher come from God.' But when Jesus told him he must be born again, must be dwelt in by the unseen Spirit of God, Nicodemus found it a hard saying:' How can a man be born when he is old?' And again: 'How can these things be?'

(c) *So now, many persons are much taken with Christ.* They are anxious about their souls for a time: and they see some glimpses of Christ as a Saviour. They love to hear the Word; 'it is like a very lovely song of one that hath a pleasant voice, and can play well on an instrument'; but when Christ says: 'Ye must be born again,' 'He that eateth me, even he shall live by me,' they say: 'This is a hard saying, who can bear it?'

First, they never saw the Spirit, and they say: 'How can these things be?' This is one of your mysteries. Therefore, they go back, and walk no more with Jesus. Is any hearing me in this condition? Oh think a moment before you go back! 'Oh! fools and slow of heart to be believe all that is written concerning Jesus.' Why should you stumble at the blessed word: 'He that eateth me shall live by me?' True, you never saw the Spirit; yet trust the word of Him that cannot lie. You never saw the wind, and yet you spread the sail; so trust to that Spirit, though you never saw him.

Second, some of you may fear that if it be true, then you would be deprived of some of your darling pleasures - your heart would be changed, and you would no more have a relish for your present enjoyments; therefore you go back, and walk no more with Jesus. Oh! how the devil blinds your understanding. Do you not see, that if you lose your relish for your present joys, it will be because you have got a taste for higher and sweeter? You might as wisely refuse to drink better wine, because you would thereby lose your relish for the worse. Oh! the joys of the Holy Ghost are sweeter than all the pleasures of sin. It is wine on the lees, well refined. 'Woe unto thee, O Jerusalem! Wilt thou not be made clean? When shall it once be?'

Many are awakened to follow Christ, but when they find that they must be drawn to Christ, that all is of free grace, by-and-by they are offended.

(a) *So here, the persons that had followed Christ had been laborious, and painstaking in following him.* They had crossed the sea, and listened to his words for many days together; and doubtless they began to think they had done well, and that they were worthy to be saved for the pains they had taken. But when Jesus told them that salvation was of mere grace, that they were helpless sinners, and needed still to be drawn to Christ by the mere good pleasure of the Father, this offended them to the quick. They turned back, and walked no more with Jesus.

(b) *So now, many persons set out in religion, thinking that they shall soon bring themselves into a converted state.* They take great pains in religion; they confess the sins of their past life, and stir up grief in their hearts because of them; they wait patiently on ordinances, and take much pains to work the works of God. But when they find out that they are not a whit nearer being saved than when they began, when they are told they must be drawn to Christ, that God is not obliged to save them, that they deserve nothing at his hand but a place in hell, that if ever they are saved it is of mere free grace, then they are offended. They cannot bear this kind of preaching; they go back, and walk no more with Jesus. Is any hearing me in this condition? Alas! proud sinner, stop one moment before you leave the divine Saviour. Is it a hard saying, that an infinitely hateful rebel and worm should be unable to buy Christ with so many tears and prayers?

Listen here to two words of warning:

First, *many go so far with Christ, who do not go the whole way.* Many hear Christ's words for a time with joy and eagerness, who yet are offended by them at last. This is a solemn warning. Do not think you are a Christian because you sit and listen to the words of Christ. Do not think you are a Christian because you have some pleasure in the words of Christ. Many are called - few are chosen. Many went back, and only twelve remained. So doubtless it will be found among you. Those only are Christians who feed upon Christ, and live by him.

Second, *those that go back generally walk no more with Jesus.* Perhaps they did not intend to bid an eternal farewell to the Saviour. Perhaps they said as they retired, I will go home and think about it; I will hear him again concerning this matter. At a more convenient season I will follow him. But, alas! that season never came - they walked no more with Jesus. Take warning, dear friends you that are anxious about your souls. Oh! do not be easily offended. Do not lose a sense of your lost condition. Oh! do not grow careless of your Bible and the means of grace. Oh! do not go back to the company of sinners. These are all marks of one who is going back from Jesus. Wait patiently for the Lord until he incline his ear and hear your cry. Still press to hear the words of Jesus. Still cry for the teaching Spirit. 'If any man draw back, my soul shall have no pleasure in him.' 'No man having put his hand to the plough, and looking back, is fit for the kingdom of God.'

2. The careful anxiety of Christ lest his own true disciples should go away: 'Then said Jesus to the twelve, Will ye also go away?' (v. 67).
I have no doubt the heart of Jesus was grieved when the multitude went away, and walked no more with him. That good Shepherd never yet saw a lost sheep running on to destruction, but his heart bled for it: 'O Jerusalem, Jerusalem, how often would I have gathered thy children together!' He could see all the future history of these men - how they would lose all their impressions, how they would harden in their sins, how, like a rolling snowball, they would gather more and more wrath around them. And I doubt not, he wept in secret over them, and said: 'If ye had known, even you, the things which belong unto your peace; but now they are hid from your eyes.' He traced their history up to that hour when he would say: 'Depart from me.' But however much Christ grieved over their departure, this only fanned the flame of his love to his own, so that he turned round and said: 'Will ye also go away?'

Observe how much love there is in these words.
When the crowd went away he did not cry after them - his soul was grieved, but he spoke not a word; but when his own believing disciples were in danger of being led away, he speaks to them: 'Will ye also go away?' - ye whom I have chosen - ye whom I have washed - ye whom I have sanctified and filled with hopes of glory - 'Will ye also go away?' Oh! see, Christians, how anxiously Christ watches over you. He is walking in the midst of the seven golden candlesticks, and his word is: 'I know thy works'. He watches the first decaying of the first love. He speaks aloud: 'Will ye also go away?'

Observe, Christ keeps his disciples from backsliding, by putting the question to them: 'Will ye also go away?'
It is probable that some of the twelve were inclining to go away with the rest. We are often deceived by example - carried away from Christ before we think of it: but Christ wakens us by the question: 'Will ye also go away?' Think of this question, you that have known Christ, and yet are going back to sin and the world. May God write it on your hearts: 'Will ye also go away?' Christians, if you would keep this word in your heart, it would keep you from the thought of going away.

3. A true believer has none to go to but Christ.
Both the Bible and experience testify, that believers do oftentimes go away from Christ. The same lips that said: 'My Lord, and my God,' are often found saying: 'I will go after my lovers.' But this passage plainly shows that it needs but the word of the tender Saviour to reach the heart of the backslider, and he says: 'Lord, to whom shall we go? Thou hast the words of eternal life.'

Two reasons are here given why the believer cleaves to Christ.

(1) 'Thou hast the words of eternal life.' To unconverted minds the words of Christ are hard sayings: to his own, they are tried words - words of eternal life. The very thing that drives the world away from Christ, draws his own disciples closer and closer to him. The world are offended when Christ says we must eat his flesh - it is a word of eternal life to the Christian. The world go away when they hear of Christ dwelling in the soul - the Christian draws nearer, and says: Lord, evermore dwell in me. The world walk no more with Jesus when they hear, It is all of grace - the Christian bows in the dust, and blesses God, who alone has made him to differ: 'Lord, to whom shall we go? Thou hast the words of eternal life.' Dear friends, try yourselves by this. Are the words of Christ to you hard sayings, or are they the words of eternal life? Oh! may God enable you to judge fairly of your case.

(2) 'We believe and are sure that thou art that Christ, the Son of the living God.' Ah! it is this that rivets the believing soul to Christ - the certain conviction that Christ is a divine Saviour. If Christ were only a man like ourselves, then how could he be a surety for us? He might suffer in the stead of one man, but how could he suffer in the stead of thousands? Ah! but I believe and am sure that he is the Son of the living God, and therefore I know he is a sufficient surety for me. To whom else can I go for pardon? If Christ were only a man like ourselves, then how could he dwell in us, or give the Spirit to abide with us for ever? But we believe and are sure that he is that Christ, the Son of the living God, and therefore we know he is able to dwell in us, and put the Spirit in us for ever. To whom, then, can I go for a new heart but unto Christ? O dear brethren! have you been thus taught? Then blessed are ye, 'for flesh and blood hath not revealed it unto you, but my Father which is in heaven.' Hold fast by this sure faith for you cannot be too sure; and then you will never, never go away from Christ.

Some of you are very wavering in your life, like a wave of the sea, driven with the wind and tossed; at one time cast upon the shore, at

another time running back into the sea. There is no decision about your Christianity or about your holiness. Why is this? It is unbelief. Oh! if you would believe and be sure, then you would never depart from him. You would say: 'To whom shall we go, because thou hast the words of eternal life?'
Dundee, 1837

42. Ye will not come unto me

'And ye will not come to me, that ye might have life' (John 5:40).

There is nothing more sad, and nothing more strange than that, when there is a Saviour that is enough for all the world, so few should come to him to be saved. If a life-boat were sent out to a wreck, sufficient to save all the crew, and if it came back with less than half of them, you would inquire, with anxiety, why the rest had not been saved by it. Just so, when Christ has come to seek and save that which was lost, and yet the vast majority are unsaved, it behoves us to inquire why so many are not saved by Christ. We have the answer in these words: 'Ye will not come to me, that ye might have life.'

Doctrine. Sinners are lost, not by reason of anything in Christ, but by reason of something in themselves. They will not come to Christ that they might have life.

1. Show that it is not by reason of anything in Christ that sinners are lost.

It is not because Christ is not sufficient to save all.
The whole Bible shows that Christ is quite sufficient to save all the world - that all the world would be saved, if all the world were to come to Christ: 'Behold the Lamb of God, that taketh away the sins of the world.' The meaning of that is, not that the sins of the whole world are now taken away. It is quite plain that the whole world is not forgiven at present. (1) Because the whole is not saved. (2) Because God everywhere calls sinners to repentance, and the first work of the Spirit is to

convince of sin - of the heavy burden that is now lying on Christless souls. (3) Because forgiveness in the Bible is everywhere attached to believing. When they brought to Jesus a man sick of the palsy, Jesus, seeing his faith, said unto him: 'Son, be of good cheer; thy sins are forgiven thee.' 'Believe on the Lord Jesus Christ and thou shalt be saved.' The simple truth of the Bible is, that Christ hath suffered and died in the stead of sinners - as a common person in their stead; and every man that is a sinner hath a right to come.

Christ is quite sufficient for all, and I would prove it by this argument: if he was sufficient for one sinner, then he must be sufficient for all. The great difficulty with God (I speak as a man) was, not how to admit many sinners into his favour, but how to admit one sinner into his favour. If that difficulty has been got over in Jesus Christ, then the whole difficulty has been got over. If one sinner clothed in Christ may come unto God, then all sinners may. If one sinner may have peace with God, and God be yet just and glorious, then every sinner may have peace with him. If Christ was enough for Abel, then he is enough for all that come after. If one dying thief may look to him and be saved, so may every dying thief. If one trembling jailer may believe on Jesus, and rejoice believing, so may every other trembling sinner. O brethren! you may doubt and wrangle about whether Christ be enough for your souls, but if you die Christless, you will see that there was room enough under his wings, but you would not.

Sinners are lost, not because Christ is unwilling to save all.
The whole Bible shows that Christ is quite willing and anxious that all sinners should come to him. The city of refuge in the Old Testament was a type of Christ; and you remember that its gates were open by night and by day. The arms of Christ were nailed wide open, when he hung upon the cross; and this was a figure of his wide willingness to save all, as he said: 'I, if I be lifted up from the earth, will draw all men unto me.' But though his arms were firmly nailed, they are more firmly nailed wide open now, by his love and compassion for perishing sinners, than ever they were nailed to the tree.

There is no unwillingness in the heart of Jesus Christ. When people are willing and anxious about something, they do everything that lies in their power to bring it to pass. So did Jesus Christ: 'What could have been done more for my vineyard, that I have not done in it?' But if they are very anxious, they will attempt it again and again. So did Jesus

Christ: 'O Jerusalem, Jerusalem, how often would I have gathered your children as a hen gathereth her chickens under her wings, and ye would not!' But if they are still more anxious, they will be grieved if they are disappointed. So was Jesus Christ: 'When he came near, he beheld the city, and wept over it.' But if they are very anxious, they will suffer pain rather than lose their object. So did Jesus Christ: The good Shepherd gave his life for the sheep. Ah! dear brethren, if you perish, it is not because Jesus wishes you to perish.

A word to anxious souls. How strange it is that anxious souls do most of all doubt the willingness of Christ to be their Saviour! These should least of all doubt him. If he is a willing Saviour to any, O surely he is a willing Saviour to a weary soul! Remember the blind beggar of Jericho. He was in your case, blind and helpless, and he cried: 'Jesus, thou son of David, have mercy upon me.' And when the crowd bade him hold his peace, he cried so much the more. Was Jesus unwilling to be that beggar's Saviour? He stood still, and commanded him to be brought, and said, 'Thy faith hath made thee whole.' He is the same willing Saviour still. Cry after him; and, though the world may bid you hold your peace, cry after him just so much the more.

A word to careless souls. You say Christ may be a willing Saviour to others, but surely not to you. O yes! he is quite willing for you too. See him sitting by the well of Samaria, convincing one poor sinful woman of her sins, and leading her to himself. He is the same Saviour toward you this day. If you do perish, it is not because Christ is willing. He wills all men to be saved, and to come to the knowledge of the truth. He pleads with you, and says: 'Turn ye, turn ye, why will ye die?'

2. True reasons why men do not come to Jesus Christ.
It is because they will not come. The reason is not in Christ, but in themselves.

Ignorance of Jesus Christ is one reason why sinners do not come to him. So it was with the Jews. They, being ignorant of God's righteousness, would not submit themselves to the righteousness of God. And so it is with many sinners amongst us. They will not come to Jesus Christ, because they do not know him. It is quite amazing the great ignorance which exists in the midst of us. Some who have lived under the preached Word for years, yet do not know who Jesus Christ is. He is an utter stranger to them. Some do not know from whence he came, or whither he has gone, or who sent him into the world, or why he came, and why he suffered and obeyed. Many more have no personal knowledge of Jesus Christ. They have had no revelation and fitness to their own case as a Saviour; and therefore they will not come to Christ to have life. In a shower of rain, you would not turn aside into a shelter unless you knew that there was a shelter there. Though you had lived at the time of the flood, if you lived in complete ignorance of the ark, it is plain you would not have fled to it; or even if you had known it, and seen it, and heard of it, yet if you did not know the use of it, you would never have fled to it. So is it with sinners now. Many do not know about Jesus Christ, though he is the only ark; and therefore they will not come to him. Many know something about Jesus Christ, but they do not know the use of him to their perishing souls; and so they also will not come to Christ to have life.

Do not live in ignorance of him, dear souls, I beseech you. Seek for him as for silver, yea, search for him as for hid treasures. Do not say you are too old to learn. If the Spirit be your teacher, he can make it quite easy. He can take of the things of Christ, and show them unto you. Do not say you are too young to learn. Happiest they who know him soonest! Happy lambs, that are soon gathered into the Saviour's bosom!

Another reason why sinners do not come to Christ is, that they have no sense that they need him.

If you had slain a man, but had no sense that the blood-avenger was pursuing you, you would not flee to the city of refuge. If your vessel were sinking, but you did not perceive it, you would not get into the lifeboat. If you were sick and dying, but had no sense of it, you would not send for the physician. Just so, if you have no sense of being under the wrath of God, and exposed to hell, you will not come to Christ, that you may have life. If you look around, you will see that the most of men have no feeling of anxiety about their souls. You will find men anxious about their families, about their money or their goods, about their character in the world; but, ah! where do you find men anxious about their souls? If you ask me why so few come to Jesus Christ, I answer, Because so few are anxious about their souls. Now, if a man be never awakened to flee from wrath, it is plain and certain that he will never come to Jesus Christ. The three thousand were pricked in their hearts, and then inquired after Christ. The jailer trembled for his soul, and then was brought to rejoice in Christ Jesus. But no one was ever brought to Christ without being convinced of sin.

Careless persons, you should seek these convictions - you should cry to God for them - you should try to get your heart made alive to the sadness of your natural condition; for if you are never awakened, you will never come to Jesus Christ - you will never be saved.

Anxious persons, you should seek to keep up these convictions. They are easily lost. You should cry to God to make them deeper on your heart. If you lose them, they may never come back. You may become another Lot's wife - a pillar of salt. If you lose them, you will never come to Christ, and never be saved.

A third reason why sinners do not come to Christ is, that the heart rises against him.

Many are brought, in some measure, to a sense of their sinful and lost condition, who yet cannot be persuaded to come to Jesus Christ. It is not anything in Christ that prevents them - it is something that rises up in their own heart. Christ is quite open - he is a door which no man can shut; and they would fain be at rest in him, and yet their proud heart rises up against him.

There may be two reasons for this:

(1) *Perhaps your anxiety has set you upon establishing your own righteousness; and, therefore, you are too proud to come to Jesus Christ.* This was the way with the Jews. They were not only ignorant of God's righteousness, but they went about to establish their own righteousness; and, therefore, they would not submit to the righteousness of God. Perhaps you thought, when you were first awakened, that you would soon find your way to peace. You thought, by tears, and prayers, and amendment of your life, to blot out past sin. You have been making a false Christ to yourself, and that is the reason you do not like the true Christ, and Christ says of you: 'Ye will not come to me, that ye might have life.' To come to Christ, you would need to forsake your own righteousness, to confess that your wisdom is folly, to lie down empty and vile and without praise, and to consent that Jesus Christ shall have all the praise. But your proud, self-flattering heart rises against this; and thus you perish: 'Ye will not come to me, that ye might have life.'

(2) Another way in which anxious souls keep away from Christ is this: 'You have been shaken off from all dependence on your own repentance, or prayers, or amendment, to make you righteous in the sight of God. You have laid you down in the dust, and confessed that, if ever you are to be justified, it must be through the obedience and

sufferings of the Son of God. Now, you have lain so long thus emptied, that you think Jesus Christ should have been revealed to you by this time. *In a word, you have been humbling yourself to make yourself worthy of Jesus Christ.* Alas! this is a still prouder thought than the one before. You are not seeking to buy forgiveness from God by your humblings and by your tears, but you are seeking to buy Christ from God by these humblings. You think that your humblings and tears deserve Christ; so that you have been attempting to buy that which buys forgiveness. This is a deep snare of the devil, which hinders many anxious souls from coming to Jesus Christ without money and without price.

There is reason to think that many souls perish in this way. They fulfil this sad word of Christ: 'Ye will not come to me, that ye might have life.' I would leave two directions with anxious souls.

(1) *You must be made willing to come to Jesus Christ, if you would be saved.* You cannot be saved against your will. Some people have hopes that they shall be lifted into Christ against their will. This is impossible. Noah was not lifted into the ark, but God said: 'Come in.' So Christ's people are a willing people. They come willingly - with all their heart and soul. Not only do they flee willingly from wrath, but they flee willingly to Jesus Christ - they choose to be saved by him rather than by any other way. If there were ten thousand other saviours, they would still choose Christ; for he is the chiefest among ten thousand, and they feel it sweetest and best to be nothing and have nothing, that Christ may be all in all.

(2) *God only can bend your will to come to Jesus Christ:* 'No man can call Jesus Lord, but by the Holy Ghost' - 'No man can come to me, except the Father which hath sent me draw him.' It is God that must beat down all your guilt and nakedness. He must make you feel the emptiness and sin of all your self-righteousness. He must reveal the beauty of Christ unto you - his comeliness - his desirableness. He must convince you that it is sweetest to have no praise, and to let Jesus have the whole. Oh! seek the teaching of God. The teaching of man is a mere dream, if you have not the teaching of God. Cry night and day for the inward teaching of the Spirit: 'Every man, therefore, that hath heard and hath learned of the Father, cometh unto me'; and, 'Him that cometh unto me I will in no wise cast out.'

3. The sinfulness of not coming to Jesus Christ.

The words of Jesus are full of pathos - enough to break the proudest heart: 'Ye will not come to me, that ye might have life.'

The greatness of the Saviour shows the sinfulness of not coming to him.
He is the eternal Son of God whom sinners are despising. John bore witness of him, his miracles bore witness to him, his Father bore witness of him, the Scriptures, on every page, testify of him; yet ye will not come to him, that ye might have life. It is the Son of God that hath undertaken the doing and dying of all in the stead of sinners; and yet you, a trembling sinner, will not honour him so much as to trust your soul upon his finished work. Ah! how shall we escape, if we neglect so great a salvation?

The loveliness of the Saviour shows the sin of not coming to him.
Methinks there is a touch of heaven's melody in these words: 'Ye will not come to me.' I know not whether they more express the high indignation of an insulted Saviour, or the tender compassion of him that wept upon the Mount of Olives, over Jerusalem. It is as if he said: I have left the bosom of the Father, to suffer, and bleed, and die for sinners, even the chief. Yet, O sinner! ye will not come unto me. I have sought the lost sheep over mountain and hill. I have stretched out my hands all the day to the gainsaying and disobedient. I have cried after sinners, and wept over sinners. And yet ye will not come to me, that ye might have life. Ah! dear brethren, if sin against love be the blackest sin under the blue vault of heaven, this is your sin because ye trample under foot the blood of the Son of God, and do despite unto the gentle Spirit of grace.

The very anxiety of some sinners increases their sin.
Some sinners are very anxious about their souls, yet will not come to Jesus Christ. They are in search of a saviour, but they will not have Jesus Christ. Are there not some of you who would do anything else to be saved: 'Will the Lord be pleased with thousands of rams, or with tens of thousands of rivers of oil? Shall I give my firstborn for my transgression, the fruit of my body for the sin of my soul?' If we would bid you pray and weep, you would do that; if we would bid you fast and use the shirt of hair, you would do that; if we would bid you afflict your soul and body, and make pilgrimage to the Holy Land, you would do that; if we would bid you live as monks and nuns, you would do that,

as thousands are doing this day; but when we say, Come to Christ, ah! you will not do that. Ah! proud, sinful, self-ruining heart, you would choose any balm but the Balm of Gilead - any saviour but the Son of God.

Oh! that these words of the sweet Saviour, whom you thus despise, would pierce to the very bottom of your soul: 'Ye will not come to me, that ye might have life.'

St Peter's, July 30, 1837.

43. Thirsting sinners called

In the last day, that great day of the feast, Jesus stood and cried, saying, If any man thirst, let him come unto me, and drink (John 7:37).

1. Christ's gracious importunity: 'In the last day, that great day of the feast, Jesus stood and cried.'

The feast here being spoken of was the great feast of tabernacles, being one of the three yearly festivals when all the males came up from the country to Jerusalem. They used to build tents, or tabernacles, of the branches of palm trees, olive, myrtle, and willows, on the flat roofs of their houses, in their courts, or in the open streets and gardens. In these they lived for seven days. The priests and Levites used to teach and preach to the people, and it was a time of great joy before the Lord. The eighth, or last day, was a holy convocation, when all the people met in the house of God before going away to their homes. On that day it was that Jesus stood and cried.

Observe, it was when the whole people of the land were met together that Jesus stood and cried: 'If any man thirst, let him come unto me, and drink.'

Jesus never thought his words thrown away, even if there were but a single soul to hear. Never did he use words of more divine power than when he spoke with Nicodemus alone by night, and with the woman of Samaria by the well; but still, when thousands came together, Jesus would not miss the happy opportunity: 'Jesus stood and cried.' O my friends! Jesus still stands in the crowded assembly. May you hear his voice this day!

Observe, the people were going home.

This was the last day of the feast. Today the courts of the temple are thronged with Jews from all parts of the country; tomorrow they will be on their way home. No time must be lost; speak now or never: 'Jesus stood and cried.' I doubt not there were many a Jew there that day who never heard the voice of the Saviour again; and therefore I can see what was in the mind of Christ when he lifted up his voice so loud: 'Jesus stood and cried.' There may be some here today who never will hear the word of Christ again. This may be the last day of the feast to some of you. Oh! then, that we might stand and cry - lift up the voice like a trumpet, and say: 'If any man thirst, let him come unto me, and drink'; and O that you would hear as for eternity!

Observe, Christ had often preached to them before, yet he 'stood and cried'.

From verse 14 we learn that it was about the middle of the feast (the middle of the week) that Jesus began to teach in the temple; and no doubt he continued preaching and teaching till the last day of the feast. Some marvelled, some murmured, some sought to lay hands on him. And was his patience not wearied out? Ah! no; who knows the long-suffering of the Son of God? How justly he might have gone away for ever, and said: 'If ye will not have me for a Saviour, then I will not be a Saviour unto you. I will go my way to him that sent me.' But no; the more careless the Jews became, the more anxious was he. On the last day he stood and cried: 'If any man thirst, let him come unto me and drink.'

Jesus is the same still. Many of you have heard his words for a thousand Sabbath days. He has stretched out his hands all the day - he has sent his messengers, rising up early and sending them. You have been always unmoved, living in sin; and now worse than you were when you heard the first of them. Does Jesus give you up? No; he stands and cries on the last day - he follows up to your dying day.

Some of you are afraid that Jesus will not receive you now, for you have so long resisted his words. Ah! it would be quite just if he were to say: 'I will not hear - I will laugh at your calamity - I will mock when your fear cometh.' But no; be not afraid. On the last day of the feast he stands and cries. He speaks more loudly, more clearly, more freely than ever. Oh! listen to his words: 'If any man thirst, let him come unto me, and drink.'

2. Christ is the smitten rock.

The feast of tabernacles was intended to be a picture of the time when the fathers of the Jewish nation lived in tents in the wilderness. It was intended to remind them that they too were strangers and pilgrims in the wilderness, and that they were journeying to a better land. But there was one thing in the wilderness which they had no resemblance of in the feast of tabernacles - the smitten rock which gave out rivers of water. In order to make up for this deficiency, it is said that on the last day of the feast the Jews used to draw water in a golden pitcher from the Fountain of Siloam, and pour it out upon the morning sacrifice, as it lay upon the altar. They did this with great rejoicing, having palm branches in their hands, and singing the twelfth chapter of Isaiah. Now it was on this very day, perhaps at that very time, that Jesus stood up in the midst of them, and, as if he wished to show them that he was the true smitten rock, cried: 'If any man thirst, let him come unto me, and drink.'

Christ is the smitten rock, because his blood has been poured out for sin.

(1) The rock was smitten before it gave out the stream. So is it with Christ. He was smitten of God and afflicted. He bore the wrath of God; and therefore his blood gushed forth, and cleanses from all sin. Oh! you that fear to be smitten of God, wash in this blood - it flowed from a smitten rock.

(2) The water gushed forth abundantly when Moses smote the rock. It was no scanty stream - it was enough for all the thousands of Israel. So is it with the blood of the Saviour. It is no scanty stream. There are no sins it cannot wash out, there is no sinner beyond its reach, there is enough here for all the thousands of Israel.

(3) It was a constant supply: 'They drank of the spiritual rock which followed them, and that rock was Christ.' We are not expressly told in the Old Testament that the waters of the smitten rock did actually follow the camp of Israel, but some learned divines are of the opinion that it was so - that the water continued to flow wherever Israel went; so that it might be said the smitten rock followed them. So is it with Christ. He is a rock that follows us. He is like rivers of water in a dry place. You may wash, and wash again.

3. All are invited to come to Christ and drink: 'If any man thirst, let him come unto me, and drink.'

Careless sinners are here invited to come to Christ and drink.
Men in their natural condition are quite careless about their souls and about Jesus Christ. They thirst after pleasure, they thirst after money, and they thirst after the world; but they do not thirst after Christ or heavenly things. Yet Christ wishes us to cry aloud in the hearing of such: 'If any man thirst, let him come unto me, and drink.' Let me speak to such. You have no anxiety of soul, no desires after Jesus Christ, no wish to receive his Holy Spirit. You are not thirsty for anything beyond the waters of this world. You are quite happy where you are, and as you are. Yet the day may come when you shall be a weary, thirsty soul. O that it may come soon! Now Jesus says: 'If ever you feel thirsty, remember, come unto me, and drink.' 'How long, ye simple ones, will ye love simplicity? and ye scorners delight in scorning, and fools hate knowledge? Turn ye at my reproof: behold, I will pour out my Spirit unto you; I will make known my words unto you.'

Anxious, thirsty souls, are especially invited to come unto Jesus:
'If any man thirst, let him come unto me, and drink.' Souls awakened by God are thirsty in two ways.

(1) They thirst after *the forgiveness of sins* - they have been awakened to know their lost condition - the weight of God's anger has been revealed to them. They go from mountain to hill seeking a resting-place, and finding none. At last they sit down, weary and thirsty. They feel that all they do just signifies nothing - that they cannot bring themselves nearer to peace. They feel as if already in that place where they shall ask in vain for a drop of water to cool the tongue. Do any of you know what this condition is? Then you are here spoken to by Christ.

(2) They thirst after *deliverance from sin*. Awakened persons generally put away all outward sin. When a drunkard or swearer is awakened, he puts away his outward sin; but he is far from being able to change his heart. On the contrary, most wicked and hateful thoughts sometimes rise into the soul. The heart is filled with such vile desires that the soul is almost driven to distraction. He goes from mountain to hill seeking a new heart, but finding none. He sits down, at last weary and thirsty. Do any of you feel this? It is to you Christ speaks: 'If any man thirst, let him come unto me, and drink.'

O thirsty souls - afflicted, tempest-tossed, and not comforted - why will ye not come unto Jesus, the smitten rock, to drink? One says: I have sinned too much - I dare not come as I am. But are you not thirsty? Christ says: 'If any man thirst, let him come unto me, and drink.' Another says: I have sinned against Christ, I have turned a deaf ear to his warning voice, I have mocked at his messengers, I have profaned his sacraments - eaten bread and wine when I was living in sin; and surely I dare not come. But are you not thirsty? Hear what Christ says: 'If any man thirst.' Another says: But I am unwilling to come to Christ, I have a proud, unbelieving heart, my heart rises against coming to Jesus Christ, surely I dare not look to Jesus. But are you not thirsty? Christ does not ask the willing or the believing, but the thirsty. He asks no more: 'If any man thirst, let him come unto me, and drink.'

Thirsty believers are here bid to come to Jesus.
Among the crowd on that great day of the feast, we are told that there were many who believed on Jesus (verse 31); and it was for their sakes also that he spake these blessed words: 'If any man thirst.' All true believers are a thirsty people. They are travelling in a wilderness, and therefore they need the rock to follow them. Oh! it is a bad sign of a soul when there is no thirst. True Christians are like new-born babes - they desire the sincere milk of the Word. They need nourishment, and need it often. They cannot live without it. Oh, then, hear the word of Jesus: 'Come unto me, and drink.'

(1) *Remember you must come to Christ before you can drink.* It is only when you have a believing view of the Saviour that you can receive the Spirit. It is only when your eye is fixed on the smitten rock that you can drink of the living water. Are there not some Christians hearing me who seem to receive very little of the Spirit of God? Are there not some Christians among you who often exhibit a mean worldly spirit? Some who are easily betrayed into a fiery, passionate spirit? Why is this? You do not come to Jesus to drink. You do not keep the eye of faith on Jesus Christ. You do not live by faith on the Son of God. You are thinking to walk holily without coming unto Jesus day by day, and hour by hour. You do not look on the Lord our strength at God's right hand; therefore you receive little of the Holy Ghost.

(2) *Remember when you come to Jesus you must drink.* O how many seem to come to Jesus Christ, and yet do not drink! How few Christians are like a tree planted by the rivers of water! What would you have

thought of the Jews, if, when Moses smote the rock, they had refused to drink? Or what would you have thought if they had only put the water to their lips? Yet such is the way with most Christians. It pleased the Father that in him should all fullness dwell. The Spirit was given to him without measure. The command is given to us to draw out of his fullness; yet who obeys? Not one in a thousand.

A Christian in our day is like a man who has got a great reservoir brimful of water. He is at liberty to drink as much as he pleases, for he never can drink it dry; but instead of drinking the full stream that flows from it, he dams it up, and is content to drink the few drops that trickle through. O that ye would draw out of his fullness, ye that have come to Christ! Do not be misers of grace. There is far more than you will use in eternity. The same waters are now in Christ that refreshed Paul, that gave Peter his boldness, that gave John his affectionate tenderness. Why is your soul less richly supplied than theirs? Because you will not drink: 'If any man thirst, let him come unto me, and drink.'

4. The change on all who drink - they become fountains like Christ: 'He that believeth on me, as the Scripture hath said, out of his belly shall flow rivers of living water' (John 7:38).

The Holy Spirit is an imperishable stream. It is not like those rivers of which you have heard, which flow through barren sands till they sink into the earth and disappear. Not so the stream of grace. When it flows from Jesus Christ, it flows into many a barren heart; but it is never lost there. It appears again - it flows forth from that heart in rivers of living water. When a soul is brought to believe on Jesus, and to drink in the Spirit, it often appears as if the Spirit were lost in that soul. The stream flows into such a barren heart, that it is long before it makes its appearance; but it is never lost. The Scripture must be fulfilled: 'He that believeth on me, out of his belly shall flow rivers of living water.'

A new motive for coming to Jesus.
If you will come to Jesus and drink, you shall become a fountain - you shall be changed into the image of Christ. Are there none of you living in a godless family? O come to Jesus and drink! You will become a fountain of grace to your family. Through your heart, through your words, through your prayers, the stream of grace will flow into other hearts. Those you love best in all the world may in this way receive grace. O come unto Jesus and drink! Many of you live in a godless

neighbourhood - come to Jesus and drink, and you will become a fountain of grace to your neighbourhood. From you shall flow rivers of living water. O if all of you that know the Lord Jesus would only drink out of his fullness, even this neglected place might become as the garden of the Lord, well watered everywhere!

New test if you have come to Jesus.
If you have believed on Jesus, then you have received the Spirit, and from you there must be flowing rivers of living water. Is this the case? Alas! how many of you must answer, No; we know not what you mean.

(a) Are there not some hearing me whose heart is more like a sink of iniquity than a fountain of living water? Are there not some who send forth from their heart rivers that pollute and poison every place where they go? Are there not some who send forth streams of horrid imaginations and impure desires? Are there not some who send forth polluting conversation - foolish, lascivious talking and jesting, which are not convenient? Ah! how plain you have never been brought to Jesus! The river of grace has never been turned into that foul bosom.

(b) Are there not some who are like a fountain sealed? They seem to come to Jesus, but they do not give out any living stream. I stand in doubt of you. Every one that believes on the Lord Jesus must receive the Spirit. Every one that receives the Spirit will make it manifest by sending forth rivers of living water. Be not deceived, my dear friends. He that doeth righteousness is righteous. If you are living a dead, useless life, you are no Christian.

'Examine yourselves, whether ye be in the faith. Prove your own selves. Know ye not your own selves, how that Jesus Christ is in you, except ye be reprobates?'
St Peter's, October 22, 1837

44. Conviction of sin

> And when he (the Comforter) is come, he will convince the world
> of sin, and of righteousness, and of judgment (John 16:8).

When friends are about to part from one another, they are far kinder than ever they have been before. It was so with Jesus. He was going to part from his disciples, and never till now did his heart flow out toward them in so many streams of heavenly tenderness. Sorrow had filled their heart, and therefore divinest compassion filled his heart. 'I tell you the truth, it is expedient for you that I go away.'

Surely it was expedient for himself that he should go away. He had lived a life of weariness and painfulness, not having where to lay his head, and surely it was pleasant in his eyes that he was about to enter into his rest. He had lived in obscurity and poverty - he gave his back to the smiters, and his cheeks to them that plucked off the hair. Now, surely, he might well look forward with joy to his return to that glory which he had with the Father before ever the world was, when all the angels of God worshipped him. And yet he does not say: It is expedient for me that I go away. Surely that would have been comfort enough to his disciples. But no; he says: 'It is expedient for you.' He forgets himself altogether, and thinks only of his little flock which he was leaving behind him: 'It is expedient for you that I go away.' O most generous of Saviours! He looked not on his own things, but on the things of others also. He knew that it is far more blessed to give than it is to receive.

The gift of the Spirit is the great argument by which he here persuades them that his going away would be expedient for them. Now, it is curious to remark that he had promised them the Spirit before, in the beginning of his discourse. In chapter 14:16-18, he says: 'I will pray the Father, and he shall give you another Comforter, that he may abide with you for ever; even the Spirit of truth; whom the world cannot receive, because it seeth him not, neither knoweth him: but ye know him; for he dwelleth with you, and shall be in you. I will not leave you comfortless: I will come to you.' And again: 'But the Comforter, which is the Holy Ghost, whom the Father will send in my name, he shall teach you all things, and bring all things to your remembrance, whatsoever I have said unto you' (verse 26).

In that passage he promises the Spirit for their own peculiar comfort and joy. He promises him as a treasure which they, and they only, could receive: 'For the world cannot receive him, because it neither sees nor knows him'; and yet, saith he, 'he dwelleth with you, and shall be in you.'

But in the passage before us the promise is quite different. He promises the Spirit here, not for themselves, but for the world - not as a peculiar treasure, to be locked up in their own bosoms, which they might brood over with a selfish joy, but as a blessed power to work, through their preaching, on the wicked world around them - not as a well springing up within their own bosoms unto everlasting life, but as rivers of living water flowing through them to water this dry and perishing world. He does not say: When he is come, he will fill your hearts with peace and joy to overflowing; but: 'When he is come, he will convince the world of sin, and of righteousness, and of judgment.'

But a little before he had told them that the world would hate and persecute them: 'If ye were of the world, the world would love his own; but because ye are not of the world, but I have chosen you out of the world, therefore the world hateth you (John 15:19). This was but poor comfort, when that very world was to be the field of their labours; but now he shows them what a blessed gift the Spirit would be; for he would work through their preaching, upon the very hearts that hated and persecuted them: 'He shall convince the world of sin.'

This has always been the case. In Acts 2 we are told that when the Spirit came on the apostles the crowd mocked them, saying: 'These men are full of new wine'; and yet, when Peter preached, the Spirit wrought through his preaching on the hearts of these very scoffers. They were pricked in their hearts, and cried: 'Men and brethren, what must we do?' And the same day three thousand souls were converted. Again, the jailer at Philippi was evidently a hard, cruel man towards the apostles; for he thrust them into the inner prison, and made their feet fast in the stocks; and yet the Spirit opens his hard heart, and he is brought to Christ by the very apostles whom he hated.

Just so is it, brethren, to this day. The world do not love the true ministers of Christ a whit better than they did. The world is the same world it was in Christ's day. That word has never yet been scored out of the Bible: 'Whosoever will live godly in the world, must suffer persecution.' We expect, as Paul did, to be hated by the most who listen to us. We are quite sure, as Paul was, that the more abundantly we love you, most of you will love us the less; and yet, brethren, none of these things move us. Though cast down, we are not in despair; for we know that the Spirit is sent to convince the world; and we do not fear but some of you who are counting us an enemy, because we tell you the truth, may even this day, in the midst of all your hatred and cold indifference, be convinced of sin by the Spirit, and made to cry out: 'Sirs, what must I do to be saved?'

1. The first work of the Spirit is to convince of sin.

Who it is that convinces of sin: 'He shall convince the world of sin, because they believe not in me.'

It is curious to remark, that wherever the Holy Ghost is spoken of in the Bible, he is spoken of in terms of gentleness and love. We often read of the wrath of God the Father, as in Romans 1: 'The wrath of God is revealed from heaven against all ungodliness and unrighteousness of men.' And we often read of the wrath of God the Son: 'Kiss the Son, lest he be angry, and ye perish from the way'; or, 'Revealed from heaven taking vengeance.' But we nowhere read of the wrath of God the Holy Ghost.

He is compared to a dove, the gentlest of all creatures. He is warm and gentle as the breath: 'Jesus breathed on them, and said, Receive ye the Holy Ghost.' He is gentle as the falling dew: 'I will be as the dew unto Israel.' He is soft and gentle as oil; for he is called, 'The oil of gladness.' The fine oil wherewith the high priest was anointed was a type of the Spirit. He is gentle and refreshing as the springing well: 'The water that I shall give him shall be in him a well of water springing up unto everlasting life.' He is called 'The Spirit of grace and of supplications.'

He is nowhere called the Spirit of wrath. He is called the 'Holy Ghost, which is the Comforter.' Nowhere is he called the Avenger. We are told that he groans within the heart of a believer, 'helping his infirmities'; so that he greatly helps the believer in prayer. We are told also of the love of the Spirit - nowhere of the wrath of the Spirit. We are told of his being grieved: 'Grieve not the Holy Spirit'; of his being resisted: 'Ye do always resist the Holy Ghost'; of his being quenched: 'Quench not the Spirit.' But these are all marks of gentleness and love.

Nowhere will you find one mark of anger or of vengeance attributed to him; and yet, brethren, when this blessed Spirit begins his work of love, mark how he begins - he convinces of sin. Even he, all-wise, almighty, all-gentle and loving though he be, cannot persuade a poor sinful heart to embrace the Saviour, without first opening up his wounds and convincing him that he is lost.

Now, brethren, I ask of you, should not the faithful minister of Christ just do the very same? Ah! brethren, if the Spirit, whose very breath is all gentleness and love - whom Jesus hath sent into the world to bring men to eternal life - if he begins his work in every soul that is to be saved by convincing of sin, why should you blame the minister of Christ if he begins in the very same way? Why should you say that we are harsh, and cruel, and severe, when we begin to deal with your souls by convincing you of sin? 'Am I become your enemy, because I tell you the truth?'

When the surgeon comes to cure a corrupted wound, when he tears off the vile bandages which unskilful hands had wrapped around it, when he lays open the deepest recesses of your wound, and show you all its venom and its virulence, do you call him cruel? May not his hands be all the time the hands of gentleness and love? Or, when a house is all on fire, when the flames are bursting out from every window, when some courageous man ventures to alarm the sleeping inmates bursts through the barred door, tears aside the close-drawn curtains, and with eager hand shakes the sleeper and bids him awake and flee - a moment longer, and he may be lost - do you call him cruel or do you say this messenger of mercy spoke too loud, too plain? Ah, no. 'Skin for skin, all that a man hath will he give for his life.'

Why, then, brethren, will you blame the minister of Christ when he begins by convincing you of sin? Think you that the wound of sin is less venomous or deadly than a wound in the flesh? Think you the flames of hell are less hard to bear than the flames of earth? The very Spirit of love begins by convincing you of sin; and are we less the messengers of love because we begin by doing the same thing? Oh, then, do not say that we are become your enemy because we tell you the truth?

2. What is this conviction of sin? I would begin to show this by showing you what it is not.

It is not the mere smiting of the natural conscience.
Although man be utterly fallen, yet God has left natural conscience behind in every heart, to speak for him. Some men, by continual sinning, sear even the conscience as with a hot iron, so that it becomes dead and past feeling; but most men have so much natural conscience remaining, that they cannot commit open sin without their conscience smiting them. When a man commits murder or theft, no eye may have seen him, and yet conscience makes a coward of him. He trembles and is afraid -

he feels that he has sinned, and he fears that God will take vengeance. Now, brethren, that is not the conviction of sin here spoken of - that is a natural work which takes place in every heart; but conviction of sin is a supernatural work of the Spirit of God. If you have had nothing more than the ordinary smiting of conscience, then you have never been convinced of sin.

It is not any impression upon the imagination.
Sometimes, when men have committed great sin, they have awful impressions of God's vengeance made upon their imaginations. In the night-time they almost fancy they see the flames of hell burning beneath them; or they seem to hear doleful cries in their ears telling of coming woe; or they fancy they see the face of Jesus all clouded with anger; or they have terrible dreams, when they sleep, of coming vengeance. Now, this is not the conviction of sin which the Spirit gives. This is altogether a natural work upon the natural faculties, and not at all a supernatural work of the Spirit. If you have had nothing more than these imaginary terrors, you have had no work of the Spirit.

It is not a mere head knowledge of what the Bible says against sin.
Many unconverted men read their Bibles, and have a clear knowledge that their case is laid down there. They are sensible men. They know very well that they are in sin, and they know just as well that the wages of sin is death. One man lives a swearer, and he reads the words, and understands them perfectly: 'Swear not at all' - 'The Lord will not hold him guiltless that taketh his name in vain.' Another man lives in the lusts of the flesh, and he reads the Bible, and understands these words perfectly: 'No unclean person hath any inheritance in the kingdom of Christ and of God.' Another man lives in habitual forgetfulness of God - never thinks of God from sunrise to sunset, and yet he reads: 'The wicked shall be turned into hell, and all the people that forget God.' Now, in this way most unconverted men have a head knowledge of their sin, and of the wages of sin; yet, brethren, this is far from conviction of sin. This is a mere natural work in the head. Conviction of sin is a work of God upon the heart. If you have had nothing more than this head knowledge that you are sinners, then you have never been convinced of sin.

Conviction of sin is not to feel the loathsomeness of sin.
This is what a child of God feels. A child of God has seen the beauty and excellency of God, and therefore sin is loathsome in his eyes. But no unconverted person has seen the beauty and excellency of God; therefore, even the Spirit cannot make him feel the loathsomeness of sin. Just as when you leave a room that is brilliantly lighted, and go out into the darkness of the open air, the night looks very dark; so when a child of God has been within the veil - in the presence of his reconciled God - in full view of the Father of lights, dwelling in light inaccessible and full of glory, then when he turns his eye inwards upon his own sinful bosom, sin appears very dark, very vile, and very loathsome. But an unconverted soul never has been in the presence of the reconciled God; and therefore sin cannot appear dark and loathsome in his eyes. Just as when you have tasted something very sweet and pleasant, when you come to taste other things, they appear very insipid and disagreeable; so when a child of God has tasted and seen that God is gracious, the taste of sin in his own heart becomes very nauseous and loathsome to him. But an unconverted soul never tasted the sweetness of God's love; he cannot, therefore, feel the vileness and loathsomeness of sin. This, then, is not the conviction of sin here spoken of.

What, then, is this conviction of sin? It is a just sense of the dreadfulness of sin.

It is not a mere knowledge that we have many sins, and that God's anger is revealed against them all; but it is a heart-feeling that we are under sin.

Again: it is not a feeling of the loathsomeness of sin - that is felt only by the children of God; but it is a feeling of the dreadfulness of sin - of the dishonour it does to God, and of the wrath to which it exposes the soul. Oh, brethren! conviction of sin is no slight natural work upon the heart. There is a great difference between knowing a thing and having a just sense of it. There is a great difference between knowing that vinegar is sour, and actually tasting and feeling that it is sour. There is a great difference between knowing that fire will burn us, and actually feeling the pain of being burned. Just in the same way, there is all the difference in the world between knowing the dreadfulness of your sins and feeling the dreadfulness of your sins. It is all in vain that you read your Bibles and hear us preach, unless the Spirit use the words to give sense and feeling to your dead hearts. The plainest words will not awaken you as long as you are in a natural condition. If we could prove to you, with the plainness of arithmetic, that the wrath of God is abiding on you and your children, still you would sit unmoved - you would go away and forget it before you reached your own door. Ah, brethren! he that made your heart can alone impress your heart. It is the Spirit that convinceth of sin.

Learn the true power of the read and preached Word. It is but an instrument in the hand of God. It has no power of itself, except to produce natural impressions. It is a hammer - but God must break your hearts with it. It is a fire - but God must kindle up your bosoms with it. Without him we may give you a knowledge of the dreadfulness of your condition, but he only can give you a just sense and feeling of the dreadfulness of your condition. The most powerful sermon in the world can make nothing more than a natural impression; but when God works through it, the feeblest word makes a supernatural impression. Many a poor sermon has been the means by which God hath converted a soul. Children of God, O that you would pray night and day for the lifting up of the arm of God!

Learn that conversion is not in your own power. It is the Spirit alone who convinces of sin, and he is a free agent. He is a sovereign Spirit, and has nowhere promised to work at the bidding of unconverted men. He hath many on whom he will have mercy; and whom he will he hardeneth. Perhaps you think you may take your fill of sin just now, and then come and repent, and be saved; but remember the Spirit is not at your bidding. He is not your servant. Many hope to be converted on their death-bed, and they come to their death-bed, and yet are not converted. If the Spirit be working with you now, do not grieve him - do not resist him - do not quench him; for he may never come back to you again.

3. I come to the argument which the Spirit uses. There are two arguments by which the Spirit usually gives men a sense of the dreadfulness of sin.

(1) *The Law:* 'The law is our schoolmaster to bring us to Christ.' 'Now we know that what things soever the law saith, it saith to them that are under the law, that every mouth may be stopped, and all the world become guilty before God.' The sinner reads the law of the great God who made heaven and earth. The Spirit of God arouses his conscience to see that the law condemns every part of his life. The law bids him love God. His heart tells him he never loved God - never had a thought of

regard toward God. The Spirit convinces him that God is a jealous God
- that his honour is concerned to uphold the law, and destroy the sinner.
The Spirit convinces him that God is a just God - that he can by no means
clear the guilty. The Spirit convinces him that he is a true God - that he
must fulfil all his threatenings: 'Have I said it, and shall I not do it?' The
sinner's mouth is stopped, and he stands guilty before God.

(2) The second argument is *the Gospel*: 'Because they believe not on
Jesus.' This is the strongest of all arguments, and therefore is chosen by
Christ here. The sinner reads in the Word that 'he that believeth on the
Son hath everlasting life'; and now the Spirit convinces him that he
never believed on the Son of God. Indeed, he does not know what it means.
For the first time the conviction comes upon his heart: 'He that believeth
not the Son shall not see life; but the wrath of God abideth on him.'

The more glorious and divine that Saviour is, the more is the
Christless soul convinced that he is lost; for he feels that he is out of that
Saviour. He sees plainly that Christ is an almighty ark riding over the
deluge of God's wrath - he sees how safe and happy the little company
are that are gathered within. But this just makes him gnash his teeth in
agony, for he is not within the ark, and the waves and billows are coming
over him. He hears that Christ hath been stretching out the hands all the
day to the chief of sinners, not willing that any should perish; but then he
never cast himself into these arms, and now he feels that Christ may be
laughing at his calamity, and mocking when his fear cometh. O yes, my
friends! how often on the death-bed, when the natural fears of conscience
are aided by the Spirit of God; how often, when we speak of Christ - his
love, his atoning blood, the refuge to be found in him, how safe and happy
all are that are in him; how often does the dying sinner turn it all away with
the awful question: *But am I in Christ?* The more we tell of the Saviour,
the more is their agony increased; for they feel that that is the Saviour
they have refused. Ah! what a meaning does that give to these words:
'The Spirit convinceth of sin, because they believe not on me.'

*Now, my friends, there are many of you who know that you never
believed on Jesus, and yet you are quite unmoved.* You sit without any
emotion - you eat your meals with appetite, and doubtless sleep sound
at night. Do you wish to know the reason? You have never been
convinced of sin. The Spirit hath never begun his work in your heart.
Oh! if the Spirit of Jesus would come on your hearts like a mighty
rushing wind, what a dreadful thought it would be to you this night, that

you are lying out of Christ! You would lose your appetite for this world's food - you would not be able to rest in your bed - you would not dare to live on in your sins. All your past sins would rise behind you like apparitions of evil. Wherever you went you would meet the word: 'Without Christ, without hope, and without God in the world'; and if your worldly friends should try to hush your fears, and tell you of your decencies, and that you were not so bad as your neighbours, and that many might fear if you feared, ah! how you would thrust them away, and stop your ears, and cry: There is a city of refuge, to which I have never fled; therefore there must be a blood-avenger. There is an ark; therefore there must be a coming deluge. There is a Christ; therefore there must be a hell for the Christless.

Some of you may be under conviction of sin - you feel the dreadfulness of being out of Christ, and you are very miserable. Now,

(1) Be thankful for this work of the Spirit: 'Flesh and blood hath not revealed it unto thee, but my Father.' God hath brought you into the wilderness just that he might allure you, and speak to your heart about Christ. This is the way he begins the work in every soul he saves. Nobody ever came to Christ but they were first convinced of sin. All that are now in heaven began this way. Be thankful you are not dead like those around you.

(2) Do not lose these convictions. Remember they are easily lost. Involve yourself over head and ears in business, and work even on the Sabbath-day, and you will soon drive all away. Indulge a little in sensual pleasure - take a little diversion with companions, and you will soon be as happy and careless as they. If you love your soul, flee these things - do not stay - flee away from them. Read the books that keep up your anxiety - wait on the ministers that keep up that anxiety. Above all, cry to the Spirit, who alone was the author of it, that he would keep it up. Cry night and day that he may never let you rest out of Christ. Oh! would you sleep over hell?

(3) Do not rest in these convictions. You are not saved yet. Many have come thus far and perished after all - many have been convinced, not converted - many lose their convictions, and wallow in sin again. 'Remember Lot's wife.' You are never safe till you are within the fold. Christ is the door. 'Strive to enter in at the strait gate; for many shall seek to enter in and shall not be able.'

Dundee, February 4, 1837

45. Conviction of righteousness [1]

And when he (the Comforter) is come, he will convince the world
of sin, and of righteousness, and of judgment (John 16:8).

In my last discourse from this passage we saw that the first work of the
Spirit on the heart of a sinner is to convince of sin - to give him a sense
of the dreadfulness of his sins, and to make him feel how surely he is a
lost sinner. And from that I drew an argument, that it is the duty of all
faithful ministers to do the same; that if the Spirit of gentleness and love
begins his work on the soul by awakening in it a deep sense of sin and
coming wrath, we are not to be called cruel, or harsh, or too plain and
outspoken, if we begin in the very same way - by convincing you of sin,
and showing every unconverted soul among you how utterly undone
you are.

But I now come to the second work of the Spirit, from which he is
properly called the Comforter: 'He will convince the world of righteousness.' When he has first *broken the bones* under a sense of sin, then
he reveals the good Physician, and makes the very bones which he hath
broken to rejoice. When he has first revealed the coming storm of wrath,
so that the sinner knows not where to flee, then he opens the secret
chamber, and whispers: Come in hither; it may be thou shalt be hid in
the day of the Lord's anger. When he has cast light into the sinner's
bosom, and let him see how every action of his life condemns him, and
how vain it is to seek for any righteousness there, he then casts light
upon the risen Saviour, and says: Look there. He shows the Saviour's
finished sufferings and finished obedience and says: All this is thine, if
thou wilt believe on Jesus. Thus does the Spirit lead the soul to accept
and close with Christ, freely offered in the gospel. The first was the
awakening work of the Spirit - this is the comforting work of the Spirit.
And this shows you plainly that the second work of the faithful minister
is to do the very same - to lead weary souls to Christ; to stand pointing
not only to the coming deluge, but to the freely offered ark; pointing not
only to the threatening storm, but to the strong tower of safety; directing
the sinner's eye not only inwards to his sin and misery, but outwards
also, to the bleeding, dying, rising, reigning Saviour.

---

1. This sermon is the second discourse on the text, delivered the following week to the previous
sermon (number 44).

Brethren, he is no minister of Christ who only terrifies and awakens you - who only aims at the first work of the Spirit, to convince you of sin, and aims not at the second work of the Spirit, to convince you of righteousness. He would be like a *surgeon* who should tear off the bandages of your wounds, and lay open their deepest recesses, and then leave you like Israel with your sores not closed, neither bound up, neither mollified with ointment. He would be like a man who should awake you when your house was all on fire, and yet leave you without showing you any way of escape.

Brethren, let us rather be taught to follow in the footsteps of the blessed Spirit, the Comforter. He first convinces of sin, and then convinces of righteousness. And so brethren, bear with us, when we first awaken you to a sense of the dreadfulness of your sins, and then open the refuge, and say: Come in hither - 'hide thee as it were for a little moment, till the indignation be overpast.'

I know there may be many of you quite offended because we preach Christ to the vilest of sinners. It was so with the Pharisees; and doubtless there are many Pharisees among us. When we enter into the haunts of wickedness and profligacy, and, in accents of tenderness, proclaim the simple message of redeeming love - that the wrath of God is abiding on sinners, but that Christ is a Saviour freely offered to them, just as they are; or when a child of sin and misery comes before us, and the minister of Christ first plainly tells of God's wrath against his sin, and then as plainly, and with all affection, of Christ's compassion, and freely offered righteousness - oh! how often the decent moral men of the world are affronted. The very imagination that the same Saviour is offered as freely to the veriest offscourings of vice as to themselves - this is more than they can bear. What! they cry; do you offer these wretches a Saviour before they have reformed their lives - before they have changed their character? I answer, Yes. The whole need not a physician, but they that are sick: and I beseech you to mark that this is the very way of the Spirit of God.

He is the Holy Spirit - of purer eyes than to behold iniquity. He is the Sanctifier of all that are in Jesus; and yet, when he has convinced a sinner of sin, his next work is to speak peace - to convince that sinner of righteousness. If you ask me, then, why I do not say to the child of sin and shame, Go and reform yourself, become honest and pure, and then I will invite you to the Saviour? I answer, Because even the Spirit, the Holy Spirit, the Sanctifier, does not do this. He first leads the soul into the wilderness, and then he allures it to come to Christ. He first shuts up the soul in prison under a sense of guilt, and then opens a door - reveals Christ an open refuge for the chief of sinners.

Brethren, do not forget it - he is the Comforter before he is the Sanctifier. Ah, then, do not blame us, if, as messengers of Christ, we tread in the very footsteps of that blessed Spirit. If even he, the Holy Sanctifying Spirit, whose very breath is all purity - if even he invite the vilest sinner to put on these beautiful garments, the divine righteousness of Jesus - do not say that we are favouring sin, that we are the enemies of morality, if we carry this message to the vilest of sinners: 'Believe on the Lord Jesus, and thou shalt be saved.'

1. What is this righteousness?
I answer, it is the righteousness of Christ, wrought out in behalf of sinners. Now righteousness means righteousness with respect to the law. When a person has never broken the law, but has rendered complete obedience to it, that person is righteous. Righteousness consists of two parts - first, freedom from guilt; and second, worthiness in the sight of God.

In the case of an unfallen angel, for example, he may be called righteous in two ways.
Firstly, he is *negatively righteous*, because he has never broken the law of God. He has never loved anything which God would not have him love, never done anything which God would not have him do. He has acquired no stain of guilt upon his snow-white garments.

But, secondly, he is *positively righteous*, because he has fulfilled the law of God. He has obeyed in all things his all-holy will. He has spread his ready wings on every errand which the Father commanded, ministering night and day to the heirs of salvation. In all things he has made it his meat and drink to do the will of his heavenly Father. So, then, he has not only kept his snowy garments clean, but he has gained the laurel wreath of obedience. He is worthy in the sight of God. God smiles on him as he approaches. Now, brethren, both of these put together make up a righteousness in the sight of God.

In the case of unfallen Adam.
Firstly, he was *negatively righteous*. He was made free from all guilt. Innocent and pure he came from the hands of his Maker. Not more truly

did the calm rivers of Paradise reflect the blue heaven from their untroubled bosom, than died the tranquil bosom of unfallen Adam reflect the blessed image of God. His soul was spotless as the white robes of angels. His thoughts were all directed heavenward. He had not once broken the law of God in thought, word or deed. His will was even with God's will. He had no conscience of sin.

But, secondly, Adam *did not acquire a positive righteousness*; that is, the righteousness of one who has obeyed the Law - who has done the will of God. He was put into Paradise in order to acquire that righteousness. He was put there in pure and holy garments, to acquire the laurel wreath of obedience - like the holy angels. But man fell without acquiring this meritorious righteousness in the sight of God. Now, brethren, both these put together - both freedom from guilt and perfect obedience - make up a perfect righteousness in the sight of God.

I come, then, to show that the righteousness of Christ, freely offered to sinners, includes both of these.
There is freedom from guilt in Christ, because he is gone to the Father. When he came to this world, he was not free from guilt. He had no sin of his own. Even in his mother's womb he was called 'That holy thing'; but yet he did not breathe one moment in this world, but under the load of guilt. When he was an infant in the manger, he was under guilt; when he was a man of sorrows and acquainted with grief, he was under guilt; when he sat down wearied at the well, he was under guilt; when he was in that dreadful agony in the garden, when his sweat was as it were great drops of blood, he was under guilt; when he was in his last agony on the cross, he was under guilt. He had no sin of his own, and yet these are his words: 'Innumerable evils have compassed me about; mine iniquities have taken hold upon me, so that I am not able to look up; they are more than the hairs of mine head; therefore my heart faileth me.'

How do you know that Christ was under guilt?

(1) *Because he was under pain.* He suffered the pains of infancy in the manger - he suffered weariness, and hunger, and thirst, and great agonies in the garden and on the cross. But God has eternally connected guilt and pain. If there were no guilt, there could be no pain.

(2) *Because God hid his face from him*: 'My God, my God.' Now, God hides his face from nothing but guilt; therefore Christ was bearing the sins of many. He was all over with guilt. He was as guilty in the sight of God as if he had committed all the sins of his people. What wonder,

then, that God hid his face even from his own Son?

But Christ is now free from guilt. He is risen and gone to the Father. When a man is lying under a debt - if he pays it, then he is free from the debt. So Christ was lying under our sins, but he suffered all the punishment, and now is free; he rose, and we see him no more. When a man is banished for so many years, it is unlawful for him to return to his country till the time has expired, and the punishment is borne; but when the time is expired, then he is free from guilt in the eye of the law. He may come back to his home and his country once more. So Christ was banished from the bosom of the Father for a time. God hid his face from him; but when he had borne all that God saw fit to lay on him, then he was free from guilt - he was free to return; and so he did - he rose, and went back to the bosom of the Father, from which he came.

Do you not see, then, trembling sinner, that there is freedom from all guilt in Christ? He is quite free - he never shall suffer any more. He is now without sin, and when he comes again, he is coming without sin. If you will become one with him, you, too, are free from guilt - you are as free as Christ is - you are as safe from being punished as if you were in heaven with Christ. If you believe on Christ, you are one with him - a member of his body; and as sure as Christ your Head is now passed from the darkness of God's anger into the light of his countenance, so surely are you, O believer, passed from darkness into God's marvellous light. O what a blessed word was that of Christ, just before he ascended: 'I go to my Father and your Father, to my God and your God!' God is now as much ours as he is Christ's.

What good is it to me that Christ is free from guilt?

Christ is offered to you as your Saviour. There is perfect obedience in Christ, because he hath gone to the Father, and we see him no more. When he came to this world, he came not only to suffer, but to do - not only to be a dying Saviour, but also a doing Saviour - not only to suffer the curse which the first Adam had brought upon the world, but to render the obedience which the first Adam had left undone. From the cradle to the cross he obeyed the will of God from the heart. When he came into the world, his word was: 'Lo! I come; in the volume of the book it is written of me, I delight to do thy will, O God; yea, thy law is within my heart.' When he was in the midst of his obedience, still he did not change his mind. He says: 'I have meat to eat that ye know not of: my meat is to do the will of him that sent me, and to finish his work.' And when he was going out of the world, still his word was: 'I have finished the work which thou gavest me to do.' So that it is true what the apostle says, that he was 'obedient even unto death.' The whole law is summed up in these two commands - That we love God and our neighbour. Christ did both.

(1) *He loved God perfectly*, as God says in the 91st Psalm: 'Because he hath set his love upon me, therefore will I deliver him; I will set him on high.'

(2) *He loved his neighbour as himself.* It was out of love to men that he came into the world at all; and everything he did and everything he suffered in the world was out of love to his neighbour. It was out of love to men that he performed the greatest part of his obedience, namely, the laying down his life. This was the principal errand upon which he came into the world. This was the most dreadful and difficult command which God laid upon him; and yet he obeyed.

But a short while before he was betrayed, God gave him an awful view of his coming wrath. In the garden of Gethsemane, he set down the cup before him, and showed that it was the cup without any mixture of mercy in it; and yet Christ obeyed: his human nature shrunk back from it, and he prayed: 'If it be possible, let this cup pass from me'; but he did not waver one moment from complete obedience, for he adds: 'Nevertheless, not as I will, but as thou wilt.'

Now this is the obedience of Christ, and we know that it is perfect. Firstly, because he was the Son of God, and all that he did must be perfect. Secondly, because he has gone to the Father. He is ascended into the presence of God. And how did the Father receive him? We are told in the 110th Psalm. A door is opened in heaven, and we are suffered to hear the very words with which God receives his Son: 'The Lord said unto my Lord, Sit thou on my right hand, till I make thine enemies thy footstool.'

So, then, God did not send him back, as one who had not obeyed perfectly enough. God did not forbid him his presence, as one unworthy to be accepted; but God highly exalted him - looked upon him as worthy of much honour - worthy of a seat on the throne at his right hand. Oh! how plain that Christ is accepted with the Father! How plain that his righteousness is most lovely and all divine in the sight of God the Father!

Hearken, then, trembling sinner! This righteousness is offered to you. It was wrought just for sinners like you, and for none else; it is for no other use but just to cover naked sinners. This is the clothing of wrought gold, and the raiment of needlework. This is the wedding-garment, the fine linen, white and clean. Oh! put ye on the Lord Jesus. Why should ye refuse your own mercies? Become one with Christ, by believing, and you are not only pardoned, as I showed before, but you are righteous in the sight of God; not only shall you never be cast into hell, but you shall surely be carried into heaven - as surely as Christ is now there.

Become one with Christ, and even this moment you are lovely in the sight of God - comely, through his comeliness put upon you. You are as much accepted in the sight of God as is the Son of Man, the Beloved that sits on his right hand. The Spirit shall be given you, as surely as he is given to Christ. He is given to Christ as the oil of gladness, wherewith he is anointed above his fellows. You are as sure to wear a crown of glory, as that Christ is now wearing his. You are as sure to sit upon Christ's throne, as that Christ is now sitting on his Father's throne. O weep for joy, happy believer! O sing for gladness of heart: 'For I am persuaded that neither death, nor life, nor angels, nor principalities, nor powers, nor things present, nor things to come, nor height, nor depth, nor any other creature, shall be able to separate us from the love of God, which is in Christ Jesus our Lord.'

2. What is conviction of righteousness?
Show what it is not.

It is not any impression on the imagination.
Just as men have often imaginary terrors, so men have also imaginary views of Christ, and of the glory of being in Christ. Sometimes they think they see Christ with the bodily eye; or sometimes they think they hear words borne in upon their mind, telling of the beauty of Christ. Now this is not conviction of righteousness. Indeed, such things may accompany true conversion. There is no impossibility in it. Stephen and Paul both saw Christ, and most of you remember a very singular example of something similar in more modern times. But, however this may be, one thing is certain, that conviction of righteousness is very different from this. It is a far higher and nobler thing - given only by the Spirit of God. Blessed are they who have not seen, and yet have believed.

It is not a revelation of any new truths not contained in the Bible.
When the Spirit revealed Christ to the apostles and prophets of old, he

revealed new truths concerning Christ. But when he convinces a sinner of the righteousness of Christ, he does it by opening up the truths contained in the Bible. If he revealed new truths, then we might put away the Bible, and sit alone, waiting for the Spirit to come down on us. But this is contrary to the Bible and experience. David prays: 'Open thou mine eyes, that I may see wonders.' Where? Not in heaven above nor earth beneath, but, 'out of thy law.' It is through the truth that the Spirit always works in our hearts: 'Sanctify them through thy truth; thy Word is truth.' Therefore, when you look for conviction of righteousness, you are not to look for new truths not in the Bible, but for divine light cast upon old truths already in the Bible.

It is not mere head knowledge of what the Bible says of Christ and his righteousness.
Most unconverted men read their Bibles, and many of them understand very wonderfully the doctrine of imputed righteousness; yet these have no conviction of righteousness. All awakened souls read their Bibles very anxiously, with much prayer and weeping; and many of them seem to understand very clearly the truth that Christ is an all-sufficient righteousness; yet they tell us they cannot close with Christ, they cannot apply him to their own case. Again: the devils believe and tremble. The devil has plainly much knowledge of the Bible; and from the quotations he made to Christ, it is plain that he understood much of the work of redemption; and yet he is none the better for it - he only trembles and gnashes his teeth the more. Ah, my friends! If you have no more than head knowledge of Christ and his righteousness, you have no more than devils have. You have never been convinced of righteousness.

What is it?
It is a sense of the preciousness and fitness of Christ, as he is revealed in the gospel.

(1) I have said it is *a sense of the preciousness of Christ*, that you may see plainly that it is no imaginary feeling of Christ's beauty; that it is no seeing of Christ with the bodily eyes; that it is no mere knowledge of Christ and of his righteousness in the head - *but a feeling of his preciousness in the heart.*

I before showed you that there is all the difference in the world between knowing a thing and feeling a thing - between having a knowledge of a thing, and having a sense of it. There is all the difference in the world between knowing that honey is sweet, and tasting that it is sweet, so as to have a sense of its sweetness. There is a great difference between knowing that a person is beautiful, and actually seeing, so as to have a present sense of the beauty of the person. There is a great difference between knowing that a glove will fit the hand, and putting it on, so as to have a sense of its fitness. Just so, brethren, there is all the difference in the world between having a head knowledge of Christ and of his righteousness, and having a heart feeling of his fitness and preciousness. The first may be acquired from flesh and blood, or from books; the second must come from the Spirit of God.

(2) Again, it is *a sense of the fitness of Christ.* It is conceivable that a person may have a sense of Christ's preciousness, without having a sense of his fitness. Some awakened souls appear to feel that Christ is very precious; and yet they dare not put on Christ; they seem to want a sense of his fitness to their case. They cry out: 'O how precious a Saviour he is to all his people! O that I were one of his people! O that I were hidden in his bleeding side!' And yet they have no sense of his fitness to be their Saviour; they do not cry out: 'He just fits my case! He is the very Saviour for me!' For, if they felt this, they would be at peace, their lips would overflow with joy. But no; they dare not appropriate Christ. Now, then, conviction of righteousness is to have such a sense of Christ as leads us, without hesitation, to put on Christ; and that I have called a sense of fitness.

It gives me no comfort to know that Christ is a precious Saviour to others, unless I know that he is a precious Saviour to me. If the deluge is coming on, the windows of heaven opening, and the fountains of the great deep broken up, it gives me no peace to know that there is an ark for others, unless you tell me that it is an ark for me. You may tell me of Christ's righteousness for ever, and of the safety of all that are in him; but if you would comfort me by the news, you must convince me that the righteousness answers me, and is offered to me. Now, this is what the Spirit does when he convinces of righteousness. This, and this only, is conviction of righteousness.

O brethren! it is no slight work of nature to persuade a soul, even an anxious soul, to put on Christ. If it were a natural work, then natural means might do it; but it is a supernatural work, and the hand of the Spirit must do it. Flesh and blood cannot reveal Christ unto you, but my Father which is in heaven. No man can call Jesus Lord, but by the Holy Ghost.

Let me speak a word to three classes.

To the unawakened.

See how far you are from salvation. Many of you may be saying just now in your heart: 'It is quite true I am not at present a saved person; but I am not very far from the kingdom of God. I have just to repent and believe on Jesus, and then I am saved. And since this is so short and simple a matter, I may do it any time. I may enjoy the world and its pleasures a little longer; and then, when death or disease threatens me, it may be good time to become anxious.' Now, all this argument proceeds upon a falsehood. You think you are not far off from salvation; but, ah! my friend, you are as far from salvation as any one can be that is in the land of the living. There is only one case in which you could be farther from salvation, and that is - in hell. You are as far from salvation as any one that is out of hell.

In my last discourse, I showed you that there must be a divine work upon your heart before you can repent. You may have much head knowledge of sin without the Spirit, but he only can convince you of sin. That Spirit is a sovereign Spirit. He is given to the children of God as often as they ask him; but he is not at the bidding of unconverted men. You cannot bid him come when you fall sick, or when you are going to die; or if you should bid him, he has nowhere promised to obey.

And now, I wish you to see that there is a second divine work needful on your heart before you can believe. *The Spirit must convince you of Christ's righteousness.* Flesh and blood cannot reveal Christ unto you, but my Father which is in heaven. God is a sovereign God. He hath mercy upon whom he will have mercy. He is not at the bidding of unconverted men. He has nowhere promised to bring to Christ all whom he awakens. Oh! how plain that you are as far from salvation as any soul can be that is out of hell. And can you be easy when you are at such a distance from salvation? Can you go now, and sit down to a game of chance - to while away the time between this and judgment? Can you go and laugh and be merry in your sins? How truly, then, did Solomon say: 'The laughter of fools is like the crackling of thorns under a pot' - a loud noise for a moment, then everlasting silence - a short blaze, and a dark eternity.

To the awakened.

Remember, unless you attain to conviction of righteousness, your conviction of sin will be all in vain. Remember anxiety for the soul does not save the soul. Sailors in a shipwreck are very anxious. They cry much to God in prayer and tears; and yet, though they are anxious men, they are not saved men - the vessel goes to pieces, and all are drowned. Travellers in a wilderness may be very anxious - their hearts may die within them; yet that does not show that they are safe - they may perish in the burning sands. So you are much afraid of the wrath of God, and it may be God has, in mercy, stirred up these anxieties in your bosom; but you are not yet saved. Unless you come to Christ all will be in vain. Many are convinced who are never converted. Many are now in hell who were once as anxious to escape as you.

Remember, God only can give you this conviction. The Spirit convinces of righteousness. It is not flesh and blood that can give you a sense of the preciousness of Christ. It is true, the Bible and preaching are the means through which God works this conviction. He always works through the truth - never without the truth. If you be truly awakened, I know how anxiously you will wait on these means - how you will search the Scriptures with tears, and lose no opportunity of hearing the preached Word. But still, the Bible and preaching are only means of themselves - they can only make natural impressions on your mind. God only can make supernatural impressions. Cry, then, to God.

But remember, God is a sovereign God. Do not cry to him to convert you, as if it were a debt he owed you. There is only one thing you can claim from God as a right, and that is a place in hell. If you think you have any claim on God, you are deceiving yourself. You are not yet convinced of sin. Lie at the feet of God as a sovereign God - a God who owes you nothing but punishment. Lie at his feet as the God who alone can reveal Christ unto you. Cry night and day that he would reveal Christ unto you - that he would shine into your darkness, and give you the light of the knowledge of the glory of God in the face of Christ. One glimpse of that face will give you peace. It may be you shall be hid in the day of the Lord's anger.

To those of you who have come to Christ.
Oh, what miracles of grace you are! Twice over you are saved by grace. When you were loathsome in your sins, and yet asleep, the Spirit awakened you. Thousands were sleeping beside you. He left thousands to perish, but awakened you.

Again, though awakened, you were as loathsome as ever: you were as vile in the sight of God as ever, only you dreaded hell. In some respects you were more wicked than the unawakened world around you.

They would not come to Christ, because they felt no need. But you felt your need, yet would not come. You made God a liar more than they, yet God had mercy on you. He led you to Christ - convinced you of righteousness. So you are twice over saved by grace. 'O to grace how great a debtor!' 'What shall I render to the Lord for all his benefits?' Will you not love him with all your heart? Will you not serve him with all you have? And when he says: Feed this poor orphan for my sake, will you not say: Lord, when I give for thee, it is more blessed to give than to receive?
Dundee, February 11, 1837

46. The unbelieving believer

And after eight days again his disciples were within, and Thomas with them: then came Jesus, the doors being shut, and stood in the midst, and said, Peace be unto you. Then saith he to Thomas, Reach hither thy finger, and behold my hands, and reach hither thy hand and thrust it into my side: and be not faithless, but believing. And Thomas answered and said unto him, My Lord, and my God (John 20:26-28).

1. When believers meet together, Jesus stands in the midst and says: 'Peace be unto you.'
It was on the evening of the day on which Jesus rose from the dead that the disciples were assembled together. He had appeared unto Mary Magdalene, and unto Peter, and unto two of the disciples on the way to Emmaus; and now they were met together to meditate, to wonder, to pray over these things, when Jesus stood in the midst, and said: 'Peace be unto you.' 'Then were the disciples glad when they saw the Lord.'

It was upon the same evening, a week after, that the disciples met again; and Jesus again revealed himself to them saying: 'Peace be unto you.' This was a fulfilment of the promise which he made long before: 'Where two or three are gathered together in my name, there am I in the midst of them.' And again he said: 'Lo, I am with you alway, even unto the end of the world.' This promise has always been, and always will be, fulfilled. Jesus still loves the assembly of his saints. If you could look into the private history of Christians, you would find that most of them have been awakened in the house of God - that they were first brought to a soul-refreshing view of Christ there - that they have been comforted there, and have received most of their heavenly joys there. Ah! it is where disciples meet that Jesus comes in and says: 'Peace be unto you.'

David says: 'My feet were almost gone; my steps had well-nigh slipped; for I was envious at the foolish, when I saw the prosperity of the wicked, until I went into the sanctuary, then understood I their end.' All his difficulties were solved, and he was enabled to say: 'God is the strength of my heart, and my portion for ever.'

So Thomas had spent a most uncomfortable week. These words, 'I will not believe', always bring pain and sorrow after them. His mind was full of misgivings and racking doubts; but he came to the meeting of the disciples, and there Jesus revealed himself to him, and he was filled with amazement and joy.

I trust this may be the experience of some this Sabbath-day. Perhaps some have spent a week of trouble instead of peace - a week of doubting when others have been rejoicing. Some of you, when others were glad, said, 'I will not believe.' Learn from Thomas not to forsake the assembling of yourselves together. Doubting, drooping, trembling souls, may Christ reveal himself to you, saying, 'Peace be unto you.'

When the doors were shut, Jesus stood in the midst, and said: 'Peace be unto you.'

When doors are shut through fear of persecution, Jesus reveals himself to the soul.

So it was with the disciples. They had shut the doors of their upper chamber for fear of the Jews. They were reproached and vilified as those who had been with Christ; nay, there was some fear that they would be made to share the same death; so they shut the doors of the place where they met. But that was the very time Jesus chose to come in. When the world was threatening them, saying, Torments and death be unto them, Jesus said, 'Peace be unto you.' So is it now. The world is just as bitter against Christians now as ever it was. Some of you who joined yourselves to the Lord last Sabbath-day may have found out by this time that the world hates you. The servant is not greater than his Lord. Some of you may have become partakers of the afflictions of the gospel, and are feeling this day that the offence of the cross has not ceased. Worldly friends may upbraid, may persecute, may reproach you. But never mind. When the doors are shut for fear, Jesus comes in, and says: 'Peace be unto you.' Remember, when you are bolting persecution out, you are not bolting Jesus out. He can come through all these bars. When the world says, Plagues be upon you, Christ says, 'Peace be unto you.' And herein is a wonder, that Christ's voice, though it be a still small voice, is yet far louder than the world. It calmed the waves of the Sea of Galilee, and, oh! it will speak peace to your soul. When the waves of persecution roar against you, he says: 'Fear not; it is I. Peace be unto you.'

When a soul is quite shut up, Jesus comes in, and says: 'Peace be unto you.'
The reason why some awakened persons are long of coming to peace, and some never come to peace at all, is that they think to find an open door for themselves. They feel shut up, by the fears of wrath hemming them in on every side, but still they hope to find some way of their own by which to escape. They are not altogether shut up. They have not been brought to despair of ever saving themselves. They have not been brought to feel and say: I never can do anything to save myself. It is impossible such persons can be brought to peace as long as every door is not shut. If God were to give them peace, they would praise themselves, and say: We did it.

Are there any such hearing me? Look here. It was when the doors were shut that Jesus came in; and so is it with the soul. It is when the mouth is stopped, and you stand lost and guilty before God - when you have no door of your own - Jesus comes in, and says: 'I am the door; peace be unto you.'

When doors of worldly comfort are shut Christ comes in, and says: 'Peace be unto you.'
So it was with the disciples. They were like a family of orphans deprived of their head. They were like a nest of unfledged birds, from whom the murderous hand had carried off the mother, beneath whose sheltering wing they used to find repose. They had left all to follow Christ - they had come to trust under his almighty wing - and now he had left them all but desolate. They shut their doors upon the cold bleak world, to show that no comfort was to be expected from the world. That was the very time when Jesus came in with the sweetest power to fulfil his word, 'I will not leave you orphans; I will come to you' by saying, 'Peace be unto you.'

So is it now. When worldly comforts abound, then the consolations of Christ do little abound. It is not when the world is full of smiles and kindness that a true believer has the sweetest visits of the Saviour. It is rather when the believer is left like an orphan - when comforts are withdrawn, when friends die or prove untrue, when the bleak world looks chillingly, and he shuts the door, saying: 'Miserable comforters are ye all' - it is then that Jesus comes in, and says, 'Peace be unto you.' The brightest gleams of sunshine are those that come through the darkest clouds; so the sweetest visits of the Saviour are when the doors of worldly comfort are shut. Are you a believer? You will have troubles; but, oh! you will have Christ with them all.

2. How kind Christ is to wayward believers!

Thomas was a most unbelieving believer, and yet Christ followed him with kindness. If the other disciples were foolish, and slow of heart to believe all that the prophets had spoken, much more was Thomas.

(a) He should *have believed the prophets*. It was written in the 16th Psalm: 'Thou wilt not leave my soul in hell, neither wilt thou suffer thine Holy One to see corruption.' He knew this to be the word of God. Thomas should have believed the witness of God.

(b) Thomas should *have believed the simple word of Christ*. Three times Christ had solemnly taken his disciples into a lonely place, and told them he must be crucified, and that he would rise again on the third day. Thomas should have believed the witness of Christ.

(c) Thomas should *have believed the words of Mary and Peter, and of the two disciples that went to Emmaus, and of all the other disciples, who told him: 'We have seen the Lord.'* But, oh! he was foolish, and slow of heart to believe all that was spoken concerning Jesus, for he said: 'Except I shall see in his hands the print of the nails, and put my finger into the print of the nails, and thrust my hand into his side, I will not believe.' He doubts the word of God - he doubts the word of Christ - he doubts the word of his brethren. Nothing but seeing and feeling will satisfy him.

Surely Christ will cast off this proud, wayward, unbelieving soul. He does not deserve any more testimony. Ah! what foolish words do I speak; he never deserved any testimony at all. But O what grace there is in Christ! How he comes over mountains of provocation toward wayward believers! He actually comes in, and offers Thomas the very evidence he asked: 'Reach hither thy finger, and behold my hands, and reach hither thy hand, and thrust it into my side; and be not faithless, but believing.' Such is the love of Christ to wayward believers. Christ may have dealt in the very same way with some of you.

To awakened souls, who yet say: 'I will not believe.'
Some of you have been awakened by God, and made anxious about your souls. You feel the guilt of a broken law, you feel the curse of a rejected gospel hanging over you. We point you to Christ, and say: 'Behold the Lamb of God that taketh away the sins of the world.' But you say you cannot, you dare not, you will not believe. You cannot believe that God has such divine compassion in his bosom to provide a ransom for one so vile as you! You cannot believe that Christ has got so strange a love that he should be willing to be the surety of such an enemy as you! Your word is just this: 'Except I see, I will not believe.' Ah! you are just Thomas over again. You are foolish, and slow of heart to believe all that has been spoken concerning Jesus.

You have rejected the testimony of God. 'You search the Scriptures, and these are they which testify of me'; yet 'ye will not come unto me, that ye might have life.' All the prophets have borne witness to you concerning Jesus, setting him forth before you as a silent, suffering Lamb - as one making atonement for sins. In the Psalms you have been led to cry: 'See, God, our shield; look upon the face of thine Anointed.' But O you have refused all this. You have still said: Christ is not for me; I will not believe.

You have rejected the witness of Christ. Christ himself has borne witness to you. He has told you that if you are weary and heavy laden, you should come to him, and find rest - that if you are thirsty, you should come to him and drink. He is the faithful and true witness, and he says: 'If it were not so, I would have told you'; and yet you have refused all this. You have still said: Christ is not for me; 'except I see, I will not believe.'

You have rejected the testimony of believers. Christian friends have borne witness to you. They have said: 'We have seen the Lord.' Christians have told you that they were in the same case as you. They had the same sins and the same heart. They had the same fears, and the same darkness; but Christ came in when the doors were shut, and said: 'Peace be unto you.' We have no better right to Christ than you. We take him because we are lost sinners, and he is the Saviour of the lost. He is as free to you as to us. But, ah! you have despised all this evidence, you still say: Christ is not for me; 'except I see, I will not believe.'

Now, it would be quite just for Christ to say: I will seek you no more. It would be quite just for Christ to leave you in your darkness - in your unbelief. But as he dealt with Thomas, so hath he dealt with you. He has tried one way more with you. Last Sabbath-day he broke bread, and poured out wine, and made a picture of his silent wounds - of his dying love; and he said: 'Reach hither thy finger: be not faithless, but believing!' O the compassion of Christ - it passeth all knowledge!

Believers, did you come to the table of Christ full of unbelief - unable to realise Christ - unable to lay hold on him? And did he reveal himself to you in the broken bread, and poured-out wine? Ah! this is the same mercy he gave to Thomas. You, of all persons in the world, should feel that Christ is a long-suffering Saviour.

Awakened souls, did you keep back from the table of Christ because you dared not say that Christ was yours? But did you look on and see Christ evidently set forth crucified? Did you see how the bread was broken - a picture of his body? Did you see the wine poured out - a picture of his blood? Ah! did your heart not burn within you when you looked around - saw, as it were, the silent, suffering Lamb of God? This is the word of Christ unto you: 'Be not faithless, but believing.' The very fact that your eyes have been permitted to see another sacrament shows plainly that Christ is seeking you - stretching out the hands to you - offering himself to you. 'Be not faithless, but believing.'

3. Thomas' appropriating faith: 'Thomas saith unto him, My Lord, and my God.'

When Thomas came to the meeting of disciples that evening, I doubt not his heart was very desolate. Unbelief and unhappiness always go together. An unbelieving believer is of all men most miserable. His brethren around him were full of joy, for they had seen the Lord. Mary still remembered the blessed tone of his voice when he said: 'Mary!' and she answered, 'Rabboni?' Peter was wondering over his amazing love when he said: 'Go tell the disciples, and Peter.' And the bosom of John was filled with a silent feeling of unutterable love. All were glad but one. That one was Thomas. But now, when Christ came in, when he revealed himself a crucified but risen Redeemer, when he showed his special kindness to Thomas, the heart of Thomas could stand out no longer, and he cried out, in words of appropriating faith, before all: 'My Lord, and my God.'

Learn two things:

(1) *To appropriate Christ - to call him your own.* It will not save you to know that Christ is a Saviour. The devils know that, and tremble. It would not have saved you from the flood to know that there was an ark. You must be in it, if you would be saved. So it will not save you that you

know there is a great and glorious Saviour, if you do not call him your own: 'My Lord and my God.'

Objection: It would be too bold in me to call him mine.

Answer: He offers himself to you. He stretched out his hands to you when you were gainsaying and disobedient. He has awakened you - followed you till now. Ah! it is daring presumption to refuse him. Take with you words and say: 'My Lord, and my God.' Is there any presumption in taking Christ at his word?

(2) *To confess him before all*. Thomas had denied Christ before all, saying: 'I will not believe'; and therefore it was right he should confess Christ before all, saying: 'My Lord, and my God.' Ah! are there none of you who have denied Christ before all? Some of you have said: I will not believe, I have kept away from the table of Christ because I dare not call Christ my own. Some of you have denied him in your life, proclaiming to all who know you that you despise the Son of God. Remember, then, I beseech you, the sight of last Sabbath-day. Remember that Christ has again offered himself to you, and is this day seeking you. Come, then, and let your acceptance of Christ be as open as your denial of him. Go home, tell your friends, tell your companions, he is 'my Lord, and my God.'

Dundee, November 4, 1837

47. Christ present, yet unknown

Have I been so long time with you, and yet hast thou not known me Philip?
(John 14:9).

Christ had been with his disciples night and day during the three years of his ministry. They had seen him in all situations - walking on the sea, feeding the multitudes, raising the dead. They had heard all his words in the synagogues, in the temple, in the fields. He had fed them with milk, and not with strong meat - giving them instruction just as they were able to bear it. And yet it is amazing how blind they were to his glory and greatness. They were foolish, and slow of heart to believe all that the prophets had spoken concerning him, and all that he had spoken concerning himself. This was the last night that Jesus was to be with his disciples, and his heart was full of a tenderness which is not of the world. But the more full and tender his holy heart became, the more dull and stupid did his disciples become. 'Philip saith unto him, Lord, show us the Father, and it sufficeth us. Jesus saith unto him, Have I been so long time with you, and yet hast thou not known me, Philip?'

Two things give this reply a peculiar tenderness. Firstly, he reminds Philip that he had been with him. He was equal with the Father - was in the bosom of God, and yet had come and dwelt with them. He had left the company of the worshipping angels to company with them - the King of glory dwelt with worms! Had he smiled on them from heaven, that would have been wonderful; but he says: 'I have been with you - with you by the way-side and by the well, with you on the sea and in the wilderness. I have been your elder brother - and yet have you not known me?' Secondly, that he had been long with them: 'So long time.' Had it been for a moment that the Son of God had visited the earth, O it would have been wonderful! But it was for years. Three years he had gone in and out with them to pray, led them like an elder brother all that time, willing to explain everything to them. O, then, what tenderness there is in this word: 'Have I been so long?'

Doctrine: When Christ has been long with any soul, he expects that soul to know him.

1. Let us speak of Christians.

Christ has been with believers.
He says to every child of God: 'I have been with you.'

(1) *In conversion.* It is the revealing of Christ to the soul which brings it to peace. When Christ revealed himself to Saul, then he fell to the ground, and cried: 'Lord, what wilt thou have me to do?' So it is still. Christ is with the soul in conversion. Are you converted? Then you have been with Jesus, and Jesus has been with you.

(2) *In the wilderness.* The soul leans on the Beloved coming up out of the wilderness. If you be believers at all, you know what it is to have the sweet, strengthening presence of the Beloved.

(3) *In affliction.* Christ is peculiarly near in the fire and in the water: 'When thou passest through the waters I will be with thee.' And again: 'I will not leave you orphans; I will come to you.' If you be Christians, you have felt that Christ is with you in the day of adversity. When doors

are shut, Jesus stands in the midst, and says: 'Peace.'

(4) *In prayer.* 'Where two or three are gathered together in my name, there am I in the midst of them.' He is near at our breathing - at our cry - to offer up our prayer with much incense. He never misses the simplest cry of the simplest believer. Christians, you know that Christ is with you in prayer. It is this which gives you boldness at the throne of grace.

Christ has been long time with believers: 'Have I been so long time with you?' he says.

Christ had been only three years with the disciples when he said this. He has been a much longer time with some of you. Look back, dear Christians, on the way by which he has led you. This day is an eminence - stand upon it, and look back. How long time has Christ been with you? Some of you who are up in years were converted in youth - you have had a lifetime with Christ. He has been with you as your surety, as your strength, as your elder brother, as your advocate with his Father. He has been with you thus for many, many years. If some great nobleman were to come and pay you a visit, and be an intimate friend with you, you would think it a great thing. But O how much greater is this! Christ has been with you. Christ knows your name. Christ has often said of you, as of Zaccheus: 'Today I must abide at thy house.'

Some of you may have been but lately brought to the knowledge of Christ. You have but lately opened the door and let him in. Still he hath been long with you. To have Christ with you for a single day is to have him long with you - it is so great an honour, it is so rich a blessing. O there is a day at hand when you will reckon a moment spent with Christ as more than all your life besides! 'A day spent in thy courts is better than a thousand.'

Christ reproves believers for knowing so little of him: 'Hast thou not known me, Philip?' The apostles knew much of Christ, and yet they were slow of heart to believe all. So is it with Christians now. They know much of Christ, yet they are slow of heart to believe all. There are many signs that Christians do not know Christ.

(1) *Little happiness among Christians.* There is very little sense of being pardoned. Some of you, who appear to be Christians, would almost start were I to ask you if you feel the forgiveness of sins. You seem to fear it, as an unlawful question - as if it were a secret not for you to know. Is this the case with you? Ah! how truly Christ may say: 'Have

I been so long time with you, yet hast thou not known me?' Has not Christ been revealed to you as a crucified Saviour - the wrath of God all poured out on him? 'O fools, and slow of heart to believe all that the prophets have spoken!'

(2) *Little communion with God.* When you stand in the sunshine, you feel the warm beams of the sun; so, when you stand in Christ, you should feel the warm beams of his love. There is little of this. Believers are said to be 'a people near to God'. Entering through the rent veil, they draw near to the Father - they dwell in his secret place, and abide under his shadow. There is little, very little of this. How truly may Christ say: 'Have I been so long time with you, and yet hast thou not known me?'

(3) *Little holiness.* If Christians had an eye on a reigning, praying, coming Saviour, O how different persons they would be! What manner of persons ought ye to be in all holy conversation and godliness, seeing ye look for such things?

(a) How much covetousness there is among some of you that seem to be Christians. How much calling your money your own, hugging it all to yourself, to please yourself, to be enjoyed by yourself. And all this when the cause of Christ calls loud for sacrifices!

(b) How much bitterness there is among some of you that seem to be Christians. How much of a proud, unforgiving spirit, keeping up the remembrance of injuries, nursing your wrath!

(c) How much likeness to the world in your feasts and luxuries, in your trifling, yea, sinful amusements; and, above all, in your conversation! Who that hears you speak would know that ever you had been with Jesus, or he with you? Why is all this? Because you know so little of Christ. For all that Christ has been so long with you, yet you know almost nothing of him.

Ah! do not let this year go without resolving to know more of Christ. He is with you still. A little while, and ye shall not see him. A few days, and you may see no more of him. Your days of grace may be nearly ended. Many of you will not see the close of another year. Walk in the light, while ye have the light. Know Christ, and then ye shall be like him.

2. Let us speak of the awakened.

Christ is with awakened souls.
He awakened them. No man is naturally anxious about his soul. It is a work of Christ on the soul. When the lightning has passed through a

wood, as you look upon one tree and another that has been split by its mighty flash, you say: Ah! the lightning has been here. So, when you see a heart split and broken under a sense of its lost condition, you may say: Christ has been here. Are any of you awakened? Christ has been with you. He saw you in your sin and folly. He pitied you, he drew near, he touched your heart, and made you feel yourself lost, in order that you might seek him as a Saviour. Do not doubt Christ has been with you.

He is seeking awakened souls, and therefore is with them. When a shepherd goes into the mountains in search of lost sheep, he seeks peculiarly those which are bleeding and torn, making the valleys resound with their sad bleatings; he bends over the wounded sheep. When a good physician enters the hospital, he hurries to the beds of the most diseased - of those who are piteously groaning under their pains; he bends over such. So does Christ seek bleeding, groaning souls, with a peculiar care. His word is: 'He hath sent me to bind up the broken-hearted; he hath given me the tongue of the learned to speak a word in season to them that are weary.' Are you an awakened soul? Then you may be quite sure Christ is with you - bending over you.

He is often with them a long time.
Some persons continue under convictions of sin for a long time; some for months and years. This year, I doubt not, has seen many souls awakened. Now Christ waits long upon these souls. He stands at the door all the day: 'I have stretched out my hands all the day to a gainsaying and disobedient people'; and then, when night comes, as he still stands and waits: 'My head is filled with dew, and my locks with the drops of the night.' Are there any awakened souls hearing me? Christ has been long with you. The Bible has been his witness; it has been with you night and day. His ministers have told you of Jesus; they have waited and been long-suffering with you. Christ himself has bended over you. Never did a beggar stand at the door of a rich man so long as Christ has stood at your door.

Still many have not known him.
Although Christ be so long with awakened souls, yet many will not know him. It is life eternal to know him. It would heal all their pains if they would only look upon him; but they will not look. Some of you are in this state. It is your sin, and it is your misery. Christ has long stood at your door and knocked. If you had opened, you would have seen a

bleeding Saviour - a surety - a righteousness. You would have looked to him, and been lightened; but you would not open. Christ has stood and cried: 'If any man thirst, let him come to me and drink.' You feel very thirsty, yet you do not come to Christ to drink. Christ has cried: 'Come unto me, all ye that labour and are heavy laden, and I will give you rest.' You are bent down with your burden, yet you will not come to Christ in order to have life. Christ has cried: 'Follow me; he that followeth me shall not walk in darkness.'

You vibrate between him and the world. You cling to the world, even though you are miserable. How long shall it be thus? Have I been so long time with you, and yet hast thou not known me, poor anxious soul? Remember, some have lived anxious, and died anxious. Remember, it will only increase your hell, that Christ was so long with you, and you would not know him. Turn to Christ now. Let not another year begin without knowing Jesus.

3. Let us speak of the unawakened.

Christ is with them.
In one sense, he is not with them. They are without Christ, and without God in the world. In another sense, he is with them: 'I know thy works.'

(1) *He is with them in the house of God.* It is wonderful to me how Christ persuades so many Christless people to come to the house of God; I never could explain it. Crowds followed Jesus; crowds follow him still. What brings you to the house of God? It is the constraining grace of Christ. Here Christ is with you. Christ unlocks his treasure, and says: 'Come, buy, without money and without price.'

(2) *He is with them in providences.* O it is wonderful to see the providences of unawakened souls! Every one of them is from the hand of Christ: 'I stand at the door and knock.' In the year now past, Christ has striven with you in his providence. To some of you he hath come once and again.

(3) *He is with them in their sins.* Christ is present at all their unholy feasts - hears all their unholy jests, is cognizant of all their desires, knows all their engagements: 'I know thy works.' Do you ever think, when you are engaged in some silly game, that Christ is by your side? He sees the smile of satisfaction on your cheek, but he sees also the deluge of wrath that is over your soul. He sees you sporting yourself with your deceivings, sitting on the brink of hell, yet 'pleased with a

rattle, tickled with a straw'. What does he say? He says: 'How long, ye simple ones, will ye love your simplicity?' and again: 'Lord, let it alone this year also.'

He is with them a long time.
There is reason to think that Jesus strives with the soul from its earliest years - that he strives on to the last. Some good men have thought that Christ doth sometimes give over striving, and leaves the soul to be joined to its idols; but perhaps it is more accordant with Scripture to say that Jesus waits all the day. How long a time Christ has pleaded with some of you! This day, another year of striving with you is finished. Think on this. O the long-suffering of Christ!

Yet they do not know him.
Ah! there is reason to think that many of you are as ignorant of Christ as the day I began my ministry among you; yea, as ignorant as the day you were born. If you knew Christ, it would break your heart with a sense of sin; but your heart is whole within you. If you knew Christ, it would drive you to seek an interest in him; but you seek him not. Hark how tenderly the Saviour pleads with you this day: 'Have I been so long time with you?' O it will be one of the greatest miseries of hell, to remember how often Christ was with you in this house of prayer - in your providences - ay, in your sins; and you would not look at him! To remember how often he was set forth a broken Saviour in the sacrament - preached by his servants a free Saviour - how often he bended over you, and wept over you, and ye would have none of him!

O sirs! I fear this year will witness against you in the judgment day! I fear there are many of you who will accuse me in that day, and say: Why did you not speak plainer, louder, oftener? Why did you not knock oftener at our doors, to tell us and our children of Christ, the way to glory? Was it not worth more effort to save us from eternal hell? Ah! dear friends, be wise. Many of you will not see another year come to a close. If there be fifty - O how dreadful! - you may be among that fifty; nay, if there be forty, thirty, twenty, ten, still you may be among the ten. If there be but one, you may be that one. O it will be an awful word in that day: 'I was a long time with you, but you would not know me!' Amen.
Dundee, December 31, 1837

48. Who shall separate us from the love of Christ?

Who shall separate us from the love of Christ? Shall tribulation, or
distress, or persecution, or famine, or nakedness, or peril, or sword?
As it is written, for thy sake we are killed all the day long; we are
accounted as sheep for the slaughter. Nay, in all these things we are
more than conquerors through him that loved us (Romans 8:35-37).

In this passage there are three very remarkable questions:
'*Who shall lay anything to the charge of God's elect?*' (verse 33). Paul
stands forth like a herald, and he looks up to the holy angels, and down
to the accusing devils, and round about on a scowling world, and into
conscience, and he asks, Who can accuse one whom God has chosen,
and Christ has washed? It is God who justifieth. The holy God has
declared believers clean every whit.

'*Who shall condemn?*' (verse 34). Paul looks round all the judges of
the world - all who are skilled in law and equity; he looks upward to the
holy angels, whose superhuman sight pierces deep and far into the
righteous government of God; he looks up to God, the judge of all, who
must do right - whose ways are equal and perfect righteousness - and he
asks, Who shall condemn? It is Christ that died. Christ has paid the
uttermost farthing: so that every judge must cry out, There is now no
condemnation.

'*Who shall separate us from the love of Christ?*' Again, he looks
around all created worlds; he looks at the might of the mightiest
archangel; the satanic power of legions of devils; the rage of a God-
defying world; the united forces of all created things; and, when he sees
sinners folded in the arms of Jesus, he cries, 'Who shall separate us from
the love of Christ?' Not all the forces of ten thousand worlds combined,
for Jesus is greater than all. 'We are more than conquerors though him
that loved us.'

The love of Christ! Paul says: 'The love of Christ passeth knowledge.' It is like the blue sky, into which you may see clearly, but the real
vastness of which you cannot measure. It is like the deep, deep sea, into
whose bosom you can look a little way, but its depths are unfathomable.
It has a breadth without a bound, length without end, height without top,
and depth without bottom. If holy Paul said this, who was so deeply
taught in divine things, who had been in the third heaven and seen the
glorified face of Jesus, how much more may we, poor and weak

believers, look into that love and say: It passeth knowledge!

There are three things in these words, of which I would speak. (1) The love of Christ; (2) The question, Who would separate us from it? (3) The truth, that whoever or whatever they are, they shall not be able.

1. I would speak of the love of Christ.

When did it begin?

In the past eternity: 'Then I was by him as one brought up with him: and I was daily his delight, rejoicing always before him; rejoicing in the habitable part of the earth; and my delights were with the sons of men' (Proverbs 8:30,31). This river of love began to flow before the world was - from everlasting, from the beginning, or ever the earth was. Christ's love to us is as old as the Father's love to the Son. This river of light began to stream from Jesus toward us before the beams poured from the sun - before the rivers flowed to the ocean - before angel loved angel, or man loved man. Before creatures were, Christ loved us. This is a great deep - who can fathom it? This love passeth knowledge.

Who was it that loved?

It was Jesus, the Son of God, the second person of the blessed Godhead. His name is, 'Wonderful, Counsellor, The Mighty God, The Everlasting Father, The Prince of Peace', 'King of kings and Lord of lords', Immanuel, Jesus the Saviour, the only begotten of his Father. His beauty is perfect: he is the brightness of his Father's glory, and the express image of his person. All the purity, majesty and love of Jehovah dwell fully in him. He is the bright and morning Star: he is the Sun of righteousness and the Light of the world: he is the Rose of Sharon and the Lily of the valleys - fairer than the children of men. His riches are infinite: he could say, 'All that the Father hath is mine.' He is Lord of all. All the crowns of heaven were cast at his feet - all angels and seraphs were his servants - all worlds his domain. His doings were infinitely glorious. By him were all things created that are in heaven and that are in earth, visible and invisible. He called the things that are not as though they were - worlds started into being at his word. *Yet he loved us.* It is much to be loved by one greater in rank than ourselves - to be loved by an angel; but, O, to be loved by the Son of God! This is wonderful! It passeth knowledge.

Whom did he love?
He loved us! He came into the world 'to save sinners, of whom I am the chief.' Had he loved one as glorious as himself, we would not have wondered. Had he loved the holy angels, that reflected his pure, bright image, we would not have wondered. Had he loved the lovely among the sons of men - the amiable, the gentle, the kind, the rich, the great, the noble - it would not have been so great a wonder. But, ah! he loved sinners - the vilest sinners - the poorest, meanest, guiltiest wretches that crawl upon the ground. Manasseh, who murdered his own children, was one whom he loved; Zaccheus, the grey-haired swindler, was another; blaspheming Paul was a third; the wanton of Samaria was another; the dying thief was another; and the lascivious Corinthians were more. 'And such were some of you.' We were black as hell when he looked on us - we were hell-worthy, under his Father's wrath and curse - and yet he loved us, and said: I will die for them. 'Thou hast loved me out of the pit of corruption', each saved one can say. Oh, brethren! this is strange love: he that was so great, and lovely, and pure, chose us, who were mean and filthy with sin, that he might wash and purify, and present us to himself. This love passeth knowledge!

What did this love cost him?
When Jacob loved Rachel, he served seven years for her - he bore the summer's heat and winter's cold. But Jesus bore the hot wrath of God, and the winter blast of his Father's anger, for those he loved. Jonathan loved David with more than the love of women, and for his sake he bore the cruel anger of his father, Saul. But Jesus, out of love to us, bore the wrath of his Father poured out without mixture. It was the love of Christ that made him leave the love of his Father, the adoration of angels, and the throne of glory. It was love that made him not despise the Virgin's womb; it was love that brought him to the manger at Bethlehem; it was love that drove him into the wilderness. Love made him a man of sorrows; love made him hungry and thirsty and weary; love made him hasten to Jerusalem; love led him to gloomy, dark Gethsemane; love bound and dragged him to the judgment hall; love nailed him to the cross; love bowed his head beneath the amazing load of his Father's anger. 'Greater love hath no man than this.' 'I am the good Shepherd; the good Shepherd giveth his life for the sheep.'

Sinners were sinking beneath the red-hot flames of hell; he plunged in and swam through the awful surge, and gathered his own into his bosom. The sword of justice was bare and glittering, ready to destroy us; He, the man that was God's fellow, opened his bosom and let the stroke fall on him. We were set up as a mark for God's arrows of vengeance; Jesus came between, and they pierced him through and through - every arrow that should have pierced our souls stuck fast in him. He, his own self, bare our sins in his own body on the tree. As far as east is from the west, so far hath he removed our transgressions from us. This is the love of Christ that passeth knowledge. This is what is set before you today in the broken bread and poured-out wine. This is what we shall see on the throne - a Lamb as it had been slain. This will be the matter of our song through eternity: 'Worthy is the Lamb!'

O the joy of being in the love of Christ! Are you in this amazing love? Has he loved you out of the pit of corruption? Then, he will wash you, and make you a king and a priest unto God. He will wash you in his own blood whiter than the snow - he will cleanse you from all your filthiness and from all your idols. A new heart also will he give you. He will keep your conscience clean, and your heart right with God. He will put his Holy Spirit within you, and make you pray with groanings that cannot be uttered. He will justify you - he will pray for you - he will glorify you. All the world may oppose you - dear friends may die and forsake you - you may be left alone in the wilderness; still you will not be alone - Christ will love you still.

O the misery of being out of the love of Christ! If Christ loves you not, how vain all other loves! Your friends may love you - your neighbours may be kind to you - the world may praise you - ministers may love your souls; but, if Christ love you not, all creature-love will be vain. You will be unwashed, unpardoned, unholy - you will sink into hell, and all the creatures will stand around and be unable to reach out a hand to help you.

How shall I know that I am in the love of Christ? By your being drawn to Christ: 'I have loved thee with an everlasting love, therefore with loving-kindness have I drawn thee.' Have you seen something attractive in Jesus? The world are attracted by beauty, or dress, or glittering jewels - have you been attracted to Christ by his good ointments? This is the mark of all who are graven on Christ's heart - they come to him; they see Jesus to be precious. The easy world see no preciousness in Christ; they prize a lust higher, the smile of the world higher, money higher, pleasure higher; but those whom Christ loves he draws after him by the sight of his preciousness. Have you thus followed him, prized him - as a drowning sinner cleaved to him? Then he will in no wise cast you out - in no wise, not for all you have done against him. 'But I spent my best days in sin' - Still I will in no wise cast you out. 'I lived in open sin' - I will in no wise cast you out. 'But I have sinned against light and conviction' - Still, I will in no wise cast you out. 'But I am a backslider' - Still the arms of his love are open to infold your poor guilty soul, and he will not cast you out.

2. Many would separate us from Christ's love.

From the beginning of the world it has been the great aim of Satan to separate believers from the love of Christ, and though he never has succeeded in the case of a single soul, yet still he tries it as eagerly as he did at first. The moment he sees the Saviour lift a lost sheep upon his shoulder, from that hour he plies all his efforts to pluck down the poor saved sheep from its place of rest. The moment the pierced hand of Jesus is laid on a poor, trembling, guilty sinner, from that hour does Satan try to pluck him out of Jesus' hand.

He did this in old times: 'As it is written, For thy sake we are killed all the day long; we are accounted as sheep for the slaughter' (verse 36). This is a cry taken from the Book of Psalms. God's people in all ages have been hated and persecuted by Satan and the world. Observe,

The reason: 'For thy sake' - because they were like Jesus, and belonged to Jesus.

The time: 'All day long' - from morning till night. The world have a perpetual hatred against true believers, so that we have to say at evening: 'Would God it were morning; and at morning, Would God it were evening.' They have no other perpetual hatred.

The manner: 'We are accounted as sheep for the slaughter.' The world care no more for ill-treating a Christian than the butcher does when he lays hold of a sheep for the slaughter. The very drunkards make a song of us. Such was the cry of believers of old. The same cry has been heard amid the snowy heights of Piedmont; and, in later days, amid the green hills and valleys of Scotland. And we are miserably deceived if we flatter ourselves that the same cry will not be heard again. Is the devil changed? Does he love Christ and his dear people any better? Is the worldly heart changed? Does it hate God and God's people any less than it did?

Ah! no. I have a deep conviction that, if God only withdraw his restraining grace, the floodgates of persecution will soon break loose again; and many of you, left unconverted under our ministry, will turn out bloody persecutors - you will yet avenge yourselves for the sermons that have pricked your hearts.

The apostle names seven forms in which trouble comes. Two of them relate to the troubles that are common to man, and five to those that are more peculiar to the children of God.

Tribulation and distress: 'Man that is born of a woman is of few days, and full of trouble. He cometh forth as a flower, and is cut down; he fleeth also as a shadow, and continueth not.' God's children are not freed from distresses - sickness, poverty, loss of friends. Jesus said to them: 'In the world ye shall have tribulation.' 'Whom I love I rebuke and chasten.' Now, Satan tries to take advantage of these times of tribulation, to separate the soul from the love of Christ; he tempts the believer to despise the chastening of the Lord - to plunge into business, or among worldly friends, or to follow worldly means of soothing sorrow. Again: he tries to make the soul faint under them - repine and murmur, and charge God foolishly - not to believe his love and wisdom in the furnace. In these ways Satan tries to separate from the love of Christ. A time of tribulation is a time of danger.

Persecution, famine, nakedness, peril, sword - all these are weapons which Satan makes use of against God's children. The history of the Church in all ages has been a history of persecution. No sooner does a soul begin to show concern for religion - no sooner does that soul cleave to Jesus, than the world talk, to the grief of those whom God hath wounded. What bitter words are hurled against that soul! In all ages this has been true: 'They wandered about in sheep-skins and goat-skins, being destitute, afflicted, tormented; of whom the world was not worthy.' Those that eat the bread of God have often been driven from their quiet meal - those who are clothed with Christ have often had to part with worldly clothing, and have been exposed to famine, nakedness, peril and sword - the last extremity. Cain murdered Abel. They killed the Prince of Life; and so all his creatures ever since have been exposed to the same.

Do not say, The times are changed, and these are the days of toleration. Christ is not changed - Satan is not changed, and, when it suits his turn, he will use the same weapons.

3. All these cannot separate us. 'In all these things we are more than conquerors, through him that loved us.'

How are we more than conquerors?

We conquer even before the battle is done.

In all other battles we do not know how the victory is to turn until the battle is won. In the battle of Waterloo, it was long thought that the French had gained; and Napoleon sent several despatches to Paris telling that he had won. But in the fight with the world, Satan and the flesh, we know how the victory is to turn already. Christ has engaged to carry us through. He will guard us against the darts of the law, by hiding us in his blood. He defends us from the power of sin by his Holy Spirit put within us. He will keep us, in the secret of his presence, from the strife of tongues. The thicker the battle, the closer will he keep to us; so that we can sing already: 'I thank God, through Jesus Christ our Lord.' We know that we shall overcome. Though the world were a million times more enraged - though the fires of persecution were again to be kindled - though my heart were a million times more wicked - though all the temptations of hell were let loose upon me - I know I shall overcome through him that loved me. When Paul and Silas sang in the low dungeon, they were more than conquerors. When Paul sang, in spite of his thorn, 'I will glory in my infirmities,' he was more than a conqueror.

We gain by our conflict.

Often a victory is a loss. So it was in that battle in Israel, after the dark night in Gibeah. All Israel mourned, for a tribe was nearly cut off out of Israel. And so, in most victories, the song of triumph is mingled with the sobbings of the widow and orphan. Not so in the good fight of faith. We are more than conquerors. We gain by our enemies.

We cling closer to Christ. Every wave of trouble for Christ's sake lifts the soul higher upon the Rock. Every arrow of bitterness shot after the believer makes him hide farther back in the clefts of Jesus. Be content, dear friend, to bear these troubles which make you cling closer to your Beloved.

They shake us loose from sin. If ye were of the world, the world would love its own. If the world smiled and fawned upon you, you would lie on its lap. But when it frowns, then Jesus is our all.

Greater is your reward in heaven. We gain a brighter crown. Be not afraid; nothing shall ever separate you from the love of Christ. O that I could know that you were all in Christ's love, that the arms of Jesus were enfolding you! Then I would know that all the hatred of men, and all the policy of hell, would never prevail against you! 'If God be for you, who can be against you?' If God has chosen you - called you - washed you - justified you - then he will glorify you. O yield to his loving hands, you that are not far from the kingdom of God! Let him wash you, for then he will carry you to glory. Amen.

Dundee, October 30, 1841 (Action Sermon)

49. Death's lessons

> Man that is born of a woman is of few days, and full of trouble. He cometh forth like a flower, and is cut down; he fleeth also as a shadow, and continueth not (Job 14:1,2).

Three things are taught us in these words.

Firstly, *the beauty of man*: 'He cometh forth like a flower' (verse 2). There is something beautiful about man. He was made at first in the image of God; and though sin has blighted and defaced that image, yet there are traces of God's workmanship to be seen in man still. His body is fearfully and wonderfully made; and the soul, though wholly averse from God by nature, is yet *a lost piece of silver*.

Secondly, *that he is short-lived*: 'Of few days - he cometh forth like a flower.' When Pharaoh asked Jacob how old he was, although he was one hundred and thirty years old, he said: 'Few and evil have the days of the years of my life been' - few compared with the life of other men. Some of the patriarchs lived nine hundred years; Methuselah nine hundred and sixty-nine. How few are our days compared with this! Few, compared to eternity - few, when we think of the work to be done.

Thirdly, *that his days are full of trouble*. If his few days were all full of joy, it would not be so sad a case, but they are full of trouble; and those that are most anxious for worldly pleasure have generally deepest troubles. Troubles of the body, and of the mind, and of the estate, come upon the back of one another like wave upon wave.

We have had solemn experience of these truths within these few days. There have been five solemn deaths, all connected with our parish, and, taken together, they form a practical commentary on these words.

Two children died, both lovely and pleasant in their lives, and in their death not far divided. They were full of promise, and their fond relatives looked forward to their being a joy and comfort to them. They came forth like a flower, and were cut down. A young man in his prime, who had reached the vigour of manhood, and thought to see many good days in the land of the living; but God changed his countenance, and he has been sent away. Another was the blooming mother of eight blooming children, beloved and admired by all around her, with all this world could give to make her happy; but the cry came at midnight. She came forth like a flower, and was cut down. The last was an aged man, called upon, after long forbearance, to give in his account. How solemn the lesson! The child, the young man, the mother, the hoary head - are all laid low this day! 'Man that is born of a woman is of few days.'

1. Learn the need of immediate conversion.

Some of you are angry that I speak so much of conversion; but, ah! when I stand beside these open graves, I am ashamed of myself for speaking so little. 'Except ye repent, ye shall likewise perish' - 'Repent, and be converted, that your sins may be blotted out.'

Children, seek conversion now, for little children die. These new-made graves are less than yours would be. Young men, seek conversion now, for young men die - they are cut down in their prime. Mothers, do not say you will seek conversion afterwards, when your family are grown, and you have more leisure - seek it now, for mothers die. Old men, do not say this is nothing to you. Others *may* die, but you *must* die; and therefore the lesson comes doubly home to you: Seek conversion now.

2. Learn the folly of living in pleasure.

There is no net by which the devil catches more souls than the silken one of worldly pleasure. It is common for worldly people to take it for granted that there is no harm in these things. Children are fond of games; young people delight in dances, and songs, and laughter; coarser spirits love the glass, and the glee, and the coarse debauch; more polished circles love the ball, and the concert, and the play; and old withered dames, and swearing captains, tottering on the brink of eternity, could hardly sleep at night without their turn at whist. Where is the harm? Sit

down upon yon grave, and ask the dead. Are you not Christless -
unpardoned - unholy - on the road to hell? Are your days not numbered?
May you not be cut down this night? Where would you be if you were
hurried away from the dance, or the play, or the card-table, to the
presence of your Judge?

'Rejoice, O young man, in thy youth; and let thy heart cheer thee in
the days of thy youth, and walk in the ways of thine heart, and in the sight
of thine eyes: but know thou that for all these things God will bring thee
into judgment.'

'Soul, thou hast much goods laid up for many years; take thine ease,
eat, drink, and be merry. But God said unto him, Thou fool, this night
thy soul shall be required of thee: then whose shall those things be which
thou hast provided?'

'She that liveth in pleasure is dead while she liveth.'

This is the time for seeking conversion.

Are we to have no pleasure, then? Yes, in Christ - holy pleasures,
such as are at God's right hand for evermore. Ah! I have tasted all the
pleasures of time, and they are not worth one drop of Christ's sweet love.

3. Learn to seek one another's souls.

Ah! there is no place for teaching ministers how to speak like the
deathbed. I often feel that I have never preached at all, when I look upon
the faces of the dying! O pray for me, that I may go out and in among
you more faithfully - that I may speak more boldly, and not fear your
anger or reproaches! You will not be angry with me when you are dead.
You will not say I preached too plainly then.

Brethren in the eldership! Come and help in this. You see our people
are dying; hundreds are now in eternity who were once under your care
and mine.

Dear teachers! Teach the children plainly, for children die. Do not
mind their impatience and waywardness. Remember they are dying
children - Death's mark is on them. The forester puts a mark round the
trees that are to be cut down. Every child has got Death's mark.

Parents! Seek your children's souls from infancy. Pray for them
before they are born. Travail in birth with them till Christ be formed in
them. Do not say they are too young, and cannot understand. God can
teach babes. O if you neglect this, will you not regret it when the green
sod lies on their breasts?

4. Learn how unable you are to bear the wrath of God.
In the time of health and strength, it is common for men to boast against God. They are not in trouble as other men, neither are they plagued like other men; therefore pride compasseth them about as a chain. They can sin with a high hand. But when they are brought to the brink of the grave by fever or wasting consumption - when they need some one to turn them on their bed, or to hold up their fainting head, or to feed them like a child - then we see that a sinner is nothing in the hands of an angry God.

And O what will it be in eternity, when he falls into the hands of the living God! Perhaps he doubted whether there was a God; but all of a sudden he sees there is a God. He thought there was no Christ - in a moment he meets his holy eye. He thought there was no hell, and laughed at those who believed it - in a moment he is tossing among its fiery waves; and now he feels it must be eternal. After a thousand years it is but beginning, and no nearer an end. The soul will sink into insupportable gloom - it will wish to die, and not be able. 'What if God, willing to show his wrath, and to make his power known, endured with much long-suffering the vessels of wrath, fitted to destruction?' O brethren, flee from the wrath to come! You cannot bear it. Can you bear a fever or the stroke of palsy, or a stroke of lightning, or wasting consumption? And these are but the little finger of the hand of God's anger.

5. Learn the preciousness of Jesus.
'Man is of few days', but 'Jesus Christ is the same yesterday, today, and for ever.' How amazing the love of Christ, that he died for us - such poor, weak flowers, and worms of a day! How safe are we in Jesus! Although we are nothing - fleeing like a shadow - yet in him we abide for ever. Our very dust is precious dust to him. Body and soul he will bring with him, and we shall reign for ever and ever. O you that are in Christ, prize him! You that are in doubt, solve it now by hasting to him. You that are out of him, choose him now.
Dundee, February 20, 1842

50. Christ, a law-magnifying Saviour

Hear, ye deaf; and look, ye blind, that ye may see. Who is blind,
but my servant? or deaf, as my messenger that I sent? who is blind
as he that is perfect, and blind as the Lord's servant? Seeing many
things, but thou observest not; opening the ears, but he heareth
not. The LORD is well-pleased for his righteousness' sake; he will
magnify the law, and make it honourable (Isaiah 42:18-21).

Observe here:

I. The name given to sinners: 'Hear, ye deaf; and look, ye blind, that
ye may see' (verse 18).

These words are applied here, first to idolaters, but they are equally
applicable to all unconverted men. All of you who are unconverted are
naturally deaf. You do not hear the voice of pastors. They are watchmen
to blow the trumpet, and warn the people - they have the tongue of the
learned; but you are 'like the deaf adder that stoppeth her ear; which will
not hearken to the voice of charmers, charming never so wisely' (Psalm
58:4,5).

Ye are blind. This word is constantly used in the Bible to describe
the stupidity of unconverted souls. Unconverted ministers are called
'Blind leaders of the blind' (Matthew 15:14). Jesus once said to a
Pharisee: 'Thou blind Pharisee' (Matthew 23:26). And again: 'Ye fools
and blind' (Matthew 23:17). 'Thou knowest not that thou art wretched,
and miserable, and poor, and blind' (Revelation 3:17). This is the true
state of every unconverted soul. You do not see your own soul - its
depravity, its guilt, its lost and ruined condition. You do not see the Sun,
the glorious Sun of Righteousness - his beauty, his glory, his excellency: 'No beauty that we should desire him.' You do not see your way.
You know not at what you stumble. Your path leads into hell, but you
do not see it, nor believe it.

Hear, ye deaf; and look, ye blind. Those of you who are deaf and
blind are generally the least attentive in the congregation. You say: The
minister has nothing for me; and so you think of something else, to
amuse your mind. But observe, God does here speak to you: 'Hear, ye
deaf; and look, ye blind.' Those of you who are careless, stupid, blind,
carnal ones are the ones that should attend, for God calls upon you.
When will you listen, if not when God is calling upon you?

But you say: This is a contradiction; 'If I am deaf, how can I hear? If I am blind, how can I look?' Leave God to settle that difficulty. Only listen and look up. There is truly no difficulty about it. He told Ezekiel to preach to dry bones: 'O ye dry bones! hear the word of the Lord'; and John to preach to men like the stones of Jordan. It is while we are speaking, and through the very words we speak, that God gives life and hearing and eyesight. Only turn your deaf ears toward God, and your blind eyeballs toward Jesus. Who can tell but some deaf and blind soul may now, for the first time, be looking up to Jesus?

2. The object pointed to: 'Who is blind, but my servant? or deaf, as my messenger that I sent? who is blind as he that is perfect, and blind as the Lord's servant? Seeing many things, but thou observest not; opening the ears, but he heareth not' (verses 19,20). Every expression here evidently points to Christ.

My servant.
This name is constantly given to Christ: 'Behold my servant' (verse 1). 'Behold, my servant shall deal prudently, he shall be exalted and extolled, and be very high' (Isaiah 52:13). 'By his knowledge shall my righteous servant justify many' (Isaiah 53:11). 'I am among you as he that serveth' (Luke 22:27). He took a towel and girded himself. 'He took upon him the form of a servant' (Philippians 2:7). The reason of the name is, that he came not to do his own will, but the will of him that sent him.

My messenger.
This name is also applied to Christ: 'If there be a messenger with him, an interpreter, one among a thousand' (Job 33:23). And again: 'The Lord, whom ye seek, shall suddenly come to his temple, even the messenger of the covenant, whom ye delight in' (Malachi 3:1). He is so called because God sent him. He came from God, with a message of eternal life to sinners.

He that is perfect: 'He is the Rock; his way is perfect.'
'As for God, his way is perfect.' It is only of Christ that these words are fully true. He did no sin, neither was guile found in his mouth. He knew no sin. He was the holy child Jesus - the perfect one - perfect in the eye of law - perfect in the eyes of the Father - perfect in the eyes of his

Church: 'Such an high priest became us, who is holy, harmless, undefiled, separate from sinners.'

Blind and deaf: 'Who is blind as my servant, and deaf as my messenger?' Also verse 20: 'Seeing many things, but thou observest not; opening the ears, but he heareth not.'

This describes the way in which he went through his work in this world. Same as verse 2: 'He shall not cry, nor lift up, nor cause his voice to be heard in the streets.' Same as Psalm 38:13,14: 'But I, as a deaf man, heard not, and I was as a dumb man that openeth not his mouth. Thus I was as a man that heareth not, and in whose mouth are no reproofs.' Also Isaiah 53:7: 'He was oppressed and he was afflicted, yet he opened not his mouth: he is brought as a lamb to the slaughter, and as a sheep before her shearers is dumb, so he openeth not his mouth.'

He was blind to the vileness of sinners. He saw, and yet did not see. Surely, if he had looked at the black hearts of those for whom he died, he could not have died for them. Surely, if he had looked only at one sin, he could not have but cast us away, or gone back to his Father's bosom. 'But who is blind as my servant?'

He was blind to his own sufferings. He hasted to Jerusalem, as if he did not see the cross before him. He saw it, but observed not. He lay in the garden of Gethsemane, as if he did not see the lanterns and torches of those that were coming to take him. 'Who is blind as my servant?'

He was deaf. He seemed not to hear their plotting against him, nor their accusations, for he answered not a word. 'Pilate said to him, Hearest thou not how many things they witness against thee? And he answered him to never a word; insomuch that the governor marvelled greatly' (Matthew 27:13,14). It is to the Lord Jesus patiently enduring all for us that you are bid to listen and to look. Consider him - study him. We have learned but little of Christ yet, brethren: and you who are Christless know him not at all.

3. The work of Christ: 'He will magnify the law, and make it honourable' (verse 21).

This is in some respects the most wonderful description of the work of Christ given in the whole Bible. He is often said to have fulfilled the law. Thus, Matthew 3:15: 'Thus it becometh us to fulfil all righteousness.' And again, Matthew 5:17: 'Think not that I am come to destroy the law, or the prophets: I am not come to destroy, but to fulfil.' But here it is said, he will 'magnify the law, and make it honourable.' He came to give new lustre and glory to the holy law of God, that all worlds might see and understand that the law is holy, and just, and good. When God wrote the law upon the heart of Adam in his creation, that was magnifying the law. He showed it to be a great and holy and happy law, when he wrote it in the bosom of so holy and happy a creature as man then was. When God spoke the law from Mount Sinai, that magnified the law, and made it glorious. When he spoke it with his own voice in so dreadful a manner, when he wrote it twice with his own finger, this was magnifying it - enough, one would think, to make our modern Sabbath breakers tremble to erase it. But most of all when Christ died, did he give lustre, and greatness, and glory, and majesty, to the law of God in the sight of all worlds.

By his sufferings.
He magnified the holiness and justice of the law by bearing its curse. When Adam sinned, he denied that the law was holy and just. The devil said to him: 'Ye shall not surely die.' He believed the devil. He thought God would not make him die - he thought God would fall back from his strict and holy law. He will not do it. Will he destroy the creatures he has made merely for taking an apple? When any man sins, he denies the holiness of God's law. When a man swears, or breaks the Sabbath, or dishonours his parents, or lies, or steals, he says in his heart: God will not see - God will not take notice - God will not cast me into hell for this. He does not believe the threatenings of God. He does not believe that the law is holy and just. If those of you who live in sin really believed that every sin you committed was to bring down another stripe for eternity, another wave of fire to roll over your bodies and souls in hell for ever, you could not sin as you do; and therefore you dishonour the law - you make it small and contemptible - you persuade yourselves that God's law will never be put in force. Thus every sin is done against God: 'Against thee, thee only.' Now God sent his Son into the world to magnify the law, by dying under its curse. He took upon him the curse due to sinners, and bore it in his body on the tree, and thereby proved that God's law cannot be mocked.

When God cast the devil and his angels into hell, this showed in a very dreadful manner the truth of his threatenings - the awful strictness of his law. If God had cast all men into hell, it would have shown the same thing. But much more when Christ bowed his head under the stroke of the law's curse. He was a person of infinite dignity and glory: 'God over all, blessed for ever.' He thought it no robbery to be equal with God. He was far exalted above all blessing and praise. God-man, the only being who ever stood on this earth who was God and man. He was one who had no personal sin. He was perfect - knew no sin - did no sin - was holy, harmless, undefiled, and separate from sinners. He was infinitely dear to God. His own Son - his only begotten Son; one who was in the beginning with God, and was God; into whose bosom the love of the uncreated God had flowed from all eternity. It was he who came and bowed his neck to the stroke of the law. He was seen of angels. Angels desired to look into the awful scene. The eyes of millions of worlds were turned towards Calvary. When Jesus died, he redeemed us from the curse of the law, being made a curse for us; and now all worlds saw that God could not be mocked. He added lustre to the holy law. Angels and archangels saw, and trembled as they saw. He that did not spare his Son will spare no other.

Learn the certainty of hell for the Christless. Which of you that are Christless can hope to escape the curse of the law, since God did not spare his Son? If you have made up your mind to refuse Christ, then you must bear hell. You say you are a person of great mind, of great power, of great wealth; but, ah! you are not equal to the Son of God, and even he was not spared. You say your sins are not many, not gross, not so bad as those of other men; ah! but Christ knew no sin; he had no personal sin - all was imputed sin. How surely will you suffer! You say God has been kind to you - has given you many mercies; ah! remember, Christ was the Son of his love, and yet when the law demanded it, God spared not his own Son. Though you were the signet on his right hand, yet would he pluck you thence - though you were a right eye, yet would he pluck you out.

Learn to flee from sin. Every sin will have its eternal punishment. The sin you are committing has either been suffered for in Christ, or will be suffered for by you in hell. Why will you fill up your cup of torment to the brim? If you will not come to Christ, at least you might spare yourself from greater damnation.

By his obedience.

He added lustre to the goodness of the law by obeying it. When Adam preferred the service of the devil to the service of God, he said that the law of God was not good. The fruit appeared good for food, and a tree to be desired to make one wise, and so he ate. And so with every sinner now. When you prefer sin to holiness - when you prefer to swear, or to break the Sabbath, or to go with the wicked, to serving God with all humility of mind, then you say: God's law is bondage. It is not good to be under it. It would not make me happy to keep it. I am happier in breaking it than I would be in keeping it. It is not good to love God with all my heart, and my neighbour as myself. Now, when Christ came and obeyed the law from the cradle to the grave - when the Son of God came and delighted to do the will of God, and had the law always in his heart, loving God with all his heart, and his neighbour as himself - this gave new lustre to the law. It showed to all worlds that it is the happiness and chief good of the creature to keep God's holy law.

Christ was the freest being in the universe - most absolutely free - doing all things according to the pleasure of his own will. He was also most wise - only wise. He knew the nature of things - knew their beginning and end. He had also tasted the joys of heaven. He had drunk from all eternity the river of God's pleasures; had enjoyed all that the Father enjoyed - the fulness of joy that is in God's presence, and the pleasures that are at his right hand for evermore; and yet, when he stood in our nature, he delighted in the law of God after the inward man; yea, God's law was within his heart. He loved God with all his heart, and soul, and mind, and strength; he loved his neighbour as himself, yea, more than himself; for he gave up his own life for ours. He was subject to parents and governors. He loved the holy Sabbath. He magnified the law and made it honourable. He gave it a new lustre in the sight of all worlds. He showed with a new clearness and a brightness before unknown that it is the chief happiness of the creature to keep the whole law.

Learn the true wisdom of those of you who are new creatures, and who love God's holy law. All of you who are really brought to Christ are changed into his image, so that you love God's holy law. 'I delight in the law of God after the inward man.' 'The statutes of the LORD are right, rejoicing the heart' (Psalm 19:8). The world say: What a slave you are! You cannot have a little amusement on the Sabbath, you cannot take a Sabbath walk, or join a Sabbath tea-party; you cannot go to a dance or theatre; you cannot enjoy the pleasures of sensual indulgence - you are a slave. I answer: Christ had none of these pleasures. He did not want them; nor do we. He knew what was truly wise, and good, and happy, and he chose God's holy law. He was the freest of all beings, and yet he knew no sin. Only make me free as Christ is free - this is all I ask. 'Great peace have they who love thy law, and nothing shall offend them.'

4. The effect: 'God is well pleased.'

With Christ.
God is well pleased with Christ for many reasons. (1) Because he is his image: 'The brightness of his glory, and the express image of his person.' (2) Because he is lovely. (3) For his dying: 'Therefore doth my Father love me' (John 10:17). He loves him with a full love; he pours out the love of his whole heart - an unclouded love, an everlasting love.

With all that are in Christ.
Whoever of you is willing to forsake your own righteousness, and to take Christ as your surety, God not only pardons, but is well pleased with you for his righteousness' sake. The same love wherewith he loves Christ, he will pour out on you; and, O! who can wonder, when you really think of the law-magnifying righteousness of the Lord Jesus? It is an ocean of divine righteousness, and those who are plunged in it are, as it were, lost in divine righteousness. It is an atmosphere of light, ready to envelop the soul, so that the sinner may be covered entirely, and thus become divinely fair, and infinitely well pleasing to God.

Invitation
He that wrought out this righteousness invites you all to get the benefit of it. To you who have no concern: 'Hear, O ye deaf; and look, ye blind' - 'Unto you, O men, I call, and my voice is to the sons of man.' You that are weary he invites still more tenderly. 'Come unto me, all ye that labour and are heavy laden;' 'Ho, every one that thirsteth, come ye to the waters.' If you come this day to Christ, you do not need to fear that God's infinite majesty will be against you; for the Lord is well pleased for his righteousness' sake, for Christ magnified the law, and made it honourable. Amen.
Dundee, March 6, 1842.

51. The obedience and disobedience of one

'For as by one man's disobedience many were made sinners, so by the obedience of one shall many be made righteous' (Romans 5:19).

There is an exact parallel between the way in which we are made sinners and the way in which we are made righteous. This is obvious at the first reading of the text; and the more our eyes are opened to see the wondrous truths that are hidden here, the more we shall discover this, that all who are justified are justified in the very same way as they were made sinners.

Unconverted men know neither of these truths. 'The natural man receiveth not the things of the Spirit of God, neither can he know them.' I am persuaded that if those of you who are carnal men get a glimpse of the meaning of this verse today, you will think it consummate folly, although it be the whole counsel of God for the salvation of a sinner. If the gospel pleased carnal men it would not be the gospel - it would prove itself to be false.

It is deeply important that you know both of these. They are life to the soul. You must know the first, how you were made sinners, in order that you may lie down as a dead, condemned soul at the feet of Christ. You must know the second, how a sinner is made righteous, in order that you may have all joy and peace in believing. O that God the Holy Spirit may open all your eyes today, and mine!

1. The way in which we are made sinners: 'By the disobedience of one.'

The one man.
Our first father, Adam - the root and spring of the human race, and also the head and representative of us all - perfect in body - perfect in soul - full of grace and truth - image of God - very good. It pleased God to deal with mankind from the very first in this way. As you heard lately, he did not deal with men as a field of corn, where every stalk stands upon its own root; but he dealt with man as with a tree, all the branches of which have but one root and stem. He seems to have dealt with the angels in the other way, each angel standing on his own root; but he dealt with mankind like a tree and its branches. So that if Adam stood, all stood; if he fell, all fell. Some may say, It is not just to deal this way with man; we were not consulted in this matter whether we would have Adam

for our head or no. I answer, 'Nay, but O man, who art thou that repliest against God? Shall the thing formed say to him that formed it, Why hast thou made me thus?' God has made us thus - the holy, wise, good, and gracious God. Whether you believe it or not, whether you like it or not, God has made man thus, and you cannot change it.

Disobedience: The eating of the forbidden fruit.
Only one sin. Some of you see little evil in one sin, or in a hundred sins; but here you see one sin cast Adam and all his children out of paradise. God did not wait till it was repeated. It appeared a small sin. The outward action was small - only stretching out the hand and taking an inviting fruit. Some of you think little of sins that make no great noise; such as breaking the Sabbath, drinking too much, speaking what is false, sitting down Christless at the Lord's table; but see here, one small sin brought a world under the curse of God. God would rather a world should perish than one small sin go unpunished.

The consequence.
'Many were made sinners.' I have said that it pleased God to deal with mankind as a tree. If you strike with the axe at the root of a tree, the whole tree falls - not only the stem, but the branches, and even the twigs upon the branches; and all the branches die and wither, and become fit for the burning. So it was when Adam fell. Satan laid the axe at the root of the tree; and when Adam fell, many fell along with him. All his branches fell that same day. One stroke brought all down. Even the branches most distant from Adam, even the tenderest twigs springing from these branches, fell, and withered, and died that day.

Death passed upon all men. From that hour man became a dying thing, the seeds of dissolution were sown, the fair, blooming creature began to wither and dissolve; and every branch came dying into the world.

Spiritual death. Just as in a tree when it is felled, the nourishment is immediately cut off from both the stem and branches; so it was with fallen man. In the day he ate he surely died. Not a spark of spiritual life remained in him, or any of his. This explains how your children come into the world utterly dead to God and divine things. They are lively in other things. The new-born babe clings to its mother's breast, but not to Jesus.

The curse of God. This is the proper meaning of 'were made sinners.' It is a judicial term - 'were held in God's sight as guilty, lost, undone sinners.' In that day the frown of God came upon all men. The holy nature of God abhorred the apostate race. The curse of the broken law passed upon all men.

Ah, brethren! here is matter for humiliation that few of you think about. Not only are you covered over with an infinite load of actual sins - not only have you got a heart like the inside of a grave, full of dead men's bones and rotten flesh, and all uncleanness; or, like the cave of hell, 'a hold for every foul spirit, and the cage of every unclean and hateful bird' - but you belong to a cursed race; you are the wicked branch of a wicked tree - you are entirely and originally a sinner - spiritually dead - disinclined from all that is good. O pray for a discovery of your connection with the first Adam, that it may make you cleave to the second Adam.

2. The way in which we are made righteous: 'By the obedience of one shall many be made righteous.'

One.

This second one is the Lord Jesus Christ - the second Adam, and the Son of God.

The first Adam was fair, exquisitely fair, as he came from the hand of God; but the second is altogether lovely - fairer than the children of men.

The first Adam was made in the likeness of God; but the second is God himself, the Lord from heaven - the brightness of the Father's glory, and the express image of his person.

The first Adam was full of heavenly wisdom, so that he named all the creatures as they came; but in the second are hid all the treasures of wisdom and knowledge. He is the wisdom of God. He spake as never man spake. He calls all the stars by their names.

The first was the head of the whole human race - the federal head; so that in him they stood, and in him they fell. Christ is offered as a head to every creature, and is actually the head of all the redeemed, and of myriads of holy angels, all gathered together in him.

O glorious one! Divine and human perfections meet in him! O that you were filled with sweet, admiring, adoring thoughts of him this day! O that he would rise upon you like the sun! He is the Light of the world, the Sun of righteousness, the bright and morning Star. It is that one who justifies the ungodly, who has power to forgive sins. He is precious to all that believe.

His obedience: Twofold:

He obeyed the holy law of God. Satan thought he had got God's law for ever dishonoured, when he got the whole human race to abhor it, to disown it, and not to obey it. But he was foiled in this very thing. The Son of God came and obeyed it. The obedience of that one was more glorifying to God, more amazing to angels, than the obedience of a world would have been. He magnified the law, and made it honourable - made it shine far brighter than ever, as a holy, just, and good law.

Look through the life of Jesus, as related in the Gospels, and you will see what it is to obey the law of God. He had no other gods before his Father. He bowed to no idols. He took not his holy name in vain. He remembered the Sabbath day to keep it holy. He came down to Nazareth, and was subject to Joseph and Mary. 'Woman, behold thy son.' He did not kill. He did not commit adultery. He did not steal. There was no guile found in his mouth. He coveted not. Or, if you sum the ten commandments, and make them into two, he loved God with all his heart, and mind, and strength; and he loved his neighbour as himself. An unquenchable love to God burned in his bosom. He regarded God in all that he did. Even when God bruised him and put him to grief - when God cried, 'Awake, O sword, against my shepherd, and against the man that is my fellow, saith the Lord of hosts: smite the shepherd, and the sheep shall be scattered: and I will turn mine hand upon the little ones' - even then he cried, 'My God, my God!' He kissed the hand that smote him. He loved his neighbour more than himself: 'Greater love hath no man than this, that a man lay down his life for his friends;' 'For my love they are my adversaries;' 'While we were yet sinners Christ died for us.' Even when they were nailing him to the cross, wagging their heads at him, railing on him, offering him vinegar, he cried: 'Father, forgive them; for they know not what they do.' Love is the fulfilling of the law. Now God is love, and Christ is God. This is part of the obedience of one, by which he makes many sinners righteous.

He laid down his life. In this he obeyed a special commandment of his Father. Adam was not only under the ten commandments, but he had a special commandment given him, to try his obedience to God's will, namely, that he should not eat the forbidden fruit. In like manner Christ was not only under the ten commandments, but under a special commandment, the most difficult that ever was given to any being - that he should die for sinners: 'Therefore doth my Father love me, because I lay down my life ... This commandment have I received of my Father'

(John 10:17,18). And a little after: 'the cup which my Father hath given me, shall I not drink it?' (John 18:11).

Therefore does he say: 'Sacrifice and offering thou didst not desire; mine ears hast thou opened: burnt-offering and sin-offering hast thou not required. Then said I, Lo, I come: in the volume of the book it is written of me, I delight to do thy will, O my God: yea, thy law is within my heart' (Psalm 40:6-8). And, 'Being found in fashion as a man, he humbled himself, and became obedient unto death, even the death of the cross' (Philippians 2:8).

This was the most amazing trial of obedience that ever was. It was a long trial: 'I am afflicted and ready to die from my youth up: while I suffer thy terrors I am distracted.' He was 'a man of sorrows' from his youth. Often, often, he sank under the dark cloud of his Father's anger, till he groaned his last on Calvary. There was nothing in the nature of things to oblige him to do it. There was nothing good or amiable in those for whom he died; they were vile sinners, not asking him to die for them, blind to his excellency and divine glory. Yet he was obedient unto death. This is the obedience by which he covers and justifies all those, however sinful, that come to God by him.

The consequence. 'Many are made righteous.'
We have seen that in the fall and ruin of man, it pleased God to deal with man, not as a field of corn, each standing on his own root, but as a tree, in which all the branches stand or fall together. We were not made sinners, each by his individual sin, but all by the sin of one. In like manner it has pleased God to justify sinners, not each by his own obedience, by his own goodness and holiness, but 'by the obedience of one.' Just as Adam by his one sin brought death, the curse of God, and total spiritual death, not only upon himself, but upon all his branches, even the most distant, even the minutest, even though unborn; so the second Adam, by his own obedience, brought pardon, righteousness, spiritual life, and eternal glory to all his branches, even the most distant, the smallest, even those unborn.

They are made righteous. Those who betake themselves to Christ are made righteous. It matters not what they have been before, they are righteous now. They belong to a righteous family, to a righteous tree; the root is righteous, and so are all the branches. They are not forgiven only - not only have their infinite sins been blotted out, but they are made righteous. They are not only made innocent, as if they had done no sin, but righteous, as if they had fulfilled all righteousness. All that Christ did and suffered is counted theirs. Neither are they made righteous as if they had obeyed, but as if they had obeyed divinely. They are made righteous all at once. We were made sinners all at once - by one blow, by one man's sin; so those of you who cleave to Christ are made righteous all at once. You have not to wait many years before you find acceptance. You find it the moment you cleave to Christ: 'He that believeth on me hath everlasting life;' 'In the Lord have I righteousness and strength;' 'In the Lord shall all the seed of Israel be justified and shall glory.'

Many, not few. The first Adam was the root of a numerous family, to whom, by his disobedience, he transmitted death and sin. The second Adam is the root of a numerous family, to whom he gives pardon and holiness. They are scattered over every country and every age, so that often they seem few, but they are many when gathered together. 'So shall thy seed be.' 'I saw a great company which no man could number', every one made righteous in this way. 'In my Father's house are many mansions' and none of them will be empty, yet every one will be righteous in the obedience of one. O will ye not be among the many?

Many, not all. The second Adam offers himself to all. He is willing to be co-extensive with the first Adam. Ruin by the fall of the first Adam extended to every creature; and so the gift of the second Adam is to every creature: 'Go, and preach the gospel to every creature.' The gospel is preached to every creature under heaven. Christ stands willing to be a root of pardon, and righteousness, and eternal life, to every creature. Yet all do not, and will not come. The most stay away, and die in their sins. I fear the most of you are now staying away from Christ. O that you were all made righteous in God's way!

3. Lessons.

Most are on the wrong way. Many people are in earnest in a wrong direction. When a ship is wrecked, and the sailors take to the long-boat, they toil hard to get to land, but often they row in wrong directions. So with sinners. Many of you are in earnest, but not in the right direction. Most are trying to be righteous in the obedience of many - each in his own. You want to stand on your own root. You will not take guilt from the first Adam, neither righteousness from the second. Are you wiser than God? If righteousness come by the law, then Christ is dead in vain. You are trying to make Christ useless. Is it not better to submit to God's way, to fall in with the divine scheme, to submit to the righteousness of God?

All believers are equally righteous before God. I have seen a family of children all dressed alike, that none might boast over the others, all being equally fair. So it is with God's family. They are all righteous in the obedience of one. One garment covers them all - the robe of their elder Brother. Believers differ in attainments, in gifts and graces, but all are equally justified before God. It is not work of their own that justifies them, it is the work of Christ alone. Ah, brethren! there is no boasting in Christ's family. 'Where is boasting, then? It is excluded.' This is what keeps most away. They cannot bear to be on the same level with a drunkard, or a publican. They cannot bear to come before God along with Mary Magdalene and the dying thief.

You may come always to God this way. It is not once only that you need this divine obedience to cover you, but all your life long. The moment you forsake Christ, you lose your righteousness before God. But you may return now. This obedience is always the same, always full, always divine. You say you are changed; Christ is not changed. You say you have got new guilt; Christ is still the same. You may still be made righteous once more in the obedience of one. Why stay away from Christ? Can you make yourself righteous away from him? Can you be righteous in any other way than by submitting to him?

Dundee, April 17, 1842 (Action Sermon)

52. The godly delivered - the unjust reserved unto judgment

The Lord knoweth how to deliver the godly out of temptations, and to reserve the unjust unto the day of judgment to be punished (2 Peter 2:9).

There are only two great classes of people in the world - the godly and the unjust; and the way in which God deals with these two classes makes up the history of the universe. To one of these classes every one of you belongs. The godly are those who have been born again, who have been made partakers of the divine nature, and live unto God. The unjust are those who are ungodly, who have never been born again, who live to themselves and to the world. God deals very differently with these two classes.

1. His treatment of the godly.

He allows them to fall into temptation.
The whole Bible shows that it is common for believers to be carried through many and great temptations. Temptations may be understood in two ways.

(1) *Solicitations to sin.* All believers are allowed to fall into these. The old nature remains; though crucified, and mortified, and hated, yet it remains. Satan shoots his fiery darts - lays snares for the soul. The world watches for our halting. No doubt Noah felt these in the old world, and Lot as he walked through the streets of Sodom.

(2) *Trials.* All kinds of trial which try the soul whether it will abide in Christ or no - reproaches and persecutions. Often the trial is fiery. The whole Bible testifies that it is common for believers to fall into these. 'There hath no temptation taken you but such as is common to man: but God is faithful, who will not suffer you to be tempted above that ye are able' (1 Corinthians 10:13). Think it not strange. James says: 'My brethren, count it all joy when ye fall into divers temptations' (James 1:2). And Paul says, that he served the Lord with all humility of mind, with many tears and temptations (Acts 20:19).

You may think it strange that God should take us by such a way to glory - by tears and temptations. Why did he let Noah live so long in a world of trials? Why did he let Lot remain in the midst of Sodom?

To manifest the reality of grace. It is said: 'For there must be also heresies among you, that they which are approved may be made manifest among you' (1 Corinthians 11:19). For the same reason there must be temptations, that those of you who are really God's children may be made manifest. In a time when there is no trial or temptation, it is easy to receive the Word with joy, and many among you appear to be Christians. But when temptation comes, many go down; many that seemed to get good at one time, to be moved, and to wait diligently on the Word. Perhaps if you had been allowed to go smoothly through life without temptations, you would have remained with a name to live all your days; but temptation came, and you sank, just to show that you were none of his. But Noah is kept in the midst of the old world, not conforming to the world, to show that there is a divine power working in him, to show that there is an electing, forgiving, upholding God. Lot is kept in Sodom to show the same thing. And you that are believers are kept by the power of God, through manifold temptations, with the same view.

To condemn the world. Noah was moved with fear, by which he condemned the world. When a poor fellow-worm and fellow-sinner was enabled to live above the world, to commune with God, and to go in and out among them, living for eternity, it proved to them that there was a Saviour, that there was a God of grace. A believer is a living demonstration of the way of salvation. Lot condemned the men of Sodom, when he vexed his soul from day to day, when he lived among them a pardoned sinner, upheld by the Holy Spirit. And so, the few believers in this place are condemning it. If you had never seen what conversion is, if you had no examples of a holy, renewed believer in your neighbourhood, you might stand with a bolder face in the judgment! But, ah! every believer in this place condemns you. Why not wash where we have been washed?

That we may be conformed to Christ: 'Think it not strange concerning the fiery trial that is to try you, as though some strange thing happened unto you; but rejoice, inasmuch as ye are partakers of the sufferings of Christ.' Christ was tempted by the devil, and hated by the world; and we must be glad to share in his sufferings. God desires us to be like our Head in all things.

The Lord knows how to deliver them.
They know not how to deliver themselves. I have no doubt Noah often said: I fear I too shall be carried away with the flood; I fear my faith will fail me; I know not what to do. And Lot often trembled in Sodom; and David, when Saul pursued him. Many of you do not know how to deliver yourselves. You are compassed about as with a flood, by old companions, old lusts, a hating world, a roaring lion.

Man knows not how to deliver you. It is common for souls under temptation to ask counsel of ministers, but they cannot deliver you. Nothing is more vain than the help of man in an hour of temptation.

'*The Lord knows.*' More is meant than the mere words imply. The Lord not only knows how to do it, but will certainly deliver the godly out of temptation. He loves them. Every godly one is a jewel in his sight; he died for them, and he will not lose one. When he puts them into the furnace, he sits as a refiner. He has promised they shall never perish: 'I will never leave thee, nor forsake thee.' He will with the temptation make a way of escape: 'I have prayed for thee, that thy faith fail not.'

It matters not what the temptation be. It matters not how great the temptation be, and how weak the believing soul. Some children of God say sometimes: If it were a lesser trial, I could bear it; if the furnace were not so hot, if the temptation were not so great, I could get through; or, if I had more strength, if I were an older and more experienced believer. Look at the words: 'The Lord knoweth how to deliver the godly out of temptations.' Is anything too hard for the Lord?

It matters not how few the believers be. There was but one Lot and one Noah. Perhaps they said: 'The Lord hath forgotten me, and my God hath forsaken me.' God is as able to deliver one as a thousand. One soul is precious in his sight: 'I will take you one of a city, and two of a family, and bring you to Zion;' 'I will sift the house of Israel like as corn is sifted in a sieve; yet shall not the least grain fall upon the earth;' 'Those whom thou hast given me have I kept, and none of them is lost, but the son of perdition, that the Scripture might be fulfilled.'

2. God's treatment of the unjust: 'God knoweth how to reserve the unjust to the day of judgment to be punished.'

The end of all the ungodly is to be punished.
Whatever be God's present dealings with the ungodly, their end is to be punished. Whatever being shall be found laden with sin, his end is to be punished. The angels sinned. They were of a noble nature, originally in the image of God. Yet God did not spare them, but cast them down to hell. The old world sinned - a great multitude; God brought in the flood upon them. An individual town sinned; God turned it into ashes, and made it an example to all that should afterward live ungodly. This will be the end of all in this congregation who live on in sin. Ah! it will be more tolerable for Sodom than for you. Your end is - to be burned.

Not now: 'God knoweth how to reserve.'
Judgment against an evil work is not executed speedily. During the French Revolution, a young man stepped forward, and dared God Almighty to strike him dead. No evil followed. Many of you have gone on in sin thus. The first time you sinned, you trembled lest you should be quickly summoned to judgment; but no evil followed, and now your heart is fully set in you to do evil. Ah! you little understand. 'The Lord

knoweth how to reserve.' God's ways are not like our ways. When a man steals, the cry immediately follows: 'Stop, thief!' else he will be out of reach. When a murder is committed, a reward is offered for the apprehension of the murderer, lest he should escape from the hands of justice. Not so with God. He is not in haste to punish. You cannot flee out of his dominions. Your feet shall slide in due time. God is reserving you to the day of judgment to be punished. He endures with much long-suffering the vessels of wrath, fitted to destruction.

It is not that you have sinned little. Many of you have sinned more than others that have been taken away. I have no doubt there are many in hell who had far less sin than some of you.

It is not that God loves your sin. God hates it infinitely. Every new sin you commit provokes him in a fearful manner. Every new Sabbath you break, every new lust you pour forth, God is more and more angry with you.

It is not that you are in health - that there are no means of your destruction at hand. God could smite in one hour. Here is the explanation: 'God knoweth how to reserve the unjust.' O employ this day of long-suffering, while Jesus waits to save you, and God refrains from destroying you! Lord, help a worm!

53. Be diligent

Wherefore, beloved, seeing that ye look for such things, be diligent that ye may be found of him in peace, without spot, and blameless (2 Peter 3:14).

1. The description of believers here given: 'Seeing ye look for such things.'

So Paul: 'While we look not at the things which are seen, but at the things which are not seen' (2 Corinthians 4:18). The unconverted among you look at things seen. All your thoughts, talk, hopes and fears, are taken up about the things of time and sense. But those of you who have anointed eyes, and hearts illumined by the Holy Ghost, look beyond the bounds of time. But the look here spoken of is more than mere knowledge: it is the look of desire, of earnest longing. It is called

'Looking and hasting unto.' It is like the look of a child for an absent parent, when he looks and runs to meet him. It is like the look of a bride for the coming of the bridegroom. What are the things for which believers look?

The second coming of the Lord.
The scoffers say, 'Where is the promise of his coming?' (verse 4). 'But the day of the Lord will come' (verse 10). 'Looking for and hasting unto the coming of the day of God' (verse 12). The great event of that day is the coming of Jesus in the clouds of heaven. The world are not looking for this, but you that are Christ's are looking for such things. The world think Christ well away, and hope he may never come back again. They believe, in some sort, that the Son of God was once born of a woman, and lay in the manger at Bethlehem; that he walked on the hills of Galilee, and did many wonders; that he died, and went to his Father. And they hope to see no more of him. They think the world is well quit of him. Certain I am, that if he were returning to this place, the most of the inhabitants would wail because of him.

But he *will* come, and like a thief in the night. He is not slack concerning his promise, as some men count slackness: 'This same Jesus ... shall so come in like manner as ye have seen him go into heaven' (Acts 1:11). 'The Lord Jesus shall be revealed from heaven with his mighty angels, in flaming fire taking vengeance on them that know not God, and that obey not the gospel of our Lord Jesus Christ: who shall be punished with everlasting destruction' (2 Thessalonians 1:7). 'Behold, he cometh with clouds; and every eye shall see him, and they also which pierced him: and all kindreds of the earth shall wail because of him' (Revelation 1:7). Even so. Amen. 'Ye look for such things.' If you are Christ's at all, you are desiring that blessed hope. Many faithful and godly men believe that the day is near; and who will venture to say they may not be right? The day of the Lord cometh as a thief in the night. Does a bride long for the coming of the bridal-day? So will you that are Christ's love his appearing.

The trial by fire: 'The heavens shall pass away with a great noise: and the elements shall melt with fervent heat: the earth also, and the works that are therein, shall be burned up;' 'All these things shall be dissolved.'
The scoffing world do not look for such things. They do not desire them, neither do they expect them. They read of them in the Bible as they

would read a terrific tale, or a tragedy; they do not read of them as coming realities. Yonder blue heaven, they think, shall always span the earth with its calm cerulean arch. The elements shall continue their sportive warfare, the wind blowing east, and then west - the summer zephyr changing with the winter blast. The green earth, they think, shall still roll on with its seed-time and harvest, summer and winter. Their houses and towers, they hope, shall last for ages; they call their lands after their own names. Ah, brethren! can you say you are looking for anything else than just that tomorrow shall be as this day, and much more abundant?

But those of you that are taught of God look for such things. You expect and desire that awful day. You are ever and anon looking up to see when the heavens shall catch fire and pass away, when the hand that stretched them out like a tent to dwell in shall roll them up like a scroll. You are waiting for the day when the heavens shall pass away with a great noise, and the elements shall melt with fervent heat. You look upon the earth as one does upon a crazy house, from which he is about to remove. You look on its mountains, trees, and fields, as soon to be burned up; and all its works, its houses, and palaces, and towers, as soon to be a smoking funeral pile. No wonder Jesus said: 'They are not of the world.' The wonder is, brethren, that we are so much of the world.

The new heavens and earth: 'Nevertheless we, according to his promise, look for new heavens, and a new earth, wherein dwelleth righteousness' (verse 13).

The promise of the new heavens and earth is contained in Isaiah 65:17, Isaiah 66:22; and Revelation 21:1: 'I saw a new heaven and a new earth.' What that glorious world shall be I cannot tell. No thunderclouds shall ever darken the sky, no lightning-flash, no blighting east wind blow, no pestilential fogs, no raging whirlwind. There shall be no more curse - thorns and thistles shall nowhere be found, paradise will be restored. All this may be - I cannot tell. But one thing is certain: 'Therein dwelleth righteousness.' 'There shall in no wise enter into it anything that defileth, neither whatsoever worketh abomination, or maketh a lie; but they which are written in the Lamb's book of life.'

The wicked shall be plucked away. The world do not look for such things. You do not believe that you shall ever be bound up in bundles, and cast away. Men of the world, you do not believe that there is a world where you will be separated from your believing friends and neighbours.

But *we* look for such things. We look for a time when you will no more scorn us, and cast out our name as evil, when you will no more hate and revile us; a world where you will never be, 'wherein dwelleth righteousness.'

2. The duty here commanded: 'Be diligent, that ye may be found of him in peace.'

The duty here commanded is *diligence*. Diligence is so living as that, when Christ shall appear, he may find you in peace, without spot and blameless. Two things are implied in this command.

Be diligent to get into Christ.
In order to be found in peace, without spot and blameless, a man must be found in Christ. If any man be out of Christ, he is not at peace with God, neither is he without spot and blameless. There is but one way of being unspotted and unblameable before God, and that is by being in Christ. By nature 'there is none righteous, no, not one: there is none that understandeth; there is none that seeketh after God; there is none that doeth good, no, not one.' You are all spotted by your constantly wicked heart; and your wicked life is a continual blot before God. Be diligent to be found in peace.

Seek it as the one thing needful: 'One thing have I desired of the Lord.' Most in this congregation have some desire to be saved. You would like not to be cast into hell; you would like to be received into glory. But not many will be diligent, or press into the kingdom of God. Get your heart so engrossed with this, that it shall be your main concern, sleeping and waking. Ah! if you knew the worth of Christ, you would be diligent to be found of him in peace.

Leave no means untried. When a man is diligent in seeking some earthly thing, he leaves no means untried to get at his end. When a merchant is seeking goodly pearls, he goes from market to market. When a beggar is seeking his meat, he goes from door to door; a hundred refusals do not daunt him, he still knocks on at the next gate. And so, if you are really in earnest, you will leave no means untried: Bible, prayer, united prayer, faithful ministers and godly friends.

Give up all that hinders. When a man is diligent in worldly things, he gives up all that would mar his success. If a man is thoroughly set upon going a journey, he leaves his bed early in the morning. If a man is running for his life, he soon throws away every weight. So, if you are diligent in seeking Christ, if your way of business prevents you, if it brings so much care as to hinder you, so that you see it will be your ruin, you will give it up. If any company is ruinous to you, destroys your seriousness, hinders your prayers, and wastes your precious hours, you will break it off. If any idol hinders your cleaving to Christ, cast it away. Be diligent, that ye may be found of him in peace. Herod would not give up his Herodias.

Be diligent to abide in Christ: 'Beware lest ye fall from your own steadfastness' (verse 17).

Abide in him, little children, that when he shall appear ye may have confidence, and not be ashamed before him at his coming.

Leave no guilt upon the conscience. Guilt mars our communion with Christ, hides the reconciled face, brings clouds, hidings, frowns. Give daily diligence to come as you came at the first. He that endureth to the end, the same shall be saved.

Be diligent to grow in grace. A growing tree is a living tree. When a tree ceases to grow, it is in danger of being blown down. So with a believer. Get more knowledge, faith, love.

Seek daily likeness to Jesus. We are not justified by our sanctification; and yet without sanctification we cannot have abiding peace or communion. We are justified entirely by the doing and dying of the Lord Jesus; and yet, when justified, he will change us into his image; so that the longer we are justified we should be the more sanctified. Study holiness, if you would have peace now, and be found of Christ in peace. The holiest believers are evermore the happiest.

3. Motives to diligence.

The most are very careless.

The most around you are living as if there were no coming Saviour, no heavens on fire, no earth to be burned up. The people of this town are like the people of Sodom, they are at ease in sin. Though they have not fulness of bread, they have abundance of idleness. The most of believers are very careless, not looking for the Bridegroom; therefore be you diligent. Let their carelessness make you the more diligent. Tremble lest you be infected with the general carelessness and slumber. It is an infectious disease.

There is need of all your diligence.
The righteous scarcely are saved. You live in a world of enemies - your own heart, the temptations of the world, the snares of the devil. Few get to heaven without desperate falls. If you were travelling in Alpine countries, among rocks and precipices, you would see your need of diligence, lest you should fall, and break your bones. Such is your journey now.

The time is short: 'What! Could ye not watch with me one hour?'
If you have yet to get into Christ, the time is short. You are like a traveller who has a long journey before him, and has slept till the day is far spent. He must double his pace, and so must you. If you are in Christ, the time is but short. You are like a sentry on guard, your hour is a short one. Do not grow sleepy, but keep awake. Watch, for ye know neither the day nor the hour.

Your diligence will be too late, if Christ find you Christless.
When the bridegroom came, the foolish virgins went to buy; but they were too late. So many of you will begin to seek when too late. When you lift up your eyes in hell, or when Jesus comes, you will cry, 'Lord, Lord'; but all diligence will then be too late. When the boat has left the shore, it is in vain for you to run. Now your diligence may be to good purpose. Yet there is room, the door is now open. 'Be diligent, that ye may be found of him in peace.'
Dundee, May 14, 1842

54. Follow the Lord fully

> But my servant Caleb, because he had another spirit with him, and
> hath followed me fully, him will I bring into the land whereinto he
> went; and his seed shall possess it (Numbers 14:24).

The children of Israel lay encamped below Mount Sinai for about a year, during which time God gave them the law and the tabernacle. Moving across the desert with the pillar-cloud before them, they soon came to

Kadesh-barnea, on the edge of the desert, and on the border of the promised land.

Here, by God's direction, they sent twelve spies to search the land, and to bring back word 'whether the people were strong or weak, few or many; and what the land is that they dwell in, whether it be good or bad; and what cities they be that they dwell in, whether in tents or in strong holds' (Numbers 13:18,19). Accordingly, the spies searched the land from one end to another, going up by the rocky dells of Hebron, and returning by the pleasant vale of Eshcol. After forty days they returned, bearing a cluster of grapes between two upon a staff; also some pomegranates, and some figs. And as they stood in the midst of assembled Israel, all eyes rested on them, all ears were open to hear their report. The land was good, they said, flowing with milk and honey; but the people were strong, and their cities walled, and very great.

Two men alone of the twelve stood boldly forward - Caleb and Joshua. And Caleb said: 'Let us go up at once, for we are well able to overcome it.' But the people wept that night, and 'bade stone Caleb with stones' (Numbers 14:10). And God was angry, and said that the congregation should die in the wilderness. 'But my servant Caleb, because he had another spirit with him, and hath followed me fully, him will I bring into the land whereinto he went; and his seed shall possess it' (verse 24).

Doctrine: It is a blessed thing to follow the Lord fully.

1. What it is to follow the Lord fully.

To follow Christ all our days.
This was the way with Caleb; he followed the Lord all his days - he followed him fully. We find it recorded of him, forty years after, when he was an old man of eighty-five, that 'he wholly followed the Lord God of Israel'. He did not follow God for a time, or by fits and starts, but all his days - he followed him fully.

There are many like Lot's wife, who flee out of Sodom for a while. She was greatly alarmed: the angels laid hands upon her, she heard the words of warning, and fled for a time; but she soon gave up, she looked back, and became a pillar of salt. So, many are awakened, and flee for their life: they weep, pray, seek salvation; but they do not hold out. They are allured by an old companion or a favourite lust, and so they draw back.

Many are like those spoken of in John 6:66. They follow Jesus for a time, and are called his disciples; they hear the gracious words that proceed out of his mouth; but by-and-by some discovery of doctrine or duty is made which offends them: 'From that time many of his disciples went back, and walked no more with Jesus.' It is those who never go back that follow him fully.

Many are like the Galatians. When Paul first preached to them, they received him 'as an angel of God, even as Christ Jesus'. They spoke of the blessedness of being in Christ, and the great salvation. They loved Paul, so that if it had been possible they would have plucked out their own eyes and given them to him (Galatians 4:15); and yet they did not follow the Lord fully. They were soon removed from the gospel of Christ to another gospel. 'O foolish Galatians, who hath bewitched you?' And now they hated Paul for speaking the truth to them. So with many of you. This is not following fully.

Many in affliction begin to follow Christ (Psalm 78:34). When laid on a sick-bed, or when some bereavement occurs, they take to their Bible, begin to weep and pray. But the world comes back upon them - temptation, old companions - and they go back. They do not follow the Lord fully.

Ah! how many in this congregation are witnesses that ye have not followed the Lord fully. Ye did run well, who did hinder you? How many of you were impressed! Divine things appeared great and precious in your eyes. You came to the Lord's table, you sat down with solemnity. And where are you now? Have you not gone quickly out of the way?

Those of you who would follow Christ fully all your days, must be like Lot: not only flee from Sodom, but flee to Zoar. You must not rest in convictions, however deep. It is a good thing to be awakened, but, ah! you are not saved. If you would follow Christ fully, you must get fully into Christ.

You must continue in his word: 'Then said Jesus to those Jews that believed on him, If ye continue in my word, then are ye my disciples indeed' (John 8:31). Remember, 'ye are saved by the gospel, if ye keep in memory what I preached unto you, unless ye have believed in vain.' *You must be like Mary,* who sat at his feet and heard his word.

You must be like aged Simeon: 'Behold, there was a man in Jerusalem whose name was Simeon, the same was just and devout, waiting for the Consolation of Israel.' Perhaps he was converted when a young man; but it was no slight work - soon over; he followed the Lord fully all his days. And now, when he was an old man, he was still waiting for the Consolation of Israel. He followed the Lord fully, and now he follows the Lamb in paradise.

You must be like the palm tree: 'The righteous shall flourish like the palm tree; he shall grow like a cedar in Lebanon. Those that be planted in the house of the LORD shall flourish in the courts of our God. They shall still bring forth fruit in old age; they shall be fat and flourishing' (Psalm 92:12-14). The palm tree and cedar have both this wonderful property, that they are fruitful to the last: and so it is with the living believer - he is a Christian to the last - full of the Spirit, full of love, full of holiness to the last. Like fine wine, the older the better. 'The path of the just is like the shining light, which shineth more and more unto the perfect day.'

You must be like Paul. From the day of his conversion, Paul was a new creature. The love of Christ constrained him, and he lived no more unto himself, but unto him that died for him and rose again. We never hear of his slackening his pace, or giving over fighting: 'Forgetting the things that are behind, and reaching forth unto the things that are before, I press toward the mark'. Even when an old man, he did not lose the fire of his love, or zeal, or compassion: 'I am ready to be offered, and the hour of my departure is at hand: I have fought the good fight, I have finished my course, I have kept the faith.' He followed the Lord fully: he never looked back, he never halted, he never slumbered. He was a second Caleb.

So must you be, if you would be saved. 'He that endureth to the end shall be saved.' Not he that has a good beginning, but he that follows fully.

To follow Christ with all the heart.

This was the way in which Caleb followed the Lord - with all his heart, fully. He had no inconsistencies, he followed the Lord in all he did.

The most of Christians do not follow the Lord fully - the most have some inconsistency. Most do not reflect Christ's image in every part. The most do not think it attainable, they are discouraged from seeking it. Many do not think it desirable; at least they think it better for the time to have this and that weakness.

Some do not follow Christ in his *lowliness*. Christ compared himself to the lily of the valleys: 'I am the rose of Sharon, and the lily of the valleys.' This was to express his lowliness - his genuine humility. Although he had no sin of his own to make him humble, yet he was humble in his own nature. He did not vaunt himself, did not seek the flattery of men. Some do not follow Christ in this. Some who seem really saved persons, yet have this unlikeness to Christ. They are proud: proud of being saved, proud of grace, proud of being different from others.

Some do not follow Christ in his *self-denial*. He was rich, yet for our sakes became poor, that we through his poverty might be rich. While we were sinners, Christ died for us. He had not where to lay his head. Yet many who seem to be Christians seek their own comfort and ease before everything else. They do not drink unto Christ's Spirit in this.

Some do not follow Christ in his *love*. Christ was love. He descended out of love, lay in the manger out of love, lived a life of sinless obedience out of love, died out of love. Yet some who are Christians do not follow him in this - do not love as he loved. Some have little compassion upon sinners, can sit at ease in their own houses, and see a world perish for lack of knowledge. How few will do anything out of love!

Many Christians have a time of decay. So it was with *Ephesus*. At one time they were 'blessed with all spiritual blessings;' 'chosen to be holy and without blame before him in love.' They were followers of God, as dear children, and walked in love, as Christ loved them. But a time of decay followed, and Christ says: 'I have this against thee, that thou hast left thy first love.' They were not like Caleb - they did not follow the Lord fully.

So it was with *David*. When he fell into gross and open sin, his whole soul seemed to decay for a time, all his bones seemed to be broken, and he feared that God would take away the Spirit from him for ever. He did not follow the Lord fully.

So it was with *Solomon*. When Solomon began to reign, it seemed as if he would follow the Lord fully. The Lord appeared to him in Gibeon, saying: 'Ask what I shall give thee.' 'God gave Solomon wisdom and understanding, exceeding much; and largeness of heart, even as the sand that is on the sea-shore.' And God enabled him to build the temple, and blessed him in all things. Yet did Solomon suffer a sad decay: he 'loved many strange women ... For it came to pass, when Solomon was old, that his wives turned away his heart after other gods: and his heart was not perfect with the LORD his God, as was the heart of David his father' (1 Kings 11:1-4). He did not follow the Lord fully.

So it was with *Asa*: 'Asa did that which was good and right in the sight of the Lord his God' (2 Chronicles 14:2). By his faith he overcame the Ethiopian army of a thousand thousand. He also made a covenant, and all Judah rejoiced at the oath. Yet he suffered a sad decay. For, when the king of Israel came against him, his faith failed him. And when he was old, he was diseased in his feet; nevertheless he sought not to the Lord, but to the physicians. He did not follow the Lord fully.

So it was with the *five virgins*. They were wise, and took oil with them in their vessels with their lamps; yet while the bridegroom tarried they all slumbered and slept. They suffered a sad decay. They did not follow the Lord fully.

Ah! this must not be the way with you, if you would be like Caleb, and follow the Lord fully. You must follow him without any inconsistency, and without any decay.

You must be like those that say: 'I am the Lord's.' 'One shall say, I am the Lord's.' God says: 'My son, give me thine heart.' Ye are bought with a price - ye are not your own. If you would be a Caleb, you must give yourself away to him. You must give away your understanding, will and affections; your body and all its members, your eyes and tongue, your hands and feet. So that you are in no respect your own, but his alone. Oh, it is sweet to give up yourself to God, to be filled with his Spirit, to be ruled by his Word; a little vessel full of him, a vessel to bear his name, a vessel afore prepared unto glory! This is to follow the Lord fully.

You must be changed into the same image. 'But we all, with open face beholding as in a glass the glory of the Lord, are changed into the same image from glory to glory, even as by the Spirit of the Lord' (2 Corinthians 3:18). Our foolish hearts think it better to retain some part of Satan's image, but, ah! this is our happiness, to reflect every feature of Jesus, and that for ever. To have no inconsistency, to be like him in every part; to love like him, to weep like him, to pray like him, to be changed into his likeness: 'I shall be satisfied when I awake with thy likeness.'

You must have his whole law written in your hearts: 'I will put my law in their inward parts, and write it in their hearts.' This is your chief happiness, to let every commandment have its proper place in your heart, to have it graven deep there, so that it cannot be effaced. This is to follow the Lord fully.

3. *To follow Christ at all hazards.*
So it was with Caleb. The congregation 'bade stone him with stones';

still he did not care, he would do his duty, whatever evil should befall him. He followed the Lord fully. Ah! there are many that follow Christ in the sunshine, that will not follow him in the storm. When the winter comes, the swallows fly away. There are many like the swallows. Many do not follow fully.

Reproach makes many stagger. As long as it is fashionable to be religious, and a man's character is advanced by it, rather than otherwise, then many follow Christ; but when it becomes a proverb and a byword, many are offended. Butterflies come out when the sun is warm; but a shower of rain makes them hide. *When men lose their worldly ease.* When Paul and Barnabas were going to Asia, they took John Mark along with them; but when the work appeared dangerous, he went back (Acts 15:38). If we would follow the Lord fully, we must go through good and bad report.

We must bear his reproach: 'Let us go out to him without the camp, bearing his reproach.' We must bear the reproach even of our nearest friends: 'He that loveth father or mother more than me, is not worthy of me; and he that loveth son or daughter more than me, is not worthy of me.' We would fain go to heaven without reproach, but it cannot be, if we go the narrow way, and follow Christ fully.

We must not think of ease if we follow Christ fully. Christ trod a thorny path: he was crowned with thorns; we must not think to be crowned with roses. Paul says: 'For whom I have suffered the loss of all things, and do count them but dung, that I may win Christ.'

We must be willing to lose our life: 'Neither count I my life dear unto myself;' 'The time cometh, when whoso killeth you shall think that he doeth God service;' 'Whoso findeth his life shall lose it;' 'Be faithful unto death;' 'They overcame him by the blood of the Lamb, and they loved not their lives unto the death.'

Oh! it is sweet to follow Christ fully, for then we shall reign with him: 'If we suffer with him, we shall reign with him. If we deny him, he will deny us.'

2. How we may be enabled to follow the Lord fully.

By keeping the eye upon him.
This was what enabled Caleb to follow the Lord fully. He endured as seeing him who was invisible; he set the Lord always before him. If Caleb had been seeking a name, or his own wealth, fame, or honour, he

would not have followed fully; he could not have followed all his days, nor with all his heart, nor at all hazards.

If you would follow Christ fully, you must know him fully.

A sight of his beauty draws us to follow him. 'He is the chief among ten thousand, and altogether lovely.' 'And I, if I be lifted up, will draw all men unto me.' There is an indescribable loveliness in Christ that draws the soul to follow him. All divine perfections dwell in him; and yet he offers to save us.

His suitableness draws us to follow him. He just answers the need of our soul. We are all guilty, he is all righteousness. We all weakness, he all strength. Nothing can more completely answer our soul than Christ doth. The chickens run under the feathers of their mother when they see them stretched out, the dove flutters into the clefts, Noah into the ark; and our soul thus follows Jesus.

His freeness draws us to follow him. 'He will in no wise cast out.' He forgives seventy times seven. It is the keeping the eye on Christ that makes you follow him. It is seeing the King in his beauty that makes the soul cleave to him, and run after him. 'My soul followeth hard after thee.' 'Run the race set before you, looking unto Jesus.'

By having the Holy Spirit.
Caleb 'had another spirit.' The other spies were carnal men; but Caleb had another spirit. He had the Holy Spirit dwelling in him, leading him, upholding and renewing. So with all who follow the Lord fully. The Spirit of God in the soul is a constant stream, a well of water springing up unto everlasting life. Lot's wife looked back; but she had not the indwelling of the Holy Spirit. He is a filling Spirit who loves to fill the heart, to fill every chamber. 'Be filled with the Spirit.' 'Now the God of hope fill you.' He loves to write the whole law on the heart, to lift the whole soul to God.

3. The motives to follow the Lord fully.
'Him will I bring into the land.' The other spies died of the plague, the people fell in the wilderness; but Caleb and Joshua, because they followed the Lord fully, were received into the land.

It is the only happy life.
There is no happier life under the sun than to follow Christ all our days. There is not a more miserable creature on earth than a backslider. Every

time we turn aside from following Christ, we are providing misery for ourselves - hidings, desertions, and broken bones. The only happy life is to follow with all our heart. We generally think it is happy to have this or that idol, but we are quite mistaken. Your true happiness is in self-surrender, in giving up your heart and all to him. Any one inconsistency mars your joy, mars communion. Are you not far happier in your times of closest walking with God? O that it were so with me always! Decays bring darkness and misery. The only happiness is to suffer the loss of all things. Many Christians are not willing to deny themselves, to suffer for Christ's sake, not willing to bear reproach or persecution. Christ will give a hundred-fold more - peace of conscience.

This is the way to be useful.
It is the thriving Christian that is the useful Christian - the one that follows Christ fully. The blessing to Abraham was: 'I will bless thee, and make thee a blessing.' This was eminently true of Paul. He followed Christ fully; and what a blessing he was! So would you be, if you followed Christ fully. If you bore all the features of Christ about with you, what a blessing would you be to this place, and to the world! Not a cumberer of the ground. How useful to your children and neighbours!

This is the way to die happily.
If you would die the death of Christ's people, you must live their life. Inconsistent Christians generally have a painful death-bed; but those that follow Christ fully can die like aged Paul - 'I am ready to be offered'; like Job - 'I know that my Redeemer liveth.'

This will insure a great reward.
Every man shall be rewarded according as his work has been. Some will be made rulers over five, some over ten cities. I have no doubt that every sin, inconsistency, backsliding and decay of God's children takes away something from their eternal glory. It is a loss for all eternity; and the more fully and unreservedly we follow the Lord Jesus now, the more abundant will our entrance be into his everlasting kingdom. The closer we walk with Christ now, the closer will we walk with him to all eternity. 'Thou hast a few names in Sardis which have not defiled their garments. They shall walk with me in white, for they are worthy.' Amen.
Dundee, 1842

55. The unworthy communicant warned

For he that eateth and drinketh unworthily, eateth and drinketh damnation to himself, not discerning the Lord's body. For this cause many are weak and sickly among you, and many sleep (1 Corinthians 11:29,30).

When it pleased God lately to pour out his Spirit in a remarkable manner on one of the parishes of Scotland, I was told by the minister that the sin that took deepest hold upon the consciences of the people was the sin of unworthy communicating. He told me it was a most affecting sight to see aged persons of threescore-and-ten sitting weeping over the broken sacraments of bygone years. If it shall please God to pour out his Spirit on the grown-up part of this congregation, I feel deeply persuaded that this dreadful sin of unworthy communicating will be like a millstone around most of your necks. Yes, my dear friends, God has a controversy with you about this matter, and he will either plead with you in time or in eternity.

There is such a thing as eating and drinking unworthily. Even in the days of the Apostle Paul this sin existed; and so it does in our day. There are many at the Lord's table who should not be there. There are many who come without the wedding garment, many who displease and provoke God by coming, many who will repent it to all eternity. They get no good by it, but great evil. They eat and drink damnation to themselves. They think they are eating harmless bread and wine; or perhaps they think they are covering the sins of the past six months by eating; whereas God says they are eating and drinking damnation to themselves. It is as if they were eating poison.

The apostle explains wherein the unworthiness of such consists: they do not discern the Lord's body. The phrase here used is evidently taken from the sense of taste in the human body, whereby we discern between different kinds of food. To discern the Lord's body is to have a peculiar taste or relish for the way of salvation by Christ and him crucified. When a heavy laden sinner feels the power of the gospel, when he sees the sweetness, freeness and fulness of Christ, he then tastes or discerns the Lord's body. But those who have not come to Christ have never got this taste, this relish for the way of salvation by Christ. They may be very decent, good-natured people, they may read the Bible, and keep up a form of godliness; but they have never tasted the honey in the clefts of the Rock. These are they who profane the Lord's table.

1. None should come to the Lord's supper but those who discern the Lord's body - i.e. have a true relish for Christ. This appears:

From the actions of the communicant.
You do not come to look at the bread and wine, but to feed upon them. You stretch out the hand, and take of the bread and eat it; you take the wine and drink it. Now, since that bread and wine represent the Lord's body, it is plain to a child, that the meaning of that action is: 'I relish the Lord Jesus Christ. He is my manna, my sweet food; my only way of pardon, peace and holiness; my Lord, and my God.' When a hungry beggar comes to your door, and you give him a piece of wholesome bread, how gladly does he catch at it, and begin to eat it! Why? Because he relishes it; it is what he requires. Such is your feeding at the Lord's table. You thereby declare that Christ is your Saviour, your manna, your all.

When the man found the treasure in the field, he was glad, and went and sold all that he had and bought that field. Such is your declaration in coming to the Lord's table: Christ is precious to me; I have left all for him.

The bride in the Song of Solomon says: 'As the apple tree among the trees of the wood, so is my beloved among the sons. I sat down under his shadow with great delight, and his fruit was sweet to my taste.' So do you say in coming to the Lord's table: I have found rest in the shade of Christ, his fruit is sweet to me; his way of pardon, his Spirit, his commands all are sweet to my taste.

When the maniac had the devils cast out, he sat at the feet of Jesus clothed, and in his right mind. Once he bade Jesus depart: 'What have I to do with thee?' Now Christ is all. Such is your declaration at the Lord's Table.

When Paul was an unconverted man, he was a blasphemer - he breathed out threatenings. But when he got a taste of Jesus, he said, 'I count all things but loss for the excellency of the knowledge of Christ Jesus my Lord.' Such is your declaration in taking that bread and wine.

Can you truly say that you have found the treasure, that you have sold all for it, that you have sat down under the shade of that apple tree, and that you delight in his holy fruit; that you were once far from Christ, but now sitting at his feet; that you now preach the faith which once you destroyed - that, like Paul, you glory only in the cross of Christ? Can you say, in the sight of God, that Christ is your manna, your sweet food, your peace, your all? Then you are welcome to the Lord's table. 'Eat, O friends; drink, yea, drink abundantly, O beloved.'

Most of you cannot say this. You have not found the treasure. Will you come to the Lord's table? To what purpose? You will eat and drink unworthily. It will provoke God in a dreadful manner. You will repent it when you die. You will grieve on account of it to all eternity. Some even perpetrate in half an hour what they will mourn for ever and ever. Judas, in eternal torments, bewails his sin and folly. So will you.

From the words of Jesus: 'This do in remembrance of me.'
An unconverted man cannot remember Christ; for he hath never seen him, neither known him. A man who never tasted honey cannot remember the taste of it; so a man who never had a saving taste of the sweetness of the Lord Jesus cannot possibly remember him. Indeed, there is a kind of remembrance of Christ that any man may have. You may remember the events of his life: that he was born in a stable, that he walked on the Lake of Galilee, that he wept over Jerusalem, that he prayed in Gethsemane, that he died on the cross on Calvary; but even the devils can remember Christ in this way. They remember all his history much more perfectly than we do. Satan has more knowledge of divine things than many doctors of divinity. And lost souls in eternal misery remember Jesus; they remember all he did, and all he suffered, and how often he would have saved them. Judas, in his place in hell, remembers Jesus. But, ah! this is not the saving remembrance of Jesus which we have at the Lord's Table.

When a labouring, heavy laden sinner is brought to the feet of Jesus, he finds a joy and peace in believing he never felt before. He gets a discovery of the love of Christ that he never had before; the love of Jesus in coming for the ungodly, and dying for them; the freeness of Christ to every creature, to sinners even the chief, to publicans and sinners, coming to him; the wisdom and excellency of this way of salvation, the amazing glory and perfection of the righteousness of God. When the Spirit thus takes the veil from the eyes, he gets a sight of Christ which he never will, and never can, forget. This is the spiritual relish and discerning of the Lord's body.

Every new exhibition of Jesus calls up again this sweet sense of his goodness and beauty. He cannot hear his name but his heart is caught away to him. His name is like ointment. When ministers preach his Word, the memory rushes back to Jesus; and when the broken bread and wine are set before his eyes, his heart is drawn away to remember Jesus. As when the widows stood by Peter weeping, showing the coats and garments that Dorcas had made, every new piece of handiwork of their departed friend called up fresh love in their bosom, and fresh tears to their eyes; so to those that know Jesus, the broken bread and poured-out wine stir up their inmost souls to remember Jesus.

Have you this sanctified memory? Do you remember when the name of Christ was all a blank to you? And is it now like ointment poured forth? Do you remember when first you saw the Lord, or if not the very time, do you feel the amazing change that has been wrought in you? Then welcome. 'This do in remembrance of me.'

But most, I fear, have no such memory. You have no gracious discovery of Christ to remember. You have never discerned the Lord's body. You say you will remember his life and death. Why, devils could do that. Would it not shock you to see devils seated at the Lord's table? And yet they have as much right to sit there as unconverted souls.

From the practice of the apostles.
One example: The Ethiopian eunuch was 'a man of great authority under Candace, queen of the Ethiopians, and had the charge of all her treasure' (Acts 8:27). By the amazing grace of God this man became concerned about his soul - a Bible had come his way, and perhaps some wandering messenger of mercy. He could not rest, but left his country to go to Jerusalem. There he found no peace, no light. Sad and weary, he proceeded on his journey home. Still his heart was heavy; he sat reading Isaiah the prophet. By the mercy of God, Philip was sent to him, and in his chariot preached to him Jesus, the Lamb of God. O what a new world now opened to the Ethiopian! He sees the way of righteousness without works. Now they come to water: 'What doth hinder me to be baptized? If thou believest with all thine heart thou mayest. I believe that Jesus is the Son of God. So they went down into the water, and Philip baptized him; and he went on his way rejoicing.' Is this your experience, beloved? Have you sought Christ as he did? Have you found him as he did? Do you believe with all your heart? Then the Lord's table is open to you, and you will go on your way rejoicing.

But, ah! it is not so with most. If some of you had been keeper of Candace's treasures, you would not have gone the length of the street to find the way to be saved. Some of you never read your Bible as that Ethiopian did. You have never sought instruction. You dare not say that you have believed with all your heart. Why, then, would you sit down at this holy table? You may come; but, alas! you will not go on your way rejoicing.

2. Unworthy communicating is very dangerous.

They who do so are guilty of the body and blood of the Lord.
There is no sin less thought of on earth - there is no sin more thought of in heaven and in hell, than unworthy communicating. Those who commit it are sharing with those who betrayed and murdered the Lord Jesus. They share with them in two respects. First, in pretending love and friendship toward him; second, in real hatred to him in their hearts, and contempt for his gospel.

When Judas betrayed the Lord Jesus, he pretended great love for him. He had followed him during all the years of his ministry, had preached in his name. He sat very reverently at the Lord's table, dipped his hand in the same dish with Christ. His words were smoother than butter; but war was in his heart. When he came to betray Christ, he said: 'Hail, Master!' and kissed him; yet all the while there was awful hatred in his heart - a deadly enmity at Christ and his gospel.

So the high priests and Pharisees pretended great zeal for God and for his cause. They pretended to be very sanctified and holy men; and yet they hated and condemned Christ to die. The soldiers of Herod pretended great respect to Christ, when they kneeled to him and said, 'Hail, King of the Jews!' but all the time they mocked and hated him. Pilate pretended much to be a friend of Christ: he washed his hands, and said, 'I am guiltless of this innocent blood'; and yet he condemned him to be crucified.

So it is with unworthy communicants. You come to the Lord's table with a great show of respect. You appear deeply solemnized. You take the bread and wine, pretending that you have been converted, that Christ is your portion. You appear to be under deep emotion. Yet all the while you despise Christ and his people, ridicule conversion, and the life of grace. 'Woe unto that man! It had been good for him that he had never been born.' You have the same heart as Judas, as the high priest, as the soldiers, as Pilate. You are guilty.

They eat and drink judgment to themselves.
This is true of unworthy communicating in two ways. First, it is adding

another sin - heaping another mountain on the burdened soul, and so bringing heavier condemnation, sinking the soul deeper. Second, it is always hardening. All sin hardens, but especially sinning in holy things. One who makes jests out of the Bible is hardly ever saved, it is so hardening. But of all sins against holy things, unworthy communicating is the most hardening; so that an unconverted man communicating does often literally eat and drink damnation to himself. Just as a child of God drinks life, so he drinks death, out of that cup.

Some of you may be saying, Though I be unconverted, I will go; for though it do me no good, it will do me no harm. Is it no harm to add another sin to your soul? Is it no harm to harden and seal your heart unto perdition? Is it no harm to eat and drink judgment to yourself?

Some may be saying, I hope I shall cover the sins of my past six months by it. Some of you, who have only been once or twice at church all that time, will be saying, I will make up for past neglect, and cover my sins. Will it cover your past sins, to add another to the heap? Will it atone for your broken Sabbaths, to come and profane the sacrament too? Will it cover sins to eat and drink judgment?

Many who are guilty of it are weak and sickly, and many sleep.
There are some sins which God visits with temporal judgments, as weakness of body, sickness, and death. When Ananias and Sapphira lied to the Holy Ghost, they fell down dead at the apostles' feet. When Herod gave not God the glory, he was eaten up of worms, and died upon his throne. So it is especially in profaning the Lord's table. This is God's word, who knows best: 'For this cause many are weak and sickly among you, and many sleep.'

The Lord Jesus, the master of the table, has all providences in his hand, and he can, and does, make use of them to bring down those who insolently profane his table. Just as God has provided a real hell of material fire that never will be quenched, in order to affect some gross sinners, who would not be moved to flee from anything but bodily pain; so in the Lord's supper it pleases God to make use of sickness and death to keep off profane hands from that bread and wine. I have often observed God doing this. I remember three deaths which took place in such a way and at such a time, that I could not doubt it was the fulfilment of this verse. Watch and see, beloved!

Take heed, then, O beloved, lest when the bread is in your mouth you should fall down dead. Ah! it is an awful thing to die profaning the

Lord's table; for you will sink lower than the grave.

'Therefore, let a man examine himself.' What are your real motives for coming to the Lord's table? Is it because you are come to a certain time of life? But are you born again? Is it because your family are coming? Is it for a name? Is it for money? Ah! Judas over again. Is it to get baptism for your child? That is to commit one sin to help you to commit another.

Is it to praise him for what he has done for your soul? (Psalm 66). Is it to show the world whom you have chosen? Is it to get near to Jesus? Come, then, and lean on his breast, and never draw back. Amen.
Dundee, 1841

56. The blessedness of giving

'It is more blessed to give than to receive' (Acts 20:35).

These words form part of a most touching address which Paul made to the elders of Ephesus, when he parted with them for the last time. He took them all to witness that he was pure from the blood of all men: 'For I have not shunned to declare unto you all the counsel of God.' It is deeply interesting to notice that the duty of giving to the poor is marked by him as one part of the counsel of God; so much so, that he makes it his last word to them: 'I have showed you all things, how that so labouring ye ought to support the weak, and to remember the words of the Lord Jesus, how he said, It is more blessed to give than to receive.' These words, which he quotes from the mouth of the Saviour, are nowhere to be found in the Gospels. It is the only traditional saying of our Lord that has been preserved. It seems to have been one of his household words, a common-place, uttered by him again and again: 'It is more blessed to give than to receive.'

I am glad of having this opportunity of laying before you this part of the counsel of God (for God knows there is no part of it I wish to keep back from you) that you ought to labour to support the weak. And the only argument I shall use with you is that of our blessed Lord: 'It is more blessed to give than to receive.'

1. We should give liberally to the poor, because it is a happier thing to give than to receive.
It is happy, because it is like all happy beings. All happy beings are giving beings. Their happiness consists not in receiving, but in giving.

Consider the angels.
The whole Bible shows that the angels are happy beings - far happier than we can conceive. They are holy beings, ever doing God's commandments. Now, holiness and happiness are inseparable. They are in heaven, always in the smile of their Father: they 'do always behold the face of my Father which is in heaven'. They must be happy, no tear on their cheek, no sigh in their bosom. They are represented as praising God, one crying to another, 'Holy, holy, holy', and singing, 'Worthy is the Lamb'. Now, singing praises is a sign of mirth and gladness. 'Is any merry? let him sing psalms.' Now, I want you to see that the happiness of these happy spirits consists in giving.

First, *they all give*: 'Are they not all ministering spirits, sent forth to minister to them that shall be heirs of salvation?' Upon the earth very few people give. Most people like to receive money, to keep it, to lay it up in the bank, to see it becoming more and more. There are only a few people that give, these often not the richest. But in heaven all give. It is their greatest pleasure. Search every dwelling of every angel, you will not find one hoard among them all. They are all ministering spirits.

Second, *they give to those who are far beneath them*. They are not contented to help those that can help them back again, but they give, hoping for nothing again. There were some poor shepherds in the fields near Bethlehem; yet a great angel did not hesitate to visit them with kind and gentle words. Nay, it would seem that there were many more that would fain have been allowed to carry the message; for no sooner was it done than a multitude of the heavenly host were with him praising God. You remember, too, how kind the angels were to the beggar Lazarus. The dogs were the only ones that ministered to him on earth; but the angels stooped on willing wing, and bore him to Abraham's bosom.

Third, *the highest love to give most*. There is reason to believe that the highest angels are those who go down lowest, and give up most in the service of God. Jesus expressly says so: 'He that is greatest among you shall be your servant.' The angels that see the face of God stoop to serve the meanest children of God. It is the happiness of the happiest angel that he can give up more, and stoop lower down in sweet humble services, than the angels beneath him. Dear Christians, you often pray, 'Thy will be done on earth as it is in heaven?' If you mean anything, you mean that you may serve God as the angels do! Ah, then, your happiness must be in giving. The happiness of the angels consists in this. If you would be like them, become a ministering spirit.

Consider the goodness of God.
We know very little of God; but we know that he is infinitely happy. You cannot add to his happiness, nor take from it. We know also many things that enter into his happiness. Everything he does must afford him happiness. As when he created the world, and said, 'All very good,' God was happy in creating. But the Bible shows that his happiness mainly consists in giving, not in receiving. His giving food to all creatures is very wonderful - not one sparrow is forgotten before God. The whole world has been cursed, and God could justly cast the whole into destruction; but he does not - he delighteth in mercy. The young lions seek their meat from God. He feeds the ravens when they cry. He gives to the wicked: 'He maketh his sun to rise on the evil and on the good, and sendeth rain on the just and unjust.' Just think for a moment how many thousands God feeds every day who blaspheme his name, and profane his Sabbath. He gives them food and raiment, he turns the hearts of people to be kind to them; and yet they curse God every day. Oh! how this shows that God delighteth in mercy. 'Be ye merciful, even as your Father in heaven is merciful.' But, most of all, he gave his own Son. God delights in giving. It is his nature. He spared not his own Son. Although he was emptying his own bosom, yet he would not keep back the gift. Now, some of you pray night and day to be made like God: 'Blessed art thou, O God: teach me thy statutes.' If you will be like him, be like him in giving. It is God's chief happiness. Be you like him in it.

Objection. Would you have me give to wicked people, who will go and abuse it?

Answer. God gives to wicked people, who go and abuse it; yet that does not diminish his happiness. God makes the sun rise on the evil and on the good, and pours down rain on the just and the unjust. It is right to give most and best to the children of God. But give to the wicked also, if you would be like God. Give to the unthankful, give to the vile. 'Give to him that asketh of thee; and from him that would borrow of thee turn not thou away', remembering the word of the Lord Jesus.

Look at Christ.

He was the eternal Son of God - equal with the Father in everything, therefore equal in happiness. He had glory with him before ever the world was. Yet his happiness also consisted in giving. He was far above all the angels, and therefore he gave far more than they all: 'The Son of Man came not to be ministered unto, but to minister, and to give his life a ransom for many.' He was highest, therefore he stooped lowest. They gave their willing services, he gave himself: 'Ye know the grace of our Lord Jesus Christ, that though he was rich, yet for our sakes he became poor, that we, through his poverty, might be made rich. Let this mind be in you which was also in Christ.'

Now, dear Christians, some of you pray night and day to be branches of the true Vine; you pray to be made all over in the image of Christ. If so, you must be like him in giving. A branch bears the same kind of fruit as the tree. If you be branches at all, you must bear the same fruit. An old divine says well: 'What would have become of us if Christ had been as saving of his blood as some men are of their money?'

Objection. My money is my own.

Answer. Christ might have said, My blood is my own, my life is my own; no man forceth it from me. Then where should we have been?

Objection. The poor are undeserving.

Answer. Christ might have said the same thing. They are wicked rebels against my Father's law: shall I lay down my life for these? I will give to the good angels. But no, he left the ninety-nine, and came after the lost. He gave his blood for the undeserving.

Objection. The poor may abuse it.

Answer. Christ might have said the same: yea, with far greater truth. Christ knew that thousands would trample his blood under their feet, that most would despise it, that many would make it an excuse for sinning more. Yet he gave his own blood.

Oh, my dear Christians! if you would be like Christ, give much, give often, give freely, to the vile and the poor, the thankless and the undeserving. Christ is glorious and happy, and so will you be. It is not your money I want, but your happiness. Remember his own words: 'It is more blessed to give than to receive.'

2. It is happier, because of the peculiar character of a Christian.

A Christian is a steward.

In every great house there is a steward, whose duty it is to manage his master's goods in such a way that every one may have his portion of meat in due season. Now you will see at once that the happiness of the steward does not consist in the receiving of more goods, but in the due distribution of what he has got. If there be any grieve or foreman hearing me, you will know quite well that your happiness consists not in the quantity of your master's goods which goes through your hands, but in the right distribution of it. The happiness of every steward consists in giving, not in receiving.

Now, dear Christians, you are only stewards of all you possess. You have not one halfpenny of your own: 'Occupy till I come' is written upon everything. The reckoning-day is near. O that you would be wise stewards! You would be far happier. It is the devil that persuades you that it is better to hoard and lay up for yourself and your children. It is far happier to be an honest steward.

Objection: I am in very poor circumstances.

Answer. Still you are a steward. Use what you have as a steward for Christ, and you will do well. He that used his two talents did not lose his reward.

Christians are members one of another.

When we are united to Christ, we are united to all the brethren. It is a closer relation than any other, for it outlasts every other. The wife of your bosom will one day be separated from you. Father and child, sister and brother, may be separated eternally; but not so Christian and Christian. They are for ever and for ever branches of the same tree for eternity, stones of the same temple for ever. Now it must be the happiness of one member to help another. In the body, when one limb is hurt or is weakly, the others help it. It is their happiness to do so. When the left hand is wounded, the right hand will do everything for it, it supplies all its need. So it is in Christ's body. It is the happiness of one member to help another. It is just like helping oneself; yea, it is like helping Christ. If Christ were to come to your door poor and clothed in rags and shivering with cold, would you feel it an unhappy thing to supply all his need? Oh, then, you may do this whenever you see a poor Christian: 'Inasmuch as ye do it to the least of these my brethren, ye do it unto me.' Woe is me! How many of you turn Christ away from your door, with a rude and angry countenance! Are you not ashamed to call yourself a Christian?

Again, if Christ lived in some poor dwelling, with not enough of fire to keep away the cold, with not enough of clothes to make the bed warm, would you not seek him out? Would you stay till he sought you? Ah, woe is me! In how many dwellings does Christ dwell thus? And yet, there are Christians hearing me that never have sought him out. Change your plan, I pray you. 'It is more blessed to give than to receive.'

3. Because Christians will be no losers.

They shall be no losers in this world by what they give away: 'There is that scattereth, and yet increaseth; there is that withholdeth more than is meet, and it tendeth to penury.'

I am going to say now what the world will scoff at. But all that I ask of you is, to be like the Bereans. Search the Scriptures, and see if these things be not so. The whole Bible shows, then, that the best way to have plenty in this world is to give liberally. 'Cast thy bread upon the waters, and thou shalt find it after many days.' This refers to the sowing of rice. The rice in the East is always sown when the fields are flooded with water. The bread-corn is actually cast upon the water. After many days the waters dry up, and a rich crop of waving rice covers the plain. So it is in giving liberally to the poor out of love to Jesus. It is like throwing away your money - it is like casting seed upon the waters. Yet fear not, you shall find a crop after many days - you shall have a return for your money in this world.

A word to Christians in humble life. You say, If I were a rich Christian, how happy would I be to give! But I am so poor, what can I give? Now I just ask you to look at the man sowing seed. When he has but little, does he keep back from sowing that little? No; he sows all the more anxiously the little he has, in order to make more. Do you the same.

How little you believe God! He says: 'He that giveth to the poor, lendeth to the Lord.' Now, I believe there is not one in a hundred who would not rather lend to a rich man than lend to the Lord. You believe man - not God. In fact, it is but the other day I heard of a child of God who was in very reduced circumstances, her husband being blind, yet who contrived not only to live, but to give to others also. She wrought with her own hands, that she might have to give. This was sowing the seed, all the seed she had, for she had no hoard. And did the crop fail? No, it appeared in India - a distant relative died, leaving £20,000 to her alone! God is able to do this every day. 'God is able to make all grace abound toward you, that ye always having all sufficiency in all things, may abound to every good work.' How easily God can give you, by the smallest turn of his providence, more than all you give away in a year! O trust the Lord! But the wicked cannot trust God. The world is an Infidel at heart.

Some will say, 'I will begin tonight. I will put your word to the test. I will give double what I ever gave, and see if I will get a return.' No such thing; keep your money, I advise you. If you give hoping for something again, you will get nothing. You must give as a Christian gives - cheerfully, liberally, and freely, hoping for nothing again; and then God will give you back good measure, pressed down, running over: 'Give, and it shall be given to you.' He that giveth to the poor shall have no lack.

Christians will be no losers in eternity.

The whole Bible shows that Christians will be rewarded in eternity just in proportion to the use they have made of their talents. Now, money is one talent. If you use it right you will in no wise lose your reward. Christ plainly shows that he will reckon with men in the judgment according as they have dealt by his poor Christians. They that have done much for Christ shall have an abundant entrance; they that have done little shall have little reward.

I thank God that there are some among you to whom Christ will say: 'Come, ye blessed of my Father, inherit the kingdom prepared for you from the foundation of the world.' Go on, dear Christians - live still for Christ. Never forget, day nor night, that you are yourselves bought with a price. Lay yourselves and your property all in his hand, and say: 'What wilt thou have me to do? Here am I, send me'; and then I know you will feel, now and in eternity, 'It is more blessed to give than to receive.'

I fear there are some Christians among you to whom Christ can say no such thing. Your haughty dwelling rises in the midst of thousands who have scarce a fire to warm themselves at, and have but little clothing to keep out the biting frost; and yet you never darkened their door. You heave a sigh, perhaps, at a distance; but you do not visit them. Ah, my dear friends! I am concerned for the poor; but more for you. I know not what Christ will say to you in the great day. You seem to be Christians, and yet you care not for his poor. Oh, what a change will pass upon you as you enter the gates of heaven! You will be saved, but that will be all. There will be no abundant entrance for you: 'He that soweth sparingly shall reap also sparingly.'

I fear there are many hearing me who may know well that they are not Christians, because they do not love to give. To give largely and liberally, not grudgingly at all requires a new heart; an old heart would rather part with its life-blood than its money. Oh, my friends! enjoy your money, make the most of it, give none away, enjoy it quickly; for I can tell you you will be beggars throughout eternity.

Dundee, February 4, 1838

57. Christ's silence under suffering

He was oppressed, and he was afflicted, yet he opened not his mouth: he is brought as a lamb to the slaughter, and as a sheep before her shearers is dumb, so he openeth not his mouth (Isaiah 53:7).

When the Jewish priests used to lead the tender fleecy lamb to be slain in the temple, it did not struggle, it did not complain. So when the shearer is clipping the snowy fleece from the sheep, it does not struggle, it does not complain. Even so, when God gave his own Son up to the death for us all, he did not struggle, he did not complain. When that gentle Lamb of God was led to the slaughter, he murmured not. When the four soldiers parted his raiment among them and for his vesture cast lots, when these cruel shearers robbed the Sheep of his snowy fleece, he was dumb, he opened not his mouth.

When he was oppressed and afflicted by man, he answered not a word. He was oppressed and afflicted by God - he murmured not. It pleased the Lord to bruise him. He put him to grief. He was stricken, smitten of God, and afflicted. Yet he spoke not. He did not turn round and say: Righteous Father, this is unjust. Why should I suffer for sins I did not commit? Lord, thou knowest that I am without spot and blameless, thou knowest that I knew no sin, neither was guile found in my mouth. He was oppressed and afflicted both by God and by man, yet he opened not his mouth. 'He was led as a lamb to the slaughter, and as a sheep before her shearers is dumb, so he opened not his mouth.'

Doctrine. Christ was silent under his sufferings.

First, the fact that Christ was really silent under his sufferings; second, why he was silent; and, third, how this is showed forth in the Lord's supper.

1. The fact that Christ was silent under his sufferings.

He was silent before man.
He was oppressed and afflicted by the wicked hands of men; and yet he did not justify himself before man. This is true when he was taken prisoner in the Garden of Gethsemane. It was night when a multitude came upon him with lanterns and torches, and swords and staves. Did Jesus flee away? No. Did he make resistance? No. His disciples said: 'Shall we smite with the sword?' and Peter actually used the sword. But Jesus forbade them. He could have called down twelve legions of angels. He could have taken away their breath, that they should die. But no; he said, 'This is your hour and the power of darkness.' 'The cup which my Father hath given me, shall I not drink it?' 'He was led as a lamb to the slaughter, and as a sheep before her shearers is dumb, so he opened not his mouth.'

This is true in his trial before Caiaphas. They had bound Jesus in the garden, and led him away to the palace of Caiaphas, the high priest. Chief priests and elders and scribes, there sat in mock trial upon the Lamb of God. Many false tongues bare false witness against him. Did he answer them? No. He answered not a word. And the high priest stood up in the midst and said: 'Answerest thou nothing?' But he held his peace, and answered nothing. He was led like a lamb - led to the slaughter; 'and as a sheep before her shearers is dumb, so he opened not his mouth.'

This is true in his trial before Pilate. From Caiaphas they led him away to the Roman governor: 'And there the chief priests stood and accused him of many things; but he answered nothing. And Pilate asked him, Answerest thou nothing? But Jesus yet answered nothing, so that Pilate marvelled greatly.' Ah! the blind Roman did not know that he was the Lamb of God, bearing the sins of many. Again: Pilate sent him to Herod. Herod questioned him, the Jews vehemently accused him, Herod's men of war made a mock of him. Yet it is written: 'He answered him nothing' - he was still the silent Lamb. Again, when Herod sent him back to Pilate, then Pilate sat down on the tribunal of justice and declared, 'I have found no fault in him.' 'He washed his hands, and said, I am innocent of the blood of this just person.' And yet he passed sentence on him that he should be crucified! Did Jesus cry, Unjust? Did he cry, I stand at Caesar's judgment-seat. I appeal unto Caesar? No. 'He was led as a lamb to the slaughter, and as a sheep before her shearers is dumb, so he opened not his mouth.'

Again: upon the cross he was oppressed and afflicted of man. The passers-by wagged the head at him, and said: 'Come down from the cross.' The priests, too, mocked him, as an outcast from God. The very thieves cast the same in his teeth, for three dark hours. Did he complain? No. He felt it to be true that he was an outcast from his God. He answered not a word. 'He was led as a lamb to the slaughter, and as a sheep before her shearers is dumb, so he opened not his mouth.'

Christ was silent before God under his sufferings.
You remember him in the garden. You remember how he was bruised there, when 'his sweat was as great drops of blood falling down to the ground.' There God set down the cup of his wrath before him, to show him what he was going to drink. He might have said: This is no cup of mine; let them drink it that filled it by their sins. But no; he only cries that it may pass from him: 'O my Father, if it be possible, let this cup pass from me.' Prayer is the cry of one who feels no right to demand. If he had seen it to be unjust to give him such a cup, he would have said: Righteous Father, this is not for me to drink. Shall not the Judge of all the earth do right? But no; he acknowledges it to be just, if the Father wills it. The second time he prays, he says: 'If this cup may not pass from me, except I drink it, thy will be done.' He acquiesces in the justice of God in giving him such a cup to drink. He is the Lamb of God. 'He was led as a lamb to the slaughter, and as a sheep before her shearers is dumb, so he opened not his mouth.'

You remember him on the cross. There God hid his face from him. For three hours did the sun refuse to shine upon that cross - darkness brooded over the land. But deeper was the darkness brooding over the Redeemer's soul. God's face refused to shine upon his Son. Yet did he say it was unjust? No. He said: 'Father, forgive them; for they know not what they do.' He said: 'Today shalt thou be with me in Paradise.' At the ninth hour he cried: 'Eloi, Eloi, lama sabachthani' - words not of murmuring, but of agony. Again he said: 'I thirst.' And again he cried: 'It is finished. Father, into thy hands I commend my spirit.' These are all the words that Jesus spake upon the cross. He did not cry: Why am here - I am the Lord of glory? Why should I hang between earth and heaven? Righteous Father, I never sinned. I was always holy, harmless, undefiled; why should I suffer thus? But no; he was silent under his sufferings, both from God and man. 'He was led as a lamb to the slaughter, and as a sheep before her shearers is dumb, so he opened not his mouth.'

2. Inquire the reasons why Christ was silent under his sufferings.

Because he knew his sufferings were all infinitely just.
When a person is undergoing a trial - when he is accused, borne witness against, and condemned - if he be really guilty of the crimes led to his charge, he is dumb, and says: I deserve it all. If he has any sense of justice left in his bosom, he will be convinced and conscience-stricken, he will answer not a word. He feels that his condemnation is just and righteous, and therefore he is dumb. Just so it was with Christ. Christ had an infinite sense of justice; therefore, both in his accusations by men and bruisings under the wrath of God, he answered not a word. He was a silent Lamb.

How was it just that Christ should suffer, when he had not committed the things laid to his charge? True, he was holy. He was the Son of God, infinitely holy. When he became man, still he was a 'holy thing'; through life he was holy, harmless, undefiled, and separate from sinners; and in his death he was a Lamb without spot and blameless. But still he was a substitute in the room of sinners. 'He who knew no sin was made sin for us.' He that was the Son of the Blessed became a curse for us. The reproaches of them that reproached us fell upon him. He stood in the place of blasphemers, and gluttons, and wine-bibbers, and deceivers, and thieves, and murderers, and outcasts from God. Therefore it was quite just that the sufferings due to these sinners should fall upon him; and so when he was accused and condemned, he opened not his mouth: 'He was led as a lamb to the slaughter, and as a sheep before her shearers is dumb, so he opened not his mouth.'

Have you joined yourself to Christ? Then there is strong consolation for you. If it was just that Christ should suffer, then it is not just that you should suffer. He was silent and opened not his mouth when wrath was poured out upon him. But, ah! he will cry aloud if wrath should be poured upon you. You have been condemned already, and buffeted and spit upon already. You will never suffer any more. 'Who shall lay anything to the charge of God's elect? It is God that justifieth - who shall condemn? It is Christ that died.'

Because he would keep his part of the covenant.
Before the world was, he entered into covenant with his Father, that he would stand as a substitute for sinners; and therefore when he did come to suffer, his very righteousness sustained him, and he set his face like a flint. When a feeble man undertakes some hard piece of service, very often he is loud and boastful before he begins; but when he comes up to the point, his courage dies, and he goes away back from his word. Not so the Son of God. He had sworn that he would bear the curse that was hanging over sinners. He had struck hands with the eternal Father he would be their Jonah, to lie down under their sea of wrath: 'Take me up,' he said, 'and cast me into that sea of wrath.' And so, when the waves and billows went over him, he did not cry nor murmur. He set his face steadfastly. He had sworn once by his holiness, and he would not turn from it. He would not alter the thing that had gone out of his lips. 'He was led as a lamb to the slaughter, and as a sheep before her shearers is dumb, so he opened not his mouth.'

To awakened souls I say, trust in Christ as a Saviour. He is worthy of all your confidence. If I had told you that the Son of God had undertaken to suffer in the room of sinners, surely that ought to give you peace; for if he undertakes it, he will perform it. But we are sent to tell you that he has finished what he undertook. He is a faithful and covenant-keeping Saviour. Come and look upon that silent Lamb. See him led from the garden to Caiaphas, from Caiaphas to Pilate, from Pilate to Herod, from Herod to Pilate again, from Pilate to Calvary. See him carrying that heavy cross upon his shoulders, see him carrying the wrath of God upon his head; and yet he murmurs not. He does not say: Father, these sins are not mine. No; he keeps truth for ever. 'He was led as a lamb to the slaughter, and as a sheep before her shearers is dumb, so he opened not his mouth.' And how do you requite all this? You say: I dare not believe it. Ah! does he deserve this at your hand, that you should call him liar? He that believeth not God hath made him a liar.

Because of his love.
It was love to perishing sinners that made the Son of God enter into covenant with his Father to bear wrath in their stead. It was the same love

in his bosom that made him keep the covenant which he had made. Ah! it was love that tied his tongue. The cords with which the soldiers bound him were tight and strong; but, oh! his love bound him more firmly than all. The nails that pierced his hands and feet held him firmly on the bloody cross; but, oh! his love was the strongest nail - it was stronger than death.

When the Jews accused him, and he answered not a word, it was love to sinners which made him hold his peace. When Herod questioned him, and Pilate condemned him, his trembling humanity said: I am not guilty. But, oh! his love said: Yes; I am guilty of all. When his Father bruised him with weights of mysterious agony in the garden and on the cross, when the infinite wrath of the infinite God was all summed up in a three hours' agony, when all that bowed down his blessed head, his shrinking humanity said, inwardly: I never sinned. This wrath is not mine; I should not bear it. But, ah! his love said: Either I or my people must bear it; I will bear it for them. Oh, believers! behold how he loved you. Surely this love was stronger than death. A deluge of wrath could not quench this love.

Can you count the drops of the ocean? Then you may fathom the depths of his love to you. Can you measure the distance between the highest throne in heaven and the lowest dungeon in hell? That is the measure of his love to you.

Some of you dare not believe in Jesus. Ah! this is the way you requite the love of the silent Lamb of God? He would not answer when he was accused. He would not murmur when condemned. When God poured wrath on him, he would not stand upon his Godhead purity, but consented to bear wrath, that every sinner looking to him may go free. And yet you will not look to this Lamb of God. Oh! you grieve him, and crucify him afresh.

He was silent, because he sought his Father's glory.
I have often tried to show you that it is more glorifying to God when sin is punished in his own Son, than when it is punished in the poor worms that committed it. If sinners bear their own sins, then they must suffer eternally, so that God's justice will never be satisfied. They will always have more to suffer, and God will never have full glory out of them. But when Christ suffers in the room of a sinner, then God is satisfied at once. He is infinitely glorified. Now, Christ knew this quite well. He came seeking his Father's glory: 'I am come to do, not mine own will, but the

will of him that sent me.' Therefore it was that he was dumb, that God might have more glory from the finished sufferings of his own Son than from the eternal sufferings of sinners. 'O the depth of the riches both of the wisdom and knowledge of God! How unsearchable are his judgments, and his ways past finding out!' Therefore did he say: 'I delight to do thy will, O my God; yea, thy law is within my heart.' Therefore did he hasten to go up to Jerusalem.

To awakened souls I say, some of you refuse to believe, lest you should tarnish the glory of God. You fear that it cannot be consistent with the glory of so pure and holy a God to receive you to pardon and peace. Are you wiser than Christ? Christ feared that God would lose some of his glory if sinners were allowed to bear their own sins, because infinite justice never could get enough of suffering out of them. Therefore was he dumb under the wrath of God, that justice might be fully satisfied out of his infinite sufferings. Be wise, I entreat of you! God is more glorified by your suffering in Christ, than by your own suffering in hell. It will be far more honouring to God if you will cleave to that bleeding silent Lamb, than if you were to bear the wrath of God for ever and ever. Give glory to the Lord, before your feet stumble on the dark mountains.

3. The broken bread represents the silent sufferings of Christ.

This day, my friends, I set before you the plainest and simplest picture of the silent sufferings of Jesus Christ, the Lamb of God. In that night in which he was betrayed, he took bread. Why bread? Firstly, because of its plainness and commonness. He did not take silver or gold or jewels, to represent his body, but bread, plain bread, to show you that when he came to be a surety for sinners, he did not come in his original glory, with his Father's angels. He took not on him the nature of angels, he became man. Secondly, he chose bread to show you that he was dumb, and opened not his mouth. When I break the bread it resists not, it complains not, it yields to my hand. So it was with Christ. He resisted not, complained not, he yielded to the hand of infinite justice. 'He was led as a lamb to the slaughter, and as a sheep before her shearers is dumb, so he opened not his mouth.'

Some of you believe not. You do not consent to take this silent Lamb as a sin-offering for your soul. Either you do not feel your need of him, or you have not faith to look to him. But if you do not truly look to him, be not so rash, so daring, so inconsistent as to take the bread and wine.

Some of you believe in the silent Lamb of God. You say: It was my sin that lay so heavy on his heart. My sins were the thorns that pierced his brow. My sins were the nails that pierced his hands and feet. My sins were the spear that pierced his heart. He loved me, and gave himself for me. Come, then, to the broken bread and poured-out wine. Feed on them. Appropriate Christ in them. And whilst you feed upon the emblems of the silent Lamb, do this in remembrance of Jesus.
Dundee 1837, (Action Sermon)

58. The panting soul

As the hart panteth after the water brooks, so panteth my soul after thee, O God' (Psalm 42:1).

These are supposed to be the words of David when he fled from his son Absalom. He seems to have been wandering in some solitary wild on the side of Mount Hermon, the stream of Jordan flowing at his feet. David seems to have been full of pensive meditation: for his enemies reproached him daily, saying: 'Where is thy God?'; nay, even God seemed to forget him, all his waves and billows were going over him; when suddenly a deer bounded past him. It had been sore wounded by the archers, or pursued by some wild beast on the mountains of the leopards. Faint and weary, he saw it rushing towards the flowing stream, and quenching its thirst in the water brook. His soul was quickened by the sight. Is not this just a picture of what I should be? Is not my God all to me that the flowing stream is to that wounded deer? 'As the hart panteth after the water brooks, so panteth my soul after thee, O God.'

I do hope that many of you have come up this day with the same panting desire in your bosom. None but gracious souls can pant after God, and Jesus Christ whom he hath sent. As the loadstone attracts nothing but what is made of steel to itself, so an uplifted Saviour, God manifest in the flesh, draws nothing but what is awakened by his own Spirit to him. May God enable me to show you shortly some of the reasons why the believer pants after God!

1. The burden of sin makes the soul pant after God.

Unawakened souls, those who feel no burden, do not pant after Christ.
'The full soul loathes the honeycomb.' Christ is the honeycomb which
God has provided for poor sinners. The sweetest honey is to be found
in the clefts of that Rock. But unawakened persons are full: full of peace,
full of business, full of pleasure. They have no desire after Christ - they
loathe the honeycomb. Unawakened persons are 'dead in trespasses and
sins'. They are as dead to Christ and eternal things as the dead in the
churchyard are to the things of this world. The dead bodies in the
churchyard are at present within reach of the preacher's voice. If they
could look up out of their graves, they would see the table spread with
the bread and the wine; and yet when we speak they do not hear, they
do not weep, their bosoms do not pant, they do not rise and come. Dear
friends, the dead souls within the church are just as dead as they.

You too are within reach of the preacher's voice, you too can see
Christ evidently set forth crucified; yet you have no desires after Christ.
Your eyes weep not, your bosoms pant not, you have no heart-longings
after Christ. When Israel was in the land of Egypt, they had leeks, and
onions, and garlic; they sat by the fleshpots, and did eat bread to the full.
They did not cry for manna, they did not seek water out of the flinty rock.
So it is with those of you who are unawakened. You have got the leeks
and the onions of this world's pleasures, and profits, and diversions; and
you care not for Christ, the bread of life. You do not pant after
forgiveness and a new birth. You have no heart-longings for the living
water, of which if a man drink he shall never thirst again.

Many awakened persons do not pant after Christ.
There are some who feel like the deer stricken by the archers; but they
think they can pull out the arrows, and heal their own wounds.

When Naaman the Syrian came to Elisha, he felt his loathsome
disease, and he longed to be cured; but when the prophet told him: 'Go
wash in Jordan seven times, and thou shalt be clean,' he did not believe
God's Word: 'Are not Abana and Pharpar, rivers of Damascus, better
than all the waters of Israel? May I not wash in them and be clean? So
he turned and went away in a rage.' So do many awakened souls among
you. You are made to feel your loathsome disease, you sometimes
tremble for fear of hell. But when we tell you of Christ's blood cleansing
from all sin, you go away in a rage.

When the flood came upon the earth, when the rain fell forty days, and the bowels of the great deep were broken up, I doubt not there were great pantings of heart. Many fled from the wrath to come. Some fled to the top of snowy Lebanon - some to the peaks of Ararat; but Noah only believed God's Word, and entered into the ark. So, many of you tremble about your souls, who yet are not believing God's word, and not panting after Christ: 'Ye will not come to me, that ye might have life.'

When Christ shall come in the clouds of heaven, it is said all kindreds of the earth shall wail because of him. There will not be one unawakened person on earth or in hell. Not the proudest and deadest of you will keep from trembling on that day. But, ah! it is only those who believe his Word that will flee under his wings. Dear friends, it is not enough that you are anxious about your souls, you must be fleeing to Christ; yea, you must be in Christ, before you are safe.

All who are taught of God long after Christ: 'Every one that hath learned of the Father, cometh unto me;' 'All that the Father giveth me shall come to me; and him that cometh to me I will in no wise cast out.'

When a sinner is convinced by God that his sins are a burden heavier than he can bear, that if he die they will crush him into an eternal hell; when convinced that God has provided a Lamb for a burnt-offering, that this Lamb is free to all, he rushes through the crowd. Others may keep back, but he cannot. He places both his hands on the head of the divine Lamb, and says: 'My Lord, and my God;' 'This God is my God for ever and ever; he will be my guide even unto death;' 'As the hart panteth after the water brooks, so panteth my soul after thee, O God.'

If there is any of you convinced that you are perishing, that heaven is like a great city with walls, that you are outside, and the storm of wrath about to fall on you? Has God also convinced you that Christ is the only gate into the city, the strait gate, and yet wide enough to admit any sinner in all the world? Ah! then I know you will strive to enter in; you will agonize; you will not rest day nor night: 'As the hart panteth after the water brooks, so panteth my soul after thee, O God.' If there is any of you convinced that sin is a mortal disease, that all other physicians are vain, that Christ is passing through the midst of us full of virtue to heal, I know you will press forward, whatever others do: 'If I may but touch the hem of his garment I shall be healed;' 'As the hart panteth after the water brooks, so panteth my soul after thee, O God.'

I would invite panting souls to close with Christ. It is a sad truth, that most of Christians in our day are rather *coming* to Christ than *come* to Christ. Most of you are like the manslayer running toward the city of refuge, rather than when he sits down within the gates. O if you feel condemned in yourself, and that God has provided a free surety for sinners, why will you not rest your soul upon his finished work? Why will you go round and round the city of refuge, and not enter in? This holy ordinance is intended to teach you appropriating faith; no more to waver, but to put out the hand of faith and close with Jesus. You do not come to look at bread and wine, but to take it. Take, eat, O panting souls! May God give you light at the same moment to venture on Christ, and say: 'This God is my God for ever and ever.'

2. Desire of holiness makes the soul pant after God.

Unconverted persons have no desire for holiness, and therefore they do not pant after God and Christ.
Indeed this is the chief reason why poor sinners do not come to Christ. They know that if they came to Christ they would get a new heart, they would bid an eternal farewell to their old companions and pleasures. But most people would rather go to hell than this. When a few Greenlanders were brought into this country, they saw no beauty in the rich corn fields, and woods, and plains; they asked for their fields of snow, and the mountains of ice glancing in the sun. When they came into our houses, they could not endure the cleanness of them; they greatly preferred their own smoky, filthy cabins.

So it is with those of you who are unconverted. You have grown up with hearts frozen to God, and to divine things; and when you come to see the heart of a Christian like a garden, with the river of life flowing through it, and beautiful flowers of meekness, love and holiness growing in it, you cannot bear the sight; you love your own frozen heart better. When you see the clean heart of a child of God, you say: I had rather have my own filthy one. Ah! this is the way with most. You do not long to be made holy, you have no panting after a new birth. It needs grace to desire grace. You do not desire to be made a new creature; you had rather remain in the image of the devil than be changed into the image of God. You are like Jerusalem: 'Woe unto thee, O Jerusalem! Wilt thou not be made clean? When shall it once be?'

But all saved souls pant after holiness: 'As the hart panteth after the water brooks, so panteth my soul after thee, O God.'

When a soul comes to close with Christ he is not made perfectly holy all at once: 'The path of the just is as the shining light, that shineth more and more unto the perfect day.' Just as you have seen the day struggling with the darkness, then with clouds, till the sun bursts forth in meridian splendour; so it is with the holiness of a Christian. Just as in the richest lands, after the deepest ploughing, weeds will still grow up among the corn; so, many roots of bitterness remain in the believer's heart.

Paul thanked God for the grace that was given to the Corinthians, that they came behind in no gift; and yet he says they had strife, and envy, and divisions, so that he could not call them spiritual, but carnal. So is it with every Christian heart. Weeds grow up in the best cultivated gardens. There is enough in Christ to supply all our need. It is our own fault that we are not holy as God is holy. It is not in Christ, but in ourselves, that we are straitened. The shower of grace is plentiful enough, and more than enough; we do not open our mouth wide.

But every soul in Christ hates sin and pants after holiness. Nothing makes him pant more after God than corruption striving within. Paul never prayed more earnestly than when he had the thorn in his flesh. The thorn in the flesh makes us pant after God.

When a vessel is left by the tide lying dry upon the sand, it cannot be moved, it is a helpless log. The mariners may try to draw it with ropes, but it only sinks deeper into the sand. They can do nothing but long for the tide, that it may again be lifted upon the waves, and sail into the harbour. So it is with a Christian. You are often like a vessel on the sand. You cannot move. You attempt duties, but it is heavy work. Without Christ you can do nothing. You wait and pant for Christ, for the full tide of the Spirit, to lift your soul above the waves, and carry you prosperously on toward the heavenly harbour.

Let me invite weary souls to come to Christ this day. Some of you are feeling the thorn in the flesh, and you are praying that it may depart from you. Some of you feel like the criminal who was chained to a dead body. You feel your loathsome body of sin, you cry: 'O wretched man!' Some of you are like the deer that has been wounded by the lion, and trembles at its roaring. You have been wounded by Satan, and you tremble to hear his roar. Come you to Jesus. He will give you rest, O panting soul. Close with Christ, feed upon Christ. Without him you can do nothing. Through Christ strengthening you, you may do all things. This ordinance is intended to teach you to feed on Jesus. You do not only look on the bread or handle it; you eat, you drink. So come into personal union with Christ, O longing soul, and he will be your strength: 'God is our refuge and our strength.'

3. Desolateness makes the soul pant after God.

Believers never should be desolate.
It is contrary to the promise: 'None of them that trust in him shall be desolate.' Christ is always the same. His righteousness is as perfect one day as another. If you are clothed in that righteousness, your peace should be like a river. It is very dishonouring to Christ for believers to be going bowed down all the day long: 'Rejoice in the Lord alway; and again I say, Rejoice.'

Still I fear some of you can bear witness that the believer is sometimes very desolate.
The moon does not always shine in a cloudless sky. The ships do not always sail on a waveless sea. The believer does not always walk in the smile of his Father.

Outward providences sometimes cause desolateness, when they come unexpectedly upon us, when we cannot see God's meaning in them, when we suspect his love, and fall into darkness. So Job: 'Let the day perish wherein I was born, and the night in which it was said, A man-child is conceived.'

Sin admitted into the heart is the most common cause. God is a jealous God. So Israel: 'She said, I will go after my lovers that give me my bread and my water, my wool and my flax, mine oil and my drink.'

The desolate soul pants after God.
So it was with Job: 'O that I knew where I might find him, that I might come even to his seat.' So it was with the bride: 'I will rise now and go about the city, in the streets and in the broad ways.' So David: 'As the hart panteth after the water brooks, so panteth my soul after thee, O God.'

When a child that has been tenderly brought up, that has been warmly clad and comfortably fed, and cared for by a gentle mother's hand, when that child is turned out on the cold world, O it is bitter indeed! - O for my father's roof! O for my mother's smile! So it is with a child of light walking in darkness.

I invite desolate souls to come to God, the living God. Some of you may be feeling like a ship tossed on a stormy sea. Deep calls unto deep, at the noise of God's waterspouts; all the waves and billows are breaking over you. Be persuaded to close with Christ, freely offered to you. Put away entirely the question as to whether you ever believed before. Believe now. This ordinance is peculiarly fitted for you. You say you cannot realise a Saviour; well, here he is set forth plainly in bread and wine: 'This is my body, broken for you.' You say: But how shall I know he is a Saviour to me? See here the bread is freely offered: 'Whosoever will, let him take the water of life freely.' You say: But how do I know he is still offered to me? I answer, 'Yet there is room.' Here is bread enough and to spare. You say: But may I really close with him? I answer, 'Take, eat.' O panting soul, come under his wings. 'The Spirit and the Bride say, Come.'

Dundee, November 4, 1838 (Action Sermon)

59. The secret of a joyful deathbed

I have fought a good fight, I have finished my course, I have kept the faith: henceforth there is laid up for me a crown of righteousness, which the Lord, the righteous judge, shall give me at that day: and not to me only, but unto all them also that love his appearing (2 Timothy 4:7,8).

How blessed it is to stand by the death-bed of God's children! How different from that of the wicked! The wicked sometimes die in anguish. Some have been known to cry out: 'Lost, lost, lost! O eternity! O for half an hour, to pray!' Some die in blasphemy, cursing God for their pains and their sores. The greater number die like a beast, without any thought or care, except for the body: 'They have no bands in their death, but their strength is firm. They are laid in their graves like sheep, and the upright have dominion over them in the morning.'

How sweet, compared with these, is the departure of God's children! They fall asleep in Jesus: 'I am ready to be offered, and the time of my departure is at hand.' Paul here compares it firstly to the pouring out of a drink offering: 'Yea, and if I be offered upon the sacrifice and service of your faith, I joy, and rejoice with you all' (Philippians 2:17). He felt so entirely dedicated and given away to God, that his death was like the pouring out of the wine offering, which already belonged to God. He compares it secondly to the departure of a ship: 'The hour of my departure is at hand.' The things of time were like the cables that bound him to this world; but soon his bark was to be loosed from the shore, to sail forward to the shore of glory, to be moored for evermore.

In these words we have the secret of a joyful death-bed: firstly, he looks back upon the life of pain; secondly, he looks forward to the crown of glory.

1. He looks back. A threefold view.
He does not look back to his life before conversion at all. He often did so, but it was to condemn it: I 'was before a blasphemer, and a persecutor, and injurious: but I obtained mercy, because I did it ignorantly in unbelief' (1 Timothy 1:13). 'For I am the least of the apostles, that am not meet to be called an apostle, because I persecuted the church of God' (1 Corinthians 15:9). 'Beyond measure I persecuted the church of God, and wasted it' (Galatians 1:13). 'Sinners - of whom I am the chief.' Paul never forgot his old life; but not one ray of comfort came from it - only condemnation. It was his life since conversion that he now looked to - not as his righteousness before God, but only as showing that he was really a sinner saved through Christ.

I have fought a good fight.
Every day since his conversion he had been fighting; he had been passing through an enemy's country, and had to fight his way.

(1) *With his corruptions.* 'When I would do good, evil is present with me. For I delight in the law of God after the inward man: but I see another law in my members, warring against the law of my mind, and bringing me into captivity to the law of sin which is in my members' (Romans 7:21-23). 'For the flesh lusteth against the Spirit, and the Spirit against the flesh: and these are contrary the one to the other: so that ye cannot do the things that ye would' (Galatians 5:17). 'There was given unto me a thorn in the flesh, the messenger of Satan to buffet me' (2 Corinthians 12:7). Paul knew what these inward fightings are. He probably experienced them more than any one here.

(2) *With the world.* As long as he was Saul the blasphemer, the world caressed him; but when he was made Paul the apostle, the world hated

him. The more he loved, the more they hated. 'I have fought with beasts at Ephesus.' His only weapons were the Word of God; and yet he fought on against a world lying in wickedness.

(3) *With the devil.* 'A messenger of Satan;' 'For we wrestle not against flesh and blood, but against principalities, against powers, against the rulers of the darkness of this world, against spiritual wickedness in high places' (Ephesians 6:12). He had experienced much of this. 'We are not ignorant of his devices.'

Still it was a 'good fight': 'War a good warfare' (1 Timothy 1:18); 'Fight the good fight of faith' (1 Timothy 6:12). Often when we are in the midst of afflictions and temptations, we grow weary of the conflict. It is a hard lot. But when we look back from eternity, every redeemed soul will be able to say: *It was a good fight.*

Because we are sure to overcome. 'We are more than conquerors, through him that loved us.' In other battles we know not how it will go until the battle is done; but in this we have a sure promise of victory. We have sweet glimpses of triumph even in the thickest of the battle - sweet confidence in Jesus.

It keeps us close to our Captain. If we had no fight, we would not keep near to Jesus; but when we suffer such fearful attacks, we are glad to hide ourselves under Jesus' wings.

Because it is glorifying to God. His glory is involved in it. Often we would wish no fight; but not so in glory. There we shall see that every trial was glorifying to God, bringing out some new feature of his grace, power and love. Are you fighting this good fight? Soon we shall look back.

I have finished my course.

The moment a soul is brought to Christ, he has a course to run: 'And as John fulfilled his course, he said, Whom think ye that I am? I am not he. But, behold, there cometh one after me, whose shoes of his feet I am not worthy to loose' (Acts 13:25). Paul says: 'But none of these things move me, neither count I my life dear unto myself, so that I might finish my course with joy, and the ministry, which I have received of the Lord Jesus, to testify the gospel of the grace of God' (Acts 20:24). 'Wherefore seeing we also are compassed about with so great a cloud of witnesses, let us lay aside every weight, and the sin which doth so easily beset us, and let us run with patience the race that is set before us' (Hebrews 12:1). Every one has a different course. Like the planets, all do not shine in the same part of the sky. So every believer has his course - a work to do. One has the course of a minister, another the course of a master, another that of a servant. Each of us has a work to do for Christ; let us do it diligently. 'My meat is to do the will of him that sent me.'

I have kept the faith.
I think the dying thief could say: I believe, and enter with joy into Paradise; but he could not say: 'I have kept the faith.' This makes the difference between a peaceful and triumphant death-bed. Paul 'bought the truth, and sold it not.' That good thing committed to him he kept, by the Holy Ghost given unto him. He held the beginning of his confidence steadfast unto the end.

Learn that perseverance in the faith is needful to a triumphant death-bed. It is Christ, and Christ alone, that is our peace in dying; yet the hand that has longest held him has the firmest hold. It is not our perseverance that is our righteousness before God, but the doing and dying of the Lord Jesus; and yet without perseverance in the faith ye cannot be saved. Alas! you that turn aside to folly, you are preparing clouds for your dying bed. Can you say you have kept the faith, poor backslider?

2. What he looked forward to.

That day.
'I know whom I have believed, and am persuaded that he is able to keep that which I have committed unto him against that day' (2 Timothy 1:12). 'The Lord grant unto him that he may find mercy of the Lord in that day' (2 Timothy 1:18). A great day of Christ's appearing, and all his saints with him. It was not merely the day of death to which he looked forward. Then he would immediately pass into glory; he would go to be in Paradise; he would be absent from the body, and present with the Lord; he would be blessed dying in the Lord. But he looked forward to that day, because it is the day of Christ's full glory, the day of the gladness of his heart. There is something selfish in merely desiring the day of death; but there is a heavenly joy in looking for the day of his appearing.

The crown of righteousness.
A crown of glory, a crown of life, an incorruptible crown, that will never die, nor shall the wearer die any more; a crown of righteousness, a crown

waiting those that have put on the armour of God and the breastplate of righteousness; a crown laid up. It is ready from all eternity. It is ready now when we are fighting. Your crown is laid up.

The Lord shall give it me.
How sweet it will be, when Christ puts on the crown on a sinner's brow! The just God and Saviour! Angels will shout for joy when they see the righteous Jesus crowning the sinners for whom he died. He will finish our redemption. He was crowned with thorns; he has been an advocate crowned with glory and majesty; but another step - he is to put on the crown of righteousness. All heaven and earth and hell own him faithful and true, and righteous in all his ways. Oh! how sweet to be crowned by Jesus.

Along with all that love his appearing.
One thing would make us sad: Am I only to be crowned? No, no, 'not to me only.' Paul could not be happy in heaven without seeing others saved along with him. It gave him joy in his death-bed to think that myriads and myriads besides him would wear the crown, many whom he had been the means of saving.
Dundee, 1842

60. Into thine hand I commit my spirit

'Into thine hand I commit my spirit: thou hast redeemed me,
O LORD God of truth.' (Psalm 31:5)

There is something peculiarly sweet in these words, because they are the words used by the Lord Jesus in his agony. For six long hours he hung upon the accursed tree, bearing the sins of many. No thought of man can imagine the load he bore: 'My God, my God, why hast thou forsaken me?' The vinegar mingled with gall was bitter, but it was nothing to the cup of wrath. The pain of his mangled body was terrible, but it was nothing to the intense agony of the sword of justice that pierced him. This was his last solemn cry: 'Father, into thy hands I commend my spirit;' and he bowed his head, and gave up the ghost. It is sweet to an afflicted sufferer to use the same words as Jesus. It is sweet to use the words of a departed friend. We treasure them in our memory, and embalm them in our hearts. But what friend is like Jesus, whose words were all gracious?

It is sweet to a heavy-laden convinced sinner to take up the words of Jesus in the 40th Psalm: 'For innumerable evils have compassed me about: mine iniquities have taken hold upon me so that I am not able to look up' (verse 12). It is sweet to a believing soul to take up his words in Isaiah 50:8: 'He is near that justifieth me; who will contend with me?'

And so it is sweet for a poor, afflicted , dying worm to take up these words: 'Into thine hand I commit my spirit: thou hast redeemed me, O LORD God of truth.'

Observe three things:

The person who speaks - a tempted, afflicted soul. Such was David: 'Pull me out of the net' (verse 4). Satan and the world had cast a net around his soul. Snare after snare, like the meshes of a net, enclosed him. He felt helpless: 'I am forgotten as a dead man, out of mind; I am like a broken vessel.' Nowhere can he go, but to his redeeming God: 'Into thine hand I commit my spirit: thou hast redeemed me, O LORD God of truth.'

Such was the Lord Jesus: 'Many bulls have compassed me: strong bulls of Bashan have beset me round. They gaped upon me with their mouths, as a ravening and a roaring lion' (Psalm 22:12,13). Where could he go but to his God? 'Into thy hands I commend my spirit.' So there may be some tempted, afflicted soul here, enclosed in the net of Satan, beset by bulls of Bashan; let him take up this sweet word: 'Into thy hands I commend my spirit.'

The person to whom he speaks - the Redeemer. On the one side there is a worm; on the other, a redeeming God. When the Lord Jesus took up this word he put in *Father*; for the Father was his redeemer. When he had finished the work which the Father gave him to do, when he had drunk the last dregs of infinite suffering, he could look up and claim full deliverance: 'Father, into thy hands I commend my spirit.' When Stephen took this saying, he said: 'Lord Jesus, receive my spirit.' The Redeemer seems to be chiefly meant - he that bore our sins in his own body on the tree, not excluding the other persons of the Godhead. It is a poor, guilty, helpless worm looking up to him that died for us: 'Into thine hand I commit my spirit, O Lord God, faithful and true.'

The thing committed - 'my spirit.' The soul of man is the most precious part. I do not mean to speak lightly of the body - far from it. It is the creation of God, and though frail, and about to crumble to dust, yet it is a dear companion, and will be raised again incorruptible. But the spirit is the precious part. 'What shall it profit a man to gain the whole world, and lose his own soul?' The soul was made in the image of God. It is this which the poor tempted soul commits to the great Redeemer's hands. The part where sin commences, and bursts forth in action; where guilt lies heavy; where the blood of Jesus giveth peace; where Satan tempts the spirit. It is this the man gives in charge to the great Redeemer of souls.

The times when we should do this.

The time of conversion.
This seems to be the meaning of Paul: 'I know whom I have believed, and am persuaded that he is able to keep that which I have committed to him against that day.' Sometimes conversion is described in the Bible from God's part in it: Jesus finding lost sheep, Jesus passing by and spreading his skirt over the soul, the Father drawing the soul to Jesus. At other times it is described from the creature's part: coming to Jesus, beholding the Lamb, cleaving to Christ, or as here, committing the spirit to his hands.

O it is a happy day when a poor sinner discovers that his spirit is wholly lost and undone; that his soul is like the leper's body, unclean, unclean; that his sins are infinite, and his heart a rock - a fountain of pollution, unsearchable, uncontrollable, insufferable! O it is a happy day when he discovers Jesus is an almighty and all-loving Redeemer, divine and glorious in his person, and yet wounded and broken under the wrath of God, borne for us! O it is a happy day when the sinner commits his poor, guilty, helpless, polluted soul into the hands of the Lord Jesus. Heavy-laden sinner, commit thy soul to Jesus. It is in great danger. The law condemns thee. Thy sins are many - thy deserved hell is beyond thought terrible. Satan is resisting thee, tempting thee, beguiling thee. Jesus alone can save: 'Into thine hand I commit my spirit.'

The time of temptation.
This seems to have been peculiarly the time alluded to in the psalm: 'Pull me out of the net.' The temptations of God's children are very dreadful. Often a child of God goes on a long time without temptation.

He is like Naphtali, 'satisfied with favour, and full with the blessings of the Lord.' Perhaps he laughs at temptation, and thinks it will never come near him. Suddenly the sky is overcast, a strong current of temptation is allowed to set upon his heart.

> Instead of this, he made me feel
> The hidden evils of my heart
> And let the angry powers of hell
> Assault my soul in every part.

The world concurs. Satan stirs up all his malice. What horrors now surround the tempted soul! He flies to his knees; but he is afraid to pray. He flies to his Bible; but it is a sealed book. Sin darkens the mind, and scares him away from prayer. All the while God's people admire and praise, though their words are like gall. What can help the tempted man? None but Jesus. O to discover Jesus in such an hour! The Redeemer that died; that lives, the Advocate with the Father! O to be enabled to commit one tempted soul into his hands! Poor tempted soul! give thyself away to Jesus. He can blot out the sin, and change the heart.

The time of affliction.
Some Christians have little affliction. They sail on a smooth sea, they enjoy health of body for years together, they never knew what it was to want a comfortable meal. Death has perhaps not once entered their dwelling. They think it will be always thus. But a change comes. The 'harp of thousand strings' becomes our tune. The 'clay cottage' gives tokens of decay, or grim want invades their dwelling, or death comes up into the window. Ah! it is hard to bear. 'No affliction for the present seems to be joyous, but grievous.' Who can comfort? None but Jesus. He knew all sorrow, deeper sorrows than we have ever known, or will ever know. His heart is not of stone. He feels along with us. He afflicts not willingly. He seeks to bring us more to himself. O afflicted believer, commit thy weeping, suffering, pining, trembling soul to Jesus: 'Into thine hand I commit my spirit.'

The time of duty.
Often at first the convert thinks only of enjoyment: of hearing sermons, enjoying sacraments and Christian converse. I have often been struck how often the inquiry is made, Did you enjoy the sacrament, or that sermon? How seldom, Did you improve it? What change has it wrought

in your life? But when God stirs up the soul, a path of duty is seen stretching before it. Often perplexed and intricate, often steep and slippery, often dangerous and terrible. Oh! what shall I do? How difficult to know the right way; and when I know it, how hard to follow it! Commit thy soul to Jesus. In him are hid treasures of wisdom and knowledge. His grace is sufficient for thee. 'He brings the blind by a way which they know not.' He has light to guide thee, strength to uphold and grace to give thee courage: 'Into thine hand I commit my spirit.'

In time of death.
Few ever think of dying till dying comes. The last enemy that shall be overcome is Death; and an awful enemy he is. We go alone. No earthly friend goes with us. We never went the way before. It is all strange and new. The results are eternal. If we have not rightly believed, it is too late to mend. These are some of the solemn thoughts that overshadow the soul. What can give peace? None but Jesus; the sight of Jesus as a Redeemer, the same yesterday, today, and for ever; the same sight we got when first we knew the Lord, when first he chose us and we chose him, when first he said, 'Seek ye my face,' and we said to him, 'Thy face, Lord, shall we seek.' To see him as a God of truth, the Lord that changes not, the unchanging One, the same Jesus; thus to see him and to cry, 'Into thy hands I commit my spirit' - this is peace.
Dundee, 1842

61. Marks, causes, and cure of backsliding

'Grey hairs are here and there upon him, yet he knoweth not.' (Hosea 7:9)

These words describe a state of secret backsliding - the most dangerous, perhaps, of any. It is a common thing for persons grown up in years to turn old and grey-headed without observing it. Most people are unwilling to be thought old. They do not love to notice the progress of decay, and the marks of old age are allowed to steal upon them unobserved. The teeth drop out one by one, the hand loses its steadiness, the limbs lose their elasticity, the eye becomes dim, and grey hairs are here and there upon the head, and we are in old age before we are aware. So is it in the decay of the soul in divine things.

It is a solemn and most affecting truth, that the life of God in the soul is subject to wither and decay. It cannot really die. If God has once given spiritual life to the soul, I know he will maintain it to eternal glory. 'The LORD will perfect that which concerneth me ... forsake not the works of thine own hands.' (Psalms 138:8) But still it is liable to many and sad decays. This is plain from Scripture. God says: 'Yet I had planted thee a noble vine, wholly a right seed: how then art thou turned into the degenerate plant of a strange vine unto me?' (Jeremiah 2:21); 'Turn, O backsliding children, saith the LORD; for I am married unto you' (Jeremiah 3:14); 'And my people are bent to backsliding from me' (Hosea 9:7); 'Nevertheless I have somewhat against thee, because thou hast left thy first love' (Revelation 2:4).

Alas! my friends, it is plain from ourselves. Though I praise God he seems to be adding to the Church among you still 'such as shall be saved', though some of you appear to be going from strength to strength, yet of how many it may be said: 'Grey hairs are here and there upon you, and you know it not.' How many have lost their relish for the house of God! It is not with you as in months past. The Thursday evening is not so prized as once it was, the private prayer-meeting is seldom if ever visited, the company of Christ more lightly esteemed. Is there not less zeal for the conversion of others, less prayer, less praise, less liberality? Ah! brethren, we as a congregation are a monument that there is such a thing as spiritual decay.

How earnest you once were in hearing the Word of God! You would not miss an opportunity, week-day or Sabbath day. You heard as for your life. Your praises were fuller and more fervent once than they are now. How careful you were in treasuring up the Word, repeating it to yourselves, and your children, and your companions! How fervent in your prayers! On many of your hearts I fear we must write, 'Ichabod. The glory is departed.'

Another solemn fact is that this decay is always secret and unnoticed. It is like the approach of old age: 'grey hairs are here and there upon him, yet he knoweth not.' Old people never observe the gradual advance of old age. In general, they do not like to think of their getting older. So it is in the decay of a believer's soul. It goes on secretly and silently: the eye of faith becomes dimmer and dimmer, the hand loses its firm hold of Jesus, the soul loses its fresh delight in Immanuel's finished work; and yet he knows it not. Sinful compliances steal upon the soul. 'Grey hairs are here and there upon him, yet he knoweth not.'

1. Let us state some of the marks which indicate declension.

The Bible neglected.
When a soul is first brought to Christ, he delights in the Word of God. He has an appetite for it 'as a new-born babe'. Just as an infant has a constant, steadily-recurring appetite for its mother's milk, so has the soul for the Word. He has spiritual understanding of the Word. It seems all sweet and easy. It all testifies of Jesus. The soul grasps the meaning or earnestly inquires from ministers and others the meaning of difficult passages. He has growth: 'That ye may grow thereby.' It is felt to be the daily nourishment of the soul, the sword to ward off temptation.

How different when the Christian is in decay! No relish for the Word. It may be read as a duty, or as a burdensome task but it is not delighted in. Other books are preferred to the Bible. There is no growing in the knowledge of the Word, no self-application, no receiving it with meekness, no frequent recurrence of the mind during the day to the chapter read in the morning, no answering Satan by 'Thus it is written' and 'Thus saith the Lord'. Ah! my friends, how is the gold become dim! 'Grey hairs are here and there upon him, yet he knoweth not.'

Prayer neglected.
'Behold, he prayeth,' was the first mark that Paul was brought from death to life. The soul enjoys great nearness to God, enters within the veil, lies down at the feet of Jesus, and there pours out its groans and tears. The believer rises, like his Lord, a great while before day; or waking in the night, he cries in secret to God. Before entering any company, or by appointment meeting a friend, or answering a proposal, his heart wings its way to the mercy-seat. He prays without ceasing. He pours forth earnest cries for the deliverance from sin; the sins he is most tempted to, he prays most against. His intercessions for others are deep, constant, wide. It is sweet and easy for him to pray for others: 'Forbid that I should sin against God by ceasing to pray for you.'

But all this secretly changes. The soul is far from God, there is no putting prayers into the golden censer, no entering within the veil, no drawing near. No early rising now to pray, no cries in the night, no prayer on sudden emergencies. He now frequently answers proposals in his own spirit, without asking counsel of the Lord. Little praying against sin, now! He durst not pray against some sin, or only feebly, and without resolving to forsake it. Little intercession now, little bearing unconverted friends on our heart before God, little prayer for the Church, for the Jews, and the Heathen. Ah! these are some of the 'grey hairs.'

Christ little esteemed.
When first we know the Lord Christ is all in all. He is the Fountain for sin, where we are continually washing our souls from sin and uncleanness. Under his white-shining robes we are continually hiding our naked souls. He is the Rock, giving out living water, which ever follows us. He is the compassionate Husband and elder Brother, on whom we lean coming up from the wilderness. He is our King, at whose feet our heart is laid down, that he may reign over it for ever and ever.

When we decay it is not so. There is much guilt on the conscience, but little travelling to the Fountain; there is a lurking doubt and dislike of the way of salvation by Christ. There is little hiding beneath the righteousness without works. There is little drinking out of the Rock; it seems dry, or we are removed from it. There is no leaning upon Christ, no sense of his presence by night and by day. Ah! this is a sad mark of 'grey hairs.'

Sin not hated.
When first we knew the Lord, how did sin appear? We had awful discoveries of the exceeding sinfulness of sin. It appeared evil and bitter, the load that had crushed the Lord Jesus to the lowest hell. We could not bear it, we fled from temptation with our whole heart, we were quick-scented in the fear of the Lord: 'The Spirit of the Lord ... shall make him of quick understanding (margin, 'of quick scent') in the fear of the Lord' (Isaiah 9:3). Like those animals that quickly scent game, so the new creature easily discovered the approach of sin, and fled from it. Now we have little conviction of sin. Dry eyes in confession, little confession or none at all, no times set apart for the confession of sin. Temptation is little feared, the soul becomes bolder and bolder in its approaches to sin.

Christians lightly esteemed.
Once we loved all that loved the Lord. The mark that Christ left as the mark of a true disciple applied to us: 'By this shall all men know that

ye are my disciples, if ye have love one to another' (John 13:35). We had all things in common with them, so that none of them could be in want. We exhorted one another daily, as iron sharpeneth iron; we would not suffer sin upon our brother; we spoke with such love, and frankness, and humility, that they could not be offended. Now we look on them with coldness; we are not so intimate with them; we fear lest they see our guilt. We are not so careful of the poor saints as once we were. We have sworn to our own hurt, and we begin to change. We do not exhort one another daily; when they reprove us, we turn angry. And we do not reprove in love, but with a bitter spirit, or we speak evil of them behind their back.

The ungodly not warned.

Once we wept over them in secret, pleaded with God night and day for their conversion, abhorred their ways: 'I hate the work of them that turn aside; it shall not cleave to me' (Psalm 101:3). Now our bowels do not yearn over them. There is little or no prayer for their conversion; nay, we perhaps guiltily smile on their wicked ways. If we do not partake in their sins, at least we do not reprove them.

2. Let us inquire into the causes of decay.

A lust allowed to prevail.

So it was with Israel: 'They are all adulterers, as an oven heated by the baker' (Hosea 7:4). This was the cause of Israel's decay. So it will be with you and me. A lust for money, a sensual lust, a lust for praise or pleasure, if tampered with, and suffered to prevail, will make the whole soul wither. For a time you begin to fight against it; then your opposition grows weaker; then you make excuses for it; then you hide it from yourself, but still obey its power. This brings guilt on the conscience, takes away your relish of the Bible, makes you weary of the mercy-seat. This makes the holy Saviour little prized, this makes sin little hated, Christians avoided, and the ungodly not pitied. O my brethren! we must either be enemies of all sin, or we shall be decaying, withering branches. One lust nourished in your heart will be a viper in your bosom.

Worldly company.

'Ephraim, he hath mixed himself among the people' (Hosea 7:8). This was the peculiar character of the Jews: 'The people shall dwell alone, and shall not be reckoned among the nations.' But when they mixed themselves among the nations, then grey hairs began to appear. So it is with Christians, they are a peculiar people. Jesus said of them: 'They are not of the world, even as I am not of the world.' We are as completely separated from the world as Christ was; we have got his blood upon us, and the Holy Spirit in us; we have peculiar joys and peculiar sorrows; we are a praying people, a praising people. But the moment we begin to mix with the ungodly, grey hairs begin to appear - our souls wither.

Do not mistake me. If God has cast your lot in an ungodly family, where God is not worshipped, where his holy name is blasphemed, where his Word is not read, where your ears are vexed with the filthy conversation of the wicked - be not cast down. This is your peculiar trial; and God, who suits the back to the burden, will give grace according to your day. But if you choose a place where God is not, if you choose companions who have no fear of God, if you venture into companies where the god of this world reigns, where the Bible is a jest-booked, and God's ministers are the song of the drunkard - then your soul will and must begin to wither.

You retire to your closet, and open your Bible; but its holy, pure words are not sweet to your taste. You kneel and fold the hands; but prayer is a burden - you have no spiritual desires. You name the name of Christ; but he does not appear altogether lovely. Sin has lost its frightful look. Lively Christians are now too exact and precise for you. Alas! it is not with you as in months past. The crown has fallen from your head. Woe unto you, because you have sinned!

3. There is a cure.
You may cured. 'O Ephraim, thou hast destroyed thyself, but in me is thine help. Thou hast played the harlot with many lovers, yet return again to me, saith the Lord.' Satan will tempt you to say, There is no hope - no for I have loved strangers; but this is a lie. Remember, in Christ there is hope.

Search out the cause of the decay. Your heart will be most unwilling to find it out, but you must find it out. If you were in a sinking ship, the first thing is to find the leak; so you must find the leak in your soul. Is it an idol? Lay it bare. Trace back your feelings till you find it out. Is it some lust you indulge? Mark it out. Is it worldly company? Note it, put your finger on it. Say, This is the Achan in my heart. This is the troubler.

Get forgiveness of it. Confess it over the head of the Scape-goat.

Plunge it into the Fountain opened for sin. Jesus is crying: 'Return unto me, for I have redeemed thee.'

Slay the troubler. Do with it as they did with Achan. Seek the Holy Spirit's indwelling power to slay the troubler, that it never rise up any more. O my friends! If we would thus seek reformation, we would be the better of our falls - we would get honey out of the lion's carcass. Awake, awake my friends! Hell is as deep as it ever was. Christ as free. Your souls as precious. Your eternity is nearer and nearer. O how foolish to deny, instead of, like Caleb, following the Lord fully! 'Be ye steadfast, immovable, always abounding in the work of the Lord, forasmuch as ye know that your labour shall not be in vain in the Lord.'

62. Not ashamed of the gospel

So, as much as in me is, I am ready to preach the gospel to you that are at Rome also. For I am not ashamed of the gospel of Christ: for it is the power of God unto salvation to every one that believeth; to the Jew first, and also to the Greek. For therein is the righteousness of God revealed from faith to faith: as it is written, The just shall live by faith. For the wrath of God is revealed from heaven against all ungodliness and unrighteousness of men, who hold the truth in unrighteousness (Romans 1:15-18).

Observe here:
Where Paul desired to preach: 'I am ready to preach the gospel to you that are at Rome also.' Rome was at that time the *mightiest city* in the whole world. Daniel compared it to a beast with iron teeth stamping other kingdoms with its feet. It was called the mistress of the world. Yet there Paul was willing to preach the gospel. It was the *most learned city* of the world. Its poets, painters, orators, historians of the Augustan age, were famed over the whole world. Some of the most perfect specimens of human composition that ever were produced were published at Rome at that very time. It was the *most wicked city* of the world. The pollution that flowed through its streets were equal to those of Sodom and Gomorrah. The emperor was one of the most cruel monsters that ever appeared in the form of a man. That was the place where Paul burned with a flame of desire to be allowed to preach.

What Paul desired to preach: 'The gospel - the gospel of Christ.' It was not to see Rome that Paul longed to be there; not to see its temples, and theatres, and statues, the wonders of the world. It was not to display his own eloquence, not to publish some new work to gain esteem and applause of the Roman people. It was to preach the gospel, the way of salvation by the righteousness of God: 'I am determined to know nothing among you but Christ, and him crucified.'

What Paul felt: 'I am not ashamed of the gospel of Christ.' More is meant in these words than is expressed. He does not mean only that he was not ashamed of the gospel, but that he gloried in it. It is very similar to Galatians 6:14: 'But God forbid that I should glory, save in the cross of our Lord Jesus Christ.' Two things are implied in this.

Firstly, Paul was not ashamed of it before God. He had ventured his own soul on this way of salvation. He could say, like David, 'This is all my salvation, this is all my desire.' The way of salvation by Jehovah our Righteousness was sweet to Paul. His soul rested there with great delight. He came thus to God in secret, thus in public, thus in dying. He hoped to stand before God through all eternity clothed in this divine righteousness. Secondly, he was not ashamed of it before men. Though all the world had been against him, Paul would have gloried in this way of salvation. He had a burning desire to make it known to other men. He felt it so sweet, he saw it to be so glorious, that he could have desired a voice so loud that all men might hear at one moment the way of salvation by Christ.

Men would laugh at the idea of a poor worm like Paul going to subdue mighty Rome with a few words of his lips; but Paul saw such a divine power in the gospel that he was not ashamed of it. He knew it could break the hardest heart, and bind up the most broken. The learned men of Rome would smile at the words of this babbler; but Paul saw such wisdom in the gospel, that all human wisdom appeared utter folly beside it. The wickedness of Rome reached up to heaven; it was a continual smoke in God's nostrils, a fire that burned all the day. But Paul knew that the righteousness of God could cover the sin of a thousand Romes. He saw it to be so vast, so immense, so free, so surpassing glorious, so divine, that it could flow over and cover the sins of the greatest sinner there.

1. Learn from this passage the reasons why worldly men are ashamed of the gospel.

Because it is foolishness.
'But we preach Christ crucified, unto the Jews a stumbling-block, and unto the Greeks foolishness' (1 Corinthians 1:23). 'But the natural man receiveth not the things of the Spirit of God: for they are foolishness unto him: neither can he know them, because they are spiritually discerned' (1 Corinthians 2:14). Unregenerate men cannot comprehend the way of salvation by the righteousness of another. It appears a foolish scheme. They do not believe it is in the Bible at all. That a man should enter heaven by his good works they can understand, this is agreeable to the pride of the natural heart. Or that God should forget to punish sin and admit bad and good into heaven, they can understand this: 'Thou thoughtest that I was altogether such an one as thyself.' But that a sinner should be covered with the righteousness of another, that he should have the sufferings and holy life of another person laid to his account so as to cover all his sins, this is utter folly to worldly men. Therefore so many of you are ashamed of the gospel of Christ. You are ashamed to hear it preached: when it is clearly set before you, you despise it in your heart. You are ashamed of it before God. You do not go to the Father this way. You do not enter into the holiest by the blood of Jesus. You do not enter guilty and loathsome in yourself, wearing only the obedience of Christ. You are ashamed of it before men, ashamed to state it to your children and servants as the only way of pardon and acceptance.

Because of the messenger.
Once when Jesus was preaching in his own country they said: 'Is not this the carpenter, the son of Mary, the brother of James, and Joses, and of Judah, and Simon? and are not his sisters here with us? And they were offended at him' (Mark 6:3). When Peter and John were before the Jewish Council, it is said: 'They perceived that they were unlearned and ignorant men' (Acts 4:13). When Paul preached at Athens, they said: 'What will this babbler say?' At Corinth they said: 'His bodily presence is weak, and his speech contemptible' (2 Corinthians 10:10). So it is still. We have this treasure in earthen vessels. Every minister I know has got some painful defect about him. Ungodly men always stumble at this, and are ashamed of the gospel because of the weakness of those who carry it.

Because they hate its holiness.

Here is the main reason why unregenerate men are ashamed of the gospel - because it is a holy-making gospel. It will not allow men to live on in their sins. If Christ had come to save men in their sins, to pluck them from hell, and let them enjoy their lusts - unregenerate men would hail the gospel. But Jesus is a holy Saviour. 'He gave himself for us, that he might redeem us from all iniquity, and purify us unto himself;' 'He shall save his people from their sins.' He first covers the soul with his white raiment, then makes the soul glorious within; he restores the lost image of God, and fills the soul with pure and heavenly holiness. Unregenerate men among you cannot bear this. The drunkard among you says: Oh! he will take me away from the tavern; the swearer: Oh! he will take away my darling oaths; the sensualist: Oh! he will make me chaste and pure. Hence your malignity against the Redeemer. Hence you see no form nor comeliness in him who is altogether lovely. You are ashamed of the gospel of Christ.

2. Reasons why believers glory in the gospel of Christ.

Because of its power.

'It is the power of God unto salvation.' To ungodly men nothing appears more weak and powerless than the gospel. They regard it as Lot's sons-in-law did his solemn warning: 'He seemed as one that mocked.' It appears an idle tale, an old wife's fable; but it is in reality 'the power of God unto salvation.' The gospel is an amazing weapon, when God wields it: 'The weapons of our warfare are not carnal, but mighty through God to the pulling down of strongholds.' When God wields the gospel, it is mighty to awaken the hardest hearts. Paul felt this in his own experience. He was a proud blasphemer, persecutor, and injurious - a proud, self-righteous Pharisee. You would have said: Nothing in the world can awaken that man. Jesus revealed himself to him, and he fell to the ground, trembling and astonished. So he had seen it in the case of others: in Lydia and the jailer, in Sergius Paulus, the deputy of Cyprus: 'He believed, being astonished at the doctrine of the Lord' (Acts 13:12). 'The power of God unto salvation!' Not God's mighty arm to destroy, but his mighty arm to save.

He knew it would have the same power on every one that believed, whether Jew or Greek. The obstinate heart of the Jew and the proud heart of the Greek would both be broken under the sharp blade of the gospel.

No wonder Paul went so boldly to Rome, when he had such a weapon in his hand. He knew that the hearts of the Romans were hard as adamant, proud as Lucifer, and full of lusts as hell is full of foul spirits; he knew that Satan held that proud city in his arms; yet still here was a power - the simple truth as it is in Jesus - by which God could bring low the proudest and hardest to sit at the feet of Jesus, clothed and in their right mind. This is what enables us to continue preaching among you. I have now some experience of the hardness of your hearts, and that it is easier to create a world than to convert one of your souls; but the gospel is 'the power of God,' and I do not despair of the conversion of any one of you. God is able to do it through his mighty gospel; 'for with God nothing shall be impossible.'

O brethren, have you felt the power of the gospel? Has the gospel come to you not in word only, but in power, and in the Holy Ghost, and in much assurance? Has it broken your heart, and bound it up? Mighty gospel! It alone can save. Awakened sinner! the gospel is 'the power of God unto salvation to every one that believeth.' Though you may have the sins of the Jew and the Greek, there is enough in Jesus to cover all. Though your heart is hard, God is able, through this mighty gospel, to subdue it.

Because of the righteousness of God revealed in it.
This reason springs out of the preceeding. It is the power of God; 'for therein is the righteousness of God revealed.' It is this righteousness which gives it all its power, makes it so attractive to sinners, so pacifying to the troubled conscience. 'The righteousness of God' is just the sufferings and obedience of the Lord Jesus, who was God, freely offered to cover sinners. The sufferings of Christ, from the manger at Bethlehem to the cross of Calvary, were all sufferings of one who was God: 'Unto us a child is born; unto us a son is given; and the government shall be upon his shoulder; and his name shall be called Wonderful, Counsellor, The Mighty God, The Everlasting Father, The Prince of Peace;' 'Awake, O sword, against my shepherd, and against the man that is my fellow, saith the Lord of hosts.' The blood of Christ is called the blood of God (Acts 20:28). It was this that gave infinite value to the sufferings of Christ. The dying of one holy man might have stood for the dying of one sinner, if God had so pleased; but it needed the dying of one who was God to stand for the dying of many sinners. The obedience of Christ, from infancy to death, was all the obedience of one who was

God. His divine will agreed with his holy human will in every act of obedience. His obedience to parents is the obedience of God; his prayers were the prayers of God; his tears, the tears of God; his holy thoughts, the thoughts of God; his holy actions, the actions of God - his whole obedience is divine. It has divine perfection in it. It has a divine fulness and excellence which no other obedience ever had, or can have - it is 'the righteousness of God.' This is what is revealed in the gospel, offered freely to every creature, to cover sin, and justify before God.

This was what nerved the arm of Paul. He knew that he was carrying this glorious righteousness into the view of sinners. What though the men of Rome were covered up to heaven with innumerable sins! He knew that this glorious righteousness was enough to cover all.

O brethren! it is this we come to offer you this day - a righteousness so vast that it is able to cover you divinely. For every sin of yours here is a stripe in Jesus. For the sins of infancy, here are the sufferings of his infancy. For the sins of youth, here are the sufferings of his youth. For the sins of manhood here are the sufferings of his manhood. For your infinite dishonour done to the law of God, here is infinite honour done to the law. His obedience is divine obedience. For your unholy life, here is his divinely holy life to cover you. Here are his divinely holy thoughts, to cover your unholy thoughts. Here are his holy words, to cover your unholy words; his holy actions, to cover your unholy actions.

There is something infinitely vast and glorious in the righteousness of God. When the deluge covered the earth, it covered the highest mountains. Looking down from above, not one mountain-top could be seen, but a vast world of waters - a vast plain reflecting the beams of the sun. So if you this day lie down under the righteousness of God, the mountains of your sins will not be seen, but only the vast, deep, glorious righteousness of your God and Saviour. If you were to cast a stone into the deepest part of the ocean, it would be lost and swallowed up by the deep waves of ocean; so when a sinner is cast down under the righteousness of God, he is as it were lost and swallowed up in Christ.

A righteousness so free - 'From faith to faith!' The meaning of this is, that it is received by faith alone. If a man would give all the substance of his house for this righteousness of God, it would be utterly contemned. It is 'without money and without price.' Christ offers himself freely to each of you, to be Jehovah your Righteousness.

St. Peter's, October 16, 1842 (Action Sermon)

63. The Christian in captivity

By the rivers of Babylon, there we are sat down, yea, we wept, when we remembered Zion. We hanged our harps upon the willows in the midst thereof. For there they that carried us away captive required of us a song; and they that wasted us required of us mirth, saying, Sing us one of the songs of Zion. How shall we sing the LORD's song in a strange land? If I forget thee, O Jerusalem, let my right hand forget her cunning. If I do not remember thee, let my tongue cleave to the roof of my mouth; if I prefer not Jerusalem above my chief joy (Psalm 137:1-6).

Israel was a typical people. In their bondage in Egypt, in their deliverance by the hand of Moses, in their passing through the Red Sea, in their journeying through the wilderness, in the manna that fed them and the smitten rock that gave them drink, in their unbelief, in their falls, in their victories, in their Jordan, and in their Land of Promise; in all of these, from the beginning to the end, Israel was a typical people. They were typical of God's Church in all ages of the world. And they were typical of the soul of every individual believer. Every believer has been in bondage in Egypt, has been brought through the Red Sea of the Redeemer's blood, has been led through the wilderness, fed with manna and water out of the rock, and is yet to pass over Jordan into a land of eternal rest.

And even God's dealings with Israel after having entered into Canaan are typical of his dealings with the believing soul. They were not able to destroy all the Canaanites, but they made them hewers of wood and drawers of water. Does not this remind you, Christian, that you have never cast out all God's enemies in your soul, that you have only brought them into bondage, that sin does not reign in you? Again, Israel and Judah were carried away captive because of their sins. Does not this remind you how often you are led captive, brought into a strange land, and into darkness by reason of sin?

This psalm is composed for Israel in her captivity. Let us go over it, taking its typical meaning.

1. When a believer is in captivity he has a sorrowful remembrance of Zion.
So it was with God's ancient people: 'By the rivers of Babylon there we sat down, yea, we wept when we remembered Zion' (verse 1). In 2

Chronicles 36:14-20, we find the melancholy tale of Judah's captivity. Many of their friends had been slain by the sword; the house of God was burned; the walls of Jerusalem were broken down; and they themselves were captives in a foreign land. No wonder that they sat down and wept when they remembered Zion.

So it is often with the believer when led captive by sin; he sits down and weeps when he remembers Zion. Zion is the place where God makes himself known. When a poor awakened sinner is brought to know the Saviour, and to enter through the rent veil into the holiest of all, then he becomes one of the people of Zion: 'A day in thy courts is better than a thousand.' He dwells in Zion; and the people that dwell therein are forgiven their iniquity. But when a believer falls into sin, he falls into darkness - he is carried a captive away from Zion. No more does he find entrance within the veil, no more is he glad when they say to him, 'Let us go up to the house of the Lord.' He sits down and weeps when he remembers Zion.

Some are hearing me who remember Zion with tears. Some of you may remember a time when you were dwellers in Zion, when you were forgiven your iniquity. Perhaps you may remember in the days of your youth that you were much affected with the things of eternity. Perhaps you remember a godly parent that prayed over you, or a godly minister who brought you into Zion. Perhaps you may remember being admitted to your first sacrament, how the minister of Christ yearned over you, how his heart filled with joy when the Word came with power upon your heart, when you were brought into the bonds of the covenant. Some of you may remember the love of your espousal, your first love when the sun shone more brightly on Sabbath days than all other days besides, when the gates of Zion were dearer to you than all the dwellings of Jacob. But these days are fled with you. You have fallen into sin. You have been carried away captive, and now you sit and weep when you remember Zion.

Do you really weep? Do you really feel it was better with you then than it is now? Do you really feel that you have been forsaking your own mercies? Ah, then, your very weeping shows that you are one of the captive children of Zion. It is only the true children of Zion that weep in their captivity. Do not say, then: 'There is no hope - no, for I have loved strangers, and after them I will go.' If you be mourning, there is hope. 'Oh, Israel! thou hast destroyed thyself; yet in me is thy help. Thou hast played the harlot with many lovers; yet, return again to me, saith the Lord.'

Do not sit and weep. Rather be like the bride: 'I will rise now and go about the city; in the streets and in the broad ways I will seek him whom my soul loveth.' Seek him in the Word, seek him by prayer, seek him by his ministers; but do seek him. 'Seek his face evermore.'

2. The world derides the believer in his captivity.

So it was with ancient Israel: 'We hanged our harps upon the willows in the midst thereof. For there they that carried us away captive required of us a song; and they that wasted us required of us mirth, saying, Sing us one of the songs of Zion' (verses 2,3).

The Chaldeans were cruel conquerors. God says by his prophet: 'I was but a little displeased, and they helped forward the affliction.' Not only did they carry them away from their temple, their country and their homes, but they made a mock of their sorrows. When they saw them sit down to shed the bitter tears by the rivers of Babylon, they demanded mirth and a song, saying, 'Sing us one of the songs of Zion.'

So it is with the world and the captive Christian. There are times when the world does not mock at the Christian. Often the Christian is filled with so strange a joy that the world wonders in silence. Often there is a meek and quiet spirit in the Christian, which disarms opposition. The soft answer turneth away wrath; and his very enemies are forced to be at peace with him. But stop till the Christian's day of darkness comes, stop till he is shut out from Zion, and carried afar off, and sits and weeps; then will the cruel world help forward the affliction. Then will they ask for mirth and song; and when they see the bitter tear trickling down the cheek, they ask with savage mockery, Where is your psalm-singing now? 'Sing us one of the songs of Zion.' Even Christ felt this bitterness when he hung upon the cross.

Some of you may be feeling this just now. You have gone away from Christ, and shut out from the light of God's countenance. You have lost all the joys of Zion, the sweet comforts of God's holy place. You shed the bitter tear when you remember Zion. But there is still another bitter, bitter dreg in your cup. The world sneers at you.

Your worldly friends deride you. There is the good of being too religious, they say; there is the end of it. It ends either in melancholy or madness. 'Come, sing us one of the songs of Zion.' Do you ask, Why must I bear all this? This is the hedge of thorns to drive you back to Christ: 'Thine own wickedness shall correct thee, and thy backsliding shall reprove thee. Know, therefore, and see that it is an evil thing and bitter that thou hast forsaken the Lord thy God, and that my fear is not in thee.'

Some hearing may be the cruel spoilers that mock at the distressed Christian. Some of you who are fathers may mock at your godly children; brothers, at your godly sisters; sisters, at your godly brothers. Alas! ye know not what ye do. Take heed that ye offend not one of these little ones that believe in Christ. It were better for you that a millstone were hanged about your neck, and you were drowned in the depth of the sea. Remember it is written: 'He that toucheth them, toucheth the apple of his eye.' Read here your doom, ye that cruelly mock at the Christian: 'Happy shall he be that rewardeth thee as thou hast served us. Happy shall he be that taketh and dasheth thy little ones against the stones.'

3. The Christian cannot sing in captivity.

So it was with ancient Israel. They were peculiarly attached to the sweet songs of Zion. They reminded them of the times of David and Solomon, when the temple was built, and Israel was in its greatest glory. They reminded them, above all, of their God, of their temple, and the services of the sanctuary. Three times a-year they came up from the country in companies, singing these sweet songs of Zion, lifting their eyes to the hills whence came their help.

But now, when they were in captivity, they hanged their harps upon the willows; and when their cruel spoilers demanded mirth and a song, they said: 'How shall we sing the Lord's song in a strange land?' So it is with the believer in darkness. He hangs his harp upon the willows, and cannot sing the song of the Lord.

Every believer has a harp. Every heart that has been made new is turned into a harp of praise. The mouth is filled with laughter, the tongue with divinest melody. Every true Christian loves praise; the holiest Christians love it most. But when the believer falls into sin and darkness, his harp is on the willows, and he cannot sing the Lord's song, for he is in a strange land.

He loses all sense of pardon. It is the sense of pardon that gives its sweetest tones to the song of the Christian: 'O Lord, I will praise thee; though thou wast angry with me, yet thine anger is turned away, and thou comfortest me.' There is a peculiar melody in the song of a forgiven soul. It is far sweeter that the song of angels, whether sung in earth or in heaven. It is called a *new* song: 'Thou hast redeemed us to God by thy blood, out of every kindred, and tongue, and people, and nation.' Do you know how to sing this new song? Then happy are you. But when a believer is in captivity he loses this sweet sense of forgiveness, and therefore cannot sing.

He loses all sense of the presence of God. It is the sweet presence of God with the soul that makes the believer sing. It is for this reason that believers love the house of God so much. God is present there, meets with them there. Is it not so, Christians? It is not the psalms, nor the prayers, nor the preaching, nor any of the creatures that make the house of God precious - it is the presence of your God. This is Bethel, the house of God. It is that which makes you sing. But when that presence is away, the Lord's house is but a howling wilderness; and you say: 'How can we sing the Lord's song in a strange land?'

He loses sight of the heavenly Canaan. The sight of the everlasting hills draws forth the heavenly melodies of the believing soul. The land of promise in sight fills the heart with joy. Hence dying saints have the sweetest song, because they stand on the top of Nebo, and say, All, all is mine. But when a believer sins, and is carried captive, he loses this hope of glory. He sits and weeps, he hangs his harp upon the willows, and cannot sing the Lord's song in a strange land.

O believers! would you keep your song? Then keep your Saviour. Would you have the harp always in tune? Then keep in sight of Christ and of glory.

4. The believer in darkness still remembers Zion, and prefers it above his chief joy.

So it was with Israel in captivity. They were now captives in a glorious land. The broad stream of the Euphrates was flowing past them, better than all the waters of Israel. The noble city Babylon was before them, with its tower reaching to heaven, its wonderful walls, its hanging gardens, and its thousand delights. Yet they looked upon all only to turn from it with a sigh, saying: 'If I forget thee, O Jerusalem, let my right hand forget her cunning. If I do not remember thee, let my tongue cleave to the roof of my mouth; if I prefer not Jerusalem above my chief joy' (verses 5,6).

So it is with a believer in darkness. He often finds, when he has fallen into sin and captivity, that he has fallen among worldly delights and worldly friends. A thousand pleasures tempt him to take up his rest there, and to say, 'Peace, peace, when there is no peace.' But if he be a true child of Zion, he never will settle in a strange land. He will look over all the pleasures of the world, and the pleasures of sin, and say: 'A day in thy courts is better than a thousand;' 'If I forget thee, O Jerusalem, let my right hand forget her cunning.'

Learn from this, that a true believer never can forget Jerusalem. Have you ever had the joys of pardon and a new heart? Then you never can forget them. Have you ever tasted the sweetness of God's favour? Then you will always remember it, and seek it above your chief joy.

Some hearing me live without one thought of Jerusalem. Some of you promised fair in days gone by. You were moved by the wrath of God, you were won by the love of God; you trembled, like Felix; you were almost persuaded to be Christians, like Agrippa; but where are you now? You are living in the busy world: in the world, and of the world; you partake of its pleasures and of its sins, and you never think of your former seriousness - you forget Jerusalem.

Ah! it is too plain that you never were a child of Zion, else you could not forget it. Oh! it is too plain that the doom of Babylon will be yours: 'Babylon the great is fallen, is fallen, and is become the habitation of devils, and the hold of every foul spirit; therefore shall her plagues come in one day; for strong is the Lord God who judgeth her. Come out of her, my people, that ye be not partakers in her sins, and that ye receive not of her plagues.'

Christians, learn to long for the heavenly Jerusalem. Do not forget it. Here we are in a strange land; be not taken up with anything that is there. But yonder is our continuing city, the heavenly Jerusalem, with its pearly gates, and streets of shining gold. Let the chief of your desires be to be with Christ, which is far better. When the world is at the brightest, when friends are at the kindest, when your sky is at the clearest, still lift up this sweet song: 'If I forget thee, O Jerusalem, let my right hand forget her cunning. If I do not remember thee, let my tongue cleave to the roof of my mouth; if I prefer not Jerusalem above my chief joy.'

St Peter's, October 1

64. The believer a blessing - the unbeliever a curse

And it shall come to pass, that as ye were a curse among the heathen, O house of Judah, and house of Israel; so will I save you, and ye shall be a blessing (Zechariah 8:13).

Doctrine. Unconverted men are a curse to all about them; but when converted, they become a blessing.

1. Unconverted men are a curse by their example. This is true, whether they be outwardly decent and moral, or be living in open sins and wickedness.

If they be outwardly decent men, then they are generally much respected in the world; and so their example is not only followed, but followed without any scruple. Though they have no love to Christ, though they have no prayer in their families, though they never gather their children upon their knees to tell them of the only way of salvation, though they have little or no secret prayer in their closets; yet, because they are outwardly honest men, and sober, respectable men, they are set up as patterns to be imitated, and even believers are tempted to think themselves and their children safe in their company. These men are whited sepulchres; men walk over them without fear. They do not know that within there is nothing but dead men's bones and all uncleanness. Oh, what a curse outwardly decent unconverted men are to every society they come into!

But still more, unconverted men are a curse by their example, if they be living in any open sin.

They are a curse to their children, to their servants, to their neighbours, by leading them into the same sins. Just as a man infected with the plague is a curse to every society he comes into, for he communicates the infection to all; so a man infected with sin infects everybody around him. Nothing teaches so soon as example. How easily do children pick up the oaths they hear their parents using! And there are no bounds to this curse; for every man stands in the centre of a circle of companions, and to each of these he communicates the hateful infection that is in his own bosom. Each of these companions stands in the centre of another circle, to each of whom he transmits the same hateful infection; so that one unconverted sinner may be a curse to thousands. Ay, even when he is lifting up his eyes in hell, the infection of which he was the origin may be raging among thousands whom he has left on earth. Oh, brethren, it is a fearful thing to think that an unconverted man in hell may yet be a curse upon the earth!

They are a curse to those that sin along with them. *Objection.* My companions are sinful already, and therefore if I sin along with them, I cannot be blamed for making them sinners. True, you cannot be blamed for making them sinners; but you can be blamed for making them worse sinners. Is it no crime, think you, to make bad worse? Is it no crime to help him to a deeper place in hell? Now, this is what all sinners are doing by their example. Nothing encourages a man in sin so much as example. When so many are on the broad way, it becomes very easy. How many a man would have been a sober man this day, if his companions had not pushed the bottle to him! How many a man would have turned at the voice of Christ, if his companions had not laughed him out of it! Oh, what a curse an unconverted man is by his example!

They are a curse to the sober, decent, unconverted men. These men will not go with them to the same excess of riot. They stand aloof and are shocked at open sin, and say inwardly in their hearts, I thank God I am not as these men are - extortioners, unjust, adulterers. Surely I must be on the right way, for I am so different from these open sinners. Ah, brethren! who knows how many unconverted souls that never came to a saving close with Christ, that never knew what it was to receive the Spirit of Christ to dwell in them, that have been hardened into a deadly peace by the sight of the openly wicked and profane! Oh, what a curse an open sinner is to all the world.

Brethren, are you unconverted? Then you have been a curse all your life long up to this day. You are decent and sober, and much respected in the world, it may be - but still unconverted. You have no love to Christ, no prayer in your family, no prayer in your closet. Do you not see what a withering blight you have cast all around you. Look at your children and your servants. Have you not frozen them into as icy coldness as yourself? Or perhaps you have lived in some darling sin. Do you not see how you have infected all around you? Have not some of your children or neighbours learned the very same sin? Nay, do you not see some who have grown more wicked since you joined them? They were like men running down-hill before; but you gave them a push, and made them run faster. Oh! how many may be in hell this day, who are cursing you for teaching them, or helping them to sin. Stop, poor soul, before you take another step in sin. Do you not think your own curse will be heavy enough, that you are heaping the curses of others on your soul? The rich man in hell did not wish his five brethren to come there; and O, have you less compassion on your friends than a soul in hell? It may be you have no compassion on your own soul, or perhaps you think you will try and bear the wrath of God; but have you no pity for your little children. You cannot bear to hear them cry on earth; oh, how will you bear to hear them cry in hell?

2. Unconverted men are a curse by being cumberers of the ground. Just as the fig tree was a curse to the other trees of the vineyard, for all the time, and expense, and care that were wasted upon it might have been bestowed upon them; so unconverted men, who bear no fruit to God, are a curse to all around them, they take up so much room and care in the church of God. Just as a boy at school who will not learn is a curse to the whole school, for he takes up so much of the master's time and care, that might all be expended on the other boys; just so the unconverted are a curse to all around, for they take up so much of the care and anxiety of ministers. Just as the criminals of a country are a great curse, not only because of their wicked example, but because of the care and expense that must be laid out upon them; the thousands of pounds that must be paid for jails, and judges, and officers, which might all be employed in aiding honest industry; so the unconverted are a curse in every parish, taking up so much of the care and time of the minister, which all might be employed in helping the dear children of God. Just as a stray sheep is a curse to all the flock, for the shepherd must leave the ninety-nine in the wilderness and go after the sheep that is lost, he must trace it over the mountains and through the valleys, and may not find it after all; so lost sinners are a curse to all the people of God by taking up so much of the shepherd's time and care to seek them.

The backward state of believers in our day is mainly to be attributed to this. So much time and labour has to be expended on the barren fig trees, that the precious vines are left unprotected and uncultivated. When a soul is brought to Christ, it is but just born again. It is but a babe in everything, and needs to be nursed and fed with milk, and tenderly cared for. But ministers cannot do everything; and how often do they leave that soul, knowing that it is saved, and expend their labours upon the unsaved and unconverted! He was a blessed man of God who made it his rule never to preach one sermon without some word for poor unconverted souls. But, see how much of our time and anxiety this takes up. And what a curse unconverted sinners thus are to the church of God!

Are you unconverted? Then you have been a curse all your life long up to this day. How many sermons have been filled up with your case! How many of the prayers of the servant of God have been taken up with you! How much of his labour has been expended upon you! And are you still unconverted? Ah, then, are you not a cumberer of the ground? Are you not a curse?

3. Unconverted men are a curse negatively, by not doing any good. Man is a social creature. It is not good for man to be alone; and, therefore, God has put us into families, and neighbourhoods, and countries, just that every one might be a blessing to every other. But unconverted men do no good to others. They do not answer the end for which they were placed in the world, and thus they are a curse. The sun was placed in the centre of our system to give light and heat to all around him; but if he were to leave the end for which he was placed there, if he were to keep all his beams to himself, instead of warming and lighting the world, then he would be a curse instead of a blessing. Such are unconverted men. They do no good, they keep all they have to themselves; like barren sands, they take in sun and shower, but give back neither flower nor fruit.

Men have a great hold on the affections of other men. This is a wonderful gift of God, given that we may lead one another to good and heavenly things. But unconverted men do not use this gift. They often use it in leading others to sin; but they never use it in leading others to Christ. An unconverted parent never uses this talent in leading his children to the Saviour. Oh! what a curse he is to them, then, instead of a blessing.

Men have money. This is a gift of God, given that we may use it all to his service. But unconverted men never use their money for Christ. God made them stewards of it; but they cheat both God and man. They pretend it is their own, and they may do what they will with it.

Men may pray for one another. God intends all Christians to be like Christ, intercessors for one another, and for the world. But the unconverted never pray for others. They have no wish to do so. Most unconverted parents never pray for their children; most unconverted children never pray for their parents. What curses they are to one another. Truly the tender mercies of the wicked are cruel.

But I hasten to show you the change that takes place when the unconverted becomes a converted man; then this word is fulfilled, and he becomes as much a blessing as ever he was a curse.

4. A converted man is a blessing by his example.

His very turning to Christ is often a great blessing in awakening others. When Naomi set out to go to God, and the people of God, then Ruth was awakened to cleave unto her. When God shall awaken the Jews in the latter day, then 'ten men, out of all languages, shall take hold of the skirt of him that is a Jew, saying, We will go with you, for we have heard that God is with you.' When an unconverted person is really awakened by God, when the heart is broken under a sense of sin, it is generally a very striking sight to those that are around him. One conversion is often the means of many more.

Objection. Conversion is a work of God. *Answer.* True, conversion is a work of God, and yet he works it by natural means. And there is no more powerful means than example. When a parent is awakened, then the children cry out, Shall we remain behind to be lost? When a child is converted, then the parents begin to think, Is our dear child going to be saved, and shall we stay behind to be cast away? In this way it is that two or three are often converted in one family, and sometimes whole families are converted.

And not only his turning persuades others to turn, but the peace and joy which he comes to in believing persuade others to believe in Jesus. Come you with us, he says, and we will do you good. Every believer is just a monument of grace, a way-mark pointing to the city of refuge. When the soul comes to close with Christ, when he comes to feel the calm delight of a forgiven soul, who can look upon the tranquillized soul, and not feel the desire rising within, Oh, that I knew that peace and joy! His very feature beaming with peace and joy, his eye so full of heavenly tenderness, pleading with poor sinners; and he says, We were once as you are. Oh, what a blessing a happy believer is to all that know him.

But most of all, by the example of his holy life is he a blessing. Often times the peace of a believer is all within, it is too tender and frail to meet the world's rude gaze. Often times the words of a believer are weak and few, and produce little effect; but still there is a power in a blameless life which is full of blessing. Just as you have seen some deep and quiet river, rolling gently onward to the sea, through deep woods and sloping banks, without the noise of rippling waves, yet enriching and gladdening the whole valley with its fertilizing waters; just such is the believer in Jesus. His voice may not be heard in the streets. He may be all unknown in the debate on the world's politics, unseen, unheard of, on his daily progress to eternity; he yet spreads the greenness of paradise around his path.

How many a believing wife gains over her husband without the Word, when he beholds her chaste conversation coupled with fear, her meek and quiet spirit, which is in the sight of God of great price!

Have you been converted? Ah, then you are a blessing. Remember the word of Christ: 'Go home to thy friends, and tell them how great things the Lord hath done for thee, and hath had compassion on thee.'

5. A converted man is a blessing, because the blessing of God is upon him.

When the ark of God was carried into the house of Obed-edom the Gittite, and remained there three months, then it is said the Lord blessed Obed-edom, and his household, and all that he had. Now, every believer is a kind of ark of God in which he hides his law, every believer is a temple of the Holy Ghost. It is a good thing to receive a believer into our house, for the blessing of God goes with him. That promise is true to him: 'Blessed is he that blesseth thee, cursed is he that curseth thee.'

As far back as the flood you remember how wicked Ham was saved in the ark, and kept from being devoured with the wicked world, because he was in righteous Noah's family. Doubtless many an ungodly son among us is kept alive, and spared a little longer because of his righteous father.

You remember how Sodom would have been spared if there had been ten righteous men found in it; and how the angel told Lot, 'I cannot do any thing until thou be escaped thither.' Doubtless, this town in which we live is spared only for the sake of the few children of God that are in it. Take them away, and God's wrath would doubtless come down immediately. How little you think, my unconverted friends, that you owe it to the children of God, whom you despise, that you are not this day in hell.

You remember how a poor widow of Sarepta received Elijah into her house, and how he was a blessing to her; for her barrel of meal never wasted, and her cruse of oil never failed; and her son was brought to life again through Elijah's prayer. Ah, brethren, be careful to entertain the children of God, you will find them angels in disguise. Wherever a child of God is, God's eye is upon that spot by night and day. Oh, it is good to be near to the children of God, that we may share in their blessing. He that receiveth them receiveth Jesus. Blessed is he that blesseth them, and cursed is he that curseth them.

6. A converted man is a blessing by his deeds and prayers.

When he was without Christ in the world, he lived only to himself; but, now brought nigh by the blood of Jesus, he lives only for others. He becomes a candle, and gives light to all that are in the house. He is changed into the image of God. God is continually giving out blessings, and so the believer feels it more blessed to give than to receive.

Abraham, before his conversion, was doubtless as selfish and ungodly as any unconverted man among us. Doubtless he thought it beneath him to have family prayer, or to teach his children and servants to know the Saviour. Doubtless he was as cold and selfish in these things as most are among ourselves. But mark the change! When Abraham becomes a child of God, he builds a family altar wherever he goes; and though he had hundreds of servants under him, yet he cared anxiously for the souls of them all. 'For I know him,' says God, 'that he will command his servants and his household after him, to keep the ways of the Lord.' Before, he had been a curse; but now he is a blessing.

Dorcas before her conversion was doubtless as selfish, and as fond of worldly things, as all unconverted people are. Doubtless she thought it beneath her to make coats and garments for the poor, doubtless she was as selfish in these things as most are amongst us. But mark the change! When she becomes a child of God, then to do good and to distribute seems to have been the pleasure of her life. This woman was full of good works and alms-deeds, which she did. Before she had been a curse; but now she is a blessing.

Paul before his conversion was as great an enemy to the truth and as keen a persecutor of Christians as most unconverted persons are: 'I thought I should do many things contrary to the name of Jesus of Nazareth; I was a blasphemer, and persecutor, and injurious.' But mark the change, when he became a child of God: 'In the bowels of Jesus Christ I long after you all;' 'I will very gladly spend and be spent for you.'

Are you converted? Then see that you be a blessing. Once you were a curse. See that you be as much a blessing.

Dear Christians, I this night bring to your remembrance the parting words of Christ: 'Go ye into all the world, and preach the gospel to every creature.' The wide world alone is to be the bound of your blessing. Once you were a curse without a bound. Now you are to be a blessing without a bound.

And not only in his deeds is the change manifest, but in his prayer. Being saved, he becomes like Christ, the intercessor; and, therefore, he bestows a blessing. Before, he never prayed for his friends, obtained no gift from God for them; even his children, he did not pray for them; but now, brought near to God, within the veil, behold, he prayeth, and his prayer availeth.

You remember how Abraham prayed for Abimelech, and God healed Abimelech and all his house. Was not Abraham a blessing?

You remember how Moses held up his hands to the going down of the sun, and Israel prevailed over Amalek. Was not Moses a blessing?

You remember how Elisha prayed unto the Lord, and the child of the Shunammite came alive again. Was not Elisha a blessing?

You remember how Elijah, a man of like passions as we are, prayed earnestly that it might not rain, and it rained not on the earth for the space of three years and six months. And he prayed again, and the heaven gave rain, and the earth brought forth fruit. Was not he a blessing?

You remember how Daniel prayed for Jerusalem, and he was answered while he was yet speaking. Was not Daniel a blessing?

Oh, my unconverted friends, how little you know how much you owe to the prayer of the despised believer. If it were not that there are some among you whom you know not, whose speech you would deem contemptible, whose prayer ascends nightly from their humble dwellings, unheard, unseen, by all but the unslumbering one, that you may be yet sought out and spared, that a blessing may attend our ministry among you, how many of you would be this day lifting up your eyes in the world where there is no preaching and no intercession - where hope is past!

In conclusion

Some of you think you have been converted. Well, have you become a blessing? Once you were a curse, now are you a blessing? Once you were like the upas tree, which casts a deadly shade over all that sit down beside it; now, if you be a child of God, you are like the apple tree among the trees of the wood: your shade will be pleasant, and your fruit sweet to the taste. Once you were like some polluted thing casting a poisonous odour round you; now your name is as ointment poured forth. Once you were the centre of a circle of friends and companions, to whom you gave the contagion of sin every time you met. Now when you come from your closet, and enter among your family, your face shines like one that has been in the mount with Christ, and when you come down into the world, 'It is even as if an angel shook his wings'. See that it be so, believing brethren. You are peculiarly saved: be a peculiar people, zealous of good works. Remember how long you were a curse; see now that ye be as much a blessing. You may have ruined many souls; see now that you save many.

And remember, unconverted souls, meddle not with believers, except to go with them. 'Touch not mine anointed, and do my prophets no harm;' 'Blessed is he that blesseth them, and cursed is he that curseth them;' 'Take heed that ye offend not one of these little ones which believe in me; it were better for you that a millstone were hanged about your neck, and you were drowned in the depth of the sea.'

LECTURES

THE TEN VIRGINS

THE TEN VIRGINS: LECTURE I
(Matthew 25:1-4)

Then shall the kingdom of heaven be likened unto ten virgins, which took
their lamps, and went forth to meet the bridegroom. And five were wise,
and five were foolish. They that were foolish took their lamps, and took no
oil with them: But the wise took oil in their vessels with their lamps.

There is not in the whole Bible a parable that applies more accurately
to this congregation than this. Like the ten virgins, you may all be
divided into two classes. Some of you are wise, I trust; and some, alas!
are foolish. Like the virgins, you all profess a great deal; and yet some
have the gift of the Holy Spirit, and some want it. And the day is fast
hastening when you will be separated. The truly saved among you will
enter in with Christ, the rest will be shut out for eternity. At present I can
overtake only three facts.

1. God's children are wise; the rest are foolish (verse 2).
Those of you who are God's children are truly wise. *First*, not worldly-
wise. This is denied: 'For ye see your calling, brethren, how that not
many wise men after the flesh, not many mighty, not many noble, are
called: but God hath chosen the foolish things of the world to confound
the wise' (1 Corinthians 1:26,27); 'the wisdom of this world is
foolishness with God' (1 Corinthians 3:19); 'I thank thee, O Father,
Lord of heaven and earth, because thou hast hid these things from the
wise and prudent, and hast revealed them unto babes' (Matthew 11:25);
'Out of the mouth of babes and sucklings hast thou ordained strength'
(Psalm 8:2). Not many of deep, profound mind are saved, not many men
of learning, not many of your sagacious, worldly men - men wise to
drive a bargain. These are often passed by; and God takes some little
child that knows nothing of the world, or some peasant from behind his
plough, and brings him to glory. Why? Just that no man may boast and
say: It was my wit that saved me. *Second*, yet God's children are wise,
the only wise in this world.

They see things as they truly are.
You that are mere professors do not see things as they truly are.

You do not see time as it truly is - the threshold of eternity. You do
not see how short it is - that three score and ten years are but a span. You

do not see how rapidly it passes - like the swift ships, like the eagle to the prey. You do not see that it cannot be recalled, and that every moment is precious, that it is the time for conversion, the only time; else you could not waste it in mere pretences to godliness. They that are Christ's see time as it really is.

You do not see yourselves as you truly are. You have never seen what it is to be by nature children of wrath. You have never seen the awful mountains of sin that are piled over your soul. You have never seen the lusts that bind your soul, the deep volcano of burning lust that is in your own bosom. They that are Christ's see this somewhat as it truly is.

You do not see the favour of God. You have never seen how precious it is. You know the value of the favour of man, and therefore you wear a cloak of profession; but you know not the value of God's favour, or you would fly to Christ. They that are Christ's know this as it is.

God's children do not rest in knowledge.

Hypocrites always rest in their knowledge. You never can tell them anything new. They say: I know that. Tell them of sin, of Christ, of judgment to come, they think they shall be saved because they have knowledge; although this knowledge has never led them to rest on Christ, to pray, to leave their sins. But you that are Christ's do not rest content with this. You not only know of Christ and speak of him, but you do the things which he says. You have turned from idols. You are the only wise.

A child of God lives for eternity.

A hypocrite lives for time. This was all Judas lived for if he could pass off for a while as a true disciple, if he could keep up appearances for a time, if he could indulge his lusts, and yet be esteemed a believer, and a true apostle. He tried to keep up appearances to the last. So Demas wanted to deceive Paul for this life - to be thought a brother. Alas, how many of you are thus foolish! Living so as to keep up an appearance of being a Christian for a little time, though you know that you are living in positive sin, and that you will be discovered before the world in a short time. You only are truly wise who live for eternity, who live as you shall wish you had done when you come to die.

A child of God is like God.

God is the only wise. In him are all the fountains of divine wisdom. God is light, and in him is no darkness at all. To become like him is to become truly wise. Those of you who have fled to Christ are becoming like God. You have his Spirit, and you are being changed into his image. You have one will with God. You fall in with God's purposes in this world. His joy is your joy. You that are mere professors have none of God's likeness. You do not seek it, nor desire it.

2. The wise and foolish are alike in many things (verses 3,4).

The virgins were alike in many things. To the eye of man they appeared the same. All were virgins, dressed probably in white, all their faces probably fair and comely. Each of the ten carried a silver lamp, bright and polished, and every lamp was lighted. Nay, all of them seemed to have one object in view. They went forth to meet the bridegroom. In one thing alone they differed. The foolish took no oil in their lamps; but the wise took oil in their vessels with their lamps. So it is with professors and God's children to this day.

In many things man can see no difference.

You enjoy the same ordinances.
You sit under the same pastor - in the same seats. You come up together to the house of God in company. You sing the same psalms. Your voices blend together, and no ear but that of God can distinguish the voice of the hypocrite from that of the wise virgin. You stand up at the same prayer, all equally reverent in appearance. You listen to the same sermons. Sometimes you will be affected together. The feeling of sympathy runs through the midst of you, and none can tell where it is like early dew, or where it is the dew of the Spirit, the sympathy of nature or the sympathy of grace. You sit down at the same Lord's table, and pass the bread from hand to hand, you pass the cup from one to another. Ah! how affecting it is to think that so many in this congregation are but foolish virgins, that you will be parted in eternity.

They use the same speech.
God's children speak the language of Canaan; but professors learn to imitate it, and at last no one can discover the difference. They speak of convictions of sin, awakening, getting light, seeking Christ, finding Christ, closing with Christ, finding peace. Yet all the time their hearts are far from God, and they are lovers of pleasure more than lovers of God. Oh! how sad it is to think that many a tongue that has spoken much

about Christ, and regeneration, and the Holy Spirit shall yet want a drop of water to cool it in the burning lake.

They utter the same prayers.
One of the great marks of a child of God is prayer: 'Behold he prayeth.' He loves to pray. But even this is imitated by professors, who have a name to live, and are dead. Often they will pray in secret with great meltings and affections; often they will pray in public with great fervour and pathos; and yet all the time they are living in sin, and know it. Alas! how sad, that many of you whose voices have often been heard in prayer may yet be heard crying, 'Lord, Lord, open to us,' crying on rocks and mountains to cover you from the wrath of God and of the Lamb!

They have the same outward behaviour.
The truest mark of children of God is their avoiding sin. They flee from their old companions and old ways, they walk with God. And yet even this is imitated by the foolish virgins. They go out to meet their Lord. They flee old sins for a time, they hasten from their work to the house of God, they seek the company of God's children, perhaps they try to save others, and become very zealous in this. O how sad that many who now cling to the godly will soon be torn from them, and bound up with devils and wicked men!

3. There is a difference: The foolish virgins have no oil in their vessels.

Professors are often striven with by the Spirit. In the days of Noah he strove long to get men to leave their sins and enter the ark (Genesis 6:3). So also with Israel in the wilderness: 'They rebelled and vexed his Holy Spirit' (Isaiah 63:10). And even in the days of Stephen: 'Ye do always resist the Holy Ghost: as your fathers did, so do ye' (Acts 7:51). In the Bible, in the ministry, by mercies, by afflictions, he strives like a man wrestling with you. He strives to make you quit your sins, and flee into Christ. Most of you have, in each or all of these ways, felt the Spirit's strivings. Still,

They are not taught by the Spirit.
All who are saved are taught by the Spirit - 'all taught of God'. Without this, no man will come to Christ for the soul is dead. He teaches our lost condition - then he glorifies Christ.

They are not dwelt in by the Spirit.
The Spirit dwells in all who come to Christ (John 7:37-39).

Firstly, as a *seal*: 'In whom also after that ye believed, ye were sealed' (Ephesians 1:13). The heart is the wax, the Holy Spirit the seal, the image of Christ the impression. He softens the heart, and presses on the sea. But not like other seals, he does not lift away, but keeps it there.

Secondly, as a *witness*: 'The Spirit itself beareth witness with our spirit' (Romans 8:16). The spirit of adoption, crying 'Abba' in the heart, is the Spirit bearing witness. When the soul is taken into the child's place, it can use a child's liberty.

Thirdly, as an *earnest*: 'The earnest of the Spirit in our hearts' (2 Corinthians 1:22). A little in hand of the full reward. The Holy Spirit in the heart is a little of heaven, all begun. Ah, my friends! be not deceived. Do not tell me you sit under this or that minister, have had those convictions, liberty in prayer. But are you changed? Have you got the new heart? Is heaven begun? Have you oil in your vessels with your lamps?

St Peter's, December 18, 1841

THE TEN VIRGINS: LECTURE II
(Matthew 25:5)

While the bridegroom tarried, they all slumbered and slept.

It is impossible to find a more solemn and awakening parable than this. I showed you last day: first, that God's children are truly wise, and mere professors truly foolish. You only who are God's children see things as they are; you live for eternity, and have the mind of God; second, in how many things the wise and foolish virgins appear to be the same: They have the same ordinances, same speech, same prayers, same outward behaviour; third, the difference between them which we shall further consider today: the one class have, the other have not, the Holy Spirit.

1. The tarrying of the bridegroom.
In that memorable discourse of the Saviour with his disciples, on the night of the last supper, Jesus said to them: 'A little while, and ye shall

not see me: and again, a little while, and ye shall see me, because I go to the Father' (John 16:16). And again, John, in Revelation 16:15, heard him say: 'Behold, I come as a thief. Blessed is he that watcheth, and keepeth his garments, lest he walk naked, and they see his shame.' And his last word, which fell like heavenliest music on John's enraptured ear, was, 'Behold, I come quickly', and, 'Surely, I come quickly.' Many of the first Christians seem to have thought that he would come in their day: so that Paul, in Second Thessalonians, had to warn them that the great Romish apostasy must happen first. And we find that scoffers, in Peter's time, used to say: 'Where is the promise of his coming?' Century after century has rolled away since then, and yet Jesus has never come. This explains the word, 'The bridegroom tarried'. Certainly he desires to come: 'His desire is toward me.' It will be the day of the gladness of his heart, the bridal day. And those that love Christ love his appearing. They cry, like John, 'Even so, come, Lord Jesus.' Yet still he tarries. Why is this?

He is not willing that any should perish. 'The Lord is not slack concerning his promise, as some men count slackness; but is long-suffering to us-ward, not willing that any should perish, but that all should come to repentance' (2 Peter 3:9).

This is the reason why he tarries: he is slow to anger. Sometimes, when I see some act of gross and open wickedness, my heart trembles within me. Then I think how the Lord sees all this, ay, all the wickedness committed over the whole world, and yet he forbears. Ah, what a sight of forbearance and long-suffering compassion is here! This is the reason why he tarries: he has compassion for the vilest, and waits long before he comes.

To fill up the number of his elect.
Christ is at this moment gathering a people from among the Gentiles. He is building up the great temple of the Lord, adding stone to stone. He cannot come till this is done. When all this is done, then he will come, and put on the top-stone, with shoutings of 'Grace, grace unto it.' He told Paul to remain and preach at Corinth: 'For I have much people in this city.' For the same reason he makes his ministers remain and preach on; for he has much people still. When he comes, those that are ready will enter in with him to the marriage, and the door will be shut. There are, no doubt, many elect ones, many that were given him by the Father

before the foundation of the world, still in the sleep of nature. He waits till these are gathered. When the last of his elect are gathered, then he will come.

To try the graces of his people.
There are many of the graces of God's people that can only grow in time of affliction. There is a plant in the garden which the gardener tramples below his feet to make it grow better. So it is with many of the graces of God's children - they grow better by being tried.

Faith in his word. The world say: 'Where is the promise of his coming? All things continue as they were.' All things seen are against it. Can you look through to the unseen world? This is what is wanted: 'We look not at the things which are seen, but at the things which are not seen.' Now this is one reason why the Bridegroom tarries: that faith may grow.

Bearing with adversaries. If he came now, and avenged us of our adversary, we would have no scope for forgiving injuries, or bearing reproaches for his name. We must be conformable to his death; therefore he bears long with us.

Compassion for souls. This was the most remarkable feature in Christ's character. This brought him from the throne of glory; this made him weep upon Mount Olivet. It behoves us to be made like him in this also. But this is the only time when we can be like him in this. When Jesus comes, we will cry, 'Just and true are thy ways, thou King of saints,' while he tramples his enemies below his feet. Do not wonder that Jesus tarries.

2. The sleep of the virgins: 'They all slumbered and slept.'
These words have been interpreted several ways. I have no doubt that the simplest interpretation is the true one, that before Christ comes all the Christian Churches will fall into a deep slumber. The Bible shows that not only do hypocrites fall asleep, but true believers also. Hence we find the apostles sleeping at the Mount of Transfiguration, and again at Gethsemane; and Paul cries to the Romans, 'It is high time to awake out of sleep.'

How Christians sleep.
The eyes begin to shut. When first brought to Christ, the eyes of sinners were opened, to see the shortness of time - that it is but a span; the vanity

of the world - all vain show; the exceeding sinfulness of sin. They saw sin covering them all over like devils, and were amazed that they were out of hell. They saw Christ in all his beauty, fulness, and glory. But now all these things become dim, as to a sleeping man. All outward objects are hidden - the soul sees no longer the shortness of time, the emptiness of the world, the vileness of sin, the glory of Christ.

The ear does not hear his knockings. Once the ear heard his voice. Amid a thousand the voice of Christ was sweet and powerful. Now the soul hears as if it did not hear: 'I have put off my coat; how shall I put it on? I have washed my feet; how shall I defile them?'

The sleeper dreams. So the soul takes up with idols, vain fancies. When first awakened, the soul said, 'What have I to do any more with idols?' But now when Christ and divine things are hidden, the soul again takes up with vain idols. Hence come, first, *deadness in prayer.* How sweet prayer is to a believing soul! There is wonderful access to the throne, pouring out of the heart, no separation, nothing kept back; but now there is utter barrenness, the soul has no desire, no free access. Second, *a fearful spirit.* A sense of guilt now lies on the conscience, a stupefying sense of having offended God, a spirit of bondage. Third, *the believer does not fear sin.* Once a sweet trembling fear of sin, a keeping far from the occasions of it, like Joseph: 'How shall I commit this great wickedness?' Now there is fearful familiarity with sin.

How hypocrites sleep.
They lose all their convictions. At one time they had deep and clear convictions of sin; but now they lose them. They have gone into some open sin and drowned conviction. They quench the Spirit.

They lose their joy in divine things. The stony-ground hearers received the Word with joy - a flash of delight. Something about the Word attracts their fancy - eloquence or imagery; or, hoping they are converted, they flatter themselves, and take great delight in hearing. This soon dies away.

They give over prayer. For a long time they prayed in a very melting manner. When under convictions, or under illuminations and a false hope, or before others, they prayed with fluency; but now they give over prayer by degrees. 'They all slumbered and slept.' They have been out in company, or they are sleepy, or they have no relish for it, and so they give over prayer by degrees.

Between the two there is this great difference, that the godly have still oil in their vessels, the others none. I would not say a word to encourage you who are godly to sleep on; on the contrary, it is high time to awake out of sleep. But I cannot but remark how different is the sleep of the two. First, the godly will waken out of their sleep. It is very sinful and very dangerous, but it is not fatal. The hypocrite seldom ever wakens out of his sleep. The rarest conversion in the world is that of a hardened hypocrite. Second, while the godly are under the displeasure of God, yet they are not under his curse; but the hypocrite sleeps over hell.

3. The coming of the Bridegroom.

The time.

At midnight, at an unexpected time, Christ will come. The whole Bible shows this: 'Of that day and hour knoweth no man, no, not the angels of heaven, but my Father only;' 'Watch, therefore: for ye know neither the day nor the hour when the Son of Man cometh.' It is compared to lightning: 'For as the lightning cometh out of the east, and shineth even unto the west; so shall also the coming of the Son of Man be.' What more awfully sudden than lightning! First an awful stillness, the black inky clouds shrouding the sky, then a bright gleam from east to west. So shall his coming be. It is like travail on a woman with child: 'When they shall say, Peace and safety; then sudden destruction cometh upon them as travail upon a woman with child; and they shall not escape.' It is like a thief: 'The day of the Lord so cometh, as a thief in the night.' It is thus in two respects:

(1) *In the uncertainty of the hour*. When a thief is going to break into a house, he does not tell the hour at which he will come. He gives no signs of his approach. If the goodman of the house knew what hour he would come, he would sit up, and not suffer his house to be broken up. Such will the coming of the Bridegroom be: 'Ye know neither the day nor the hour when the Son of Man cometh.'

(2) *A thief comes at the hour of rest*. When the family have all gone to rest, when the goodman of the house has locked and barred the door, when every candle is put out, and every eye is sealed in sleep, then the thief comes and forces the bar, and enters in. Such will the coming of the Saviour be. When the world is steeped in slumber Jesus will come.

Some of you will say: 'Surely we shall have some guess of the time of his coming.' Now, if there be one thing plainer than another, it is that you know neither the day nor the hour: 'In such an hour as ye think not, the Son of Man cometh.' If I were to go round you all, and say, 'Do you think the Son of Man will come tonight?' you would all say, 'I think not'. Well just in such an hour he will come. Are you ready?

A word to the unconverted.

Some of you *live in dishonesty.* In buying and selling, some of you, perhaps, use the light weight and the false balance, or in some other way you deceive your neighbour. O how dreadful if Christ should come and find you thus! It is said men will be buying and selling when he comes.

Some *live in deeds of darkness.* Perhaps you say, Surely the darkness shall cover me: 'At the window of my house I looked through my casement, and beheld among the simple ones, I discerned among the youths, a young man void of understanding, passing through the street near her corner; and he went the way to her house, in the twilight, in the evening, in the black and dark night.' Some of you commit those things of which it is a shame even so much as to speak. How awful will it be to you when his holy face appears!

Some of you *stifle convictions.* Like Agrippa, you are almost persuaded to be a Christian. Like Felix, you tremble, and say, 'A more convenient season.' Some of you put off your convictions with a little gaiety, a little worldly pleasure, saying, Plenty of time before I die. Ah! what will you do when the cry comes at midnight? No time for a prayer, no time for your Bible then, no time for conversion. 'At midnight there was a cry.'

THE TEN VIRGINS: LECTURE III

(Matthew 25:6-9)

And at midnight there was a cry made, Behold, the bridegroom cometh; go ye out to meet him. Then all those virgins arose, and trimmed their lamps. And the foolish said unto the wise, Give us of your oil; for our lamps are gone out. But the wise answered, saying, Not so; lest there be not enough for us and you: but go ye rather to them that sell, and buy for yourselves.

There is something sweet in that midnight-cry, 'Behold, the Bridegroom cometh.' It will be an awful day even to a child of God.

First, all sudden changes are dreadful. Many persons have been killed by the sudden news of something joyful. How awfully joyful, then, will be that cry, when we hear that all our toils and cares are past, that sin shall no longer reign in the world!

Second, the fate of our ungodly friends will be dreadful. All of us have ungodly friends, for whose conversion we pray. When that cry comes, it will be the knell of their souls; and yet for all that it will be a joyful day. In Matthew 24:32, it is compared to summer. It will be the summer of the soul - the winter will be past. 'But unto you that fear my name shall the Sun of righteousness arise with healing in his wings' (Malachi 4:2). 'And he shall be as the light of the morning, when the sun riseth, even a morning without clouds' (2 Samuel 23:4). 'He shall come down like rain upon the mown grass: as showers that water the earth' (Psalm 72:6).

But most of all, the cry, 'The Bridegroom cometh,' will revive the drooping hearts of his own chosen ones. It will remind us of the time that he chose us to be his own - the time of love, when he wooed us, and said: 'Thou shalt be for me, and not for another man.' He that loved us, and died for us, and promised to return and receive us to himself - 'Behold the Bridegroom cometh.' Ah! consider, beloved friends, whether it will be a time of joy to you, or of wailing. Careless sinner, what shall then become of thee? Mark here:

1. The discovery: 'Our lamps are gone out.'
A dry wick has often a great blaze for a while. So hypocrites often keep up their profession to the last; often it is very showy and evident. Many things might awaken hypocrites.

Their case is described in sermons. Often the minister is directed by God to speak exactly to their case. Often the Word comes very close to their conscience. We say, Surely that man will take the Word home. No; it slips past some way or other.

Seeing others converted. Often hypocrites see others beside them undergo a saving change. They see them convinced of sin, made to lie in the dust, brought to Jesus, filled with joy, living a new life, overcoming the world. This might open their eyes to see that their professed change is false and hollow.

The death of others. It must be a solemn thing to a hypocrite to see others cut down. Death tears away every mask for it calls the soul before the heart-searching one. Pretended convictions, pretended grace, words of put-on godliness, will not avail now. When hypocrites see others cut down, I have often thought, surely they will turn now. Yet it is not so: they often burn on to the last.

They have got a name to live, and they do not like to lose it. They have made a profession, and they do not like to draw back from it. Ministers have been pleased and satisfied, or godly persons have esteemed them, and they do not like all at once to give up this. So Judas was long esteemed a true disciple, and kept up his profession to the last.

Often do they delude themselves. They have some inward light and knowledge, which they mistake for grace. They have a form of godliness, pray in secret and in the family, and so deceive themselves as well as others. But their lamp will go out at the coming of Christ. 'Our lamps are gone out.' Not one blaze more, not one spark more. What is the reason?

There is no indwelling grace.

Their lamps went out because they had no oil. They burned for a while, as a dry wick will do, often with a great blaze; but soon the flame decays, and it goes out for want of oil. This is the case with hypocrites. They have no spring of gracious oil within their hearts. The Spirit of God often comes upon them, but he does not dwell in them. So it was with Balaam. His eyes were opened, he saw much of the joy of God's people, he longed to die the death of the righteous (Numbers 23:10); but he had no oil in the lamp, and his lamp went out. So with Saul. 'God gave him another heart' and 'the Spirit of God came upon him' (1 Samuel 10:9,10); but he had no oil in the lamp, no gracious indwelling of the Spirit, enabling him to cleave to Jesus, and so his lamp went out.

Often, in a rainy season, there are large pools of water gathered in the field where there is no spring or fountain. At first they appear large and deep, but when the summer comes, they dry up and disappear. So it is with hypocrites in this congregation. Many of you have had the Spirit poured on you as it was on Balaam and on Saul. Your eyes have been opened, you have had deep convictions, wonderful discoveries, panting desires after Christ and divine things; and yet you have never been brought, by the working of the Spirit of God to cleave to Christ. Ah! your lamp will go out and leave you in the blackness of darkness.

Dear friends, make sure of a deep and real work of grace upon your hearts. Remember it is said, that the man, who built his house upon the rock, digged deep and laid his foundation on the rock. It is not every change that is saving conversion. Of many it is true, 'They return, but not to the Most High' (Hosea 7:16). Do not be contented with being civilized, if you are not converted. It will not stand you in stead in the great day.

They have to appear before Christ.
It is an easy thing to appear Christian before men: 'Man looks only on the outward appearance, but God looketh on the heart.' As long as hypocrites have to appear only before men, they can keep up appearances. They can talk, and read, and pray, as if they were God's children; but when the cry comes, 'Behold, the Bridegroom cometh', then they know that they must appear before Christ, the searcher of hearts. When Jesse brought in his seven sons, Samuel looked on Eliab, and said: 'Surely the LORD's anointed is before him.' But God said: '... I have refused him: for the LORD seeth not as man seeth; for man looketh on the outward appearance, but the Lord looketh on the heart' (1 Samuel 16:6,7).

Ah, brethren! There are many of you that can now come in boldly before men, though you know yourselves to be graceless, never born again, living in sin. You can sit down at a sacrament, without fear or shame. But when Christ comes, your lamp will go out, you will not be able to bear the glance of his holy eye. O pray for such an interest in Christ now, that you may stand before the Son of Man at his coming!

2. The anxious application: 'Give us of your oil; for our lamps are gone out.'

Hypocrites will then see the difference between them and the godly. Their lamps will be out, but the lamps of the truly godly will be burning bright and clear. At present hypocrites think they are as good as anyone. They think there is no real difference between them and God's people. In that day they will be convinced that there is a great gulf fixed between.

They will see what a happy thing it is to have oil in their lamp. At present many among you do not see your need of grace. You do not see that you would be any happier with grace in your heart. You are willing rather to remain as you are. But in that day you will cry: 'Give us of your oil.' You will see the peace of the godly in that day. They will be unmoved amid a falling universe. The blood of Christ on their conscience will give them abiding peace. You will see their joyful faces, as they hear the cry, as they hear the footsteps, of the coming Bridegroom.

You will hear their song of praise as they welcome their Lord and Redeemer. At present the godly are poor and despised, often in trouble, and chastened every morning, and you would not join them; but in that day they will be like the stones of a crown, like the children of a king.

They will apply to the godly. At present hypocrites despise the godly and would not apply to them for anything. When a truly godly person warns you or advises you, you are offended. But in that day you will be in despair - glad to apply to any one. You will be glad to apply to godly friends and godly ministers in that day. You that wonder what makes people go to speak to ministers, you that mock and deride the truly godly, you will say: 'Give us of your oil.' At this day ministers and godly friends knock at your door, beseeching you to get the oil of grace into your hearts; but at that day you will knock at their door, crying, 'Give us of your oil; for our lamps are gone out.'

O what folly to rest in desires after grace, when even hypocrites will have this in that awful day!

3. The disappointment: 'Not so, lest there be not enough for us and you.'

It is not in their power to give grace. It pleases God to use the godly as instruments, but he has not given them to be fountains of grace: 'I have planted, Apollos watered; but God gave the increase' (1 Corinthians 3:6). Rachel said to Jacob: 'Give me children, or else I die. And Jacob's anger was kindled against Rachel: and he said, Am I in God's stead?' (Genesis 30:1,2). So grace is not in the hand of man. Those who receive Christ 'are born, not of blood, nor of the will of the flesh, nor of the will of man, but of God' (John 1:13). It is in vain, then, that you look to the means to give saving grace to your soul. The axe cannot hew without the hand of the forester. The pitcher that carries water is not the well. It will be in vain that you apply to God's children in that awful day. Go to Jesus now.

They have none to spare. The righteous scarcely are saved. Every child of God gets just so much grace as will carry him to heaven, and no more. Even now every child of God feels that he has nothing to spare. He has not too much of the Holy Spirit, helping him to pray, to mourn over sin, to love Christ. In time of temptation a believer feels as if he had nothing of the Holy Spirit. He has more need to receive, than ability to give away. When Christ shall come in that solemn hour, he will feel that he has none to spare.

Oh, dear brethren, go and buy for yourselves! You that know yourselves graceless, go, before the cry is made, to Jesus, and get grace for yourselves. The saints cannot give it you, ministers cannot give it you. All our springs are in Jesus. In him the Spirit dwells without measure. Lord, incline their hearts to run to thyself!

THE TEN VIRGINS: LECTURE IV
(Matthew 25:10-13)

And while they went to buy, the bridegroom came: and they that were ready went in with him to the marriage: and the door was shut. Afterward came also the other virgins, saying, Lord, Lord, open to us. But he answered and said, Verily I say unto you, I know you not. Watch therefore, for ye know neither the day nor the hour wherein the Son of man cometh.

1. Who are ready?
All are not ready. This parable shows that all who make a profession of being Christ's are not ready. The foolish virgins appeared to be ready. They had their robe, their lamp, their wick and flame; yet they were not ready. Many of you come to the house of God, and sit down at sacraments, and make a profession of care for your soul; yet you are not ready. Not all who are anxious are ready. The foolish were anxious now. They had a throbbing heart. They went to buy - their cry was loud and bitter, perhaps they shed bitter tears; and yet they were not ready. Many of you are anxious - going to buy. You have wet cheeks when you go to seek the Lord; and yet you are not ready. If you were to die tonight, or if Christ were to come tonight, you would not be found ready. Who, then, are ready?

Those who have the wedding garment.
This you see in Revelation 19:7,8: 'For his wife hath made herself ready. And to her was granted that she should be arrayed in fine linen, clean and white: for the fine linen is the righteousness of the saints.' And so Psalm 45:9,13: 'Upon thy right hand did stand the queen in gold of Ophir.' ' The king's daughter is all glorious within: her clothing is of wrought gold.' And in Matthew 22:11, we find this was the first thing that struck the eye of the king, that the man had not on a wedding

garment. This wedding garment is the righteousness of God, the skirt of Jesus cast over the soul, the imputed righteousness.

This is the first part of readiness to meet the heavenly Bridegroom. Have you been shown your own utter loathsomeness, that you are all as an unclean thing, all vile and filthy? Have you got a glorious discovery of the way of righteousness, by what Christ has done being reckoned to us? Have you lain down under the blood and white robe of the Lord Jesus? Then you are ready.

Do not mistake.

It is not the knowledge of this imputed righteousness. Many people hear and know a great deal about this robe of righteousness, who never put it on, and are not a whit the better. Knowledge will but condemn you, and sink you deeper.

It is not a desire to have this righteousness. The sluggard desires, and hath nothing. Many have lazy desires after Christ, that are never satisfied, and they are none the better for them - like beggars wishing they were rich.

It is not having it once put over us, and then something else afterwards. This fine linen must be granted unto us for ever. It is not that Christ is our righteousness at first, and our own holiness after; but it is Christ to the end. Our wedding garment in heaven must be Christ's blood-washed robe; we must have it granted to us every day - every moment. Happy soul, who daily beholdest thine own vileness, and daily receivest that wedding garment to hide thy nakedness.

Those who have the new heart.

Can two walk together except they be agreed? It is impossible that two souls can be happy together if they love opposite things. It is like two bullocks in the yoke drawing different ways. Hence the deep wisdom of the command which forbids God's children to intermarry with the world. What fellowship hath light with darkness? In the same way with Christ's bride, she must be of one mind with him, if she would enter in with him to the marriage.

Suppose one of you who has an old heart were to be admitted with Christ to the marriage. Your heart is enmity to God, you hate God's people, the Sabbath is a weariness, you serve divers lusts and pleasures. The Lamb that is in the midst of the throne would lead you, and God would wipe away tears from your eyes. But you hate God and the Lamb. How could you be happy there? None but God's children or companions (psalm-singing hypocrites, as you used to call them) - could you be happy with them? An eternal Sabbath! My highest notion of heaven is an eternal Sabbath with Christ. Could you be happy? Could you enjoy it? Ah, my friends, there shall in no wise enter in any that defileth, any that maketh or loveth a lie. If you are still unborn again, you are not ready.

Those whose lamps are trimmed.
While the wise virgins slept, they were not ready. True, they had the wedding garment and the oil in their vessels, although their lamps were dim - their eyes were closed. But when they heard the cry, they arose and trimmed their lamps, and now they are ready to meet and enter with the Bridegroom. It is not every child of God that is ready. Is a backslider ready - one that has gathered fresh guilt upon the soul, and not got it washed away; one that is still lying under guilt, and not hastening to the Fountain; one that is standing with his back to the house of God, and his face toward his idol? Is an idolater ready - one that once loved Christ, and now puts an idol in his place, entangled with some unlawful affection? Is the soul ready that has left its first love, grown cold in divine things? Was Solomon ready, when his heart went after many wives? Or Peter, when he denied his Lord?

Ah! learn, dear friends, to stir up the grace that is in you. Stir up your faith in Jesus, your love to him and to the saints, if you would be ready. Watch! Live among divine things. Keep the eye open to the coming glory.

2. The reward of those who are ready: 'They went in with him to the marriage.'

Christ will own them.
Christ will take them in with him before his Father, and say: 'Behold, I, and the children whom thou hast given me.' These are they for whom I died, prayed, reigned. At present Christ does not publicly own his people, or put a difference between them and hypocrites.

The world does not know them. The sun shines on the evil and on the good. Worldly men think we are like themselves.

Saints do not know us. Often they suspect us. Often the children of God suspect one another unjustly. They have not this or that experience, this or that mark of God's children.

Often we know not ourselves. When the war of corruption is strong within, when we have fallen into sin, when grace is low in the soul, 'Can I deem myself a child?'

But then Christ will own us, and that will put an end to all doubt for ever and ever. The scoffing world will then know that Christ loved us, they will then wish they had cast in their lot with us. The saints will see that we are Christ's as well as they, they will have no more suspicions of us. We will have no more doubts of ourselves: no more deadness, inconsistency, corruption, darkness, sin. Christ will confess our name before his Father. He will say: 'Come, ye blessed of my Father; inherit the kingdom prepared for you.'

Saints shall be with Christ: 'Went in with him.'
The greatest joy of a believer in this world is to enjoy the presence of Christ - not seen, not felt, not heard, but still real - the real presence of the unseen Saviour. It is this makes secret prayer sweet, and sermons sweet, and sacraments sweet, when we meet with Jesus in them: 'I have set the Lord always before me. Because he is at my right hand, I shall not be moved.'

Often Jesus hides his face, and we are troubled. We seek him whom our soul loveth, but he is gone. We rise and seek, but find him not. At the best, it is but half bliss to feel after an unseen Saviour. Suppose a husband and wife parted by many seas. It is sweet to have letters and love tokens, and to see a friend who left him well; but this will not make up for his presence. So we mourn an absent Lord.

But when he comes we shall be with him. 'In thy presence is fulness of joy; at thy right hand there are pleasures for evermore' (Psalm 16:11). Here we have drops and gleams of pleasure. Christ could not be happy without us. We are his body. If one child of God were wanting, he would not be complete. We are his fulness. Hence his prayer: 'Father, I will that they also, whom thou hast given me, be with me where I am; that they may behold my glory, which thou hast given me' (John 17:24).

We could not be happy without Christ. Take us to the golden pavement, the pearly gates, the songs, the thrones, the palms, the angels, we would still say, Where is the God-man that died for me? Where is the Angel that redeemed me from all evil? Where is Jesus? Where is the side that was pierced? 'We shall see his face.' The Lamb is the light thereof. We shall stand with the Lamb upon mount Zion. We shall never be parted more.

3. The fate of hypocrites: 'The door was shut.'

The door of Christ stands wide open for a long time, but shuts at last. When Christ comes, the door will be shut. Now the door is open, and we are sent to invite you to come in. Soon it will be shut, and then you cannot. So it was at the flood. One hundred and twenty years the door of the ark stood wide open. Noah went forth, and preached everywhere, inviting men to come in. The Spirit strove with men. But they only mocked at the coming flood. At last the day came. Noah entered, and God shut him in. The door was shut. The flood came and carried them all away. So it will be with many here. The door is wide open now. Jesus says: 'I am the door: by me if any man enter in, he shall be saved, and shall go in and out, and find pasture.' Christ does not say, I was, or I will be, but, I am the door. At present any man may enter in. Soon Christ will come - like a thief - like a snare - like travail on a woman with child - and you shall not escape. Enter in at the strait gate.

They prayed, 'Lord, Lord, open to us.' At present hypocrites do not pray, or not in earnest. They have a cold, formal, dull prayer; but in that day they shall cry in real earnest. At present many of you would be ashamed to be seen in earnest about your soul - weeping, or praying, or going to a minister; in that day you will lose all shame - you will weep and howl, and run to Christ's door in agony of spirit. At present many of you are sought after by Christ: 'He is come to seek and to save that which was lost.' He is the shepherd seeking the one sheep that was lost. He stands at your door and knocks - stands and cries: 'Unto you, O men, I call;' 'Turn ye, turn ye;' Sinner, sinner open to me.

In that day it will be the very reverse. You will seek after the Saviour in that day, and not find him; you will stand and knock at his door; you will exert your voice, and cry: 'Lord, Lord open to me.' What a scene this parish will present in that day! Those who come not to the house of God, old men and old women greyheaded in carelessness and sin, young persons mad upon pleasure, children who live without Christ, you will be all in earnest on that day. May this not rebuke some of you that pray not, or pray in a cold, dull manner, or in a form? Ah! you will pray in that day, when too late. Why not antedate that anxiety, and begin to pray now?

They were disappointed. The Lord answered: 'I know you not.' Christ will own his own people: 'I know *them.*' The poor despised believers he will own. Though the world knew them not, Christ will know them. Not one shall be passed over in that day. But not so with the foolish virgins, who have no oil in their lamps. Christ will not own them. Ah! it will be a fearful thing to be denied by Christ before his Father and the holy angels.

'Watch, therefore; for ye know neither the day nor the hour when the Son of Man cometh.' See that ye have true grace in your hearts, that Christ is your righteousness, that your soul is alive.

THE FAMILY AT BETHANY

BETHANY: LECTURE ONE
(John 11:1-4)

Now a certain man was sick, named Lazarus, of Bethany, the town of Mary and her sister Martha. (It was that Mary which anointed the Lord with ointment, and wiped his feet with her hair, whose brother Lazarus was sick.) Therefore his sisters sent unto him, saying, Lord, behold, he whom thou lovest is sick. When Jesus heard that, he said, This sickness is not unto death, but for the glory of God, that the Son of God might be glorified thereby.

'Man is born to trouble, as the sparks fly upward.' Sickness goes round, it spares no family, rich or poor. Sometimes the young, sometimes the old, sometimes those in the strength of their days, are laid down on the bed of sickness. 'Remember those that suffer adversity, as being yourselves also in the body.'

The reasons why God sends sickness are very various:

In some *it is sent for the conversion of the soul.* Sometimes in health the word does not touch the heart. The world is *all.* Its gaieties, its pleasures, its admiration, captivate your mind. God sometimes draws you aside into a sick-bed, and shows you the sin of your heart, the vanity of worldly pleasures, and drives the soul to seek a sure resting-place for eternity in Christ. O happy sickness, that draws the soul to Jesus! (Job 33; Psalm 107).

Sometimes it is *for the conversion of friends.* When the Covenanters went out to battle, they kneeled down on the field and prayed and this was one of their prayers: 'Lord, take the ripe, and spare the green'. God sometimes does this in families. He cuts down the praying child, the child that was half-ridiculed, half-wondered at, that the rest may think, and turn, and pray.

Sometimes it is *a frown of judgment.* When worldly people go long on in a course of sin, against the light of the Bible and the warnings of ministers, God sometimes frowns upon them, and they wither suddenly. 'He, that being often reproved, hardeneth his neck, shall suddenly be destroyed, and that without remedy' (Proverbs 29:1). 'For this cause many are weak and sickly among you, and many sleep (1 Corinthians 11:30).

Another case is now before us - that of a child of God, sick, that Christ might be glorified in him.

(1) The case - the person.

'A certain man was sick named Lazarus.' Lazarus was evidently a child of God, and yet Lazarus was sick. How he had come by his grace we are not told. His name is not mentioned before. If we may be allowed to guess, it seems probable that Mary was the first in the family who knew the Lord (Luke 10); then perhaps Martha left her 'much serving' to come also and sit at Jesus' feet; and both prevailed on their brother Lazarus to come also.

At all events he was a child of God. He was in a godly family. All the house were children of God - one in nature and one in grace. Happy family at Bethany, going hand in hand to glory! Yet here was the hand of sickness entered in - Lazarus was sick. He was peculiarly loved by Christ: 'he whom thou lovest' (verse 3); 'Jesus loved Martha, and her sister, and Lazarus' (verse 5); 'Our friend Lazarus sleepeth' (verse 11). Like John, the disciple whom Jesus loved, so Jesus had a peculiar love for Lazarus. I cannot tell you why. He was a sinner, like other men; but perhaps when Jesus washed and renewed him, he gave him more of his own likeness than other believers. One thing is certain: Jesus loved him, and yet Lazarus was sick.

Learn not to judge others because of affliction. Job's three friends tried to show him that he must be a hypocrite and a bad man, because God afflicted him. They did not know that God afflicts his own dear children. Lazarus was sick; and the beggar Lazarus was full of sores; and Hezekiah was sick, even unto death; and yet all were peculiarly dear to Jesus.

God's children should not doubt his love when he afflicts. Christ loved Lazarus peculiarly, and yet he afflicted him very sore. A surgeon never bends his eye so tenderly upon his patient, as when he is putting in the lancet, or probing the wound to the very bottom. And so with Christ; he bends his eye most tenderly over his own at the time he is afflicting them.

Do not doubt the holy love of Jesus to your soul when he is laying a heavy hand upon you. Jesus did not love Lazarus less when he afflicted him, but rather more - even as a father correcteth a son in whom he delighteth (Proverbs 3:12). A goldsmith when he casts gold into the furnace looks after it.

(2) The place.

'Of Bethany, the town of Mary and her sister Martha.' Bethany is a sweet retired village, about two miles from Jerusalem, in a ravine at the back of the Mount of Olives. It is at this day embosomed in fig-trees and almond trees and pomegranates. But it had a greater loveliness still in the eyes of Christ. It was 'the town of Mary and her sister Martha'.

Probably the worldly people in Jerusalem knew Bethany by its being the town of some rich Pharisee who had his country villa there or some luxuriant noble who called the lands after his own name. But Jesus knew it only as 'the town of Mary and her sister Martha'. Probably they lived in a humble cottage, under the shade of a fig-tree; but that cottage was dear to Christ. Often, as he came over the Mount of Olives and drew near, the light in that cottage window gladdened his heart. Often he sat beneath their fig-tree telling them the things of the kingdom of God.

His Father loved that dwelling; for these were justified ones. And angels knew it well, for night and day they ministered there to three heirs of salvation. No wonder he called the place 'the town of Mary and her sister Martha'. That was its name in heaven.

So it is still. When worldly people think of our town, they call it the town of some rich merchant, some leading men in public matters, some great politician, who makes a dash as a friend of the people; not the town of our Marthas and Marys. Perhaps some poor garret where an eminent child of God dwells gives this town its name and interest in the presence of Jesus.

Dear believers, how great the love of Christ is to you! He knows the town where you live, the house where you dwell, the room where you pray. Often he stands at the door, often he puts in his hand at the hole of the door: 'I have graven thee on the palms of my hands: thy walls are continually before me'.

Like a bridegroom loving the place where his bride dwells, so Christ often says, There they dwell for whom I died. Learn to be like Christ in this. When a merchant looks at a map of the world, his eye turns to those places where his ships are sailing; a soldier looks to the traces of ancient battlefields and fortified towns; but a believer should be like Jesus, he should love the spots where believers dwell.

(3) The message.

They 'sent unto him'.
This seems to have been their very first recourse when the sickness came on - 'his sisters sent unto Jesus'. They did not think a bodily trouble beneath his notice. True, he had taught them that 'one thing was

needful', and Mary had chosen that good part which could not be taken from her. Yet they knew well that Jesus did not despise the body. They knew that he had a heart to bleed for every kind of grief; and therefore they sent to tell Jesus. This is what you should do: 'And call upon me in the day of trouble: I will deliver thee, and thou shalt glorify me' (Psalm 50:15). Remember there is no grief too great to carry to him, and none too small: 'In every thing by prayer and supplication, with thanksgiving, make your requests known unto God.' 'Cast thy burden on the Lord.' Whatever it be, take it to Jesus. Some trust Christ with their soul, but not with their body; with their salvation, but not with their health. He loves to be sent for in our smallest troubles.

The argument: 'He whom thou lovest is sick.'
If a worldly person had been sending to Christ, he would have sent a very different argument. He would have said: He who loves thee is sick. Here is one who has believed on thy name. Here is one that has confessed thee before the world, suffered reproach and scorn for thy sake. Martha and Mary knew better how to plead with Jesus. The only argument was in Jesus' breast: 'He whom thou lovest is sick.'

Jesus loved him with an electing love: freely from all eternity Jesus loved him. Jesus loved him with a drawing love: he drew him from under wrath, from serving sin. Jesus loved him with a pardoning love: he drew him to himself, and blotted out all his sin. Jesus loved him with an upholding love: 'Who could hold me up but thou?' He for whom thou died, he whom thou hast chosen, washed and kept till now, 'he whom thou lovest is sick'.

Learn thus to plead with Christ, dear believers. Often you do not receive, because you do not ask aright: 'ye ask, and receive not because ye ask amiss, that ye may consume it upon your lusts.' Often you ask proudly, as if you were somebody; so that if Christ were to grant it, he would only be fattening your lusts. Learn to lie in the dust, and plead only his own free love. Thou hast loved me for no good thing in me:

> Chosen, not for good in me;
> Wakened up from wrath to flee;
> Hidden in the Saviour's side;
> By the Spirit sanctified.

Do not deny thy love. 'Have respect unto the work of thine own hands.'

A holy delicacy in prayer.
They lay the object at his feet, and leave it there. They do not say: Come and heal him, come quickly, Lord. They know his love, they believe his wisdom. They leave the case in his hands: 'Lord, he whom thou lovest is sick.' They 'cast them down at Jesus' feet; and he healed them' (Matthew 15:30). They did not plead, but let their misery plead for them. 'Let your request be made known unto God' (Philippians 4:6). Learn that urgency in prayer does not so much consist in vehement pleading, as in vehement believing. He that believes most the love and power of Jesus will obtain most in prayer.

Indeed, the Bible does not forbid you using all arguments, and asking for express gifts, such as healing for sick friends. 'My little daughter lieth at the point of death: I pray thee, come and lay thy hands on her, that she may be healed; and she shall live' (Mark 5:23). 'Lord, I am not worthy that thou shouldest come under my roof: but speak the word only, and my servant shall be healed' (Matthew 8:8). Still there is a holy delicacy in prayer, which some believers know how to use. Like these two sisters, lay the object at his feet, saying: 'Lord, he whom thou lovest is sick'.

(4) The answer.

A word of promise: 'This sickness is not unto death'.
This was an immediate answer to prayer. He did not come, he did not heal; but he sent them a word enough to make them happy: 'This sickness is not unto death.' Away the messenger ran, crossed the Jordan, and before sunset perhaps he enters breathless the village of Bethany. With anxious faces the sisters run out to hear what news of Jesus. Good news! 'This sickness is not unto death.' Sweet promise! The hearts of the sisters are comforted, and no doubt they tell their joy to the dying man.

But he gets weaker and weaker; and as they look through their tears at his pale cheek, they begin almost to waver in their faith. But Jesus said it, and Jesus cannot lie: if it were not so, he would have told us, 'This sickness is not unto death.' At last Lazarus breathes his last sigh beside his weeping sisters. His eye is dim, his cheek is cold, he is dead; and yet Jesus said: 'Not unto death!' The friends assemble, to carry the body to the rocky sepulchre; and as the sisters turn away from the tomb, their faith dies, their hearts sink into utter gloom. What could he mean by saying, 'not unto death'?

Learn to trust Christ's Word, whatever sight may say. We live in dark times. Every day the clouds are becoming heavier and more lowering. The enemies of the Sabbath are raging. The enemies of the Church are becoming more desperate. The cause of Christ is everywhere threatened.

But we have a sweet word of promise: 'This sickness is not unto death'. Darker times are coming yet. The clouds will break and deluge our country soon with a flood of infidelity, and many will be like Mary, heart-broken.

Has the Lord's Word failed? No, never! 'This sickness is not unto death.' The dry bones of Israel shall live. Popery shall sink like a millstone, widowhood and loss of children shall come to her in one day. The kings of Tarshish and the isles shall bow their knee to Jesus. Jesus shall reign till all his enemies are put under his feet, and the whole world shall soon enjoy a real Sabbath.

The explanation: 'But for the glory of God, that the Son of God might be glorified thereby.'

Some might ask, Why, then, was Lazarus sick? The reason: 'For the glory of God.' Christ was thereby in an eminent manner made known. First, his amazing love to his own was seen, when he wept at the grave. Second, his power to raise the dead. He was shown to be the resurrection and the life when he cried, 'Lazarus, come forth'.

Christ was far more glorified than if Lazarus had not been sick and died. So in all the sufferings of God's people. Sometimes a child of God says: Lord, what wilt thou have me to do? I will teach, preach, do great things for thee. Sometimes the answer is, Thou shalt suffer for my sake.

It shows the power of Christ's blood, when it gives peace in an hour of trouble, when it can make happy in sickness, poverty, persecution and death. Do not be surprised if you suffer, but glorify God.

It brings out graces that cannot be seen in a time of health. It is the treading of the grapes that brings out the sweet juices of the vine; so it is affliction that draws forth submission, weanedness from the world, and complete rest in God. Use afflictions while you have them.

BETHANY: LECTURE TWO
(John 11:5-10)

Now Jesus loved Martha, and her sister, and Lazarus. When he had heard therefore that he was sick, he abode two days still in the same place where he was. Then after that saith he to his disciples, Let us go into Judea again. His disciples say unto him, Master, the Jews of late sought to stone thee; and goest thou thither again? Jesus answered, Are there not twelve hours in the day? If any man walk in the day, he stumbleth not, because he seeth the light of this world. But if a man walk in the night, he stumbleth, because there is no light in him.

(1) 'Jesus loved Martha, and Mary, and Lazarus.'

These are the words of John.
He knew what was in the heart of Christ, for the Holy Spirit taught him what to write, and he leaned upon Jesus' bosom, and knew the deepest secrets of Jesus' heart. This, then, is John's testimony: 'Jesus loved Martha, and Mary, and Lazarus.'

You remember they had sent this message to Jesus: 'He whom *thou lovest* is sick'. Some would have said, That was a presumptuous message to send. How did they know that Lazarus was really converted, that Jesus really loved him? But here you see John puts his seal upon their testimony. It was really true, and no presumption in it: 'Jesus loved Martha, and Mary, and Lazarus'.

How is it saints know when Jesus loves them? Christ has ways of telling his own love peculiar to himself: 'The secret of the Lord is with them that fear him.' How ridiculous is it to think that Christ cannot make known his love to the soul! I shall mention one way, by drawing the soul to himself: 'Yea, I have loved thee with an everlasting love: therefore with lovingkindness have I drawn thee' (Jeremiah 31:3). 'Now when I passed by thee, and looked upon thee, behold, thy time was the time of love; and I spread my skirt over thee, and covered thy nakedness: yea, I sware unto thee, and entered into a covenant with thee, saith the Lord GOD, and thou becamest mine' (Ezekiel 16:8). 'No man can come unto me except the Father draw him' (John 6:44).

Now when the Lord Jesus draws near to a dead, carnal sinner, and reveals to him a glimpse of his own beauty, of his face fairer than the sons of men, of his precious blood, of the room that there is under his wings; and when the soul is drawn away from its old sins, old ways, away from its deadness, darkness, and worldliness, and is persuaded to forsake all, and flow toward the Lord Jesus, then that soul is made to taste the peace of believing, and is made to know that Jesus loves him.

Thus Lazarus knew that Christ loved him. I was a worldly, careless man, I mocked at my sisters when they were so careful to entertain the Lamb of God, I often was angry with them. But one day he came and showed me such an excellence in the way of salvation by him. He drew me, and now I know that Jesus has loved me.

Do you know that Christ loves you? Have you this love-token, that he has drawn you to leave all and follow him, to leave your self-righteousness, to leave your sins, to leave your worldly companions for Christ, to let all go that interferes with Christ? Then you have a good token that he has loved you.

Jesus loved all the house.
It seems highly probable that there was a great difference among the family: some of them were much more enlightened than others, some were much nearer Christ and some more like Christ, than others. Yet Jesus loved them all. It would seem that Mary was the most heavenly-minded of the family. Probably she was brought first to know and love the Lord Jesus Christ. She sat at the feet of Christ, when Martha was encumbered about much serving. She was also evidently more humbled under this trying dispensation than her sister was, for it is said: 'She fell down at his feet'. She seems also to have been filled with livelier gratitude for it was she that took a pound of ointment of spikenard, very costly, and anointed the feet of Christ, and wiped his feet with her hair. She did what she could. She seems to have been a very eminent believer, very full of love, and of a teachable, meek, quiet spirit. And yet Jesus loved them all - Jesus loved Martha, and her sister, and Lazarus. Every one that is in Christ is beloved by Christ, even weak members.

Good news for weak disciples.
You are very apt to say: I am not a Paul, nor a John, nor a Mary. I fear Jesus will not care for me. But remember he loved Martha, and Mary, and Lazarus. He loves the weakest of those for whom he died. Just as a mother loves all her children, even those that are weak and sickly; so Christ cares for those who are weak in the faith, who have many doubts and fears, who have heavy burdens and temptations.

Be like Christ in this.

'Him that is weak in the faith receive ye, but not to doubtful disputations;' 'We then that are strong ought to bear the infirmities of the weak, and not to please ourselves' (Romans 14:1; 15:1). There is much of an opposite spirit, I fear, amongst us. I fear that you love our Marys and Pauls and Johns, you highly esteem those that are evidently pillars. But can you condescend to men of low estate? Learn to stoop low, and to be gentle and kind to the feeble. Do not speak evil of them, do not make their blemishes the subject of your common talk. Cover their faults. Assist them by counsel, and pray for them.

(2) Christ's delay: 'When he had heard therefore that he was sick, he abode two days still in the same place where he was.'

Here seems a contradiction - Jesus loved them, and yet abode two days. You would have expected the very reverse; Jesus loved them, and therefore made no delay, but hastened to Bethany. This is the way with man's love. Human love will not brook delay. When you love anyone tenderly, and hear that he is sick, you run to see him, and to help him.

These were two important days in the cottage of Bethany. The messenger has returned, saying: 'This sickness is not unto death.' They knew that Jesus loved them, and loved their brother tenderly; and therefore they expected him to come every hour.

Martha, perhaps, would begin to be uneasy, saying, 'Why does he tarry? Why is he so long in coming? Can anything have kept him?' 'Do not fret,' Mary would say. 'You know that he loves Lazarus, and he loves us; and you know he is true, and he said: "This sickness is not unto death".' The dying man grew weaker, and at length breathed his last sigh into their affectionate bosoms. Both the sisters were overwhelmed: *he loved us, and yet he tarried two days.* So with the woman of Syrophenicia, he delayed helping her. Such are Christ's dealings with his own still. Although he loves, he sometimes on that very account tarries. Do not be surprised, and do not fret. Why does he delay:

Because he is God.

He sees the end from the beginning. Known unto him are all his works from the foundation of the world. Although absent in the body, he was present in the sick man's room at Bethany. He saw every change on his pale features, and heard every gentle sigh. Every tear that stole down the cheek of Mary he observed, put into his bottle, and wrote in his book.

He saw when Lazarus died. But the future was before him also. He knew what he would do, that the grave would yield up its dead, and that he would soon turn their weeping into songs of rejoicing. Therefore he stayed where he was, just because he was God. So, when Christ delays to help his saints now, you think this is a great mystery, you cannot explain it; but Jesus sees the end from the beginning. Be still, and know that Christ is God.

To increase their faith.
First of all he gave them a promise to hold by. He sent word by their messenger: 'This sickness is not unto death'. This was an easy and simple word for them to hold by; but, ah! it was sorely tried. When he got worse and worse, they clung to their promise with a trembling heart; when he died, their faith died too. They knew not what to think. And yet Christ's word was true, and thus their faith was increased ever after. They were taught to believe the word of Christ, even when all outward circumstances were against them.

One evening Christ gave commandment on the Sea of Galilee to depart to 'the other side'; and as they sailed he fell asleep. Here was a simple word of promise to hold by in the storm. But when the storm came down, and the waves covered the ship, they cried, 'Master, save us; we perish.' And he said: 'Where is your faith?' By that trial the faith of the disciples was greatly increased ever after (Matthew 8:18-27). So it is with all trials of faith. When God gives a promise, he always tries our faith. Just as the roots of trees take firmer hold when they are contending with the wind, so faith takes a firmer hold when it struggles with adverse appearances.

To make his help shine brighter.
Had Christ come at the first and healed their brother, we never would have known the love that showed itself at the grave of Lazarus, we never would have known the power of the great Redeemer in raising from the grave. These bright forth-shinings of the glory of Christ would have been lost to the Church and to the world. Therefore it was good that he stayed away for two days. Thus the honour of his name was spread far and wide. The Son of God was glorified. 'This people have I formed for myself; they shall show forth my praise.' This is God's great end in all his dealings with his people - that he may be seen. For this reason he destroyed the Egyptians: 'That the Egyptians may know that I am the Lord.'

If Christ seems to tarry past the time he promised, wait for him; for he will come, and will not tarry. He has good reason for it, whether you can see it or not. And never forget that he loves, even when he tarries. He loved the Syrophenician even when he answered her not a word.

(3) Christ's determination: 'After that saith he to his disciples, Let us go into Judea again.'

The time: 'After that...'
After the two days were over. Christ waits a certain time without helping his own, but no longer. Christ waits a certain time with the wicked before destroying them. He waited till the cup of the Amorites was full, before he destroyed them. He waited on the fig-tree a certain time. If it does not bear fruit, then, 'after that, thou shalt cut it down'. Oh, wicked man! you have a certain measure to fill; when that is filled, you will sink immediately into hell. When the sand has run, you will be cast away. So Christ has his set time for coming to his own: 'After two days will he revive us: in the third day he will raise us up, and we shall live in his sight' (Hosea 6:2).

First, *in conversion*: 'Humble yourselves therefore under the mighty hand of God, that he may exalt you in due time' (1 Peter 5:6). When God awakens a soul by the mighty power of his Spirit, he takes his own time and way of bringing the soul to peace. Often the sinner thinks it very hard that Christ should be so long of coming; often he begins to despair, and to think there is something peculiar in his case. Remember! wait on the Lord. It is good to wait for Christ.

Second, *in answering prayer*. When we ask for something agreeable to God's will, and in the name of Christ, we know that we have the petitions which we desire of him. But the time he keeps in his own power. God is very sovereign in the time of his answers. When Martha and Mary sent their petition to Christ, he gave them an immediate promise; but the answer was not when they expected. So Christ frequently gives us the desires of our heart, though not at the peculiar time we desired, but a better time. Do not be weary in putting up prayers, say for the conversion of a friend. They may be answered when you are in the dust. Hold on to pray. He will answer in the best time. 'Be not weary in well-doing; for in due season we shall reap, if we faint not.'

Third, *in his own second glorious coming*. Christ said to the church long ago: 'Yet a little while, and he that shall come will come, and will not tarry.' And still the time is prolonged. The Bridegroom seems to tarry; but he will come at the due time. He waits for infinitely wise reasons. And the moment that he should come, the heavens shall open, and he will appear.

The objection.
The objection was, that it was dangerous to him and to them, because the Jews had sought to stone him before. Another time Peter made objection to Christ, saying: 'Be it far from thee, Lord. This shall not be unto thee. But he turned and said unto Peter, Get thee behind me, Satan; thou art an offence unto me, for thou savourest not the things that be of God, but the things that be of men.' How selfish are even godly men! The disciples did not care for the distress of Martha and Mary. They did not care for the pain of their friend Lazarus. They were afraid of being stoned, and that made them forget the case of the afflicted family. There is no root deeper in the bosom than selfishness. Watch and pray against it. Even the godly will sometimes oppose you in what is good and right. Here, when Christ proposed that they should go into Judea again, the disciples opposed it. They were astonished at such a proposal. They, as it were, reproved him for it. Think it not strange, dear brethren, if you are opposed by those who are children of God, especially if it be something in which you are called to suffer.

Christ's answer.
The path of duty Christ here compares to walking in the daylight. 'If a man walk in the day, he stumbleth not.' As long as a man has got a good conscience, and the smile and the presence of God, he is like one walking in the daytime; he plants his foot firmly and boldly forward. But if a man shrink from the call of God, through fear of man, and at the call of worldly prudence, he is like one walking in darkness: 'He stumbleth, because there is no light.'

Oh, that you who are believers would be persuaded to follow Jesus fearlessly wherever he calls you! If you are a believer, you will often be tempted to shrink back. The path of a Christian is narrow, and often difficult. But what have you to fear? Have you the blood of Christ upon your conscience, and the presence of God within your soul? Are there not twelve hours in the day? Are we not all immortal till our work is done?

BETHANY: LECTURE THREE
(John 11:11-16)

These things said he: and after that he saith unto them, Our friend Lazarus
sleepeth; but I go, that I may awake him out of sleep. Then said his
disciples, Lord, if he sleep, he shall do well. Howbeit Jesus spake of his
death: but they thought that he had spoken of taking of rest in sleep. Then
said Jesus unto them plainly, Lazarus is dead. And I am glad for your
sakes that I was not there, to the intent ye may believe; nevertheless let us
go unto him. Then said Thomas, which is called Didymus, unto his fellow
disciples, Let us also go, that we may die with him.

(1) Christ's love to a dead Lazarus.

He calls him friend.
An eminent infidel used to say that neither patriotism nor friendship was
taught in the Bible. He only proved that he neither knew nor understood
the Bible. How different the sentiment of the Christian poet, who says,

> The noblest friendship ever shown,
> The Saviour's history makes known.

Ah! it is an amazing truth that Jehovah-Jesus came and made friends
of such worms as we are. True friendship consists in mutual confidence
and mutual sacrifices. Thus God dealt with Enoch: 'Enoch walked with
God three hundred years.' Enoch told all to God, and God told all to him.
Blessed friendship between Jehovah and a worm! So God treated
Abraham. Three times in the Bible he is called 'the friend of God' (2
Chronicles 20:7; Isaiah 41:8; James 2:23). 'He raised up the righteous
man from the East and called him to his foot.' The God of glory appeared
unto Abraham, and we find God saying, 'Shall I hide from Abraham that
thing which I do?' (Genesis 18:17). So God dealt with Moses: 'the LORD
spake unto Moses face to face, as a man speaketh unto his friend.' And
God 'said to him, My presence shall go with thee, and I will give thee
rest' (Exodus 33:11, 14). 'And when Moses went in before the LORD to
speak with him, he took the veil off' (Exodus 34:34).

Thus did Christ deal with his disciples. Though he was the holy
Lamb of God, yet he says: 'Henceforth I call you not servants; for the
servant knoweth not what his lord doeth: but I have called you friends;
for all things that I have heard of my Father I have made known unto

you' (John 15:15). He admitted them to the closest fellowship; so that one leaned on his breast at supper, and another washed his feet with ointment. He told them freely all that he had learned in the bosom of his Father - all that they were able to bear of the Father's glory, the Father's love. Thus he dealt with Lazarus: 'Our friend Lazarus.' Often, no doubt, they had sat beneath the spreading fig tree at the cottage of Bethany, and Christ had opened up to them the glories of an eternal world.

This is what you are invited to, dear friends - to become the friends of Jesus. When men choose friends, they generally choose the rich, or the wise, or the witty; they ask those that will invite them back. Not so with Christ. He chooses the poor, the foolish, babes, and makes them friends - those of whom the world is ashamed. *The world changes friends.* In the world, if a rich friend wax poor, if overtaken by a sudden failure, and plunged in deepest poverty, friends, like butterflies in the rain, fly quickly home; they look cold and strange, as if they did not see you. Not so Jesus, the friend that sticketh closer than a brother. A true friend does not hide anything from another which it would be good for him to know. Neither does Christ: 'Shall I hide from Abraham that thing which I do?'

Even when dead: 'Our friend Lazarus.'
Few people remember the dead. They are 'a wind that passeth away, and cometh not again;' 'The place that knows them shall know them no more for ever.' In some of the countries where I have been, there are immense burying-grounds where cities have been, but where not a living being now remains. There is not one to remember their name, or to shed a tear over their memory. Even among yourselves, how soon are the dead forgotten! Although you loved them well when living ('lovely and pleasant in their lives'), yet when they are out of sight, they are soon out of mind. But Christ's dead are never forgotten. There is one faithful Brother, who keeps in mind the sleeping dust of all of his brothers and sisters. Death makes no change in the love of Christ; death cannot separate us from his love; death does not take us off his breastplate. 'Our friend Lazarus sleepeth.'

Ah, my friends! this is how to take the sting away from death. You will, no doubt, be forgotten by the world; if you are Christ's, they never loved you, and will be glad when you are gone. Living sermons are no pleasant objects in the world's eye. They will be glad when you are under the sod. Even believers will forget you. Man is a frail creature, and memory is fading. But Christ never will forget you. He that said, 'My faithful martyr Antipas!' when all the world had forgotten him, remembers all his sleeping saints and will bring them with him.

(2) The mistake (12,13).

In the last lecture we had a specimen of the selfishness of the disciples - here of their stupidity. They were beloved disciples who had left all to follow Christ and sincerely believed his word and loved his person; and yet what remains of blindness in the understanding! 'If he sleep, he shall do well.'

To *sleep* was the common expression for the death of saints in the Old Testament. Thus God said to Moses: 'Thou shalt sleep with thy fathers.' And to Daniel: 'Many of those that sleep in the dust of the earth shall awake.' To King David: 'Thou shalt sleep with thy fathers.' 'Now shall I sleep in the dust' (Job 7:21). 'Lest I sleep the sleep of death' (Psalm 13:3). Surely if they had thought a little, they might have found the meaning!

What would have been the use of going to awake him out of a refreshing sleep? Did they think so lightly of their Master, as that he would run into personal danger to awaken a sleeping man? Do not wonder when disciples mistake the meaning of Christ's words. They have done so before, and may do it again. Every gracious man is not an infallible man. Learn to search patiently into the meaning of Christ's words, by comparing Scripture with Scripture, and especially going to him for light. When you are reading in a dark room, and come to a difficult part, you take it to the window to get more light. So take your Bibles to Christ.

What was the cause of their mistake? *Fear.* They did not want to go into Judaea again. They were afraid of being stoned. They saw their Master was bent upon going, and they wanted to dissuade him. They misunderstood his words, because of the averseness of their hearts to his will. This is the great reason of all blindness in divine things: 'Through the blindness of their hearts;' 'If any man will do the will of God, he shall know of the doctrine.'

The reason why many of you do not understand your lost condition, is not that it is not taught in the Bible, not that the words are difficult (the Bible is a plain, simple book) but it is that you do not wish to be convinced of sin; you do not want your fine dreams of your own goodness and safety to be dashed to pieces. The reason why many of you do not understand the way of forgiveness is that you do not like it.

Your heart is averse from God's way, you cannot bear to have all your righteousness accounted rags, and to be beholden entirely to the righteousness of Jesus. The reason why many saints among you cannot see your rule of duty plain, is that you are averse from the duty. You want to have your own way, and you cannot understand the Scriptures that contradict it. This was the case with the apostles. This is frequently the case in entering into marriage, or a servant fixing on a place. When once a strong desire is formed in the heart, it blinds the mind to the Scriptures.

Pray for a pure heart, that you may be filled with the knowledge of his will, that you may walk worthy of the Lord to all pleasing!

(3) The explanation (14,15)
Christ here explains two things: his words and his absence.

Jesus said plainly, 'Lazarus is dead!'
His disciples had shown great selfishness, great blindness of heart, great stupidity, and yet he was not angry, neither did he turn away. But he said plainly, 'Lazarus is dead.' When he had been teaching them many things, he said, 'Have ye understood all these things?' (Matthew 13:51). Another time, when he had been telling them of the Father's house, Thomas said: 'Lord, we know not whither thou goest.' With the same admirable patience and gentleness he said: 'I am the way, and the truth, and the life: no man cometh unto the Father, but by me.' He 'can have compassion on the ignorant, and on them that are out of the way.' Perhaps some of you feel dead and ignorant - you need not keep away from Christ on that account. Take your blind eyes to him, that he may give you sight. He wants you to understand his way and his will.

He explains his absence: 'I am glad I was not there.'
The objection would immediately arise in the breast of his disciples, If Lazarus be dead, why did our Master stay these two days? Therefore he explains that it was for their sakes. Had Christ been there, he felt that he must have healed Lazarus. Had he been there, Lazarus had not died.

Christ could not have stood in the cottage of Bethany, and looked on the face of his dying friend, and seen the silent tears of Mary, and heard the imploring words of Martha without granting their desire. Therefore he says: 'I am glad I was not there.' Ah! learn the amazing love of Christ to his own. He cannot deny their prayer. When Moses was pleading with God, God said: 'Let me alone.' God could not destroy Israel so long as

Moses pleaded for them. So God had to tell Jeremiah, 'Pray not for this people.' And so when God wants to destroy, he shuts up his saints that they cannot pray. Jesus kept away, that he might not be overcome by their prayer. The uplifted hand of a believing Mary is too much for Jesus to resist. The tearful eye of an earnest believer is 'terrible as an army with banners'. 'Turn away thine eye from me, for thou hast overcome me.' But why was he not there? 'For your sakes, to the intent ye may believe.'

In the last lecture, we saw he delayed for the sake of the cottagers at Bethany; here is another reason - 'For your sakes.'

'All things are for your sakes' (2 Corinthians 4:15). For the sake of believers this world was created - the sun made to rule the day, and the moon to rule the night; every shining star was made for them. All are kept in being for your sakes. Winds rise and fall, waves roar and are still, seasons revolve, seed-time and harvest, day and night - all for your sakes. 'All things are yours.'

All events are for your sakes. Kingdoms rise and fall to save God's people. Nations are his rod, his saw and axe to hew out a way for the chariot of the everlasting gospel; even as Hiram's hewers in Lebanon and the Gibeonite drawers of water were building up the temple of God. The enemies of the church are only a rod in God's hand. He will do his purpose with them, then break the rod in two, and cast it away.

Specially all the providences of believing families are for your sakes. When Christ is dealing with a believing family, you say, That is no matter of mine. What have I to do with it? Ah, truly if you are of the world, you have no part or lot in it! But if you are Christ's, it is for your sake, to the intent that ye may believe. The dealings of Christ with believing families are very instructive, his afflictions and his comforts, his way.

O learn to bear one another's burdens, to see more of Christ's hand among you, to the intent that ye may believe!

> There's not a plant that grows below
> But makes his glory known;
> And thunders roll and tempests blow
> By order from the throne.

(4) The zealous disciple

'Let us also go, that we may die with him.' What voice is that? It is Thomas, unbelieving Thomas.

There is true love to Christ here. He saw that Christ was determined to go; he saw the danger, he counted the cost. Well, says he, 'Let us go also.' Strange, that following the Lamb of God should endanger our very life; yet in how many ages of the Church it has been so! 'The time will come when whosoever killeth you, shall think that he doeth God service.' What a cloud of witnesses has Scotland seen, all saying, like Thomas, 'Let us go and die with him!' Ah, we do not know the value of Christ, if we will not cleave to him unto death!

True zeal toward others: 'Let us go.' He does not say, like Peter, 'I am ready to go with thee'; but, 'Let *us* go.' Whenever we clearly apprehend the path of duty, we should persuade others to come along with us. It is not enough for a believer to go in the way himself; you must say, 'Let us go.' So Israel: 'Come, and let *us* join ourselves to the LORD' (Jeremiah 50:5). So Moses to Hobab: 'Come thou with *us*.' So the converted Gentiles: 'O house of Israel, come ye and let *us* walk in the light of the Lord.' A Christian should be like a river that fertilizes while it runs, carrying ships and all that floats upon its bosom, along with it to the ocean.

Yet there is sin mingled with it. Jesus spoke not of dying; on the contrary, he spoke of 'not stumbling'. But Thomas was full of unbelief, and full of fear. He heeded not the word of Christ. Learn how much sin and weakness mingles with our love and zeal, and what infinite need we have of one who bears the iniquity of our holy things.

BETHANY: LECTURE FOUR
(John 11:17-27)

Then when Jesus came, he found that he had lain in the grave four days already. Now Bethany was nigh unto Jerusalem, about fifteen furlongs off. And many of the Jews came to Martha and Mary, to comfort them concerning their brother. Then Martha, as soon as she heard that Jesus was coming, went and met him: but Mary sat still in the house. Then said Martha unto Jesus, Lord, if thou hadst been here, my brother had not died. But I know, that even now, whatsoever thou wilt ask of God, God will give it thee. Jesus saith unto her, Thy brother shall rise again. Martha saith unto him, I know that he shall rise again in the resurrection at the last day. Jesus said unto her, I am the resurrection, and the life: he that believeth in me, though he were dead, yet shall he live: And whosoever liveth and believeth in me shall never die. Believest thou this? She saith unto him, Yea, Lord: I believe that thou are the Christ, the Son of God, which should come into the world.

(1) Christ orders all events for his own glory.

One day, when Christ had healed a man deaf and dumb, the multitude cried: 'He hath done all things well.' Ah! this is true indeed of the Lord Jesus Christ. 'He is head over all things to the church.' He that died to redeem us from hell, lives to make all things work together for our good. 'He healeth the broken in heart, and bindeth up their wounds. He telleth the number of the stars; he calleth them all by their names' (Psalm 147:3,4). The same hand that was nailed to the cross for us brings out Arcturus and the Pleiades, and guides the sun in his journey - and all for us. A striking example of this we have now before us.

In the time: 'He found that he had lain in the grave four days already' (verse 17). We saw that when he heard that Lazarus was sick, he remained two days in the same place where he was. Then slowly and calmly he left the secluded glens of Mount Gilead, and, crossing the Jordan, came on the fourth day to the village of Bethany. The shady ravines of Mount Olivet wore an aspect of gloom. The village was silent and still, and perhaps around the cottage door of Lazarus a group of mourners sat upon the ground.

Jesus and the disciples halted a little way from the village, as if unwilling to break in upon the scene of deep sorrow. At length a passing villager tells them that Lazarus is dead, and this is the fourth day he has been lying in the cold rocky tomb. The disciples looked at one another, and wondered. Four days dead! Why did our Master tarry? Why did we lose two days on the other side of Jordan? The sisters also thought Jesus came too late. 'If thou hadst been here, my brother had not died.' The Jews also wondered.

Yet Jesus came at the right time. Had he come later, the sensation would have passed away, the death of Lazarus would have been forgotten in the whirl of the world. We soon forget the dead. Had he come sooner, the death of Lazarus would not have been known. He came in due time. He orders all things for his glory - he doeth all things well.

In the place: 'Bethany was nigh unto Jerusalem' (verse 18). The place of this wonder of grace was also chosen with infinite skill. Bethany was a retired village, in a shady, secluded ravine entirely removed from the bustle and noise of the city. So that there was opportunity for Christ to exhibit those tender emotions of pity and love, weeping and groaning, which he could not have done in the bustle of a crowded city.

And yet Bethany was nigh unto Jerusalem, about fifteen furlongs, or two miles, so that many Jews were present as witnesses; and the news of it was carried in a few hours to the capital, and spread all over Jerusalem and Judaea. Had it been done in a corner, men would have derided and denied it. But it was done within half an hour's walk of Jerusalem, so that all might ascertain its reality. Christ chooses the place where he does his wonders wisely and well, all to show forth his own glorious name. He chooses the spot where to break the alabaster box, so that the ointment may be most widely diffused.

In the witnesses: 'Many of the Jews' (verse 19). From verses 45, 46 we learn that the company were far from being all friends of Christ. Perhaps they would not have come if they had known Christ was to be there. But they were friends of Martha and Mary, and though they did not like their serious ways, yet in an hour of affliction they could not but visit them to give them such comfort as they were able. This is the way of the world. There is much natural kindness remaining in the bosom even of worldly men. Christ knew this, and therefore chose this very time to arrive. Ah, friends, he doeth all things well. You often wonder, often murmur, at the way that he takes you.

Learn that if you are his, he will make all things work together for your good, and his own glory. Learn to trust him, then, in the dark, in the darkest frowns of providence, in the most painful delays. Learn to wait upon him. 'It is good for a man both to hope and quietly wait for the salvation of God.' He is good to the soul that waiteth for him.

(2) See here the weak believer.

Jesus and his disciples had halted a little way from the village, under the shade of the trees. But word soon came to the ear of Martha that the Saviour was come. She immediately hastened to meet him. Ah! who can tell what love and compassion must have appeared in his eye, what holy calmness on his brow, what tenderness upon his lips? He was the Rose of Sharon and the Lily of the valleys. Yet Martha is not hushed at the sight. She bursts out into this impassioned cry: 'Lord, if thou hadst been here, my brother had not died.' Observe:

Her presumption. 'If thou hadst been here, my brother had not died.' How did she know this? What promise of the Bible could she name upon which this expectation was grounded? God had promised that his own shall never want bread nor any good thing, that he will supply all their need, that they shall never perish, that he will be with them in time of trouble. But nowhere has he promised that they shall not die. On the contrary, 'Israel must die.' David prays: 'Make me to know mine end, and the measure of my days.' And Job: 'I would not live alway.'

Her limiting of Christ: 'If thou hadst been here.' Why so? Am I a God at hand, and not afar off? 'Is my hand shortened at all, and have I no power to redeem?' She forgot the centurion of Capernaum: 'Lord, I am not worthy that thou shouldest come under my roof: but speak the word only' (Matthew 8:8). She forgot the nobleman's son at Capernaum: 'Sir, come down, ere my child die ... Go thy way, thy son liveth' (John 4:49,50). Her grief and anguish kept her from calmly remembering the works and power of Jesus.

Her unbelief: 'But I know that even now' (verse 22). This was faith, and yet unbelief. She believed something, but not all, concerning Jesus. She believed in him as an advocate and intercessor, but not that all things were given into his hands, that he is Lord of all, head over all things to the church. Her grief and confusion and darkness hid many things from her.

And yet she came to Jesus. Though grieved, she was not offended; she did not keep away from him. She poured out all her grief, darkness and complaint into his bosom. This is just the picture of a weak believer: much of nature and little grace, many questionings of Christ's love and power, and yet carrying their complaints only to him. It was not to the Jews Martha told her grief, it was not to the disciples, it was to Jesus himself.

Learn that afflicting time is trying time. Affliction is like the furnace, it discovers the dross as well as the gold. Had all things gone on smoothly at Bethany, Martha and Mary had never known their sin and weakness; but now the furnace brought out the dross. Learn to guard against unbelief. Guard against presumption, making a Bible-promise for yourself, and leaning upon a word God has never spoken. Guard against prescribing your way to Christ, and limiting him in his dealings. Guard against unbelief, believing only part of God's testimony. 'O foolish, and slow of heart to believe all that God hath spoken.' Remember, whatever your darkness may be, to carry your complaint to Jesus himself.

(3) Jesus reveals himself (verses 23-26).

Not a feature of Christ's face was ruffled by the passionate cry of Martha. He was not angry, and did not turn away, but opened up more of himself than he had ever done. 'Thy brother shall rise again.' He comforts her by the assurance that her brother shall rise again, and then leads her to see that all the spring and source of that is in himself. Two things he shows in himself.

First, *I am the resurrection*: 'He that believeth in me, though he were dead, yet shall he live.' Christ here reveals himself as the head of all dead believers.

He shows what he is: I am the author or spring of all resurrection. The fountain of the resurrection is in my hand. It is my voice that shall call forth the sleeping dust of all my saints. It is my hand that shall gather their dust and fashion it like my own glorious body. All this is mine. At my command Enoch was translated. I also carried away Elijah. I will raise the myriads of sleeping believers also. Believest thou this? Believest thou that he who has sat so often under thy roof and fig-tree, at thy table, that he is the resurrection?

He shows the certainty that all dead believers shall live: 'He that believeth on me, though he were dead, yet shall he live.' If I am the resurrection, then surely I will raise every one for whom I died. I will not lose one of them. Here is comfort for those of you who, like Martha, weep over the believing dead. Thy brother shall rise again. Jesus, who died for them, is the Resurrection. That great work of gathering and raising their scattered dust is committed to Jesus. 'They shall be mine, in that day when I shall make up my jewels.'

Oh, what unspeakable comfort it will be to be raised from the grave by Jesus! If it were an angel's voice we might wish to lie still; but when the voice of our Beloved calls, how gladly shall we arise!

> Sweet thought to me!
> I shall arise,
> And with these eyes
> My Saviour see.

Oh, what unspeakable terror it will give to you that are Christless, to hear the voice of Jesus breaking the long silence of the tomb!

Second, *I am the life*: 'He that liveth and believeth in me shall never die.' Christ here reveals himself as the head of all living believers.

He directs her eye to himself: 'I am the life.' This name is frequently applied to the Lord Jesus: 'In him was life; and the life was the light of men' (John 1:4); 'When Christ, who is our life, shall appear, then shall ye also appear with him in glory' (Colossians 3:4); 'For the life was manifested, and we have seen it, and bear witness, and shew unto you that eternal life, which was with the Father, and was manifested unto us (1 John 1:2).' And therefore Jesus says: 'Ye will not come unto me that ye might have life.' In my hand is the source of all natural, spiritual and eternal life. Every thing that lives derives its life from me, every living soul. Every drop of living water flows from my hand. I begin, I carry on, I give eternal life.

He shows the happy consequence to all living believers. 'They shall never die.' Their life suffers no interruption by the death of the body. Death has no power to quench the vital flame in the believer's soul. If I be the life, I will keep all mine, even in the valley of the shadow of death. They shall never perish. Believest thou this? Here is comfort to those of you who, like Martha, tremble at the sight of death. Ah! it is a ghastly sight when it comes, the terror of kings and the king of terrors. There is something dreadful in the still features, the silent lips, the glazed eye, the cold hand that no more returns our fond pressure, but rather sends a chill through the blood. Ah! you say, must we all thus die? Where is the gospel now? *Answer*: Jesus is the life, the spring of eternal life to all his own. Believe this, and you will triumph over the grave.

(4) Martha's confession.

When her faith flowed out. When the south wind blows softly upon a bed of spices, it causes the fragrant odours to flow out. So when Jesus breathed on this believer's heart, saying: 'I am the resurrection and the life,' it drew from her this sweet confession: 'Yea, Lord, I believe.'

This shows how faith and love spring up in the heart. Some of you seek for faith much in the same way as you would dig for a well. You turn the eye inward upon yourself and search amidst the depths of your polluted heart to find if faith is there; you search amid all your feelings at sermons and sacraments to see if faith is there; and still you find nothing but sin and disappointment.

Learn Martha's plan. She looked full in the face of Jesus; she saw his dust-soiled feet and sullied garment, and his eye of more than human tenderness. She drank in his word: 'I am the resurrection and the life;' and in spite of all she saw and all she felt, she could not but believe. The discovery that Jesus made of his love and power, as the head of dead believers and the head of living believers, revived her fainting soul, and she cried: 'Yea, Lord, I believe.' Faith comes by hearing the voice of Jesus.

Upon what her faith flowed out: upon the person of Jesus. It seems probable that Martha did not comprehend all that was implied in the words of the Lord Jesus. Something she saw, but much she did not see. Still on this one thing her faith fastens - that Jesus is the Christ, the Son of God. So do you, brethren, when glorious promises are unfolded, whose full meaning you cannot comprehend. Embrace Jesus and you have all: 'for all the promises of God in him are yea, and in him amen, to the glory of God by us.' Much you cannot comprehend, for it doth not yet appear what we shall be; yet take a whole Christ into the arms of your faith, and say: 'Yea, Lord, I believe that thou art the Christ, the Son of God, which should come into the world.'

BETHANY: LECTURE FIVE
(John 11:28-35)

And when she had so said, she went her way, and called Mary her sister secretly, saying, The Master is come, and calleth for thee. As soon as she heard that, she arose quickly, and came unto him. Now Jesus was not yet come into the town, but was in that place where Martha met him. The Jews then which were with her in the house, and comforted her, when they saw Mary, that she rose up hastily and went out, followed her, saying, She goeth unto the grave to weep there. Then when Mary was come where Jesus was, and saw him, she fell down at his feet, saying unto him, Lord, if thou hadst been here, my brother had not died. When Jesus therefore saw her weeping, and the Jews also weeping which came with her, he groaned in the spirit, and was troubled, and said, Where have ye laid him? They said unto him, Lord, come and see. Jesus wept.

(1) The calling of Mary.

Martha is the messenger.
Martha had got a little comfort from that sweet word of Jesus, 'I am the resurrection and the life.' Her faith had been revived by the question, 'Believest thou this?' The swelling tide of sorrow in her breast was calmed: 'And when she had so said, she went her way, and called Mary.'

Those who have been comforted by Christ themselves are the fittest messengers to bring comfort to others: 'Blessed be God, even the Father of our Lord Jesus Christ, the Father of mercies, and the God of all comfort; who comforteth us in all our tribulation, that we may be able to comfort them which are in any trouble, by the comfort wherewith we ourselves are comforted of God' (2 Corinthians 1:3,4).

God takes his ministers through divers trials and consolations, just that he may make them fitting messengers to comfort others. O! it is then we can tell others of the excellence of the apple-tree, when we have been sitting under its shadow and eating its pleasant fruits. Martha was but a weak believer compared with Mary, and yet she is made the channel of conveying the joyful news to her. It is a great mistake to think that none but eminent believers are made useful in the church of God. God often feeds eminent believers by a weak ministry. The minister has often less grace than those to whom he ministers. Especially when eminent believers are cast down and perplexed, frequently a very small means is used to lift them up again.

She called her secretly.
The last time the Saviour was in Judea, they took up stones to stone him to death; and probably some of the Jews who were sitting beside Mary were among his bitter enemies. Martha therefore came in, and whispered softly into Mary's ear, 'The Master is come and calleth thee.' She feared the Jews. Jesus had done much for her, and she was tender of his safety and of his cause. Thus does it become those of you for whom Jesus has done much to be tender of his honour, tender of his name and cause. You will feel as a member of his body, and that you have no interest separate from him.

The message: 'The Master is come, and calleth for thee.'
Mary was sitting sad and desolate in the cottage at Bethany. It was now the fourth day from the funeral, and yet no comfort came. The place of Lazarus was empty; the house looked desolate without him, and Jesus had not come. He had sent them a message that this sickness was not unto death. Yet his word was broken, and he had not come. Mary knew not what to think. Why does he tarry beyond Jordan? She would say to herself, Has he forgotten to be gracious? Suddenly her sister whispers, 'The Master is come and calleth for thee.' Christ was near the cottage before she knew. So it was that morning at the Lake of Tiberias, when

'Jesus stood on the shore, but the disciples knew not that it was Jesus'; or that evening when the two disciples went to Emmaus and Jesus drew near, but their eyes were holden that they did not know him.

So does death come upon the believer in Jesus. 'The Master is come, and calleth for thee.' So will Jesus come to his weeping, desolate church, and this cry shall awake the dead. 'The Master is come, and calleth for thee.'

(2) Mary's going (verses 29-31).

She arose quickly.
It is evident that Mary was the more deeply affected of the two sisters. Martha was able to go about, but Mary sat still in the house. She felt the absence of Christ more than Martha. She believed his word more, and when that word seemed to fail, Mary's heart was nearly broken. Ah! it is a deep sorrow when natural and spiritual grief come together. Affliction is easily borne if we have the smile of Jehovah's countenance.

Why does the mourner rise, and hastily drying her tears, with eager step leave the cottage door? Her friends who sat around her she seems quite to forget. 'The Master is come.' Such is the presence of the Lord Jesus to mourners still. The world's comforters are all physicians of no value. Miserable comforters are they all. They have no balm for a wounded spirit. 'The heart knoweth its own bitterness.' But when the Master comes and calls us, the soul revives. There is life in his call, his voice speaks peace. 'In me ye shall have peace.' Mourners should rise up quickly, and go to Jesus. The bereaved should spread their sorrows at the feet of Christ.

The place: 'Now Jesus was not yet come into the town' (verse 30). Jesus had probably come far that day, perhaps all the way from Jericho. He had journeyed onwards on foot, till he came to the foot of the Mount of Olives, and halted beneath the trees that skirt the village of Bethany.

He did not go into the town till he had finished the work for which he came. Perhaps he was hungry and thirsty, as he was that day when he sat beside Jacob's well, and said, 'Give me to drink.' But he did not mention it now. His mind was intent upon his work - the raising of dead Lazarus, and the glorifying of his Father's great name. 'I have meat to eat that ye know not of.' 'My meat is to do the will of him that sent me, and to finish his work.'

Christ's delight in saving sinners, and doing good to his own, overcame his sense of hunger and thirst and weariness. Oh! see what a ready high-priest we have to go to. And see what is our true happiness, namely, to do God's holy will, not much minding bodily comforts. They have most of the mind of Christ, and most of the joy of Christ, who prefer his service to bodily rest and refreshment.

The Jews followed Mary.
We saw that it was natural kindness that brought them to Bethany; and so natural kindness makes them follow Mary now. They could not comprehend her spiritual grief, and thought she was going to the grave to weep there. Yet this was the means of leading some of them to the spot where they were born again. 'Many of the Jews believed on him.'

How wonderful are God's ways of leading men to Christ! 'And I will bring the blind by a way that they know not: I will lead them in paths that they have not known.' One soul is led by curiosity, like Zaccheus, to go and hear a particular minister, and the word is sent home with power. Another goes in kindness to a friend, and is arrested and sent home with a bleeding heart. His name is Wonderful - his ways are wonderful, his grace is wonderful. Learn that it is good to cleave to the godly, and to go with them. They may lead you to where Jesus is.

(3) The meeting with Jesus (verses 32-35).

Mary's tender humility.
With eager footstep Mary hurried over the rocky footpath. Jesus was standing in the same place where Martha met him; and as Mary approached, he bent his compassionate eyes upon her. Mary saw, and fell at his feet. What a crowd of feelings were in her breast at that moment! She wondered why he had not come sooner. That was a dark mystery to her. She knew he was her Saviour, and the Son of God. She knew that he loved her. And yet she fell at his feet. She felt that she was a vile sinner, worthy to be trampled on. She felt that she was a worm, and that all her hope was in Jesus. Ah! brethren, it is sweet to be able to take Mary's place. The most eminent believers are the lowliest. Paul said: 'I am the chief of sinners' and 'I am less than the least of all saints.' The nearer you take anything to the light, the darker its spots appear; and the nearer you live to God, the more you will see your own utter vileness.

Mary repeats Martha's complaint: 'Lord, if thou hadst been here, my brother had not died' (verse 32).

From this it is plain that the two sisters had been often conversing upon Christ's absence; and they had agreed upon this, that if Christ had been there, their brother had not died. It was both presumptuous and unbelieving. Perhaps Mary learned it from Martha. We are very apt to learn unbelief from one another. The Bible says: 'Exhort one another daily, while it is called today.' But believers frequently discourage one another.

Jesus' compassion.

When he saw, he groaned in the spirit, and was troubled. This is humanity. His eye affected his heart, when he saw her weeping - her whom he loved so well, so eminent a believer, one whom he had washed and justified. When he saw the Jews weeping, mere worldly friends, he groaned within himself. So when he came near, and beheld the city, he wept over it; when he saw the widow of Nain, he had compassion on her; when he saw the multitudes of Galilee, like sheep without a shepherd, he had compassion on them. All this shows his perfect humanity. He is bone of our bone, and flesh of our flesh.

He asked, Where have ye laid him? This also was human. As God he knew well where they had laid him; but he wanted them to lead him to the grave.

Jesus wept. When he saw the cave, and the stone, and the weeping friends, 'Jesus wept'. He wept because his heart was deeply touched. It was not feigned weeping, it was real. He knew that he was to raise him from the dead, and yet he wept because others wept. He wept as our example, to teach us to weep with one another. He wept to show what was in him: 'For we have not an high-priest which cannot be touched with the feeling of our infirmities; but was in all points tempted like as we are, yet without sin. Let us therefore come boldly unto the throne of grace, that we may obtain mercy, and find grace to help in time of need' (Hebrews 4:15,16).

BETHANY: LECTURE SIX
(John 11: 35-42)

> Jesus wept. Then said the Jews, Behold how he loved him! And some of
> them said, Could not this man, which opened the eyes of the blind, have
> caused that even this man should not have died? Jesus therefore again
> groaning in himself cometh to the grave. It was a cave, and a stone lay
> upon it. Jesus said, Take ye away the stone. Martha, the sister of him that
> was dead, saith unto him, Lord, by this time he stinketh: for he has been
> dead four days. Jesus saith unto her, Said I not unto thee, that, if thou
> wouldest believe, thou shouldest see the glory of God? Then they took
> away the stone from the place where the dead was laid. And Jesus lifted
> up his eyes, and said, Father, I thank thee that thou hast heard me. And I
> knew that thou hearest me always: but because of the people which stand
> by I said it, that they may believe that thou hast sent me.

In the last lecture, we considered briefly, these wonderful words, *Jesus
wept.* When he saw Mary weeping, and the Jews weeping, he groaned
within himself, and said, 'Where have ye laid him?' They said, 'Come
and see.' And as they led him along the path to the cave in the rock,
'Jesus wept.' Amazing sight! 'Jesus wept.' He was the Son of God, who
thought it no robbery to be equal with God, infinite in happiness, and
yet he weeps, so truly does he feel the sorrows of his own.

(1) The feelings of the Jews at this sight.

Wonder at his love. 'Behold how he loved him!'
These Jews were as yet only worldly men, and yet they were amazed at
such an overflow of love. They saw that heavenly form bowed down at
the grave of Lazarus, they heard his groans of agony, they saw the tears
that fell like rain from his compassionate eyes, they saw the heaving of
his seamless mantle. But, ah! they saw not what was within. They saw
but a little of his love, they did not see its eternity. They did not see that
it was love that made him die for Lazarus. They did not know the
fullness, freeness, vastness of that love of his.

And yet they were astonished at it. 'Behold how he loved him!'
There is something in the love of Christ to amaze even worldly men.

When Jesus gives peace to his own in the midst of trouble, when the
waves of trouble come round the soul, when clouds and darkness,
poverty and distress overwhelm his dwelling, when he can yet be glad

in the Lord, and say: 'Although the fig-tree shall not blossom, neither shall fruit be in the vines; the labour of the olive shall fail, and the fields shall yield no meat; the flock shall be cut off from the fold, and there shall be no herd in the stalls: yet I will rejoice in the Lord, I will joy in the God of my salvation'; then the world are forced to say, 'Behold how he loved him!'

When Jesus is with the believer in death, standing beside him so that he cannot be moved, overshadowing him with his wings, washing him in his blood, and filling him with holy peace, so that he cries, 'To depart, and be with Christ, is far better,' then the world cry, 'Behold how he loved him!' 'Let me die the death of the righteous, and let my last end be like his!'

Another solemn day is coming when all of you who are believers shall be separated, and stand on the right hand of the throne, and Jesus shall welcome you, poor and hell-deserving though you be, to share his throne, and to share his glory. Then you who are unbelievers shall cry, with bitter wailing, 'Behold how he loved them!'

Some doubt his love.
'Could not this man, which opened the eyes of the blind, have caused that even this man should not have died?' (verse 37). It was but a little before that Jesus had given sight to a man that was born blind; and the Jews that now stood around had seen the miracle. Now they reasoned thus with one another: If he really loved Lazarus, could he not have kept him from dying? He that opened the eyes of the blind, could also preserve the dying from death. They doubted his tears, they doubted his words. This is unbelief. It turns aside the plainest declarations of the Lord Jesus by its own arguments. How many of you have turned aside the love of Christ in the same way!

We read that he wept over Jerusalem. This plainly showed that he did not want them to die in their sins - that he does not want you to perish, but to have everlasting life. And yet you doubt his love, and turn aside his tears by some wretched argument of your own. Jesus says: 'Come unto me, all ye that labour, and are heavy laden, and I will give you rest.' This is a simple declaration, but you turn it aside thus: If Christ had really wanted to give me rest, would he not have brought me to himself before now? Unbelief turns the very exhibition of Christ's love into gall and wormwood. Some men, the more they see of Christ, the harder they grow. These Jews had seen him give sight to the blind, and weep over

Lazarus, and yet they only grew harder. Take heed that it be not so with you. Take heed lest the more you hear of Christ, and of his love to his own, the harder you grow.

(2) The scene at the grave.

The command: 'Take ye away the stone.'
Christ's ways are not as our ways, nor his thoughts like our thoughts. One would have thought that he would have commanded the stone to fly back by his own word.

When he rose from the dead himself, 'the angel of the Lord descended from heaven, and came and rolled back the stone from the door and sat upon it'; but he did not do so now. He said to the men, 'Take ye away the stone' for two reasons. First, he wanted to bring out Martha's unbelief, that it might be made manifest. Unbelief in the heart is like evil humour in a wound - it festers; and therefore Jesus wanted to draw it out of Martha's heart. Second, to teach us to use the means. The men around the grave could not give life to dead Lazarus, but they could roll back the stone. Now Jesus was about to use his divine power in awaking the dead, but he would not take away the stone.

Have any of you an unconverted friend for whom you pray? You know it is only Christ that can give him life, it is only Christ that can call him forth. Yet you can roll away the stone - you can use the means, you can bring your friend under the faithful preaching of the gospel. Speak to him, write to him. 'Take away the stone.'

Martha's unbelief: 'Lord, by this time he stinketh, for he hath been dead four days.'
Mary was silent. She did not know what Jesus was going to do; but she knew that he would do all things well. She knew that he was full of love and wisdom and grace. But Martha cries out. She forgot all the words of Christ. She forgot his message: 'This sickness is not unto death, but for the glory of God, that the Son of God may be glorified thereby.' She forgot his sweet saying, 'Thy brother shall rise again' and 'I am the resurrection and the life; he that believeth on me, though he were dead, yet shall he live.' She forgot her own declaration that Jesus was the Son of God. And see how she would have hindered her own mercy. She loved her brother tenderly, and yet she would have the stone kept on the mouth of the cave. She was standing in her own light.

Learn how easily you may fall into unbelief. A few minutes before, Martha was full of faith; but now she sinks again. Oh, what marvellous blindness and sin there is in the human heart! Learn how unbelief shuts out your own mercy. 'He did not many mighty works there, because of their unbelief.' Martha had nearly hindered the restoration of Lazarus. Oh, do not forget the words of Jesus, nor his wonders of love and power! 'Is anything too hard for the Lord?'

Christ's reproof: 'Said I not unto thee, that if thou wouldest believe, thou shouldest see the glory of God?' (verse 40) Christ had sent this message: 'This sickness is not unto death'; now he recalls his word: 'Said I not unto thee?' as if he had said, Martha, have you forgotten my words? Am I a liar, or like waters that fail? Am I a man that I should lie, or the son of man that I should repent? See how unbelief wounded Jesus. 'He that believeth not God, hath made him a liar.' You will have a deeper hell than the heathen. They will be cast away because of their sins, but you because of your sin and unbelief. 'He that believeth not is condemned already.'

(3) Christ's prayer and thanksgiving.

His prayer was secret.
We are not told any words that he prayed; but no doubt during his groans and tears he was praying to his Father in secret. Even in the midst of the crowd, Jesus was alone with his Father, praying for his own that their faith might not fail. The tears of Christ were not mere tears of feeling, they were the tears also of earnest prayer. His is no empty fellow-feeling, but real intercession. Christ teaches you to pray in sudden trials. Even when you cannot get any secret place, lift up your heart to him in the midst of the crowd. Ah, brethren! a sincere soul is never at a loss for a praying place to meet with God.

If you are a child of God, you will find some secret place to pray. It will not do to say, you will pray when walking, or at your work, or in the midst of company. It will not do to make that your praying time through the day. No; Satan is at your right hand. Get alone with God. Spend as much time as you can alone with God every day; and then, in sudden temptations and afflictions, you will be able to lift your heart easily even among the crowd to your Father's ear.

His thanksgiving.

'Father, I thank thee that thou hast heard me, and I knew that thou hearest me always; but because of the people which stand by I said it, that they may believe that thou hast sent me.'

See what *speed* Christ comes in his prayer: 'Thou hearest me always.' Every intercession that Christ makes is answered. The moment he asks he is answered. If we know that Christ prays for us, then we know that we have what he desires.

He *thanks.* So entirely one is Christ with his own, that he gives thanks in our name. This should teach us not only to pray, but also to give thanks.

He does this *aloud*, that all around might believe on him. Christ was always seeking the conversion of souls, even here, in praying and giving thanks to his Father. He does it aloud, that those around him might believe on him, as the sent of God, and the Saviour of the world. Yea, brethren, he records it here, that ye may believe on him. For this end is Christ set before you in the gospel as the sent of God, the compassionate Saviour, the Mediator and Intercessor, that ye may believe on him.

BETHANY: LECTURE SEVEN
(John 11: 43-46)

And when he thus had spoken, he cried with a loud voice, Lazarus, come forth. And he that was dead came forth, bound hand and foot with graveclothes: and his face was bound about with a napkin, Jesus saith unto them, Loose him, and let him go. Then many of the Jews which came to Mary, and had seen the things which Jesus did, believed on him. But some of them went their ways to the Pharisees, and told them what things Jesus had done.

(1) The raising of dead Lazarus.

The time: 'When he thus had spoken.'

When Jesus first heard that Lazarus was sick, he abode two days in the place where he was. Slowly and calmly he moved toward Bethany, so that when he arrived beneath its fig-trees, the passing villager told him that Lazarus had lain in the grave four days already.

Still Jesus did not hurry, but waited till he had drawn forth the unbelief of Martha and Mary, waited till he had manifested his own tender, compassionate heart, waited till he had given public thanks to the Father to show that he was sent of God. 'And when he thus had spoken, he cried with a loud voice, Lazarus, come forth.'

His time is the right time. So will it be in giving life to Israel. Israel, like Lazarus, have been lying in their graves eighteen hundred years. Their bones are dry and very many. Since he spake against them, he earnestly remembers them still; and there is a day coming when he will pour the Spirit of life upon them, and make them come forth, and be life to the dead world. But this in his own time.

Jesus does not hurry. He waits till he has drawn out the unbelief of men, and manifested his own tender heart. Then when his time is come, he will cry, Israel, come forth. So in the deliverance of the church; so in the deliverance of individual believers: 'For yet a little while, and he that shall come will come, and will not tarry.'

The work: 'He cried with a loud voice, Lazarus, come forth.' And he that was dead came forth, bound hand and foot with grave-clothes.'

What a strange scene was here! It was a retired part of the narrow ravine in which Bethany lies, and the crowd were standing beside the newly-opened sepulchre of Lazarus. It was a cave cut in the rock, and the huge stone that had been rolled to the door was now rolled back. The Jews stood around, wondering what he would do. The hardy peasants of Bethany leaned over the newly-moved stone and gazed into the dark cave. Martha and Mary fixed their eyes on Jesus, and a deep silence hung upon the group. Opposite the cavern's mouth stood the Saviour, his tears not yet dried, his eye looking up towards his Father. 'He cried with a loud voice, Lazarus, come forth!' The hollow cave rang with the solemn sound.

The ear of Lazarus was dead and cold, the limbs stiff and motionless, the eyelids closely sealed, and the cold damp of death lay on his forehead; the grave-clothes were round him, and his face bound with a napkin, when the sudden cry, 'Lazarus, come forth,' awoke the dead. It pierced down into the deep cave, and through the close damp napkin into the dead ear. The heart began suddenly to beat, and the warm current of life to flow through the dead man's veins. The vital heat and the sense of hearing came back. It was a well-known voice. 'The voice of my Beloved,' he would say, 'he calls my name.' So he arose: 'And he that was dead came forth, bound hand and foot, with grave-clothes.'

How simple, and yet how glorious! Jehovah speaks, and it is done. 'The voice of the Lord is powerful, the voice of the Lord is full of majesty; the voice of the Lord breaketh the cedars, yea, the Lord breaketh the cedars of Lebanon.' Now were the words of Christ fulfilled: 'This sickness is not unto death, but for the glory of God, that the Son of God may be glorified thereby.' Christ manifested forth his glory as the resurrection and the life.

(2) The resurrection.

This is the way in which Christ will raise all that have died in the Lord. 'Marvel not at this: for the hour is coming, in which all that are in their graves shall hear his voice, and shall come forth; they that have done good, unto the resurrection of life; and they that have done evil, unto the resurrection of damnation' (John 5:28,29). There is a day near at hand, in which every dead ear shall hear the same voice crying, Come forth! Come forth!

Learn not to sorrow over departed believers as those who have no hope: 'For if we believe that Jesus died and rose again, even so them also that sleep in Jesus will God bring with him.' The dust of Lazarus was dear to Jesus; he would not leave it in the rocky tomb. So is the dust of every Lazarus dear in his sight. He will not lose so much as one of them. Wherever they lie, it matters not - beneath the deep blue sea, or on some distant battlefield, or consumed in flame and smoke - the Lord Jesus will yet collect their scattered dust, and make them like his own glorious body.

Learn not to fear the grave. There is nothing that we naturally shrink back from more than the grave. Ah! it is a fearful thing to leave the company of living men, and lie down in the narrow house, with a shroud for our only clothing, a coffin for our couch, and the worm for our companion. It is humiliating, it is loathsome. But if you are one of Christ's, here is the victory: 'In a moment, in the twinkling of an eye, at the last trump: for the trumpet shall sound, and the dead shall be raised incorruptible, and we shall be changed. For this corruptible must put on incorruption, and this mortal must put on immortality. So when this corruptible shall have put on incorruption, and this mortal shall have put on immortality, then shall be brought to pass the saying that is written, Death is swallowed up in victory. O death, where is thy sting? O grave, where is thy victory?' (1 Corinthians 15:52-55).

Fix your eye on Jesus at the grave of Lazarus; so will he stand over the grave of a sleeping world, and cry, 'Come forth!'

O Christless man! you too will hear that voice. Your soul will hear it in hell, your body will hear it in the grave; and death and hell will give up the dead which are in them. You will not hear his voice now, but you must hear it then. You will come forth, like Lazarus, and stand before God. Perhaps you would like to lie still in the grave. Oh! let the rocks fall on me, and the mountains cover me. Perhaps you will cling to the sides of the grave, and clasp your frail coffin in your arms. Perhaps your soul would wish to lie still in hell. Oh! let me alone! Let the burning wave go over for ever, let the worm gnaw and never die. But you must come forth to the resurrection of damnation. You must rise to shame and everlasting contempt.

(3) The life.

This is the way in which Christ gives life to dead souls. 'Verily, verily, I say unto you, The hour is coming, and now is, when the dead shall hear the voice of the Son of God: and they that hear shall live' (John 5:25).

The soul of the unconverted among you is as dead to divine things as the body of Lazarus was to common things. There is a total death in every unconverted bosom. It is not a mere figure of speech. It is not figurative death, but real - as real as that of Lazarus. Your eye does not see divine things, your ear does not hear them, your heart does not feel them.

It is the voice of Christ that wakens the dead soul. Jesus speaks through the Bible, through ministers, through providences. His voice can reach the dead. He quickeneth whom he will. They that hear, live.

Learn that it is right in ministers and godly friends to give warnings, and calls, and invitations to those that are spiritually dead. It appears strange to some that we should believe men to be spiritually dead, and yet warn them, and call them, and invite them to repent and believe the gospel. But this is the very way Jesus did to a dead Lazarus; and the way he does still to dead souls. It is through these very warnings, and calls, and invitations that Jesus speaks to your dead hearts. All that have been saved in this place heard the voice of Christ when they were dead. Godly persons among you should continue these calls and warnings, even though your friends appear as dead as Lazarus was.

Learn where to look for spiritual life. It was not the voice of Mary, nor the voice of Martha, nor the voice of the Jews that raised dead Lazarus. They could roll away the stone, but they could do no more.

They could not raise the dead. It was the voice of Immanuel - of him who is the life of all that live. So it is still, dear friends. It is his voice alone that can awaken you. It is not my voice, nor that of your loving Marthas and Marys - it must be the voice of Jesus, or you will sleep on and die in your sins, and where Christ has gone you will never come. Many a time the voice of ministers has rung through this house, and through your ears, and you have lived on in sin. But when the voice of Christ speaks through the Word, then you will arise, and leave all, and follow him.

(4) The effect on the bystanders.

Many believed on him.
It was a happy day in Bethany. He turneth the shadow of death into the morning. Martha and Mary had their bitter grief turned into a song of praise. Their buried brother was once more restored to their arms safe and sound; and I can imagine the feelings with which they sang that evening at their family worship: 'Return unto thy rest, O my soul, for the Lord had dealt bountifully with thee.'

Another joy was this: all their unbelief was now cleared away; Christ was like a morning without clouds. His tarrying, his promise, his trial of them - all was now explained; and as Mary sat at his feet that evening and heard his words, she felt more than ever that it was impossible for Christ to lie.

But a greater joy still remained: 'Many of the Jews believed on him.' It was a birth-night for eternity. The Shepherd found some lost sheep that night. The voice that called Lazarus forth pierced many a heart. The cottage at Bethany would be like a little heaven that night.

Observe what made them believe: 'When they saw the things that Jesus did.' It was not the sight of one thing, but of all that Jesus did. Just as the dying thief believed on Christ, not from seeing one thing but all that Jesus did. When he saw his holy person, his calmness, his love, his pity, he could not but feel that this was the Son of God, and the Saviour of the world. So with these Jews. They saw the amazing love of Jesus to Lazarus, and Martha and Mary; they saw his tears, they heard his groans, they saw him thank and praise his Father; and they could not but believe on him.

Two things especially they saw: divine power and divine love to sinners. It is the same thing which persuades sinners now to believe on him. It is seeing such love in him that he is willing to save; and such power that he is able.

And O how happy it would make us if many of you believed on him! If you were constrained this day to lay hold on him as your surety, elder brother and friend!

Some went and told the Pharisees. Some were saved and some were hardened.

Their companions were saved, yet they were not. They left Jerusalem together, strangers to God and to conversion. Some were taken, and some were left. So it is ever. I have often thought when sinners have been stricken and saved in this place, surely their neighbours will be saved also. Often it is the very reverse. Are there not many of you that have been hardened, while others have been saved by your side?

They loved Martha and Mary, and yet were not saved, but hated Christ. They were friends of Martha and Mary; they seem even to have loved Mary best, and yet they did not love Christ. So it is now. Some among you love our Marthas and Marys, and yet do not love Christ. Ah! those whom you love will soon be eternally separated from you.

Their objections were answered, and yet they were not saved. 'Could not this man who opened the eyes of the blind, have caused that even this man should not have died?' They objected that his love was not true, or he would not have suffered Lazarus to drop into the grave. Here their objection is taken away. Lazarus is raised, so that it is proved to them that Jesus loved him. Their mouth is shut. Still they do not turn. Alas! it is the same still. Many say, If I knew that Christ was willing to receive me, I would come. Remove the objection, still they do not come. If I had clothes, if I were free from family cares, I would begin to care about my soul. Still, remove the objection, and they are as careless as ever.

They hated Christ, the more they saw of him. Not only did they not believe on him, but they went and told his deadly enemies, they went and plotted his destruction. Ah! this is almost incredible. What a diabolical heart is a natural heart! Not only do you refuse to be saved by Christ, but you hate his name and cause. 'Behold, I lay in Zion a stumbling-stone and rock of offence; and whosoever believeth on him shall not be ashamed.'

THE GOOD SHEPHERD

LECTURE 1: THE GOOD SHEPHERD
(John 10:1-6)

Verily, verily, I say unto you, He that entereth not by the door into the
sheepfold, but climbeth up some other way, the same is a thief and a
robber. But he that entereth in by the door is the shepherd of the sheep.
To him the porter openeth; and the sheep hear his voice: and he calleth his
own sheep by name, and leadeth them out. And when he putteth forth his
own sheep, he goeth before them, and the sheep follow him: for they know
his voice. And a stranger will they not follow, but will flee from him: for
they know not the voice of strangers. This parable spake Jesus unto them:
but they understood not what things they were which he spake unto them

We may learn from verse 6 that this parable is difficult and dark to the
natural eye: 'They understood not what things they were which he spake
unto them.' How much need, then, have I of a fresh baptism of the Holy
Spirit while I open it to you! And how much need have you to have the
face of the covering destroyed from off your hearts, and to receive the
unction from the Holy One, that you may know all things!

1. The thief and robber: 'Verily, verily, I say unto you, He that
entereth not by the door into the sheepfold ... the same is a thief and a
robber' (verse 1).

There can be no doubt that this chapter is a continuation of the
preceding. Jesus was showing the Pharisees what blind and guilty
teachers they were. They were deeply offended at him. In this chapter
he goes on to show them the marks and defects of false teachers. It seems
plain, however, that Jesus speaks mainly of one thief and robber. He
calls him 'a stranger' (verse 5), 'the thief' (verse 10), 'the hireling'
(verse 13); and he contrasts him with the good shepherd, who gives his
life for the sheep. Who is this thief and robber, who climbs over the wall
of the sheepfold? This stranger, who tries to lead away the sheep of
Christ? This thief and robber, who comes not but for to kill, and to steal,
and to destroy? I have no doubt that it is Satan, the god of this world,
the prince of the power of the air; he that entered into Judas, he who filled
the heart of Ananias and Sapphira.

Satan has three ways of attacking the sheepfold.

Through Antichrist. There can be no doubt that Satan is the grand
master-mover of all the workings of Antichrist. We are told so in 2

Thessalonians 2:8,9: 'And then shall that Wicked be revealed, whom the Lord shall consume with the spirit of his mouth, and shall destroy with the brightness of his coming: even him, whose coming is after the working of Satan with all power and with signs and lying wonders.' Again, Revelation 12:9: 'And the great dragon was cast out, that old serpent called the Devil, and Satan, which deceiveth the whole world.' And again, Revelation 13:1,2: 'And I stood upon the sand of the sea, and saw a beast rise up out of the sea, having seven heads and ten horns, and upon his horns ten crowns, and upon his heads the name of blasphemy ... and the dragon gave him his power and his seat, and great authority.' This is Satan's grand plan for killing and destroying the sheep of the sheepfold. Thus he wears out the saints of the Most High.

Through the world. Satan is the god of this world. From the days of Cain the world has come over the walls of the sheepfold, to kill, and steal, and destroy. The world, whether it smiles or frowns, hates the Christians, and seeks to leap over the wall of the fold.

Through worldly ministers. Satan entered into Judas, and no doubt enters into many ministers still: 'For such are false apostles, deceitful workers, transforming themselves into the apostles of Christ. And no marvel: for Satan himself is transformed into an angel of light.' There is no way in which Satan has done more damage to the church than by thrusting unfaithful shepherds over the wall of the fold. Such were the Pharisees of old. Such are careless ministers to this day.

The mark of the false shepherd.
The false shepherd 'entereth not by the door, but climbeth up some other way.' The door of the fold we know to be Christ: 'I am the door: by me if any man enter in, he shall be saved' (verse 9). This is the sure mark of Satan, and all his underlings; they do not enter in, and are not saved through Christ. It is so with Satan himself. Unhappy spirit of evil, the strait gate of life was never opened to him. He leaps over the wall into the fold, seeking to devour the sheep; himself lost and unholy. So is it with Antichrist and all his ministers. They have never themselves entered by the door. They deny Christ to be the door. They would have men climb over some other way.

The object of the false shepherd: 'The same is a thief and a robber ... The thief cometh not but for to steal, and to kill, and to destroy' (verse 10).
The object of Christ in coming to this world was to seek and to save

that which was lost: 'For the Son of Man is not come to destroy men's lives, but to save them' (Luke 9:56); 'I am come that they might have life, and that they might have it more abundantly' (John 10:10). So with all his ministers. Our heart's desire and prayer to God for you all is, that ye may be saved. We cease not from 'warning every man, and teaching every man in all wisdom; that we may present every man perfect in Christ Jesus' (Colossians 1:28). 'I am made all things to all men, that I might by all means save some' (1 Corinthians 9:22). But the object of Satan and all under him is 'to steal, and to kill, and to destroy.'

First, they seek to rob God. Antichrist robs God of his throne, changing the very law of God; he robs Christ of the glory of being the only Mediator between God and man. The world robs God of his throne in your hearts; and worldly ministers rob God of his glory by concealing it, by keeping back the counsel of God for man's salvation. The same are thieves and robbers.

Second, they seek to rob man. Antichrist robs man of the Bible, of the preached gospel, of the way of pardon and peace. The world tries to rob you of your peace, of your way to holiness and eternal life. Worldly ministers seek to rob you of your precious, never-dying souls.

Awake, my friends! You are in a dangerous time. Beware of false shepherds, which come to you in sheep's clothing. Beware of Antichrist, in whatever form he may come to you. Beware of the world, whether in its frown or in its bewitching smile. Beware of cold worldly ministers.

2. The good shepherd: 'The shepherd of the sheep.'
The shepherd of the sheep is the Lord Jesus Christ.
'I am the good shepherd' (verse 11); 'I am the good shepherd, and know my sheep, and am known of mine' (verse 14). Why does he get this name?

First, because he died for the sheep. He is not a thief nor a robber, he is not a stranger nor an hireling, but the shepherd of the sheep: 'All we like sheep have gone astray; we have turned every one to his own way; and the LORD hath laid on him the iniquity of us all' (Isaiah 53:6).

Second, because he finds the sheep: 'What man of you, having an hundred sheep, if he lose one of them, doth not leave the ninety and nine in the wilderness, and go after that which is lost, until he find it? (Luke 15:4). Every sheep in the fold has been found by Jesus.

Third, because he carries the sheep: 'And when he hath found it, he lays it on his shoulders, rejoicing' (Luke 15:5). He gathers the lambs with his arm, and carries them in his bosom.

Fourth, because he leads and feeds the sheep. They 'go in and out, and find pasture' (verse 9). 'The LORD is my shepherd; I shall not want. He maketh me to lie down in green pastures: he leadeth me beside the still waters' (Psalm 23:1,2). 'For the Lamb which is in the midst of the throne shall feed them, and shall lead them unto living fountains of waters; and God shall wipe away all tears from their eyes' (Revelation 7:17).

The marks of the good shepherd.
He entereth by the door. You may be surprised at this. Is not Christ himself the door? How can he enter by himself? It was just by himself that he entered. Compare Hebrews 9:12, 'By his own blood he entered in once into the holy place' with 10:19,20, 'Having, therefore, brethren, boldness to enter into the holiest by the blood of Jesus, by a new and living way, which he hath consecrated for us through the veil, that is to say, his flesh.' Christ himself entered in by this way to the Father, namely, by his own blood; and by this way every faithful servant of Christ enters in: 'He that entereth in by the door is the shepherd of the sheep.' O that God would raise up many such in Scotland, men who have entered in by the door into the sheepfold, men who can speak of sin because they have felt it, of pardon because it is sweet to them.

He calleth his own sheep by name. In the eastern countries, the shepherd frequently speaks to his sheep. He calls upon them, and they hear and know his voice. So is it with Christ. He is not a stranger shepherd nor a hireling. He calls his own sheep by name.

This intimates first, *his knowledge of them.* When Zacchaeus, a lost and wandering sheep, was straying far away from the fold, Jesus called him by his name: 'Zacchaeus, come down.' When Nathanael was wandering under the fig tree, Christ saw him, and called him by his name. When Mary did not know Jesus, he said unto her, 'Mary': she turned herself and saith unto him, 'Rabboni.' Christ knows all in this congregation who are his. He could name them over. He does often name them. Man does not know you, ministers do not you, you may not know yourself; but Christ knows you: 'He calleth his own sheep by name.'

Second, he *deals in a very endearing manner* with his own sheep. This is implied. When you love a person, you love his name for it has music in it. So Christ loves to call his own sheep by name. He loves the names of those for whom he died. He holds sweet and daily communion with them.

Third, *he changes their nature.* When Abram became a believer, Christ gave him a new name; so with Peter. So, when the Jews are brought to Christ, it is said, 'Thou shalt be called by a new name, which the mouth of the LORD shall name' (Isaiah 62:2). 'But now thus saith the LORD that created thee, O Jacob, and he that redeemed thee, O Israel, Fear not: for I have redeemed thee, I have called thee by thy name; thou art mine' (Isaiah 43:1). 'Him that overcometh will I make a pillar in the temple of my God, and he shall go no more out: and I will write upon him the name of my God, and the name of the city of my God, which is New Jerusalem, which cometh down out of heaven from my God: and I will write upon him my new name' (Revelation 3:12).

If one of you were brought to Christ this day, you would get a new heart and a new name. You would no more be called worldling, swearer, drunkard, wanton; but disciple, child of God, heir of glory, Christian indeed. Has Christ called you by your name?

He goeth before them. He did so while on earth. He went through all that he calls us to follow him in. He went before us in faith and holiness. He went before us in labours of love, in reproaches, in necessities, in sufferings, in death. He does not ask you to go through anything that he did not go through. He still goes before his sheep; often unseen, often unfelt and unheeded, but still present. He will not leave you orphans: 'When thou passest through the waters, I will be with thee; when thou walkest through the fire, thou shalt not be burned; neither shall the flame kindle upon thee' (Isaiah 43:2).

My dear friends, are you following Jesus, the good shepherd, or a stranger? Ah! flee from strangers. Flee from the company of the world, where you cannot hear the voice of Jesus. It is not safe to be there. Flee from those houses where the voice of Jesus is not heard, but the voice of strangers. Follow Jesus. Keep your eye on the Master. Believe on him, and do not let him go.

LECTURE 2: CHRIST THE DOOR
(John 10:7-10)

Then said Jesus unto them again, Verily, verily, I say unto you, I am the
door of the sheep. All that ever came before me are thieves and robbers:
but the sheep did not hear them. I am the door: by me if any man enter in,
he shall be saved, and shall go in and out, and find pasture. The thief
cometh not, but for to steal, and to kill, and to destroy: I am come that
they might have life, and that they might have it more abundantly.

Christ is a kind teacher. He was speaking to stupid, prejudiced and
ignorant Pharisees; and, as we have seen from the context, 'they
understood not what things they were which he spake unto them' (verse
6). They did not understand his first parable, and here he explains it over
to them. He showed them the difference between the true and false
shepherd: that the true shepherd enters by the door, but the other climbs
up some other way. The two points they did not understand were, first,
what is the door? and, second, who is the true shepherd? These he now
proceeds to explain: 'Verily, verily, I say unto you, I am the door of the
sheep.'

Christ is a kind teacher still. He can have compassion on the
ignorant, and on them that are out of the way. How long he bears with
those of you who are stupid and prejudiced by your lusts! He gives
'precept upon precept, precept upon precept, line upon line, line upon
line, here a little and there a little' (Isaiah 28:10). He will readily explain
his word to those of you who are seeking after him. He will open your
understanding to understand the Scriptures.

1. Christ is the door into the sheepfold: 'I am the door of the sheep.'
All that ever came another way were thieves and robbers; but the sheep
did not hear them. 'I am the door.' There is no way of entering into the
church of God, but by conversion and faith in Christ.

There is no other way for shepherds.
Many, in all ages of the church, have entered into the ministry by
another way than by conversion and saving faith in Christ. Jesus says
here, they are thieves and robbers.

Many have entered in by their learning; masters of sciences and of
many languages; many who have written learned volumes in defence of

Christianity. Now, learning is good, and not to be despised; but it is not the door. Christ is the door of the sheep; and unless a minister enter by this door, he is but a thief and a robber.

Many have entered in by their gifts; men of human eloquence, mighty in word, either for good or evil; men of rich imagination, strong judgment and fluent tongue. The world runs after them. Still these gifts are not the door, and the men are but thieves and robbers.

Many have entered in by the favour of the great, by the patronage of the rich and powerful. They have great influence, and are held in esteem. Still this is not the door: 'I am the door of the sheep.' All who are faithful shepherds enter in by this door. As poor, lost sinners, they come in through the blood and righteousness of Christ. Ah! none can speak of sin, but those who have been taught by the Spirit to feel the load. None can speak of Christ's beauty, but those who know and love him. None can speak of forgiveness, but those who have tasted it. Hold such in reputation: 'Esteem them very highly in love for their work's sake.'

Flee from others. The sheep do not hear them. Whatever be their gifts, their learning, their eloquence, flee from them. They are strangers - thieves and robbers. They come not 'but for to steal, and to kill, and to destroy.'

There is no other way for the sheep.
Many enter into the church in other ways: many come into the fold of the Lord's table by another door; many enter by their *knowledge*. They have learned the plan of salvation through Christ. They can answer questions upon it. They have a form of sound words, but nothing more. Ah! this is not the door. Conversion to Christ is the only true door.

Many enter by their *blameless character*. Many are members of the visible Church because of their blameless character in the sight of men, though unconverted in the sight of God. You do not live in any way of open sin, and, therefore, you think you have a good right to sit down at Christ's table. Alas! you are but wolves in sheep's clothing. Christ is the door. Unless you have entered in by him, by his obedience and blood, you are but a thief and a robber.

'Friend, how camest thou in hither?' may be addressed to multitudes. How did you come to the Lord's table among the sheep of Christ? Was it by a true conversion and faith in Christ? Or was it in some other way? If you came in by your knowledge, by your serious air, by your blameless character, and not by Christ, you are but a thief and a robber.

You have stolen into the fold. You will soon be cast out among the liars.

Christ is the door at present: 'I am the door.'
There is plainly an emphasis on the words, *I am*. All to whom the gospel comes have a short time in their existence when the door is open to them, when the rent veil is open, when the way into the holiest, the way into the Father's love, is made manifest to them. *That time is short.* Compared with the long eternity that is to follow, it is but a moment, it is but a breathing-time. The few short years that each sinner has the open door before him will soon pass away; and then the door will be shut to all eternity.

Each of you, in eternity, will look back upon this sweet time when the door stood open before you: '*I am* the door.' Oh! my brethren, if I could promise you that the gospel door would stand open for you an hundred years, still it would be the part of true wisdom to enter in now; or, if I could say, for fifty, or twenty, or ten years, it would still more be the part of true wisdom to enter in. But I cannot say for one year, nor for one month, nor for one day. All I can say is, that *Christ is now the door.* Today there is a way of pardon and eternal life open before you. Tomorrow it may be closed for ever.

2. The invitation.

To whom?
'Any man.' Some of the sweet invitations of Christ are addressed to the *thirsty*: 'Ho, every one that thirsteth, come ye to the waters;' 'If any man thirst, let him come unto me and drink.' Some are addressed to the *burdened soul*: 'Come unto me, all ye that labour and are heavy laden, and I will give you rest.' Some are addressed to the *hungry*: 'Blessed are they which do hunger and thirst after righteousness; for they shall be filled.' Some are addressed to those who feel themselves *prisoners*: 'Turn you to the stronghold, ye prisoners of hope.' But here is the freest invitation possible. It is addressed to any man: 'If any man enter in, he shall be saved.'

It is not like the door of some of the great people of this world, open only to the great and the rich, and the beautiful and the gay. This door is open to all people, and any man may enter in. The beggar Lazarus was laid at the rich man's gate. He was not allowed to enter in. But Christ was an open door to him. It is not like the door of some churches, where none but the rich and the gay must enter, none but those who wear fine clothes, that have a gold ring on their hand, and a fine robe. No; Christ says: 'If any man enter in, he shall be saved;' 'To the poor the gospel is preached;' 'Go out into the highways and hedges, and compel them to come in, that my house may be filled.'

Some may say: I have committed open sins, sins of which it is a shame even to speak; so that if men knew, they would stone me. Still Christ says: 'If any man enter in, he shall be saved.' Some may say: I have despised Christ all my days, sinned against godly parents, godly teachers, against my Bible, against my conscience, against the Holy Ghost striving with me. Still this is his word who cannot lie: 'If any man enter in, he shall be saved.' Of whatever rank, or age, or sex, you be - of however deep a dye your sins may be - you are invited to enter in.

What?

'Enter in.' Many content themselves with hearing about the open door. They like to hear the gospel preached. They know about the way of salvation. They can talk about it. Still they do not enter in. They do not experimentally go through the door into the sheepfold. They do not forsake all their sins, all their worldly companions, for Christ. They do not appropriate Christ. They do not wash in his blood. They do not put on Christ as their righteousness. They are never at rest, never taste forgiveness. Oh! mark the word: 'If any man *enter* in.'

Many come up to the door. Like Agrippa, they say: 'Almost thou persuadest me to be a Christian.' They see the folly and vanity of the world. They feel deeply their lost and ruined condition. They desire to be saved through Christ. But, when they come to the door, they do not enter in. When they come to the point when they must forsake all, when they must cut the cord that binds them to the world, when they must leave Pharaoh's palace and bear afflictions with the people of God, they pause and draw back, they do not enter in. They do not choose Christ for better for worse, for life and for death.

Many see others enter in. Many not only hear about the door, and come near it, but see others enter. Still they do not enter in. They see a brother or sister or friend giving up all for Christ; and yet they do not enter in. Ah! my brethren, do not rest in mere convictions. Conviction is not conversion. Concern about your soul is not faith in Christ. Many look in at the door, who go away sorrowful.

3. The promise: 'He shall be saved, and shall go in and out, and find pasture ... I am come that they might have life, and that they might have it more abundantly.'

Salvation.
All who are without are unsaved. 'Walk in wisdom toward *them that are without*' (Colossians 4:5). 'Without Christ, being aliens from the commonwealth of Israel, and strangers from the covenants of promise, having no hope, and without God in the world' (Ephesians 2:12). 'For without are dogs, and sorcerers, and whoremongers, and murderers, and idolaters, and whosoever loveth and maketh a lie' (Revelation 22:15). All who come short of Christ come short of salvation. All who do not come to God through the blood and righteousness of Christ, must come naked, guilty, exposed to everlasting wrath, and shall be frowned away into outer darkness.

But he that entereth in *shall be saved*. Jesus here gives his word for it. Enter in by me, and you shall be saved. Immediate pardon, immediate entrance into the love and smile of God, is the portion of all that enter in. You will be pardoned all the sins that you have done the moment you receive the Lord Jesus Christ. Free, full, immediate salvation is what Jesus gives.

Liberty: 'He shall go in and out.'
This alludes to the sheep. When sheep are gathered into the fold, then they are at perfect liberty under the care of their shepherd. They go in and out. They are cared for and treated as dear sheep. Ah, brethren! 'If the Son therefore shall make you free, ye shall be free indeed' (John 8:36). There is no freedom like that of Christ's flock. As long as you are of the world, you think that to be a Christian is to live a dull, strict life, to give up all pleasure. But the reverse is the truth. The pleasures of this world are not to be compared with those of the Christian. 'Whosoever committeth sin is the servant of sin.' It is true slavery, to serve sin. Sin is the hardest of all slave-masters: 'The wages of sin is death.' But Christ's sheep go in and out. They have true genuine liberty, the same freedom that God and Christ have, freedom from the power of sin.

The pasture: 'Shall find pasture' - more than life.
The soul that enters in by the door is not only saved, but sanctified - set free, filled, enriched for eternity. Jesus will never suffer you to want,

here or hereafter. The saved soul shall verily be fed. Even though under-shepherds be removed - though Scotland be made desolate, the witnesses slain, and God's people scattered - still verily they shall find pasture.

LECTURE 3: I AM THE GOOD SHEPHERD
(John 10:11-15)

I am the good shepherd: the good shepherd giveth his life for the sheep. But he that is a hireling, and not the shepherd, whose own the sheep are not, seeth the wolf coming, and leaveth the sheep, and fleeth: and the wolf catcheth them, and scattereth the sheep. The hireling fleeth, because he is hireling, and careth not for the sheep. I am the good shepherd, and know my sheep, and am known of mine. As the Father knoweth me, even so know I the Father: and I lay down my life for the sheep.

In the preceding verses, we have seen that Christ is the door into the sheepfold. Now let us regard him as the shepherd of the sheep. Christ is represented to us in Scripture under a great variety of names and titles. There are more than a hundred different names applied to Christ in the Bible. He is the rose of Sharon, the apple tree, the plant of renown, the bridegroom, the husband, the friend of sinners, the door, the way, the true vine, etc. The reason is that no one name fully describes Immanuel. He is so full, so wonderful, so filled with treasures of grace to the needy soul, that all the names in the Bible do not half describe him. Here is one of the sweetest: 'I am the good shepherd.' May God draw you this day to put your lost souls in his hand!

We understand things best by contrast. For this reason Christ here contrasts himself with the hireling.

1. The hireling.

He is an hireling.
It is quite right for ministers to preach for hire: 'Thou shalt not muzzle the ox that treadeth out the corn;' 'Even so hath the Lord ordained, that they who preach the gospel should live of the gospel' (1 Corinthians 9:14). It is not desirable that God's ministers should waste their strength in other occupations, so that they must needs be maintained. But unfaithful ministers make hire the end of their ministry. So they did long

ago: 'Yea, they are greedy dogs which can never have enough, and they are shepherds that cannot understand: they all look to their own way, every one for his gain, from his quarter' (Isaiah 56:11); 'For from the least of them even unto the greatest of them every one is given to covetousness; and from the prophet even unto the priest every one dealeth falsely' (Jeremiah 6:13). 'Woe be to the shepherds of Israel that do feed themselves: should not the shepherds feed the flocks?' So Paul complains of those in his day: 'For I have no man like-minded, who will naturally care for your state. For all seek their own, not the things which are Jesus Christ's' (Philippians 2:20, 21). Ah! this is the black mark of every unfaithful minister. He is an hireling, he seeks his own: his own ease, his own profit, his own honour.

Whose own the sheep are not (verse 12).

He has neither part nor lot in the sheep. Faithful pastors have a peculiar relation to the sheep. There is a peculiar tie between a minister and the people saved under him, a tie that will never be dissolved. They are fathers: 'For though ye have ten thousand instructors in Christ, yet have ye not many fathers; for in Christ Jesus I have begotten you through the gospel' (1 Corinthians 4:15); 'My little children, of whom I travail in birth again until Christ be formed in you' (Galatians 4:19); 'Unto Timothy, my own son in the faith' (1 Timothy 1:2); 'I beseech thee for my son Onesimus, whom I have begotten in my bonds' (Philemon 10). Those saved under them are to be their crown: 'For what is our hope, or joy, or crown of rejoicing? Are not even ye in the presence of our Lord Jesus Christ at his coming? For ye are our glory and joy' (1 Thessalonians 2:19,20). Not so careless ministers, whose own the sheep are not. Instructors they may be, but not fathers. God, in general, does not own them in the conversion of souls. They have no sons in the faith. They shall have no crown in the presence of the Lord Jesus at his coming.

He careth not for the sheep (verse 13).

Faithful pastors have a peculiar care for the sheep. How remarkably is this exemplified in the case of Paul?

He prayed for them: 'I would that ye knew what great conflict I have for you' (Colossians 2:1); 'For God is my witness, whom I serve with my spirit in the gospel of his Son, that without ceasing I make mention of you always in my prayers' (Romans 1:9); 'We give thanks to God and the Father of our Lord Jesus Christ, praying always for you' (Colossians 1:3).

What labours he underwent for them: 'Ye know, from the first day that I came into Asia, after what manner I have been with you at all seasons' (Acts 20:18); '... remember that by the space of three years I ceased not to warn every one day and night with tears' (Acts 20:31); 'And I will very gladly spend and be spent for you; though the more abundantly I love you, the less I be loved' (2 Corinthians 12:15). 'So being affectionately desirous of you, we were willing to have imparted unto you, not the gospel of God only, but also our own souls, because ye were dear unto us. For ye remember, brethren, our labour and travail: for labouring night and day, because we would not be chargeable unto any of you, we preached unto you the gospel of God' (1 Thessalonians 2:8).

What tears did he shed for them: 'For, out of much affliction and anguish of heart I wrote unto you with many tears' (2 Corinthians 2:4); 'I fear ... lest, when I come again, my God will humble me among you, and that I shall bewail many that have sinned already' (2 Corinthians 12:20,21); 'For many walk, of whom I have told you often, and now tell you even weeping, that they are the enemies of the cross of Christ' (Philippians 3:18).

What joys over them: 'For now we live, if ye stand fast in the Lord. For what thanks can we render to God again for you, for all the joy wherewith we joy for your sakes before our God?' (1 Thessalonians 3:8,9).

Not so the unfaithful pastor. He cares not for the sheep. They are not his brothers and sisters. He may call them brethren; but they are not his joy and crown. They are not his spiritual children: 'He careth not for the sheep.'

He fleeth.

The wolf in the Bible means either false teachers, or a persecuting world: 'For I know this, that after my departing shall grievous wolves enter in among you, not sparing the flock' (Acts 20:29); 'Behold, I send you forth as sheep in the midst of wolves' (Matthew 10:16); 'behold, I send you forth as lambs among wolves' (Luke 10:3). Heresy and persecution are the two great dangers to which the sheep are exposed. These are the very times when faithful pastors stand most firmly to their post, though it should cost them life itself. But the hireling fleeth. He does not defend the flock from heresy by sound teaching; nor does he stand between the flock and the arrows of a God-hating world.

O, my brethren! pray for a faithful ministry to be given and continued in Scotland; not hirelings, whose the sheep are not, who care not for the sheep, but flee at the approach of the wolf. Pray for holy self-denied pastors, who will spend and be spent in the cause of Christ, and not count their lives dear.

2. The good shepherd: 'I am the good shepherd: the good shepherd giveth his life for the sheep' (verse 11); 'I am the good shepherd, and know my sheep, and am known of mine' (verse 14). Our Lord here lays down the marks of his excellency as a shepherd.

In giving his life for the sheep.
This is the chief point of his excellency. Herein he excels all others. Jacob was a faithful shepherd: '... in the day the drought consumed me, and the frost by night; and my sleep departed from mine eyes' (Genesis 31:40). But the good shepherd gave his life for the sheep. David was a faithful shepherd. A lion and a bear took a lamb out of the flock, and David went after them, and delivered it out of the mouth of the lion, and caught him by the beard and slew him (1 Samuel 17:34,35). But what was this to Christ? 'I lay down my life for the sheep.' The sheep were condemned to die. This sentence was suspended over every one of them: 'Thou shalt surely die.' All were ready to be cast into hell, when he cried, 'Lo, I come.' He laid down his life for the sheep.

Observe, it was not merely temporal death. His death was equal to the eternal death of sinners. He died under the wrath of God: 'Awake, O sword, against my shepherd, and against the man that is my fellow, saith the LORD of hosts' (Zechariah 13:7); 'All we like sheep have gone astray; we have turned every one to his own way; and the LORD hath laid on him the iniquity of us all' (Isaiah 53:6). He himself 'bare our sins in his own body on the tree.' He was made a curse for us.

Observe, he did it freely: 'I lay down my life;' 'No man taketh it from me, but I lay it down of myself' (verse 18); 'as Christ also hath loved us, and hath given himself for us' (Ephesians 5:2); 'Who gave himself for us' (Titus 2:14); 'Who gave himself a ransom for all' (1 Timothy 2:6).

Herein consists the goodness of the shepherd. He was such an one as to lay down his life freely. There will be much in Jesus to admire when we shall see him as he is. But that which will draw out the loudest notes of the new song will be the sight of the prints of the nails, and of the wound in his side: '... thou wast slain, and hast redeemed us to God by thy blood' (Revelation 5:9). This makes Christ the most attractive of all objects now: 'And I, if I be lifted up from the earth, will draw all men unto me' (John 12:32). Ah! brethren, what are you made of, that you are not drawn to give up all for Jesus?

In knowing his sheep: 'I know my sheep.' Christ knows the sheep, as the Father knows him.

The Father knew the Son from all eternity: 'Then I was by him as one brought up with him: and I was daily his delight, rejoicing always before him' (Proverbs 8:30). He was in the bosom of the Father. So did this good shepherd know his sheep from all eternity: 'Chosen before the foundation of the world.'

The Father knew the Son with a knowledge of most perfect delight and love: 'I was daily his delight.' At his baptism, a voice from heaven was heard saying: 'This is my beloved Son, in whom I am well pleased' (Matthew 3:17). So does Christ know his sheep: 'Thou art all fair, my love; there is no spot in thee;' 'The King is held in the galleries;' 'How fair and how pleasant art thou, O love, for delights!' 'Turn away thine eyes from me, for they have overcome me.'

The Father knew the Son through all his sufferings. So Christ knows his sheep: 'I know their sorrows;' 'In all their afflictions, he was afflicted.' He knows their decays: 'I know thy works, that thou art neither cold nor hot.'

The Father will know the Son to all eternity; and so the Son will know his sheep for ever and ever. They shall soon 'hunger no more, neither thirst any more; neither shall the sun light on them, nor any heat' (Revelation 7:16).

I am known of mine.

Christ knows the Father perfectly: 'No man knoweth the Father but the Son;' 'O righteous Father, the world hath not known thee; but I have known thee.' So do Christ's sheep know Christ. He gives them 'the Spirit of wisdom and revelation in the knowledge of him.' He manifests himself to them in another way than he doth to the world. He gives them an understanding to know him that is true. This is the perfection of our shepherd, that he reveals himself to us, that he lets out his fragrance and draw us after him: 'I am known of mine.'

Brethren, do you know the Lord Jesus Christ? Has he opened up his unsearchable riches to you, and drawn you to leave all for him?

LECTURE ON CAPERNAUM

LECTURE ON CAPERNAUM

Then began he to upbraid the cities wherein most of his mighty works were done, because they repented not: Woe unto thee, Chorazin! woe unto thee, Bethsaida! for if the mighty works, which were done in you, had been done in Tyre and Sidon, they would have repented long ago in sackcloth and ashes. But I say unto you, It shall be more tolerable for Tyre and Sidon at the day of judgment, than for you. And thou, Capernaum, which art exalted unto heaven, shalt be brought down to hell: for if the mighty works, which have been done in thee, had been done in Sodom, it would have remained until this day. But I say unto you, That it shall be more tolerable for the land of Sodom in the day of judgment, than for thee (Matthew 11:20-24).

On the north-west border of the lake of Galilee, there is a beautiful little plain, which was called in ancient times 'the land of Gennesaret'. It is in the shape of a crescent, and is about four miles in length, and two in breadth at its broadest part. It has two fine streams which rush down from the mountains, and it has, besides, two large fountains; so that it is well watered and very fertile. On that little plain stood long ago the three cities of Chorazin, Bethsaida and Capernaum. At the northern corner, almost at the sea, there is a fine fountain, and beside it a heap of ruins half buried by the reeds and thorny bushes that spread over them. This is believed to mark the site of Capernaum. Of the other two not a vestige remains, and no man can tell in what part of the plain they stood. And yet it was there in that little plain that Jesus did most of his mighty works. But the woe which he pronounced over them has fallen with silent but exterminating power. It is more tolerable for Tyre and Sidon than for Chorazin and Bethsaida; and Capernaum, long exalted to heaven, has been brought down to hell. Tell me, brethren, is there no voice of warning rising from these blasted ruins addressed to this favoured land? Is there no warning here for you and me? You, too, have been favoured like Capernaum, and if you do not repent, you will be brought down to hell.

I. Capernaum was exalted to heaven.
The reason why Capernaum is said to have been exalted to heaven was because of Christ's preaching and performing so many of his miracles there. When the people of Nazareth rejected him, and wanted to cast him over a precipice, 'he came and dwelt in Capernaum'. Whenever he came

to Galilee, he seems to have dwelt in Capernaum. It was his home more than any town on earth, so that it is frequently called 'his own city' (Matthew 9:1). He seems to have loved that spot more than other places.

Here he performed most of his miracles.
He healed the centurion's servant here (Matthew 8:5-13). Here he raised up Jairus' daughter, and cured the woman of the issue of blood. Here they brought their sick friends, and laid them down at his feet, and he healed them all.

Jesus preached here.
He spoke the most of his parables here. The parable of the sower, and those that follow, were spoken in the hearing of the people of Capernaum.

He prayed here (Mark 1:35).
So that it was a glorious opportunity to be saved. It was a day of salvation. It was an effectual door. The gate of heaven was, as it were, thrown open there. The Son of God, and the Saviour of the world, was living among them, healing and preaching among them.

Because the Holy Spirit descended here.
The Holy Spirit is the author of conversion in the soul, and without his work even the preaching of Christ does not convert souls. Now we know that the preaching of Christ in Galilee was not in vain. Though many were not converted, yet some were. Where did the centurion get that great faith that made Jesus marvel? Where did the woman, who came at last to Christ, get grace to leave all other physicians? Doubtless there were many drops of the Spirit given around that silent lake. Although the Spirit was not fully given, because Christ was not yet glorified, yet drops of the Spirit were given, upon the credit of his laying down his life a ransom. Many a time when Jesus rose a great while before day, and went up into some of the deep ravines of the mountains around, he obtained showers of the Spirit, which came down at evening as he taught the people out of the boat on the lake. I believe there are many in heaven that were born again during these sermons, under the open canopy of heaven, beside the Lake of Galilee. It was this that exalted Capernaum to heaven - the presence of the Saviour, and the falling of the Spirit.

Scotland, in like manner, has been exalted to heaven.

By the preaching of the gospel.
We have not had the personal presence of Christ, like Capernaum, but we have had the same message which he carried. Faithful ministers come from Christ. They are his gift. They are sent by him. Wherever they go, they go in his name; so that Christ may be said to dwell where they dwell.

Never, since 1560, has Scotland wanted faithful pastors. There were nearly a hundred years of spiritual death; but even then there were here and there a believing remnant. I suppose this town has never since then wanted some faithful pastors, even in its worst times. Dundee has been exalted to heaven. When Christ went to Sychar, he stayed only two days among them; and yet many of the Samaritans of that city believed on him. These were two days of merciful visitation. Jesus spent but a single day in the coasts of Syrophenicia, and yet that was the birth-day of the Syrophenician woman's soul. You have had a thousand such days of mercy, yet how few of you have improved them!

If you take up a map of the world, it is wonderful to mark how few spots have a preached gospel. Almost all Asia is sunk under the wicked delusions of Mahomet, or under the idolatries of Paganism. Africa is given over to Mahomet and witchcraft. South America, to idolatry and Popery. Europe is, for the most part, covered with the thick darkness of Popery. Oh! what grace is it to pass over the fairest provinces of the world, and come to this bleak island, with an open Bible, a quiet Sabbath, and a preached gospel! My friends, you will never know till eternity the greatness of the mercy of having a regularly preached gospel. It is the gate of heaven thrown open.

By the pouring out of the Spirit.
We have had more of the Holy Spirit poured out than ever Capernaum had. I do not know that any country in the world has been visited this way, as Scotland has been.

The first remarkable time in Scotland was from 1625 to 1630, when for five years there was an open window of heaven over Scotland. Under the ministry of David Dickson at Irvine and Stewarton, hundreds were brought to Christ; and under John Livingston, at Kirk of Shotts, five hundred in one day.

The second time of love was exactly a hundred years ago, in 1742, when the windows of heaven were opened over Kilsyth and Cambuslang, and about twenty or thirty other parts of Scotland shared in the blessing.

The third time of love in Scotland was from 1798 to 1800, when the parish of Moulin and some neighbouring parishes were visited in a remarkable manner.

The last is in our own day, beginning in 1839, when God opened the windows of heaven and poured down a blessing, till there was no room to receive it. This congregation has been exalted to heaven. You have had such an opportunity of being saved as you may never have again. Christ has done mighty works in the midst of you. Every sinner converted is a greater miracle than all external miracles put together.

By the Spirit being poured on your heart.
No doubt this was the case with many in Capernaum. The Holy Spirit strove with them; but they vexed him, so that he was turned to be their enemy, and fought against them. This has been the case with some of you. The Spirit has been poured on you, convincing you of sin, making you lie in the dust because of sin, giving you glances of desire after Christ. Ah! this is an amazing opportunity for being saved. If ever any man was at heaven's gates, it is that man with whom the Spirit has been striving.

2. Capernaum repented not (verse 20).
It would be interesting to know the secret history of the people of Capernaum. When Christ came among them, they were 'a people that sat in darkness, in the region and shadow of death.' A few were taken out of them, jewels for the Redeemer's crown; but the most repented not.

Some would not go to hear.
Their neighbours told them that a great prophet had come to dwell in their town; that he spoke as never man spake; that gracious words proceeded out of his mouth; that he spoke with majesty, and heavenly power, and holy love; that he healed all that came. They heard of the centurion's servant being healed, of Jairus' daughter being raised, and the nobleman's son. The whole town rang again. Their neighbours said, Will you not go and hear him? They made light of it, and went their way - one to his farm, another to his merchandise. 'I have bought five yoke of oxen, and I go to prove them; I pray thee to have me excused.' And

so they repented not. In darkness he found them, in darkness he left them.

Some went for a while.
They wondered when they saw his miracles. They followed him from place to place. They sat down on the grass to eat the bread he gave. They stood on the shore and listened to his preaching, and for a while they seemed taken with it. But when he pressed them that they must eat his flesh and drink his blood - a personal closing with Christ - they said: 'This is a hard saying, who can bear it?' They went back, and walked no more with Jesus. They repented not.

Some followed him all the time.
They would not miss a sermon by the lake for all the world. They ran on foot round the lake when he sailed to the other side. They stood breathless to hear; and yet they lived in some damning sin. They were hearers of the Word - not doers. They repented not. So it is in this place. If Christ were now where I am, he would upbraid this nation, because it has repented not. Instead of repenting, our nation is evidently like Capernaum, becoming more dark and wicked.

But with regard to this place:

How many will not come to hear, but live on in their unrepented sins!
Although God has opened his house of mercy here, although the door is open, notwithstanding all that God has done in this place, notwithstanding all the souls that have been saved, notwithstanding all the mighty works Jesus has done, multitudes have never come. They repent not. The taverns are as many as ever, these dens of iniquity are not diminished; the number of brawlers on the Saturday night and Sabbath is not smaller. If Jesus were here, he would upbraid you.

Some have come, and gone away offended.
Many came for a while, but when pressed to close with Jesus, were offended. It seems as if ministers must not speak the truth nowadays, but mince their words and make them sweet and sugary, that sinners may swallow them without offending their palate. We must not call black, black, and bitter, bitter, or some will be offended. All this shows that you have not repented.

Some have done many things, but still have not repented.
Some follow from sermon to sermon, and, like the multitudes that stood by the lake, drink in the word greedily. You have wondered at Christ's mighty works; but still you have not left your sin, your idol, your unlawful attachment. You are still a covetous man and an idolater who shall not enter into the kingdom of heaven. You repent not.

3. Capernaum was brought down to hell.
The inhabitants of these cities have long since passed away, and now the woe of Christ has taken hold of them. You must either have Christ's blessing or his woe. These cities were to sink lower than other cities, lower than Tyre and Sidon, lower than Sodom.

The whole Bible shows that there will be degrees of suffering in hell. Some will suffer more, some less, and yet all eternally. Just as there are degrees of blessedness in heaven; some being scarcely saved, some having an abundant entrance; others having an exceeding weight of external glory; one having authority over five cities, another over ten cities; all vessels being full of glory and joy, but some being more capacious: so in hell, there will be degrees of agony. 'He that knew his Lord's will, and did it not, shall be beaten with many stripes. But he that knew not, and did it not, shall be beaten with few stripes.' Those who have sinned against gospel light shall receive greater damnation. The people of Capernaum went far deeper into the lake than the people of Tyre and Sidon and Sodom. 'It shall be more tolerable.' The hell of these people will be infinitely dreadful, but it will be more tolerable than yours.

According to justice.
It is to satisfy justice that there is a hell at all: 'Because the righteous Lord loveth righteousness.' If it be just that there be a hell, then justice demands that those who have sinned against greater light should have a deeper place. So that as surely as gospel sinners go to hell, so surely will they go to the deepest place of all.

According to truth.
God says it will be so; therefore it must be so. Some people please themselves with the fancy that there is no hell, that God is too kind and merciful. But is he a true God? If he be a true God, then there is a hell, and the deepest part is for gospel sinners.

In the nature of things.

One of the bitterest parts of a sinner's eternity will be memory. As it will increase the joy of God's people when they sing the song of Moses, so it will increase the misery of the damned, when they remember all God's kindness and their own sin. And, oh! what kind of memory will you have who have lived on under this ministry unconverted and unsaved? Oh! if you could pluck memory from its seat. Oh! if you could blot out the memory of these quiet Sabbaths. Alas! it may not be.

'It shall be more tolerable for Tyre and Sidon at the day of judgment, than for you. And thou, Capernaum, which art exalted unto heaven, shalt be brought down to hell: for if the mighty works, which have been done in thee, had been done in Sodom, it would have remained until this day.'

Index of Scripture verses